D910

nothing ventured

DISABLED PEOPLE TRAVEL THE WORLD

KT-234-586

Hereward College
Bramston Crescent
COVENTRY
CV4 9SW

other available rough guides

ITALY • VENICE • SICILY • TUSCANY & UMBRIA • GREECE • CRETE
TURKEY • FRANCE • PARIS • PROVENCE & COTE D'AZUR
BRITTANY & NORMANDY • THE PYRENEES • SPAIN • PORTUGAL
GERMANY • BERLIN • HOLLAND, BELGIUM & LUXEMBOURG
AMSTERDAM • EASTERN EUROPE • YUGOSLAVIA • HUNGARY
POLAND • CZECHOSLOVAKIA • SCANDINAVIA • IRELAND • NEPAL
HONG KONG • ISRAEL & THE OCCUPIED TERRITORIES
WEST AFRICA • ZIMBABWE & BOTSWANA • MOROCCO • TUNISIA
KENYA • GUATEMALA & BELIZE • PERU • MEXICO • BRAZIL
CALIFORNIA & WEST COAST USA • SAN FRANCISCO • NEW YORK
WOMEN TRAVEL • MEDITERRANEAN WILDLIFE

• forthcoming titles

EGYPT • USA • CANADA • EUROPE • THAILAND • ROMANIA
FLORIDA • BARCELONA • WORLD MUSIC

Acknowledgements

Initial inspiration for the format of this book came from another Rough Guide Special, *Women Travel*, edited by Natania Jansz and Miranda Davies: thanks to them, and to Mark Ellingham, who helped shape the original idea.

The task of attracting contributions was made easier by the media folk who gave the project column space and air time: Frank Barrett, Andy Bull, Victoria McKee, Bernice Davison; the producers of *Same Difference* and *Does He Take Sugar?*; and the editors of all the newsletters and magazines produced by disability organisations. This publicity was vital and greatly appreciated.

Thanks to the hundreds of people who contributed accounts, information, anecdotes and know-how: those whose accounts have been included are acknowledged in the text; their hard graft produced the core of the book. Those who submitted material for the *Travel Notes* are also acknowledged in the text; thanks to them for taking time to put thoughts on paper. And to the many whose accounts were not included, thank you for making the effort and for your patience when decisions seemed to take forever. Special thanks to The Rev. Dr Dietrich Schuld, Ro Impey, Eva Falk, Malby Goodman, Jenny Brown, Sally Owen, Gilbert Vaux, Eric Roberts, Frances Sheridan, David Seagrave, Polly Higgins, Jeanette Huber, Adrian Mencarelli, Terry North, Christine Moir, Lesley Fildes and Dorothy Dalton.

For valuable facts, figures, opinions and encouragement, I am indebted to an army of knowledgeable people, especially Maundy Todd, Jackie West, John Stanford, Peter Duncan, Gordon Couch, Gerry Kinsella, Ken Ewart, Helen McAuley, Michelle Hill, Louise Hendriksen, Jennifer Johnston, Debbie Reynolds, Dave Atherton, Sue Brinkerhoff Bland, Margaret Jackson, Louise Henson, Paul Dicken, Sonja Lindhe, Yasmina Ashrat, Valerie Saunders, John Bradley, Rita Harvey, Philip Wright, and all those in the travel trade who answered my pleas for information.

All at *Rough Guides* have given a great deal in the making of *Nothing Ventured*, not only by sharing their expertise, but also with their enthusiasm for, and interest in, the book. In particular, I thank John Fisher for his calm control of the whole project, his steady flow of ideas, editorial genius and good humour; Susanne Hillen, Kate Berens, Gail Jammy and Andy Hilliard for their fine, painstaking production and typesetting work; Jack Holland for some hard sales talk; and Richard Trillo for energetic publicity work.

Illustration requests were beautifully interpreted by Sally Davies. Su Huntley, Donna Muir and Chris Shamwana produced a fantastic cover.

Finally, my thanks to Jeremy Round, Jeremy Trevathan and Katharine Hinton for advice in the very early stages, and to family and friends (in particular Adam and Eva Gordon, Michael and Valerie Walsh) for preserving my sanity throughout with a mixture of love, support, criticism and inspiration – plus the odd reminder that there is life after *Nothing Ventured*.

The publishers and authors have done their best to ensure the accuracy and currency of all the information in *Nothing Ventured: Disabled People Travel the World*; however, they can accept no responsibility for any loss, injury or inconvenience sustained by any traveller as a result of information or advice contained in the book.

Published by Harrap Columbus, Chelsea House, 26 Market Square, Bromley, Kent BR1 1NA.
Design by Gail Jammy, Greg Ward and Andrew Oliver.
Map artwork and illustrations by Sally Davies.
Printed in the UK by Cox & Wyman, Reading, Berks.

© Alison Walsh 1991.

No part of this book may be reproduced in any form without permission from the publisher except for the quotation of brief passages in reviews.

560p.

British Library Cataloguing in Publication Data
Nothing ventured: disabled people travel the world - (The Rough guides)
  1. Handicapped persons. Travel
I. Walsh, Alison II. Series
  910.910240816

ISBN 0–7471–0208–2

nothing ventured

DISABLED PEOPLE TRAVEL THE WORLD

Edited by

ALISON WALSH

Rough Guide editor

JOHN FISHER

HARRAP COLUMBUS ■ LONDON

Contents

Introduction

1 MEDITERRANEAN EUROPE

4 Spain
Jill Rann *Poppies in Spain*
Joan Cooper *Hell on Wheels*
Julie Smethurst *Lessons in Communication*
Jean Dyke *The Au Pair Network*
Spain Travel Notes

18 The Balearics
Judy Page *Feeling Square in Mallorca*
Rosalind May *Grounded in Menorca*
Balearics Travel Notes

25 The Canaries
Peter Stone *December Cocktails*
Maxine Smith *Still Searching for the Perfect Holiday*
Canaries Travel Notes

32 Portugal
Theodora Hampton *An Ideal Hobby*
Portugal Travel Notes

37 Italy
Stephen Hunt *Roman Style*
Anna Thomson *The Italian Cure*
Sian Williams *Venice For All*
Italy Travel Notes

47 Yugoslavia
Margaret Lees *Red Soil, Mishmash and Folk Songs*
Muriel Smith *Package Tour vs Independent Travel*
Yugoslavia Travel Notes

57 Greece
Julie Smethurst *Welcomed in Greece*
Jo Austen *A Rough Ride in Crete*
Allan Green *Somewhere Warm and Somewhere New*
Greece Travel Notes

69 Cyprus

Jack Tulley *Still Good for a Holiday*
Liz Crow *A Divided Island*
Jane Hutchinson *At Home in Cyprus*
Turkish Cyprus: Another View
Cyprus Travel Notes

82 Malta

Barry Atkinson *Digging Deeper in Malta*
Christine Warburton *A Prize Worth Winning*
Enid Jasper *Multicoloured Malta*
Malta Travel Notes

95 NORTHERN EUROPE

98 Ireland

Annie Delin *Sidetracked in Ireland*
Helena O'Keefe *Abandoning Ship in Galway*
Nancy Bower-Meale *Sibling Rivalry*
Ireland Travel Notes

110 Scotland

Paul Cox *High Expectations North of the Border*
Charlotte Billington *First Trip to Scotland*
Scotland Travel Notes

117 England and Wales

Isobel Williams *Wild Eric and the Devil's Chair*
Caryl Lloyd *It Rains in the Lakes*
Vivienne Adcock *English Country Holiday*
Vivienne Adcock *Bird-watching in Nottingham*
Mickie Nixon *Halfway round the World*
Jane Nyman *Leicestershire Bells*
Veronica Smith *Cornish Adventure Holiday*
Eileen Cross *Lashings of Cornish Cream*
Marion Embury *Loaded Camel and Laughing Man Rock*
England and Wales Travel Notes

144 The Channel Islands

Jill Brown *A Very Accessible Island*
Bryan Smith *Operation Jersey*
Channel Islands Travel Notes

151 France
Pete Kendall *Je Vais Chercher un Parachute*
Ian Marshall *Savoie Fare*
Ian Marshall *The Dordogne*
Alison Walsh *A Strange Phenomenon*
Sian Williams *Independent Living in Nancy*
Mairene Gordon *Half a Loaf*
Enid Fisher *Wintering in Roussillon*
France Travel Notes

176 Switzerland
Ian Marshall *A Long Love Affair*
Beryl Bristow *The Eiger on my Doorstep*
Switzerland Travel Notes

185 Austria
Eric Leary *Setting out for Mars*
Ron Cottrell *An Improbable Ski Party*
Margaret Hides *And for the Non-skier*
Austria Travel Notes

194 Belgium
Jane Nyman *There is Nothing like a Nun*
Belgium Travel Notes

199 The Netherlands
Philippa Thomas *Put your Money on a Good Hotel*
Barry Atkinson *Falling for the Countryside*
Netherlands Travel Notes

207 Scandinavia
Charlotte Billington *Sweden under Scrutiny*
Dorothea Boulton *High Mountains, High Prices*
Scandinavia Travel Notes

216 Germany
James Franey *The End of East and West in Berlin*
Germany Travel Notes

222 Poland
Annie Delin *A Survival Guide for Poland*

226 Czechoslovakia
Joyce Benson *An Empty Hillside*

230 The Soviet Union
Biddy Haines *Russian Cruise*
Joy Schwabe *Art Appreciation in Moscow and Leningrad*
Eastern Europe & Soviet Union Travel Notes

239 NEAR AND MIDDLE EAST
242 Israel
Barry Atkinson *The View from Masada*
Israel Travel Notes

249 Egypt
Stephen Hunt *Ups and Downs*
Maxine Smith *Sand, Flies and Holes in the Ground*
Egypt Travel Notes

257 Oman and the UAE
Betty Layton *Boiling Oil and Velcro*
Oman and the UAE Travel Notes

263 AFRICA
266 Morocco
Ivy Geach *A Meeting in the Desert*

270 Sierra Leone
Kate Margrie *Nor Touch Arata*

275 Tanzania
John Bignell *I Felt Like a King*

279 Zimbabwe
John Myall *Silent Zimbabwe*
Africa Travel Notes

287 ASIA
290 India
Daphne Pagnamenta *India at Last*
Robin Reeley *Getting around India*
Alison Walsh *Visit India*
Hugh Chetwynd-Talbot *The Valley of the Gods*

308 The Maldives
Sue Kelley *Stuck in the Sand*
India & the Maldives Travel Notes

315 Singapore
Susan Preston *Looking for Excellence*

320 Thailand
Barbara Horrocks *A Prayer to the Emerald Buddha*

324 Bali
Veronica Smith *A Taste of Bali*

327 The Philippines
Alfred Azzopardi *No Concessions, no Prejudice*

331 Hong Kong and Macau
Sue Kelley *The Pied Piper of Fushan*

335 China
Betty Layton *Fame at Last*
Far East Travel Notes

345 AUSTRALIA AND NEW ZEALAND

348 Australia
Andrew Healey *Wheeling around Queensland*
Barbara Horrocks *Old Haunts, New Thrills*
John Moore *Honeymoon First*
Donald Crowther *Tasmania to the Tropics*
Roger Elliott *A Spirit of Adventure*
Lorna Hooper *Family Matters in Sydney and Perth*
Sheila Murray *An Outdoor Life*

374 New Zealand
David Gray *Going for the Big One*
Australia & New Zealand Travel Notes

387 NORTH AMERICA

390 USA
Carolyn Lucas *Drama on the East Coast*
Carolyn Lucas *Another America*

Carolyn Lucas *Drama on the West Coast*
Frances Hill *One of the Crowd*
Arthur Goldthorpe *Bargain Breaks in Southern California*
Stephen Latham *It's OK to Scream in Orlando*
Shirley Lihou *Corinne's Choice*
Christine Panton *Whirlwind USA*
Angela Deakin *USAir Go to Court*
USA Travel Notes

429 Canada
Dee Hopkins *Satisfied Customers*
Christine Swan *Canada: Second to None*
Steve Veness *Large Marge Steals the Show*
Dorothea Boulton *Proud to be a Montrealer*
Rod Semple *Transportation Issues in Vancouver*
Frieda Maguire *A Helper's View*
Canada Travel Notes

455 SOUTH AMERICA

458 Venezuela
Sue Kelley *Success in South America*

462 Ecuador
Hugh Chetwynd-Talbot *A Golden Wedding Anniversary*
South America Travel Notes

471 TOURS AND CRUISES

474 Expeditions
David Bonnett *Sand in my Callipers*
Jack Davidson *Personal Everest*

482 Touring
Roderick MacDonald *A Giant Buffet*
Michael Turner *Coming Home*

490 Cruises
Terence Wilson *A Dose of Romantic Escapism*
Betty Parkin *To the Edge of the Polar Icecap*
Betty Airlie *And the Sun was Shining!*

499 Working

Frankie Armstrong *Memories and Magic*

Tours and Cruises Travel Notes

507 PRACTICALITIES

509 Planning
511 Booking
516 Insurance
517 Health and comfort
520 Holiday helpers
521 Red tape
522 Getting there by air
529 Getting there by land and sea
532 Sleeping
533 Eating and drinking
534 Getting around
537 Work and study
538 After your trip
539 Books
540 Directory

Nothing Ventured

A s a celebration of travel for its own sake, as a demonstration of the desire to "get away" and to travel widely, freely and independently, these stories speak for themselves. In addition, they provide a source of reference, containing a wealth of experiences, hints, opinions, recommendations and criticisms that will not only be valuable to other disabled travellers, but also provide food for thought for all those involved in the travel industry – worldwide.

The division of the book into **sections** has been based on the nature and numbers of accounts received, rather than on geographical boundaries or political definitions. The Soviet Union, for example, is included in the Northern Europe section because the few accounts that cover travel there relate to the western parts, close to Europe.

The **Introduction** to each section summarises the findings of the following accounts and gives an overview of the picture for disabled travellers in the countries covered. It picks out the problems and may offer some suggestions for change. It highlights the good points and describes the new initiatives.

The **Travel Notes** are essentially a postscript to the account(s) for each country, expanding on points mentioned in the account and with some additional information included if it is available and relevant to the contributors' stories. There may be some mention of tour operators recommended by other contributors; perhaps some discussion of different means of transport or types of accommodation; some addresses, contacts and books for further research; some general points on access and facilities.

The *Travel Notes* are not standardised because every country has a different approach to providing facilities and information for disabled visitors: indeed, many have an indifferent approach, making this section at times very brief. Sometimes the notes for a number of countries are grouped in one section. The Scandinavian countries are covered in this way because accounts of travel in Denmark and Finland were not received but some information and comments were submitted. In Asia the *Travel Notes* have been gathered into two sections, and in Africa and South America into one, largely because there is very little information available on these parts of the world (this does not mean they are totally inaccessible, but a wheelchair symbol is definitely a rare sight in the tourist literature).

The **Practicalities** section comes after the accounts and is the place to find a mixture of hard facts, comment and criticism. There are comparisons of airline and airport facilities, a discussion of the pros and cons of group travel, a selection of competitive insurance policies, some thoughts on accommodation, a few tales from the travel industry, a list of useful books and all the addresses you are likely to need.

All who work for the agencies which disseminate information for disabled holiday-makers know that the gathering of accurate information, and committing it to print, is a nightmare task, not least because of the speed with which changes in facilities and services are being introduced. It's hard to keep up, and this book is no different from any other in that apologies must be made in advance for information which will be out of date before publication.

There have been other problems. The members of the travel industry who *do* make efforts to accommodate disabled people – and their numbers are increasing – very often do not adequately advertise their facilities or services; they do not define them, they do not ensure that all their staff know of them, and simply do not get their message across. Rather than state that certain disabilities are not catered for they imply this by omission, which makes research difficult, and does not inspire confidence in the industry's *genuine* desire to integrate tourists with handicaps into its programmes.

Although the travel industry is waking up to the disabled section of the market, many operators are still unwilling to delve deeply enough to ensure *full provision* for people with *all* types of disability. Their excuse – that it is impossible to provide facilities which suit all disabled people – does not hold water. Every holidaymaker is different, with different likes and dislikes: no expense has been spared in researching the needs of able-bodied tourists; it is no less commercially sound, particularly in the light of recent downturns in some parts of the business, to explore thoroughly another section of the market.

There is plenty of help available for this research, numerous organisations of disabled people, as well as individuals, to turn to for advice. In the UK, *Tourism for All*, a joint venture involving the English Tourist Board and *Holiday Care Service*, has taken the initiative, laying down four minimum criteria which have to be met before an establishment can be awarded the *Tourism for All* symbol, and backing this up with two comprehensive handbooks for proprietors.

A common claim is that treating a disabled person like any other traveller is physically impossible – on aircraft ("we just don't have the space to provide a bigger toilet cubicle") and on public buses ("we have schedules to keep, there's no time to load and unload wheelchairs on a hydraulic lift"), to name but two examples. These are debatable claims, and the writers of this book make a good case for attempting the impossible, but in the meantime it is surely not too much to ask that procedures for disabled customers are, at least: developed in consultation with disabled people; made known in honest, regularly updated, crystal-clear literature which is easy to obtain; and constantly reviewed and improved.

Perhaps most important of all, these procedures must be **flexible**. The root cause of an enormous number of problems experienced by disabled travellers is the rigidity of officialdom: employees who insist that this is the way they have to do it and if it's inconvenient and uncomfortable, too bad. The air passenger who wants to remain in his or her own wheelchair and potter about in the duty free shop or have a drink before take-off is told by an airline official to transfer to an uncomfortable chair with small wheels and attendant attached. The railway traveller is *told* where to sit – either in the goods van or the vestibule, or park your chair in this special space in the carriage.

All travellers are different, and the only way to treat them is to ask how each one wishes to play it. Too often, disabled travellers are bundled off to distant recesses of vehicles or stations, simply because that's company policy. By asking first if the disabled person *needs* any help, an opening is made; the traveller can state where he or she wants to go, and how, and the operator – who is, after all, providing a service – can make the arrangements, the fewer the better (and cheaper).

The *Tourism for All* philosophy extends beyond accommodation to include accessible public buildings, transport, tourist attractions, countryside and information, as well as provision of holidays for people in financial difficulty. It has begun to attract the attention and support of some powerful bodies in the travel trade. There are the first signs of a move towards more coherent policy and more acceptable procedures, with the ultimate aim of total integration of everyone, whatever their disability or preference, into the general marketplace of holidays and travel.

With that aim in mind, input from anyone with an interest in travel for disabled people must be useful; every disabled person, every holiday helper, every tour operator has a contribution to make. This book airs some of those contributions, albeit mainly from the consumer's viewpoint. It is a collection of opinions, facts and experiences to throw into the melting pot.

The achievement of true integration of disabled people into the travel scene will be cause for some celebration. Even more exciting would be the sight of people with any handicap – related to mobility, senses or intellect – travelling anywhere in the world, unrestricted by their environment. That may sound like a pipe dream, but there was a time when finding an accessible public toilet was a hopeless task.

When the pipe dream is realised, this book will be redundant as a source of reference – no information will be necessary because disabled people will set off in the knowledge that they will reach their destinations in reasonable comfort, find suitable accommodation, enter all the museums, shops and art galleries on their itineraries, be able to use the public toilets, and explore the local countryside. *Nothing Ventured* will be nothing more than entertainment – a collection of travellers' tales, indistinguishable from those of travellers without disabilities.

HELP US UPDATE

Nothing Ventured aims to give disabled travellers space to share their experiences and air their opinions. If this one works there will be a **second edition,** for which we will need new accounts and updated information for the *Practicalities* and *Travel Notes.* Anyone wishing to write, or contribute in any way, should contact Alison Walsh, c/o The Rough Guides, 149 Kennington Lane, London SE11 4EZ. Please send a brief letter first, stating where you intend to travel or what you'd like to write about.

We are keen to develop a worldwide network of people who can gather access information on their own region, so that the *Travel Notes* will be more accurate and immediate. Articles from foreign contributors will also be welcomed.

PART ONE

MEDITERRANEAN EUROPE

Introduction

The kindness of both climate and people is a strong theme in these reports of holidays in Mediterranean countries. Judging by the number of accounts received, the warmer, southern parts of Europe are as popular amongst disabled travellers as they are with the able-bodied and there are good reasons for this.

First must be the lure of the **sunshine**. The cold, damp weather of Britain depresses us all at times but for so many people with disabilities it is a serious drain on physical wellbeing and morale. Most of the year it's possible to find more congenial temperatures somewhere in Mediterranean Europe, whilst those who find extreme heat intolerable can also be satisfied, either by heading for higher ground or by travelling out of season. The benefits – of spending all day out in the fresh air without feeling chilled, of exercising rarely used limbs in warm and buoyant sea water, of slowing down mentally to the pace of life in warmer climes – are obvious.

The second big draw is the **low cost and speed of travel** to these parts of the world – no expensive long-haul flights to different time zones, less outlandish travel insurance premiums to pay, and for many people the freedom and independence of using their own transport, adapted to their needs. For those who fly, of course, the journey may be lengthened by delays at airports at peak times, but this is an occupational hazard for all travellers.

Cost is an important consideration for most but especially for those organisations, such as *Winged Fellowship* and *Project Phoenix Trust*, which arrange holidays abroad for groups of disabled people. Many are charities and some offer help to group members who are unable to pay for a holiday; this naturally restricts their choice of destination. Even if they could afford to send a group further afield, there are some airlines that refuse to take groups of disabled people on long-haul flights.

Weighing against the low cost of getting there is the high cost of **getting about** once there, unless you are in your own car. Public transport in these countries is for the fit and agile – there are no concessions to the disabled traveller, although some people do manage, with help which is usually cheerfully given. Car hire is expensive and adapted cars are not always available. Although taxi rates in most places are cheaper than in the UK, fares soon mount up.

However, if you overcome the transport problem, the cost of eating and drinking well is still low in most areas. **Food** – fresh, simple and delicious – features often as a highlight of the holiday in these accounts; even those on restricted diets find no difficulties in countries where eating is a pleasure, to be drawn out, and every meal an occasion. Being able to eat outside adds to this pleasure, especially for the wheelchair user accustomed to manoeuvring in crowded restaurants and coping with steps at the entrances.

The final attraction is **variety**: there is more to Mediterranean Europe than sun and sand. Lazing on the beach can be combined with visits to ancient sites and historic buildings, or escapes into remote rural villages. Nightlife can consist of tranquil meals under the stars, or all-night partying in bars and nightclubs. Access to many of these places is difficult and toilets for the disabled visitor are few and far between, but this is not a problem peculiar to Mediterranean Europe, and with the best will in the world it would be impossible to make a craggy Greek island into a paradise for wheelchair users.

It's probably fair to say that the countries covered in this section are behind those of northern Europe in terms of provision for disabled tourists; indeed, there is widespread ignorance of the fact that people with disabilities *do* travel, particularly in the more remote areas. Attitudes to disability vary from friendly indifference in Rome to muttered prayers in Cyprus, but always there is kindness, always an offer of help without embarrassment to either party. And there *are* hopeful signs, such as the accessibility project in Venice and an increasing number of new hotels offering rooms for disabled clients. Most of the airports can deal with disabled passengers, even if their methods seem somewhat primitive when compared with those in the north.

All things considered, the barriers that prove too much for the disabled traveller in Mediterranean Europe are surprisingly few. If disabled holidaymakers continue to be undeterred by these and their numbers increase, then it's probably not hopelessly optimistic to expect a gradual growth of facilities, in the same way that earlier waves of tourists have been adapted to and provided for.

Spain

Poppies in Spain

Peter and Jill Rann took their two small children to the Costa Brava in 1983. Peter has an unremitting form of multiple sclerosis and is completely wheelchair-bound.

If it hadn't been for an attack of pneumonia we might never have gone abroad again. Young children and multiple sclerosis put a stop to any thoughts of travel outside Britain. But after a long dark winter and three weeks in hospital for Peter with pneumonia, we wanted some fun and sunshine.

So in May the four of us set off for three weeks in a Costa Brava that not everyone sees. The fields were awash with wild flowers, including the scarlet poppies of my Norfolk childhood; now gone from East Anglia, they were everywhere in northern Spain. There were few tourists then, so we were greeted like the first swallows of summer. The beaches were clean and empty, and the shopfronts smelled of fresh paint. And if the sea was a bit cold for the adults, that made Peter – too disabled even to want to swim – equal.

But back in March we looked at our restrictions. Peter was unable to walk or stand, and his arm weakness meant that he needed help to cut his food and sometimes feeding at the end of a meal. The children were aged three and six. Beyond everything, there were the finances: after three years on income support our savings were gone, so we

did something terribly rash – we paid for as much as we could by credit card.

We planned the trip around our car, though it did not honour the trust we placed in it, and for four days each way it became our little world. It was small – a Vauxhall Chevette – and we were packed tight. The children lived in the back with buckets of Lego and crisps, wedged in by "Green Hippo" and "Blue Blanket". There they fought (mostly), played and slept, and learned to say "Yes, lovely" without looking up as we passed spectacular snow-tipped mountains or golden eagles on the high plains stretch between the Atlantic and the Mediterranean. We had our tapes in the front, though the sound of that holiday will always be an old Arthur Lowe recording of "Mr Men" stories, "Silly old Wizard"...

The car, bought through the *Motability* scheme and still under warranty, broke down two days before our departure date. The garage we were contracted to specialised in splendid apologies and poor repairs. Collecting it the day before leaving, we sat open-mouthed as the manager cheerfully explained that due to some hitch at the factory we would have to drive without keys, stopping and starting with a screwdriver. This was to cause dark looks at Spanish filling stations, which are all service only.

We just about made it home before all the electrics blacked out. A desperate telephone call caught the departing manager who, kinder than he was proficient, gave up his evening to finding the fault – a mysteriously unlisted fuse. Nothing was going to stop us now, we'd remembered to pack the wheelchair pump and Peter's drugs, plus all those extra bits and pieces which you need if disabled.

We set off the next day but by Chiswick Roundabout the car was faltering and before Bristol the engine died, with luck as we passed a motorway service station. We ground to a halt outside a repair shed and a mechanic coming off duty saw our desperate faces and the Orange Badge. He poked and scraped under the bonnet, talked of distributors, refused payment and said "Get 5-star, but that'll see you to Plymouth". And so it did, plus a couple of thousand miles and back to our front door, admittedly with a top speed of 58mph but at least we got to look at the scenery. Apart from an earth-mover knocking us off the road on our way to buy fresh Spanish bread one morning, there was no more trouble with the car.

After an overnight stay in a family room at the *Holiday Inn*, which was one of the few hotels in Plymouth to cater for wheelchair users, we used a *Brittany Ferries* 24-hour crossing to northwest Spain to save us the long drive through France. Travelling in May gave us the advantage of out-of-season prices and a special offer – two free nights in a *parador*, the state-run Spanish hotels in National Trust-type properties.

The ferry was marvellous and the staff were exceptionally helpful. I'd forgotten that I get seasick and couldn't leave the cabin, reserving my energy for Peter's needs – meals, assistance to the loo and physiotherapy. The crew knew our situation and looked after Amy and Tom, who ran free and happy all over the ship. The ship's cinema had well designed seating and Peter was able to enjoy films in comfort for the first time in years. Sadly, the *Bretagne*, which came into service in summer 1989 and has taken over the Plymouth–Santander route, has two cinemas only accessible by steep stairs. (But there are lifts to all decks, accessible toilets and special cabins for disabled passengers.)

I was nervous about driving in Spain; before our trip I had never driven at night, on a motorway or on the "wrong side of the road" and I'd passed my test only two months ago. Peter had lost all use of his legs and had limited arm movement. In fact, my inexperience gave him the chance to drive again: although I turned the wheel, he talked me through the entire journey, including his bad driving habits such as overtaking by slipping through the L-shape of a lorry tortuously negotiating a tight bend near Santander.

"Arriving at our destination ... at nearly midnight, we found that I'd left the address of our villa in London"

We'll never forget the luxury of arriving that first evening at our *parador*, a rosy brick building in gardens with fine views. The children, released from the back seat, ran to the playground. The hotel had no special thoughts for the disabled, but apart from two steps at the front and an inaccessible lounge it proved perfect because of the large scale on which it was built. It had lifts and a huge bathroom with great fluffy towels. For me the floor would not stop moving, a strange aftereffect of the ferry crossing, but we slept like logs and awoke in the morning to geese cackling in a small yard across the road. Breakfast was extraordinary (we were last, of course, after the long process of getting Peter ready for the day): the table was arranged with rings of cakes and brioches, and the children were given something like hot chocolate blancmange to drink. It was all both very comforting and very foreign, after a journey more fraught than expected.

Out of season, the Spanish motorway across the country is almost deserted, with the lorries taking A-roads to avoid the tolls. We trundled at 58mph past the foothills of the Pyrenees to the north and saw Zaragoza – half medieval turrets, half tower blocks – shimmering on the distant plain. Arriving at our destination, Estartit, in the dark at nearly midnight, we found that I'd left the address of our villa in London.

"We were led with blue lights blazing, through red traffic lights, right across Santander"

By sheer luck the owner of the first bar we went into knew our landlady, who was also a singer in the summer season, and left his bar to lead us to the villa. On our return journey, I'd unforgivably done the same thing with our overnight *parador* in Santander. There we asked at the fire station (Peter thought they'd know all the hotels because of fire checks) and were led with blue lights blazing, through red traffic lights, right across Santander. Disability can bring some rather special experiences as well as the more dreary quests for loos.

The villa, which we'd seen advertised in our neighbouring Borough of Brent's newsletter, had some drawbacks. The flat was small and furnished with awful mattresses and excruciating armchairs. But the personality of the owner, who lived upstairs, made up for this. She was a retired English actress, whose magnificent bosom had caused car crashes in her youth. She threw mats on the old enemy gravel, entertained the children while we slept late in the morning, took us out to dinner and quietly spooned the regional sheep's milk pudding into Peter's mouth when he tired. Amy and Tom loved the villa so much that they sometimes refused the beach, preferring to play with our landlady's collection of pets – many dogs, a monkey and a parrot – or to net butterflies in the lane at the back.

The local beach was wide and sandy but a little breezy; we drove miles through the pretty countryside exploring hilly towns and finding new bays and fishing villages. If a beach was inaccessible people would always help if asked, though they were often too shy to volunteer. At first we were uncomfortable at the locals' tendency to stare at us but we later learned that the Spanish don't have a tradition of holidaying away (who needs it with their wonderful climate?) and they thought us mad to travel with small children, never mind disabilities.

We found the climate in May just warm enough and the sun strong enough to burn quickly if we weren't careful. We ate out cheaply some evenings in an uncrowded restaurant overlooking the harbour. Simple fish, paella, roast pork and salad, escalopes or pasta did not unnerve the children. We visited a local potter and sculptor, a small farmer who lived in a series of cement forms which he'd created – his Renault was garaged in a large concrete dinosaur.

We had to cope with difficulties. Peter wouldn't drink during part of the day to avoid searching for loos and we carried a bottle for emergencies. If disabled you have to plan harder than most; you are not allowed the indulgence of forgetting vital equipment or leaving things to the last minute, at least in theory. But disasters fuel one of the best parts of any holiday

– recounting it afterwards. After all, no one really wants to hear what a wonderful time you had.

In fact, we are left not with a catalogue of woes, nor with a credit card debt (help is available from many sources, in this case mainly a charity, but a good Local Authority will also help, relatives may chip in, or try auctioning something that you can live without) but with very rosy memories – and the photos don't betray them.

Hell on Wheels

Joan Cooper is a regular volunteer with charities which organise holidays for the disabled in Britain and abroad. Her trip to Spain in 1989 was arranged by Winged Fellowship (see Directory).

"Torremolinos for a fortnight in a group of eighteen people, with nine confined to wheelchairs. Sounds like hell on wheels, and this is your Easter holiday from teaching. You must be mad."

With these cheering words from a colleague ringing in my ears, I arrived at Gatwick two hours before departure to Málaga and met, for the first time, the rest of the group. The ratio was one voluntary helper to one severely physically handicapped "guest" and the eighteen members of the group came from all over Britain. Everyone makes their own way to the airport, although a list of names and addresses is sent out in advance, in case it is possible for people to double up on transport.

My experience of group travel from Gatwick is good, with priority loading onto the aircraft and paramedical help to carry the disabled passengers to their seats. However, foreign airports vary enormously in size and facilities: passengers at Málaga disembark down a flight of steps and those who are disabled must be carried down to the tarmac by companions and reluctant Spanish paramedics.

On the plane the helpers sit intermingled with guests to assist with meals, drinks and trips to the loo; by now polite conversation is over and the ice well and truly broken. The disabled travellers are always last off the plane – just as well for their fellow passengers. Once the wheelchairs are waiting on the tarmac (they travel in the hold) the helpers have their work cut out identifying which wheelchair, cushions and footrests belong to each guest, but they learn quickly! The *Winged Fellowship* driver is waiting with a specially adapted luxury Mercedes coach to take us to our hotel.

The *Don Pedro* has lifts and ramps, accessible public rooms and a buffet-style dining room. Three steps to the swimming pool and sunbathing terrace aren't a problem for a group. The staff are accustomed to looking after wheelchair users, those travelling in family groups as well as in groups like ours, and they are amenable even when they find that a bathroom door has been lifted off its hinges.

Torremolinos is a large, commercial resort, frequented by most European nationalities. It is busy – something like Blackpool – so a quiet and restful holiday isn't really on! However, there are hotels at all ratings and all the amenities of any large holiday centre, including numerous "free" discos, with drinks at exorbitant prices. There is plenty to do but help is needed for the disabled visitor. Attractions include Tivoli World (an amusement park), where disabled people are welcomed on rides but the place is set on the side of a hill. The Aquapark, with open-air jacuzzi, is popular and good fun, a welcome relief for bodies aching after too many rides on cobblestones.

Torremolinos makes an ideal base from which to tour the Costa del Sol. And talk about tour – you name it, we saw it, visited it, ate it, drank it and had a go on or at it! For two weeks our party covered more of Andalucía than the average single traveller or package deal family would ever see. With good transport, an experienced driver and plenty of help, everyone had their money's worth.

"There are plenty of experienced people to carry wheelchairs in situations where one helper would have no chance"

There are obvious drawbacks to group travel but it does have its advantages. As the holiday is booked and organised by an experienced charity, paying great attention to wheelchair access, much of the worry of quizzing travel agents (often inexperienced in handling disabled clients) is removed. Insurance is arranged and an itinerary drawn up – all you need to do is supply medical details, pay up (help is often available for those on very low incomes) and turn up with luggage, money and passport. There are plenty of experienced people to carry wheelchairs in situations where one helper would have no chance.

On *Winged Fellowship* holidays abroad, helper and guest share a hotel room and private bathroom. The helper provides any personal care needed, as well as assistance with meals. While the matching up of guests and helpers can be a bit of a hit-and-miss affair, it is surprising how often it works out well. People seldom change "partners" during the holiday, although this is possible if there are difficulties on either side, whether in care given or as a result of personality clashes. The cour-

ier assigns roommates, using medical notes, any available knowledge of personalities and a lot of "gut feeling".

Apart from sharing accommodation, roommates do not have to stick together as a couple. The best fun is had if guests choose a different helper every day; this means a change of conversation and viewpoint and the arrangement is less demanding for any one helper. Undoubtedly this sort of holiday is physically hard work and can be mentally and emotionally demanding – just when you feel like a rest, it's time to be up and off again. And there are not only your own postcards to write and suitcases to pack, there are your roommate's too!

Ideally, the group is located in a block of rooms, rather than scattered throughout the hotel, so that helpers can move easily between rooms to help with lifting. One of the volunteers is a registered nurse, providing daily medical care – a luxury denied to the individual traveller.

It is made clear in the literature that as it is a group holiday, everyone is expected to fit in with the planned activities and general wishes of the group, which some might find off-putting. However, it is possible to opt out of a particular activity if desired, and something which you wouldn't normally choose may turn out to be an enjoyable experience. In Torremolinos, 79-year-old Bob revelled in his first ever nightclub and revisited it twice!

One of the best parts of the Costa del Sol, probably never seen by many of its tourists, is reached by spectacular drives, leaving behind the busy coastal road and climbing high above the crowded beaches to the mountain villages. Casares is one much-photographed example, its whitewashed houses with orange-tiled roofs built haphazardly on the rocks. The narrow streets are hard to negotiate in a vehicle and wheelchair pushing is impossible, but the views from the restaurant terraces are well worth the effort of carrying nine wheelchairs and their occupants in the baking heat of the midday sun. We enjoyed the welcome breeze as we lingered for two or three hours over our lunch, in true continental style, eating delicious ice cream desserts to build up our strength for carrying the wheelchairs back down to the bus. I have to admit to creeping off on my own for ten minutes for a quick look at the village. Two old men sat weighing whitebait in a balance scale and a woman was making lace – if I'd seen it on a travel programme I'd have dismissed it as a put-up job!

Another mountain village worth a visit is Mijas, usually combined with a wander around Fuengirola market, which is a large weekly affair, very crowded and hot. Pushing a wheelchair in a busy market has its advantages – you can "ankle bash" a few folk to reach the front of a stall – but handbags slung on the backs of wheelchairs provide easy pickings for thieves. Not that we gave anyone a chance to steal our money – what better place to keep it safe than under your bottom!

Probably the best and most hilarious way to see the winding streets of Mijas is by donkey-taxi. This is a typical tourist trap and quite expensive, but good fun and just another obstacle course for the helpers. The buggy has a canopy overhead and seating for two adults, and the owner walks alongside, leading the donkey. Try manoeuvring stiff legs between the shafts of the cart and the donkey's backside! I spent the tour of Mijas keeping Margaret's legs out of the way of the donkey's. But Margaret enjoyed the adventure – it's not something she does every day. I did panic a bit when the donkey slipped on a steep hill but the owner didn't bat an eyelid. He was probably sleepwalking – it was siesta time.

There is a magnificent vantage point over the Mediterranean at Mijas. A ramp is thoughtfully provided next to the steps, but be warned that it's slippery; we worked as a team and took the wheelchairs up the steps.

"Even the most enthusiastic helper would find the going tough with the temperature touching 100°F"

Another fascinating day was spent in Ronda, one of the most ancient cities in Spain, where Celts, Phoenicians, Romans and Arabs have left their mark. They obviously didn't plan for wheelchairs – the cobblestones proved a challenge for the helpers, while guests tried to "grin and bear it". The usual way to tackle cobblestones is to tilt the chair onto its back wheels but even the most enthusiastic helper would find the going tough with the temperature touching 100°F and a passenger wearing a huge sombrero – try looking round the side of that!

A day trip to Gibraltar is possible from Torremolinos, about three hours' drive through Marbella, Puerto Banús (where the other half live, with their palatial apartments, yachts and fast cars) and Estepona. The journey is one long traffic jam, but more interesting than the M25. Crossing over the border from Spain is a culture shock – British bobbies, cars, petrol stations and red telephone boxes.

Gibraltar is busy, crowded and dirty, but fascinating. The highlight is definitely the view from the top of the rock, accessible by cable car. Wheelchairs can be loaded straight onto the cable car, which is like a lift with windows. This is fine except for the long, narrow flight of concrete steps up to the boarding stage. There is no way that anyone with only a single helper could negotiate them, and no chance of asking the public to help – it's far too difficult. Our group managed it, though it was hot work. The café, bar, shop and toilets at the viewing area are all inaccessible, reached via a staircase. Never mind, our disabled group members all agreed that the views were marvellous, and helpers get their exercise that way – fetching drinks, ice creams and souvenirs.

The main street in Gibraltar, popular for duty free purchases, is narrow with deep kerbs, but the locals are friendly and helpful. Alcohol, perfume, jewellery and electrical goods are on sale everywhere. Pushing a wheelchair with bottles hanging off the back is no joke! But we were only in training for the biggest assault course yet – Granada.

The skyline at Granada is dominated by the Alhambra, palace of the Nasrid Sultans, rulers of the last Spanish Moorish kingdom. It is defended by a series of towers and walls – and cobblestones and steps. The Alhambra is an architectural marvel: the ornate stonework and the lattice windows, the symmetry of the courtyards and the reflecting pools are magnificent, but it is hot, dry and dusty, and exploration is a real test of strength. Everyone cooled off by wetting T-shirts and hats with water from the drinking fountain; this time the usual holiday splashing and water-play was a serious business, not just a silly prank.

It *is* possible to achieve more on a group holiday and in spite of the disadvantages it is a great way to travel and meet people from a wide social range. The problems of group dynamics may develop as people relax, as personalities unwind and friendships grow. A fortnight among people who were originally strangers can be a long time, particularly as it is almost 24 hours a day intensive interaction – probably more than most of us see our loved ones! Yet there are surprisingly few problems. I don't see the helper as a self-denying citizen, a martyr to the cause of the disabled. Able-bodied and disabled on holiday together help each other to enjoy themselves; they simply make different contributions. And that's what holidays are about, isn't it?

Lessons In Communication

Julie Smethurst's first experience of holidaying abroad alone, in July 1989, was arranged by ONCE, the Spanish National Organisation of the Blind, a care foundation dedicated to improving the quality of life for all handicapped people.*

I have found that one of the greatest pleasures of travelling alone is that I almost always get into conversation with the most interesting people. From its very beginning my first solo trip abroad proved to be no exception: by the time I reached Birmingham airport I had already met a West Indian who was spending three months in England studying agriculture, and a Liverpudlian whose sister lives within a stone's throw of my parents back in Yorkshire. These encounters, plus a straightforward journey from Sheffield to the airport, augured well, and my spirits were high as we soared through the sunshine, bound for Barcelona.

There I was met by Esther, one of the ten "hostesses" whose job it would be for the next ten days to help the visually handicapped members of our holiday party in any situation where sighted assistance was necessary. I was next introduced to Juan Jesus Torres, like

---

*Julie has also written about her travels with sighted companions in the Greek Islands (on p.57), and the two pieces make an interesting contrast.

myself totally blind, and the organiser of the whole holiday project. As we drove down the coast to Segur de Calafell, I tried to convey to Juan and Esther how excited I was about the trip and how happy I felt about this my second visit to Spain. Luckily their English was far superior to my Spanish, so they were able to come to my rescue when vital but unfamiliar words eluded me.

"I encountered no other English people until I returned to Barcelona airport"

Although this holiday, about which I was waxing so enthusiastic, was primarily geared to the needs of visually handicapped people, a number of fully sighted friends and relatives were also present. The party was international, with visitors coming from as far away as Japan and Norway. I was somewhat daunted to discover that I was the only English participant; indeed, I encountered no other English people until I returned to Barcelona airport on my homeward journey.

Juan's perfect understanding of what might present difficulties for a blind person meant that practical concerns had been well thought out in advance, thus minimising our anxiety about them. He had chosen a small hotel whose layout was easy to assimilate, and the first activity on my arrival was a conducted tour with Esther. This included not only learning the way round the interior of the hotel, but also such minute yet important details as the location of light switches, lift buttons and those eminently breakable tooth-glasses, which often balance precariously on the end of a glass shelf and are the bane of my life when exploring a hotel room without sighted help.

Even at this early stage I was greatly impressed by the hostesses' attitude: whilst offering us the most thorough and constructive help they never for a moment patronised or underestimated

our capabilities. They and the hotel staff demonstrated clearly what I am coming to regard as the "Mediterranean" approach to visually handicapped visitors: very helpful, very thoughtful, but absolutely matter-of-fact. As with many other aspects of life, the Spaniards seem to treat blindness in a much more relaxed, laid-back manner than do the English. This produces – in me, at any rate – a reciprocal feeling, so that I am more at ease and less inhibited than when among strangers at home.

Naturally enough, Juan had not underestimated our collective independence either, and the programme was structured so as to give us the maximum amount of freedom – including freedom from anxiety. The main responsibility for achieving this marvellously Utopian aim fell to the hostesses, who worked very hard as guides, interpreters and troubleshooters. They were always there and on the lookout in case they were needed, yet they also managed to integrate and become our friends too. It would have been so easy for them to band together, and for an "us and them" situation to develop – the carers and the cared-for. But their warm and spontaneous manner, and the fact that they seemed to be enjoying themselves and having just as good a time as we were having, set us all at our ease.

Notwithstanding all this, I don't think my first night in Segur was exactly what the organisers had intended. After a dinner over which I made the acquaintance of Wolfgang, Lydia and Meike from Germany, we were all asked to introduce ourselves to the party in our own language. In the ensuing hubbub of conversation two of the hostesses approached me: there was a problem, they said; would I mind changing rooms for one night only? Inwardly a little reluctant – I'd just got nicely unpacked – I nevertheless complied, and with their help moved my things across the landing to a room already occupied by

Nabuko (from Japan) and Meike. I then retired to the bar.

It was quite late when I returned to find my two roommates asleep. The room was stiflingly hot, and examination of the window revealed that the outside metal shutter had been lowered to within six inches of the floor. I didn't fancy trying to raise it – the noise would probably disturb the others and anyway I wasn't sure how the thing worked. I lay in my folding bed, trying not to toss, for with every movement it let out groans and squeaks of protest. Finally, in desperation, I took to the floor and spent the remainder of the night there. It was cool to the touch and made no noise, however much I wriggled and fidgeted. I placed my pillow as close to the few inches of fresh air as possible, and slept intermittently. Not quite what the hotel management had in mind for its guests, I fancy, but I've slept in and through much worse conditions, and it was a good ice-breaking story to tell at breakfast!

It was at mealtimes that the international dimension of the holiday really asserted itself. In the early days the hostesses did their best to find us tablemates who had at least one language in common. But as time went by and we all knew each other better they linked us up with friends. For example, it became known that I wanted to improve my Spanish, and increasingly I found myself sharing a table with some of the Spanish visitors. One particular lunchtime stands out in my memory as a perfect example of the meeting of nations: besides myself at our table there was my roommate Ana Maria (Argentinian but now living in Sweden), Nathalie (French) and Elisa (Italian). Under such circumstances it was hard to know which language to adopt and we found ourselves conversing in a curious fragmentary mixture!

Holidaymaking began in earnest on the first morning, with most of us eager to go to the beach. Relays of hostesses made it possible for us to come and go more or less as and when we wanted to, and a large area of beach had been cordoned off for our exclusive use. I took a long swim in the delightfully warm sea and discovered that a rope extended far out into it, acting literally as a "landmark" when we wanted to relocate our party. Then, with the help of one of our attentive hostesses, I found my things and settled to the pleasurable business of drying off in the sunshine.

It was at this point that I met Pilar and Tere, and immediately embarked on what became my daily impromptu Spanish lesson. From then on Pilar always sought me out after the morning swim and we ensconced ourselves in the shade to study idioms and for me to copy down quantities of irregular verbs. I'd tell her in English what I wanted to say and we'd then translate into Spanish. Sometimes, however, our conversations became so involved and interesting that we hadn't the patience to wait while I laboriously attempted the translation; on these occasions we simply relied on Pilar's excellent command of English.

"Where music is concerned language barriers cease to be important"

Juan had made every effort to overcome the problems presented by language barriers. All the hostesses spoke at least one language in addition to Spanish, and several spoke two or three. During a quite formal discussion about employment they actually worked as interpreters, while we listened in on the Simultaneous Translation Facility provided by the *ONCE* Educational Resource Centre. Many of the participants themselves spoke more than one language and it is surprising how many tactile signals can be devised. We found that for some – the Japanese, for example – who were using a second language (English) as their main communication medium, English spoken with a non-English accent could be quite difficult to understand. I was amused and somewhat intrigued to find myself translating for them from quite complex English spoken with, say, a Spanish accent, to quite simple English spoken with an English one.

Where music is concerned, however, language barriers cease to be important. There were several excellent singers, guitarists and pianists among the participants and many an evening ended with a group on the terrace – or once on the beach – making music into the small hours. On other evenings there was live music for dancing; one particular musical highlight was the visit of a well-known student group, who played and sang for us during dinner and then stayed on to share a few more beers with us while we all continued the singing late into the night.

One of the most delightful evening events was the so-called "Dinner on the Beach", which took place behind the Nautical Club on a large terrace overlooking the sea. We feasted on fresh sardines barbecued over the fire, fresh mussels, huge hunks of bread, potato salad and as much *sangría* as we wanted. This was followed by enormous slices of watermelon and a typical Catalan drink called *ron cremat* – a sort of rum punch *flambé*. A Catalan folk group played and sang for us during the meal then afterwards for dancing and, as we were leaving, the Nautical Club presented each of us with a *poron* of Muscatelle wine.

Juan had tried hard to include some "new experiences" in the programme and one of these was the opportunity for us to learn flamenco dancing. The venue was a club at Villanova – about fifteen minutes' drive from Segur – and after some champagne, dry sherry (billed as "typical Andalucian wine") and splendid entertainment, the professionals and hostesses took us in hand and did their best to teach us the rudiments of the dance. I can now say that I

have rarely tackled anything so energetic or exhausting as ten minutes of flamenco!

Segur de Calafell is a typical Spanish "summer village", where Spaniards go to spend their holidays and where the wealthier ones keep summer houses. The town of Calafell itself lies some miles inland, and one evening Ana Maria and I, together with Esther and some other Spanish friends, made an abortive attempt to visit the Roman remains there. After a lengthy wait for the bus, we gave up and went for a walk in the smart area of Segur, with its imposing houses, large gardens and parkland. As an inveterate seeker after authenticity, I was particularly thrilled by the experience which followed.

"It is amazing how close a bond of friendship can be forged in ten short days"

On our walk we met Marie-Carmen – one of our party – and her friend Jaime, both exercising their guide dogs. The upshot was an invitation for us all to go to Jaime's summer house for drinks. Via Esther I explained what a special pleasure it was for an English person to visit a Spanish home. After that, Jaime's wife gave me a thorough conducted tour of this palatial establishment: I explored every room, I examined all the fruit ripening in the garden, and I inspected the football and basketball areas, where the children of this large family were playing noisily.

All too soon the final-night party was upon us. I was one of the last to leave Segur, which was nice because it meant I could enjoy the pleasures (and share the sorrows) of this last social get-together without having to worry about my packing or the catching of an early-morning flight. Many addresses, gifts and promises to keep in touch were exchanged; many warm farewells were said, and not a few tears shed. It is amazing how close a bond of friendship can be forged in ten short days. As the various parties left, the hotel became quiet. Meals took on a calm gentility distinctly absent from our riotous lunches and dinners. It was as if all concerned were drawing a deep breath after the onslaught of a whirlwind.

Reflecting on a holiday which offered me many new sensations, I have now discovered another advantage of solo travel: when one is alone among a group of strangers one *has* to make the effort to form new friendships, thus extending one's circle in new and potentially interesting directions. There is nothing better than sharing a holiday's rich harvest of experience with a trusted and like-minded friend, but sharing experiences with a whole new set of friends is just as exciting and rewarding. It is important that disabled people, like non-disabled people, should have the choice of travelling and holidaying independently if that is what they wish to do. Juan and *ONCE* have taken a major step towards making this possible for visually handicapped people, and I very much hope that others will follow their lead and provide further such opportunities. If there was one Spanish word which we all learned and remembered during our holiday, it was *Vamos!* (Let's go!) – need I say more?

The Au Pair Network

In 1970, at the age of 37, Jean Dyke was told she had multiple sclerosis (MS). Over the next ten years her mobility became progressively restricted and she is now confined to a motorised wheelchair which she operates with her chin. In 1988 Jean and her husband Stanley travelled in an adapted Volkswagen camper van to the Navarra region of northern Spain.

Over the years we've had a number of au pair girls from many different countries helping in our house; although I'm able to move around the house in my wheelchair, I rely on others for almost everything else. Since there is such close contact between the girls and myself, most have become part of the family and many keep in regular contact with us. When Stanley retired we accepted invitations to stay with two of our recent au pairs, Isabel and Fernanda, in Spain.

We discovered that campers and motor homes could be purchased free of VAT by disabled people; servicing and extra fitments are also exempt. After a few months we decided on a Volkswagen and had the vehicle fitted with a permanent ramp for the wheelchair and clamps inside to secure the chair when we were mobile. A number of other features made the van ideal: a swivel passenger seat, central heating and a portable toilet. This last was to prove invaluable during the drive through France – although all the campsites we stayed on were well maintained, they rarely had special facilities for wheelchairs.

So that our visit coincided with the annual festivals, we planned our trip for August–September and took the less busy ferry route from Poole to Cherbourg – the channel ports are often congested in the height of the summer.

After an unhurried journey through France and across the magnificent Pyrenees, we descended into Pamplona, the capital of the Basque territory of Navarra.

The city has retained much of its original charm, so that it has the feel of a much smaller place. Many of the old streets are very narrow, with most of the older buildings formed around attractive courtyards. The skyline is also relatively uninterrupted, unlike many other Spanish cities.

"The phrase Invito yo, roughly translated as "I'll get it", invariably beats you to the bar"

There are many churches, the typical bullring and a beautiful Gothic cathedral to admire, as well as one of Hemingway's old haunts – *Marceliano*. The bar is full of character, a "spit and sawdust" place in one of the oldest parts of the city centre. It was a bit of a struggle with the wheelchair, because of cobblestones and uneven steps, but with Stanley's expert handling and manoeuvring we managed.

Just outside of Pamplona there are some excellent sights, in particular the spectacularly set Monasterio de San Salvador de Leyre, which overlooks the artificial lake, Embalse de Yesa. A few kilometres south is the castle of Javier, birthplace of saint Francisco Xavier. It is of the fairy-tale kind and intact, but steps have to be tackled!

The real charm of Pamplona, however, is supplied by the people, who display admirable patience towards "interested" foreigners, not to mention great generosity. The phrase *Invito yo*, roughly translated as "I'll get it", invariably beats you to the bar. It is unusual to find so many people proud to offer better than professional explanations of their traditions, culture, sights and cuisine.

Isabel's parents gave us their wooden summerhouse for the duration of our stay. This was ideal as it was close to the city centre but secluded and with a small attractive garden. From here Stanley could easily take me in the wheelchair to all the sights of the town, as well as to our evening entertainments with our hosts and other friends. The climate was perfect at that

time of year – constant sunshine but not insufferably hot because of the altitude.

After a week in Pamplona we travelled on to the sleepy village of Cortes, which is set in a beautiful valley just beyond Tudela, halfway between Pamplona and Zaragoza. The cluster of picturesque white houses with terracotta tiling lies dormant for most of the year, but comes to life when the September festival begins.

We were put up by Fernanda's family, who had taken great trouble to convert one of their ground-floor rooms into a bedroom for Stanley and myself. There was also a ground-floor toilet, which made life much easier. We were the only foreigners in the village and in such a small place news travels fast; soon everyone knew who we were and where we were from.

The *fiesta*, a tribute to the village *patrón* (patron saint), is the perfect excuse for the villagers to enjoy themselves. The men gather in the bars before entering into one of the major events – the "bull-run". This is not a bloodcurdling affair but a display of male bravado, with men running in front of the young bulls and darting aside at the last minute. The spectators cheer from safe vantage points and the balcony of the town hall is reserved for those with some form of disability. I watched some of the day's events from here while Stanley dressed in red and joined the men diving from one bar to the next. In the evening there was a free party, with a simple and delicious meal of beef stew (*not* the bulls that appeared earlier!), bread, beer and soft drinks, finishing off with a firework display in one of the village squares.

Leaving Fernanda, family and friends behind, we moved further into the hills to the spa resort of Fitero, which lies along the Pamplona–Soria road. The thermal baths (Baños de Fitero) are well known throughout northern Spain and are particularly popular with

Basques from the industrial towns of San Sebastián and Bilbao. The resort is 3.5km from the village of Fitero and is state-run, consisting of two hotels, the *Spa Hotel Bequer* and the *Spa Hotel Palafox*. We were now in for a period of inexpensive luxury, staying in a double room with en suite facilities (even the loos are flushed with thermal water!) and all meals included in the price (£23), dinner being a six-course affair inclusive of wine. There are lifts to all levels in both hotels.

Fitero advertises itself as a centre for thermal treatment for the relief of rheumatism, arthritis and circulatory, nervous, digestive, urinary and respiratory system disorders. The resort doctor prescribes the temperature and length of immersion in the waters.

Our consultation with the doctor was an interesting experience since he spoke no English and our Spanish is minimal. We muddled along with the help of the receptionist who was the only person in the hotel to speak a little English.

Stanley took me to the baths and two assistants lifted me from the wheel-chair to the large walk-in bath where I soaked for nearly an hour. As well as being a pleasurable activity, the thermal bath is particularly helpful to MS sufferers because it encourages some degree of muscle relaxation. (For severe MS sufferers like myself, limbs are "locked" because of muscle taut-ness, so the warmth and buoyancy of a hot bath assist in limb movement.)

We spent four days in the resort; there is a range of activities to enjoy, including swimming in the heated outdoor pools and playing tennis. The village of Fitero provides an ideal base for exploring the hills of Sierra de Alcarama to the west and the mountains of Sierra del Moncayo to the south.

Our first trip in the camper was a great success, enabling us to see some out-of-the-way parts of Spain and to visit good friends. But that was just the beginning: it was southern Austria in 1989 and Portugal in 1990 – our European au pair network continues to serve us well!

SPAIN: TRAVEL NOTES

Sources of information

Spanish National Tourist Office (*SNTO*), 57/58 St James's Street, London SW1A 1LD; ☎071/499 0901. Produces excellent pamphlets (including good maps) on the all the major Spanish towns and a fact sheet for disabled tourists which lists useful addresses and some accessible accommodation.

Organización Nacional de Ciegos de España (*ONCE*), Calle de Prada 24, Madrid; ☎1/4311900. Julie Smethurst's trip was through the Delegación Territorial de Cataluña, Calabria 66–76, Barcelona 08015. Write to them for details.

Winged Fellowship Trust, Angel House, Pentonville Road, London N1 9XD; ☎071/833 2594. Write for details of their holiday programme, or for a Volunteer Application Form.

Getting there

Iberia Airlines of Spain are not recommended. Find an airline that does not make a fuss about wheelchairs (see *Practicalities*). The major Spanish **airports** are reasonably accessible, and in recent years facilities have been adapted for wheelchair users. The *Holiday Care Service* has a fact sheet on access at Spanish airports.

SPAIN: TRAVEL NOTES

The 24-hour **ferry** crossing from Plymouth to Santander with *Brittany Ferries* (The Brittany Centre, Wharf Road, Portsmouth PO2 8RU; ☎0752/221321) aboard the *Bretagne*, is a relaxing way to start a motoring holiday, and there are facilities on board for disabled passengers (p.5).

Transport

Facilities on trains are not ideal, but wheelchairs are available at major Spanish stations, and even wheelchair space in some carriages. Overall, though, there is no long-term policy to make the service fully accessible to passengers with any type of disability.

It is possible to **hire cars** with hand controls, from *Hertz* in Madrid and Barcelona. Remember that road surfaces in rural areas are rough, and the coastal roads in high season dangerous. Toilet facilities for disabled motorists are a rare sight.

Buses are generally difficult for those with mobility problems, but taxi drivers are usually helpful and the odd day excursion or short ride to the airport won't break the bank.

Accommodation

Although hotel owners are waking up to the idea of providing for disabled guests, the choice of well-known, fully accessible accommodation in Spain is fairly limited and tends to be in the busiest areas. The *Holiday Care Service* has inspected hotels in the popular resorts; ask for their fact sheet. The *RADAR* holiday guide offers more ideas.

The situation off the beaten track – whether in hotels, pensions, rented villas or *paradores* – is far from hopeless, and accommodation can often be rendered suitable with some minor modifications. This is on the whole more satisfactory than staying in a hotel in the "concrete jungle" which purports to be accessible but is blighted by lifts that don't work and noise that makes sleep impossible.

A list and map of Spanish ***paradores***, many of which are converted from castles, palaces and monasteries, is available from the *SNTO*. Although not converted with the disabled guest in mind, these properties tend to be on a grand scale, with plenty of room to manoeuvre a wheelchair inside. *Paradores* are not cheap, but there are special rates for a minimum of two nights out of season. Malby Goodman, a regular visitor to Spain, recommends a *parador* a few miles southeast of Teruel, in southern Aragón, for motorists: *Euro-Ruta Restaurante y Hostal* (La Puebla de Valverde, 44450 Teruel; ☎74/670136); the bar, restaurant and bedrooms are all on the ground floor.

There are numerous **spa resorts** in Spain. Jean and Stanley Dyke stayed at *Baños de Fitero* (31594 Fitero, Navarra, Spain; ☎48/776100, 776275). Opening dates are, for *Hotel Becquer*, June 15 to October 14, and for *Hotel Palafox*, July 1 to September 30.

Maxine Smith recommends the *Hotel Poseidon* in Benidorm (☎6/5852355) for good accessibility.

Access and facilities

Ramps are not unheard of in these parts, but exploration of many tourist attractions involves considerable muscle power – Joan Cooper describes a visit to the Alhambra at Granada as a "test of strength" (p.10) – and a number of sights are simply inaccessible without a team of helpers.

Public transport is not wheelchair friendly and roads are not particularly well maintained. Uneven pavements, cobblestones and steps make walking/wheeling heavy going, particularly in the high-season heat of southern and inland Spain.

That said, Spain, the Balearics and the Canary Islands are all popular destinations amongst our contributors – there must be some compensations, perhaps the *tapas* or *sangría*, the beauty of the Moorish architecture (which can be admired in spite of sometimes tricky access), the scenery, the charms of the people. Active and forceful groups of disabled people, especially *ONCE*, offer hope for improvement. Perhaps the staging of the 1992 Paralympic Games in Barcelona will provide added impetus. As well as opening up more of the tourist attractions and widening the choice of accessible accommodation and transport, more guides for disabled visitors and more printed information would be a great help.

The Balearics

Feeling Square in Mallorca

For someone with renal failure secondary to diabetes the real problem in travelling is not mobility but the availability of dialysis. The British Kidney Patient Association (BKPA) runs a dialysis centre in Cala Mayor, Mallorca, and Judy Page made this her base for her first venture abroad as a person on haemodialysis.

Mallorca would not have been my natural choice for a holiday, partly because I'd already been there and I like to explore new territory, but also because I favour uncrowded, uncommercialised areas. Cala Mayor, described in the brochures as a lively spot for funseekers, with a nightclub on every corner, would suit the type of person who likes Englishness abroad. It ranked pretty near the bottom of my choice of resorts, but it was where the *BKPA* dialysis centre was situated and at least it promised to satiate my desire for hot sun and warm sea.

The island does have its unspoilt areas and if I were to return I'd make my base in San Augustin (within walking distance of Cala Mayor) or perhaps Illetas, or even further away if I was travelling with a driver. The ideal way to explore the island is by car on the very good roads but there are also alternative, quieter resorts on the bus route. It is worth checking thoroughly what kind of resort you are committing yourself to before booking.

For such a small island – it is the largest of the Balearics but measures only 502 square kilometres, with a population of 363,000 – Mallorca has a surprisingly colourful history. It has centre-staged in several disputes, being conquered in turn by the Phoenicians, Romans, Vandals and Moors before falling to the Spanish Aragons in 1229. They created the Balearics as a territory in their own right but resumed sovereignty in 1349, only to cede the islands to the British in 1713. However, they were restored to the Spanish monarchy in 1802 and the royal family maintain a holiday home there to this day. There is a degree of animosity in some parts between Mallorcans and Spanish, which is noticeable on the altered road signs: the Mallorcans have a language of their own which differs from Spanish and causes a clash over spellings – hence the red paintbrush corrections.

Although the traditional industries are farming (fruit and vines), fishing and quarrying, tourism has largely taken over. The island caters for all tastes, with the natural beauty of its coastline and mountains, the historic buildings, museums, crafts and untouched villages, in addition to the purpose-built tourist attractions – Marineland, El Dorado (a Western town, Hollywood-style), Aquapark and Aquacity (giant water complexes) and endless nightclubs, including *BM's* at Magaluf, reputedly the biggest in the world. The area around Palma is rather built-up and commercial but it's easy to find places where life plods on as it did a hundred years ago and locals regard you with a complacent curiosity that says "Well, the wind didn't blow anything very exciting our way today, then".

Lorraine and I arrived in Cala Mayor in the close heat of August. It was about 2am and appeared to be rush hour. Between dawn and midday, I later discovered, all was quiet – people slept late in Mallorca. Unlike some of our keen fellow travellers, who instantly hit the local nightspots, Lorraine and I went tamely to bed.

At the Welcome Party the next morning (a small gathering of young women) we could not have felt more square had we been wearing twin-sets and pearls and doing our knitting. What was with these people, complaining that Cala Mayor was dead by daybreak? Hadn't they heard of sleep? We exchanged nervous glances and sipped our "champagne" dubiously, wondering whether our loud shorts and tops would disguise the secret of our inward fuddy-duddiness. Sleep was going to feature on our itinerary, and not in precious sunshine hours.

We had chosen self-catering accommodation because hotel food and mealtimes don't suit me and I wanted a fridge for drugs and drinks. What we unwittingly selected was an apartment in the local high-rise hooligan blocks – a pair of characterless towers largely occupied by the deservedly notorious

Club 18–30. One fondly imagines tales of such folk to be greatly exaggerated. They are not. To be fair, they seemed generally good-natured, if somewhat antisocial and definitely not my scene, and there would be a lull around six or seven in the morning when an uneasy peace descended during the Hooligan Recuperation Period.

"I probably appeared quite ordinary next to the hordes of permanently tipsy holidaymakers"

We encountered a universal friendliness amongst our fellow British, an eagerness to chat and relate experiences. With regard to my "disability" we met only enthusiastic support, but I should point out that I am fully mobile and the only visible sign of not being totally "normal" is the scarring on my arm from the access graft. However, I also have peculiarly limited sight (as a result of diabetic retinopathy) and I found the number of steps around Cala Mayor slightly alarming. It's not ideal for wheelchairs, although some people were coping admirably in them. As I made my precarious way around I probably appeared quite ordinary next to the hordes of permanently tipsy holidaymakers. The beach at least was quite hazard-free and there I was in my element. There were times, moreover, when my inability to alter my focus quickly was an advantage – while my fellow passengers clung nervously to their seats during some of the more hair-raising mountain car journeys, I was quite unperturbed, gazing at the distant crags.

The bus service from Palma and Cala Mayor proved both efficient and economical, enabling us to sightsee at far less extortionate prices than the organised tours. The drivers are used to linguistic incompetents and have a level of patience and a mastery of English that would win over the most cynical or cautious traveller. The buses are spacious enough to take wheelchairs on board but a strong helper is required to lift it up the steps.

Palma, the bustling capital which nestles around a busy harbour, was one place we visited by bus. The rain could not disguise totally the appeal of this city, with its mixture of modern apartment blocks, tall grandiose buildings, elegant marble-floored squares and fountains, and the intriguing warren of dark, narrow backstreets where the filthy, tightly shuttered houses almost meet overhead.

We accidentally toured the old palace – built by the Moors, once the official royal residence and now a military headquarters – because, like most of the British in the queue, we thought we were lining up for the cathedral. At the top of the steps from the harbour path the cathedral is on the right, the palace on the left. The simple, austere palace, though sparsely furnished, will give a fair insight into the island's history.

Having located the correct queue, we made our last destination in Palma the cathedral. For many people this is the highlight of Mallorca. I found the magnificent and very ornate monument somewhat dark but Lorraine assured me that it was quite special! Even I could appreciate the stunning stained-glass windows and the cool tranquillity of the hushed atmosphere. A word of warning: like so many of the sights, the cathedral is closed from midday to 4pm; during this period there is little to do but eat and sleep, so you might as well resign yourself and adapt your lifestyle accordingly.

Although the Caves of Drach are highly publicised and said to be very beautiful, we were recommended those at Genoa, only 3km up the road from Cala Mayor. We set off, only to encounter the usual problem of prolonged siesta closing. We wandered around the village and sat in a café but the caves proved well worth the wait. The tour group was small and informal and conducted in a charmingly amateurish way. The caves were amazing, a hidden treasure trove lurking behind a shabby door and a sign on the wall marked *CUEVAS*. Genoa also had some genuine Mallorcan restaurants within a reasonable taxi fare of the resort and this made a pleasant change from the fast-food atmosphere of Cala Mayor.

"I sat too close to an obnoxious little boy who would rather have gone to Butlins"

There are various boat trips available, offering the two basic alternatives of viewing the coast (a bit monotonous but relaxing) or getting drunk (I hate being seasick and have a 500ml a day fluid restriction, even if Spanish wine were allowable; dry white wine and certain spirits are permitted in moderation but most alcohol is too high in potassium for someone on a renal diet). We went on a cruise to a "genuine fishing village": I spotted no fishing boats at all and sat too close to an obnoxious little boy who would rather have gone to Butlins. By the end of the three-hour cruise I wished he *had* gone to Butlins. What I enjoyed most was the hunk of Mallorcan cake that comes in a flat hexagonal box and tastes like a cross between a croissant and a Danish pastry.

Most of the postcards sold in our hotel would have deterred all but the strangest type from visiting Mallorca, but there was one exception – an inspirational view of a place called Torrente de Pareis. Lorraine and I spent some time locating it on the map and pondering how to get there. It happened to be the destination chosen by two affable Welshmen with a car, who offered to take us us out for a day. The drive through the barren beauty of the island's mountains took some time but we were rewarded as we dropped into the valley above the dazzling coves of Torrente de Pareis. The cliffs fell steeply into the turbulent blue sea and to reach the secluded pebble beach we had to grope through a narrow, dimly lit cave. I was content to relax to the hypnotic sound of the sea while my companions battled with the waves.

Two factors contributed greatly to my enjoyment of this holiday: the first was the dialysis centre, with its excellent staff. The Charge Nurse was very proficient and managed to create an atmosphere such that I felt like a person, not a patient. It is hard to express the significance of that and how much I gained from stress-free dialysis, thanks to his attitude and approach. The dialysis room itself helped too – overlooking the sea, light and airy, with up-to-date facilities, pictures on the wall and pleasant furniture. It's not surprising that some people come back year after year.

The other highlight was my lilo! I was content to drift for hours. The lilo was my escape from people – out there on the scarcely undulating water I could retreat into a world of undisturbed daydreams. These times of relaxation alone would have justified the holiday in terms of the psychological benefits, but to find in addition that Mallorca is a fascinating and enchanting island was an unexpected bonus.

Grounded in Menorca

Rosalind May is 66, with considerable weakness in right arm and leg caused by polio; steps are very difficult, walking is unsteady. She booked a holiday in Menorca through Horizon Holidays and found them not geared up to dealing with disabled clients, although they advertise that they are.

Drystone walls surrounding small green fields, black and white cows grazing long tough grass, meadow flowers of mauve and pink – it could be England, except that the modest roads are almost bereft of cars. This is Menorca in May, before the island is scorched by summer heat.

I studied the *Horizon* brochure closely, trying to work out from the photographs which apartment satisfied all my requirements: flat terrain, easy access to beach or pool, lifts to all floors, restaurant or shop in the apartment buildings. My friend, Dora, was not worried about any of these but insisted on separate bedrooms. Hotels were out, then – we could find no single accommodation in the entire Mediterranean region.

The *Lord Nelson* apartments at Santo Tomás on the south side of the island seemed to meet most of my needs. Our apartment had balcony, bedroom, living room, fully equipped kitchen and bathroom and the brochure said it would sleep four. Since we were only two, we each had to pay a supplement.

I quizzed my local travel agent about the site of the apartment: were there steps up to the front entrance? Did the lifts work? Was the route to the beach flat? All such queries were met with astonishment. The attitude was that if I couldn't manage steps I shouldn't be going abroad. I pointed out that the *Horizon* brochure carries a note at the end to the effect that handicapped clients could be catered for, and that there was space on the booking form in which to state any special needs. The travel agent seemed puzzled but wrote down my requirements and assured me that transport would be provided from the airport to Santo Tomás and all luggage would be handled for me and safely delivered to my apartment. I rang the *Horizon* head office in the hope of checking the facilities in greater detail. I was passed from one office to another, discovered nothing, and finally gave up because my phone bill was mounting.

I was able to leave my car for ten days at the Gatwick Airport Services car park – cheaper than the long-stay car park. At the Airport Services office there was only one shallow step to negotiate; I registered my car while my luggage was unloaded and put on a waiting coach.

"Don't worry about your car; we'll park it. Do you need help up the steps?"

I needed a shove from behind. There were only five other passengers on the coach. "Wait until the others have got off," said the driver. "I'll see you're all right." Once outside the departures building, he lifted me down from the coach and parked me on a seat with my luggage at my feet. Then he phoned for an airport official and five minutes later a buggy glided down the slope towards me.

"The paths were steep and narrow, something which had not shown up on the brochure"

After checking in, I pushed my trolley to the office for disabled passengers, meeting Dora on the way – she had travelled from the south coast by train. We were ushered to a special section of the departure lounge reserved for disabled passengers. There was a two-hour delay but when the flight was called two buggies appeared and whisked all disabled passengers down long corridors to the aircraft. I was offered a sling chair lift when we reached the steps up to the aircraft but I opted to attempt them on my own. However, they were steeper and longer than I thought: one official heaved me from behind and another held out a helping hand from above;

finally I made it to my seat, ready for the first drink of the flight.

A wheelchair was waiting at Mahón airport (this was in contrast to the return journey, when there was no wheelchair in sight and no *Horizon* rep to help). Dora piled all the hand luggage on my lap and we were first through customs. The coach ride passed through various resorts and ours was the last one. I viewed with misgiving many hotels and apartments with steep steps and no handrails, but the *Lord Nelson* apartments weren't bad – only three steps to the entrance and in lieu of handrails a large palm plant pot, which I used to haul myself up.

We had a quick meal in the apartment restaurant before unpacking and remaking the beds in separate rooms. It was colder than England, the beds were damp and with only one blanket apiece we spent an uncomfortable first night. But in the morning the sun shone and we breakfasted on the balcony overlooking the sea and the swimming pool.

Outside the apartments there was a flat grassy area surrounding the pool and, beyond this, paths winding through scrubby vegetation down to the beach. The paths were steep and narrow, something which had not shown up on the brochure photograph, but there was a pleasant café at the top with panoramic views of the coastline.

On the third day I ventured into the pool. Dora is a non-swimmer but gave moral support. The swimmers – mostly young families – looked a little surprised when I approached the pool with my stick. Getting in was no problem. The water was freezing and space to swim was limited but no holiday is complete without a swim. I persuaded the nearest man at the edge of the pool to give me a hand getting out. I was obviously not part of the Mediterranean seaside scene, but no more strange than the topless girls stretched out on towels around the pool.

We had booked one full-day excursion by coach and as we set off the guide explained Menorca's English appearance. The British occupied the island between 1713 and 1782, but it was lost briefly to the French in 1756 by Admiral Byng, who was executed by the British government for his carelessness. The island was retrieved from the French in 1763. Spain regained possession in 1782, although a new British naval base was established under Admirals Nelson and Collingwood when Napoleon became a threat in the Mediterranean.

During the British occupation, one of the governors imported some black and white cows in order to provide fresh milk for his family. There is a reservoir of water in the rock structure of the island, so the cows thrived on the long winter grass, particularly in the valleys on the south side, and agriculture flourished. Menorca is savaged by the *tramontana* (a north wind) so drystone walls were erected to prevent erosion of the topsoil. Most of the fields are barren now, since tourism left agriculture behind, and the island is dotted with windmills.

The British moved the capital from Ciudadela to Mahón. The coach took us to Port Mahón, one of the world's largest natural harbours and ideal for the eighteenth-century British navy; Nelson spent short periods here and lived in a house now known as Golden Farm. The centre of Mahón, reminiscent of a Georgian square in Bloomsbury or Dublin, was where the coach left us to shop before proceeding to the harbour. I declined the trip around the harbour because it meant a steep descent on slippery steps to a bucking boat, but Dora enjoyed the half-hour trip.

Our next stop was for lunch at a waterside restaurant in Biniancola, passing on the way the elegant Villacarlos, patronised by the rich and famous. Next we went north, skirting Monte Toro, the island's highest point, which is topped by a convent. The road

led to Fornells, a delightful town with faded Regency houses along the waterfront and a multitude of brightly coloured yachts moored in the shallow marina. The town is jealously protected by the tourist authorities, who refuse most plans for modern buildings.

"I drove off confidently but soon realised that I was on the wrong side of the road"

We hired a Ford Fiesta for three days. The hire company owner looked dubiously at my international driving licence as I struggled up the steps to his office. I drove off confidently but soon realised that I was on the wrong side of the road. The gears and handbrake were also on the wrong side; I need them on the left and was unable to book an automatic. I stuck in third gear as much as possible and asked Dora to put on the handbrake when necessary.

Our first destination was a petrol station. There are only about four on the island and we had been directed to the nearest, at Alayor. In this small town delicious ice cream and *Roque Rico*, Menorca's famous white cheese, are manufactured.

From Alayor we drove west towards Ciudadela, centre of the shoemaking industry and a town showing greater Moorish influence than British. Menorca has been occupied by many dominant Mediterranean powers, including Greeks, Romans, Vandals and Moors. On the way we were sidetracked first by the beautiful countryside, which we stopped frequently to admire, and then by an enormous Andalucian-style building at the top of a long hill. We were seduced by this Aladdin's cave and spent two hours browsing amongst all manner of things, from smutty dolls to pink stone bottles full of Menorcan gin. After tea in a vine-covered ornamental garden it was too late to go on to Ciudadela, so we returned to Santo Tomás, planning to make the trip the next day.

We never did reach Ciudadela. The next morning whilst shopping for a picnic at our local supermarket I tore my leg on a rough metal ledge. Blood poured out over the supermarket floor but a charming girl from behind the cold meat counter rushed to my aid. She bandaged my leg roughly and took me in her car to the local doctor. A trail of blood followed me to the surgery.

"No driving, no walking, no swimming," said the doctor. "You must keep your leg up."

So that was the end of my swimming and our explorations by car. We would have liked to investigate more of the bays on the southern coastline, perhaps by bus, but there is no coastal road and bus routes are limited, sticking mainly to the M1 of the island, the British-built road from Mahón to Ciudadela, and occasionally branching off to the major coastal towns. Perhaps this lack of a comprehensive road network accounts for the lack of developed resorts: Menorca is peaceful and relatively unspoilt; if you can reach them on foot, by moped or four-wheel drive car, there are beautiful and sparsely populated beaches to be enjoyed.

THE BALEARICS: TRAVEL NOTES

For main sources of information and tour operators, see the Spain *Travel Notes*, p.16. Maxine Smith recommends *Hotel Santa Lucia*, Palma Nova, Mallorca (☎71/681358). *Horizon* now have the benefit of information stored in *Factfile*, set up for the companies owned by the *Thomson* group (see "Booking", *Practicalities*), so, in theory, Rosalind May's experiences should not be repeated.

The *BKPA* **dialysis centre** in Cala Mayor has been running for seven years and is open, free to *BKPA* members, from May to October. The services of a renal specialist are available if required. The efficient running of *BKPA* (*BKPA* HQ, Bordon, Hants; ☎04203/2021) reduced Judy Page's part in the arrangements to filling out and posting two short forms and ringing the centre when she arrived.

The Canaries

December Cocktails

At the age of 39 and with multiple sclerosis (MS), Peter Stone had been using a wheelchair for three years when he first arranged a holiday in Lanzarote. He has since been back twice, and this account is compiled from tape recordings of his thoughts on the island.

Lanzarote is the most easterly of the Canary Islands and lies about 160km off the west coast of Africa. Less than 60km long and only 26km across, the island is the result of enormous volcanic eruptions from the Atlantic sea bed. The majority of the landscape is barren and in parts more akin to a moonscape. Nevertheless, the land is farmed and there are successful crops of grapes, lemons, melons and tomatoes.

Strict planning regulations mean that there are no multistorey buildings, and all housing is painted white, with the woodwork left natural or painted green or blue. Lanzarote seems to be the least commercialised of the three main Canary Islands, and it was because of this, and the fact that it offered the warmest winter temperatures in my price range, that I chose the island for a holiday.

The native tongue is Spanish, despite the distance from mainland Spain, its governing country. I found that the local people serving in the shops, banks and restaurants spoke some English but treated my attempts at basic Spanish (memorised from a crash course of cassettes from my local library) with a mixture of delight, amusement and encouragement.

Puerto del Carmen, the major resort, stretches for about three miles along a huge sandy beach and there is a great variety of shops, bars and restaurants along the roadside. (Resist the duty free shops at airports and on the plane; much better value can be found in the shops on the island.) Nightlife centres around Puerto del Carmen and ranges from a quiet drink or meal to a lively bar or disco. Not my scene anyway, the three discos are all inaccessible to wheelchair users. Another problem in this town is that the kerbs are generally very high, but I've found that there's always someone to lend a hand when an extra push is required.

For those, like me, who prefer a quieter seaside resort, there is Playa Blanca, an ex-fishing village on the southern coast of Lanzarote. There have been building developments nearby but Playa Blanca remains unspoilt. In the centre of the village there is a small sandy beach and an attractive promenade. I particularly relished sitting in the sun outside one of the two seafront bars, drinking a spectacular-looking cocktail in the middle of December!

On the coast between Playa Blanca and Puerto del Carmen is *Las Salinas* – the salt works. This is a large bay containing desalination beds, from which the island obtains its domestic water, profiting from the resulting salt. If you don't fancy desalinated water, bottled mineral water is readily available in the shops.

I visited Lanzarote for the second time in December 1988, accompanied by a female care-assistant friend. As I wanted to taste the local restaurant food and not be restricted to hotel eating times I booked seven days in a self-catering apartment in Puerto del Carmen. I asked for a ground-floor apartment and taxi transfer from the airport. Most of the taxi-drivers I've had dealings with on Lanzarote have been helpful and patient, but you may encounter the odd impatient misery. We got him! Never mind. We arrived safely at our apartment, which stood in a complex of about thirty buildings, surrounded by beautiful flowers – bougainvillaea, hibiscus and poinsettia.

"The heat from the mountain is used to cook, barbecue-style, in the large, circular restaurant"

Taxi fares and car hire are very reasonable. Since my companion had past experience of left-hand driving we chose to hire a car for three days, at a cost of about £10 per day. During our stay only one day was cloudy, and even then the temperature reached 65°F; we chose this day to drive to Fire Mountain, at Timanfaya. This is a National Park, reached by travelling inland through miles of barren volcanic terrain, interrupted occasionally by a small village or hamlet, the houses distinctive with their white paint and Moorish design.

There was much activity in the car park, caused by a long line of camels that were taking the tourists for twenty-minute rides across the hillside. Although I'm sure I'd have been given all the help I needed to mount the camel and climb into the chair on its back, there were no restraining straps and as it looked like a bumpy ride I gave this one a miss. It turned out, however, that riding a camel was one of my companion's unfulfilled ambitions, so for just under £4 she was helped on, and I watched her bounce off into the distance. I spent a very entertaining half-hour sitting in the car, watching groups of people loading onto the kneeling camels, hooting with laughter as the camel jerked to its feet and clinging on to their seats as they wobbled off.

We travelled on to Fire Mountain which, as its name implies, is a volcano, albeit dormant. The summit can be reached by road and when we showed the car-park attendant my wheelchair we were waved on to the top of the slope. The heat from the mountain is used to cook, barbecue-style, in the large, circular restaurant standing on the summit. Further demonstrations of the heat beneath us were given at regular intervals by a guide who poured water into a hole in the ground and shouted, "Ready with your cameras!" – at which point a powerful jet of steam shot into the air.

We returned via the village of Yaiza, where we stumbled on a wonderful old restaurant set amongst orange and palm trees. As with other restaurants that I've experienced on the island, the waiter was very friendly and I particularly enjoyed the feeling of not being hurried through my meal. On another occasion we went to a restaurant in Puerto del Carmen which I'd visited twice on my previous trip, in 1987, and I was greeted by the waiters like a long-lost friend, with much shoulder slapping and shaking of hands.

We spent most of our remaining days relaxing in the warm sunshine, although we did enjoy the colourful Sunday market at Teguise. The cobblestone marketplace was a little rough on wheelchair pusher and occupant but it was well worth it for the fun of haggling over prices in the busy, cosmopolitan atmosphere. On our return to England we were delayed for an hour at Lanzarote airport. The facilities were quite adequate and the disabled persons' toilets were larger, better equipped and cleaner than those at Gatwick. By the time I arrived for my third holiday, in October 1989, the airport had an adapted minibus to ferry disabled passengers between the aircraft and terminal, even though this is only a distance of a hundred yards or so.

We hired a car for a few days to explore the northern half of the island, taking the easterly coast road to the northern tip and returning by the mountainous westerly route. Our first impression of the north was that it is greener than the rest of the island; this is mainly because large areas are being used to grow prickly pears. Twenty minutes into our journey we reached the large resort of Costa Teguise, which has been highly developed for the holidaymaker. Despite the lack of rain there is a golf course here with nine highly watered greens, standing out in shiny contrast to the surrounding landscape.

Preferring to get away from it all, we left behind the complex of luxury hotels and apartments and drove to Arrieta on the northeast coast. As we entered the village we spotted a beautiful sandy beach and turned off the main road towards it. The road petered out at the edge of the village and after a few yards of bumpy track we parked on a fairly flat surface, virtually on the beach. We had the beach to ourselves, apart from a few local children swimming and surfing in the sea. My companion went in for a swim and we sunned ourselves for an hour or so before driving back into the village and parking on the quay.

There were two cafés on the quayside and we lunched at one of them, a new culinary experience for both of us – limpets with garlic dressing. After a cool drink we set off northwards again. There are three tourist attractions in the area, only one of which is wheelchair accessible. The two inaccessible spots are the Grotto Jameos del Agua and the nearby Green Caves.

"Lanzarote is a perfect place for doing very little: a bit of drinking, sampling the local cuisine"

The accessible attraction is *Mirador del Rio*, situated on the northernmost point of the island. The journey from Arrieta took us past what I consider to be the most attractive coastline on Lanzarote. For two or three kilometres there are white sand dunes and several beaches accessible by car. The area is quiet, with no facilities, but ideal for relaxing beside the turquoise sea.

Mirador del Rio used to be a fortification, commanding the most magnificent views of the island of La Graciosa. The fortification has been tastefully converted into a belvedere from which to admire this breathtaking scene. There is a snack bar and a good parking area, with totally flat access throughout.

Our return journey took us through the more familiar volcanic landscape of the western and central areas. We passed many vineyards (easily identifiable by the semicircular walls which protect them from the northeasterly winds), where vines are cultivated in a unique way. Small holes are dug, deep in the soil. The vines are then planted inside and covered in layers of black lava granules. Being porous, the granules absorb the dew at night and dripfeed it down to the roots below. They also screen the vines from the harsh rays of the sun. That evening we enjoyed the fruits of these labours – a good bottle of local red wine!

Lanzarote is a perfect place for doing very little: a bit of drinking, sampling the local cuisine, lounging in the sun, some unhurried exploration of the island. Bearing in mind the time of year of my visits, it was very satisfying to be able to wear T-shirts and shorts; the temperatures were in the mid-seventies and humidity was low – an exhilarating climate for someone with MS.

Still Searching for the Perfect Holiday

Maxine Smith developed Still's disease (childhood rheumatoid arthritis) at the age of seven, and has been confined to a wheelchair for 36 years, although she can hobble a few steps with a crutch and someone to help her. Accompanied by her mother, Maxine has travelled extensively and tried several travel agents and tour operators, including a "specialist" company for disabled holidaymakers, none of which have been completely satisfactory. In January 1987 she spent three weeks in Puerto de la Cruz, Tenerife.

The shriek of the engines reached a crescendo, then slowly faded as the plane taxied to a halt. Now I could relax and begin to enjoy our holiday on Tenerife. I developed a fear of flying after only my second flight, which was particularly turbulent, throwing meal trays all over the floor. My mother and I had just wedged ourselves into the tiny toilet when the stewardess cried, "I'll have to leave you, we're landing!" and dashed away. I looked at my watch, realised that we couldn't possibly have reached our destination yet and became hysterical, convinced we were crash-landing into the sea. Unbeknown to us, a heavy tail wind had cut forty minutes off the flight time. There we were, locked in the loo until the plane landed and all the other passengers had disembarked.

My travelling companions for Tenerife were Bill and Dorrie, my parents. We try to have a holiday abroad every year and for the last six years we've taken winter breaks to avoid disrupting my Open University study. We have experienced a nightmare car journey in blizzards across the Pennines to reach Manchester airport, and endured a long rail–Carelink–Airbus journey from Cleveland to Heathrow, so we much prefer to fly from our local airport, Teeside, or even Newcastle. Both are convenient for a relative or friend to drive us there and back, but unfortunately the choice of resorts serviced by these two airports is very limited, particularly in winter.

As public transport is inaccessible to me, we generally choose fairly flat resorts with plenty of shops, nightlife and interesting places to visit within walking distance of a suitable hotel. We'd already run through the list of resorts recommended by friends or travel agents as suitable for me – Benidorm, Lloret, Mallorca, Rimini, Budva, Sliema – so we decided on Tenerife. Travel agents advised against the more hilly resorts in the north of the island, and suggested Los Cristianos or Playa de las Americas – flat, with better beaches, in the sunnier south. Neither appealed to us, however

– the former appeared to be a small, quiet village and the latter a concrete jungle, specially built for tourists and with no chance of getting a wheelchair on the beach.

A few months later friends returned from a holiday in Puerto de la Cruz with the names of three hotels which they assured us were suitable and in a flat area. Once again we studied the brochures, discovered which company used these hotels, checked with the company for the most accessible hotel, and booked three weeks at the *Hotel Las Vegas*. Normally we take four or five weeks in winter, as the cost per week reduces as the length of stay increases, but each extra week in Tenerife cost £140, so three weeks it had to be.

At last we'd arrived! Patiently waiting for the airport porters to lift me off, while the cleaners hoovered around me, I had visions of the plane returning to England with me still on board. One of these days it will happen. Eventually I was reunited with my wheelchair. The staff at all the airports we've used have been very helpful, escorting me and my companions to the baggage carousels and straight through customs.

As the taxi drove us along the main road from south to north Tenerife the scenery changed dramatically. At first the landscape was bleak and barren, no trees or greenery, only parched earth, interspersed with steep grey cliffs dotted with caves – some apparently inhabited, as lines of washing were strewn across the entrances. My parents and I became apprehensive and wondered if we'd made a mistake in coming to Tenerife. Was it going to be like Malta – barren and monotonous, all churches and pale boxy houses? Our holiday spirits returned, however, as the scenery became more colourful the further north we travelled: tropical trees, vineyards, fruit plantations, exotic flowers, all able to flourish in the kinder, more humid climate of the north.

Our anger and dismay at seeing several steps at the hotel entrance quickly evaporated when we were directed to a side door with only one step. Although there were three lifts, only one was large enough to accommodate my four-foot-long wheelchair; needless to say, this was the one which broke down several times a day. During the first four days we became increasingly angry, frustrated and tired of hearing "Sorry, lift kaput, only five minutes please" which in Spanish time meant one to two hours. However, once our request to change to a bedroom on the first floor (the same floor as the dining room, thus reducing the number of times we used the lift) had been granted, we found the hotel very pleasant and convenient. The staff were friendly and helpful, and one of them even repaired a puncture on my wheelchair. Why does that always happen on holiday and never at home?

"The old town was only a few minutes away from our hotel – for walkers"

We'd only booked half-board but the self-service breakfast and first-course buffets offered such a huge and tempting variety of delicious dishes that we wanted only a cake or ice cream (every flavour under the sun and a meal in itself) during the day. The hotel provided two types of entertainment: a resident musical trio for nightly dancing in the bar-café, while in the salon a compère organised "do-it-yourself" entertainment, which entailed hotel guests entering competitions or playing silly games – actually, some were quite funny. Professional artists appeared three times a week, including flamenco dancers, an excellent group playing South American music, and local folk singing and dancing (a cross between Morris dancing and Austrian thigh-and bum-smacking).

Puerto de la Cruz is V-shaped: one side is the old town, very hilly, and the other side, where our hotel was situated, is flatter and has gradually developed to cater for the tourists – hotels, apartments, bars, restaurants, cafés and shops lie along gently sloping side-streets leading from the long, level promenade, or Playa, as the locals call it.

That may sound like a typical commercialised resort but it is the other side of the Playa, the seaward side, that makes Puerto such a popular resort. At one end of the Playa steep hills provide natural shelter for the small area of beach, which is not golden sand but black volcanic ash, dirty and unpleasant for children to play on. However, to compensate for the poor beach and the fact that the very strong tides and numerous rocks make swimming dangerous, a huge lido has been constructed on the lower level of the prom.

The Lido contains several swimming pools, sunbathing areas, fountains, pretty gardens and areas for evening entertainment. The developers have managed to provide what holidaymakers want in an attractive way which harmonises perfectly with the natural beauty of the area. One can spend all day there for less than a pound. Although the Lido is not very accessible to disabled tourists, some might think it worthwhile to accept the offers of help and be carried down the few steps at the entrance, and see how far they can get.

Both in the Lido and along the Playa are numerous groups of seats, facing different ways, some with small thatched canopies, and everywhere an abundance of trees, flowers and exotic purple birds of paradise. Plants, boulders, seats and trees are artistically and strategically placed to provide colour, beauty and a feeling of privacy.

The old town was only a few minutes away from our hotel – for walkers. Down a flight of stone steps, across a level path, then up another flight of steps – impossible for wheelchairs. A bridge linking "our side" to the old town would be ideal. Dorrie and I tried

several detours, unsuccessfully, but Bill discovered a way through an alley and up a steep road (strong pusher required). Although many of the streets in the old town are hilly, with narrow, bumpy pavements and high kerbs, it's well worth the effort to see the highly decorative architecture, the market and the bazaar, and simply to see where the locals live.

"During twenty years of travel we've noticed little improvement in facilities for disabled people"

We intended to visit the volcano, Mount Teide, but were warned that it is cold and the air is very thin up there, not advisable for people with breathing problems (Bill). The trip involves a bus or taxi ride through spectacular scenery, then a cable car that almost reaches the top. Those disabled tourists who can manage buses might enjoy some of the "free" bus trips available – to a fashion show or leather factory, banana plantation or parrot park – but be warned, some require passengers to pay an entrance fee or purchase something. One couple in our hotel decided to save on taxi fares by using a "free" bus to a time-share complex, in a village where their friend lived. They were left stranded when the bus driver refused to take them back to Puerto because they hadn't looked round the time-share complex.

As Tenerife is part of the Canary Islands, which are governed by Spain, we expected the people and customs of Puerto to be Spanish. We've noticed over the years that many Spanish resorts have become increasingly commercialised: muggings and bag snatching have multiplied, making us nervous when walking at night, and shopkeepers are quite rude if tourists walk out of their shops without buying anything. We were, therefore, surprised to find Tenerife different; in fact, the islanders detest being referred to as Spanish. They are extremely polite and courteous, and we were able to browse without buying, or sit all day over a coffee in a crowded café. We enjoyed many late-night strolls, feeling completely safe. The only unpleasantness that we encountered was the exploitation of tiger cubs, monkeys and parrots, doped and hawked around by photographers who harassed the tourists, urging them to have their pictures taken with these poor animals.

Puerto is not ideal for wheelchairs, but we enjoyed a very pleasant and relaxing holiday and encountered no more difficulties there than anywhere else. Special facilities for wheelchairs are virtually non-existent in Europe – at most, small ramps – and Puerto is no exception. We've not found one special loo for the disabled in any of the eighteen resorts in ten different countries that we've visited.

During twenty years of travel we've noticed little improvement in facilities for disabled people. A few travel agents and holiday companies are slowly becoming aware of the needs of disabled holidaymakers but their definitions of accessibility are inadequate. No matter how much preparation we make, problems always occur. Airlines rarely inform stewardesses about my unbending legs and some argue that I should book two or three seats. Quite rightly, I'm not allowed to sit near the exits, but airlines have not made any alternative arrangements. Until travel agents, tour operators and airlines realise that disabled people have a right to a holiday too, travel will not become any easier. We have yet to find a foolproof method, but so far we've always managed to overcome the difficulties without too much suffering. Looking back, it's the disasters that make a holiday memorable – such as arriving in Rimini at 4am to be locked out by the hotel manager as soon as he clocked my wheelchair.

My advice is, if you are adventurous, have a sense of humour, are prepared to put up with inconveniences and the occasional disaster, *and* have a good helper, go and pester your nearest travel agent tomorrow!

THE CANARIES: TRAVEL NOTES

For general sources of information, see the Spain *Travel Notes*, p.16.

Lanzarote Villas Valentine House, Ilford Hill, Ilford, Essex IG1 2DG (☎081/514 4455) are local specialists who will attempt to advise individual enquirers on suitability of accommodation.

Allan Green booked a holiday with *Thomson* on Tenerife, staying in the *Hotel Vulcano*, Playa de las Americas (☎22/792035). The hotel has some special rooms for disabled guests – large, with spacious bathrooms and wide doorways – and can cope easily with large groups of disabled people.

Portugal

An Ideal Hobby

Theodora Hampton has rheumatoid arthritis and has had both hips and knees replaced in the last ten years. In 1988 she went wine tasting in Portugal.

As a hobby for a disabled person – drugs, doctor and transport permitting – wine tasting has a lot to offer. It can be enjoyed from a wheelchair, does not involve much walking and enables one to meet a wide variety of people. I've been wine tasting for years but it was not until recently that I considered going with a friend on an organised wine tour abroad.

The tour base was a large hotel in Ofir, a resort on the Costa Verde. Transport was by coach and only one night was spent away from the base hotel. Two "rest days" were written in to the tour and this appealed to me – I felt that two days beside a swimming pool with a good book would enable me to cope with coach travel on the remaining five days. I also hoped to swim but unfortunately the pool turned out to be very cold, so I had to make do with a deck chair in the sunshine.

The prospect of coach travel was rather daunting for two reasons: I was worried about the steps and I was not sure how stiff I'd become sitting in one position for longish stretches. In the event both worries proved unfounded. The coach driver was somehow always present when we were getting in or out of the coach and unobtrusively gave me a helping hand. The other tourists on

the trip – mainly older but not disabled – were quick to realise that I needed more time than most to negotiate the steps. As for stiffening up, the trips all included frequent stops to stretch legs and, since the coach was by no means full, for much of the time I had a double seat to myself. For anyone who can manage a few steps – with a stick, perhaps – this means of transport should not be automatically rejected.

The first wine visit was to Brejoeira Palace in the *Vinho Verde* area. The owner escorted us on a tour of the estate, much of which was wooded, with grottoes, artificial streams, small fountains and occasional rustic bridges. After about ten minutes we reached the edge of the woods and ahead lay the vineyards, stretching away into the distance.

I found the walk back a bit of a struggle and while the rest of the party were shown around the state rooms of the palace I sat outside in the shade of a large tree. There was no time to get bored, however, as very shortly a procession of servants emerged from the palace and began preparations for our buffet lunch. Long trestle tables were spread with shining white tablecloths, chairs were set up and then came the food – tray after tray of small edibles to be eaten with the fingers. Just as the rest of the party began to wander back, the wine was brought out.

Vinho verde is a light white wine, with almost a touch of green to it (as its name suggests). It is slightly sparkling and, like many light white wines, is best drunk on its home ground. Somehow in London it seems to lose some of its sparkle and become just another slightly fizzy wine, enjoyable but hardly memorable. The *vinho verde* produced at Brejoeira Palace, however, is the famous Alvarinho, acknowledged to be one of the best, if not *the* best of the *vinho verde* wines. Set out on the lawns of the estate, the long green bottles in their ice buckets looked very welcoming indeed. The wine made an excellent accompaniment to the food – smokey bacon with dates, fish and meat balls, cheese and, when we tired of savouries, some delicious almond cream tarts.

Our second outing was a moderately gruelling two-day trip, stopping first at the Quinta de Avalida at Peñafiel. Again we started with a stroll through the grounds. We inspected the goat enclosure – rather like an enormous dovecote, with small brown and white goats trotting up and down the rickety wooden steps and looking down at us out of their strange pale eyes. Nearer the house, the woods gave way to gardens, with large colourful flower-beds, masses of red and pink geraniums, petunias and great swathes of purple bougainvillaea on the walls of the house itself.

We tasted the *vinho verde* standing on the verandah which ran along the back of the house, overlooking the rose bushes and, behind them, the vines, shimmering in the midday sun. At Avalida we had what was without doubt the best meal of the trip. Vegetable soup, roast pork and crème brulée were expertly served on fine china, in a large, airy dining room. We were very impressed and later discovered that the *patrona* provides meals only two or three times a year; this was the first time *Blackheath Wine Trails* had qualified for the full treatment!

Our visit to Avalida preceded the drive to Lamego, where we were to spend our one night away from Ofir. It was a long day, finishing with a tasting and tour of the production lines of a sparkling wine estate. Made by the *méthode champenoise*, the samples were excellent but I think we were all a little too tired to give them the appreciation they deserved.

"The Douro is one of the few regions in which some of the estates carry on the practice of trampling the grapes by foot"

The *Hotel de Parque* at Lamego is set in the grounds of the Sanctuary dos Remedios, high above the small town. We could see the lights twinkling below as we waited for dinner. I seem to recall an excellent trout but by that stage I was more interested in my bed.

The following morning, most of the party were keen to walk down to Lamego, which could be reached down more than a hundred steps through a series of terraced gardens. I decided that this would have to be a "miss" for me but when the hotel porter realised that my friend and I were thinking of taking a taxi he offered to take us down in his car. We were happy to accept and although he had hardly more English than we had Portuguese (none!) he chatted away cheerfully, pointing out the sights as he drove and enjoying the short trip as much as we did.

From Lamego our coach took us up the winding roads above the Douro valley, each bend revealing a fresh panorama of steep terraced slopes covered with vines. We were heading for Quinta do Noval, probably one of the best-known producers of port and for many the highlight of the tour.

The grape harvest in the Douro is in September. When we finally reached Quinta do Noval we found that the grapes had already been gathered and were in the process of being crushed in large granite *lagars*. The Douro is one of the few regions in which some estates carry on the practice of trampling the grapes by foot. The human foot is considered the ideal "crusher". It releases the colour from the grape skin and frees the juice from the grapes without piercing the pips, whose bitter flavour would ruin the wine. It is thought that the warmth of the human body helps the fermentation of the grapes. The men normally wade knee-deep in grapes and "trample" in four-hour shifts.

"We were given more port to taste"

When the juice reaches the right colour and about halfway through the fermentation process, it is drawn off into barrels, called *toneles*, in which a quantity of grape spirit (similar to cheap brandy) has been placed. This arrests the fermentation and the wine is then left to mature. The short period of fermentation accounts for both the rich colour and the sweetness of the port.

We tasted both red and white port at Quinta do Noval, standing outside the estate house and overlooking the vines which covered the hillside in every direction. The meal here was again a buffet and we finished with some fine green figs.

Later in the afternoon the coach took us down to the town of Regua, where we joined the local train to Oporto. The train was fun, rather old-fashioned, with hard seats and a shrill whistle. We meandered along the side of the Douro valley, following the river all the way to Oporto. Another of my worries proved groundless as the train, unlike many continental trains, had doors that opened level with the platform – no steep steps to climb.

Between the early eighteenth century and the beginning of the twentieth more port was drunk in England than any other wine, and the British influence remains strong in Portugal, where many of the Port Lodges are British owned or part-owned. *The Factory House* in Oporto, a club and business premises combined, was established by the British merchants. We were given an informed tour by Signor Delaforce, the current president of the club and the senior member of one of the oldest port firms. One of the most interesting rooms to me was the kitchen, a relic of the Victorian era and situated on the top floor but one! A more modern kitchen has been installed in the last few years – within easy walking distance of the dining room!

In Vila Nova de Gaia, on the banks of the Douro, we saw a line of *rabelos* at anchor, the square sail on each bearing the name of a Port Lodge. These ancient river boats used to carry the pipes of new wine from the Quintas downstream to Vila Nova de Gaia, where the wine was stored. However, the river is now dammed in several places for the generation of hydroelectric power and the voyage, always hazardous because of the rapids, is no longer possible. Now the pipes of wine are brought down by lorry and, sadly, the boats are mainly decorative.

In Vila Nova we went first to Sandeman and watched the process of storing and bottling port, starting with the cooperage sheds, where the oak barrels are still made by hand, and finishing at the bottling plant. At Calém, another long-established firm, we were given more port to taste and an unexpectedly enjoyable lunch. I say "unexpectedly" as the dish provided was a local speciality, the basic ingredient of which was tripe – after a hesitant start our party cleared the lot!

We made this tour during the first week of October and were lucky to have sunny weather throughout. It was never too hot, just right for a holiday of this kind, and the scenery in this part of Portugal is particularly pleasing. Apart

from the plunging slopes of the Douro valley, with thousands of vines clinging to the narrow man-made terraces, the countryside is scattered with farms and small villages, cattle grazing peacefully, the occasional pig, some hens and heavily laden apple trees. With luck the area may remain unchanged a little longer – it is relatively undeveloped as a tourist area, and away from the coast much of the land is a protected nature reserve. In October the trees made a bright splash of autumn colours; a month later and everything might look a little bleak.

PORTUGAL: TRAVEL NOTES

Sources of information

Portuguese National Tourist Office, 1–5 New Bond Street, London W1Y 0NP; ☎071/493 3873. Supplies general tourist information and details of *Portuguese Railways* services, but the only reference to disabled visitors is a contact list of disability organisations and some hotel recommendations (see below). On the spot you'll find a *tourismo* office in almost every town of any size – these can be very helpful.

National Rehabilitation Secretariat (*Secretariado Nacional de Reabilitacão*), Av. Conde Valbom 63, 1000 Lisbon; ☎1/761081. Portuguese-speakers can make use of their guide to transport facilities and Lisbon access guide.

Transport

The major **airports** are reasonably accessible, and getting better. Facilities on **trains** are not ideal, although one contributor found that access from the platform to train, at least, was level. There are some accessible toilets on Portuguese stations, but no apparent concerted policy to improve disabled access.

For **hire cars** with hand controls, try *ARAC* (Rua Dr Antonio Candido 8, 1097 Lisbon; ☎1/

563836). As in Spain, road surfaces in rural areas can be tough going, and toilet facilities for disabled motorists are rare. Buses are not easy, but taxis are relatively cheap, and their drivers generally helpful.

Accommodation

Accessible accommodation is scarce and tends to be in the busiest areas. The *Holiday Care Service* and the *RADAR* holiday guide have some suggestions. As in Spain, though, places off the beaten track are often more adaptable.

Portuguese *pousadas*, the local version of the Spanish *parador*, are again often former castles and palaces, and again fairly pricey. The network covers the country and rates are reduced out of season. A list and map may be obtained from the tourist office in London.

The *Institute for the Promotion of Tourism* (*IPT*, Rua Alexandre Herculano 51, 1200 Lisbon; ☎1/681174) and the *National Rehabilitation Secretariat* (see *Sources of information*) have produced a list of hotels that are rather vaguely classified as being "without barriers or with few obstacles to wheelchair users". It can be obtained from the *Portuguese National Tourist Office*, or by consulting the *RADAR* holiday guide.

PORTUGAL: TRAVEL NOTES

Spas abound in Portugal: again you can get details from the tourist office in London, or locally.

Books

As an introduction to her passion, Theodora Hampton recommends the *Pocket Guide to Wine Tasting*, by Michael Broadbent (Christies Wine Publications). *Hugh Johnson's Wine Companion* and the *World Atlas of Wine* (both by Hugh Johnson and published by Mitchell Beazley) and *The New Wine Companion* by David Burroughs and Norman Bezzant (Heinemann) contain detailed accounts of the various wine regions, including those in Portugal.

Italy

Roman Style

Stephen Hunt, who sees his wheel-chair as a tool for travel, took a City Break in Rome in 1988 with friend and helper, Tim.

The plane banks steeply and the Eternal City slides briefly past the window opposite my customary aisle seat. For most of the two-hour flight I've been resting forward with a cushion on my meal table in a pleasant doze of anticipation; a packed charter flight is cheap and cheerful and the seats don't recline. The cost of only four nights off-peak B&B for myself and Tim in a central hotel would have taken me halfway round the world in my hitchhiking days. Looking at freedom in those terms, though, wouldn't have got me across the road to the travel agent.

We land at Ciampino and passengers slowly struggle out to a waiting coach. Some have enough luggage to spend their entire City Break indoors, changing clothes. I sweep past them with our two small bags on my lap and Tim pushing; better mobility than gentility.

The airbrakes release with a hiss and we pull out, into the sunburnt Italian countryside. At last I'm getting away from it all – the four walls, the familiar streets, the routines and regimes. Soon we're entering Rome and heads are swivelling faster than a tennis umpires' convention.

The interior of the hotel that Tim and I have chosen is in the grandiose "palazzo" style but with monetarist

innovations: we glide across the marble floor to what had once been a single generous lift but is now two miserly cost-effective lifts, which my wheel-chair won't fit into. The plan, then, is for me to wedge myself upright just inside while Tim belts upstairs and calls the lift from our floor, luckily the first, quickly unfolding the wheelchair in time for my arrival. Unfortunately we forget the vital role of the "HOLD" button in such a plan. Tim has hardly installed me before the door slides shut. I ascend rapidly to the third floor, where I'm confronted by a group of camera-festooned Japanese. Thinking that I'm trying to get out, the men enthusiastically rush forward while their wives and mothers bow encouragingly in the background. I fend them off, struggling to keep my balance until at last the door closes and the lift descends to the first floor. But Tim isn't there. Within seconds the door has closed again and the lift is reascending, this time to the fifth floor. Here, more Japanese await me and rush forward, helpful as ever. Holding them at bay, I call out for Tim. Before the door closes his answering voice comes from below, rising past me as the lift starts descending again. I arrive back in the lobby just as Japanese reinforcements are checking in. Tim and I are now at opposite poles of the building, my legs are starting to give way and I am wondering if we will ever come back together again. But the gods are with me, in their own way, and the lift mercifully ascends to the first floor, where a dishevelled Tim is waiting for me to collapse into the wheelchair.

Our room is of course palatial, though in the vertical rather than the horizontal sense, so we get down to some urgent furniture rearrangement. In the bathroom, the lavatory prevents access to the washbasin, but at least it's not the other way around.

By now the afternoon is closing fast and Rome still lies undiscovered outside. Hurrying back to the lift we put Plan B into operation and I meet Tim almost instantly in the lobby. In front of a classical fresco a giant electronic guide-map shows us that the famous Trevi fountain is hardly a coin's throw away. We set off into Rome's burgeoning evening rush and arrive three hours later. I'd imagined straight roads. They are, but so enmeshed in a maze of narrow streets and alleys that in the end it's impossible to know which way up to hold the street guide. Not that it matters. There's so much to see that we even pass through one little piazza three times from different directions and only realise later. The Trevi fountain is also a surprise. This is no municipal park goldfish-squirter. It is said that Rome's numerous fountains provided ideal places for plots and intrigues to be discussed discreetly. Conspirators at the Trevi fountain

would have needed ear trumpets to hear anything against the background deluge, gushing and cascading triumphantly from every orifice of this half-human granite mountain.

Back at the hotel, while Tim is trying to reach his wife on the phone before she goes to bed, I watch an old movie on TV. It's a dubbed Hollywood World War II drama: gum-chewing Italian soldiers fearlessly charge a Nazi stronghold. Things are definitely not as I've been led to believe.

"The Vatican's answer to Disneyland: a vast indoor theme park of the spirit"

Going up the wide Via della Conciliazione towards Saint Peter's, it's impossible not to feel self-conscious. How many wheelchairs have flowed in prayerful hope along this Pilgrim's Way before me? I even feel a strange tremor of anticipation myself, although I hardly qualify for a new set of tyres. In Saint Peter's Square our eyes automatically go up to The Balcony – focus of the hopes and fears of a quarter of civilisation.

The interior of the basilica is the Vatican's answer to Disneyland: a vast indoor theme park of the spirit, designed to fill the soul rather than empty the pocket. Emerging disorientated, back into the mortal world, we head for the Papal post office to buy "Sunset over Saint Peter's" postcards and are accosted by women and children selling newspapers or begging. Suddenly I feel prying hands fumbling in the folds of my jacket. At first they have the advantage: my reaction has to change from sympathy to disbelief to outrage before I lash out. Rob a poor defenceless invalid and his harassed attendant, would they! In fact they try it twice more before we leave Rome. But forewarned is forearmed and they don't know that I'm already trained to a peak of fitness by the street hustlers of Morocco.

So we continue unmolested on our way across the river in the vague direction of the Villa Borghese. Although most of Rome would fit onto two pages of my London A to Z, our constant rambling makes the Eternal City go on and on. Again we wander into Piazza Navona, once Domitian's athletic stadium, where exuberant Bernini fountains now sport against a background of mellow ochre-washed houses, all chariot-free thanks to the City Council. The Villa Borghese is another haven for the fugitive pedestrian: originally a Goth campsite, now Rome's largest public park, it houses fine collections of paintings and sculptures.

Back at the hotel that night, while Tim is trying again to get through to his wife, I stretch out and unpleat after a day on the cobbles. To relax me on TV a soap opera that – even with my meagre Italian – makes "Neighbours" look like a towering intellectual achievement.

Next morning we risk our one and only taxi ride, as far as the tower blocks of the suburbs. The careful and friendly assistance we receive when getting into and out of the car somehow doesn't relate to the homicidal maniac at the wheel. The guidebook mistakenly lists Porto Portese as an antique flea market but at similar venues all over Britain the same milling Sunday morning crowd is shuffling past the same stalls of second-rate domestic clutter and mass-produced fashion.

Yet Porto Portese is a must for the dedicated tourist. Just over the street lies the sort of contrast that guidebook clichés are made of. Crossing into Trastevere is truly "a step back in time". The faithful are now at lunch, the tourists still at Saint Peter's. We trundle through peaceful medieval streets, vine-hung and flower-scented. Dappled by the warm October sunshine, the stonework has the faded opulence of old Persian carpets. Here is Santa Maria in Trastevere, said to be the oldest Christian church in Rome. Nearby, from a pair of open doors,

comes the soft rasp of a saw. In the gloom amongst the cobwebs a man is working on an ornamental balustrade; around him are stacked chairs, gilt picture-frames and other antique furniture and fittings. In Rome there must be as many restorers as taxi-drivers.

From Trastevere on to the island in the Tiber to rest and eat, as usual resisting the pasta blowout. To wallow like stranded whales at the hour when Rome is most free of traffic would be a waste. Instead we end up later for another snack at a pavement café in the Piazza della Rotunda (the Pantheon). Built under Hadrian, it's one of the most impressive and best-preserved relics of Imperial Rome. The interior of the great building is hollow, almost featureless, its encircling walls rising up to the dome from where the only light appears. Visitors seem subdued and expectant in the strangely empty space.

"Here, as elsewhere in Rome, I'm regarded with the same friendly indifference as any other tourist"

That night, while Tim is trying to get through to his wife, I watch "Culpo Grosso", a deregulated TV "Play your cards right" strip-quiz, during which gas-fitters and receptionists lose their clothes and win money.

It could be a seriously vandalised multistorey car park. But, next morning, as we approach from the Piazza Venezia, the emotions are already stirred by an air of melancholy glory. As we slowly circumnavigate the Colosseum's battered walls I'm almost sad that the days of bread and circuses are over.

On our way to the Forum the clouds thicken; it looks like rain and there's barely time to see the sights before it starts. We find a sidestreet bar, just an ordinary place for ordinary Romans. Yet its style makes my local wine bar look like a bus shelter, and the barman and the blokes arguing football exude that sophisticated panache which TV commercials labour after. Among strangers I'm used to being stared at rudely, ignored politely, or smiled on sympathetically. But here, as elsewhere in Rome, I'm regarded with the same friendly indifference as any other tourist. It's relaxing for me and must be how the inhabitants survive the year-round invasions: Italy is the most visited country in the world, I'm told.

After consulting our wallets, our last evening is spent window-shopping around the nightlife of Rome. Back at the hotel, Tim finally connects with his wife and tells her that we've arrived safely and will be returning the next day.

We have only the morning left for the Sistine Chapel. "No one can leave Rome without seeing the Sistine Chapel" say the brochures. Well, I can. On the coach going up the Appian Way to the airport I no longer feel the pang of disappointment. After all, if I'd wanted somewhere with ramps and walkways I could have gone to Milton Keynes. A holiday for the disabled person is about possibilities and Roma has more than enough to offer the independent traveller. Imagine your local grocer's in a lofty temple, the post office a stately palazzo, the church a Renaissance art gallery . . . and that's just one street!

The Italian Cure

Anna Thomson is 52 and has had rheumatoid arthritis for about twelve years. In June 1989 she travelled alone to Abano Terme, a spa in northeast Italy.

After years of trial and error, I know that a holiday on my own suits me. I'm better able to relax and appreciate my surroundings while alone; only in the evenings do I occasionally feel lonely. My ideal companion would be someone with whom I was madly in love, or a loner like myself who would disappear until supper time; in the absence of both I go it alone.

I have loved Italy since my first visit there when I was a healthy eighteen-year-old and I have long been aware of the existence of spas, where vast numbers of Italians take the "cure" for just about every ailment under the sun, but for arthritis in particular. Information from the Italian State Tourist Office helped me to decide on Abano Terme, which has a worldwide reputation, has been a centre for hot thermal mud and water treatments since Roman times and is approximately 25 miles from Venice.

Although a few tour operators do feature holidays to Abano and other spas, none offered flights from Edinburgh, and I couldn't find a two-centre holiday incorporating Venice, so I booked a flight only and reserved the hotels by telephone. This turned out to be surprisingly easy – but I do speak some Italian.

Over the years I have been taking less and less luggage on holiday: while assistance with luggage at airports is generally very good, sometimes it is not forthcoming or is begrudged, and on two occasions my suitcase has disappeared altogether. Taking only absolute basics, I can dispense with the suitcase and swing a travel bag, weighing only about ten pounds, over my shoulder. The sense of freedom is marvellous – there are no long drawn out inner conflicts over what to wear, nor are there any agonising waits at airport carousels.

It was in such a carefree state that I stepped off the Edinburgh–Venice flight early in June to be confronted by a torrential downpour, but at least the air was warm after the frozen north. I knew there was a bus service to Abano but no one seemed to have any information on it until I asked a friendly road-sweeper, who had all the time in the world to give me directions.

"I had a feeling that a special healing power was present in this place"

By the time we reached Abano, the sun's rays were penetrating the last of the storm clouds, bathing the town in a mysterious golden light. I had a feeling, the first of many, that a special healing power was present in this place. The bus stopped very close to my hotel, where I received a warm welcome. As lunch had just started, I was soon enjoying delicious pasta with local red wine and reflecting that the early rise in Edinburgh had been well worth the effort.

Abano, with its relaxing ambience and beautiful gardens, appealed to me immediately, so there was no "settling in" period: I arrived, I relaxed – it was as simple as that. More than anything, I was looking forward to swimming in the warm thermal pool. Swimming eases my arthritis but it is never easy to find warm water in the UK. The hotel had two swimming pools, one outside in an attractive garden and one inside on the fourth floor, with a view of the surrounding hills. As I descended the shallow steps of the still, blue indoor pool, the soft touch of the slightly oily water soothed me immediately, and memories of swimming movements gradually returned to my stiff joints. At first I felt very weak, so I tried not to push myself too hard, taking breaks from swimming to float or do simple exercises. As the holiday progressed, my swimming became decidedly stronger and I was able to swim underwater for the first time in years. Many of the pool users were non-swimmers

and some were quite severely disabled; all seemed to benefit from the thermal water, which was kept at a temperature of 86°F.

Before too long I realised that I was the only British person at the hotel, although I did see the occasional fellow countryman in the cafés and shops. Most of the guests were Italian, some German and a few Swiss, Belgian and Austrian. Not everyone was disabled – I'd say around fifty percent – but Abano Terme is certainly an ideal place for disabled people. The town is very flat, the pavements are in excellent repair, with no high kerbs, and there are no steps or bridges. In the evenings many streets are closed to traffic. There are gardens everywhere and plenty of seats for resting. Naturally the hotels are very much geared up to serve the needs of disabled guests, and the staff are kind and sympathetic. There are many attractive cafés and the Italian custom of sitting with a coffee or a glass of wine, simply to watch the world go by, can very easily become an addiction. At night there is a programme of entertainment, often at open-air venues, including street parades and folk dancing. There is a marked absence of discos and wild young people, but the Italians do tend to be boisterous and I found a pair of earplugs invaluable when getting off to sleep.

Before commencing the hot thermal mud treatment, I had to be examined by the hotel doctor, who was very charming but with not a word of English. However, arthritic joints are fairly obvious things and I remembered the Italian for some parts of the body, so we were able to communicate fairly well. The treatments take place in the morning and I was given a choice of times, the earliest being 4am! I settled for the last one, at 9am.

The chambermaid gave me a white towelling bathrobe with a hood to wear before and after the treatment. Even in the lift, on the way down to the treatment centre, I could smell the hot mud; somehow it felt comforting. The centre reminded me of a hospital clinic. I was shown to a small, tiled room with bed, chair, sunken bath and shower. Two large buckets of steaming mud lay on the bed. They call the mud *fango*, and the attendant who gives the treatment is a *fangina*. My *fangina* – Leonora – was young, strong, cheerful and over-weight. As she prepared my "bed" of thick, grey mud, I couldn't help think-ing that it looked terribly hot.

My bathrobe had been threatening to slip off since I put it on (it was large and long and I am small and thin), so I let it go and stepped bravely forward. Leonora asked me to sit on the edge of the bed first, while she rubbed hand-fuls of *fango* into my back, giving me a chance to judge the temperature. Finding it just bearable, I reckoned it could only get cooler, so I eased my body into the oozing mass. Leonora wrapped me tightly in the strong linen sheets which had been under the mud, put a wool blanket on top, and disappeared.

"The pool was my constant delight"

With only my head sticking out and my arms imprisoned in the sheets, I felt like an Egyptian mummy. The heat was actually very pleasant and the mud was soft and soothing against my body. As I had no idea how long I was supposed to lie there, the first treatment was slightly unnerving but I did hear a clock ticking away in the background and Leonora appeared occasionally to wipe the sweat from my face with a rough towel (the Italians are wonderful people but their towels have the texture of pliable crispbread).

The alarm went off after twenty minutes and I was freed from my cocoon. After removing some excess mud from my body with her strong hands, Leonora led me to the shower where I was given a good hosing down. The sunken bath had been filled with

thermal water and I was led down the steps to relax in the warmth and to enjoy the free movement of my limbs in the water – this was a lovely part of the treatment.

After the bath I felt pretty good. Leonora helped me to dry off and wrapped me up in my bathrobe, making sure the hood was over my head to conserve the heat. As I walked to the lift I could feel new strength in my limbs. I was told to return to my room to await yet more treatment – a massage. I immediately warmed to my masseuse, Adriana, and we were soon chatting like old friends as she put my reluctant joints through their paces. She called me *uccelino*, which means "little bird".

Each morning followed the same pattern, except on Sunday when there was no treatment. The pool was my constant delight and I'd be in the water for about an hour before lunch and again before dinner. All were equal in the pool and people talked freely about themselves and their lives. I learned that many Italians enjoy spa holidays, all expenses paid, through the equiva-lent of our National Health Service or through their companies. They were most surprised to hear that I had to pay for everything. Some were regulars who had been coming for twenty years or more. Everyone said the same thing – it's best to have the treatment every year to maintain the benefit.

Although Abano is an excellent centre for touring, and the surrounding countryside is very beautiful, I was content to have a mostly lazy holiday, enjoying the sunshine and the wonder-ful food and wine, or taking little walks through parks and gardens. I did try the local bus service, which reminded me of the buses back home – not designed with the disabled passenger in mind. But there were usually plenty of people willing to assist.

Towards the end of my stay, I took a bus close to the foot of a wooded hill with a monastery on top, which I had admired every day from the breakfast terrace and which at first looked unattainable but, as the treatment began to take effect, presented both a possibility and a challenge. I'll never forget my joy as I climbed the winding road to the top with the sun shining and the birds singing. The views were superb and my body felt healed and strengthened. I knew then that the treatment had worked for me and that I would return.

Venice For All

While spending nine months in Nancy, France, studying for her degree in French and European literature, Sian Williams (a wheelchair user) was one of a party of about twenty people who took an Easter break in 1987. They travelled in convoy – two cars and two minibuses – to Lido di Jesolo, a resort not far from Venice.

The idea was originally dreamt up by some workers for the regional branch of *APF* (*Association des Paralysés de France*), an organisation which aims to promote and improve the integration of people with disabilities into the community. Not surprisingly, we jumped at the chance to explore Venice – a city that I expect many disabled people would steer well clear of. The party included about ten people with different types of disabilities; the others were the "enablers" – some who worked for *APF*, others who also had experience of living and working with disabled people, and a few students for whom this trip would be their first contact with the likes of us!

The grey skies and drizzle that accompanied us through France and Germany in the early hours of the morning were soon forgotten when, emerging from one of Switzerland's many tunnels, we were met by brilliant sunshine which stayed with us throughout our week in Italy. Arriving at the hotel in the evening, our surprise at seeing steps outside was nothing compared with our surprise when we saw the size of the lift! With a bit of quick thinking, however, the problem of where some of us were to spend the night was solved . . .Those whose wheelchairs were too big to fit in the lift spent the night with the Space Invaders and fruit machines in a makeshift dormitory on the ground floor. The following day, after telephoning a good proportion of the local property owners, we tracked down a villa with an accessible ground floor. Those whose vital statistics were bigger than those of the lift packed their bags and moved four hundred metres around the corner.

In spite of this initial inconvenience, which arose from being misinformed, for most of us the facilities in the hotel were adequate and the staff proved to be some of the friendliest and warmest people we had ever met. They were always ready to help and they showed exceptional openness towards the disabled members of our party. We encountered similar attitudes among the locals: when asked by one of us to change a rather large bank note, the owner of a pizzeria didn't hesitate – on seeing us all outside, eagerly awaiting our Italian currency, he invited us in and gave us a round of drinks on the house.

We had our own means of transport – the minibuses were adapted to take wheelchairs – so that on the mainland we didn't have to rely on public transport and could come and go as we pleased. One day we drove to Aquileia to visit the basilica, which dates from

1031. From the outside it is not particularly impressive but inside the architecture is breathtaking. Huge stone pillars are surrounded by brightly coloured mosaics with elaborate designs, such as peacocks and fishing scenes. There is a tape-recorded account, in many different languages, of the historical origins and architectural design of the basilica; this is especially useful for blind or partially sighted visitors. At the far end of the basilica there is a crypt containing Carolingian pillars and its walls and ceiling are covered in well-preserved frescoes. In common with many ancient buildings, though, this one provided considerable access difficulties and some of us could not enter it. I wonder whether total accessibility could be achieved without damaging the looks of such buildings.

In Venice we expected 160 canals and 118 islands, connected by 411 bridges, to present insurmountable barriers, but we successfully visited sights that had once been mere pictures in books or images on TV: the Bridge of Sighs and Saint Mark's Square, with its cathedral and Doges' Palace – and its pigeons. Venice is often swamped with tourists; wandering through its streets full of expensive restaurants and shops selling leather goods, jewellery and glassware, it is easy to forget that the city is also home to many people, but we had only to glance upwards at the rows of washing strung across the streets to remind us.

Whenever we had to travel across stretches of water, we made use of the *vaporetto*, or water-bus. This form of public transport is suitable for those with mobility difficulties because the deck of the water-bus is at the same level as the quay, so that wheelchairs can board and alight quite easily. It was the sights themselves which posed the access problems, but these were usually overcome with the help of our enablers.

In future, however, disabled visitors may be able to manage without the muscle-power of their companions. An architectural establishment has recognised the need to improve the accessibility of Venice and has launched a project called

"Venice and its surroundings do present problems for the disabled tourist"

VENEZIAPERTUTTI (Venice For All). A city map and guide have been produced, indicating those islands which are accessible and giving details of facilities in the accommodation on each of these islands. The aims of the project include construction of retractable ramps between those islands which can only be reached on foot, and production of a detailed map showing places of historical and cultural interest with descriptions in Braille. Fingers crossed that there are also plans to build some accessible toilets! This was the nightmare during our stay – we sometimes spent over an hour looking for a suitable spot!

We took the opportunity to visit two other islands in the region: Burano and Murano. The former is famous for its lace goods and many islanders rely on this trade for their livelihood. Fishing is another important source of income and the canals throughout Burano were lined with fishing boats as brightly coloured as rows of terraced seaside cottages. There were far fewer tourists on this island than in Venice; it was quiet and clean, with the atmosphere of a close-knit community.

Murano is renowned for its production of glassware and I was amazed at the variety of styles and colours of the samples that decorated the shop windows. We visited one of the workshops and were able to see some of the craftsmen at work. Although some of us were unable to negotiate the steps of most of the craft shops on these islands, the shopkeepers willingly allowed their merchandise to be taken outside for inspection.

Venice and its surroundings do present problems for the disabled tourist but on the whole our week's holiday was an enjoyable experience. The Italians were very friendly, facilities *are* improving and our enablers eliminated many of the difficulties that we encountered. It was interesting to see the changes in attitude that occurred in the enablers who had had little previous contact with disabled people. At the start of our holiday, there were those who presumed that we enjoyed waiting on pavements while everyone else went into a bank or souvenir shop; some did not hesitate to decide what time some-

one with a speech difficulty should go to bed; others were surprised to hear that one of us who uses a wheelchair has two children! By the end of the week, however, there was much greater awareness not only of our personal needs, since some members of the group require help for daily activities such as dressing and eating, but also of those attitudes and barriers which hinder the integration of people with disabilities. Our companions came to realise that even if some of us cannot eat spaghetti without assistance we are nevertheless capable of leading fulfilling and independent lives!

ITALY: TRAVEL NOTES

Sources of information

Italian State Tourist Office, 1 Princes Street, London W1R 8AY; ☎071/408 1254. No brochures for disabled tourists; some regional accommodation guides use the wheelchair symbol but these cannot be totally relied upon.

Progetto VENEZIAPERTUTTI, Unitá Locale Socio Sanitaria, 16 Venezia. Send for the city map and guide that have been produced for the *VENEZIAPERTUTTI* project.

Ufficio Informazioni API (*Azienda Promozione Turistica*), San Marco, Calle dell'Ascensione 71c, Venezia. Write and ask for their magazine *Un Ospite di Venezia* (A Guest in Venice). Published weekly in summer and monthly in winter by the local tourist board, this includes much useful information, although it's not aimed specifically at tourists who are disabled. It can also be picked up in Venice at the **EPT** (*Ente Provinciale per il Turismo*) offices or in the receptions of the larger hotels.

Tour operators

Project Phoenix Trust (Overseas Study Tours for the Disabled, 68 Rochfords, Coffee Hall, Milton Keynes MK6 5DJ; ☎0908/678038) is a non profit-making organisation with a good track record in providing special interest holidays for adults who need some physical assistance. Send large SAE for details.

Try the *Thomson Factfile* (see "Booking", *Practicalities*) for information on the accessibility of their Citybreaks and other Italian holidays.

CIT (England) Ltd (Marco Polo House, 3–5 Lansdowne Road, Croydon CR9 1LL; ☎081/686 0677) offer a wide range of holidays and are reported to have considerable experience of advising disabled clients. Their advice is based on information (covering resort and accommodation) submitted by their operators at the beginning of each season.

Getting there

Bad reports of *Alitalia*'s service to disabled passengers include one from an unaccompanied wheelchair user (a seasoned traveller with full use of his arms) who was refused a ticket unless he took a companion on his trip. See *Practicalities* for advice on choice of airline. Anna Thomson flew with *Air Europe* and was well looked after at Venice airport. Full assistance, with wheelchairs if required, is available at the major **airports**.

ITALY: TRAVEL NOTES

Transport

Italian State Railways (*FS*) provide no special facilities for disabled passengers, although there is an assistance centre for disabled passengers at Rome station, open from 7am to 10.30pm. Buses are out of the question for lone wheelchair users, and the **car** is probably the best form of transport within Italy. In town centres the private car comes a poor second to public transport but local authorities are required to make some arrangements for disabled drivers to **park**, and reserved parking spaces are marked with the international symbol.

Accommodation

Wheelchair-accessible hotels are few and far between, especially in cities such as Rome, Venice and Florence, where steps, both inside and out, are features of most buildings. But Sian Williams found that the warmth of the hotel staff more than compensated, and her group quickly tracked down alternative, more suitable accommodation by telephone. It's definitely worth looking into villa accommodation – large, airy, ground-floor rooms with smooth marble floors shouldn't be too difficult to come by.

Anna Thomson stayed at *The Aurora Hotel* (Via Pietro d'Abano, Abano Terme; ☎49/66 90 81). She returned in 1990 and paid around £35 per night for full board and use of the swimming pool; there was a supplement for the mud treatment.

Access and facilities

If asked which city in Italy might present most barriers to a visitor in a wheelchair, most people would think of Venice, with its hordes of visitors, waterborne transport, bridges, narrow streets, old buildings and steps. But the *vaporettos* were accessible, and Sian Williams reports some good initiatives from the *Venice For All* project; with strong helpers, the wheelchair users in her group were able to see most of the sights. Their main difficulty was the lack of toilet facilities for disabled people, and this is not a problem confined to Venice.

In Rome, Stephen Hunt was thwarted only by the Sistine Chapel, but again he had a fit companion to help with busy narrow streets, steps and cobbles (not to mention an inaccessible hotel lift). It seems that visitors in wheelchairs must be tough if they are to explore these cities without companions, not only to cope with the difficult surfaces and awkward access to buildings, but also to face Italian drivers when struggling across the wider streets.

In more peaceful Abano Terme, Anna Thomson found the terrain ideal for wheelchairs – the town is flat, the pavements well maintained, and there are plenty of resting places for those with limited stamina for walking.

As far as physical access is concerned, there is room for many more *VENEZIAPERTUTTI*-type projects, but general attitudes toward people with disabilities appear to be excellent – a relaxing blend of disinterested acceptance and cheerful readiness to offer assistance.

Books

Access in Rome and *Access in Florence* are published by the *Project Phoenix Trust*. Stephen Hunt used the Rome guide, which was helpful "even though they don't supply the team of body-builders pictured lugging wheelchairs up and down the steps".

Yugoslavia

Red Soil, Mishmash and Folk Songs

Margaret Lees and her husband Donald are both physically disabled, she with rheumatoid arthritis and he with a polio-type disorder. They have visited northern Yugoslavia three times, travelling to Istria in 1987, Krk Island in 1988 and the lakes and mountains of Slovenia in 1989.

ISTRIA

Four hundred years of Venetian rule left the Istrian region with gracious buildings, pleasant piazzas and an Italian air to many of the towns. The town centre of Pula encircles a Venetian fortress but the skyline of the town is dominated by a spectacular Roman amphitheatre, and there are other Roman remains scattered throughout the town: the Arch of Sergius, a small theatre, the Roman forum (now the main square of the old town) and the Temple of Augustus, inside which there is an exhibition of the best of Pula's Roman treasures.

I enjoyed the friendly atmosphere of the outdoor market, with its bright canopies and colourful stalls of fruit and wild flowers. Anything from underwear to fish could be bought here at reasonable prices. While walking along one of the old streets in Pula we decided to try some of the local ice cream from one of the *sladoled* (ice cream) shops. Inside, the sellers were throwing scoops of ice cream from one to another and catching the icy globes

in their metal spoons. They caught them behind their backs and over their heads, chatting all the while in Serbo-Croat and laughing – great fun to watch and the ice cream was delicious!

Istria differs from other Yugoslav regions that I've seen in that it has an abundance of poplar trees. Olives and grapes are grown here and the Istrian peninsula is commonly known as "Red Istria" because it is the only region in the country to have bright red soil. The contrast between the red soil and the green fields and trees is most spectacular when seen from the air while coming in to land at Pula airport.

We travelled to Pula in May; the sun shone almost every day and the temperatures stayed in the high sixties. We saw many beautiful sunsets, although they only lasted about ten minutes – the sun goes down very quickly at this time of year. Donald and I stayed at the *Hotel Park*, situated in a pine forest on a cliff a mile or two from Pula. We woke every morning to the fresh smell of pine and the sound of jays singing; from our balcony we could watch the red squirrels scurrying from tree to tree.

The *Hotel Park* catered very well for the physically disabled. The entrance had no steps and there were two lifts inside the hotel. A larger modern complex, about twenty minutes' walk from the hotel, incorporated hair and beauty salons, shops and a supermarket. The noise emanating from the ten-pin bowling alley was deafening and accompanied by flashing neon lights, electronic scoreboard and bar – not the place to go for a romantic evening drink!

We took advantage of two organised trips: a day trip to Venice and a tour of the Istrian peninsula. We travelled by hydrofoil to Venice on an early-morning two-hour crossing. My image of gracefully skimming over the waves was shattered as the hydrofoil charged noisily through them, giving a very bumpy ride.

> *"A café owner stood at his front door enticing passers-by to sample his "real" Nescafé coffee and Mr Kipling cakes!"*

But Venice was wonderful. At noon the Piazza San Marco was filled with the sound of bells, and lines of black-robed nuns wound their way into the Basilica di San Marco where midday mass was held. My mobility was limited severely by the vast numbers of steps: crossing the road in Venice means crossing a bridge and the bridges have steps either side. In the afternoon, though, we were taken on a tour of the canals and were able to see many of the sights, including the "Bridge of Sighs" and the hospital and cemetery islands.

Our second trip was by bus, visiting Rovinj, Poreč and a "traditional" farm. The bus driver lifted me on and off the bus at every stop. Rovinj is a lovely town but I found it difficult to get around, again because of the steps.

Like Rovinj, Poreč is a beautiful harbour town. It is the largest resort in Yugoslavia and swamped with tourists in the summer, many there to visit the sixth-century Byzantine Basilica of Euphrasius with its superb mosaics. But I liked Poreč for its picturesque promenade. We walked along narrow cobbled streets, passing various market stalls selling oil paintings, silver filigree jewellery and handmade wooden marionettes. The marionette seller sang while he walked his puppets up and down the street. A café owner stood at his front door enticing passers-by to sample his "real" Nescafé coffee and Mr Kipling cakes! We resisted his kind offer and made our way to a shop selling delicious homemade cakes.

Our tour of Istria finished with a visit to a traditional Istrian farm, where we were served refreshments and entertained with live accordion, guitar and balalaika music. The farm had the expected stock of goats, sheep and cows, but most unusual was the collection of white rabbits and peacocks!

One of my favourite memories of this holiday was an afternoon when Donald, Dragan (our *Yugotours* courier) and I sang and played guitar together in the sunshine. We talked and drank espresso coffee while watching the little grass lizards basking in the heat. Occasionally, the lizards would "dance", lifting a front foot and diagonally opposite hind foot, then hopping onto the other two feet and back again – a neat way of avoiding burnt feet.

KRK

Krk is one of the most developed of the Adriatic islands and the scenery is unexciting except in the south. We spent two weeks in July in Njivice, on the northwestern coast. The *Hotel Beli Kamik* was large, accommodating over 600 guests, and very few of the kind and helpful staff spoke English. Most had very good German and almost every guest in the hotel was German. We don't speak German, so were glad of the extra company provided by my parents, who travelled with us.

The weather was glorious but not for the faint-hearted, with temperatures topping 100° F. Donald and I felt somewhat restricted on this holiday, being based on an island, albeit linked to the mainland by a bridge. Most of the local trips were by boat and we decided to attempt only one of these because I find it difficult to clamber in and out of boats.

"Drinking tall chilled glasses of 'mishmash' was the best way to keep cool in the intense heat"

Njivice village is very "touristy", more so than any other town I've visited in Yugoslavia. The fishing industry has been superseded by the tourist trade and many of the local people run market stalls or cafés. Topless sunbathing is very popular, much to my husband's delight. There are numerous cafés, restaurants and open-air grills. Donald developed a great love for *razjnici* (grilled kebabs of pork, chicken or beef, sometimes all three) and I found that drinking tall chilled glasses of "mishmash" (orange juice and red wine) was the best way to keep cool in the intense heat.

We joined an organised bus trip to the Plitvice Lakes, about 40km inland from Senj which is on the mainland opposite the southern end of Krk. On arriving at the lakes we informed our tour guide that we would sightsee independently, rather than follow the organised walking tour, and we arranged a pick-up time when we would rejoin the rest of the group. The sixteen lakes lie in two areas, the upper lakes in the south and the lower northern lakes. The park is very carefully laid out, with numbered walkways and regular boat trips.

Donald and I explored the lower lakes, spending a long time admiring the roaring waterfalls that feed them. The colour of the water in these lakes is a brilliant turquoise, almost luminous in

its intensity, and iridescent dragonflies hovered about our heads as we walked. There are beautiful wildflowers to be spotted, including wild lilies, and an impressive variety of animal life – bears, deer, foxes and many insects and birds.

We took another day trip, this time by plane, from Rijeka airport (sited on Krk, though the town of Rijeka is just north of the island, on the mainland) to Dubrovnik. Different coloured mimosas in full bloom lined the central reservation of the dual carriageway leading into Dubrovnik. Most of the buildings making up the old town were built in the fifteenth and sixteenth centuries. The streets are very light and airy, probably because the building material is limestone, which dazzles in the sunlight. The locals keep the old town clean by the washing the streets down with buckets of water twice a day.

We went by cable car to the top of Mount Srdj, which overlooks the town and the island of Lokrum. The Fort Imperial on the summit was built by Napoleon's forces in 1808. On the way up in the cable car, I stood by the door taking photographs of the scenery below. The car supervisor smiled at me and opened the door, "so as you get good pictures", he said. I stood rooted to the spot while trying not to look down. Finally I persuaded him to close the door by smiling back and saying that I had no film left in my camera.

The flight back to Rijeka was no less frightening as we had to land during a violent thunderstorm. Forks of lightning flashed all around us and the turbulence was very bad, causing the forty-seater twin-propeller plane to shake and plunge steeply. The pilot made two approaches but was forced to climb back up through the storm to try again. We landed on the third attempt, 45 minutes after being told to fasten our seat-belts for landing. A row of fire engines stood by on the landing strip, red lights flashing. The next day our courier told us that our landing had featured in the local newspapers!

SLOVENIA

I still love flying, though, and the following June returned to Yugoslavia on a package holiday to Kranjska Gora, a small town near the Austrian border, in the northwest corner of Slovenia. We travelled from Glasgow to Ljubljana (Slovenia's capital); neither airport poses problems for the disabled traveller. At Glasgow there are excellent toilets for disabled people and lifts to all floors. All shops, restaurants and bars are accessible and the staff are very helpful and friendly. I was taken in my wheelchair through a separate security check and boarded the plane by automatic lift.

"The local people seemed to have a pleasantly open attitude towards disabled people"

The toilet facilities on the plane were reasonable for a semi-ambulant person such as myself but probably unsuitable for wheelchair-bound passengers. On arrival at Ljubljana airport I was carried down the boarding stairs by a member of the airport ground staff (very handsome he was too!) and I was lifted in a very professional manner, causing no discomfort. There are no steps at any entrance or exit to the airport, and passport control, baggage collection and check-in areas are all on the ground floor, as are shops, restaurant and toilets.

We asked the *Yugotours* courier to help lift me onto the bus; there are three or four very steep steps into Yugoslav buses, and a further step up to the seats. However, before the courier had time to arrange anything, a fellow traveller lifted me on! Our journey took about one and a half hours, stopping off at Lake Bled to deliver some passengers to their hotels.

We arrived at our hotel, the *Prisank*, at 11pm and were met by another *Yugotours* courier, who settled us in quickly. The hotel has no lift but we had specifically requested a ground-floor room. There is only one small step to negotiate at the entrance and clear access to the dining room. Our room was fairly basic and the bathroom was small, but it was comfortable and the beds and chairs were a good height.

In the morning we woke to a spectacular view of Mount Triglav, at 2700m the highest mountain in Yugoslavia. By 6am we were walking down the narrow main street towards the beautiful church. We passed a man shaving in the wing mirror of his lorry and he smiled and said *"Dobar dan"* (good day). The lorry opened up to form a market stall from which he sold wicker baskets, chairs and small tables, as well as a selection of handmade wooden farming tools. Most families in Kranjska Gora farm some land. At other market stalls we found fruit, hand-knitted jumpers and handmade leather slippers. The local people seemed to have a pleasantly open attitude towards disabled people, willing to help us when asked, but never pushy or patronising.

Kranjska Gora is a winter ski resort and perfectly situated for those interested in spectacular scenery, zoology, botany and walking. The town lies in a long valley, fringed by rugged mountains, and there are many lakes and waterfalls in the area. An enormous variety of wildflowers add colour, and there are no less than four species of orchid in the fields around the town. There are eagles, deer, many species of butterfly, and a huge selection of well-signposted, numbered trails to follow; some paths are very rough but we found most of the main routes quite easy and walking surfaces were good.

The choice of eating places in Kranjska Gora is wide, ranging from restaurants serving speciality meats such as roast boar and bear, to spaghetti houses and pizzerias. There were no great difficulties with access but people in wheelchairs might have problems with toilet door widths.

Service was excellent, staff friendly and prices low: we ate steak for £3 and pizza for £1 a head; a good bottle of wine cost £1. The town has a high proportion of British tourists, which may explain why many of the hotel and restaurant staff, villagers and shop assistants could speak at least a little English. The lack of language difficulties went a long way to solving such minor problems as obtaining directions and asking about items on the menus. That said, knowledge of a few words of Serbo-Croat is greatly appreciated by the locals.

We went to a concert of traditional folk songs held in the local church. The singers, all in traditional dress, came from Kranjska Gora and the surrounding villages. The music was so romantic, the clear voices swelling to fill the beautifully decorated little church; I was sorry when the concert came to an end.

We also attended a classical guitar recital at a nearby hotel. A couple from Newcastle came with us and lifted me up the steps to the hotel. The guitarist was a student of Segovia and played in front of large windows overlooking the mountains. We watched, captivated by the music, as dusk fell on this magnificent backdrop. A magical night and just one of the memories that helped me get through the long winter months at home on our return.

Package Tour vs Independent Travel

Muriel Smith and her husband spent the month of November, 1988, in Yugoslavia on a Saga holiday for The Over 60s. In October 1989 they set off for Yugoslavia again, this time by car and towing a specially adapted caravan, eventually returning to England in April 1990. Muriel has rheumatoid arthritis; she could walk short distances on her first trip but needed a wheelchair on the second.

The day began at 4am in the dark and cold, rheumaticky fingers fumbling as I dressed whilst half asleep. "Is it all worth it?" I wondered. Our son took us by car to Coventry, where I was bundled into the lower back half of the coach, the driver pushing and my husband pulling me up the steps. How much easier to travel from Birmingham or East Midlands airports, but no flights in November, so Gatwick it had to be.

There the fun began. The computer at the check-in desk had broken down, so there were long queues, hardly moving. A *Saga* rep adopted me and found me a seat until a jolly porter collected me on a buggy. I'd made no special arrangements but the airport personnel put about eight of us in an ambulance and airlifted us into the plane, only an hour and a half late. The plane looked ancient but it was a smooth flight and a perfect landing at Split in beautiful sunshine. Once again I was pushed and pulled into the coach, with many ribald remarks from other members of our party.

We'd chosen Yugoslavia out of curiosity: so many cultures and religions combined in one country. Populations of Albanians, Hungarians and Romanians live alongside the Slav majority of Serbs, Croatians, Macedonians and Slovenians. The official religions are Orthodox Christian, Roman Catholic and Muslim. The first thing our courier told us was "everyone is equal – no chauvinist pigs here!" Subsequent weekly lectures gave us an outline of local history: how the pirates used to run the next village, how local mountain villages were wiped out by an earthquake some years ago. We also learned that all the employees at our hotel owned a share and that it was run by a committee; no one earned more than £25 a week but profits were shared at the end of the year.

Our seafront hotel (the *Meteor*) was in Makarska, a lively town on the Adriatic coast, and our room was comfortable, with the most glorious view of mountains and sea. Most of my days were spent on the sun terraces at the hotel; I had a favourite corner and a lizard used to keep me company. The sun was warm, 60–70°F, and I had plenty of books, my painting and art work, and my tapestry. Unfortunately I became very sunburnt, probably because I take steroids – the only other person to suffer sunburn was also taking these drugs. We searched unsuccessfully for a sunhat and sunblock cream, so I retreated to the shade.

> "I lunched with friends from the hotel, after which the local boatman ferried us back to the hotel"

To anyone like me, crippled with arthritis, the indoor swimming pool was too deep and had very few hand-holds. I would like to have exercised my limbs in the water daily and next time will search for a hotel with a suitable pool. I prefer winter holidays because we can afford to stay longer, and we found the climate ideal, but the outside pools in Yugoslavia are closed in winter.

My husband could go walking or swimming as he pleased but I found the 450m to the town too far to walk, even though it was a level path through the pine trees along the seafront. Sometimes we hired a taxi to drop me

off near the shops and harbour. Looking back, I could perhaps have borrowed a wheelchair from the local hospital. These shopping trips always ended in a local bar where I lunched with friends from the hotel, after which the local boatman ferried us back to the hotel.

Boat trips to the islands of Hvar and Brač, both beautiful and very peaceful at this time of year, were worthwhile as there was little walking for me. We were told that the flowers in summer are a sight to behold and the small bays are good for swimming; we were also told that the hotels give you your money back for each day that it rains! The boatman we used was very popular, possibly because he handed round sweets and large glasses of local brandy. In spite of this I found it very cold on the water – the active people always grabbed the sheltered spots on the boat first.

Organised coach trips were too difficult for me because, apart from the high steps on the coach, these outings usually involved a lot of walking. Local buses were frequent and cheap but, again, not for me. I listened instead to other travellers' tales of golden eagles and chamois, seen in the Biokovo mountains which tower behind Makarska.

The hotel staff were dignified and quiet, except for the lady who cleaned our room: she would throw her arms around me every morning, kiss me and then run to summon the lift. We had a warm welcome from other Yugoslavs, especially some of my husband's business contacts. They sent a car and chauffeur to fetch us several times – once for a day trip to the medieval city of Dubrovnik, and two or three times to take us to lunch and sightseeing.

One memorable day we were taken miles along unmade roads, past trees laden with ripe tangerines, to a country inn. It looked like a peasant's cottage to me and I was a bit dubious when I saw the rickety chairs and tables, and candles stuck in the tops of bottles. There were some queer-looking bearded men sitting in the corners and Marshall Tito stared down at me from the walls. The local wine came in Coca-Cola bottles and I looked Tito straight in the eye as I tasted some special brew brought to us in tiny thimble glasses.

"I remember singing along with the tapes in the car . . ."

In a haze I tried all the various broths and pork dishes, each one flavoured with wild grasses and herbs. After about five different courses and several more thimble measures of wine we ended up with lamb roasted in a charcoal oven, served with steaming pasta rolls and more wine. I forgot that I was the only woman in a room full of men. I was even introduced to the Regional President of Trade and his minions. I vaguely remember the chauffeur picking us up and the car having a puncture somewhere in the mountains. And I remember singing along with the tapes in the car. . .

From Makarska we followed the coast road, with high mountains to one side, all the way to Dubrovnik. There were a few grim reminders of the war: memorials to villagers wiped out by the Germans because of the activities of resistance groups in the mountains; one village destroyed in retaliation for the sinking of a submarine in the bay; a huge memorial to the mountain resistance fighters.

Motor vehicles are banned from the centre of Dubrovnik's old town, so we were dropped at one of the two main entrances, Pile Gate and Ploče Gate. The main thoroughfare (Placa) is wide and lined with tourist shops; I didn't sense the antiquity of the place until I saw the narrow, cobbled side streets, with buildings almost touching overhead, murky and dark – even the cats and dogs looked sinister as they slipped quietly by. My husband was able to tour the remarkably well

preserved city walls, most of which were constructed in the twelfth and thirteenth centuries to protect the city-state of Ragusa, which developed from seventh-century settlements of Greeks, Romans and Slavs.

Much of the city was destroyed by an earthquake in 1667 but the subsequent rebuilding has left plenty to enjoy: the Baroque-style church of Sv Vlaho (Saint Blaise, the patron saint of Dubrovnik), built in 1714, and across the Luža square the Sponza Palace, once the customs house and mint, with its mix of Venetian, Gothic and Renaissance looks and a magnificent courtyard inside. The cloister of the fourteenth-century Franciscan monastery is decorated with rows of double arches topped with bizarre gargoyles.

We had lunch in an old dark bar, where the stools were so high that I had to have a leg-up. The cafés and shops were full of Japanese tourists. I had to wade through thirty or forty of them to reach the counter when buying a few souvenirs for the grandchildren. Dubrovnik is the most popular tourist destination in Yugoslavia and it seems that you cannot escape the crowds even in winter.

My husband's Yugoslav friends wanted to take him into the mountains to see a power station, so we travelled north for a weekend. While they struggled with snowdrifts I enjoyed warm sunshine in the town of Mostar, which straddles the Nerevta valley. Although the roads were made from round cobblestones and very difficult to negotiate with two wobbly legs and a stick, I was able to wander around, marvelling at some of the forty Turkish mosques and minarets. The Turks governed Hercegovina from Mostar in the fifteenth century. They built mosques, public baths and caravanserai, but their most famous contribution was the bridge, a beautiful arch built in 1566. I found the bridge, which the local lads dive off for money, but I couldn't negotiate the steep, slippery steps on my own.

The Yugoslavs joined us for dinner at the hotel and afterwards we watched the Holland vs Yugoslavia football match on TV. Unfortunately the beds in the hotel were only eighteen inches high – I was quite unable to cope and spent most of the night in a chair. The hotel was full of Americans and very noisy but our friends steered us away to quieter places. We were shown their pride and joy – the new blocks of flats and the supermarkets. Our trip by coach to the airport at daybreak, as the sun rose over the mountains, was beautiful. We made plans to return, to explore a different part of Yugoslavia, perhaps the deep south.

A year later we left home with a fully laden car, a caravan, my doctor's permission, plenty of tablets, a wheelchair, and an extended walking frame with armrests, which my kind physiotherapist had suggested would be much better for my walking attempts.

After staying overnight in Dunkirk we whizzed through France and Belgium and into Luxembourg. Two nights there and two in Germany and we were enjoying the vivid autumn colours in the Black Forest, picking our own sweet chestnuts. Into Austria and soon we were climbing up to the high Lörbl pass and entering Yugoslavia. Another day's journey and we were enjoying the sunshine on the island of Krk, where we stayed for a month and made friends with several German families on the campsite.

Itchy feet made us travel further down the Dalmatian coast to Split and beyond, to Omiš, where we found a campsite completely surrounded by mountains. The family there were so friendly that we stayed another month, until just before Christmas. Meanwhile, we had made friends with a young Yugoslav who lived in Makarska, and he invited us home for coffee. We were

then invited to take our caravan there in time for Christmas with the family – parents, grandmother, aunts, uncles and cousins.

Christmas Day was spent enjoying Dalmatian cooking and much local wine. We conversed with a little English, even less Serbo-Croat and plenty of sign language. We were taken to the family's other house in the mountains, where 68 villagers had been shot in World War II.

"One million dinars for half a tank of petrol!"

We stayed three months in Makarska with this family, sleeping in the caravan and using the bathroom in one of their summer apartments. Our diet was much better than during our 1988 visit, as fresh vegetables and fruit were readily available – unfortunately these are a rare sight in hotels. Meat and groceries were easy to buy, and we had great fun with the language, but it was difficult to cope with the rampant inflation. One million dinars for half a tank of petrol! The situation eased after Christmas, though, when the government knocked four noughts off all currency!

We met another mad English couple who were wintering in Makarska and we were soon great friends, meeting for morning coffee and lunches, out in the sunshine and watching the world go by. I was a source of amusement with my strange walking frame, and we were soon well known to the waiters and waitresses. We spent long, leisurely days on the beaches and had many picnics in the mountains with no one but goats for company.

Another invitation that we took up was to visit a farm about 60km away in the hills. We had a hilarious day amongst a three-generation family, with only one person apart from the school-children speaking English. The wine flowed and everyone enjoyed themselves – I even acquired a "second husband", who took over helping me about and cutting up my meat. We were urged to stay the night, or to visit again, even to holiday in their shooting lodge, but the sight of a large wolfskin put me off this idea. Instead we'll post back our photographs and hope to soon meet them all again one day.

We travelled back through Italy and were amused at the border guard's reaction to us: he couldn't understand why we'd stayed so long in Yugoslavia rather than Italy. In Austria we stayed five days in the glorious hot sunshine and two nights up in the forests, where we met an English teacher walking her dog. She stayed for hours talking to us and returned the next day for an English cup of tea. I was presented with a box of Austrian chocolates and we gave her a book on English cricket, as she'd been describing the game to her students.

After a few more days on the road we arrived home full of pleasant memories. We were travel weary but five grand-children (one a new baby not yet seen) soon put us right, and the doctor says I've taken no harm. This last trip put the *Saga* holiday in the shade, and in future we won't hesitate to travel under our own steam. The rewards are many, including discovery of out-of-the-way places and much greater contact with the locals. It is infinitely more satisfying to travel independently than to place yourself in someone else's hands. Now we have a stack of library books on Greece, Turkey, Spain and Portugal – where next?

YUGOSLAVIA: TRAVEL NOTES

Sources of information

Yugoslav National Tourist Office, 143 Regent Street, London W1R 8AE; ☎071/734 5243. Their only relevant offering is a guide to spa resorts, which usually offer some facilities for disabled people.

Tour operators

Yugotours Ltd (Chesham House, 150 Regent Street, London W1R 6BB; ☎071/734 7321; plus offices in Birmingham, Manchester and Glasgow) have a team of helpful couriers. The brochure is straightforward: it states which hotels are least accessible and reminds clients what to look for when selecting a suitable hotel in a suitable area. Further advice on hotel accessibility is given on request, basing judgements on past experiences with disabled holidaymakers. Enquiries are dealt with by one member of the staff who takes care of all disabled clients and is happy to telex hotels for specific dimensions if necessary, although reasonably detailed information about each of the hotels is kept in the office.

Transport

You are unlikely to come across any specially adapted toilets or sophisticated lifting devices for boarding and disembarking at Yugoslav **airports**, but you'll be able to get about the terminals in a wheelchair, and airport staff seem to be well practised in the art of lifting and pushing.

If you have the time, the long **drive** south is quite feasible, especially in a camper van or with caravan in tow, so that you are not totally reliant on finding accessible washing and toilet facilities *en route*.

Yugoslav **trains**, on the other hand, are not only inaccessible, but also tend to be dirty and overcrowded.

Although **buses** may have three or four steep steps at the entrance, the drivers on organised tours are not averse to lifting a disabled passenger on and off at stopping points. **Taxis** are not too expensive for getting around towns, and will carry a wheelchair in the boot, but ensure that the meter is started when you set off.

YUGOSLAVIA: TRAVEL NOTES

Accommodation

If the *Yugotours* brochure and the tourist board information are anything to go by, fully accessible accommodation is hard to find. But it's not impossible – either using an operator who is conscientious in the use of past experience with disabled clients, combined with carefully acquired details of hotels and resorts, or travelling independently, perhaps taking your own adapted accommodation with you.

Access and facilities

There are many difficulties for Yugoslavs with disabilities – in housing, education, training and employment. Patience and persistence are required to make any progress in these areas, and even the most basic equipment has to be fought for. It is not uncommon for a wheelchair-bound person to live in a flat on one of the upper floors in a block with no lifts or ramps, where he or she is imprisoned unless a squad of friends can be organised to help. There is no question of changing flats because of the nationwide housing shortage.

Disabled people in Yugoslavia do receive a small disability benefit. They can obtain a new wheelchair or power-chair every few years, and disabled car owners may **park** their cars in places where parking is usually prohibited. But there is no reciprocal arrangement for tourists who display the Orange Badge on their windscreens.

There are few concessions to the disabled tourist as far as physical barriers are concerned – no specially adapted toilets, no ramped entrances, wide doorways or lowered telephones. In many places assistance will be needed and those with very limited mobility won't manage everything, but more than enough – judging by these reports – to make the holiday worthwhile.

Greece

Welcomed in Greece

Julie Smethurst is totally blind and an enthusiastic Greek island-hopper. Three of her favourites – Sími, Tílos and Kárpathos – are in the Dodecanese, southeast of mainland Greece. Here she travels with sighted friends; her account of visiting Spain alone appears on p.10.

SÍMI

Sími announced herself to me by means of an overwhelmingly powerful aroma of herbs: after a hot day, the mingled fragrances of wild thyme, sage and oregano rose from the hills in great waves and were carried to us on the evening breeze. In the gathering dusk the *Sími I*, which plies daily between Sími and Rhodes, left Turkey astern – we had come within yards of the coastline – and rounded the headland into Sími harbour.

Sími lies closer to Turkey than to any part of the Greek mainland. The island is very small and very hilly – probably not the ideal place for someone with walking difficulties, as reaching anywhere beyond the two main centres of population involves a long walk, a rough climb, a boat journey, or a combination of all three. For example, the tiny community of Nimborios, where we once spent a whole day on the beach and saw only two other people, can be visited by boat or on foot along a rough track which follows the coastline. But the most interesting route is via a tough climb over the headland, where carpets of wild flowers blossom

in their season and you might meet a herdsman minding his goats, their bells gently tonking as they move.

During my first two visits to the island we lived in the *Villa Katerína*, one hundred and nine steep and irregular steps up from the harbour. What was once a quite grand Simiote house, in the wealthy days of the nineteenth century, has been converted into a villa and a studio, both with perfect views over the whole harbour area. From the balcony we could watch all its varied comings and goings: the arrival of the VIPs' launch on a festival day; the daily tripper boats from Rhodes; the inter-island ferries and the Rhodes "waterboat", rising higher and higher as its vital cargo was discharged into the Sími water system. There is now a desalination plant near Emborió but the still limited supply of water is probably the very factor which has protected Sími from over-rapid growth as a tourist centre.

The main thoroughfare around the harbour is horseshoe-shaped, following the quayside, and a walk along it takes you past all the boat moorings plus many shops, cafés and tavernas. One of my companions had been to Sími before and his return not only meant several warm reunions but also kept us in free drinks for most of the holiday. My first encounter with this particular brand of Greek hospitality was in a quayside café – with our order of coffee and cakes came three enormous brandies ("a present from Sotíris") and from then on we rarely left his café without something in the way of a "present": free coffees, lemonade to take to the beach, the loan of a bottle-opener. We passed many a blissfully idle hour at our favourite table on the edge of the quay.

I rediscovered an old but neglected love of swimming as a result of another reunion, with another Sotíris, who owned a boat in which he would take visitors for day trips to different parts of the island. To leap from the boat into unknown depths of clear, invigorating water was sheer delight. The Aegean is very salty and therefore extremely buoyant, so that there is little or no danger for a confident swimmer – if you become tired it is easy to float until rested. Swimming from this boat is one of the most "independent" experiences I've ever had, for Sotíris generally had some loud music playing on board, so that I could swim freely and alone, using the sound as a beacon for my return.

I found the Greeks very willing to accept my independence and very matter-of-fact about the presence of a blind person. At the same time they were thoughtful when helping, so that the help was practical rather than "fussy" as it often is in England. In a supermarket which I used regularly on

Sími the manager was always careful to sort out my change so that it was easy for me to handle and know which notes and coins I'd received. When I scrambled in and out of boats the Greeks were very quick and adept at conveying where I should place a foot or hand in order to be safe and manage in the easiest way. On the whole, I found their assistance less clumsy than that proffered by my English fellow tourists.

TÍLOS

We used the Sími travel agency to book a few days on the island of Tílos, about two hours' journey on the inter-island ferry. So it was that we found ourselves aboard the *Panormitis*, the tiny ship which visits all the smaller islands of the Dodecanese at least once a week throughout the year, sailing across a misty sea. There are always interesting people on such ferries if one has a mind to chat: on this one we made the acquaintance of a taxi driver on his way home to Kálimnos. He corrected my halting Greek and told us that we must visit his beautiful island one day!

"Music poured out of the quayside taverna and it seemed that everyone had turned out to meet the ferry"

Our arrival at Livádhia, the port of Tílos, was like something out of a romantic novel. The late afternoon sun shone on white houses and little boats, music poured out of the quayside taverna and it seemed that everyone had turned out to meet the ferry. As we stepped ashore we were greeted by our hotel manager, Panagiótis, who loaded our bags into his truck and said "Have a drink here, and come whenever you are ready".

Sími is not exactly noisy but Tílos seemed almost silent. We discovered a beach taverna (the *Irrína*) at which we had supper and breakfast within a few yards of the rippling sea. When we told the owner that we should like to visit

Megálo Horió (Big Village) and the beach at Éristos Bay, he simply phoned his friend who owned a truck.

Our driver was something of a raconteur and, like most Greeks, was proud and pleased to show off his island to interested visitors. He had been in the merchant navy and besides Greek could speak English, Italian and Turkish. Now he had settled to look after his farm, whose ripening oranges he pointed out as we passed. He also showed us one of the ruined crusader castles and an archaeological site which he graphically described as a "cemetery of elephants" – a cave where the fossilised remains of dwarf mammoths have been found. Reaching Megálo Horió he showed us a good place to eat and then dropped us off at the beach with a promise to pick us up at the taverna later.

The beaches on Tílos are more extensive than those on Sími but, perhaps because of the time of year, we were badly plagued by flies, which lurked in ominous swarms at the edge of the sea and started biting the moment we emerged. After a swim and lunch in the shade of the recommended taverna's orange trees, we returned to the beach to find a strong wind swirling the sand about in stinging showers. So we contented ourselves with a walk and were back at the taverna in time to meet our truck driver.

Waiting for inter-island ferries can be a very relaxed and pleasant occupation. We ate a late lunch of red mullet and sat out the heat of the day under the awning of a quayside taverna, then strolled around the harbour as the people of Tílos gathered for the arrival of the ferry. She slid into place exactly on time and our new friends waved us off – our truck man, and Panagiótis and his crusty old uncle from the hotel. Two hours later we were once again disembarking in front of Sotíris' café, glad to be back and receiving the "welcome" treatment all over again.

KÁRPATHOS

I arrived on Kárpathos – one of the larger Dodecanese islands – in a tiny, nineteen-seater, *Olympic Airways* skyvan. It taxied to a halt and spilled its handful of passengers onto the sliver of tarmac which until very recently served as the only runway. A short minibus ride brought us to some huts – the airport buildings – and a hearty welcome from George Philippides, the island's "Mr Tourism".

It was our good fortune to be allocated by George to Minás' taxi for the half-hour journey to our apartment, which was just outside Pigádhia, the main village on Kárpathos. When I complimented him on his music his face immediately lit up (so my friend Sandra told me later). From then on the conversation proceeded happily in a mixture of our two languages. As he said goodbye, after helping with our bags, he gave us his card: "If you want to go anywhere, just ring me up!"

First, though, we explored on foot. As we returned from a long walk, George's hitherto clear instructions seemed to run out about a mile short of home. At what appeared to be a dead end, we were hailed by a friendly man who we assumed would set us on our way. So he did, but only after he'd invited us onto his neighbours' verandah for coffee and a chat. I was reminded, not for the first time, that in Greek "stranger", "guest" and "traveller" are the same word (*xenós*).

Northern Kárpathos is rugged and mountainous, characterised for me by a blustery wind which the villagers of Ólimbos assured us "blows all the time". We visited Ólimbos on one of George Philippides' coach trips via a precipitous coastal road which was closed the following week due to fear of landslips! Luckily there is an alternative route by sea via Dhiafáni. The old windmill in the village still grinds flour, and we tasted the distinctive bread which is made from it – so rock hard that it has to be soaked in water before it can be eaten. The wind, the rocky terrain and the absolute remoteness led me to feel that life in Ólimbos must be tough. Yet the house into which we were invited for cakes gleamed with cleanliness, the people were as friendly and hospitable as ever, and the well-cared-for condition of the churches bore testimony to much love and attention.

"When told that we were visitors she presented each of us with a beautiful fresh artichoke"

It is helpful, and altogether much more relaxing, if one can adopt a flexible approach when participating in Greek island life. A day dawned when the boat trip we had planned proved not to be running. Everyone (except us) knew that the boat was not going to Dhiafáni but no one seemed able to say quite why. The islands can be like that – it usually has something to do with the state of the sea, or the fact that the Greeks do not consider it summer until the beginning of June. If you visit the islands in May – which is not too hot and is the best time to see and smell the flowers – it is likely that some places will not be open and some excursions will not be running yet.

Faced with a suddenly empty Sunday we found Minás and drove from Pigádhia on the east coast of Kárpathos to Arkássa on the west. On the way we frequently drew up to greet Minás' friends – he appeared to know everyone. One of them, an old lady carrying a large basket of vegetables, was given a lift. When told that we were visitors she presented each of us with a beautiful fresh artichoke.

As we arrived, about an hour later, Minás drew our attention to the priest, quietly drinking coffee outside one of the cafés in the village square: "If you ask him, he will show you the museum – he has the key". The priest did indeed show us the museum. Not only must I handle all the objects which defied his or Sandra's description –

various measuring devices and articles used in the Greek Orthodox liturgy – but I must also be shown how all the farming and domestic implements worked. From a jumble of Greek, German and English we learned that our guide's daughter had studied at the University of Essex and that there was a magnificent mosaic which we must not miss seeing on our way to the beach. This was in fact a section of the floor of the Byzantine church of Saint Anastasia, of which it is the only remaining part. Finally, he picked us a bunch of wild flowers and delightedly we repeated after him the Greek names for moon-daisy (*margaríta*) and carnation (*garifalló*).

Before leaving us, Minás had pointed out a track through some rough land which led to the most exquisite sandy beach, long, totally deserted and bordered by a sparkling sea of exciting rolling waves, in which it was impossible to swim but delightful to play. A major practical advantage of being befriended by an islander with a car is that one can reach places such as this, not normally on the tourist trails. Prices are generally reasonable (a full day out with Minás cost us about £40) and many taxi drivers are enthusiastic guides, pointing out interesting features and giving information about their island.

For our last day Minás took us to the three remaining principal villages which we had not so far seen. First, Apéri, said to be one of the richest villages in Greece, populated by Greeks who, once or twice a year, bestir themselves from their olive or lemon groves to travel west and inspect their New York stores.

Next came Mesohóri (Middle Village), remote and primitive, where the women were busy washing clothes in the spring. Greek courtesy being what it is, they immediately removed their bowls of blankets and packets of Omo, inviting us to drink from the spring, which we did. No one spoke any language but Greek, except for the schoolteacher, who could manage French. As we paused to watch some workers laying paving stones, a man appeared with a tray of hot, freshly cooked *loukoumades* – something like a hot doughnut. The workers gathered round, pressing us to eat. Soon my stumbling Greek and Sandra's sign language were being severely tested under a barrage of friendly questions. When they were certain that we could manage no more cakes we headed back to the car, meeting a traffic jam of donkeys blocking the narrow streets on the way. The streets were all made up of steps, so that the donkey is the only "vehicle" which can successfully negotiate them.

We spent the rest of that perfect day in the tiny village of Léfkos – just a few houses and tavernas strung out along the edge of a bay which is almost a lagoon. A swim, a delicious lunch of sea bream at Maria's taverna, siesta under a large tree and another long swim brought our stay on Kárpathos to an end.

I've heard it said that if you've seen one Greek island you've seen them all, but with more than two thousand islands scattered over an area of ten thousand square miles this has to be untrue. Every one has its own individual colour and personality, and I hope to have the privilege of getting to know many more of them, as well as revisiting old friends. For there is no sensation in the world quite comparable with being welcomed as a "guest" by the Greek islanders.

A Rough Ride in Crete

Jo Austen is spastic, severely disabled, wheelchair-bound and has no speech. In September 1989 she went with her able-bodied husband to northwestern Crete.

We flew from Gatwick, where the hand-luggage checkers were baffled by my light pen, which I wear on my head to point to letters on a card – that's how I communicate. With its plastic casing, long wire and battery charger it was bound to arouse the curiosity of the security men!

At Haniá airport a taxi driver managed to cram four people's luggage plus my wheelchair into his boot and we set off for Plataniás, 10km west along the coast. We had a choice of two available apartments in the *Villa Dora*; we chose the one up seven steps, not from sheer cussedness but because in the other one it was impossible to get my chair anywhere near the loo.

Our first few days were spent being thoroughly lazy. We used a technique we had perfected on other Mediterranean holidays for getting me in and out of the sea: John would put our lilo at the sea's edge, pull me in my chair backwards across the sand and then dump me on the lilo. Next he walked backwards into the sea, pulling the lilo behind him (fortunately I am fairly light!) until he could stand waist deep; then he'd tip me off the lilo and hold my head while I swam for five or ten minutes using my peculiar doggy-paddle. When I'd had enough he'd dump me back on the lilo, where I'd warm up in the sun while he had a swim. He'd tip me off for another swim as many times as I wanted before towing me back to the shore to sunbathe. Using this method I could have four or five swims a morning without John having to work too hard. This was ideal except for the day when a well-meaning gentleman, with whom we didn't share a common language, approached while John was tipping me off the lilo and assiduously tried to put me back on!

We hired a car for a week; it's awfully expensive but that or taxis (much cheaper) are essential to us for sightseeing – on the organised coach trips we wouldn't have had time to get around with the wheelchair. On our first day out, we went to the lovely sheltered bay at Falasarna, in the far west of Crete. This part of the island is for the moment unspoilt by tourism: the villages are isolated and roads often no more than rough tracks.

Another day we drove past Haniá to a hilltop called Aptera, where there are ruins dating from the fifth century BC and from early Christian times. Like many ancient sites in Greece, it was almost deserted and virtually inaccessible to wheelchairs. But John tipped the chair up on its big back wheels and we charged off down a precipitous track – my question was whether I was more likely to fall out of the chair sideways or forwards! Our reward was to see a vast Roman edifice which looked like three arches of a London railway station and whose use remains a mystery.

Luckily, two other tourists arrived and they were dragooned into helping us back up the path. After that we swam at Kalíves, where we were able to park on the sand three feet from the water's edge. We decided to have an early supper before driving back, so John pushed me along the main road, looking for a taverna. The road was quiet at this time and it was clear that none of the villagers who watched us from their doors had seen a wheelchair in Kalíves. This didn't surprise me but I was embarrassed later on when an old man approached me, muttering in Greek and making the sign of the cross – I couldn't tell whether he was praying for me or warding off the evil eye!

The ancient site I'd always wanted to visit was Knossós, but since it was over 150km away we decided to make our visit a two-day event, renting a room for the night. We took the best road in Crete, to Réthimno and Iráklio; Knossós is just 5km southeast of Iráklio. The site is vast, much bigger than the modern village in which we found a suitable room – three steps up to the entrance and no way of squeezing my chair into the loo but we coped for one night.

"Royal Road, probably the oldest road in Europe and definitely not built for wheelchairs"

The palace of Knossós is a relic of the Minoan civilisation that thrived over 3500 years ago. It was excavated by Sir Arthur Evans, who made some dubious reconstructions but at least they provide fuel for the imagination and give some idea of how the palace might have looked. It is certainly like the legendary labyrinth (built by Daedalus to contain the Minotaur: half-bull, half-man) and I can only describe things as I remember them, between being hauled up and down flights of steps by more or less willing tourists (Knossós is not recommended for wheelchairs, especially if you or your pusher are shy of asking for help, but with determination you can go anywhere).

I remember looking down from the reconstructed first floor onto a row of storerooms with giant *pithoi* (jars) which would have held grain, wine or oil – they were certainly bigger than me! I liked the Throne Room, which has a reconstructed fresco of two griffins just visible on the far wall and a tiny throne complete with footstool, whether for a ruler or a priestess is unsure. The Queen's Suite is luxurious, leading off the Hall of the Colonnades and with a dolphin fresco along one wall of the main living room. Down a short passage is the Queen's bathroom, with its clay tub protected behind a low wall. My last memory is of the Hall of the Double Axes, where this symbol is carved into every block of masonry. We came out to the theatre, with its two tiers of seats, and I sat on the podium which is thought to be the site of the royal box. From there we walked along what remains of the Royal Road, probably the oldest road in Europe and definitely not built for wheelchairs.

The Archaeological Museum in Iráklio houses many treasures from the palace of Knossós and the other ancient sites of Crete. There were tiny models of goddesses with serpents climbing their arms, long swords with handles inlaid with gold and many small Minoan clay coffins. But the most interesting collections for me were upstairs, so we pounced on a passing tourist (no lift, of course) and struggled up. It was the Hall of Frescoes that I wanted to see – carefully reconstructed wall paintings from Knossós and other sites. My favourite was the depiction of bull-leaping, in which acrobatic young men and women leapt and somersaulted over the backs of the sacred bulls.

Heading south from Iráklio through fields of drying grapes we drove over the mountains to Festos, a ruined palace much smaller than Knossós and surrounded by hills. Here, reconstructions were kept to a bare minimum but plenty remains, including most of the storerooms. The central court is huge and, now that the two-storey buildings on each side have crumbled, the views across the plain of Messará are spectacular. The north corridor leads to the spot where you can look down on the royal apartments; the Festos disc, which we had seen in the museum, was found nearby. Made of clay, it is marked with hieroglyphic characters that are still undeciphered. Before we left Festos, I downed two mugs of the deliciously cool drinking water which is provided free at the main sites.

The sea was rough for our last two days in Plataniás – that can be a problem on Crete – but we found a small harbour where the water was always calm enough to swim. On our last day John packed while I lay in the sun, and at midday, which was really too early for the taverna, we had our last meal, served by our favourite waiter.

Crete is not for the unadventurous, but if you have a strong companion and are willing to ask others for assistance it is a wonderful experience.

Somewhere Warm and Somewhere New

As the result of an operation, Allan Green has the symptoms of a stroke victim: he is unable to walk or use his right arm and his speech and vision are also affected; in addition he suffers from polymyositis. Allan and his wife, Lorna, went to Greece in 1988.

As a comparative newcomer to the ranks of the disabled, I didn't know what a wheelchair user could expect when travelling by air. So for the first trip after I came out of hospital, Lorna and I chose the short flight from Bournemouth to Guernsey, which took only half an hour. The aircraft was small and it was my first experience of being carried aboard, in one of the airline's narrow, portable seats. The journey and the staff, both on board and at the airports, were very pleasant and we had no difficulty at all, so we thought we'd venture a little further afield.

Since Lorna has taken premature retirement to look after me, we can go on holiday when it suits us. We wanted to avoid the busiest time of year, to fly from a local airport, to go somewhere warm and, preferably, somewhere new. It didn't take us long to decide on the Greek island of Rhodes (Ródhos) in September. The travel agent knew of my condition and we took a hotel recommended by the tour operator (*Thomson*). We were told that the travel agent would see to everything but we rang the airline a few days before departure to explain our requirements and book a front seat.

"We sat in the shade where, we are told, Hippocrates taught medicine in the fifth century BC"

When the day came, we were helped through the few formalities at each airport and helped when we were on the plane, so we arrived without any trouble. As I cannot board a coach we had to take a taxi to our hotel – a pleasant, unhurried ride of about twenty minutes. The *Hotel Metropolitan Capsis* is large, with several lifts, no steps at the front or inside, ramps to the two pools and to the restaurant in the grounds, and even a toilet for disabled guests on the same level as the pools. As in many hotels, the beds were low and it would have been difficult for Lorna to lift me from mine. We asked for an extra mattress and it was supplied immediately.

The hotel is in Ixia, a short distance from Ródhos town; anyone feeling energetic could walk it in half an hour, but we were on holiday and there was no pavement along one section of the road, so we went by taxi for about a pound each way. Ródhos town has two distinct parts, the old and well preserved medieval town, and the spreading new town with its hotels, bars, casinos, discos, restaurants, shops and banks. We

particularly liked the old town, and its narrow cobbled streets did not defeat my wife and the wheelchair. It's true that the shops in the main street (Odhós Sokrátous) of the old town were of the type seen in most holiday resorts, but they don't destroy the charm completely and there is much to see away from the shops, and much pleasure to be had from simply wandering the attractive lanes.

Two or three times we enjoyed strolling round the smaller of the two harbours (Mandhráki), where small boats and ferries were moored. The temperature was in the eighties (I still think in Fahrenheit) and after walking for a while in that heat we'd accept the hospitality of one of the many bars, and watch the world go by. Here, too, we booked ferries to other islands; we could have arranged these with *Thomson* but we wanted to check the boats for access.

Our first trip was to Kós, which is smaller than Ródhos but has a similar relaxed and friendly atmosphere and a similar Knights of St John castle overlooking the harbour. The ferry took three and a half hours (hydrofoil is quicker) so we had only a few hours on the island and saw only Kós town. There are many Greek and Roman remains here, and a very old plane tree at the entrance to the castle. We sat in the shade where, we are told, Hippocrates taught medicine in the fifth century BC. (The tree is not *that* old, but certainly one of the oldest in Europe.) The gangway of the ferry to Kós was wide enough to take my wheelchair, but on the *Sími I* it wasn't. This was easily overcome, though, by two crew members who carried me (in the wheelchair) on and off. Sími is even smaller and something of a contrast to Ródhos and Kós. The houses seemed to scramble up the steep slopes rising from the harbour. I saw Sími town described in a travel book as "like a film set" and that's how it appeared to me. There were stalls along the quayside, some selling sponges, for which the island is famous. It also had a reputation for boat-building at one time, but is now just home to several old seafarers.

Being unable to board a coach, we missed out on the organised coach trips on our own island, so we hired a taxi for the day. It cost about £48, or the equivalent of two coach trips each. Most tourists on Ródhos pay a visit to Líndhos, about 50km south of Ródhos town, and this was our first stop. It is a picturesque, whitewashed town, with winding pebble streets. Lorna managed to manoeuvre my chair around the town, but I stayed chatting to our driver in the shade of a café while she climbed higher to the ancient acropolis, with its Doric Temple of Athena (sixth-century BC).

We crossed to the other side of the island, passing through one or two small villages, and after a delicious fish lunch headed back towards Ródhos town. On the way we stopped at the "Valley of the Butterflies" (*Petaloúdhes*), which was well wooded with a stream running through it. In fact it is the valley of the Jersey tiger moths – orange and black striped, well camouflaged when stationary on a tree.

"It brought home to us the advantages of hiring a taxi"

Our last stop was the Filérimos monastery, about 5km inland from Triánda, amongst the pines on Filérimos hill. There were a number of steps here, so I was unable to go in, but Lorna looked around. We came across a party from a cruise liner being unceremoniously herded onto their coaches and told to board without delay; it brought home to us the advantages of hiring a taxi – we could go where we liked and linger as the fancy took us.

Most evenings we ate at our hotel, for the food was good. There was always a selection of cold dishes to start with, all sorts of salads and

perhaps stuffed vine leaves and squid. The main dishes were rather international but always included a fish dish, presumably local and usually tasty. Dessert could be anything from fresh fruit to treacly *baclavá*. There was a vast choice at breakfast, hot and cold; my favourite was peaches with Greek yoghurt, followed by salami with feta cheese. We usually finished the night off in our favourite bar, appropriately called *The Sea House* as it's almost on the beach, where we met up with some of the friends we'd made.

Talking of people, throughout our stay everyone, including hotel staff, taxi drivers, boat crews and bar staff, was very helpful. In addition, though I find British people at home very kind, if anything they were even better on holiday. For example, there were some public toilets in Ródhos town, not specially for disabled people but whenever I wanted to use them there was no shortage of willing helpers.

When the time came to fly home, we arrived at the airport early, checked in and made ourselves known to our rep. Passport control and departure gates are on the first floor, up a flight of stairs, and there is no lift. The rep took our passports, had them stamped and asked us to wait on the ground floor until someone came to collect us. We'd be the last on the aircraft, so we were not to worry about the other passengers boarding. Lorna asked a few questions and was assured that we'd not be forgotten as all the important people knew about the arrangement.

I suppose we waited about an hour until our flight began boarding. We assumed that someone would collect us shortly but we waited and waited and no one came. Then we heard an announcement: "Will the last two passengers for Cardiff please report to Gate Five." We knew the message was for us but what could we do? There was no way of getting me up to the first floor. We couldn't find a rep, from *Thomson* or any other tour company, so we approached a desk and tried to communicate with the Greek member of staff behind it. Another announcement blared out: "This is the last call for the two passengers for Cardiff. Please report immediately to Gate Five." We were speaking, gesticulating, pointing to the speakers and, somehow, our Greek friend must have realised our predicament. He wandered off, in no particular hurry, and came back two or three minutes later with a colleague.

This one did hurry. Taking a firm hold of the handles of my wheelchair, he shouted for a way through the milling crowd, and raced me in and out of a baggage handling section, through passport control for arriving passengers, and out onto the tarmac, with my wife running behind. I was quickly transferred to an airline chair, carried up the steps and installed in my seat. Almost immediately we taxied onto the runway and I could imagine the other passengers wondering what on earth we'd been up to. Lorna explained what had happened to one of the stewardesses and she was very sympathetic – we were supplied with free drinks all the way. So the plane didn't leave us behind, which was a pity in a way because we wouldn't have minded a little longer on Ródhos.

GREECE: TRAVEL NOTES

Sources of information

National Tourist Organisation of Greece (*Ellinikós Organismós Tourismóu*, or *EOT*), 195–197 Regent Street, London W1R 8DR; ☎071/734 5997. Supplies maps and information about ferries, but nothing specific on disability.

Mobility International Hellas, 101 Egnatia Street, 8th Floor, Thessaloniki GR-54635; ☎31/234489, 206667. *MI Hellas* grew from a specialist travel agency called *Lavinia Tours*, managed by wheelchair user Eugenia Stavropoulou, and is much involved in disability issues both in Greece and at an international level through the *MI* programme of meetings, leisure weeks and exchanges (☎071/403 5688 for the 1991 programme).

Tour operators

Grecofile (Sourdock Hill, Barkisland, Halifax, West Yorkshire HX4 0AG; ☎0422/375999) act as a consultancy for Greek holidays and as a straight travel agency (*Abakos Worldwide*) for trips to other parts of the world. They do their best to suggest suitable destinations but stress that they are bound by what the tour operators have to offer and by the physical restrictions of Greece itself.

Julie Smethurst obtained advice from *Grecofile* on which tour operators cover the small islands. *Laskarina Holidays* (Saint Mary's Gate, Wirksworth, Derbyshire DE4 4DQ; ☎062982/2203) and *Twelve Islands* (Angel Way, Romford, Essex RM1 1AB; ☎0708/752653) were most efficient in making her travel arrangements, particularly for the transfers within Greece itself.

Jo Austen explained her needs to *Grecofile* and asked for accommodation very near the beach, close to a village and tavernas, and fairly accessible. *Grecofile* recommended a set of apartments available through *Sunvil Travel* (7–8 Upper Square, Isleworth, Middlesex TW7 7BJ; ☎081/568 4499), who point out in their brochure that most of their holidays are unsuitable for wheelchair users – they are often built on sloping ground, with many steps to negotiate. But they will try to help, if consulted well before bookings are made.

In a country of craggy islands with villages clinging to cliffsides, there must be give and take between tour operator and disabled client.

GREECE: TRAVEL NOTES

If both parties are honest, and all efforts are made to find manageable accommodation, there should be no recriminations. Jo was satisfied with both *Grecofile* and *Sunvil*. The *Sunvil* rep in Haniá was very helpful, and Jo feels that this company is one of the more caring small tour operators.

Allan Green was given good advice on accommodation by *Thomson*, and with the introduction of *Thomson's Factfile* (see "Booking", *Practicalities*) it should be possible to obtain some access details on properties in *Horizon* and *Thomson* brochures.

Getting there

The flight to Greece is short enough to bear even a charter flight, and most airlines should provide adequate service. Take the cheapest deal you can find. If you encounter any problems on a flight to Greece, they'll be at **Athens airport**, where a few travellers have reported less than friendly handling, and where if you are flying onward from the domestic terminal you may be taken along subterranean passages or have to fight for a taxi outside the international terminal (if you are changing planes in Athens, flying in with *Olympic* saves a long trek from one terminal to the other). For some islands you can avoid flying to Athens altogether: there are direct flights to Rhodes, Crete, Lesvos and more; Kárpathos is reached via Rhodes.

Driving to Greece is feasible and enjoyable if you have the time, aiming for ferry ports in Italy or Yugoslavia (consult *The Rough Guide to Greece* for suggested routes and details of ferry services). Taking a camper van or caravan will solve potential accommodation headaches as well as transport difficulties, but don't expect to find a network of motorways.

Transport

Olympic Airways operate all **internal flights**, using small aircraft. Be prepared to be carried up and down the steps from the plane. The island airports are tiny, with no special facilities, but they can be negotiated, even if passport control and departure gates are on the first floor with no lift (p.65).

The width of gangways varies but **ferry** travel is always possible for wheelchair users with help from the crew, and it's an important part of many holidays in the Greek islands. A blind person can obtain a free ticket for a companion on Greek ferries run nationally.

Buses are inaccessible and often overloaded. **Taxis**, though, are cheap, especially when shared, and they tend to be enormous, ancient Mercedes saloons with plenty of room for luggage and wheelchair in the boot. The roads are terrible in many areas so don't expect a smooth ride. Cars can be hired, without hand controls, but it's no fun driving on Greek roads and better to befriend a local taxi driver (see p.58).

Accommodation

On the larger, more developed islands some of the modern hotels may have suitable facilities. The *Hotel Metropolitan Capsis* (Ixia, Rhodes; ☎241/25015), recommended by Allan Green, has lifts, no steps, ramps to the swimming pools and even a public toilet for disabled guests.

But staying in village rooms, villas or small hotels will require compromise – taking a room in a house with several steps at the entrance because you can get into the toilet, using chair-to-chair transfer to get through the bathroom doorway – and some assistance. That said, there has been one report from a paraplegic who arrived on a rugged, sparsely populated island, with no accommodation booked in advance, and fell into a fully accessible village room only minutes from the beach.

Access and facilities

Jo Austen's account proves that some of the roughest ground to be found in Greece can be covered in a wheelchair, but not without strong helpers and a pioneering spirit. Remember to take a puncture repair kit. (There are a few hints on coping with rough ground in the *Tours and Cruises* section on p.505.)

Those who are not wheelchair users but are unsteady on their feet or have limited stamina for walking should study the terrain of their chosen destination with care. If your island is hilly and you need good ankle support, don't

GREECE: TRAVEL NOTES

plan to wear flimsy sandals simply because you expect hot weather: steep and winding streets, composed of large, uneven stone slabs or cobblestones, put great stress on arthritic joints, for example. Feet, ankles, knees and hips will take a pounding, so pack your Doc Martens rather than your flip-flops.

Of course, Greece isn't all rocky outcrops and ruins, and there are accessible pastimes, including pottering around the quaysides and eating outside one of the numerous restaurants. You won't find too many public toilets, let alone accessible ones, but Greek hospitality is justly renowned (p.58) and our contributors report a practical, unpatronising approach to their disabilities. It's one of those countries in which the charms of the people make light of the physical obstacles.

Although there are no signs of government recognition of access as a right for disabled people, there is a thriving disability "movement", typified by *Mobility International Hellas.*

Health and insurance

State-run outpatient clinics, found in rural areas and attached to public hospitals, are fine for most problems that cannot be sorted out with the pharmacist. But get there early to avoid the queues. This report is from a paraplegic, Nic Fleming: "In 1987 I suffered a severe burn on my left heel, by stupidly letting my bare foot rest on the floor of the car whilst I was driving in very hot weather. The blister was bigger than a golf ball, and the whole heel went black after a few days. The head of a local medical clinic treated it brilliantly."

For complaints that require hospitalisation it is wise to use private hospitals because nursing care is not adequate in state hospitals. So make sure that your insurance policy will cover the costs of private medical treatment.

Take a copy of the prescription for your drugs, using the generic name. This will not only enable you to obtain fresh supplies, but also smooth the way with customs officials, who may wish to confirm that none of the drugs contain codeine – it's recently been banned in Greece.

For more information see *The Rough Guide to Greece* and form E111 (available from any post office).

Books

Breakthrough Greek (Pan: two cassettes and a book) and *Modern Greek,* by S.A. Sofroniou (seven cassettes), as well as the modern Greek Braille code, can be obtained from the *RNIB* (Customer Services, PO Box 173, Peterborough PE2 0WS; ☎0733/370777).

The Rough Guide to Greece and *The Rough Guide to Crete* are essential.

Cyprus

Still Good for a Holiday

Now in his late sixties, Jack Tulley contracted polio over fifty years ago. His legs and back muscles were weakened by the disease and he has used a wheelchair for the past twenty years. In this account of holidaying in Cyprus, he encourages those whose mobility is restricted late in life to travel, even though they may find it more difficult to face a journey than younger disabled people, who perhaps do not have the same trepidation or inhibitions.

Cyprus was under Greek and Phoenician influence in 709 BC. The antagonism between Greece and Turkey began in 1570, when the island was conquered by Ottoman Turks. In more recent times it was annexed by Britain in 1914. After World War I, since Turkey had fought on the German side, Britain backed Greece in taking over part of Turkey and the islands in the near vicinity. Although Turkey regained much of this territory, the British remained in Cyprus. Greece wanted to take over the island, but the Greek Cypriots wanted independence, which they attained after much bitter fighting in 1960. Archbishop Makarios became their first president and the British maintained two sovereign bases on the island by agreement.

There was still a strained relationship with Turkey, who claimed that

Turkish Cypriots were being persecuted. Turkey invaded in 1974 but the UN stepped in and set up a buffer zone. The island is now peaceful but no satisfactory political settlement has been reached and many mainland Turks have moved into the northern part of the island. Settlement is difficult because of the deep religious divide between the Greek Orthodox Church and the Muslim Turks. In addition, there is tension over the possession of many islands off the Turkish coast as these waters may be rich in oil.

It's possible to fly direct to the south of the island, which is in Greek Cypriot hands, and where tourism is more developed than in the north. However, the attraction of Cyprus for me is that it is still possible to find unspoilt places and people. Although I've visited a number of hotels, the one I find most functional is the *Cypria Maris* in Paphos, which has special rooms with wide-door bathrooms reserved for disabled clients. It's worth paying a little extra for a room with a sea view, so that you can relax on the balcony if the sightseeing wears you out. Studio rooms allow more space for wheelchairs.

Pavements outside the town centres are uneven and this prevents access to some sites. On one visit, after my wife had taken me over some rough ground, both wheels of my chair had punctures. Our taxi driver found, in a remote village, a small garage owned by one of his friends who repaired the wheels in fifteen minutes for less than a pound.

"One driver picked some grapefruit for us while filling up with petrol!"

Public transport is good but not accessible. I recommend the organised sightseeing trips for the less severely disabled tourist; some companies provide a minibus, which is better than a large coach, but I'm able to take a few steps and have found the coach trips well worthwhile. If you can make up a party of three or four and take a taxi, you can enjoy a day with your own driver at little more than the cost of a coach trip. Your tour rep can arrange this for an agreed price. Taxi drivers are generally very helpful with loading the wheelchair and they will take you to places inaccessible to coaches. It is not uncommon for them to stop and dive off to pick flowers or fruit for their passengers. One driver picked some grapefruit for us while filling up with petrol! The island is well cultivated and self sufficient, with superb fresh fruit and vegetables.

Car hire is another alternative but you will not be able to obtain a car with hand controls. Driving on the left (as in Britain) makes life easier, particularly in strange towns. Many of the side roads are rough but the main roads are well maintained and there is one motorway running from Nicosia to Limassol, which speeds up the journey for nearly half the length of the island.

Cyprus has plenty of historic sights, but some are not accessible to wheelchairs or to those unsteady on their feet. When faced with this, and if my companions are eager to explore, I find a quiet bar, rest there and enjoy a chat with the locals. That said, a wheelchair can be used in most parts of the island and I would encourage people who can walk only a short distance with difficulty to use a lightweight folding chair on holiday even if they don't use one at home. So many people with walking difficulties regard the wheelchair as an invalid carriage when really it is no different to taking to a car for longer journeys.

Nicosia, the capital since the twelfth century, lies roughly in the centre of the island and is divided into Turkish and Greek Cypriot sections, although only a small, less interesting part is in Turkish hands. The fascinating part is the old city, surrounded by Venetian-built walls which are in an excellent state of preservation. There are many places of historic interest, including the Cathedral of St John, with its famous wall paintings, the Cyprus Museum, the Makarios Cultural Centre and the Cyprus Handicraft Centre. Every year at the end of May the International State Fair and the Nicosia Art Festival are held in the city. To the south and west are the modern hotels, restaurants, shops, supermarkets and nightclubs.

Limassol, situated about the middle of the south coast, is a busy modern city and not my scene. However, there are excellent shops which attract tourists looking for leather goods at bargain prices. Other bargain hunters go for spectacles! A qualified optician here will provide prescription glasses at very low cost.

I find the west of the island, with a base at Paphos, the most attractive. This is the wine growing area and many types of local fish are served in the restaurants. A short drive along the coast from Paphos northwards leads to Coral Bay with its superb bathing beach, but this area is undergoing rapid development. A little further on is a much quieter fishing village, Ayios

Yioryios (St George), with an excellent fish restaurant and an early Christian basilica.

One of the nicest trips from Paphos is to go north through Cedar Valley, stopping at the monastery of Ayios Neophytos, founded in 1220 AD, where the monks make and sell their own wine. Further north is the little town of Polis and the fishing village of Latsi. The beach here is totally unspoilt and beyond it is a grotto known as Fontana Amorosa, where Aphrodite is said to have bathed. From here a single dirt track leads to the tip of the Akamas Peninsula, Cyprus' first designated national park.

Running through the centre of the island is high ground – the Troodos Mountains. Mount Troodos (also known as Olympus) is rather commercialised and far less beautiful than the lower slopes to the west. From November to April the peaks are snow-covered and there is skiing while the southern coast is still quite warm. I've enjoyed good sunshine in October, February, March and April; November to January may be wet.

In spite of the past fighting, the present tensions and the division of the country, Cyprus remains a beautiful island and it *is* possible for the tourist to be blissfully unaware of the political problems. Access is difficult in places but the people are friendly, there is much to see and the pace of life is pleasantly slow.

A Divided Island

Liz Crow, a 27-year-old wheelchair user, spent a month in Cyprus with a friend in 1989.

The number of visitors to Cyprus every year is roughly twice the population of the island. Tourism has only recently (in the last ten years or so) become a major industry and tourist information was not widely available prior to our departure, particularly with respect to women or disabled travellers. The advantage of this was that we arrived with relatively few preconceptions.

The priority during my stay was convalescence. We developed a vague and flexible routine – a bit of culture in the morning after an early swim, home for lunch and siesta, return to the pool for a tea-time swim and sunbathe, home for pre-prandials, supper and early, early bed.

At Paphos airport we were met by the architect and builder of our villa. Unfortunately he couldn't remember where he'd built the villa, so in the early hours of the morning we had a two-hour mystery tour, discovering dead-ends, dirt tracks and numberless houses before we came across the villa we wanted, more by luck than by design. The villa belonged to a friend of a friend of a friend and was part of the *Leptos Kamares Village* (estate), about 11km from Paphos. Michael Leptos must be a multimillionaire, judging by the number of developments that bear his name. Immediately next door to our villa, about ten yards from my left ear when I was in bed, another villa was being built. The bulldozers started at 6.30 each morning – a rude awakening but a good incentive to get up and out before the main heat of the day.

We would have preferred to have stayed in Cypriot accommodation with a local family but in order to ensure that I had at least a minimum of wheelchair access and could also rest or swim as needed, we were reduced to two options: a hotel at the more expensive end of the range, or a villa arranged through personal contacts. The villas and plots of land are predominantly owned by foreigners, mainly British. The *Kamares Club* (restaurant, bar, pool table, swimming pool) is very British, very colonial, and frequented by some swanky Brits full of superiority and condescension towards the locals employed there. Perhaps the advantage of this arrangement is that the negative impact of outsiders is relatively confined.

"As a rule, poor access didn't prevent us from visiting the places we chose"

Access was a constant issue. The villa had fifteen steps down to the front door, so that although I could circumnavigate them by scaling a very low wall and being collected at the bottom, we had to be very organised in our comings and goings. This meant that I was made very dependent and all of our time outside the villa had to be spent together. We hired a car but only manual transmission was available so I could not drive. The hire charge almost doubled the cost of the holiday for the two of us, but the car was essential since we were situated so far from town.

Very few places were adequately wheelchair accessible, although the situation is improving as tourism becomes established. As a rule, poor access didn't prevent us from visiting the places we chose but at times it did demand a fair degree of initiative, determination and biting of tongues.

Our trip to the Tombs of the Kings, a burial ground with underground chambers for Roman VIPs, required great staying power. To say that the terrain was rough is an understatement. We tackled the vast area, stretching for over 2km down steep hollows and over boulders and scrub, through sheer will power. As we went, my friend shoving and me pushing with all our might,

there must have been a hundred people – hulking, fit, healthy – just watching us. Spectator sport. At times the people watching us outnumbered those looking at the tombs.

In contrast to this, the Department of Antiquities curators at the House of Dionysus and Paphos District Museum were particularly helpful, organising competent people-lifts.

Another constructive approach was shown by the leader of *Exalt* (*Excursion Alternatives*), a team offering jeep excursions to remote and often uninhabited areas of western Cyprus. I had read about the tours but decided to commit myself only if the tour guide was prepared to think in terms of solutions rather than problems. Imagine my delight when the guide was both honest and practical: "never taken a disabled person on a tour before but you tell me what you need and let's get on with it!" I was concerned about distorting the itinerary or demanding too much of other group members but the tour leader set the tone and everyone joined in. With people willing to haul me over boulders and piggy-back me down cliff faces, the whole experience was made possible.

We took the coastal road from Paphos and when the tarmac petered out continued along dusty tracks and over fire breaks. We were surprised throughout our stay at the variety of landscape within such a small area: limestone to volcanic rock, plains to mountains, different qualities and colours of the sea, and changing village structure.

We stopped high above Lara beach, now a protected area because of the tourist threat to turtle breeding. The café lights mirror the phosphorescence of the sea, so that the baby turtles, after hatching on the beach, set off in the wrong direction and die. Lara is one of the few sandy beaches and the main turtle breeding ground in Cyprus. The protection laws ban beach umbrellas and sun-loungers from the sand and the mooring of pleasure cruisers. However, pleasure-boat trips are a boom trade and the law is flouted. Whilst there we watched a cruiser approach the beach, closer and closer until the scientists on the beach leapt into their dinghy and rushed out to fend it off. Shades of James Bond.

We drove through the British military firing range to the most northerly tip of the peninsula, complete with panoramic views of shore and sea. I've never seen such vibrant colours – blue, turquoise, ultramarine, in patches and swatches, with a pale purple tint where sea met sky. The cliff dropped down to a black shingle beach and the sea bed was black and white sand. The salt-buoyancy made floating effortless and I'd have been happy to spend all day swimming and bobbing up and down!

Our return journey took us through a Turkish-Cypriot village, abandoned in the 1974 war. A few houses were occupied by Greek-Cypriot refugees, on a non-ownership basis so that if and when the conflict is resolved Greek Cypriots cannot be accused of taking over Turkish villages. Meanwhile the rest of the village falls into ruin.

"The performance was in Greek but I soon stopped trying to recognise the odd word and instead listened to the melody"

The second jeep excursion was specifically to explore an abandoned village. During the Turkish invasion UN troops removed occupants from either "wrong" side of the Green Line, which divides the country, on a temporary basis which has stretched to fifteen years. Weathering and occasional vandalism are reducing homes to ruin – sagging and split bamboo roofs, trees growing into rooms, main supporting arches leaning and cracking. The village must have been a thriving community – winding cobbled streets, coffee shops, solidly built

houses. Now it is used by shepherds as a staging post for their animals. We found cats and dogs roaming, and the floors of people's homes slippery with goat dung. Amongst some tall grasses were a rusting tricycle and a plastic doll's head.

We went to the local high school dance-drama dedicated to occupied (Turkish) Cyprus. The Roman amphitheatre had been half-restored on its original site at the seashore, below a lighthouse. Warm sea breezes wafted through clear air on a dark and star-twinkling night. I sat on a little plinth at the end of the bottom row, feeling like a Grecian urn on a pedestal, especially when the spotlights were being tested. The performance was in Greek but I soon stopped trying to recognise the odd word and instead listened to the melody, lamenting lost homes and lives and renewing promises to continue the struggle.

What struck me overall was the push-me-pull-you state of Cyprus: an exquisite island, smaller than Wales, with a tradition of hospitality, low crime rate, glorious scenery and idyllic climate, invaded from all sides and throughout history. If it's not the British it's the Turks, or the Arabs or Venetians, and if it's none of these it's the tourists and developers. The Turkish issue, however, appears to subsume other concerns and the implications of development are consequently not approached critically or comprehensively.

The pressures on the landscape are immense. The huge building developments stretching for miles along the coast rarely benefit the local communities and are often detrimental. Many Cypriots used to make ends meet by providing bed and breakfast to the once small number of tourists. Now the large complexes poach visitors and local people lose revenue.

Proposed ecological legislation is announced without interim restrictions. This allows developers to make their mark quickly before the laws are finalised. A large area next to "our" beach had been purchased by the owner of a multinational corporation. He had chopped down large tracts of indigenous woodland, replacing it with fruit trees so that under the guise of agriculture he can stay the wrath of the law. Just before the Akamas becomes a protected area (if it does), his building will commence. Goodbye to the perfection of the northwest peninsula.

I still find it hard to believe that governments can be so naive or negligent as to allow this to happen. The situation feels acute in Cyprus because of its scale: a small amount of development can squeeze the whole country; one misplaced villa can destroy an entire coastline. The developers benefit whilst the "real" people are often forced to compromise their lifestyles to accommodate the tourist invasion.

"It was during our tour that I began to understand the significance of the reactions which I had received as a disabled person"

A concerted effort is now being made to preserve Cypriot culture, not – it is hoped – just for the sake of tourism. There are Roman sites, mountain monasteries, restored frescoes and museums, including a folk art museum. The most outstanding of these, for me, was the Ethnographic Museum in Paphos, a "living" exhibition of Cypriot civilisation. It was our final visit and drew together the threads of what we had seen and learnt.

The museum was set up by Professor Eliades, who married into a family home which turned out to have second-century tombs in the garden, now partly excavated. The whole operation is critically underfunded but is kept going by his wife, Chryso Eliades, who runs the museum on sheer devotion. She gave us a personal detailed tour, explaining everything from traditional baskets and bed-linen to carts and chapel. The

family squeezes into about a third of the first floor of the house, with at least half of the rooms they inhabit open to museum visitors. Mrs Eliades gives tours from 10am to 7pm, with a couple of hours off in the afternoon, seven days a week. In her spare time she runs the home and family.

It was during our tour that I began to understand the significance of the reactions which I had received as a disabled person throughout my stay: consternation, averted eyes, a physical drawing back, sometimes accompanied by muttering, particularly amongst middle-aged and older people. Not that I don't receive similar reactions in Britain but these were somehow deeper, more impenetrable. In Cyprus, what I initially interpreted as hostility stems from the Greek Orthodox view of disability. Reactions were muttered prayers and sorrow for my "sickness", prayers for healing and counting personal blessings. I don't pretend to feel comfortable with such behaviour but understanding its origins places it in perspective.

The religious influence is deep. Even in the most remote and derelict church we found wax effigies of limbs or heads, or whole babies, offered up to ensure healing or a safe passage after death. For the same reasons, bits of fabric from the ill or disabled person's clothing, or even bits of plastic carrier bags are tied to holy trees in church grounds.

Other disabled people were a very rare sight during my month in Cyprus, although of course there must be some somewhere, if only as a result of the 1974 war. We did eventually find an accessible (tourist) toilet down by the harbour in Paphos and I couldn't have been alone because there were tyre tracks before me! I looked up "Disability" (handicap, invalid, health, blind, etc) in the Yellow Pages but found not a single reference, direct or indirect. I then learnt that Cyprus has no state welfare system for disabled people, leaving them entirely dependent on family and benefactors. The tiny number of segregated institutions are privately funded. There are no government-issue wheelchairs or other equipment – small wonder, then, that a disabled woman out of doors, wheelchair and all, caused much consternation.

As two women unaccompanied by men, and one of us disabled, we often felt conspicuous and found it surprisingly difficult to make contact with Cypriot women. It is a very macho society. In all the villages we passed through, day or evening, the cafés were full of men, talking, always talking, with not a woman in sight. As men we could have stopped off for a drink and discovered more of the "real Cyprus", but as women it is unlikely that we would have been welcomed. Reading between the lines, though, there are the beginnings of a women's movement, evident a few months earlier in a march of 3000 women to the Green Line.

Like so many countries, Cyprus is undergoing rapid change. The issues affecting the country are similar to those in other parts of the world but the scale of change and sense of urgency seem particularly visible in such a compact geographical area. Even in the space of a month I was able to experience and learn a great deal, and I left inspired both to return and to travel further afield.

At Home in Cyprus

Islands have always fascinated Jane Hutchinson and she has many happy memories of island holidays. The only one she has felt the urge to revisit, however, is Cyprus.

The sense of relief which I experienced on arrival in Cyprus was related to the absence of anxiety and tension which beset the partially sighted traveller. From the minute a journey commences, to the return home a few weeks later, the stresses and strains of coping with the unknown can prove to be exhausting. In short, you need a rest to recover from the holiday!

For some inexplicable reason, however, Cyprus felt familiar. Standing in the passport queue, chatting to a couple of locals who had returned from the UK, I felt none of the usual worries as to whether I would spot our luggage as it came through on the carousel, or how I would identify our coach. Relaxed and happy, I almost skipped about the small airport building looking for a trolley; for once they were in abundance, as were the offers of assistance from eager porters. In no time at all my partially sighted companion and I were ushered into a waiting taxi by an understanding and helpful tour representative and whisked off to the most luxurious hotel in Paphos: the *Annabelle*.

Nowhere have we been treated with such care and kindness as we received in Cyprus. On their own initiative, hotel staff willingly completed registration forms, read menus and bills (as did the staff in all the bars and restaurants that we frequented). They moved obstacles out of the way as we walked down stairs and along corridors, offered to give us conducted tours of the buildings and grounds and continually expressed concern about our general wellbeing. Instinctively they seemed to appreciate the needs of people with a visual handicap, constantly reassuring us that nothing was ever a problem or too much trouble. Their only request was that we adopt the same philosophy of life as their own: everything must be taken *siga, siga* (slowly, slowly!). Heard often enough, these exhortations inspire inner calm and a sense of security.

Not that the *Annabelle* posed many mobility problems for us: far from it. In terms of both interior and exterior layout, conceptualisation is easy and guests with little or no sight should experience few orientation difficulties. However, although equipped with lifts to all floors, the hotel would pose problems for wheelchair users: the bathrooms and parts of the grounds and outdoor facilities are not accessible and there are various flights of steps leading to the taverna and grotto bar.

The *Paphiana Hotel*, on top of a small hill overlooking the village of Yeroskipos, provides more suitable accommodation for guests with wheelchairs and would appeal to anyone seeking a quiet holiday location. Yeroskipos (Sacred Garden – once dedicated to Aphrodite) lies just over 3km east of the main town of Paphos; the eleventh-century church of Ayia Paraskevi in the central square and the nearby Museum of Folk Art make a visit well worthwhile.

At no time did we see a Cypriot wheelchair user or anyone with a visual disability. Apparently they only venture out when members of their families can accompany them. This reflects the belief in the importance of the family as a unit; if one of its members is disabled, it is the family's duty to care for that member. It appears that no statutory organisations exist to provide help and support to the families of disabled people, and the state offers no financial assistance.

In education, segregation seems to be preferred, unless the disability is so slight that the individual can cope in mainstream education. The specialist schools are in Nicosia and the pupils have to board unless they live in the immediate vicinity. I suspect that some people with severe disabilities do not attend school but are "educated" at home. We were told that disabled people do obtain employment, though, for example blind people as telephonists or typists.

"It was clear that the concept of 'charity' finds far more favour amongst the Cypriots than that of 'rights'"

Socially, segregation is again the rule. We were given to understand that able-bodied people do occasionally organise social gatherings for people with disabilities. It was tacitly implied that segregation was preferable to social integration, at least from the point of view of able-bodied people! This view was rationalised by the argument that people with similar disabilities are better able to relax and enjoy themselves when separated from the stresses and strains of the "normal" world. They are more likely to find friendship amongst people with whom they can identify than with able-bodied people whose understanding must be limited. These notions were not expressed with overt and hostile prejudice but it was clear that the concept of "charity" finds far more favour amongst the Cypriots than that of "rights". This is also reflected in the way in which the Cypriot men treat the local women – and the female tourists for that matter!

The name "Paphos" is derived from two Greek words: *pan* and *phos*, translated as "everywhere light" – a perfect description of the entire district. There are two main towns. The capital, Ktima (Upper Paphos), is a modern, bustling town, built on a rocky plateau some 40m above sea level; Kato (Lower) Paphos is situated about 3km south of Ktima and combines the ancient city around the harbour and the new tourist area lying to the east, with its welcoming beaches, hotels, tavernas and nightlife.

Whilst strolling along the generally clean and well-made pavements of Kato Paphos you should stop for cocktails and a delicious fish lunch or supper at one of the many restaurants overlooking the harbour. Here you can sit for hours, mesmerised by the gentle swaying of the boats. If mobility and energy levels permit, the magnificent thirteenth-century medieval castle commands spectacular views of the surrounding area. Nearby is a seventh-century Byzantine castle, originally designed to protect the port and town against Arab raids.

There are countless other attractions within walking distance of Kato Paphos. The impressive second-century stone amphitheatre (Odeon) has been restored and can accommodate 1200 spectators. Performances of Greek drama take place during the summer but access could be difficult for wheelchair users. Furthermore, the surrounding terrain is somewhat uneven, though with care and perseverance we managed to walk to the adjacent Asklepeion (a building dedicated to the god of healing, Asklepeios) and to the Acropolis, on top of which stands a lighthouse.

A walk around the busy streets of modern Ktima can incorporate a visit to the colourful market (*agora*), the Byzantine Museum and the Bishopric Palace. Stress levels are reduced for the visually handicapped pedestrian by the surprisingly courteous motorists, who wait patiently while you cross the road, and by the alacrity with which unsolicited assistance is offered by the friendly locals. Some of the pavements are narrow, with irregularly placed steps, and in some areas there are no pavements at all, but even in this lively town the pace is leisurely and the disabled visitor remains remarkably unhassled.

This is in contrast to Limassol or Nicosia, where the action is fast and furious, but stimulating, with lots to see and do. The high noise level, coupled with the abundance of uneven steps, haphazardly arranged along extremely narrow pavements, may render these places less pleasurable for disabled travellers.

Cypriots generally speak good English and this talent is an asset to British visitors whose visual disabilities render them unable to read travel guides or decipher maps and who therefore rely on verbal directions. In Limassol, for example, every local can describe the way to the beach or to one of the town's three breweries, where you can sample many varieties of beer, wine and spirit. Try to remain sober enough to visit Kolossi Castle and the ancient kingdom of Curium, both situated to the west of Limassol. Curium's archaeological sites – the house of Efstolios with its interesting mosaics, the sanctuary of Apollo Hylates and the huge amphitheatre – are all worth seeing, in spite of the relatively difficult access. The terrain around these sites is peppered with protruding rocks, potholes, steep inclines and irregular steps but, predictably, the Cypriot guides are eager to offer help where it is needed.

"If you opt for the 'des res', the bottle of Ouzo comes free"

No one can spend a holiday on Cyprus and ignore the legend of Aphrodite, goddess of love and beauty. She was born out of the sea at Petra Tou Romiou, a beautiful part of the coast about 11km east of Paphos; this momentous event is signified by an impressive rock formation close to the beach. Her sanctuary is at nearby Kouklia, her baths are near Polis on the northern coastline.

It is also difficult to spend a holiday on Cyprus and ignore the separation of Greek and Turkish communities, emphasised by the regulations governing access to the allegedly beautiful northern Turkish territory. At present, access to the north of the island from abroad is via the Turkish mainland and permission to enter the country is given only to non-Greek nationals. It is possible for non-Greek tourists to visit the Turkish area while on holiday in the south but this requires a special entry visa and the maximum length of stay is one day.

Although talks to date have failed to secure an agreement on a united Cyprus, there are signs that the political climate is changing for the better. Both Greek-occupied Cyprus (under George Vassiliou) and Turkey have applied to join the EEC. Greek Cypriots believe that in order to secure membership, the Turkish government in Ankara will be required to put pressure on the Turkish Cypriot leaders to arrive at an amicable agreement with George Vassiliou, the result of which will ideally be the formation of a federal republic of Cyprus.

At present, then, the political situation appears to be stable. The Greek Cypriots still bear the scars of the 1974 war, when many arrived in the south as refugees, leaving thriving businesses behind, but they now seem generally optimistic and proud of their country. Their entrepreneurial zeal has fostered a burgeoning tourist industry, in spite of the territorial limitations imposed by the 1974 war and the recent moratorium on new hotel development. They are quick to show off the luxury hotels, villas and apartments, to advertise local crafts, to offer boat trips and taxi rides; they are keen to do business.

Shopping in Cyprus is fun and need not present insurmountable difficulties for visitors with sight problems. Whether you are looking for a bottle of Ouzo with which to dull the senses or a bijou pad in which to drink it year after year, the Cypriot vendor is eager to guide you carefully around the premises, satisfied only when you've made what is always hailed as a "very good deal"! Of course, if you opt for the "des res", the bottle of Ouzo comes free, compliments of the multimillionaire property developer. When we arrived in Cyprus, we little thought that we'd be able to abandon our British reserve, caution and suspicion, as well as the mistrust which is often thrust upon us, so to speak, as visually handicapped shoppers. But we did, and after being skilfully guided around numerous properties and building sites the deal was completed on the morning of our departure and we returned to London with a free bottle of Ouzo and a holiday flat!

Turkish Cyprus: Another View

The above three accounts are of holidays in the Greek Cypriot part of Cyprus. The following few paragraphs give a different perspective on the political situation and are written by a frequent visitor to the Turkish Republic of Northern Cyprus.

"When the British annexed Cyprus in 1914, they inherited an island which was struggling for its identity. For more than four centuries she was governed by a benevolent Ottoman empire, the Greek-speaking majority and a Turkish minority living together more or less peacefully. The nineteenth century, however, brought a wave of Greek nationalism which spilt over from the Greek mainland to all Greek-speaking islands and areas of the Aegean. The idea of "enosis" was born: the unification of all Greek-speaking people in one state. This meant that in Cyprus the Greek nationalists had two enemies: the British and the Turkish minority. The failure of the British to involve the Cypriots in the government of their island, and to raise the living standards of the islanders, led eventually to riots and terrorist attacks against government institutions. The British also failed to protect the Turkish minority against attacks from Greek "enosis" fighters.

It must be stressed that most of these terrorists came from the Greek mainland or were in the pay of mainland organisations. In the 1950s the Greek Cypriots formed EOKA (National Organisation of Cypriot Fighters) under ex-general Grivas (known as Dighenis). In 1960 Cyprus became independent and the guarantors of the new constitution were Britain, Turkey and Greece. The president of the new republic was to be a Greek Cypriot, the vice-president a Turkish Cypriot; seven ministers were to be Greek, three Turkish. Accordingly, the House of Representatives was to consist of seventy percent Greek Cypriots and thirty percent Turkish Cypriots.

This constitution did not work. The Greek majority under President and Archbishop Makarios began systematically to undermine it. Attacks on the Turkish minority increased steadily, in spite of protests by the Turkish Cypriots to the international community and to the guarantors of the 1960 constitution. Eventually, in 1974, the overthrow of a democratically elected government in Athens by a fascist military junta brought tensions in Cyprus to a head.

The junta ousted President Makarios and put Nikos Sampson in his place. Sampson immediately unleashed an unprecedented persecution of both the Turkish minority and his own opponents within the Greek Cypriot community. Acting in accordance with the guaranties given in 1960, the Turkish government in Ankara sent troops to Cyprus for the protection of the Turkish minority. The resulting establishment of the Turkish Republic of Northern Cyprus guaranties the freedom and cultural identity of the Turkish-speaking minority in Cyprus."

CYPRUS: TRAVEL NOTES

Sources of information

Cyprus Tourism Organisation, 213 Regent Street, London W1R 8DA; ☎071/734 9822. Provides helpful general advice and books, including brief notes for the disabled visitor, but some of their maps are unreliable. Since these tend to be supplied to tour reps, prospective travellers should buy a good map of their own before departure.

Tour operators

Jack Tulley deals direct with a small company specialising in Cyprus, *Cyplon Travel and Holidays* (Cyplon House, 563 Green Lanes, London N8 0RL; ☎081/348 9142). He finds the service efficient and caring, provided that all disability-related requirements are clearly stated.

Jane Hutchinson books all her trips abroad through a Cypriot travel agent whose "unstinting personal attention and advice extends far beyond the bounds of professional duty": *Cyprus Travel (London) Ltd* (42 Hampstead Road, London NW1 2PH; ☎071/580 0581).

In April 1989 an EC grant was matched by a group of charities including Friends of the Earth, the Leventis Foundation and other Cypriot supporters, to set up the **Laona Project**, designed to bring controlled tourism to the dying villages of the Akamas Peninsula. Crafts were to be revived and old homes restored to provide tourist accommodation. *Sunvil Travel* (7–8 Upper Square, Isleworth, Middlesex TW7 7BJ; ☎081/568 4499) has taken up this village-based tourism and doesn't rule out these holidays for disabled tourists, especially as hire cars are included in the pack

CYPRUS: TRAVEL NOTES

age, but offers the following cautionary notes: travellers must disclose *all* restrictions imposed by their disabilities; *at least* one able-bodied person per disabled person is the recommended ratio; most of the accommodation is in old houses, up in the hills, and most have steps or narrow staircases, but *Sunvil* will attempt to provide rooms to suit individual cases. "A sense of adventure is essential!"

In Cyprus, *EXALT* (*Excursion Alternatives*, PO Box 337, Paphos; ☎6/243803) offer fascinating day trips by Land Rover (p.72) from March to December; off-season excursions can be organised if sufficient notice is given. Prices for 1990 were £18 per person, including all transport arrangements, elaborate lunch and drinks; cheaper rates can be negotiated for groups. David Pearlman, the American leader of *EXALT*, believes that very little has been done to open up the possibilities for disabled travellers in Cyprus, and is keen to rectify this. His approach is highly praised by Liz Crow.

Getting there

There are regular **flights** to Cyprus, both charter and scheduled, from Glasgow, Birmingham, Manchester and the London airports. Larnaca and Paphos are the two main airports in the south of the island, although more flights stop at Larnaca. If heading for Paphos try to book a flight that lands there as transfer time by coach from Larnaca is two and a half hours.

Both **airports** are equipped with lifting gear to carry a number of wheelchairs and people who cannot manage the steep steps from the aircraft. There are no steps inside either terminal and Jack Tulley has received better handling here than at many larger international airports, which he often finds intimidating and impersonal. Special toilets for disabled passengers have been constructed at both airports.

Cyprus Airways (Euston Centre, 29–31 Hampstead Road, London NW1 3AJ; ☎071/388 5411) have a modern fleet of airbuses and provide good service to their disabled passengers. Jack Tulley suggests that by using a scheduled airline, rather than joining a charter flight, there is more flexibility if you have to change your return flight, and you can still get a package deal.

Transport

Public transport is inaccessible for wheelchair users, and **car hire** is expensive. No hand controls are available. **Taxis**, however, can be quite reasonable for day excursions, particularly if shared between four people. *Kem Taxis* (2 Byron Avenue, PO Box 2276, Nicosia; ☎2/472062) have a 53-seater, air-conditioned coach for hire with space for about fifteen wheelchairs, loading via a ramp through the rear door; it costs £90 per day, including evening use.

Accommodation

The *Cyprus Tourism Organisation*'s annual *Guide to Hotels, Travel Agencies and other Tourist Services* indicates those hotels which offer "facilities for disabled persons" but this does not mean that they are accessible. Jean Lewis, who has multiple sclerosis, has this to say about one such hotel, the *Dionysos* (1 Dionysou Street), in Paphos:

"There were many residents using sticks, wheelchairs or having some walking difficulty at the hotel, in spite of the fact that there were steps to negotiate at all three entrances. These were decorative marble steps – no handrails – into the lounge, the reception area and to the front entrance. Since I use a battery-powered BEC Scoota this was bad news, and had it not been for the tolerance of my menfolk in disassembling said Scoota in order to carry it in and out of the hotel, in reassembling it and in finding more reserves of strength to help yours truly up and down, the holiday would have been an expensive disaster."

The *Cypria Maris* (Posidonos Street, PO Box 456, Paphos; 6/238111) has rooms with wide-door bathrooms for disabled guests and is recommended by Jack Tulley. Prices for a double room with breakfast in 1990 were around £60 per night.

Jane Hutchinson stayed at the *Annabelle* (Posidonos Street, PO Box 401, Paphos; ☎6/244000) which is listed as having facilities for disabled guests in the tourist board guide. Jane found several potential problems for wheelchair users (p.76) and suggests that the *Paphiana* (Konia, PO Box 314, Paphos; ☎6/235252) provides more accessible accommoda-

CYPRUS: TRAVEL NOTES

tion; it is also considerably cheaper (£24.50 in 1990 for a double room with breakfast) – about a third of the *Annabelle*'s prices.

Liz Crow's observations suggest that, on the whole, accessible hotels are at the top end of the price range, in which case it's worth noting that many hotels offer off-season (November–March) discounts, varying between ten and forty percent.

Access and facilities

It is interesting to compare the tourist board's views ("Most towns in Cyprus are flat and most places are easily accessible with a wheelchair") with those of Liz Crow ("Very few places were adequately wheelchair accessible, although the situation is improving as tourism becomes established.") and Jane Hutchinson ("The abundance of uneven steps, haphazardly arranged along extremely narrow pavements, in Limassol and Laranaca may render these places less pleasurable for disabled travellers").

The tourist board is probably a little premature in its judgement, and although none of our contributors were totally defeated in their attempts to see the sights, considerable exertion was often needed. There is much to be done, but it is cheering to see some attempt to produce information (in English) for tourists with disabilities, and to see adequate facilities at the airports, and a growing number of hotels making efforts to accommodate guests in wheelchairs or with other handicaps.

Although Liz found no reference to disability organisations in the Yellow Pages, there are a few listed in the tourist board's notes for disabled visitors: *The Cyprus Paraplegic Organisation* (PO Box 4094, Nicosia; ☎2/462441) might prove a useful source of information before you go; *The Pancyprian Organisation for Disabled Persons* (50 Pendelis Street, Dasoupolis, PO Box 8627, Nicosia; ☎2/426301) and the *Vocational Rehabilitation Centre for the Disabled* (28th October Street, PO Box 3526, Nicosia; ☎2/305005) may be able to help with loan or hire of aids and equipment; *Saint Barnabas School for the Blind* (28th October Street, PO Box 3511, Nicosia; ☎2/422131); *School for the Deaf* (Makedonitissis Street, PO Box 4738, Nicosia; ☎2/302613).

Attitudes to disability may be tied up with religious beliefs, with emphasis on the "sickness" aspect and prayers for a miracle cure, but this does not detract from the general desire to help. Concern, patience, and willingness to make everything possible, even where the terrain is difficult, were encountered from locals by our correspondents, sometimes in sharp contrast to the apathy of fellow tourists.

Books

Liz Crow recommends *Journey into Cyprus* by Colin Thubron (Penguin), which was written before the 1974 war: "It's a bit sexist, but still gives an interesting perspective, especially once you've seen a bit of the island for yourself."

Malta

Digging Deeper in Malta

To Barry Atkinson, Malta is more than a holiday island. Since his first visit in 1983 he has returned often, sometimes staying for months at a time.

On the edge of Europe, in the Mediterranean Sea between Sicily and the Barbary Coast of Africa, lies the tiny country of Malta. The archipelago consists of Malta itself, the sister island of Gozo (about half its sibling's size), Comino, uninhabited little Cominotto and, off the southern edge of Malta, the nature reserve rock of Filfa. The total area is approximately equal to that of the Isle of Wight.

Almost since Neolithic times the land has known violence. Its strategic position and its superb harbour have long made it sought after. The Arabs came here in 870 AD, in the course of their Muslim jihad, and medieval times found Malta tied to Sicily by the Normans, caught in the complexities of the Crusader era. In 1530 the Knights Hospitaller of St John, originally formed in the Holy Land of the Crusades, were allocated the island and, in the Great Siege of 1565, defeated Suleiman's hordes in a long and terrible battle. The heritage of the Knights is still very much alive today. So, too, is the memory of the devastating Italian bombing raids of World War II.

Now the vulnerability remains but the criteria have changed and the pressures are economic, not strategic. The

magnificent Grand Harbour is reaping the benefit of the Mediterranean shipping trade but its zenith is gone. Some industry has come to the island but it is nothing to speak of. Today, sadly, Malta's economic survival depends on tourism.

And the tourist will find many treasures here: historical, from which there is no escape, scenic and climatic. The flora in spring is breathtaking in its beauty – the flowing mimosa, the sorrel, the red and yellow splashes of marigold and daisy dotted with poppies, the breaking out of the vines and fig trees, the giant fennel, the alkenite, the orchids.

It is natural that the casual visitor will follow the tour operators on a restricted circuit: first, the Rotunda Church of Saint Mary, which dwarfs and dominates the busy town of Mosta. Completed in 1860 and built largely by a voluntary labour force who used no scaffolding, the dome (the fourth largest in Europe) is a landmark for miles around. During World War II three bombs hit the church. Two bounced off the dome, whilst the third crashed through to interrupt a service. It failed to explode and, now defused, stands on show in the vestry.

Next comes Golden Bay on the north-west coast. The busy road from Mosta crosses the Victoria Lines (a long fortification built by the British in the 1880s to defend the harbours from enemy landing in the open northern bays) and twists down past the statue of St Joseph to St Paul's Bay and Xemxija (pronounced "Shem-shia"). The road then follows the fertile valley at the foot of Bajda Ridge, past fields of potatoes, tomatoes, melons, vines or asparagus, according to the time of year. In April the alfalfa – a purple-flowered plant used for animal fodder – is harvested. Golden Bay has one of the most popular of Malta's few sandy beaches.

"It's a spooky, lonely place on a dank winter's day"

Mdina, the capital of Malta's ancient past, is justly thrust upon every visitor. The Romans made the first lasting impression here. Their city (Melita) was three times as big as the present-day version and it was the seat of their government. When the Arabs conquered the island, they reduced this "silent city", with its narrow streets and grille-covered windows, to its present size and encircled it with defensive walls. They put a moat at its southern front and renamed it Mdina (the medina is the ancient native quarter of many North African towns). It's a spooky, lonely place on a dank winter's day but the view from the bastion, across terraces and fields to the sea, is one of Malta's finest.

Tours always include the fishing village of Marsaxlokk (*marsa* means "harbour"; *xlokk* is derived from "sirocco" – the gritty wind that blows from the Sahara) on the southern bay, where Turks disembarked in 1565 and Napoleon landed his troops in 1798. Although host to many tourists,

Marsaxlokk is a working village. The gaily painted *luzzus* and fishing smacks are not for show and the visitor has to tread carefully to avoid the fishing nets spread across the little promenade.

Few people will feel the need to discover Gozo, the island which mythology has cited as Calypso's abode. Calypso may have captivated Ulysses into remaining here for seven years but many tourists visit for just a day. It is not enough. Gozo is a greener, more agricultural land than its busy sister because of deposits of blue clay and the abundance of springs. Its slow charm is not immediately obvious but worthy of investigation.

Similarly, few visitors will see Xghajra (pronounced "Shara"), the village east of Malta's capital, Valletta, best reached via Zabbar. From the terrace of the little bar overlooking the rocky shore, the Arab influence can be seen in the row of squat houses with their tight doorways and small windows. As I write this, a road is under construction, running from the film studios at Rinella to Marsascala, via Xghajra. It will make a beautiful coastal drive but what will it do to Xghajra?

The region of Bahrija, west of Rabat, is often forgotten except by those who are able to visit the Bronze Age village remains along a difficult path. Yet it's an area of natural beauty and a contrast to the rest of the island: a place of solitude, sparse in population and vegetation. The roads ramble past tiny fields and wind-torn barrenness. Find the coast and sit on top of the cliff – perhaps in spring, amid clusters of scarlet pimpernel and miniature iris – to stare across the empty Fomm ir (Rich Bay).

The village of Ghaxaq (pronounced "A-shar"), situated between Valletta and Marsaxlokk, is not on the tourist map. The main road runs by the newer buildings, so that the old village surrounding the church of St Mary is seldom seen. But it is a delightful piece of old Malta that will put much of the crass modernity into perspective. The narrow streets bind the church and the tight-packed houses and shuttered windows have an air of timeless serenity.

Whatever it may admit, Malta owes much to the Arab. The language is basically Arabic, although English is spoken, to some degree, everywhere and is still taught in the schools – a result of the general pro-British feeling which has remained since the old British rule (1800–1974). The buildings, even the new villas on the edge of Bugibba, are decidedly Moorish in style. Other signs of the Arab influence are seen unexpectedly: in the begging gesture of an old man (begging is now forbidden in Malta and only happens occasionally, away from towns); in the use of derelict war buildings as shelters on an outing (like the Bedouin in Israel), ignoring the beauty of the flower-filled environment outside.

"The concepts of independent living and integration into the community are alien here"

The attitude to disability is also very different. In 1986, having never seen a local wheelchair on the streets, I visited the main centre for the handicapped at Siggiewi. It was sorely understaffed and the workers seemed content to lock the disabled away. I was dispirited then and, sadly, the position is largely unchanged. The concepts of independent living and integration into the community, which have become such common issues in western Europe, are alien here: a disabled person is bound to the family, the institution, or both.

However, there is now a government committee for the disabled and things have improved, if slightly. Over the age of sixteen a disabled person gets fifty percent of the minimum wage; the family of a child under sixteen receives a small supplement to the family allowance. Good lump sums are given for adaption of homes and for stair lifts. Vehicles used by disabled people are exempt from road tax and help is given

for purchase of imported cars. Adapted cars are almost unheard of.

In January 1986 I'd been forced to give up my work because of the progression of my illness, and a separation from my wife was shortly to end in divorce. I decided to seek solitude and warmer climes for the winter and wrote to the *PHRE* Rehabilitation Centre in Corradino (see *Travel Notes*), who suggested an appropriate hotel. Unfortunately it was in Bugibba but I was in no state to argue. The DHSS agreed to pay my money into the bank (which they still do every year), a bank loan paved the way and I made a three-month booking at the hotel.

Those three months taught me a great deal that has been useful in the ensuing years of travel, the foremost being a positive mental approach to dealing with new, untried situations. There are certain criteria to be met for such a stay alone. I am able to propel myself and transfer from my wheelchair into bed and onto the toilet. The mental approach will not help you if you cannot do either of these or have not arranged for someone to be on hand to help. In addition, my arms are strong enough to lift me into a coach or car once my wheelchair is in the right position. If I'm not an expert at these things and some are done with painful slowness, so what?

My first morning in the hotel was not easy. I'd made sure, in one of my many letters, that my wheelchair would fit into the lift, and I now headed down to the breakfast room. When the lift opened I was confronted by a stern room-maid clutching a pile of towels to her ample bosom. She looked at me and shook her head. "Shitter," she hissed, twice, and taking my place in the lift ascended slowly. Now wary of my reception and wondering where the Maltese kindness had gone, I went to breakfast.

Of course, it was all a mistake. Maria, who soon began to "mother" me, had simply been telling me that it was raining. The Maltese for rain is *xita*, pronounced "shita". After a month Maria began telling me off about the amount of wine I was consuming and I took to leaving the empties in waste baskets around the hotel, trying to keep the peace. Finally she left to look after her grandchild, by which time my social life had improved, but her stolid influence helped me through the early weeks.

This was my first experience of a Mediterranean winter. Many people believe that the summer temperatures continue throughout the year. The well-known spring flora shows that this is false – the plethora of growth means rain! Temperatures are usually quite a bit higher than in Britain but not always. I spent December of 1988 in Malta with London temperatures and a lot of rain. The local northeasterly wind (*gregale*) can bring atrocious storms and I've seen the sirocco keep everyone indoors in Bugibba, covering parked cars with sand and clogging the swimming pool.

Lack of mobility was naturally a constant difficulty. Finances would not allow me to hire taxis often. Maltese taxi drivers have always been good to me but the fares are slightly above London rates and money soon goes. The frequent buses are cheap and far reaching but have no adaptions whatsoever. I've used them with friends – as I pulled myself in they coped with the wheelchair. We managed, but I cannot recommend the buses to a non-ambulant disabled person, especially alone. For some reason the drivers are always in a hurry and often have little patience. There are no trains on the island. I would advise a disabled person to travel with someone who can drive because car hire rates are among the lowest in Europe and if you have time to shop around you can find a good deal. But beware of Maltese driving – go into the countryside to get used to the vehicle.

All in all, the 1986 venture worked well. Since then I've returned many times, staying with friends, in rented houses or in hotels. I now keep my power-chair on the island and have learned to use it over difficult terrain and amid the notorious traffic. Because I have known the country over a number of years I have, so far, been able to adapt to the increasing demands of my disability. The growth of knowledge of the country has been the important thing for me, but for those who simply want to get away, the Maltese archipelago makes a superb holiday destination. Facilities for the disabled are limited but a surprising number of limitations can be overcome by the friendly people. And I do believe that every time an able-bodied person helps a disabled person it is an act of education.

A Prize Worth Winning

Christine Warburton is hooked on entering competitions. In 1988 she won a holiday for two in Malta and set off with her husband, Arthur, from Manchester airport one miserable, wet evening in October. Christine has had rheumatoid arthritis since early childhood and her mobility is severely limited: she is able to walk a few paces on crutches but cannot bend her hips or knees.

Having fixed hips and knees undoubtedly creates the biggest problem when travelling, especially by air. However, our journey started smoothly and I was wheeled across the wet tarmac into a high-lift loading vehicle which gently deposited me at the aircraft's open door. Arthur lifted me aboard and succeeded in squeezing me into an end seat, which if not exactly comfortable was tolerable for the three-and-a-half-hour flight. In any case, I was so euphoric that I was past feeling any pain and could have flown without the aid of the aircraft!

After disembarking at Luqa airport on a much older lift, we were whisked away through passport control by a friendly porter, who quickly found us a Mercedes taxi with reclining seats to take us to the *Preluna Hotel* in Sliema. The warm sultry night after the recent squalls in Manchester increased my excitement, as did the fleeting glimpse of palm trees.

A few hours sleep and we were ready to view Malta by daylight – and what incredibly bright light it was. The early morning sun bounced off the limestone buildings and warmed my outstretched legs. We set off along the attractive wide promenade, occasionally stopping to rest on the seats along the water-front. Here we could watch the fisher-men with their gaily coloured boats (*dghajjes*), and chat to the young man selling his catch at the roadside. We continued on to Msida Creek and the marina, full of exotic-looking yachts, pausing to watch the tiny lizards warm-ing themselves on the rocks, or a horse patiently standing in the shallow water, cooling down before resuming his duties with the grocery cart.

Realising that we'd need a car to explore Malta's 95 square miles, and sadly unable to use the apple-green, Fifties-style buses, we arranged to hire a Ford Fiesta for seven days. Armed with maps, guidebooks, wheelchair and cameras, we set off to investigate Malta's rich supply of megalithic temples, complex fortifications, historic palaces and churches.

Driving along the somewhat bumpy roads we soon left the town, passing through ochre and white countryside with low stone walls crisscrossing terraced fields, and occasional carob trees dotting the rocky landscape. We climbed up towards ancient Rabat and Mdina, impressively outlined against a cloudless sky. Leaving the car under the shade of a convenient tree, Arthur pushed me through a fine stone gate-way and across a moat into the beauti-ful walled "Silent City" of Mdina, once the capital of Malta. With the coming of the Knights Hospitaller of St John in 1530, the status of the city was reduced as the new Order, a maritime power, established itself by the waters of the Grand Harbour. With the building of Valletta, Mdina became "Citta Vecchia", the Old City, inhabited then as now by the old nobility and leading Maltese families, plus the nuns of St Benedict. Despite Mdina's popularity with the tourists, we met hardly a soul as we wandered through the tiny alley-ways flanked by high, mysterious, shut-tered fourteenth-century buildings.

"Whenever I need to relax I conjure up this scene and am never disappointed by its calming effect"

We eventually found ourselves in a square dominated by a magnificent Baroque cathedral, distinguished by a huge dome which crowns the city's skyline. There are several steps to cope with, but the cathedral is accessible with help. On either side of the west front are two impressive seventeenth-century bronze cannon, on which a group of young tourists climbed to have their photographs taken. A pass-ing priest appeared unperturbed as he nodded and smiled, obviously well used to the oddities of foreigners.

On another memorable day we took a Grand Harbour cruise. The crew manfully pulled and pushed my chair up the gangway, positioning me, Cleopatra-style, in the stern of the launch, where I had a superb view of Sliema's colourful waterfront and the tiny fishing boats rocking furiously in our wake. In and out of the creeks we sailed, passing the Black Pearl – reputed to have been Errol Flynn's yacht and now a restaurant. We headed briefly out to the rougher waters of the Med before turning into Grand Harbour, to be greeted by the unforgettable sight of the Fortifications of the Knights of St John, and tiers of honey-coloured churches and houses overlooking the deep blue waters. Whenever I need to relax I conjure up this scene and am never disappointed by its calming effect.

Turning into Dockyard Creek, once kept busy with the pride of the British navy, we passed Libyan tankers being refitted and refuelled, and a Russian cruise liner in for repairs, her passengers gaily waving to us as we sailed by. Our guide told us that Grand Harbour, with its strategic position at the heart of the Mediterranean, was the reason for the domination of Malta by successive invading forces, but it is also the source of her prosperity. Returning past Fort St Elmo, originally a watchtower guarding the entrance to the harbour, we sailed back into Sliema Creek.

In spite of the steep streets and many steps, the capital –Valletta – *is* negotiable with a healthy escort. When Grand Master La Valette decided to build a fortified city in the 1560s, it was originally proposed to level the ground and foundations. But this proved too expensive, so the streets and the bastions are on different levels. We left our car outside the city gates and began a leisurely exploration of the main streets, curio and souvenir shops, bars, fabulous street markets and open-air cafés. We watched fascinated as women high up on their enclosed balconies lowered baskets to ground level to be filled with groceries by youngsters before being hauled up again. Washing was strung out to dry

across the narrow streets to the balconies opposite, creating a carnival effect: very picturesque, but it struck us how hard life must be for the elderly and disabled – do they have to rely on a rope and basket as their only escape route?

Following a pleasant lunch at a pavement café in Queens Square, we moved on to the Grand Master's Palace, with its cool courtyards and bronze statue of Neptune; there was level access to the main courtyard only. After brief stops at the Fine Arts Museum (ground floor accessible) and the Cathedral (access difficult but possible with help) and Museum of St John, we doubled back down Republic Street to make our way on to the Bastions and the War Museum. Here, there was level access throughout, and we photographed the Cheshire Regiment wall plaque to show to my father, who served with them during the war. The emotive photographs and artefacts illustrated the terrible deprivation that the Maltese people suffered throughout the war, and their pride in the George Cross subsequently awarded to the islanders.

The twenty-minute crossing by car ferry to Gozo, which lies just over 6km to the north across the Fliegu Channel, was comfortable and enjoyable as passengers were allowed to remain in their vehicles; with all the windows open we found the sea breeze most welcome on such a hot day. Gozo is greener, with more trees and vines than Malta; otherwise the islands are very alike, with the honey-coloured stone, ornate churches, fishing boats and small farming communities. Tourism is expanding here, too, though not as noticeably as on Malta.

In Victoria, the capital of Gozo, we explored the streets of the old town before deciding to take a look at the citadel and cathedral. Arthur did a recce and reported back: "a bit steep, but manageable". This turned out to be a gross understatement! As we struggled up the almost vertical hill, with my stalwart husband bent double with the effort of pushing my not inconsiderable weight, and desperately trying not to slip, I prayed silently for the gift of levitation and that Arthur would not suffer a heart attack or sunstroke – both possibilities, given the conditions. We finally made it to the top, where we regained breath and admired the impressive architecture (the cathedral was inaccessible – many steps) before venturing down again. This proved to be equally hair-raising, not least for the black-clad elderly ladies stood gossiping at the bottom of the hill, who glanced up to see us charging towards them. Fortunately we skirted round them and came to a halt in the tree-lined square, collapsing at the nearest café to gulp down several refreshing drinks.

The Maltese people impressed us greatly with their friendly, courteous nature; they were quick to offer assistance or refreshment, and clearly pleased when complimented on their homeland. Who could forget the cheerful optimism of the drivers of the horse-cabs (*karrozzini*), who from their high perches frequently cried, "Want a ride, lady?" (getting me up there would have required a crane, plus removal of my lower limbs!), and George, the hotel gardener, who not only showed us every kindness but presented me with a fresh flower daily.

Our departure was not to be without incident: at the airport there was a "breakdown in communications" and after my fellow passengers had boarded for the return flight I was stuck aloft in an ancient, shaky platform lift whilst the cabin crew gazed from afar and puzzled over what to do with me. Just as panic was about to take over, a decision was made and to my intense relief I was carried onto the aircraft and laid across the width of *three* seats, firmly belted down with *three* seat-belts. With a cushion placed beneath my head I was not only very comfortable but could actually look out of the window for the first time (I am unable to turn my head). Would that I could travel in this fashion all the time, but airlines usually demand payment for a seat taken to give extra legroom. And in the very seats which provide sufficient room – near the exits – I am not allowed to sit; understandable but surely provision could also be made for those of us with fixed knees? As it was, I rejoiced in my good fortune and lay happily watching the lights of Malta recede.

Multicoloured Malta

Enid Jasper is an artist with an unbendable right leg. She travels with a tiny folding stool to hold her painting materials whilst working, and a National Trust walking aid which opens out to form a canvas seat. In early March 1989 she went to Malta with another artist, staying in the self-catering Burlington Apartments in Saint Julian's Bay.

On aircraft, there isn't enough room for me to sit on the edge of my seat, in order to rest my foot on the floor, and if I sit well back in the seat my leg sticks out horizontally, for which there is no room for my length of leg or for a small stool – necessary if I am to keep my leg in mid-air for three hours or so. I thought I'd solved the problem on my trip to Malta – I had a front seat to allow me to rest my foot flat against the bulkhead. Ideal.

However, on the return flight the aircraft was much smaller, with less room between seat and bulkhead. My friend and I were separated as the plane was full but I was glad enough to have the front seat, even though my leg was at such a sharp angle upwards that my foot was way above my head. The steward warned that if the pilot braked sharply on take-off or landing I would break my leg, so for these two manoeuvres I had to rest my leg across the lap of the man in the next seat (either that or through the window). Anyway, he couldn't remain a stranger after that, and I learned a lesson – wear trousers for travelling.

Another hazard is the lavatory – plenty of manoeuvring required to close the door. Thank goodness I'm not a six-footer. Cornerways is the answer.

There are, of course, three gorgeous seats with unlimited legroom on any plane, by the exit doors. I'm told I'd be a hazard in emergencies, as each passenger rushing for the exit would first be tripped up by my leg. But why not throw me out first?

We arrived in the early hours and were efficiently assigned to our buses. All the buses in Malta seem to be museum pieces. We sat in the back row (for extra legroom) and what a mistake. The driver drove like a madman and the roads were full of pot-holes; we clung on for grim life but frequently almost hit the roof.

When booking our holiday through *Richard Staples Travel* (the tour operator was *Global*) we did our utmost to secure an apartment without steps. Some of the apartments *are* free of steps; ours wasn't. There were eight steps from the lift down to the landing, while inside the flat was a flight of twelve deep steps to kitchen and sitting room, and a further six or so up to the main bedroom. We protested strongly and after two nights (Sunday intervened) the courier moved us to a more suitable flat.

The Maltese people, almost without exception, seem to be happy, carefree types, and they love the British, which is rare enough these days. I think one holidaymaker put it in a nutshell when he said, "The Maltese are lovely, but get them behind a wheel of a car and they turn into maniacs". I'm afraid so. We didn't venture to drive but hired a taxi for several journeys. The driver would happily position his taxi astride the white line on main roads, gesticulating with both hands off the wheel. But everyone was smiling – hooters blaring, yes, but all smiles.

"I felt so sorry for you, I was about to bring you both a mug of tea."

On several occasions, when we were sitting painting, a car would pull up behind us and there would be furious hooting. I'd turn round, expecting perhaps that we were in someone's way, but not at all – just interested, with wide smiles all round. Once a minibus stopped immediately behind us so that the driver could explain the finer points of watercolour and oil painting to his busload of small children.

Art leads to some interesting conversations: always when painting in public one attracts "lookers on" (less in cities than in the countryside). People gather behind and of course many, if they don't paint themselves, have a relative who does, and we hear all about that. Mostly we're engrossed, and ignore the comments – if we talked to everyone we'd never get anything done. Distracted by a discussion with two men behind me about the potential closure of the Carlisle–Settle railway, I once painted almost half a seascape with palm trees and cacti in the foreground; I found that I just could not concentrate on splashing blue waves onto the paper whilst thinking about railway lines!

The weather was mainly very comfortably warm, occasionally very hot and sometimes cold and windy. We were determined to paint the brightly coloured boats bobbing about in the green waters of St Julian's Bay. It was blowing a gale and very cold. I wore trousers, sweater, headscarf, anorak and plastic mac, but my eyes watered so much that I could hardly see to paint. My friend secured huge rocks to all three legs of his easel – we feared we might be blown into the harbour. I poured water from my bottle into my painting jar, but the stream of water was blown into my paintbox instead. When we finally left, beaten by the weather, a Maltese man called over: "I felt so sorry for you, I was about to bring you both a mug of tea." We painted a narrow street in the old part of St Julian's Bay: colour-washed houses, their distinctive, jutting, square bay windows, huge cactus plants and geraniums in the tiny front gardens, and deep shadows slanting across the scene. A Maltese lady emerged from a nearby doorway and, in faultless English, insisted that we come inside for coffee and biscuits. The house interior was rather heavily furnished, with religious icons and crucifixes displayed. The Maltese are a religious race and there are holy pictures in the drivers' cabs on buses, in the banks, everywhere. On Sundays everything except church is suspended.

The food in Malta is simple but very good. Excellent fish, of course, especially the swordfish steaks. Lorries selling fresh produce park on street corners until late evening. On our forays into the countryside we saw lorries in the fields being loaded with broad beans and carrots. The countryside was much greener and more colourful than we expected: palm trees, tamarisks, enormous cacti, fields of yellow daisies and giant red clover, interspersed with poppies, all feature in our paintings.

Painting is very time-consuming, so we generally avoid organised excursions, but we do try to cover a representative range of subjects. We went by ferry to Gozo, which remains a rustic, unspoilt outpost. There are about thirty parish churches, not to mention the little chapels, and church bells punctuate the day in every settlement. Life here carries on at a very slow tempo, centred on agriculture and fishing. We saw farmers leading their flocks of goats, and women bent double under loads of red clover grass, staggering up rocky hillsides. We ate a simple tuna fish salad overlooking the bay at Xlendi, a tiny fishing village, where the inevitable statue of a saint looked out to sea. Pink tamarisk blossom leant against the base, and a little donkey was tethered to the tree trunk. The midday sun ensured that this scene was deserted, except for a group of old men talking, and a couple of women making lace in a shadowed doorway.

In Victoria there are good shops, shady squares and the cathedral, with its convincing *trompe-l'oeil* "dome", painted on a flat surface. The Bondi Palace houses the Gozo National Museum and was once owned by a wealthy family. There are exhibits of Roman finds and a good introduction to the nearby prehistoric temples.

"Dazzling yellow daisies, mauve and scarlet poppies and pink blossoms against an azure sea"

Back on Malta, I was keen to paint a mosque, so we went to a farming district of drystone walls and many terraces, with a mosque on the horizon. We sat in dense undergrowth, just in front of a tiny stone block building, with two minute slits in the wall; I assumed it was a wood store. It started to rain and being entirely without shelter (spots of rain on a watercolour ruin it), I tried to shield my sketchbook in the doorway – the building seemed derelict and the door didn't budge. A man approached and passed very close to us. We greeted him, since his feet were almost in my paintbox. I was surprised to see him go into the building, after which he kept passing to and fro. I said that I hoped we weren't in his way. He indicated not, but spoke no English. Then I noticed a small number six above the door – this was his home, and we were more or less in his front garden! I tried to imagine what it would be like inside – almost total darkness, but the view, if he could see out, was of dazzling yellow daisies, mauve and scarlet poppies and pink blossoms against an azure sea.

Valletta should be visited on foot as the streets are narrow and many are closed to traffic. The main street is about a mile long and reminiscent of a street in San Francisco. It takes about two hours to walk along the top of the capital's fortifications but if you can manage it the views are spectacular. From the Barracca Gardens, with their vivid hibiscus blossoms and statues, there's a stunning vista across Grand Harbour.

In Freedom Square are the ruins of the old opera house, bombed in World War II, and nearby is Valletta's oldest church, completed in the sixteenth century to commemorate the Great Siege. A large number of the palaces and stately buildings have rather blank facades; privacy and security were of prime importance in the past and many buildings were entered only by an arched doorway at the side. The characteristic brightly painted wooden enclosed balconies – seen even in the humblest houses – were for the benefit of the strictly cloistered women of Moorish times, to allow them to glimpse the outside world and, presumably, to catch a breath of fresh air.

Nowhere is the cloistered style of architecture more apparent than in Mdina, where several of Malta's aristocratic families live in enclosed palaces behind high walls. Colossal heavy doors with iron grilles and ornate door knockers hint at the luxury behind. One of the palaces houses Malta's oldest titled family: no windows visible, and massive walls support a door with an outsize pair of brass Neptunes – I doubt anyone can lift them. The Natural History Museum is inside the Vilhena Palace and nearby is the convent, another blank-walled building.

The cathedral in Mdina is lavishly Baroque and its museum contains a most marvellous coin collection in mirrored cases. Upstairs the paintings include works by Dürer, Rembrandt, Van Dyck and Goya, to mention a few. After all this, it was a relief to sit on the ramparts and take in the magnificent patchwork of fields and minute farms, stretching all the way to the spires of Valletta. Before departure I'd made sure to include in my watercolours a good supply of yellow ochre, which I'd anticipated to be the main colour required for the honey-coloured buildings. How wrong I was: Malta in the spring is multicoloured indeed.

MALTA: TRAVEL NOTES

Sources of information

Physically Handicapped Rehabilitation Fund (*PHRF*), Rehabilitation Centre, Corradino, Paola, Malta; ☎222221, 227518. Any advice on your stay can be obtained from John Micallef at *PHRF*: tours for visiting groups of disabled people are organised using adapted transport, and *PHRF* will try to fit in individuals whenever possible. They hire out wheelchairs, walking aids and toilet adaptions according to availability (write as soon as possible). However, many of the centre's wheelchairs are of the older type; if you are staying at the *Grosvenor* or *Seabreeze* you'll need removable footrests and will have to

MALTA: TRAVEL NOTES

advise the centre of this. Barry Atkinson recommends that you take your own chair, for which there is a repair service. For a small fee (£10 in 1989) *PHRF* will meet you at the airport and convey you to your destination, then return you to the airport at the end of your stay.
Malta National Tourist Office, Suite 300, Mappin House, 4 Winsley Street, London W1N 7AR; ☎071/323 0506. Supplies only general information.

Tour operators

It's easy to make your own arrangements, by contacting the hotel direct and fixing the flight separately. If you want to go through an operator, steer clear of *Global* (p.89). Try *Meon Villa Holidays*, *Horizon Holidays* or *Thomson*.

Getting there

There isn't much to choose between the **airlines** (*Air Malta* and *Monarch Airlines*) that operate scheduled flights to Malta. *Air Malta* (314/316 Upper Richmond Road, London SW15 6TU; ☎071/785 3177) is the only one to fly from Heathrow (as well as Gatwick and Manchester). Choice of flight should be based on price and proximity of departure airport.

All aircraft will be cramped, particularly tricky for those with unbendable leg(s), but Christine Warburton was treated well on her return flight by *Air Malta* – she was given three seats to stretch out on. For most people the flight is probably just short enough (under four hours) to survive the lack of space.

There is a (somewhat antiquated) lift at Luqa **airport** for disembarking wheelchair passengers, and adapted toilet facilities in the terminal.

Transport

On Malta, the **buses** are of roughly the same vintage as the airport lifts, and with deep steps at the entrances are not recommended for non-ambulant disabled people travelling alone. **Taxis** are surprisingly expensive and **car hire** (no hand controls) is a better option, especially if you shop around the local firms.

The **ferry** crossing to Gozo is short and passengers can remain in their cars. Christine

Warburton managed a Grand Harbour cruise with help from the crew when boarding.

Accommodation

There are no fully adapted hotels in Malta but five are better equipped than most. Barry comments on these below, having stayed in two and visited them all. Any other type of accessible accommodation is very difficult to find.

The cost of a long-term, off-season stay will be between you and the hotel; it's best to deal direct and then book a flight separately. Barry now always uses the *Grosvenor Hotel* (Pope Alexander VII Junction, Balzan; ☎486916) in old Balzan, one of the "three villages" (Attard, Balzan and Lija), which are worth exploring. The friendly staff here will sort out any difficulties. The steep ramp, round the corner from the stepped front entrance, has recently been made less steep but is still narrow. Inside, good ramps take you via the central lobby to the rooms, which are spacious; even the bathrooms are reasonably suited to wheelchair use. A lift, which requires the footrests to be folded to one side, goes to the restaurant. The only access to the reception is via steps but this problem is easily overcome by the staff. A small lip to the outside pool area is the only minor fault and this area is mostly wide and flat. A bonus is that the hotel backs onto the San Anton Gardens. However, be warned that the hotel is inland and not easy to find – a hire car is recommended.

The most expensive of the five hotels is the *Suncrest Hotel* (Qawra Coast, Qawra; ☎4477101), situated opposite the sea in a very accessible, if busy, position in Qawra. The tourist haunts of Bugibba and the tranquillity of Salina Bay are close at hand. There are built-in ramps to most places and spacious lifts. Request a bedroom in which the wardrobe won't hinder a wheelchair turning into the bathroom.

There is little thought of disability at the *Jerma Palace Hotel* (Marsascala; ☎823222), but it happens to be fairly accessible and is in a quiet area outside Marsascala on the east coast, a very nice part of the island. Few troubles for the wheelchair except an exasperating lip at the entrance. Doors to the bedrooms and

MALTA: TRAVEL NOTES

bathrooms are a tight fit, except for one "special" room.

The *Seabreeze Hotel* (Pretty Bay, Birzebbuga; ☎871256), recommended by the Rehabilitation Centre because of its cost and friendliness, is small and in a lovely area. However, the main problem of a high-stepped entrance, reached across a narrow pavement and gutter, overcome by a portable ramp, is not helped by the hotel's difficult position round a busy corner. The lift to the bedrooms is only just wide enough for a wheelchair (you'll have to take the footrests off) and the bathrooms are extremely compact, with only just enough room between bath and wall for a wheelchair to reach the toilet.

Barry wouldn't return to *The Complex*, Bugibba, where he stayed for three months in 1986, despite the helpful staff. The rooms are reasonably suited to wheelchairs and the outside ramp is now permanent but there was little interest in the requirements of disabled tourists when he visited recently. When Barry was there the main bar was reached down steep steps and the staff carried him down. Perhaps things have changed though — it's worth a letter to find out.

Christine Warburton stayed at the *Preluna Hotel* (124 Tower Road, Sliema; ☎334001). It has a ramped entrance, lift to all floors, plus nightclub. Measurements are given in the *RADAR* holiday guide, as is a short list of other accessible hotels.

Access and facilities

A reasonable number of the historic sights of Malta are at least partially accessible with the aid of a strong companion, or a friendly islander. But there is a long way to go in the fight for accessible public transport, cars with hand controls, adapted accommodation, easy access to buildings, provision of wheelchair-accessible toilet facilities and so on.

The disabled inhabitant of the islands must rely on the work of the government committee for the disabled and of organisations such as the *PHRF*. There have been improvements in living standards and disability allowances (p.84), but Barry Atkinson's impressions suggest that the concepts of independent living and integration of the disabled person into the community are far removed from Maltese thinking.

Most handicapped people in Malta spend their lives in institutions. An interesting recent development aims to provide relief from this form of imprisonment: *Ir-Razzett Tal-Hbiberija* (A Park of Friendship) has been founded by Janatha and Paddy Stubbs near Marsascala Bay. The aim is to create a leisure centre for handicapped islanders — with farmhouse, barn (for social events), swimming pool, sports ground, adventure playground, children's zoo and gardens. Funds are being raised through the *Janatha Stubbs Foundation* and the founders are happy to show visitors around the park (Zinzell Street, Marsascala; ☎684412).

Although the enthusiasm and work of the people involved in this project cannot be faulted, and accessible leisure facilities will greatly enhance the quality of life for those who are confined to institutions, it would be good to see the same degree of enthusiasm directed towards provision of better access all over the island. In a sense, this is the creation of another institution, albeit a very pleasant and enjoyable one.

PART TWO

NORTHERN
EUROPE

Introduction

The whole of northern Europe is covered in this section, but although the differences may soon start to fade, there is still a huge gulf between Eastern and Western Europe as far as facilities for disabled travellers go. One indication of awareness of the disabled traveller's needs is the quality and quantity of literature available, from either the tourist boards or specialist organisations. The **East European** countries fail this test with flying colours, although tourist board staff do try their best to answer individual enquiries. Two accounts of trips to the **Soviet Union** are included here as they cover travel in the western edge of this vast collection of states, nearest to Europe.

Although conditions for many disabled Eastern Europeans are grim, it is a time of great upheaval in Europe, with the reunification of Germany and the toppling of old regimes. New associations of disabled people are forming almost daily in the Soviet Union and East European countries. Links are being forged with similar associations in the West and exchange visits are taking place. All this will have spin-offs for travellers to the East – they will find more and more facilities and better access, resulting in a wider choice of destination and discovery of a different face of Europe.

There's more money in northern, western Europe than in the eastern and Mediterranean countries, and evidence of differing attitudes to disability. Here our expectations are high – we discover a fully accessible museum or art gallery and see that it *can* be done, so we want to see it done everywhere. In the south, on the other hand, we demand less and are pleasantly surprised if we find an accessible self-catering apartment or museum. Unfortunately, awareness of the requirements of disabled people remains abysmally low and changes come slowly and almost grudgingly.

In some areas, such as **access to public buildings**, tourist attractions and transport, Europe as a whole has a long way to go to catch up with the USA, where disabled people are generally well organised into vociferous groups capable of forcing through far-reaching legislation. In her account on p.164, Sian Williams stresses the importance of passing laws – rather than simply making encouraging noises to the planners – to ensure maximum independence for disabled people.

In Europe the age of the building often works against attempts to make it accessible to wheelchair users. It is perhaps unfair to compare the totally accessible Metrorail in Washington DC with the London Underground. But improving access, even in old buildings and antiquated transport systems, does not have to involve unsightly alterations or be prohibitively expensive. In Sweden, Gripsholm Castle in Mariefred, which dates back to the sixteenth century and houses the Swedish State Portrait Collection, has been made fully accessible by the purchase of a stair-climbing wheelchair – much cheaper than lift installation and causing no damage to the fabric of the building.

There *are* accessible **underground systems** in northern Europe – in Lille, Berlin, Amsterdam, Stockholm, Helsinki, Newcastle-upon-Tyne – but many partially accessible systems are spoiled by fiercely sprung gates, long distances to cover at interchanges, difficult door handles on trains, no facilities for blind passengers. There is still much to be done. The cheapest form of transport in cities – the **bus** – remains largely inaccessible. On the **trains**, it's not good enough to plan new rolling stock for the Nineties that only sometimes makes provision for wheelchairs in the carriages (p.140); wheelchair users should be given the choice to remain in their chairs without having to sit in the vestibule or the goods van. Specialist taxi or minibus services for disabled people cannot be a substitute for a totally accessible public transport system unless they provide a full, scheduled service covering the entire network; they should be considered a stop-gap measure until new, accessible rolling stock is introduced, lifts are installed, and the necessary changes made to station platforms.

Reports of **air travel** in northern Europe have been generally optimistic. But there are some gripes, in the main resulting from airport officials who insist on channelling every disabled passenger through exactly the same "special" handling procedure. Swedish airports seem to have the most civilised approach, allowing the wheelchair user the freedom to behave like any other passenger – shopping, eating, drinking – until ten minutes before the other passengers are called to the gate.

Boarding and disembarking may have to be performed without lifting vehicles or airbridges because of the size of the aircraft and lack of facilities at regional airports. If the human lifting service is well trained and prepared to adopt the carrying technique that best suits each passenger, this need not cause problems, but for those who cannot maintain their posture it is an unpleasant experience (p.151).

The **ferry companies** operating routes to continental Europe and to Ireland have incorporated facilities for disabled passengers on their newer ships. *Sealink Stena Line*, *P&O* and *Brittany Ferries* are singled out for praise. Many people like to take their cars or camper vans, and there are substantial reductions to be had for members of disabled drivers' motoring organisations (*DDMC*, *DDA*).

Driving conditions in the north of Europe are reasonable and there are reciprocal parking arrangements in most countries for Orange Badge holders. The number of motorway service stations with accessible facilities is on the increase; several countries supply lists of them, making route planning easier. On minor roads, however, it is often difficult to find any toilets, let alone wheelchair-accessible ones.

Accommodation, more often than not, is far from totally accessible, but the situation is not impossible and it's getting better. We received many accounts from people who travelled through Europe without pre-booking accommodation (see also *Practicalities*, "Sleeping"). However, there is much confusion over the use of the wheelchair symbol in hotel lists or guidebooks, and a rather cavalier over-use of the phrase "clients must check details of accessibility with the hotel before booking", or words to that effect. In Britain it is hoped that the use of the *Tourism for All Accessible* symbol will encourage progress in this area.

The amount of **information** which is out of date is also disturbing – material published in the early Eighties is still sent out by tourist boards. It's almost as though the International Year of the Disabled (1981) spurred a few energetic groups into action and they've now lost enthusiasm. This is a pity because outdated information can be worse than no information.

Ireland

Sidetracked in Ireland

As a result of a combination of achondroplasia and restricted growth syndrome, Annie Delin is not much more than a metre tall. The practical effects of this are that she cannot walk very far or stand for long. Although she doesn't use a wheelchair ordinarily she takes a Major Buggy when she travels, and a companion to push it. In August 1989 she went with three friends to Ireland.

When I told people my summer holiday was to be in Ireland, a particular tone of caressing warmth came into the voices of those who'd already been. "Oh, you'll love it," they all said.

Nevertheless, we went away with a certain set of ideas in our heads. Ireland would be beautiful and green. The west coast would have cliffs and wildlife – it would be a little like Wales or the wild parts of Scotland. Only at the last minute did we remember to take our passports. This was, after all, a foreign country. Until we disembarked at Dun Laoghaire, it hadn't entered our heads how foreign somewhere as close as Ireland might be. It's almost England, isn't it? They speak the same language, share our history, have the same climate.

By the end of a week, we found that we were fundamentally wrong on all those counts. No English person could use the language in such an unashamedly poetic way – we could only guess that the Gaelic language, spoken for preference in most of the places we visited, must be as beautiful. Our history is shared only because we rode roughshod over their own history to impose ours onto it, but the countryside speaks of a different past, of traditions and people.

And the climate is the most surprising part. It rains, which makes Ireland green, and in the mountains the mists are ever present, but the warmth of the air on wet and dry days encourages yucca trees to reach a height of thirty feet in gardens all over the country. On the Dingle Peninsula the hedgerows are of shocking pink fuschia flowers, and the heather and gorse on the moors form a startling carpet of purple and gold. If rain alone does this, why does it only happen in Ireland?

Four of us travelled together, jammed into one car with luggage and two tents, a box of Sainsbury's foodstuffs and a Calor-gas stove. My concessions to essential comfort (to reduce the risks of stiff joints and rheumatism) were an air-bed, which attracted universal contempt because the foot pump was slow and had to be operated by everyone except me, a stool to sit on and a quantity of warm clothes, even though it was August.

We thought of taking my wheelchair in case we needed to cover distances that I couldn't walk, but I decided against it for reasons of space and self-image. We could always use the car, even if only for short hops around towns, from one parking space to another. Travelling with three girl-friends who knew me well, I didn't need to feel worried about stating my requirements forcefully if I was too tired or stiff to walk.

Camping isn't the ideal style of accommodation if sitting in the damp, constantly bending down, or wriggling around trying to get dressed in a two-man tent are likely to aggravate your physical problems. On the other hand, how can you beat sitting on a cliff top, swaddled in sleeping bags and jumpers, drinking the contents of a three-litre wine-box and then simply rolling into the tent? The sea air blows in and the waves still whisper as you fall into drunken sleep. You couldn't do it in a warm, dry B&B.

"We went into Kelly's Bar and tried Irish Guinness. Everything they say is true"

The cliff top was our first night's camp, near the tiny town of Wicklow. We had crossed from Holyhead on a ferry which arrived at 6.30am (for cheaper tickets). The amazingly Mediterranean look of Dun Laoghaire woke us up for a bit, but we still needed to sleep. Fortune made us drive further than we intended, ignoring a large and impersonal caravan park, until we came to Silver Strand.

We found, on waking up, that we had a private beach of clean, soft sand with a gentle slope into the sea. The steps leading down the cliff became steeper as we descended but there was a handrail, and the way back up was a lot easier because my friends carried me!

We booked for two nights, thus giving ourselves time to spend the next day in Dublin. The National Gallery there had a wheelchair to lend us, giving me the chance to absorb Irish Art without a backache. The poet W.B. Yeats had a brother called Jack, we discovered, whose paintings hold the same magic as the poetry. We bought far too many books and pictures, and transformed our tarpaulin dining area into an open-air reading room when we got back to camp.

Wicklow itself doesn't seem big enough to have named a whole county, but its quiet ways and quaint appearances charmed us. Every shopfront had been hand-painted in a style which was not quite as professional as sign-writing, making it attractive in an idiosyncratic way. In the evening we went into Kelly's Bar and tried Irish Guinness. Everything they say is true.

Since our intention had been to spend the week in County Kerry, we set off the next day. Nothing had prepared us for the fact that Ireland has no major roads – or none that you would call major in England. By the time we reached Limerick – which didn't live up to the poetic implications of its name – we were tired and fed up of travelling behind slow vehicles on single-carriage roads. The drivers do tend to pull over to allow you to pass, but they cannot do much if the road winds or is overloaded with oncoming traffic.

The result of our arduous journey was that we camped at Killarney, fifty miles short of our intended destination (the Dingle Peninsula). The campsite was not as enchanting as the first, and much busier; we had by then discovered that campers are a strange breed in Ireland, where bed and breakfasts in what seems like half the nation's houses cater for the tourist trade.

Camping at Killarney did mean that the following day we were tempted to stop and look at Muckross Abbey, within a mile of the town. It was then that we noticed what a delightful place Killarney is, nestled in a valley against the Ring of Kerry mountains, its church spire rising from the town.

Muckross, a fourteenth-century abbey destroyed by Cromwell, is set in a huge expanse of lakes, holy islands and wild parkland. It is closed to vehicles, which makes for a tranquil setting but leaves only two options for getting there – walking or taking one of the horse-drawn gigs for which Killarney is apparently famed. These are sold hard by men who have scant regard for charity, and feel that your inability to walk is not their problem. Not allowing myself to feel annoyed, I paid £5 (Irish) for one mile to the abbey, and reasoned that this was the whole point of Mobility Allowance – to spend it on getting places.

Fortunately, it was a place worth getting to. We spent a good part of the day around the lakes and ended up driving only about twenty miles to our third and final camp – down an unmade road in the heart of the Ring of Kerry. Here was another advantage of camping. There wasn't a B&B for miles and we were camping in country silence, mist-shrouded mountains all around us and the sheep kept out of the camp only by ditches. These, incidentally, were not enough to keep the cows out at night – as we found when we woke to a cowpat so close to the tent flap we wondered why we hadn't been trampled in our sleep.

The Ring of Kerry campsite catered for the real traveller. A communal games and dining room offered two electric cookers operated by coin meters, and this was clearly a luxury for the cyclists we encountered – from

Germany, France, even New Zealand – who were "doing" Ireland by bike.

In this camp, as in the others, the showers would have been impossible for me to use alone. Their six-foot-high coin meters and ludicrously small compartments were almost made up for by the therapeutic effect of streams of very hot water, but I had to do most of my dressing in the open because I couldn't sit down in the cubicles.

"You're as welcome as the flowers in May"

Our nearest town was Kenmare, where we decided to treat ourselves to a meal out. The previous night we had drunk Guinness and listened to Irish music in Killarney. This time, in the Ivy Leaf, we ate a combination of traditional Irish and modern French cuisine – wild Irish salmon marinaded in honey and dill, yam pie and pistachio ice cream with raspberry sauce, and an Irish cheeseboard with a fiercely pungent odour.

When we'd eaten, the chef came to tell us that Ireland's finest folk musician was playing across the road in the hotel where the Kenmare Folk Club meets. Noel Hill was on his way to Tralee, where the Rose of Tralee festival started the next day. There he played to support Van Morrison and tickets cost £16. We saw him in an upstairs room in Kenmare for £4 and had a rousing good time.

There was just a day left to reach Dingle – which we'd expected to be our holiday base. We made it in a day trip and glimpsed spectacular cliff-top views through the shifting mists. When the sun burst out it lit the sea round the islands in an ultramarine glow. The islands, inhabited for centuries, were abandoned less than forty years ago and are now populated by birds and seals. In the evening we got caught in the traffic and ribaldry of Tralee as the festival started. Perhaps more time would have allowed us to enjoy it; as it was, we couldn't wait to leave it behind.

Knowing that the next day we'd be speeding back to the east coast – glancing at Cork, bypassing Blarney Castle, talking through Waterford – we all felt that we'd done Ireland an injustice. A week was more of a whistle-stop taster than a holiday. On our last night we stayed again at Wicklow, with a few hours in the blazing sunshine on the silver beach, and our first sea bathe of the holiday – we hadn't had time elsewhere.

Waiting in the morning for the ferry to start loading, we spent our last Irish pennies on tea from a quayside stall. When my friend thanked the stallholder, he replied, "You're as welcome as the flowers in May." We felt Ireland had been glad to have us.

When I go back to Ireland, as I surely will, there are several things I will know. My reception there was almost unblemished by prejudice or short-sightedness – partly, I believe, because the Irish are kind and welcoming whatever the circumstances. The only difficulty came

at Dublin Castle, where an attendant wouldn't let us park in the inner area under the castle "because we had English number plates".

If I travel by car I know I'll be sidetracked by sights and views and opportunities at every turn. To travel west it would be better – for those who can afford it – to fly to Shannon and hire a car, allowing as much time in the west as originally planned. Perhaps, taking the sensible option, I'd also decide to use B&Bs next time – for the comfort of a warm, dry bed and a hot bath. At least I will know that wherever I go there will most definitely be accommodation available.

There hasn't been space to mention the ancient forests, the stone "beehive" huts built by Christian hermits, the famed solo dolphin at Dingle (is he really called Fungi?) and the way people enquired with genuine interest what we thought of Ireland at every chance encounter. Ireland deserves plenty of time from every traveller, both to get to know the country and to enjoy its many charms.

Abandoning Ship in Galway

Although born in Ireland, Helena O'Keefe had not been back since spending many months in hospital and taking early retirement as a result of disabilities caused by rheumatoid arthritis.

My sister said that sailing up the west coast was the perfect way to appreciate the miles of bays, cliffs and mountains, but she thought the wheelchair would be a problem. So did I. We considered renting a cottage but did not want to be

confined to one area. Mum, who is in her seventies, still had a Sprite caravan and awning – would a touring holiday be appropriate?

There are a set of problems when I am away from home: how high is the bed, how far is the toilet, are there steps or stairs, can I choose when to rest or eat and – just as important – will the wheelchair pusher enjoy the holiday too? My brother was able to take time off in September and offered to help with arrangements and the hard work. As I weigh less than eight stone he is able to lift me about and is skilled at getting me, in the chair, down flights of stairs, to the astonishment of passers-by. By towing the family caravan we were able to take special equipment, including an adapted Porta-potti, all of which took the strain out of travelling. The wheelchair is standard DSS issue; it folds quite easily but takes up most of the boot. The spares kit wasn't needed, but I wouldn't travel without it – and a pump.

"When planning what to do and see once there we made good use of the tourist information offices"

We used the Irish Tourist Board information to plan our route, going first to County Waterford, visiting relatives and seeing how much it had altered. From there it was the N24 to Limerick, N18 to Galway and the Atlantic coast, and on up the N59 to Westport to explore County Mayo. When planning what to do and see once there we made good use of the tourist information offices in the larger towns; these are always well signposted, they supply plenty of free information, and they recommend accommodation and make reservations.

Although the Fishguard to Rosslare crossing is only three and a half hours, the total journey time from southern England is much longer. The M4 gives way to local roads, and the Welsh hills go on and on. It helps to check in early and be settled before the majority of passengers arrive.

We made our reservations through the *Disabled Drivers' Motor Club* and wrote to *Sealink* explaining that we'd need access to the lift. At Fishguard we repeated this to everyone who checked our tickets and we were given a distinctive windscreen sticker. I have found all the ferry operators cooperative as long as they are fully informed. We were directed to a parking place by the service lift and escorted to the main deck along with cases of duty free goods. Some of the smaller, older ferries do not have passenger lifts, so it is important to arrange for help back to the car deck later – this avoids competing with the kitchen garbage at the end of the voyage.

We booked a cabin, so that we had space to relax, but the high sills made the toilet difficult to use. All the ladies' toilets on board seemed very tricky for wheelchairs, but the bar, restaurant and self-service were accessible.

Customs formalities were brief and we did not need passports. Finding our way out of Rosslare harbour, into Wexford and onto the N25 was not so easy. Distances did not look odd once we realised that they were in kilometres on the newer signs; the place names were in Irish and English. The main routes (N roads) were quite well signposted and partly dual-carriageway. The maximum speed limit was 55mph (88km) and in the countryside there was very little traffic.

As we approached Waterford a car began flashing at us. Mum said, "I think it's all right. I bet it's Eamon Cusack come out to meet us." She was right. When we stopped, our cousin explained that he had been waiting to escort us through the city and along the narrow, unlit country lanes to the caravan site on the cliffs at Dunmore. There were special problems as Maeve Binchey's book, *Echoes*, was being filmed for TV, and most of Dunmore had been blocked off or altered to the style of the 1950s.

"It seemed that the wheelchair was rather a novelty"

During our visit we looked at about a dozen campsites, none of them really suitable for wheelchairs. Washing and toilet facilities were basic, with few adapted toilets or shower cubicles. When shopping we often encountered surprise at seeing a wheelchair and, although we were always welcomed, access would have been a real problem without my brother and sister to push. Anyone using a manual chair on their own would need to be very fit to cope. The tourist board leaflet,

Accommodation for the Disabled, listed accommodation suitable for disabled people but we were unable to find specific information on access to the sights or to public buildings.

The newer visitor attractions are well adapted for wheelchairs. In County Clare, Aillwee Caves, where prehistoric bears had wintered with the stalactites and stalagmites, are accessible throughout, as is the Burren Display Centre. The Burren is a limestone area, startlingly beautiful with many rare alpine and arctic plants and, surprisingly, Mediterranean species growing alongside. Spectacular when viewed from a car, this would make fascinating back-packing country. The upland limestone pavements must be eerie by moonlight – even at noon they felt inhabited, although they were quite empty and silent, not a tree for miles.

Also in County Clare, the visitors' centre, toilets and café at the Cliffs of Moher (198m) are accessible with help, but parking is difficult. There is a very long, gravel path from the car park to the cliff top, where protective walls obstruct the views. Visitors require agility to enjoy this place, and to escape the crowds – it was the only site on our tour that was overrun with tourists.

Further along the coast we stopped at Galway, the busiest town we visited and the only one with any nightlife apart from pubs and restaurants. Many of the streets and pavements were narrow, but the harbour area and tourist information office were accessible. Most of the shops were quite small but happy to accommodate a wheelchair. Many were craft or gift shops, selling Irish linen, pottery, alcohol, Donegal tweed, Aran knitwear and Waterford glass. We were welcomed in cafés and pubs, even when tables or chairs had to be moved to make space. It seemed that the wheelchair was rather a novelty, which perhaps explains the special attention we received.

Our second caravan site was at Spittal on Galway Bay. It was flat and exposed,

giving clear views across the bay to the Burren. We parked beside metre-high boulders marking the edge of the strand and wondered why no one else had chosen to enjoy such views. The answer came during the night: the wind kept rising, the sea roared, the van shook and spray covered the windows. We slept badly and woke feeling damp. After arranging to leave the caravan in a safer spot we phoned a little place Mum remembered in Dugort, Achill Island, to see if they could put us up.

"As we travelled through the Connemara mountains the twentieth century faded"

Driving along the edge of Lough Corrig below a bare granite ridge, we stopped to photograph a donkey cart loaded with turf. (Remember to take plenty of film with you – it's very expensive and can be difficult to find.) The cart-driver said he was the only one left – the rest of the turf was moved by lorry. The lough was dotted with rowing boats, each holding two fishermen; it's a good area for coarse fishing.

There were few cars or houses. As we drew closer to the mountains the small fields gave way to bogs, then scrub and stones, and finally bare rock. We learned to fill up whenever we saw a petrol station; they close after tea and on Sundays and, like human habitation, are scarce in the west. Obtaining cash was also a hit and miss affair and although sterling was accepted it was on a pound-for-pound basis, ignoring the (favourable to us) exchange rate.

As we travelled through the Connemara mountains the twentieth century faded. Apart from the road and telegraph poles, everything we saw had existed for thousands of years. The silver streak on top of a high peak near the coast puzzled me at first. It turned out to be St Patrick's chapel on top of Croagh Patrick (754m), reached by a 1000-year-old track winding up the mountain.

We drove for miles along the edge of Clew Bay, passing huge areas of bog and the occasional ruined stone cottage. From the quay at Newport the goods for Achill Island used to be loaded onto boats, until the bridge was built 30km up the coast. The once busy town has shrunk, and a four-storey warehouse that used to store wool from the island's sheep is now the convent home of a small group of nuns. We were attracted to it by a large mural of Mary the Queen of the Sea above the door, and by a sign saying "TEAS, SWEETS, GIFTS". Inside the massive stone walls we found a small shop with locally made toys and knitwear, and a spotlessly clean tearoom and toilets. The Filippini Sisters provided sustaining homemade food and everything was accessible. As we went back outside, into the sunshine, the convent suddenly became busy as local people hurried in for a religious service.

"The few houses are small and huddle together, their backs to the Atlantic gales"

On the approach to the bridge connecting Achill Island with the rest of County Mayo, the patches of grass and heather were so sparse that even the sheep had lost interest. There must have been trees once – we saw stumps and broken trunks in parts of the bog where turf had been cut and stacked.

My grandparents had come to Achill Island eighty years ago to manage the post office; it must have seemed the furthest outpost of civilisation. The few houses are small and huddle together, their backs to the Atlantic gales. In sheltered spots trees have rooted and the narrow valleys are packed with rhododendrons; flowers dot the hedges of wild fuschia like specks of blood. With its seal caves, wild cliffs and amethyst-bearing mountains, the island is a retreat for lovers of solitary pursuits or walking holidays.

The hotel (*Grays*) is really a row of converted cottages. Luckily there is a ground-floor room with a toilet beside it. The dining room is on the same level. We found it comfortable and hospitable, but I wouldn't recommend it for unaccompanied wheelchair users.

We took the coast road back to Galway, staying at Clifden, a popular town in summer and the centre for west-coast sailing. It lies in a sheltered estuary surrounded by tree-covered hills which rise gradually to the mountains. The little harbour is always busy and there are lots of places to stay and to eat. We found the same holiday atmosphere all along the Connemara coast, all without coachloads of tourists.

My sister left us to return to work. She said later that the journey by coach and train was difficult, with poor connections and delays. We made our way back to the caravan at Spittal and dried everything out. When the rain started again we hitched up and drove about 300km across the country. Most of it was flat. It kept raining. At Rosslare we found a place to eat but it was all rather dull and cheerless after the west coast.

Back in Wales it was still raining. By the time we reached the M4 it had stopped. I'd advise anyone going to Ireland to take waterproofs and an umbrella!

Sibling Rivalry

Nancy Bower-Meale gave up work because of rheumatoid arthritis in 1966. In 1977 she made the trip to Belfast alone (plus wheelchair) and since then has been back many times.

A phone call from my sister set the ball rolling. With her husband she was planning a week away in the Cotswolds. They would travel over by ferry with their car, and on their way home would collect me for a much needed holiday, she told me. It was a large, comfortable car and I could have a cabin on the boat from Liverpool to Belfast. She was obviously very pleased with her offer. After all, for over three years my only outings had been a weekly trip to church and I could no longer get into our garden. It was, she considered, an offer not to be refused, especially since I'd have two able-bodied travelling companions.

But refused it was. I reacted with horror and dread, not only to the idea of the sea crossing (I'd only had to stand on Tower Pier during my city lunch hours to feel seasick), but also to the thought of moving out of my cosy little orbit and having to cope in an entirely new situation. How would I manage washing, or the loo? Would the chairs be right? What about the Ulster bombs and shootings? How would I face getting out of bed in a strange house to start a different kind of day? I firmly declined the offer with thanks.

My sister replied that it was a great opportunity – perhaps the only one I'd get – to see her and my nieces and nephew in their own home, and she was surprised that I was chickening out! Stung into reaction, I retorted that I'd travel by air, making my own arrangements. There was no going back after that affirmation, and the following days were spent in wondering exactly *how* I was going to travel solo by air.

I eventually phoned the local travel agent and discovered that *British Airways* really would "take good care" of me. I arranged for the Red Cross to take me by car (at minimal cost) to Heathrow and meet me on my return. Since then I've used the local mini-cab firm for such trips, always explaining my circumstances, and have found their drivers to be consistently helpful and courteous. This mode of transport gives a great boost to the desire for independence and is, after all, what the Mobility Allowance is for.

Arriving at Heathrow I found that *BA* have a special check-in desk for wheelchair-bound travellers, where I waited for a porter to wheel me through security checks to the departure lounge. I was the first passenger aboard, in a roomy bulkhead seat. Then one of the cabin crew gave me my first shock – we would be delayed for anything up to two hours. But would I like a pot of tea and some biscuits? I felt like royalty, although I did think about the problem of access to the toilet should I indulge in an extra cuppa. As if reading my mind, the steward added that I should press the nearby button or just call out for the stewardess if I required help.

"I realised that being able to communicate is far more important than mobility"

Before long the seat next to me was taken by a young girl. I was pleased to have someone to talk to, hoping to keep panic at bay, but to my opening remarks she replied, "Je suis Française" and for the rest of the flight, which mercifully started sooner than anticipated, my mind was fully taken up in practising the French conversation I'd been studying at home on cassettes. This worked like magic – I realised that being able to communicate is far more important than mobility. By touchdown at Belfast's Aldergrove airport I was elated with a new-found confidence.

The day after my arrival we drove along the shore road of Strangford Lough to do some bird-watching. Named by the Vikings "Strong Ford" because of the strong currents, the area attracts many species of migrating birds and at low tide presents a fascinating scene of bird activity. For those, like myself, who have a problem handling weighty binoculars, I recommend the use of small opera-glasses. Like the proverbial half loaf, they are better than none at all, and I find mine adequate for a distance of about 30m.

> **"Northern Ireland, more than most places, learned to provide good wheelchair access, through the tragedy of 'The Troubles'"**

Moving southeast to Downpatrick we viewed the reputed burial place of Saint Patrick. We were the only visitors and were able to enjoy a few moments of quiet reflection on the life of this fifth-century saint. Born somewhere along the west coast of Britain, the story goes that at the age of sixteen he was carried off by raiders to become a slave in Ireland. He managed to escape to the continent, where he underwent religious training, but was then called in a dream to return to Ireland to preach the gospel of Christ. He arrived in Ireland as a missionary priest in about 432 AD, and through his preaching and ministry overcame all pagan opposition to establish Christianity throughout the island.

In County Antrim, north and west of Belfast, I saw the distinctive Slemish Mountain, with its flat top, where (legend has it) the enslaved Patrick was a herdsman and grazed his master's sheep. The sheep were our only companions as we toured the quiet hills of Antrim; the only sounds when we stopped came from the sheep nibbling at the grass or the clear waters of a stream running over stones. Everywhere we went in Northern Ireland the road traffic was minimal compared to that in the Home Counties, and we often stopped beside the sea or halfway up a hill to enjoy the view with no worries about obstructing the road.

We made a memorable trip along the scenic Antrim coast road, with the sea often just a few yards away and good views over the Irish Sea to Scotland's mountains. Rounding Torr Head in the north we glimpsed Rathlin Island and, beyond it, the Atlantic Ocean stretching away to the Arctic and the North Pole. Our homeward journey took us through some of the Nine Glens of Antrim, wild country where Flora Macdonald is said to have brought Bonnie Prince Charlie to her kinsfolk after their flight from Scotland. Fairy thorns were pointed out to me, bringing to mind the opening lines of the very first poem I'd had to learn at school. My sister and I chanted in unison:

Up the airy mountain
Down the rushey glen,
We daren't go a-hunting
For fear of little men.
(William Allingham: "The Fairies")

Cut down or mutilate a fairy thorn, it was believed in years gone by, and you'd bring down the wrath of the wee folk on your head and your family. Much to my disappointment, I didn't spot any "little men" – perhaps I should have taken the opera-glasses.

The social history of Northern Ireland is encapsulated in the Ulster Folk and Transport Museum at Cultra, east of Belfast, where a typical village has been reconstructed using original buildings. The low thatched cottages are genuine, down to the pots and pans and intricately patterned patchwork quilts, and a peat fire burning in the hearth completes the authentic atmosphere.

Belfast provides a contrast to these rural scenes but it is not the city of violence depicted on our TV screens. As with the violence and mugging in English cities, "The Troubles" are for the most part restricted to a tiny minority in particular areas, which are easily avoided. There are streets where a car cannot be parked without a sitter but I have only once seen armed soldiers, on the outskirts of Belfast. Ringed by hills, the capital of Northern Ireland seems dominated by the large number of church spires and towers, as well as the old mill chimneys, reminders of the linen which brought Belfast its nineteenth-century prosperity. Samson and Goliath, the huge gantries in the Harland & Wolff shipyard, stand guard over the Lagan river as it widens into Belfast Lough; from here the *Titanic* sailed on her disastrous maiden voyage.

My day in Belfast would not have been possible without my wheelchair and the Orange Badge (a pleasant change from London's West End, where the Orange Badge is not officially recognised). Of course, I was fortunate to be with my sister and brother-in-law who knew the city, but I was impressed by the friendliness and courtesy shown by members of the RUC concerning parking and by the hotel waitress who expertly accommodated my wheelchair and me at the table. Access to the *Europa Hotel* (Great Victoria Street) for lunch was good, and I was thrilled to recognise one of the well known Irish folk groups, The Chieftains. I was delighted with the ease of access to Crane's Bookshop in Rosemary Street, where rows of bookcases are widely spaced and no shelf is out of the wheelchair occupant's range of vision. Since my first visit three new accessible bookshops have opened in Royal Avenue.

"I realised that in some respects air travel for the unaccompanied wheelchair user is more relaxing than for the average traveller"

Northern Ireland, more than most places, learned to provide good wheelchair access, through the tragedy of "The Troubles" which have not only killed but also maimed. New building has taken place later than on the mainland – at a time when the importance of access, for the able-bodied as well as disabled, had been recognised. For example, the new shopping complex in Royal Avenue has been built with an adjacent car park.

Perhaps access seemed simpler in Northern Ireland because geographically it is smaller than the mainland and people there seem very much more aware of their neighbours and their needs. They show a great warmth and kindness, and give a tremendous welcome to visitors, so that any obstacles for the wheelchair traveller are quickly overcome. At my brother-in-law's golf club one evening three strong young men volunteered to carry me in my wheelchair up a flight of steps to the restaurant so that the visitor from "across the water" could appreciate the magnificent view over the Ards Peninsula and Strangford Lough.

My flight to Heathrow on the way home was uneventful, and I realised that in some respects air travel for the unaccompanied wheelchair user is more relaxing than for the average traveller. No baggage to carry and no long walk from check-in desk to aircraft, also a reserved seat close to the toilet!

Back in my own home I felt the richer for having gained a new interest in Irish history and literature, and an awareness that I could again read the travel pages, knowing that with a little homework beforehand I could once more indulge in the luxury of a holiday – the next time with my husband.

Since that first trip I've returned to Northern Ireland several times and my sister and brother-in-law have retired to County Antrim. If speed turns you on there is some lovely driving to be had on the new, relatively uncrowded motorways. But one of the features which I find most attractive remains – I can still enjoy leisurely drives down quiet lanes, stopping to admire the view or to sit by a hedgerow scented with honeysuckle and bright with wild fuschia.

IRELAND: TRAVEL NOTES

Sources of information

Irish Tourist Board (Bord Fáilte), 150 New Bond Street, London W1Y 0AQ; ☎071/493 3201. Will always make an effort to answer specific queries. There is a fact sheet for disabled visitors, and the main accommodation guide uses the wheelchair symbol.

National Rehabilitation Board (write to the Access Officer, 24–25 Clyde Road, Ballsbridge, Dublin 4; ☎010 3531/684181). Two free guides, *Accommodation for Disabled Persons* (1989) and *Dublin: A guide for disabled persons* (1990), are produced in conjunction with the tourist board.

Northern Ireland Tourist Board, River House, 48 High Street, Belfast BT1 2DS; ☎0232/246609. The wheelchair symbol is used in their accommodation guide, *Where to Stay: Northern Ireland*. They plan to replace the booklet *The Disabled Tourist in Northern Ireland – Things to See, Places to Stay* with a new guide, prepared by the **Northern Ireland Council on Disability** (2 Annadale Avenue, Belfast BT7 3JR; ☎0232/491011) but there has been some wrangling over funding. Meanwhile, the council will send what printed information it has on receipt of an SAE, and help with accommodation queries where possible.

Northern Ireland is also included, of course, in many of the publications which cover the whole of Britain: see the England and Wales *Travel Notes*.

Getting there

The major **ferry** companies that offer concessions to members of the *DDMC* or *DDA* (see "Getting There By Land Sea", *Practicalities*) are *B&I Line*, *P&O* and *Sealink Stena Line* (see "Directory", *Practicalities*). The shortest crossing is from Stranraer or Cairnryan to Larne, Northern Ireland (2hr 20min), operated by *P&O* and *Sealink Stena Line*.

B&I Line sail to Ireland (Pembroke–Rosslare and Holyhead–Dublin) and their ships are equipped with a service lift and accessible toilet. *P&O*'s *Ionic Ferry* (Cairnryan–Larne) is better suited for disabled passengers than the *Europic Ferry*: it has accessible toilets, lifts to all main passenger areas and wide entrances to

bar, restaurant and lounges. *Sealink Stena Line* covers routes to Ireland (Holyhead–Dun Laoghaire; Fishguard–Rosslare) and Northern Ireland (Stranraer–Larne). The *Saint Christopher* (Stranraer–Larne) and the *Saint Anselm* (Holyhead–Dun Laoghaire;) have the best facilities for disabled passengers.

All these ports are reasonably accessible, but Rosslare's new terminal stands out, with smooth walkways, excellent signs, both audio and visual announcements, adapted toilets and wheelchair-friendly cafeteria. The design, layout and ambience here greatly impressed judges in the 1990 *European Year of Tourism* competition for best facilities for disabled tourists in Europe.

Travel to Ireland **by air** is relatively expensive but all the airlines offer APEX and budget round-trip fares. *Air Lingus* and *British Airways* (see "Directory", *Practicalities*) are well known for their smooth treatment of disabled passengers (see "Getting There By Air", *Practicalities*) other possibilities include *Air UK* (recommended by Jill Brown, p.144), *British Midland* (☎071/589 5599), *Britannia Airways* (☎0582/405737), *Capital Airlines* (☎0345/800777), *Dan Air* (☎0345/100200) and *Ryan Air* (☎071 435 7101). Facilities at Dublin and Belfast International airports are very good: Belfast even has an accessible Airbus service into the city centre (wheelchair space can be booked in advance on ☎0232/320011 ext 419).

Transport

Dublin **airport** is fully accessible and boarding or disembarking is usually by airbridge. Facilities at other airports vary and you are likely to require some sort of assistance; consult the Aer Rianta Duty Officer at the airport you wish to use.

On the Irish **railways**, accessible toilets and mobile rails for boarding wheelchairs are available at most mainline stations, but the aisles in the carriages are too narrow for wheelchairs, and passengers who wish to remain in their chairs must sit in the vestibule (which is at least air conditioned). Refreshments can be obtained from the travelling food trolley.

Dublin's suburban rail system (*DART*) is for the most part accessible, but at stations situ-

IRELAND: TRAVEL NOTES

ated on a bend there may be a wide gap between train and platform, and assistance may be required. Gates have to be locked at some stations for security reasons (a special key can be obtained from the *National Rehabilitation Board*) and this may make access difficult for passengers in wheelchairs.

Irish **buses** are generally inaccessible to wheelchair users. In Dublin, new vehicles added to the *Bus Ath Cliath* (*Dublin Bus*) fleet from 1990 onwards have improved identification; a public address system; easily reached bell pushes; more hand-rails; and less mountainous steps which are better illuminated and with clearly defined edges, at entrance and exit – but no hydraulic lift and no wheelchair spaces.

Driving is an attractive and easy alternative here. Cars with hand controls can be hired from *Hertz* (19 Hogan Place, Dublin 2; ☎010 3531/765921). The Orange Badge is recognised by the Irish authorities, but in Dublin it only entitles the holder to park free on metered spaces – parking on single or double yellow lines is not allowed. Parking in Dublin during office hours is tricky.

Along the way you'll find a fair number of accessible toilets, although some require a special key. This can be obtained from the *National Rehabilitation Board* or the *Irish Wheelchair Association* (Blackheath Drive, Clontarf, Dublin 3; ☎010 3531/338241).

Accommodation

Several useful publications have been listed under *Sources of Information*, although one contributor who used *Accommodation for Disabled Persons* stopped consulting it after the second day of her trip because "almost every B&B we stopped at was wheelchair accessible as long as someone was there to help – and we never ran short of people more than willing to lend a hand".

For accompanied wheelchair users, Helena O'Keefe (p.101) liked *Grays Guesthouse* (Dugort, Achill Island, County Mayo, Republic of Ireland; ☎98/43244).

In Northern Ireland, the *Share Centre* (Smiths Strand, Lisnaskea, County Fermanagh BT92 0EQ; ☎03657/22122) enables both able-bodied and disabled people to take a very reasonable holiday on the shores of Lough Erne, where they can sail, canoe or learn traditional crafts, as well as enjoying the social life and exploring the surrounding countryside. In addition to the central guesthouse, there is a caravan and camping site, all designed for use by disabled people. Funds to build this residential activity centre were raised by small groups and schools throughout Northern Ireland and it was opened in 1981.

Few campsites in Ireland have any special facilities, but contributors did manage.

Scotland

High Expectations North of the Border

Paul Cox is a quadriplegic, the son of a Yorkshire miner. His paternal grandfather was Scottish, a professional footballer whose services were bought towards the end of his playing career by a pit owner who also had a stake in Doncaster Rovers FC. In September 1989 Paul chose Scotland for a holiday in the hope of discovering not only something of his grandfather's life, but also some signs of the centuries-old struggle between Scotland and England.

Apart from all that, I'd just bought a new car and was dying to try it out on a long run. Sue Baker, *The Observer*'s excellent motoring correspondent, has referred to the north of Scotland as a driver's dream in comparison with the rest of Britain.

My holiday north of the border almost didn't get the chance to fulfil these expectations. After making detailed enquiries of its facilities, I'd booked a self-catering chalet in Aviemore with a girlfriend. This, the car and the aids I could pack into it would, I felt, minimise the inconveniences of "making do" with other transport, hotels and their facilities. But between booking and departure the girlfriend had gone and I was stuck for someone to accompany me.

RADAR had already sent me a list of addresses matching the type of holiday I wanted; next they suggested a number of care attendant agencies. Some of these are voluntary and require notice; some ask for full payment but can often supply help immediately. Circumstances dictated the latter option in my case. The risk in using such agencies is that you're not going to get on with your helper. But it's a small risk: people attracted to this type of work, whether volunteers or professionals, are almost by definition not unpleasant. My helper was competent with the basics, nice and interested, and we got on.

She was also Scottish, which meant that she knew what wasn't worth seeing – helpful, since it was soon apparent that I'd underestimated the size of the country. Perhaps it only felt big because of the relative lack of people in the parts we touched; the bulk of the population are crammed into the neck of land between the Glasgow and Edinburgh conurbations. We were based in the Highlands, well north of this, where there was room to move. And what a place to move in! Such variety of landscapes: elemental, geological landscapes – peaks and plateaux, hard rock and soft glens, peat and pine – in which people and buildings appear as afterthoughts. Here the earth dominates, with its look, its feel and its smells.

Aviemore is a touristy ski centre with the spartan feel of a North American pioneer town. It's in the heart of the Cairngorm mountains, car-stopping in themselves, but chosen principally as a strategically placed starting point – this was always going to be a motoring holiday. I'm glad the roads *were* as good as Sue Baker said because we covered an awful lot of them: 3700km in a week. Whether long and straight, winding sharply or softly, flat or hilly, they were superbly maintained. North of Pitlochry I don't recall a pothole, and we glided from place to place, above the road surface rather than on it, chewing gum, listening to Ry Cooder and the wind whistling through the sun-roof, feeling like stars in a road movie.

Road atlas and *Good Food Guide* in hand, we set off each morning with the day half planned, half left to chance. Often we were pleasantly surprised, much less often disappointed. What remains clearest is the drive through Glencoe Pass. I was vaguely aware of the English-instigated massacre there in 1692 of 38 MacDonalds by the Campbell clan. I was also aware that the Scottish tourist industry has cashed in on the legend grown from this event and positively promotes the place as one cloaked in perpetual gloom. Undoubtedly the closed-in mountain formation lends itself to overcast conditions at certain points on most days. But we happened on particularly fine

weather and although I did feel a "Wuthering Heights" gloom when high on desolate Rannoch Moor, the descent from there into the broad valley of a rolling, tumbling River Coe was a descent into relief.

It's hard to turn around anywhere in northern Scotland and not be struck by the physical geography. One day stands out in this respect, a day spent travelling along and around the Caledonian Canal. When completed in 1847, this 100-kilometre chain of lochs and canals joined the Irish Sea to the North Sea and cut the northwest Highlands from the rest of Scotland. It's a prime example of the Scots adding to Nature, making her work better for them. The artificial 37km of canal finished off what the Great Glen Fault almost achieved, and enabled vessels to avoid the dangerous route via the Hebrides and Pentland Firth. Fishing boats and pleasure craft can now float in safety from a western coastline deeply indented by fjords, or sea lochs, and fragmented by islands and peninsulas, to a lower, straighter eastern coastline characterised by several great drowned inlets, or firths. These boats pass Lochs Linnhe, Lochy, Oich and Ness; particularly impressive is Loch Ness, forbidding in its size and cold bronze feel. It's easy to see why the legend sticks.

"The spectacularly glacial northwest coastline, hewn and heaved high out of the sea"

High up on the west coast is the unspoilt fisherman's village of Ullapool. Although there are the odd souvenir and trinket shops, the folksy heart of the place seems self-contained. From Ullapool we drove down the spectacularly glacial northwest coastline, hewn and heaved high out of the sea. We caught sight of the Isle of Skye and stopped for coffee at a fine little folk museum in Gairloch; we stayed for two hours, fascinated as it bared Scotland's soul from the time of the aboriginal

Picts and the immigrant tribe of Scots (who were actually Irish), through myriad bloody clan feuds, right up to the almost-as-primitive early twentieth century.

"Because we saw and did and felt so much, I can offer only my impressions"

After that it was back to the visual drama of the coastline (or coast-zigzag) – a dream of a drive, jarred awake by the blemish that is the US military; I knew that the Clyde Firth is infested with them, but to come across an armed-to-the-teeth superpower this far north was not just chilling, it was incongruous. It's easy to forget such things – too easy I fear – when the next day you discover a place of such simple, peaceful beauty as the hunting lodge which we found on Loch Tummel. I wanted to take the place home with me. It was perfect, down to the unreal stillness of the silver-surfaced loch and, inside, where we ate earthy smoked salmon, the slightly eccentric, not-quite-of-this-century maître d'.

Because we saw and did and felt so much, I can offer only my impressions: the lack of litter and graffiti; the clearness of the air (I saw a rainbow the colours of which were so distinct it looked artificial); the unobtrusive hydroelectric works, tucked neatly away in hillfolds or amid trees, keeping environmental disturbance to a minimum; superb food almost everywhere we stopped (usually recommended by the *Good Food Guide*, which is good on wheelchair access); the people no more or less friendly, the streets and buildings no more or less accessible than in my home area.

John O'Groats was disappointing, not so much because of the busloads of tourists queuing to be photographed under the sign to Land's End, but because after the seeming endlessness of the A9 up there I could see land out north – I wanted to have arrived at the

end of the world. The sheep – laid out in the road, cool as nightclub bouncers, chewing grass and staring us out – were the nearest thing to wildlife we saw, which was a shame. Also missing was the sound of the bagpipes, one of the few things that can give me goosepimples and make me shiver. That would have been nice, so too the sight of a stag.

I didn't sit in the middle of that field on Culloden Moor, where the Duke of Cumberland's army slaughtered one thousand Jacobite rebels – in forty minutes! – in 1746. Seeing the name on a signpost was enough to make me think about it, and that's all one can do now. Believing that an extended stationary stare would bring me no nearer to the past than a glance from the car, I sped homewards on the M9 past the Bannockburn Monument near Sterling, scene of Robert Bruce's routing of a huge English army in 1314. For the same reason we didn't stop at other battle sites: Dunbar (1650, Cromwell, aftermath of the English Civil War); Flodden (1513, James IV, an attempt to assuage his own Scottish baronage); Killiecrankie (1689, another Jacobite revolt). If any of these events *are* relevant to an understanding of my history – any more relevant than, say, the Highland clearances or the countless unmarked border feuds – this holiday didn't clarify how.

But perhaps I expected too much. I chose the Highlands not to find the "real" Scotland, but to escape people and cities. In doing so I was avoiding history in the making, for it is people who make history. If I'd gone to the cities I'd have come across a different Scotland, one that would evoke different feelings in me, probably more immediately meaningful feelings given that where most of the people are is where most of the coalfields were. No, despite all my talk of the atavistic pull of Scotland, a holiday for me is ultimately a "getting away". It was a wonderful escape, and I'll be going back.

First Trip to Scotland

Charlotte Billington has cerebral palsy and has written two accounts of organised group holidays. On p.207 she describes a Project Phoenix Trust Study Tour in Sweden. Here she writes about her holiday with the Disaway Trust in June 1989. Her group was based at Crieff, near Perth, on the edge of the Highlands.

We travelled to Scotland by coach from Victoria, London (I picked it up in Newport Pagnell). The journey took nearly fifteen hours, mainly because of the number of stops on the way, and we arrived at our hotel at 11pm feeling absolutely exhausted. The hotel had expected us three hours earlier, so the salad with which we were presented was a bit on the dry side!

After playing with a couple of lettuce leaves, our only desire was to hit the sack as soon as possible. Once we'd sorted out which suitcase belonged to whom, and returned missing jackets to their rightful owners, we all piled into the two lifts and headed upstairs for our rooms.

But not for us a quick collapse into our beds! Many of the wheelchairs could not fit through the bathroom doorways, and this resulted in most of us changing rooms, including my helper and myself. What the other residents thought of all the noise is not recorded – probably just as well – but by 2am peace had descended and we at last got some sleep.

The first thing on the agenda in the morning was to have a carpenter take the bathroom doors off their hinges for the duration of our stay. The hotel staff did make a genuine effort to be helpful towards disabled guests. Apart from two lifts which went to all floors, there was a specially equipped bathroom on the ground floor, with all necessary attachments to enable us to have a bath or shower in comfort, as well as a raised loo for those who have difficulty in getting up from a low seat.

All sports facilities were accessible for a wheelchair user, and there was a choice of table tennis, snooker, tennis, golf and swimming in a heated pool. To gain access to the pool it was necessary to inform the staff, who placed two planks over the six steps leading into the pool and were very willing to help with wheelchairs. The sauna could be booked in advance.

The hotel grounds offer an interesting if rather hilly stroll through a wide selection of flowers, shrubs and trees – enough to keep keen gardeners talking for weeks! As the hotel stands on a hill above Crieff, it commands a superb view over Strathearn to the Ochil hills, and west to the Grampians. It is also a stone's throw from *Gleneagles*.

The food was very good: buffet-style breakfast, lunch from the sandwich and salad bar for the full-boarders, and five-course dinner with wine. Vegetarians and those on special diets were catered for if advance notice was given. Men were expected to wear a tie for dinner as well as on the dance floor. Regular dances took place in the hotel ballroom (but mainly for the over 60s) and other leisure facilities included the TV and cinema room, the drawing room and loggia, the Winter Garden and library.

"The gradients were such that each wheelchair would have needed a team of shire horses"

Our first visit of the week was to Scone Palace in Perth. Known as the Crowning Place of the Kings of the Scots on the Stone of Scone, the palace is also the home of Lord Mansfield (a descendant of the first Scottish laird to be accepted into the House of Lords) and is famous for its 400-year-old collection of rare porcelain, clocks, needlework and furniture. Only the ground floor is open to the public and is accessible to wheelchairs apart from half a dozen steps leading into the main entrance hall. Our coach driver overcame this problem by manoeuvring the coach so that the tail-lift came to rest on the top step and we could wheel straight in. We were met by the tartan-clad guides who conduct the tourist groups around the house, delivering a well-practised history of its treasures.

After the tour we emerged onto the beautifully manicured lawns, admiring the peacocks in all their finery. We wandered around the magnificent grounds, then disappeared round the back of the palace, through a courtyard to a small teashop. Once the staff had got over the shock of seeing eighteen of us in wheelchairs plus our helpers, they were very amenable, moving tables and chairs aside so that we could settle down to tea, cakes and sandwiches. Next door was a souvenir shop, also a loo for disabled visitors – since most of us wanted to use it, this was a long stop.

We headed back to the hotel via Perth, which is an unremarkable town sitting at the mouth of the River Tay. The squat, austere, granite buildings nestle cheek by jowl with the earlier architectural pomposity of the Victorian era, but the beauty of the surrounding hills provides a redeeming feature. The town itself is also very hilly, making it difficult for wheelchairs.

For the same reason, an exploration of Crieff was abandoned. The gradients were such that each wheelchair would have needed a team of shire horses to pull it. Visits to the Weaver's House and to the Highland Tryst Museum were cancelled as both places had very difficult access and room for only one wheelchair inside (heat and tiredness also dampened our enthusiasm). We again had access problems at the Glen Turret distillery – Scotland's oldest – but we were able to see an interesting video of the distilling process, as well as taste a wee dram of the golden liquid.

A trip to the Stuart Crystal Factory, just outside Crieff, was more successful in terms of access. We watched the fascinating process, stage by stage; it was also displayed on video in case we missed anything. In the shop where the crystal is sold the prices ranged from £5 to £500 – something for all tastes and pockets.

Across the road, at the Crieff Visitors' Centre, we watched the creation of Britain's premier *millefiori* and lampwork paperweights, and toured the famous Thistle Factory, centre for production of hand-painted pottery. The centre is equipped with a good café and a disabled persons' loo.

We took advantage of the facilities and then drove to the Scottish Deer Centre at Cupar, in Fife. The farm is situated in fifty acres of beautiful parkland in the Howe of Fife. The visitors' centre is housed in an early nineteenth-century courtyard made fully accessible for wheelchairs. We were allowed to go down into the pens, where the red deer clambered about over bales of hay, showing off, it seemed, for the benefit of the human onlookers. They were so tame and friendly that we were able to pat and stroke them, after which we watched a video explaining the deers' life cycle and the activities of the local conservationists who are working to preserve the species.

"Most of us decided to take a spin in our wheelchairs on the dance floor"

The day was rounded off with a production of Agatha Christie's *Witness for the Prosecution*, performed at the Pitlochry Festival Theatre. It was an excellent evening's entertainment. The theatre is relatively new – it was opened by Prince Charles in 1979 – and combines modern architecture with good facilities which are accessible to all members of the community.

Our day trip to Edinburgh took in a guided tour of Holyrood House, including some of the magnificent state rooms and apartments used by the royal family when visiting Scotland. We had a picnic in the grounds of the house before boarding the coach for a quick trip to the shops on Princes Street. The Royal Mile would have been impossible to negotiate in a wheelchair (the gradient is one in two) but we did at least drive along it.

That evening we returned to the hotel to discover that a dance had been arranged. Most of the younger females in our party, including myself, thought that this would be an opportunity to meet some of the local "talent". We couldn't have been more wrong. I'm not sure whether our hotel made a point of catering for old people, or the population of Scotland really is severely lacking in younger folk, but it wasn't the first time on this holiday that we'd noticed a preponderance of senior citizens around us. However, after swallowing our disappointment, most of us decided to take a spin in our wheelchairs on the dance floor and we ended up hugely enjoying ourselves.

A bright, hot and sunny Thursday was perfect for a cruise on Loch Katrine. The coach ride to the Trossachs took about two hours and we arrived at a pretty little bay which was picturesque as well as functional, providing accessible tea shop, souvenir shop and toilet facilities. The *SS Sir Walter Scott* was fully accessible and there was a choice of remaining in our wheelchairs or transferring to one of the wooden benches placed at strategic vantage points all round the deck. The captain pointed out the parts of the dramatic landscape around us which featured in the history and literature of Scotland, particularly in the novels of Sir Walter Scott. This was a fascinating and inexpensive trip, well worth the two-hour journey from Crieff.

Our last full day was spent in Pitlochry, where mountains, lochs and rivers make a spectacular setting for the town. Pitlochry was still attractive when we visited but is fast losing its charm in the race to woo the tourists. The High Street is full of souvenir shops, selling tacky Scottish memorabilia, and large numbers of cafés and teashops, most of which are reasonably accessible. The only accessible toilet is in the car park at the back of the town.

> ### "You need to make sure that your wheelchair is in good nick if you want to go exploring in those wild landscapes"

The Strathearn regional hydroelectric plant is based in Pitlochry, and the visitors' centre offers an exhibition using maps and diagrams to explain how electricity is generated and distributed to different parts of the region. The exhibition is free and accessible for those in wheelchairs but two strong helpers are needed for the steps in the entrance hall. We were also able to see the Fish Ladder and watch the salmon leaping.

The last evening was hot: some people went for a swim, some grabbed a last-minute sunbathe, others went to their rooms to contemplate the gaping mouth of an open suitcase. Sunday saw us wend our way back to London. Scotland had scored highly with all of us. To say that the scenery is spectacular is an understatement; the shapes and colours defy the most skilled photographer, and you need to make sure that your wheelchair is in good nick if you want to go exploring in those wild landscapes. I cannot say that I got to know the Scots people, but it takes more than one visit to do that, and I'm sure to go back.

SCOTLAND: TRAVEL NOTES

Sources of information

Scottish Tourist Board, 23 Ravelston Terrace, Edinburgh EH4 3EU; ☎031/332 2433. Access information is included in all major accommodation and sightseeing guides. Four grades of accessibility are awarded to accommodation, for wheelchair users with or without assistance, for ambulant disabled people and for residents only.

Disability Scotland (formerly *Scottish Council on Disability*), Information Service, Princes House, 5 Shandwick Place, Edinburgh EH2 4RG; ☎031/229 8632. This organisation works closely with the tourist board and is a mine of information for prospective holidaymakers in Scotland.

Forestry Commission, 231 Corstorphine Road, Edinburgh EH12 7AT; ☎031/334 0303. Provide useful information on their accessible forest trails, campsites and picnic areas.

Accommodation and Transport

On the whole the situation with accommodation and transport in Scotland is the same as that for the whole of Britain, so see the England and Wales *Travel Notes*. One specific recommendation, however, is a retreat house, the *Macleod Centre* (The Abbey, Iona, Argyll PA76 6SN), which was designed to be accessible to disabled guests and opened in 1989. Write to The Warden for further information.

England & Wales

Wild Eric and the Devil's Chair

Isobel Williams has multiple sclerosis. In the summer of 1987 she took her three-wheeled trike on holiday to Wales and Shropshire.

I've never felt the urge to sunbathe on some foreign beach or to sample the delights of Blackpool's Golden Mile. I like peace and quiet, and so does my husband. For some twenty years we found it for a fortnight every summer with some old friends, the Johnsons, who had moved from the Midlands to a dairy farm in what used to be Cardiganshire (now Dyfed).

We travelled by car, taking our four terriers, breaking the journey in Shropshire. I had suffered from what I thought was back trouble for years, but in 1981 multiple sclerosis was diagnosed. Although I still drive, I can manage only short distances; my husband doesn't drive so Wales seemed out of reach.

In 1987 Mrs Johnson had been recently widowed and I was anxious to see her. To increase my mobility I had purchased a battery-operated trike and I read that *British Rail* could accommodate passengers in wheelchairs. Why not go to Wales by train? I knew that my husband wouldn't leave his garden or his dogs (not to mention his rabbits and canaries), so I resolved to go alone.

The first step was to buy a *Disabled Person's Railcard*, which makes the fare much cheaper. The procedure then is to phone the station of departure the day before the journey commences. I arranged to be met at the other end, and a friend took me to Rugby station in her car. The trike easily takes to pieces to stow in the car and was soon reassembled at the station. There are no steps at Rugby, only a slope, so we bought my ticket and waited for the train. When it arrived a small portable ramp was placed at the entrance to the guard's van and I was asked to enter. I was a bit taken aback at this but was assured that there was a window, so I rode the trike up the ramp into the van. Several parcels were loaded, the ramp was removed and we were on our way.

It was surprisingly comfortable, with a good view out of the window. No fighting for the best seat, I could sit at whatever angle I chose and there were no other passengers to bother me. But it would have been far too cold in winter.

I had to make two changes, first at Birmingham New Street, then at Shrewsbury. The guard seemed to know all about my journey so I didn't worry about missing the connections. As far as Birmingham the train followed much the same route as the road I knew so well. When we arrived at Birmingham someone was there to meet me, as promised. He carried my suitcase, taking me up in the luggage lift to the platform for the Shrewsbury train. It was a busy station, the largest junction in Europe, I was told. Thank goodness *BR* treated me as a parcel – let loose on my own I would have been hopelessly lost!

When the Shrewsbury train pulled in, another ramp was put in place, and with a bit of pushing I was in my second, much bigger guard's van. I had a box of day-old chicks for company, cheeping and chattering all the way to Shrewsbury. There I was met as before and transferred to a dear little local train. As there was no guard's van they somehow squeezed me into the carriage. This line was a single track and the engine hooted mournfully at every bend.

As we drew into Aberystwyth station I could see my friend's son, Jim, waiting for me. The journey had taken about five hours and I had expected to feel exhausted, but I was in quite good form. Only about twenty miles to go, this time by road.

At Cilrhyg the farmyard slopes steeply down from the road. The farmhouse is old and square, built of stone with a slate roof. About 200m below there is a shallow river, which the cows cross twice a day in summer as they come in to be milked. Over the road the ground rises steeply to the wooded *vron* (sloping field). In winter, water rushes down through the yard to the river.

The 31-hectare farm stands alone, a couple of kilometres from the tiny village – two shops, a pub and a post office. There is no sound except from a passing car or tractor and, of course,

the birds. There are red kites about – once or twice I've spotted one. The verges at the side of the lanes are not sprayed and are full of wild flowers never seen by the roadside at home – foxgloves, meadowsweet, flag irises and wild strawberries.

"The unfenced road winds through the mountains, where a few long-tailed sheep snatch a living from those barren pastures"

Mrs Johnson didn't go out but there weren't many days that passed without a caller. Everything came to the door – I even bought a pair of trousers while I was there! A neighbouring farmer brought the daily paper together with any local news that he'd heard. The butcher brought the meat and put it away in the fridge; there was a baker, a mobile grocer and a man with fresh mackerel. We were very slow to answer the door; Susie the springer spaniel beat us to it every time. She would stand on her hind legs, turn the doorknob with her paw and step back, opening the door – rather disconcerting for strangers!

I spent much of my time at Cilrhyg in the sunroom on the south side of the house. It was full of plants and always warm, even on a dull day. Mrs Johnson and I sat there talking endlessly. If it was a fine day I sat outside on my trike but the yard was too steep for me to go far.

In Wales the land is so hilly that any flat land is highly prized. At Cilrhyg the pasture bordering the river is completely flat, about 90m above sea level. Jim's brother David and his wife live on a much hillier farm, about 50ha at 200–300m above sea level. David took me to see it one afternoon, after a struggle to get me into the Land Rover. They keep some horses, milking cows and sheep, and were having a go at strawberry growing.

Our mealtimes were arranged to suit Jim's milking. He worked alone, and cows have to be milked twice a day, every day of the year. He came in for his breakfast at about 10am and we would sit at the table for hours, unless he wanted to get away to the "Mart". Any work about the farm had to be done between milkings.

Jim didn't have much time to spare from his Guernsey cows, but he did find time to take me to Aberystwyth, a fine seaside town twenty miles west of Cilrhyg, at the centre of the gentle curve of Cardigan Bay. We drove to the seafront and watched the large ships passing on the horizon. The tall, narrow hotels on the esplanade give a rather dignified air to the seafront. There is a pier and a sandy beach, but there weren't many bathers that day, despite the June sunshine.

My week at Cilrhyg was soon over. I was to spend the second week with Mrs Johnson's daughter, Rachel, in Shropshire. Rachel and I are old friends (we were bridesmaids at each other's weddings) and she drove down to the farm to fetch me.

The drive from Cilrhyg to Bishop's Castle is most enjoyable, first passing Tregaron bog, some 400ha, said to be the largest in Europe and surely one of the last really wild places left on our island. Then the unfenced road winds through the mountains, where a few long-tailed sheep snatch a living from those barren pastures. Hill farmers cultivate impossible slopes and little streams rush downhill.

There are vast, gloomy Forestry Commission plantations, the trees in straight lines like so many soldiers, the fire brooms stacked ready, just in case. On past little Welsh houses, paint gleaming in colours we'd never think of using. Then on to the main road, through Devil's Bridge with its tourists and ice-cream stalls, and through Newtown into Shropshire with its prosperous farms and half-timbered houses.

Rachel's home is approached along narrow lanes with high banks. The old farmhouse was built of local stone and the beautiful garden created by Rachel. It stands on level ground surrounded by hills, the largest being the Long Mynd, 2225ha of which is owned by the National Trust. There is good access to viewpoints on the Long Mynd and to the information centre, shop and café at Carding Mill Valley.

Cyril manages the 400-hectare farm, growing corn and fodder on the lower 113ha. The rest is hillside and moor, where heather and windberries grow and the sheep and cattle graze in the summer. There are several milking cows, hens and sometimes geese being fattened for Christmas. A shepherd and a tractor driver work with Cyril, and Rachel does the books and anything else that needs doing.

"On December 22 all the ghosts in Shropshire are said to meet on the Stiperstones"

There is a large concrete farmyard, ideal for my trike, and I was even able to go up the road. I also sat outside listening to the curlews and watching the clouds scudding over the Long Mynd. Rachel's capuchin pigeons strutted importantly on the lawn and if I sat still enough one would fly onto my lap.

This part of Shropshire is full of legends of witches and ghosts. Rachel took me up to the Stiperstones hills, a wild and lonely place. On December 22 all the ghosts in Shropshire are said to meet on the Stiperstones. Wild Eric is there with his wife Godda, his men and a pack of yellow-eyed hounds. Should Wild Eric be seen at any other time, soldiers will perish far away. The last time he was seen was three days before the Falklands War. Nearby is a rock formation known as the Devil's Chair; when cloud covers the Stiperstones, the Devil is said to be in his chair!

The second week of Wimbledon was in full swing and I found it difficult to tear myself away from the TV, but we visited the butterfly farm at Country World, Yockleton, near Shrewsbury.

There were plenty of benches so I managed quite well without my trike (I can still walk a little); wheelchair users will find the farm quite accessible. The butterflies live in a huge greenhouse amidst many exotic plants, including a six-metre-high abutilon – I have one about a metre high, so I thought that was big! I'd like to have watched the butterflies for longer but I couldn't stand the heat in the greenhouse.

After a farewell barbecue it was time to go home. I phoned Shrewsbury station and the journey went smoothly as before; *BR* certainly looked after me well. It was good to get home and see my husband and the dogs. It's grand to go away but even better to come home.

It Rains in the Lakes

Self-catering in the Lake District might seem an improbable choice of holiday for a severely disabled couple. Caryl and Pete Lloyd managed it in 1989 with a great deal of careful planning and two very willing helpers.

My husband and I live in our own flatlet in a large residential centre run by *The Spastics Society*. We are as independent as our disabilities allow, and fully responsible for organising our holidays. This means writing lots of letters and finding suitable helpers, which can be very difficult but is not impossible.

We are fortunate as far as transport is concerned because we own a small van which has been adapted to take our chairs and all the other necessities for a comfortable holiday. But we do have to find helpers who are willing to drive it as well as give us complete daily living care.

In past years we have been abroad with organisations such as *The Across Trust* but this meant that we had to go with a group and share helpers. We much prefer to take holidays as a couple with our own escorts, mainly because of the circumstances in which we live – we have independence at home, so we like to enjoy it as far as possible when we travel.

I wrote to the *Disabled Living Foundation* asking for information on suitable self-catering accommodation for two severely disabled people in wheelchairs plus at least two helpers. From their information we discovered that the *John Grooms Association* owns, amongst other properties, a bungalow in Ambleside, on the north shore of Lake Windemere. I'd never been to the Lakes, so this was the one we chose.

We didn't have to find helpers on this trip because our friends Jo and Jane, whom we met in 1988, had already offered to help us again. We found Jo and Jane through an organisation called *Holiday Helpers*, which matches up able-bodied helpers with disabled holidaymakers. You meet up before the holiday and if you don't get on you have to try again – it's important not to give up at this stage.

When you need as much help as we do, it's vital to state your requirements clearly. If possible, spend at least 24 hours with the helpers, so that you can decide whether or not they can cope. Don't make things too easy for them on this first meeting – remember that when you are on holiday you will be in strange surroundings and even simple tasks will be more difficult. And a piece of advice for both helper and disabled person: don't be afraid to say no! This will save both parties from a potentially disastrous holiday – and I speak from experience.

That's most of the hard work done, apart from saving the money. Unless you are travelling with family, friend or an organised group, you have to pay for your helper's holiday, including food and in some cases spending money. This must be sorted out before you set off. Going on holiday is a costly business, but we think it's well worth it as long as you go through the preparations realistically and with care.

Jo and Jane joined us on the evening before our departure to help with the packing. For a self-catering holiday this is no small task and involves clothes, food, kitchen utensils and bedding, to name but a few. Finally everything was ready, and as we had over 400km to travel we set off early the next morning.

We made good time, although it was a Saturday morning in the height of the holiday season. We stopped twice at motorway service stations and the only difficulty was the usual one of not being able to get our wheelchairs close to the cafeteria tables because all the seats are fixed to the floor. So we had to sit at the end and this meant that we were in the way, but most people were understanding.

"We had only ourselves to please"

Thanks to clear instructions from *John Grooms*, we had no problems finding "Nationwide", which was to be our home for the next two weeks. When I first saw the bungalow, all kinds of thoughts were spinning round my head: would we be able to get on the toilet, would Jane like the kitchen, would the bedroom be big enough? But the bathroom was huge, there was plenty of room for us to move around in our chairs, and there was a colour TV which worked!

It didn't take us long to sort ourselves out and find things in the kitchen. I could hardly believe that for a whole fortnight this lovely bungalow was ours! We could lie in bed, have a drink whenever we wished, have a hot

bath every morning – absolute bliss. No waiting around for someone to come and put you on the toilet. We had only ourselves to please. It was peaceful and the views from most of the windows were beautiful.

"We rarely get a chance to be right out in the wilds"

The summer of 1989 was dry and sunny but, let me tell you, it rains in the Lakes! This didn't stop us having a good time – far from it! Because it was mid-August the traffic was extremely heavy, so we stayed around Ambleside over both weekends. But we weren't confined to the bungalow: Jo and Jane were quite happy to push us to the town, although with steps and crowds to negotiate we had to sit outside nearly all the shops. We were able to get down to the lakeside and we had a very enjoyable boat trip on Lake Windemere. There was plenty of room for people in wheelchairs on board the pleasure boat, and the crew were very helpful.

In the bungalow we found much information on the local sights, and in the lakeside newsagent we bought *A Guide to the Lakes and Surrounding Areas for the Disabled Tourist*, a useful booklet. From this we found out about footpaths for wheelchairs just outside Ambleside and we managed to locate the shorter one. It was a bit rough and therefore hard work for our pushers, but exciting for us as we rarely get a chance to be right out in the wilds.

With our own van we could go out whenever we wished. There is a tail-lift at the back and the only tricky part is clamping the chairs down to the floor, but Jo soon mastered it. He also liked driving, so we planned circular routes, often involving two or three hours on the road.

One day we went to the Scottish border and stopped at the first house in Scotland. After refreshments Jo and Jane pushed us to Gretna Green's famous smithy. We were able to get in through the back way and didn't have to pay. The other tourists were very friendly and did not mind making space for us. That interesting visit and the journey there through beautiful scenery made a lovely day out – I felt good to be alive!

We made a tour of the lakes, starting with a drive round the north end of Lake Windemere and continuing north past Grassmere and Thirlmere. The weather restricted our views to some extent – it was very misty and rained heavily at times – but we were able to appreciate the beauty of the thick woods surrounding the lakes, and the mountains rising from beyond the tree line.

"Cream all over my face and a grin from ear to ear – this is my idea of having fun!"

We climbed into the hills, past Bassenthwaite and Ullswater, with sheep grazing on the higher ground. Skirting Derwentwater we drove up through a rough pass with the crags disappearing into the clouds. Then we crept down a winding, steep road from the rocky scree and boulders to the gentler slopes, all shades of green, and the trees around Lake Buttermere. We ended up at Cocklemouth, where we explored the town until the heavens opened and we hurried back to the van. The rain kept up all the way back to Ambleside and our cosy home.

Towards the end of our holiday we decided to spend a day at the seaside. So off we went to Morecambe, but the sea was nowhere in sight – just miles of rather dirty brown sand! There was a brisk wind blowing onshore and the sun was in and out all day. Much to our surprise there were no crowds there,

so we had plenty of room to be wheeled along the seafront. We found a pleasant, quiet snack bar on the front; everyone was friendly and helped to hold the doors open. In the indoor shopping area I spotted my favourite cream cake. I bought one and ate it there and then, cream all over my face and a grin from ear to ear – this is my idea of having fun! I did see the sea in the end, as it was high tide by the time we left, which made my day!

In order to allow our helpers to recover their strength, we usually went for a long drive one day and then stayed close to Ambleside the next. We spent most evenings watching TV or playing Scrabble, enjoying a very strong nightcap! This may sound rather boring but for us it was fun and we could all drink knowing that we didn't have far to go to bed.

We did go out for one meal but it was not a good area for eating out, unless you count the hotels which were a bit costly for us. Jane and I went to the local cinema in spite of a flight of steps at the front entrance – there was a back entrance on the level. The staff said they'd move a seat for me but I am able to transfer from my wheelchair. We stopped off after the film to collect some chips to take to the men of our party who stayed home at "Nationwide".

Our memories of our holiday in the Lakes are the marvellous company of Jo and Jane, the wild and dramatic scenery, and the delightful freedom of being able to do just what we wanted when we wanted. None of it would have been possible without our wonderful helpers, who had to do everything for us apart from think. It is hard work helping people 24 hours a day for two weeks, but with give and take on both sides it can be rewarding for everyone.

English Country Holiday

Vivienne Adcock's disabilities arise from a condition which she contracted at the age of two. She was hospitalised for five years with TB hip and spine, during which time an accident occurred when a nurse was taking a full-length plaster cast off Vivienne's right leg. The nurse cut through tendons from hip to knee, and as a result Vivienne has a considerably shorter leg, stiff hip, permanently bent knee and curvature of the spine. But she and her husband love to travel: here she enjoys life on a Wiltshire farm, which they visited in 1988.

At the very edge of a little village called Kington St Michael, near Chippenham, lies Priory Farm, and on it a converted granary, purpose built for persons with disabilities, where there are no hazardous steps or any other obstacles to overcome. The granary sleeps two in separate beds of the "three bears" variety, both as comfy as Goldilocks' Mamma Bear's bed. It is tastefully decorated and furnished with antiques. There is an intercom to the farmhouse, and a spacious and thoughtfully equipped bathroom, plus a small kitchen area where you can make drinks and prepare picnics. This is bed and breakfast accommodation, with evening meals by arrangement. A car is necessary for exploration of the surrounding area and can be parked almost directly outside the granary.

Priscilla and Colin Labouchere, who own the farm, are out to provide very special holidays. They keep Belted Galloway cattle and Friesland sheep, and opposite the granary is a landscaped pond, which is the home of ornamental wildfowl. Another resident is Totty, a pony previously owned by a rag merchant. These days she responds to a quieter voice, with dignity and a sense of humour. "Tell her a joke and she'll laugh," urges Cilla – and she does! Totty will gladly pull you along in her trap which is adapted for wheelchairs. Cilla wins hearts with her endless tales of animal adventures, and – usually before breakfast – she carves ducks! These are so realistic that my husband couldn't resist constantly fingering them to assure himself that they weren't covered with real feathers!

There is a limited number of beds available at *Priory Cottage*, should your extended family or friends be coming with you, and the farmhouse is only a few yards from the granary, with easy access to the dining area and sitting room. Also available is an electric scooter which allows you to go where the mood takes you, up and down the lanes or over the fields to the brook.

As we spent so many happy hours seated around the pond we were interested to learn how it had materialised. Cilla patented an invention – a structure for taking the backache out of attending to sheep – and with the proceeds financed the building and stocking of the pond. The entire family gave a hand with the digging, using the farm tractor, and finally introducing their precious new family of a dozen pairs of waterfowl, including rare breeds. We never tired of watching the antics of these ducks, sharing our picnics with them and listening to duck anecdotes from our hostess.

Apart from the area around the farm there are many interesting and pretty places to visit within a 25-kilometre radius. We travelled as far as about 50km, covering a good bit of the Cotswolds. The River Windrush flows through the village of Bourton-on-the-Water under picturesque low stone bridges. There is a riverside path which leads to some quiet corners, and beyond the green you can enjoy secluded lanes with cottages of golden Cotswold stone.

But if you need a change from the quiet life, Bourton-on-the-Water is a bustling place with lots to see and do. I enjoyed a visit to the model village of Bourton, which even includes a model of the model! Although it is suffering from the ravages of time, I was enchanted by the attention to detail in miniature trees, shrubs and flowerbeds. Go there half an hour before closing time, when you can hear strains of music from the church on one side and the chapel on the other. Sadly, the paths are too narrow to take wheelchairs.

"We stayed all afternoon, painting and watching the occasional horse passing over the bridge"

Also worth visiting is Birdland, in the grounds of a Tudor manor, where you can see and speak to brightly coloured parrots and macaws, their plumage flashing as they fly among the trees. There are penguins swimming in a glass-sided pool, toucans in the aviary and hummingbirds in the tropical houses. Wheelchairs are available here.

For contrast in the Cotswolds we recommend lunch at the ancient Mill Inn, in the small village of Withington. The building is of great historical interest and the atmosphere and menu are a rare treat. We had one of their home-made steak, kidney, bacon and mushroom deep pies – every mouthful a joy. On a warm day you can eat in the garden with its miniature low bridge over a stream. We stayed all afternoon, painting and watching the occasional horse passing over the bridge.

Slimbridge Wildfowl and Wetlands Centre is another good place to make for, with every concession to the disabled visitor, including a taped guided tour (free of charge) for blind or partially sighted people. We spent about six hours there watching the largest and most varied collection of

wildfowl in the world. We had lunch outdoors beside the beautifully landscaped lake, home to six species of flamingo. Hundreds of geese and ducks wander the grounds, ever hopeful of sharing the visitors' picnics; seed can be purchased for feeding them. There is a visitor centre with fine exhibitions of paintings, a cinema, gift shop and restaurant, and an observatory.

My first visit to Slimbridge was with my husband soon after we were married. It was a bus ride from where we were staying and having missed the one bus of the day we were rescued by the local milkman. He took us all the way perched on the back of his float, with legs swinging in time with the clanking bottles. The centre was very new then and quite different; the path surfaces were of rough gravel which spoilt the visit for me, but the memory makes me thankful for the improved access today, at Slimbridge and at many other places of interest.

Stourhead garden, laid out in the eighteenth century with lakes, temples and rare botanic specimens, is rated among our favourite National Trust properties and we've been there three times. The path around the edge of the main lake is about 2km long, wide enough for wheelchairs and has a good smooth surface. We stopped at the tearoom before starting on our walk and booked a cold lunch for our return – it gets very busy, especially at weekends. Wheelchairs are available at the Stourton village entrance to the garden and inside the house; there are thirteen steps up to the ground floor of the house.

Back at the farm there is a large folder of information and many written comments and suggestions from previous disabled visitors, with stress on easy access and adapted toilets. It's a delightful area, with far too much to fit into a week.

Bird-watching in Nottingham

In this passage, Vivienne Adcock (see p.123) describes a bird-watching holiday based at a Winged Fellowship centre in Nottingham, in 1989.

Perhaps Nottingham seems an unlikely spot for bird-watching, but John Wyatt, organiser and leader on behalf of the RSPB, knows better. In 1989 he had been running this sort of holiday for two years, and we were impressed by his careful planning and efficient organisation.

Following a warm welcome over a pot of tea on our arrival at *Skylarks Holiday Centre*, any physical help that would be needed during our stay was discussed. The centre is modern with bright decor and plenty of space. Most of the bedrooms overlook beautiful lawns and a well-kept, secluded garden with seats tucked away in patios and in nooks and crannies near a small pond. We saw quite a bit of wildlife here with minimal effort.

The centre adjoins the National Water Sports Centre and Nature reserve at Holme Pierrepoint, which was created out of an area of worked-out gravel pits. The reserve is managed by the Nottinghamshire Trust for Nature Conservation and all the different types of habitat on the reserve can be seen from the nature trail.

"We had what I would call an 'action-packed holiday'"

The trail paths are excellent both for wheelchair users and for those with walking difficulties. There are several places for a sit and the first time I visited I managed almost the whole circuit with the aid of elbow crutches. The habitats for wildlife include two lakes, reed beds, dense areas of willow (a haven for warblers) and carpets of orchids in the summer, with clearings attractive to butterflies. Three hides allow close-up views of birds; from one of them we watched activity at the tern table and – a special treat for us – the courtship dance of the great crested grebe.

On our second visit to the reserve I went by wheelchair and was able to see tiny frogs. The bonus of the day was that the Wildlife Management team had rigged up netting the previous evening in order to catch a few species for ringing. We were able to touch and hold – as well as see at close quarters – reed warbler, reed bunting, willow warbler and song thrush.

We had what I would call an "action-packed holiday". By 10am each day we set off in a specially adapted *Winged Fellowship* van, returning in time to freshen up before the evening meal. In the evenings the bird-watching group (which in this instance was small – five disabled visitors and five helpers) met in a separate lounge for slide shows of what we were hoping to see the next day, then what we had seen, and check-lists of the day's sightings.

Not all of the bird-watching was done in Nottingham. On our first venture to Leicestershire's Rutland Waters the rain tipped down unmercifully, but once inside the Egleton Interpretive Centre at the southernmost point of the village we were welcomed with steaming hot drinks. We looked at slides of the reserve and were given a potted history of the huge area (1214ha) of open water. Since it was constructed in 1975 it has become one of the most important wildfowl sanctuaries in Britain, with its purpose-built islands, shingle banks and three lagoons. We later had time to look at the displays of information at the centre, and an attractive shop.

John and company had come fully equipped for all eventualities, and when we returned to our bus we were handed extra waterproofs. I hit the record by wearing fourteen items of clothing! But we arrived at the hide to find it surprisingly comfortable, with moulded plastic chairs (what luxury!) and two telescopes rigged up for our use. Before long the rain lessened and we made some unexpected and unusual sightings. About an hour later the picnic was distributed – attractively arranged salads, pies, crisps, fruit, biscuits, cake, and as many hot drinks as we could wish for. The reserve wardens joined us and it was one big party! I have since discovered that many bird lovers take their lunch into the hides and stay for several hours. I didn't imagine it could be so exciting.

The next day we drove to Welbeck Park and Clumber Park, hoping to see honey buzzards at the first venue. We were disappointed but carried on to Clumber Park where I had my first experience of being pushed through woods in a wheelchair. I am usually very limited as regards rough ground and distances, walking slowly with elbow crutches, and most of my time is spent looking down rather than up. My particular delight in the woods was being able to look up at the cathedral-like canopies of spring leaves while listening to the symphony of woodland birds.

"78 species were spotted at these sites, out of which I claim to have seen 66"

In Derbyshire, on another outing, we made first for Swallow Moss, a reserve which is not open to the public except down one track. We picnicked at one end of this moorland in the hope of seeing red and black grouse.

Unexpected entertainment, similarly coloured, arrived in the shape of a company of cadets with blackened faces, whose leader, distinguished by his red beret, crouched, stalked and beckoned them on until they took cover by our bus. We tried hard to contain our amusement as many of the cadets looked self-conscious and some-what sheepish. At the other end of the track we were rewarded with sightings of grouse and wheatear.

At Wetton Mill we walked along an old railway track by the Manifold river. This is a good hard track for wheel-chairs, with no traffic passing. The scenery is beautiful and the track has a slight incline, leaving the fast flowing river just below to the right, and steep banks on the left, eventually ending in dramatic cave mouths, marking an ancient level of the river. The area is rich in wild flowers and birds, and we learned to look to the higher slopes for goldfinch, linnet and whinchat, while lower down we sighted tree pipits, spot-ted flycatcher, whitethroat and black-cap. On our return we scanned the river from the bridge in vain for the promised kingfisher, but were consoled with a long study of the habits of the dipper.

During our five-day stay 78 species were spotted at these sites, out of which I claim to have seen 66 – not bad for a beginner, although whether or not I'd recognise them again is questionable! Our leader and helpers were with us throughout each day, including meal-times, and their patience seemed limit-less. Those of us who were slower or didn't know very much about the subject were embraced as equal with the "old hands", and we had a lot of fun together.

Halfway round the World

As a result of a severe stroke at the age of 48, some 16 years ago, Mickie Nixon can hardly walk, is paralysed on her right side, has a useless hand and very little voice. But she has acquired an unexpected zest for adventure, a feeling that everything she achieves is a bonus and that she must accomplish as much as possible to the best of her physical ability. In 1988 she decided to visit relatives in Wigan, Lancashire, travelling alone by train from Ashford in Kent.

The journey entailed crossing London but, having heard that *British Rail* operate a free escort service for disabled passengers, I was determined to undertake it alone. This may not sound very special, nor particularly glamorous or exciting, to an able-bodied person, but to me it was a major expedition. My first obstacle was to persuade my husband that I was capable of making the journey on my own. Being unable to express my feelings in words this was no easy task, but he is very cooperative, and knowing how stubborn I am he agreed to do all he could on my behalf.

The first step was to contact the stationmaster at our nearest mainline station, Ashford. My husband made an appointment and went along to discuss the situation with him. He intended to drive me the 10km to Ashford but needed to find out my route from there, as well as the times of the trains. Although I would need a wheelchair during the stay with my relatives, I did not want the added worry of having to take one with me. My husband was assured that *BR* staff would meet me at each station as the train arrived and convey me to the next point of departure either by wheelchair or other

means. I was to travel from Ashford to Charing Cross, where I would be met and put on a taxi, with instructions to the driver to take me to Euston. There I would be met and seen on to the Intercity train direct to Wigan, where I would again be met.

My husband impressed on the stationmaster the need for assistance, particularly in view of my inability to converse, in getting on and off trains, carrying luggage, and making the connection between stations in London. He left feeling confident that I would be in safe hands. Although sure that nothing could go wrong, I took the precaution of thinking through what might happen and carried in my pocket several typed "HELP" notes which, as it turned out, proved invaluable.

My husband took me to Ashford station, where we made ourselves known. We were told that everything had been arranged. By sheer chance I met a friend waiting for the same train, so my husband was relieved of any worries, at least for the first leg of the journey.

When we arrived at Charing Cross, to my consternation the promised porter did not appear. I was escorted by my friend to the exit barrier, where enquiries were made for my promised assistance. Soon a porter arrived and escorted me to a taxi, requesting the driver to take me to Euston. So far so good.

"My main interest was studying the passengers as they passed along the aisle"

When the taxi pulled up at Euston, a railway buggy was waiting for me and I was transported in style and comfort to the train. The porter found my reserved seat and was extremely kind, making sure I was comfortable and knew exactly where he had stowed my suitcase. Nothing was too much trouble. Incidentally, no tips are accepted by porters, and it is a good idea to travel light – it is difficult for porters to manage you and your baggage if you need a wheelchair.

It was a very pleasant ride and although I couldn't really converse, one of my travelling companions – a complete stranger – offered to help with refreshment. I had taken some sandwiches and a carton of orange juice but this sort of fare was available on the train and could have been supplied to me at my seat. The Intercity trains waste no time covering as much ground as possible in the shortest time, so it was difficult to catch the names of stations as we sped past, but I could appreciate the beautiful countryside.

My main interest was studying the passengers as they passed along the aisle, and exchanging a few words with a lady opposite who was returning to her children in Liverpool, having left her family for the first time to visit friends in London. She was very interested in my exploits! I had to write everything down on a pad, which was no mean feat with the train moving at such a pace and with my right hand out of action! This lady also helped to extricate my luggage and hand it to the porter at Wigan.

"I had arrived, and felt that I'd achieved a miracle"

On arrival at Wigan I spotted three porters with wheelchairs, so *BR* are well equipped for disabled folk. As my relatives were waiting to greet me they took my luggage while the porter pushed me through the station and into the lift. So, I had arrived, and felt that I'd achieved a miracle! And, of course, I received a hero's welcome which did great things for my ego! I was then able to spend two glorious weeks enjoying the love and affection of my cousins on the Costa Lancs!

My cousins live in a cosy terraced house on a main road, Frog Lane, with a small backyard, brimming with flowers, and an outside toilet framed with

runner beans. Since I live in a bungalow I was not used to coping with stairs, but the outside loo was a godsend. My welcome was overwhelming, almost as if I'd travelled halfway round the world (as indeed it seemed) and to celebrate my "victory" one of their close friends had sent a basket of flowers.

Unfortunately, my cousins do not find a car necessary as they can easily walk – although both in their seventies – and they have buses, trains and taxis close at hand. To enable me to get about they had obtained a brand new wheelchair, free of charge, from the Red Cross; that was much appreciated and much used.

Wigan is very built up but the natives are friendly, and the surrounding countryside is lovely; living as I do in the heart of the country in Kent, I found the change of scene refreshing. Of course my first request was to visit the famous Wigan Pier, which we did by taxi (very cheap in this part of England). We hired one which was equipped with a ramp, making life easier with the wheelchair, and a very obliging driver who was quite willing to carry me upstairs if necessary.

We also made many shopping trips to the brand new, enclosed market and shopping centre, which were still in the process of being completed, and by rail to Southport and Blackpool, which are both nearby. In Blackpool I met up with a pen friend, made through our disability (stroke). I was also able to make contact, via my church at Canterbury, with the church in Bolton where I made more friends.

I made the return journey midweek and I was fortunate with the weather, which was dry and comfortably warm. I wore a trouser suit which is best for relaxing in and manoeuvring in and out of wheelchairs. Again I had booked a seat, which the porter found for me, but this time the train was rather full – I strongly recommend reserving a seat on these Intercity trains.

I sat opposite a very friendly lady who told me that she was involved with deaf and dumb people; she introduced me to sign language through letters that I could convey with one hand. That was an added bonus, and we still correspond with each other, having much in common. It is interesting that all the passengers who spoke to and helped me were female and middle-aged; perhaps this group is more likely to be sympathetic to folk such as myself?

One other person who joined the train on my return journey was a drunk, who insisted on talking to everyone. I understood him as well as he understood me, but it didn't bother him and he talked ceaselessly. The encounter was short-lived, however, as he soon staggered away on the arm of a railway official, to the relief of the other passengers.

When I arrived at Euston, *BR* let me down and there was no porter to help me. I took out my "HELP" note and was able to attract the attention of a passenger who found assistance for me, and I was eventually taken to a taxi. This time the taxi driver was foreign: out came "HELP" note with the name of the station I wanted, and we finally set off.

At Charing Cross once again the system failed and it was another passenger, not a porter, who came to my aid.

She found a porter who took me to the Ashford train, although it turned out to be an earlier train than intended. I arrived safely, but being on a different train I was not met. Another passenger kindly helped me off with my luggage and soon after that my husband arrived to collect his tired but elated wife.

"I advise anyone who is doubtful about embarking on such a journey not to hesitate"

On reflection it seems I overestimated *BR*'s service, which is in fact advertised not as an escort service but as "Disabled Assistance" – perhaps more apt, and certainly more non-committal. I did not complain as I really should have done, mostly because I was so relieved to arrive home in one piece. By the time I came down to earth and life was back to "normal" it was too late to do anything about it. I'm afraid life moves forward at a much slower pace since the stroke, and I tend to be thankful for small mercies. And, besides, the whole experience was like a tonic to me. I advise anyone who is doubtful about embarking on such a journey not to hesitate: people are so very kind, especially fellow travellers, and, having done it once, the world's your oyster!

Leicestershire Bells

Jane Nyman, who has Parkinson's disease, has spent many holidays in convents (she writes about the English Convent in Bruges on p.194), but she was rather nonplussed when it was suggested that she try a holiday in a Trappist monastery in deepest Leicestershire.

I knew very little about Trappist monasteries, except that this order was originally French and that the monks spent the greater part of their days in silence. As far as I could gather, they led a very frugal existence shut away from the world.

I then encountered a Trappist monk in Belgium and he turned out to be a dapper little man from Zaire with an elegant short beard, impeccably dressed in a pin-striped suit. He was studying at the University of Brussels and, somehow, he did not fit the image. He questioned me minutely about aspects of the Anglican faith, and either I did not know or had forgotten the answers. Panic-stricken, my French failed me, and I decided that in future I would avoid Trappist monks.

"There was a lovely pub ... in case I could not stand the Trappist regime and needed to decamp at short notice!"

As for taking a holiday in a Trappist monastery, I had visions of a great many church services, a cold stone cell, and bread and cheese meals, so I arranged for a friend to take me over for a sneak preview of the monastery before I committed myself. It was a cold spring day, with a piercing wind, and despite directions from the Guest Master, who had assured me that we could not miss it, we had some difficulty in locating the monastery and its large bell tower.

However, I was delighted to find that there was a lovely pub, not a hundred yards from the gate. Since this is "Quorn country", famous for its hunting, the bar was filled with hunting horns (genuine) and hunting prints. It was warm and welcoming; the food was excellent and reasonably priced. I made a note of their weekly terms and their phone number, in case I could not stand the Trappist regime and needed to decamp at short notice! The monastery was built in the 1930s but the solidity of its walls suggested a far earlier tradition. The monks derive their income from a number of enterprises on the premises, thus ensuring that they spend a maximum amount of time in prayer, while at the same time being self-sufficient. There is a farm, a guesthouse and a shop which is open for about three hours a day. The monks also run a pottery and a printing press, although these are out of bounds to guests.

The shop sells a marvellous mixture of items, ranging from Catholic bric-à-brac to postcards and homemade honey. There is a good selection of pottery at very fair prices, and some nicely carved Nativity scenes in the Austrian tradition. They also sell printed stationery and a wide range of religious books. As the monks who run the shop are relaxed and possessed of a good sense of humour, I found myself returning again and again. The silence rules certainly did not apply there. I still do not know whether or not they were pulling my leg when they assured me that they sold teapots with three spouts, but were temporarily out of stock ...

The monastery caters for people who are on retreat, or for people who simply need a holiday. I met Catholics as well as non-Catholics, and some who did not seem to belong to any persuasion but simply liked the atmosphere. I met two elderly sisters who had been going there for years, as it was a convenient place for them to meet, geographically about halfway between their two homes.

I discovered that the single men and married couples were housed in the monastery itself, and the single ladies slept in a building about a hundred yards away, down the drive. Whilst it is the Guest Master who books you in and answers any queries that you may have, there is also a warden for the women's guesthouse, who gives you a warm welcome.

The Guest Master, who I discovered had been a keen cricketer in the past, produced a list of regulations for me to read. I found that very helpful: if you decide to come here for a holiday, you cannot inadvertently break the rules. He checked that I was not on any special diet, and I asked if I could be put in a room near the bathrooms. It was also explained that I would need to be able to climb one flight of stairs. Having settled the details, I felt quite happy to book a five-day stay.

Although there are some rules, attendance at church is not one of them. The main rules are that there is silence after the last office (about 7.30pm) until breakfast time, although this was not strictly observed in the ladies' guesthouse, and that the main gates are locked at this time. In practice, I did not find it difficult to observe this rule, as my day tended to start very early and by 7.30pm I was glad to be in bed.

I arrived in the middle of a heatwave in May. My room was tiny but adequate, and only three of us had to share the bathroom. I heaved a sigh of relief when I unpacked and found a hot-water bottle in the drawers. There was a radiator in my room but I assumed (wrongly, as it turned out) that it would not be turned on if we had a couple of chilly days. There was a small sitting room downstairs, containing one of those weird and wonderful machines for making tea and coffee with ten variations. The first night I was there I learned the reason for the embargo on nightlife. The monks begin their devotions at 3.30am and guests are welcome to join them. You do not have to worry about an alarm clock, as a huge bell tolls at 3.30am and again at 4am. From where I slept I could look out over rolling farmland and see the bell tower looming out of the morning mist. Soon, when my body had adjusted to the different routine, I enjoyed being woken so early.

"Despite their old-fashioned way of life and clothing, the monks went in for modern technology in a big way"

After meals, the guests join in the washing-up and this is quite a good way of getting to know your fellow guests. Indeed, the rules positively enjoin guests to talk to each other. Although most of the monastery is out of bounds to guests, the monks came flocking across to greet and have tea or coffee with their particular friends.

At first it sounded a little odd to listen to these elderly monks in their traditional white habits with enormously long sleeves (two feet longer than their arms) discussing the merits of various computers. But I soon discovered that despite their old-fashioned way of life and clothing, the monks went in for modern technology in a big way. While the Guest Master was welcoming me, his bleep went off and this happened again when I was talking to a saintly 84-year-old monk who was quite happy to discuss the merits of abortion with me. These men might seem to lead a life cut off from the modern world, but they are as up to date in their thinking as anyone outside the monastery. As the monastery is enormous, the bleep system made perfect sense; it was just that I had never linked saintliness and modern technology in my mind.

The church is huge and the monks sing their office at one end, like an invisible choir. As I am the nosy sort, I found this disappointing, but at Mass the monks and guests make a large circle and you can gawk to your heart's content.

In addition to a bedroom, each guest is allocated a private sitting room, so that if you wish to be alone to read or write, or to talk to a monk, you have complete privacy. Although guests who are on retreat are expected to get on with it by themselves, if you have any sort of problem there is always someone available for a chat.

I sometimes needed help with cutting up food, but this was always done without fuss. Occasionally, I needed help to walk to my seat in church, but again help was immediately given. The atmosphere was very peaceful and I felt myself gradually unwind. The monastery provides three cooked meals a day, as well as tea and coffee, which is too much for me. It was so hot that at lunchtime I nipped off to my devotions in the pub, for a cooling drink.

I got up early and went to church, after which I was glad of my "English" breakfast. I read, lounged about in the lovely garden on comfortable wooden benches, did embroidery and periodically went for a run in the car in the very beautiful countryside. There is a village about three miles away, with a railway station and a selection of shops. Loughborough is only about 16km away, if you hanker for a town, but most people had come to escape "civilisation" and were content with the quiet life.

One night, we had a tremendous thunderstorm while we were in church. The lights went out half a dozen times but the emergency lighting functioned well. The problem was, how to get back to supper, in the torrential rain, without getting soaked to the skin . . . I drove back to find the Guest Master assembling a collection of large, black brollies, and monks with towels at the ready, to dry our hair. When I returned to my room after supper, my windows had been closed and the radiator was warm.

Although I normally use a wheelchair outside, I found that I did not need one and instead used my car to move between the ladies' guesthouse, the monastery and the church. The accommodation would not be suitable for an indoor wheelchair user. If you are handicapped you need a car to get out and about.

If you do not like being woken early, take some earplugs or just close the window to prevent the bell from waking you. If you are a "single" and you cannot face a holiday on your own, this offers a way of meeting people in a relaxed way. My fellow guests were a very mixed bunch, ranging from a lad from the northeast who had been out of work for several years, to an amateur weather-forecaster, who worried when we had a storm that he was not at home to take the rain readings. There was also an ex-nun, with a delightful sense of humour, who wore glamorous clothes, a few deacons and parish priests, as well as others who were difficult to fit into any category.

If you have very little money, you make a donation to the monastery and you do not receive a bill. It is tactfully indicated how much your stay costs the monks (in 1989 it was £10 a day) and you may give more or less according to your circumstances. For total board, I thought it excellent value for money. If *haute cuisine* and a lively nightlife are what you require, this holiday is not for you, but as a restful break in lovely countryside it is ideal.

Cornish Adventure Holiday

In May 1989 Veronica Smith, herself a wheelchair user, was one of eight members of staff who took a group of children to the specially adapted Churchtown Farm Field Studies Centre at Lanlivery in Cornwall.

We met outside the school in Cambridge at 8.30am: sixteen children between the ages of eleven and sixteen (ten wheelchair disabled, two ambulant disabled, four able-bodied) and eight members of staff (six able-bodied and two wheelchair disabled). To transport all of us and our luggage we had hired a coach with a lift. Getting us all safely aboard was a work of art; some children transferred to coach seats, but those in electric chairs stayed put and their chairs were clamped to the floor of the coach. Extra space had to be found for spare wheelchairs and for two hoists.

"It was curious to see a boy in an electric wheelchair with a pitchfork or broom wedged down the side, mucking out a dirty stall!"

We set off only a few minutes later than intended and, initially, apart from Linda's chair coming unclamped, the journey was uneventful. After an hour or so, we became aware of an unpleasant smell – the coach was belching out clouds of pungent, black fumes. Next the engine began to stall – something was definitely wrong! We stopped at a service area, unloaded everyone and headed for food and much needed coffee, leaving the driver to phone for advice. He managed to make temporary repairs and we continued on our way, arriving at the centre in time to unpack before the evening meal.

The centre is superbly equipped for disabled people and has a large number of staff, including a resident night nurse, who was able to turn the boys with muscular dystrophy, thus enabling the staff to have an uninterrupted night's rest.

For daytime activities we split up into two groups, each with eight children, four of our staff and between two and four staff from the centre, depending on the nature of the day's activities. On our first full day my group was based at the centre's own farm. The children were able to participate in many new activities, including bottle-feeding the lambs, feeding the pigs, collecting eggs, grooming ponies and mucking out cows and horses. It was curious to see a boy in an electric wheelchair with a pitchfork or broom wedged down the side, mucking out a dirty stall! We had a chance to inspect and handle the small animals kept at the farm, including snakes. All of the children were

happy to hold a snake or have it draped around their necks; some of the staff were not so keen!

Our group then had to plan our evening meal, cooking their own food in the open, over a campfire. The wood collecting expedition was successful and we soon had a suitably large pile, at which point ominous black clouds began to gather and we returned briefly to the centre to don warm clothes and waterproofs. On the way back to the field, Jeremy managed to slide off the bumpy grass track and tip his electric wheelchair over, landing underneath it. But he was quickly righted and no damage sustained, by Jeremy or his chair.

"Abseiling and rock climbing were our activities for the next day"

When we arrived back at the field it was tipping down, so the children cooked their food on camping stoves in the shelter of an open-sided barn. By the time we'd finished our meal the rain had stopped and we were able to light the fire, have a somewhat tuneless sing-song and play silly games.

Abseiling and rock climbing were our activities for the next day. We set off in two minibuses across Bodmin Moor to a disused quarry. There we unloaded and played a hectic wheelchair chase game on the quarry floor, which involved much laughter and hitting members of the opposing team with rolled-up newspapers. This worked up an appetite for the picnic lunch, after which the serious business of the day began.

Rock climbing was first on the agenda. Robert, who has cerebral palsy but is ambulant, decided to accept the instructor's invitation to climb up the almost sheer rockface of the quarry. He was kitted out with a safety helmet and connected securely to a rope; looking slightly less confident, he set off with the instructor amid shouts of encouragement from the others. All went well until Robert had reached the halfway point, when he seemed to realise the enormity of what he was doing and "froze". After considerable help and cajoling, he completed the climb, feeling justifiably pleased with himself but leaving me with a few more grey hairs!

"The quarry walls were too steep for wheelchair abseiling"

Meanwhile, David had got out of his chair and, with some help, was scrambling delightedly over the boulders and rocks of the quarry floor. Neil was driving around in his electric chair, whizzing through puddles, hitting the water with sticks and generally getting into a very pleasurable mess.

Next came the abseiling, in which all the group took part. The quarry walls were too steep for wheelchair abseiling but there was a very steep grassy hill which proved ideal. It was a complicated business roping up chairs and children safely, but well worth the effort. Even those who were apprehensive to start with enjoyed the experience; most had more than one go, and everyone learned to control their own descent, with varying degrees of assistance.

After supper that evening the children tried one of two craft activities – pottery or making a collage. This was relaxing after an energetic day and provided a good opportunity for boasting of their achievements.

The centre has its own specially adapted cruiser moored in the small, picturesque port of Fowey. The boat is flat bottomed and the bow lets down to allow loading of wheelchairs. We headed out of the harbour towards the open sea. It was a fresh day and the wind was strong, creating sizeable waves. The noise, the splashing and bouncing across the waves were all greatly enjoyed, and once back inside the harbour the children were each able to have a go at controlling the boat – at times we must have resembled a wildly tacking yacht!

After lunch it was time for canoeing. Some of the centre staff had paddled out to join us in two Canadian canoes. We cruised up a quiet creek and began loading them up. This involved hauling each canoe up the partially lowered bow and into the boat; transfer of children into the canoes was then safe and relatively easy. All of the children except Linda were able to take part; Linda and I stayed on the motor boat, enjoying a quiet coffee, while the others paddled off, in high spirits, up the creek to explore.

The canoeists were tired when they returned and we all headed back to the centre. After supper, those with enough energy left made good use of the indoor swimming pool.

We had one "day off" during our stay, when we could choose our own activity. Our two groups joined together and after much debate we decided to drive to Flambard's Theme Park, near Helston. The park has a range of attractions, including funfair rides, remote controlled model vehicles and various indoor theme exhibitions – an excellent one portrays life in the Blitz. Everything is fully accessible, so that the children were able to go off without needing a member of staff with them. There is a large gift shop, a highly popular "clotted cream by post" centre and a great deal of junk food on sale, all of which was relished by the children – the food provided at *Churchtown Farm* was very good but, for the children, did not have the same appeal as ice cream or chips!

Towards the end of our week we had the help of four naval ratings from a nearby training ship: their assistance was welcomed by us all, but particularly by some of the older girls! We decided to make good use of the extra muscle power and spend part of the day at a local cove. Great strength was certainly needed when dragging the wheelchairs across the sand to a pleasantly sheltered picnic spot. After lunch most of the children got out of their chairs and sat chatting, played in the sand or went for a paddle. David and Neil did not want to transfer from their chairs but did want to paddle, so they parked at the edge of the sea with feet and wheels just in the water – like a couple of King Canutes! Later in the afternoon we left the beach, drove to a bluebell wood and went for a delightful scent-filled walk; the entire wood was a mass of blue.

On our last day we set off once more for Fowey and the motor cruiser, but this time we towed two sailing boats behind us. These boats had been cleverly adapted so that even the most severely disabled children could control them independently. Each boat held six people and could be powered by sails or motor.

There was a strong breeze and the boats cut through the water at exhilarating speed. To begin with the sails were used, with the children working the ropes and controlling the rudder. Later the engines were put to use and the most severely disabled were able to sit strapped securely into a specially constructed seat in the stern of each boat. From here they took charge of the boats, controlling speed and direction by using a joystick in the same way as for manoeuvring their electric chairs. This was an enormous success and quite made the children's holiday.

Lashings of Cornish Cream

Eileen Cross, a St Ives artist, had a severe stroke in 1979 and lost the use of her right hand. She learnt to paint with her left hand and still produces saleable pictures. Now 90 years old and living in a residential home, she has been twice to Newquay for a holiday with the St Ives and District Disabled Club.

When the club offered me a holiday in Newquay, I thought I'd risk it as long as I could share a room with my friend, who is more mobile than I am. After all, St Ives is not so far away if I couldn't cope! So off we went in the County Disabled bus, picking up other people en route. We soon found ourselves in *The Western Hotel*, perched on the cliff of Fistral Bay with a wonderful view of beach and sea.

There were two very helpful resident nurses on call day and night. Two Red Cross ladies – a different pair each day – came to dress and undress me, morning and night. In my residential home I have to do these things for myself with the help of my frame, but I let them do it as I felt it was good training for them! For the gentlemen in our group the St John's ambulancemen were there in the same way. In the late afternoon two senior schoolgirls arrived to see if we wanted any shopping.

I felt that the hotel toilet facilities were not too good – I managed with difficulty, but we all lodged a complaint with the manager and he promised to improve them. The food was super, far too good really, with a wide choice of menu. The old-fashioned breakfast was available if you wanted it – porridge, bacon and eggs, sausages. Lunch was as substantial as dinner, with lashings of Cornish cream on all sweets. And to work up an appetite, guests can swim in the basement pool; there is also a jacuzzi in the basement.

We were taken on several trips; Newquay is an ideal base for exploring if you have your own transport. Further up the coast is Padstow, on the estuary of the Camel river, where on May Day you can watch the ancient Hobby Horse dance festival, originally a fertility rite, which celebrates the passing of winter. A traditional figure, the Teaser, and a band of attendants lead the Hobby Horse through the streets in a boisterous parade. The Floral Dance at Helston is also worth seeing, on or about May 8. The nearby Flambards Triple Theme Park (Aero Park, Victorian village and "Britain in the Blitz") won an award for its facilities for disabled visitors.

Dobwalls Theme Park, another award winner, is near Liskeard (east of Newquay). Among the attractions are a forest railroad and a collection of fine wildlife paintings. The art gallery is equipped with information cards in Braille, and the park is fully accessible.

"We were taken on a trip to Woolworth's and given a cup of tea in the staff room"

An easy drive down the coast towards Land's End (now very commercialised) is Godrevy Point, near Portreath. This is National Trust land, a series of coastal car parks with sea views. At Reskajeage an enclosure with low walls allows wide-angle viewing of the coast. Another accessible National Trust property is Trerice, about 5km southeast of Newquay. A small, secluded Elizabethan manor house, Trerice contains tapestries, oak and walnut furniture and some interesting fireplaces. The gardens, though, are tricky for wheelchairs. For more accessible gardens (but loose gravel paths) try Trelissick Garden, near Truro, where there are woodland walks beside the Fal river, rare plants and beautiful views over the estuary.

When on holiday with a group of thirty, the decisions are made for you, so we went to Praa Sands, said to be a smugglers' cove. It was raining. All we saw was sea, sand and rain! And everything was closed in October, so we turned round and went back to Newquay! There we were taken on a trip to Woolworth's and given a cup of tea in the staff room.

We visited the Newquay Disabled Club; the members were making some wonderful things. I bought a Tom and Jerry knitted cat and mouse, just the job for my great-grandson's third birthday. I also found a "wrist purse" (fastened with a Velcro strip around the wrist), only 30p but indispensable for someone with only one useable hand.

It is often very windy in Newquay – one night a large window in the lounge was blown in. This explains the popularity of the town with surfers – the north coast of Cornwall is a favourite haunt of theirs. The waves are always good and the surfing competitions held there attract international stars. We had a good view of the surfers carrying their gear down to the beach past our lounge windows.

For evening entertainment the hotel laid on a different act each day, always with a Cornish theme. One night a choir from Newquay church sang for us, another a young man sang Cornish songs and funny poems. On the last night a trio of musicians played the sort of music that the more mobile amongst us could dance to. An exciting thing happened that night: just as we were thinking of bed the band started up with "Happy Birthday to You"; it was my 88th birthday weekend, also that of three other people in our party. The group had clubbed together to buy us a large birthday cake and a bottle of wine. Each of us was taken into the centre of the room and then the St John's ambulancemen pushed us round and round in a sort of dance – great fun!

I haven't laughed as much for years as I did in that week. It's the best medicine, and I went home feeling much more cheerful and ready to struggle on again. That holiday also taught me a lesson – there are people in more serious trouble than I am, and they were still enjoying themselves. I feel lucky that I did all my foreign travelling before my stroke. To me, Venice is the most delightful place, but for a learner traveller I'd advise Switzerland. The air is fresh, the Swiss are a kindly people, and everything is beautifully decorated – houses, furniture, even the people themselves. And oh! The wild strawberries and cream! But there was plenty of cream in Newquay, and my trip there was almost as good!

Loaded Camel and Laughing Man Rock

Marion Embury was born on St Mary's, the largest of the Scilly Isles, and lived there until 1960. She's been back a few times, but her visits stopped in 1980 when increasing leg disability limited her walking to very short distances on crutches. In 1988 Marion bought a battery-operated scooter and returned to the islands with a friend, Liz, and her dog, Pebble.

Although it is possible to travel to the Isles of Scilly by helicopter or small, fixed-wing aircraft from Penzance, in order to accommodate scooter and dog we had to cross by ferry. In the past I've booked through *Renwicks* travel agency but this time chose to deal direct with the *Isles of Scilly Steamship Company*, Penzance; I told them that I am a disabled traveller and would have a scooter with me.

On arrival at Penzance quayside, where we were to board the *RMV Scillonian*, I was alarmed by the angle of the gangway, but the officer in charge of boarding assured me that if the scooter could not manage it he would find two or three crew members to give me a push. I need not have worried because the Everest and Jennings Runaround swept up the gangway and only required assistance at the top, where we met the deck.

The Isles of Scilly are situated about 50km southwest of Land's End. There are five inhabited islands – St Mary's, Tresco, St Martin's, Bryher and St Agnes – with a total population of about two thousand. The largest uninhabited island is Samson, which consists of two grassy hills. It was inhabited until the mid-nineteenth century, and my ancestors were the last to move off, when they could no longer earn a living from fishing and kelping. There are many smaller uninhabited islands and rocks in the archipelago and it is possible to land on some of these, but with no quays or paths the terrain is very difficult for the disabled.

Our accommodation on St Mary's was on the ground floor of the guesthouse, but there were two steps from the road into the garden and another two into the sun lounge, where the scooter was to be housed and recharged. The proprietor was very helpful and provided a wooden board to be used as a ramp; throughout our stay I could ride straight in and out. Earlier in the year I had written to the Tourist Information Office at the Town Hall on St Mary's. As well as sending me a list of accommodation addresses and a map of the islands, they were able to suggest one or two guesthouses which they thought would be suitable; I then telephoned direct to the owners. Unfortunately our guesthouse was permanently closed at the end of the 1988 season, to be turned into flats and sold.

We wanted to visit the other islands in the group and this meant travelling by small motor launches. The local boatmen were only too pleased to help Liz to dismantle the scooter, load it onto the boat and reassemble it on arrival at our destination.

St Mary's is the only island to allow cars, so there are no tarmac roads on the other islands. There are tractors, but the lanes are narrow, and several times it was quite comical to meet a tractor in a narrow lane with no room to pass. Naturally it was much easier for me to reverse, but once or twice the farmers insisted on going back, much to the amusement of onlookers!

The beautiful subtropical gardens on the island of Tresco have a well-deserved reputation. It is impossible for the wheelchair-bound visitor to see all of the plants at close quarters, as some are situated on terraces approached by steps, but there are plenty that *can* be reached, including huge cacti, agapanthus, eucalyptus trees and many varieties of mesembrianthemum. Many plants cannot be grown anywhere else in the UK because the climate is unsuitable.

"I'm still not sure how I clambered into the very small aircraft, but I made it, and it was certainly worth the effort"

Less than a kilometre away from the gardens is a beautiful beach – Pentle Bay – which is usually deserted and its fine, white sand is sprinkled with shells. Another island with beautiful beaches is St Martin's, most parts of which were accessible to me and my scooter.

My favourite islands are the two smallest inhabited ones – Bryher and St Agnes – each with a population of about sixty. St Agnes is the furthest from St Mary's, and not always possible to reach, but it is this remoteness

which appeals to me. Bryher is a very pretty island, and on the northern coast, which is exposed to the Atlantic, there are often very spectacular seas pounding into Hell Bay.

"Now I know that my scooter can cope with the often rough terrain I cannot wait to go again"

Apart from inter-island ferry services the boats run pleasure trips, and on one of these we were lucky enough to see the first of the baby seals – very fluffy and yellow, and kept well above the high tide mark by the proud mum. We also took a marvellous flight around all the islands and saw the famous Bishop Rock Lighthouse, the first or last point of England for countless sailors. I'm still not sure how I clambered into the very small aircraft, but I made it, and it was certainly worth the effort.

On St Mary's I visited many people whom I'd known when I lived there, and I explored some of my old haunts. One of these is the rugged headland of Peninnis, which is on the south of the island and covered with heather and sea-pinks. I was thrilled to drive out there on my scooter in a very bracing gale! There are some dramatic rock formations to be seen, many with appropriate names – Giant's Tooth Rock, Kettle and Pan Rocks, Pulpit Rock, Loaded Camel and Laughing Man Rock.

On the other side of the island is Pelistry Bay, another much-loved spot. This lovely beach makes a good stop for cream teas and wonderful views of the Eastern Isles. Equally good views of the Western Isles can be had from the walk (about 3km) to the Garrison; this is also the place for watching magnificent sunsets. I was disappointed that my scooter could not cope with the steep gravelly hill approaching the Garrison.

One evening we attended a film show about shipwrecks around the islands. It was held in a church hall with a large step at the entrance, and as I couldn't leave my scooter outside in the rain I borrowed my improvised ramp from the guesthouse and transported it, with Liz's help, balanced on the back of the scooter (more amused glances from passers-by). The film was very interesting: there have been many ships lost on the notorious rocks around the Scillies, but with radar and improved navigational aids there are very few these days. There was a film shown in the hall most evenings; other subjects included the bird life of the islands and local history.

There are no cinemas or bingo halls, but the Scillonian Entertainers regularly put on good variety shows, and dances or discos are held once or twice a week. There are two pubs on St

Mary's, both with good local atmosphere, and several restaurants.

Since I left the islands in 1960 the most obvious change has been in the number of holiday homes owned by people living in other parts of the UK. Houses and flats seem to have sprung up everywhere but, surprisingly, do not detract from the beauty and peace of Scilly. The islands have not become commercialised and you will not see ice-cream vans, hot dog stalls or candy floss anywhere.

I am biased, I suppose, but to me the Isles of Scilly are very special. Now I know that my scooter can cope with the often rough terrain I cannot wait to go again, but I do think it best to take a companion to help, even if only to balance the ramp on the scooter.

ENGLAND AND WALES: TRAVEL NOTES

Sources of information

Wales Council for the Disabled, Llys Ifor, Crescent Road, Caerphilly, Mid-Glamorgan CF8 1XL; ☎0222/887325. Good for specific queries on holidays for disabled people in Wales.

Land & Leisure Ltd, Pas y Ffynon, Cambrian Way, Brecon, Powys LD3 7HP; ☎0874/3181. Information on access to sailing, fishing, bird-watching and nature trails on and around the Welsh reservoirs: ask for a free copy of *Reservoir Recreation with Special Interest to the Disabled*.

Wales Tourist Board, Brunel House, 2 Fitzalen Road, Cardiff CF2 1UY; ☎0222/499909. At present their publications contain no access information. There is a new guide for disabled visitors in the pipeline, but it has a long way to go and publication is unlikely before the end of 1991.

English Tourist Board, Thames Tower, Black's Road, London W6 9EL; ☎081/846 9000. A well-researched and readable report,

Tourism for All (£5, published September 1989), was produced for the English Tourist Board by a working party led by Mary Baker, chairman of the *Holiday Care Service* (see *Practicalities*), and including representatives from voluntary organisations, national tourist boards and the tourism industry. Many of the report's findings are supported by the accounts in this book; *Tourism for All* deserves to be widely read and its recommendations acted upon.

Addresses of the twelve English **regional tourist boards** are given in the excellent *RADAR* guide, *Holidays in the British Isles* (see *Books*). Most of them supply information for disabled visitors.

Transport

Public transport bodies have been notoriously slow to respond to the needs of disabled passengers, but the outlook for the Nineties is pretty good for travellers using trains, domestic airlines and ferries. It remains bleak for bus users and travellers on London's Underground.

ENGLAND AND WALES: TRAVEL NOTES

British Rail have made significant progress in improvement of access and facilities for disabled passengers on trains and at stations. However, some conflicting reports of *BR*'s service have been received, in spite of the fact that staff receive instruction from a detailed training video which explains how to meet the differing needs of all disabled customers. Provision of wheelchair-accessible toilets on trains is still poor, and wheelchair users are still frequently forced to travel in the vestibule or in the guard's van.

By May 1991, all regular Intercity services will have a space (67cm wide) for a wheelchair in the passenger saloon. Wide doors, automatic interior doors and grab-rails are standard facilities. A wheelchair-accessible toilet is provided on London–Glasgow services, and all new mainline stock will have one adapted toilet per train. There are no plans to introduce larger compartments on Intercity Sleepers to allow disabled passengers to transfer comfortably from wheelchair to bed.

Modern Sprinter and Pacer trains will be in service on most regional routes by 1992, replacing stock of 1950s vintage. Trains serving long-distance routes will be equipped with a wheelchair-accessible toilet. Wheelchair-bound passengers will either travel in the vestibule or, "in some cases", in the seating area – this is not very cheering, and certainly not in line with *BR*'s stated aim, "to enable wheelchair users, if they so wish, to travel in their wheelchairs throughout their journey within the public saloon alongside other passengers and not in guards' vans or special compartments".

Network Southeast is served by some older trains, which *BR* claims have up to fifteen years' life in them; restructuring to accommodate wheelchairs is deemed uneconomical, and as a stop-gap solution guards' vans are being "upgraded" to provide a more comfortable environment – heat, light, wheelchair restraints and a tip-up seat for a companion. Accessible, sliding-door stock is being introduced on inner and outer suburban routes. On long-distance routes, trains have Intercity-type facilities.

BR has equipped more than 130 principal stations with facilities for four main categories of disabled rail travellers: ambulant disabled,

wheelchair users, sight impaired and hearing impaired. Further stations are being upgraded to full accessibility. Facilities include conveniently sited parking spaces, signing to indicate easiest routes and call-for-assistance facilities, adapted toilets (fitted with National Key System locks; keys available from *RADAR*), passenger lifts, induction loops at booking office windows and travel centres, inductive couplers fitted to public phones, access to catering facilities, medium-level phones, white markings on platform edges and stairs, and portable ramps for access to trains.

There are special fares for a wheelchair user or visually handicapped person and one companion. You can also apply for a *Disabled Persons Railcard* (application form from stations, travel centres and main post offices) which costs £12 and gives concessions on a range of tickets, including Saver, AwayBreak and Cheap Day Return fares.

Careful planning and advance warning is necessary if you are travelling alone and require assistance on your journey, and the assumption seems to be that disabled people never need to travel at short notice and are expert at preplanning. Those who are should write to the Area Manager of their nearest mainline station (addresses supplied in the passenger care leaflet *British Rail and Disabled Travellers*, available at any station). Even the prescribed advance notice doesn't always guarantee a smooth journey (see p.127)

Probably the best means of public transport for the handicapped person – **air travel** – is unfortunately the most expensive, and there are no fare concessions for disabled passengers here. For a review of facilities at domestic airports, see *Practicalities*.

Facilities on older **ferries** may be barely adequate, with high sills to negotiate, no passenger lifts and inaccessible toilet facilities, but the newer boats are better equipped. Access at ferry terminals and on ferries is discussed in *Practicalities*, "Getting There by Land and Sea". Our contributors report reasonably trouble-free crossings to Ireland and the Scilly Isles. Obtain details of fare concessions from the *Disabled Drivers' Motor Club* or the *Disabled Drivers' Association. Sealink Stena*

ENGLAND AND WALES: TRAVEL NOTES

Line will give discounts to non-members of the *DDMC* or *DDA*, but you'll need a signature from the director of your local authority social services or social work department.

Several companies offer accessible **coaches** for hire – see *Getting Around by Bus and Coach* (available from the *Bus & Coach Council*, Sardinia House, 52 Lincoln Fields, London WC2A 3LZ; ☎071/831 7546) and the *RADAR* holiday guide. But it's access to *National Express* that's needed, with hydraulic lifts installed as standard on *all* public buses. In 1990 a petition with 38,000 signatures was presented to Parliament by the *London Dial-a-Ride Users' Association*, pressing for legislation that would require all new buses and coaches purchased from 1992 by UK operators to be accessible to people with disabilities, including wheelchair users. By early 1991 there was no sign of action.

Driving is a popular method of holiday transport, and finding accessible toilets should not be too difficult in Britain. Apply to *RADAR* for the key to about 3000 toilets covered by the National Key Scheme; for £3.75, you get a key plus a complete list. The *AA Guide for the Disabled Traveller* includes a useful survey of the facilities at motorway service areas. *Shell UK Oil* (Shell-Mex House, The Strand, London WC2R 0DX; ☎071/257 3045) produces a free directory of facilities available at *Shell* garages, *Easier Motoring for Disabled Drivers*.

The **Orange Badge Scheme** is effective everywhere except parts of London (City of London, boroughs of Westminster, Kensington and Chelsea).

If you require more information and ideas on the subject of transport, the *RADAR* holiday guide covers all eventualities: air, sea and rail travel, car and coach hire; escort, taxi and private ambulance services; caravans for adaptation. The *Holiday Care Service* can also assist.

Accommodation

The range of accessible accommodation in Britain is limited, particularly at the cheaper end of the scale. This is an acute problem in London, where hotel rates are ludicrous. But there are encouraging signs of change.

The introduction of the *Tourism for All Accessible* symbol is a giant step in the right direction, with properties being inspected and awarded the symbol on the basis of specific accessibility criteria: a public entrance to the building must be accessible to disabled people from a setting-down point or car-parking place; where an establishment has a car park, a space should be reserved for a disabled guest on request; disabled people must have access to public areas in the building, including reception, dining room, lounge and bar; and a minimum of one ground-floor bedroom (per twenty rooms) with bath or shower and toilet facilities suitable for wheelchair use must be provided.

Managers of accommodation wishing to display the symbol must apply to the *Holiday Care Service*, the *Hotel and Holiday Consortium* or the relevant national tourist board. The first four awards of the symbol went to *The London Tara Hotel* (Scarsdale Place, Kensington, London W8 5SR; ☎071/937 7211), *Hospitality Inn, Irvine* (46 Annick Road, Irvine, Ayrshire KA11 4LD; ☎0294/74272), *Gorslwyd Farm* (Tan-y-Groes, Cardigan, Dyfed SA43 2HZ; ☎0239/810593) and the *Trusthouse Forte Travelodges*, details of which can be obtained from the *RADAR* guide.

Consort Hotels (see *Practicalities*) has adopted the *Tourism for All* "Model Policy Statement", setting out the intention to provide facilities for disabled people, and their brochure, *UK Holidays & Short Breaks: Nice 'n Easy*, lists forty accessible hotels. The *National Trust* has also adopted the Model Policy Statement, welcoming disabled visitors at most of its properties and offering nine fully accessible cottages in its range of holiday accommodation.

The following accommodation is recommended by our contributors. Vivienne Adcock stayed at *Priory Cottage* (Kington St Michael, Chippenham, Wiltshire; ☎024975/222). Contact Colin and Priscilla Labouchere for bookings.

Christine Warburton recommends one place (self-catering) in Wales and three in England. The owner of *Hen Ysgol Holiday Homes* (Rhoscolyn, Isle of Anglesey, Gwynned LL65 2RQ; ☎0407/741593), himself disabled, built the two bungalows (six-berth), which are fully

ENGLAND AND WALES: TRAVEL NOTES

accessible, with wheel-in shower, handrails, "monkey bars", bed blocks, wheelchair-height electrical switches and kitchen, and level patio. The views are stunning, the beach is about 3km away and it's an ideal spot for a quiet break or as a base for touring North Wales.

A country inn and restaurant situated on the A683, the *Fat Lamb Hotel* (Ravenstonedale, Kirkby Stephen, Cumbria; ☎05873/242) has ground-floor rooms with access for most wheelchairs, but the bend in the corridor is difficult for chairs with extended leg-rests to negotiate.

For B&B only, *Alexa House Hotel and Stable Cottages* (26 Ripon Road, Harrogate HG2 2JJ; ☎0423/501988) offers accessible, *en suite*, ground-floor rooms in converted stables. Breakfast is served in the main house, which has a couple of steep steps. The ramp could not be found on Christine's visit, but help was willingly given.

Again for B&B only, *Leasow House* (Laverton Meadows, Broadway, Worcester WR12 7NA; ☎0386/73526) has a large, comfortable, *en suite*, ground-floor room in a converted barn. Breakfast served in main house – no steps at entrance. If necessary, Mrs Meeking will serve breakfast in guests' own room, which has table and chairs and facilities for making tea or coffee.

There are a number of religious establishments in Britain, most of them set in beautiful countryside, which offer the sort of holiday described by Jane Nyman on p.129. These are listed in *Away From It All*, by Geoffrey Gerard (Lutterworth Press). Jane stayed at Mount St Bernard, Coalville, Leicestershire; write to the Guest Master.

Veronica Smith stayed at the *Churchtown Farm Field Studies Centre* (Lanlivery, Bodmin, Cornwall PL30 5BT; ☎0208/872148).

Facilities for disabled **campers and caravanners** are far from perfect, but better on the newer sites. Contributors generally found that they could cope, perhaps with a folding stool for use in the shower, or with help from a companion. Contact *The Forestry Commission* (see p.116), the *Camping and Caravanning Club* or *The Caravan Club* for details of sites which have accessible toilet and washing facilities.

Many accommodation addresses, with access details, are given in the *RADAR* guide. The *RAC* hotel guides are another source; there is more skimpy information in the *AA* guide. Use the regional tourist boards and the *Holiday Care Service*.

Access and facilities

It is impossible to list all the **new initiatives**: the opening of a new lakeland walk along the shore of Derwentwater by the *National Trust*; the publication of a guide for less mobile birdwatchers in and around Suffolk; the provision of good access to the recently reopened Imperial War Museum, London; the awarding of a *Tourism for All Accessible* symbol to another hotel; the inclusion of access details for arts and entertainment venues in the London telephone directory; the launch of a new *Hoseasons* narrowboat, fitted with a wheelchair lift and accessible toilet facilities . . .

To keep up to date with these developments (and other matters of concern to disabled people) it's a good idea to subscribe to disability magazines and newspapers such as *Disability Now* (12 Park Crescent, London W1E 3HU) and *The Disabled Driver* (the magazine of the *Disabled Drivers' Motor Club*).

Several operators deserve praise for their efforts, but there is still much room for improvement and development of better access and facilities in all areas. Perhaps most important, there must be better **communication** – between holidaymakers and operators, between designers or planners and disabled people, between hotel or tourist attraction managements and the market they hope to attract.

Books

Holidays in the British Isles. A Guide for Disabled People (£4.50) is published annually by *RADAR* and available by mail order or from major bookshops. It is a substantial reference book, well worth spending a few pounds on. Other *RADAR* publications (see "Books", *Practicalities*) include *A Guide to British Rail for Disabled People* (1991), and *The Countryside and Wildlife for Disabled People* (1990), which

ENGLAND AND WALES: TRAVEL NOTES

lists facilities at nature sites all over Britain and the Channel Isles. Locally compiled access guides to many towns throughout Britain are available from *RADAR*; some are free.

Access guides produced by the *Pauline Hephaistos Survey Projects* are recommended. *Access in London* (Nicholson, £3.50) was updated in 1989 and a supplement will be available during 1991 – key sections (such as accommodation) have been revised, and new buildings and facilities listed. It is a detailed guide, comprehensive and written with a sense of humour, and the access symbols used in the guide are explained in French and German – quite a departure from the normal assumption that everyone speaks English.

AA Guide for the Disabled Traveller (see "Books", *Practicalities*) is designed to be used in conjunction with other *AA* publications. It contains some useful information but not enough detail on access to accommodation and places of interest.

The *RAC* guide for disabled motorists, On the Move, makes use of access information supplied by disabled researchers. The two accommodation guides (see "Books", *Practicalities*) use the wheelchair symbol; in the main hotel guide some 600 hotels are listed, with an indication of those with reserved parking spaces, level or ramped entrance, level access to public areas, accessible rooms with adjacent or *en suite* adapted bathrooms.

Channel Islands

A Very Accessible Island

Since developing a myopathy and thinning of the bones, and becoming a wheelchair user, Jill Brown had never quite plucked up the courage to travel abroad or by air. In July 1989 she took the plunge.

When a friend invited me to stay at her home in St Peter, on the island of Jersey, I decided that I must overcome my hesitation. I booked with a local travel agent (*WH Smith*, Salisbury), who were most helpful but seemed to ask numerous questions about my disability; I now realise how essential this is – I found that as long as I told people what help I needed, they were happy to assist me without any fuss. Friends took me to and from Eastleigh airport, which made the journey more pleasant and less tiring, and gave me a good start and a welcome home at the end. The airline staff (*Air UK*) provided a thoughtful and caring service.

As soon as we landed at Jersey airport I felt I was abroad! Most of the street names are in French; Jersey has its own language but sadly this is dying out. Even the telephone boxes are different – they are painted yellow. I immediately noticed the narrow lanes with their high banks and colourful flowers in the hedgerows, and the numerous hanging baskets and window boxes on most of the houses made a cheery first impression. I had been told that the climate is better on Jersey than

in England, and I did enjoy warm sunny weather throughout my stay, with a refreshing breeze which made it comfortable to be outdoors.

From my reading matter (supplied by the local library and the States of Jersey, Tourism Department) I had discovered some fascinating customs which date back many years. Each parish had a sanctuary path, called *perquage*, from the church to the beach, along which criminals had safe passage to escape from the island. Many of these paths remain but it would be wise to check their suitability for wheelchairs with a local resident before attempting to follow one.

I noticed the "marriage stones" on some of the houses, mainly old farmhouses, and I was told that these commemorate a wedding. The stone is usually inscribed with the date of the marriage and initials of those married.

If the house has been a wedding gift, it is the custom to name it *La Rosière* (rose garden or place where reeds grow), which accounts for the large number of houses in Jersey bearing that name.

Branchage is another custom which amused me. The occupier of each residence is required to keep the frontage of his or her property tidy, and twice a year the Parish Constable, who is a member of the rather feudal State system, makes an inspection with a special measuring stick. If the hedges and trees are not trimmed back to the required standard, the Constable imposes a fine of 50p. This is considered a disgrace – perhaps it would be a good idea to adopt this on the mainland! In Jersey it is certainly necessary, as most of the lanes are very narrow, and I think it does improve the appearance of the island.

Judging by my own encounters with the islanders, and from my enquiries about Social Services for disabled people living in Jersey, I formed the opinion that it is a very caring community. I was told that many facilities for disabled people have been donated by residents of the island, and I found the shop assistants in St Helier particularly helpful. There were an adequate number of dropped kerbs in St Helier, as well as parking spaces for disabled drivers, although these get filled up very early in the day. Facilities are being improved constantly, which is encouraging, and I certainly found that using a wheelchair was not too difficult. Of course there were places that had steps and no ramps, but life is never perfect and as long as we planned our visits we encountered few problems.

I was fortunate to have a friend with a car. I relied on her entirely for getting around, as the bus service has not yet been adapted for disabled passengers. However, there is a taxi service which takes wheelchairs, and car hire and petrol are relatively cheap, although there are no adapted hire cars. You will need some form of transport in order to explore the scenic coastline and beautiful countryside.

There are numerous places to visit but my stay was limited to one week, so I had to be selective. We chose to keep to outdoor pursuits as the weather was so favourable, and I used the comprehensive booklet *Access in Jersey* (supplied by Jersey Tourism) to choose those which interested me and those which are most accessible for the wheelchair – there's no sense in selecting places which you know are going to present problems when you are out to enjoy a holiday, and there are plenty which are both interesting and easy to visit.

I thoroughly recommend spending a day at Gerald Durrell's zoo at Trinity, in the north of the island. The animals are very well cared for, in spacious enclosures, and it was a pleasure to wander around the well laid out grounds. The paths are reasonable and the restaurant is very comfortable and accessible. The zoo authorities are clearly aware of the needs of disabled visitors – those paths which are not suitable for wheelchairs are marked and there are many that are easy to traverse. The flowers in the grounds are as pleasing as the animals. A guidebook makes the visit more interesting, as well as serving as a reminder of the zoo, and there is a fully accessible gift shop (a little cramped in places) if you want to buy other mementos.

"The zoo authorities are clearly aware of the needs of disabled visitors"

On the east coast is Gorey, which is very attractive and set at the foot of the splendid Mont Orgueil castle, built as a defence against the French. On a clear day you can see the coast of France from this part of the island. If you are not very mobile I think it wise to admire the castle from a distance as I was told that it has many steps. The pottery at Gorey is open to the public during working hours. It is fascinating to watch (free of charge) the craftspeople at work, making and painting the pots which can be bought at the factory shop. The pottery and shop are both accessible. The restaurant is excellent, though rather expensive, and you can eat indoors, under cover or in the open air. At this restaurant, as at all the others we used, I had no problems obtaining food which I am able to eat and enjoy in spite of a digestive disorder; the chefs were willing to make me a meal from the food available although it was not always listed on the menu.

"I wanted to test the claim that Jersey sea is warmer than English sea"

No holiday on Jersey would be complete without a visit to St Helier and the Victorian covered market, with its colourful and enticing displays of fresh flowers, fruit and vegetables, meat and cheese. The centre of the town is traffic free, making shopping a pleasure, and it is worth looking for goods which you can buy free of VAT. I had a look inside antique shops, jewellery shops and picture galleries, and was glad of the good choice of cafés – some with outdoor tables – in which to relax and take a coffee break. One evening I was taken to a very enjoyable piano recital at the Art Centre, at which there is a full programme of concerts and events throughout the year, and disabled members of the audience can sit in comfort in their wheelchairs on the ground floor.

St Brelade's Bay, west of St Helier, is wide and sandy, ideal for sunbathing if that's what you enjoy. We chose to visit the Fisherman's Chapel, at the far west of the bay. Fourteenth- and fifteenth-century murals are being revealed on the walls of this tiny chapel, and it is an oasis of peace, but beware – there are a couple of steps at the entrance. Better for wheelchairs is the fully accessible lavender farm at St Brelade, where we followed the process from lavender bush through distillery to bottling. There is a pleasant café and a shop selling some of the lavender products.

The next bay, going east, is St Aubin's, another attractive wide sweep of the coastline. There is a fascinating harbour, with much entertaining activity on the boats. From here you can see St Aubin's Fort, which was used as a landing-place for the boats bringing goods from France – the goods were then shared amongst Captain and crew at the pub on the quay!

My friend and I had a walk (wheelchair push) in Val de la Mare, St Peter, a nature reserve which includes a beautiful reservoir. An arboretum has been planted on one side of the main path and this is gradually being developed with trees from different countries. The paths are fairly flat and we found one around the reservoir suitable for the wheelchair. It was a peaceful contrast to some of the busier tourist attractions on the island.

The glass church of St Matthew at Millbrook was recommended to me, and it is indeed worth a visit. The interior of this church is decorated with glass designed and made by René Lalique, and it is the only church in which he decorated throughout. The glasswork bears the design of the lily – symbol of purity – on the cross, the communion rail, the screens and the windows, and the simplicity of the design is beautiful.

The coastal scenery of Jersey is magnificent and varied. St Ouen's Bay, just north of La Corbière lighthouse (with a strong helper it is possible to reach the lighthouse if you don't mind a bumpy ride), is a paradise for bathers and surfers, and the sandy beach stretches along the west coast of the island. It is generally more difficult to reach the northern beaches, but there are plenty of vantage points from which to view the rocky harbours. The road to

Bouley Bay is particularly attractive and descends steeply to the shore and sheltered harbour typical of this stretch of coast.

I wanted to test the claim that Jersey sea is warmer than English sea, and I had a blissful swim in clear blue water at St Ouen's Bay. The water temperature was certainly higher than I've experienced in England! I was also able to use the small pool at the *Maison des Landes Hotel*, after making prior arrangement to do so. There is a public pool at Fort Regent, the large entertainment complex at St Helier, but I avoided this as it becomes very crowded in high season.

I had no time to visit the German Underground Hospital, nor any museums, but I already have a list of places that I'd like to see if I return to Jersey as I hope to. Of course, my holiday was made special by the understanding and hospitality of my friend and her family. But I recommend a holiday in Jersey to anyone, whatever their physical state. The journey is easy and there is no need for passport or foreign money. There is a great variety of accommodation available, some catering especially for disabled people, and the people are remarkably friendly and helpful. And it *is* a very accessible and very beautiful island.

Operation Jersey

It all started in June 1988, after Bryan Smith and his wife had spent another enjoyable holiday at the Maison des Landes Hotel in Saint Ouen, Jersey. Some friends at the Rowans Unit for the Young Disabled, Plymouth, were looking for a suitable holiday destination: the Maison des Landes seemed ideal.

The first letters were sent out in August 1988 to book twenty places, ten disabled people and their helpers, with one large motorised chair and a six-foot stretcher bed; no problems with either of these last two items for the hotel. After many phone calls, it was decided that the ambulance carrying the motorised chair and stretcher bed would travel by *British Channel Island* ferry from Poole in Dorset. To ensure that all the gear was at the hotel when the main party arrived, the Poole party had to leave in the afternoon a day earlier. This meant an overnight crossing, so a suitable

cabin was booked for the two disabled passengers. The other eight disabled people, with the smaller wheelchairs, crossed by *Condor* hydrofoil from Weymouth. Transport to Weymouth was by two ambulances, which became separated en route, and an hour was lost in locating each other; luckily we had left Plymouth with plenty of time to spare.

After a smooth crossing in the hydrofoil, we arrived at St Helier and there were plenty of hands to help us all up the gangplanks and steps. Of course, I had told everyone that the hotel minibuses would be waiting for us: they were not! Black looks on Bryan. A quick phone call and they were soon with us. (We had arrived an hour earlier than the time given to us by *Condor*.) We reached the hotel just as the evening meal was being served, so with no fuss we were seated and enjoying a very welcome meal, ready to hear the tales of our night travellers.

They had arrived at Poole without mishap and ahead of schedule, but the cabin which had been reserved to accommodate the stretcher bed and wheelchair users had a doorway too narrow for the stretcher bed – plenty of room inside, if only they could get in through the door. However, the wheelchair did fit, so one person slept in the cabin and the other in the lounge on the stretcher bed. Fortunately it was a very smooth crossing and there were no problems with disembarking at St Helier, where the hotel minibus was waiting on the quayside.

Jersey is the most southerly (hence the warmest) of the three largest British Channel Islands, the other two being Guernsey and Alderney. The islands are situated in the Gulf of St Malo, so geographically speaking they are French. France is visible from each island and French names are used.

The *Maison des Landes Hotel* has room for about forty people and caters for disabled people and their families. Our general routine was that we all had breakfast together and then went out in the hotel minibuses for the day. The seating allocations in the bus were sorted out on the first morning and we kept to these seats for the rest of the holiday, as well as keeping the same driver; this arrangement allows friendships to develop and causes great fun and rivalry between the buses. The hotel supplies packed lunches and we spent each day visiting places of interest, returning in time for dinner and the evening entertainment, either in-house or "out on the town".

On our first morning the minibuses took us into the centre of St Helier and parked in Royal Square, an attractive paved area ringed by trees, and a good base to explore from. A visit to The Market is well worthwhile for two reasons: first, to admire the variety of vegetables and fruit and the mass of flowers; second, to make use of the only toilet for the disabled that we found in St Helier centre! This was the only place on the island that was poorly represented for loos; everywhere else it was clear that disabled people were expected.

We all reported back to the minibuses for our packed lunch. As the weather was good we were able to sit outside and have a drink at one of the two pubs on the edge of the square. The Jersey law which prevents pubs from allowing their customers to take their drinks out onto the pavement is waived in the case of people in wheelchairs. So we had only pigeons for company – hundreds of them, very friendly, jumping onto our hands and helping themselves to our rolls.

It was very noticeable that the shop assistants in St Helier always came to our aid when we were entering the shops, and they spoke to *us*, rather than our helpers – it made a pleasant change not to be ignored. We came to the conclusion that since tourists provide a major source of income on Jersey, the philosophy was to make *everyone* welcome, in order to encourage the tourist trade.

For those who are not so keen on shopping there is the harbour to explore, and the seafront with its long promenade around St Aubin's Bay. On our way back to the hotel we made a stop at the *Plemont Stores*. This was to be a regular stop each night as the hotel is not licensed; most people liked to drink something during and after the evening meal, and drink is certainly much cheaper over there. On some evenings the heated swimming pool (complete with ramp) was opened up for a quick dip before dinner.

The food at the hotel was excellent and the nightlife action-packed. On our first night we were kept in stitches by three musicians, one of whom was the "chat man" with the jokes. We spent an evening at the *Caesar's Palace* nightclub, where four resident dancers and a terrific main act called Cedric of the Three Monics entertained us. For a family cabaret night we visited the *Château Plaisir*, and for a more restful evening in the hotel we were fascinated by a magician whose act is something we still talk about.

The hotel is very near St Ouen's Bay, which makes up virtually the entire west coast. It is a magnificent bay, very popular for surfing and sand yachting, and the views out to sea to the north and west are breathtaking. The road along the bay is called the Five Mile Road (actually only three miles long) and it is the only straight road on the island. It was built by the Germans when they occupied the islands during World War II. All the other roads are narrow and twisting – no wonder the speed limit is only 40mph and in places down to 20mph.

Travelling along the Five Mile Road we saw other reminders of the war. Some of the coastal batteries have been converted into canoe and surf clubs, some into museums, one into a scout troop headquarters and the one nearest the hotel is a fresh fish shop. They are all on the beaches so out of bounds for those of us in wheelchairs. But we did see the German Underground Hospital, which shows the extensive network of tunnels that the Germans constructed for use as operating theatres, wards and staff quarters. Some of the medical equipment used is still in position. It was very cold down there – take an extra jumper.

"I could see by the look on the booking clerk's face that we were going to cause a problem"

We visited the butterfly farm, pearl centre and gold centre, as well as the pottery at Gorey (and its mouthwatering seafood restaurant). There is a pleasant, if sometimes very breezy, walk out to the coastguard tower at Gorey Harbour. In the evening the floodlit castle (Mont Orgueil) makes a striking picture. Like most castles, though, there are plenty of steps and narrow corridors, so wheelchairs are out, but the views must be superb.

The hotel had crammed a great deal into our week, and on our last day we were taken into St Helier for last-minute shopping. The group on our bus didn't fancy a whole day shopping, so we arranged to return to the bus for lunch and then drive to St Brelade's Bay, another great sandy bay, edged by a promenade and flower gardens. We took a leisurely stroll in the sunshine before returning to the hotel to pack. It was a lovely end to the week – much better than shopping!

The *Condor* hydrofoil party was in trouble before we reached the docks the next day. We were held up by a road accident in St Helier and eventually booked in twenty minutes late, at 8.40am. By this time the hydrofoil was steadily filling up and I could see by the look on the booking clerk's face that we were going to cause a problem. However, we agreed to go on the next sailing, at 9.10am, on a smaller hydrofoil than the one we travelled over on. Our hotel drivers were still with us and Gerry, the hotel manager, was not too happy that we had a smaller boat – the gale warning cones were flying.

We soon realised that Gerry's concern was justified, as the crossing turned out to be very rough. The hostesses were kept busy with seasick passengers, although our party had few problems (disabled people are hardier than most!); no chance of reading anything on this ride. At Guernsey we were told that there would be a delay of nearly an hour whilst some repairs to one of the stabilisers were carried out. In fact it was nearer two hours before we were under way again.

By this stage, after a busy week and a very early start that morning, we were all beginning to feel very tired. The last leg, from Guernsey to Weymouth, seemed endless; fortunately the sea was much calmer. At Weymouth, after a slight hiccup at customs caused by the fact that our luggage had travelled separately (apparently we are always to pass through customs with our luggage), we were at last reunited with our own transport and our one thought was Plymouth. The original plan was to have lunch but we decided to call in somewhere for sandwiches and drinks, not unload, and press on home. Just outside Weymouth we pulled in to a *Happy Eater* restaurant. One driver had just jumped out of his cab when a woman appeared, waving her hands and saying, "I don't want you, I'm short of staff, you've got to go!" After a super week, we chorused, "Welcome back to England!"

If organising another trip, I'd make two improvements: ensure that all vehicles travel together, and double-check when booking that the boat meets all requirements. However, having been twice to Jersey by air, I'd much prefer to travel this way. You can be in Jersey within an hour of take-off and this gives you almost two more days there, which in my book is a good thing.

THE CHANNEL ISLANDS: TRAVEL NOTES

Sources of information

States of Jersey, Tourism Department, Weighbridge, St Helier, Jersey; ☎0534/78000). Distribute a free booklet, *Access in Jersey* (also available from *RADAR*), five years old but still useful. It's one of a fine series of access guides (see *Books*).

Access in Guernsey (1990) is also free, either from *RADAR* or the **States of Guernsey Tourist Board**, PO Box 23, White Rock, St Peter Port, Guernsey; ☎1481/26611.

Getting there

The **sea crossing** with *British Channel Island Ferries* is generally accessible but longish (6hr from Poole to Guernsey, 9hr to Jersey). DDMC/DDA members' vehicles are carried free; cabins should be booked well in advance. *Condor's* "wave-piercing catamaran" is for foot passengers only: Weymouth to Guernsey, 2hr 10min; to Jersey, 3hr 40min. Passengers who cannot walk must be lifted manually on and off the ship. A limited number of wheelchair users can be accepted with advance warning, and passengers will be seated near the accessible toilet.

All terminals have good access: there are accessible loos at Poole, Weymouth, and Channel Island, unisex cubicles at Jersey and Guernsey.

You can travel **by air** from many British airports: flights from Bournemouth and Southampton Eastleigh are popular, taking less than an hour. Boarding and disembarking will be by carry-chair or by fork-lift on large planes. Access and toilet facilities at Bournemouth, Jersey and Guernsey airports are good.

Jill Brown flew from Southampton Eastleigh, which has an accessible toilet and plenty of wheelchairs. Assistance from the railway station, about 100m away, can be arranged, and disabled drivers can park in the short-stay car-park for as long as they need. In the exisiting terminal the bar and café are situated on the first floor and there is no lift (staff will bring refreshments down), but a new, fully accessible building is scheduled for completion in 1993.

Airlines operating to the Channel Islands include *Air UK, British Airways, British Midland* (☎071/589 5599), *Dan Air* (☎0345/100200) and *Jersey European* (☎0392/64440).

Transport and accommodation

On Jersey there is a choice of **car hire** without hand controls, local buses or taxis. **Bus** and **taxi** drivers are reported to be extremely helpful. *Yellow Cabs* driver Dave Rankin (☎0534/44897) drives an adapted taxi with tailgate, allowing the wheelchair passenger to wheel straight in; book well in advance. For **parking** concessions in Jersey you must obtain a standard parking disc from the Town Hall, St Helier, and display that as well as your Orange Badge.

The *Maison des Landes Hotel* (La Rue des Landes, Saint Ouen, Jersey; ☎0534/81683) is 14.5km from St Helier, with views of St Ouen's Bay, the Atlantic and the headlands of *Les Landes* (sandy moors). A charitable trust managed by the *Lions' Club of Jersey, Maison des Landes* runs the hotel for disabled guests and their families or escorts.

The *Holiday Care Service* has fact sheets on hotel accommodation in Jersey and Guernsey.

France

Je Vais Chercher un Parachute

As a result of polio in 1953, Pete Kendall is unable to stand or walk, or sit without support. She travels on her own every year by taxi to Gatwick and thence by air to Lancashire and Scotland. Less often, she makes the journey to France, and in 1988 she stayed in the Cévennes with her sister, who is married to a Frenchman.

It was time I visited France again: my last trip was over ten years ago. I couldn't conduct a single-handed poll, but I wanted to know what at least some French people were thinking. I wanted to explore, to visit new places and, above all, to see my sister and her husband, as well as assorted nephews and nieces and their families, some French, some English, all living in France.

Having made my usual preparations for travelling, I sat in the taxi bound for Gatwick, thinking gleefully of the letters accumulating on the mat and the phone ringing in vain. I had packed my belongings into one suitcase and one zip-bag with pockets; cheques and credit cards were in my money belt; passport and tickets were in a pocket of the bag. My shoes were sellotaped on to prevent them from dropping off during lifting, and I carried spare sellotape and scissors. Bright orange labels adorned my luggage: one on the wheelchair was marked, "Please do not unload wheelchair with luggage, but

leave by aircraft for use of passenger". It is best to mention this to the cabin crew as well; otherwise, the wheelchair may be left, reduced to its component parts, circulating with the baggage, while you are obliged to use an airport chair – cushionless and possibly lacking footrests.

At Gatwick I rang the appropriate airline using a special phone for disabled travellers. This time, a helper came quickly but no porters or trolleys were free, so we managed with my bag on my knees and my suitcase perched across the arms of my chair. Once I'd parted with the suitcase and been issued with a boarding card, I had only my bag to keep an eye on while it went through the X-rays and I received my body check. Then came the only part of a journey that I dislike – being lifted up the steps into the plane in a carry-chair. My knees fall apart, my feet fall off the narrow footrest, and sometimes there is no safety-belt. Sellotape for feet and knees can help. (Some airports do provide carry-chairs with safety-belts and wide footrests.) However, the ordeal was soon over and I was deposited in my seat.

"Seven litres of mussels were barbecued and consumed with garlic butter, saffron rice, salad and wine"

In no time, it seemed, we were landing at Montpellier. Only one man, with no carry-chair, awaited me. He looked at me quizzically.

"Il faut que je tombe?" I asked.

"Mais non," he replied, "Je vais chercher un parachute!" Luckily, I am light and flexible, and he carried me down the steps to my chair. He said that I was fortunate with the weather this was the first fine day for a week.

My sister and brother-in-law were there to meet me, Bertha slowed down by Parkinson's disease, Jean-Pierre diminutive, sprightly, very bald, unable to lift as a result of an accident years ago. It was lovely to see them, and soon we were on our way to Aumessas, a village in the Cévennes, in the southeast corner of the Massif Central. The route is beautiful, through the spectacular scenery of the Causses – great limestone plateaux deeply dissected by gorges, full of underground streams and caverns, and sparsely covered with vegetation. We followed the gorge of the Hérault river, which rises amongst the older rocks (schists and granites) on Mont Aigoual in the Cévennes. We passed through small villages and the town of Ganges, which from the time of Louis XIV was famous for the manufacture of silk stockings, replaced more recently with rayon and then nylon.

Presently, we turned west along the valley of the Arre (from the Latin *aurum*, gold, which was panned in many valleys hereabouts). To the north

are the old hard rocks of the Cévennes, to the south the abrupt limestones of the Causses. Dizzily perched at the summit of a hill is the tiny village of Esparon, so named because it is on a spur (*éperon*) of the Causses. The valley of the Rivière d'Aumessas runs southward through the Cévennes to join the Arre, and the village of Aumessas huddles in the valley. The lower parts of the Cévennes are clothed in sweet chestnuts, the waysides yellow with broom. Sometimes the rocks are bare, sinuously folded and glistening with mica flakes.

We passed through Aumessas, with its viaduct, Catholic church and Protestant temple, then darted suddenly up a steep track full of potholes and mini-cliffs. There at last was the house, surrounded by cherry trees and conifers. Lower down on the long strip of garden was the "chalet" – a smaller house still occupied by Bertha and Jean-Pierre because the new one, after endless problems with builders, was incomplete. I was given a finished room in the house, and a cordless phone for communicating with the chalet.

"I could do nothing but stare through my camera and think hard about f-stops"

After lunch, we sat on the balcony of the house, with a fine view over the valley to the mountains. Large, pale swallowtail butterflies were moving with a beautiful gliding flight amongst the trees, and lizards sunbathed on the stones. We could hear the sound of sheep-bells mingling with the call of the cuckoo. A gnarled old lady greeted us. I didn't understand a word she said. "I don't either," said Bertha. "She's the shepherdess, and every day she takes her flocks to a different pasture. She's of Italian origin but speaks the local dialect."

The next day, members of the family, young and old, converged from all parts of France. Seven litres of mussels were barbecued and consumed with garlic butter, saffron rice, salad and wine; Bertha produced her brandied cherries. Some of the family gossiped, some swam in the little pool by the chalet, some went out and caught fish for supper. We talked far into the twilight.

In the following days I was taken on too many excursions to count. One day after lunch we crammed into two cars and set out to explore the upper part of the Aumessas valley. There were fine views from the sharply bending road, and the roadside was bright with flowers – a small, vividly mauve cranesbill, broom, orchids, vetch, periwinkles, sainfoin and many others unknown to me. We passed a waterfall making its way down a steep hillside to a stream bridged by the road, and so came to the hamlet of Le Travers, where the houses were of stone with red pan-tiled roofs. Some were deserted, testimony to rural depopulation.

We left the cars and followed the road above the village for a view down the valley, marvelling at its extent and at the variations from green to blue as cloud shadows passed over the waves of trees in its depths, or slightly darkened the paler heights where grass and bare rock prevailed. In the distance, tiny blocks of colour indicated the buildings of Aumessas. The ground sloped steeply away below the road and a few trees grew along its margin. From time to time a shaft of light would illuminate their branches, revealing every leaf and twig against the slate blue of the hills behind. Then, all would be reversed; dark trees would be silhouetted against the pale wall of the valley, across which, improbably suspended, ran a tiny thread of red-roofed houses – the hamlet of Le Caladon.

On another excursion we viewed this hamlet from above. We drove down a track through chestnut woods to an open space with a precipice on one side and, set at the cliff edge, a rambling house where until the twelfth century there had been a castle; this was Le Haut Caladon. My nephew, Pierre, pushed me to the top of the cliff to look down the valley and see the rooftops of Le Caladon immediately below. "Just fifty centimetres further," he said, while Bertha hung on to the back of my chair. Pierre pushed aside a broom tree so that I could look down past my feet at the hamlet. I could do nothing but stare through my camera and think hard about f-stops.

"Sometimes the hippies come down here from the mountains"

Several times I joined shopping parties to Le Vigan, a small town at the confluence of two tributaries with the Arre. It is at the heart of a fertile agricultural area and was the centre for the manufacture of silk thread. There are parks, a great avenue of chestnut trees, memorials to military heroes, houses of character and a lovely stone bridge, the single semicircular arch of which meets its reflection to form a perfect circle.

Through the bustle of the market-place we would push our way to buy long sausages, vegetables, organically produced honey-cake, spices or meat. "Sometimes the hippies come down here from the mountains," said Pierre. After shopping we would stop for coffee or cassis under the trees in the main square, comparing notes about our lives or discussing stories in the newspapers of varying political hue, bought by Pierre in a nearby shop.

We visited the Cirque de Navacelles, a natural amphitheatre formed by a deeply incised "abandoned meander" of the Vis river in Causse country. On our way there, we stopped for a fine peasant lunch at a farm, where the dining room was reached by a long, outside flight of stone steps. Sundry nephews and strangers hauled my chair to the top and made way for me to sit near a welcome log fire.

The Cirque is a spectacular bowl some 275m deep, approached by a series of hairpin bends. Nephews and nieces carried me, chair and all, over a steep humpbacked bridge and up a rocky path for a better view. They also pushed me out onto a slab of rock jutting terrifyingly over the river, so that I could take a photograph. "Je sais que Pete aime des précipices!" said Pierre. (I don't!)

"There were many places from which one could fall right out of Esparon with no trouble at all!"

Another outing took us to the little village of Esparon, which I'd seen during the drive from Montpellier. The streets are extremely narrow and punctuated by flights of steps, up or down which Pierre and his wife, Marie-Noëlle, pushed me, at the same time carrying their seven-month-old baby, Juliette. There were views of the Causses to the south, the Cévennes to the north. At the village fountain we met an old lady using elbow crutches, but carrying a pail of water. She told us that during the last nine years of her husband's life he had been in a wheelchair, and she'd found it difficult to manage in the steep streets. To me, it looked impossible – there were many places from which one could fall right out of Esparon with no trouble at all!

We visited La Couvertoirade, too, a tiny walled town with turrets, built in the heart of Causse country, begun by the Knights Templar and completed by the Knights Hospitaller of St John. Once again, nephews and nieces humped my chair along narrow cobbled streets and up flights of stony steps, but not, I'm glad to say, up onto the town wall, which was topped by an unfenced path only a metre wide!

In Aumessas itself I was shown *clèdes*, small buildings in which chestnuts used to be dried before treading or beating off their shells. The best nuts were for human consumption, the inferior ones for pigs and other animals. Silk production later superseded chestnut growing, after a cold winter killed many of the trees, which were then replaced by mulberry trees. The eggs of the silk moths were hatched in incubators, or sometimes in little bags kept warm between women's breasts! There were special buildings for rearing the silkworms and for processing the silk.

Crowds of us would go for walks in and around Aumessas. Sometimes the children would stop to play on swings and slides in a grassy area near the old railway station, where games of *pétanque* were in progress. On July 14, dancing takes place here – "the only time Maman has ever been known to dance!" One walk took us along a steep, rocky path above the river valley. We looked down over gardens and roofs to the valley bottom, where beehives were set out in rows. Among the butterflies we saw a few black-veined whites, extinct now in Britain. Afterwards, we walked up the valley. The sun was hot. I saw ivy-leaved toadflax, white campions, red clover and white, hop trefoil and cleavers. *Robinia* trees were white with their heavy-scented blossom and the hawthorn bushes were strewn with hammock-like cobweb shelters, full of caterpillars.

One night, Jean-Pierre, with all the younger members of the family, took off to help a radio ham in difficulties with his computers. (Jean-Pierre is unofficial consultant to innumerable computer users – the district nurse, the baker and many others make detours during working hours to seek his advice!) They were away until the small hours, helping to set Bernard to rights. A few days later, Bernard and his "radio widow", accompanied by a similar couple, turned up bearing an enormous gâteau and a bottle of champagne, as a gesture of thanks. Elections were in progress, and Bernard expressed some fairly racist views. I was cheered, and a little surprised, to hear Jean-Pierre contesting these vigorously. One of the radio widows spoke out against Monsieur Le Pen and his followers.

Another day, the valley echoed to the roars of high-powered cars taking part in a rally. I felt it wrong to disrupt the peace and put animals and people at risk on the roads, but found no support for my opinion. "It's the great event of the year in Aumessas. All the old women love it; they gather by the cemetery to watch. If you look through the binoculars you'll see them!" Sure enough, there they were, and I retreated in the face of the evidence.

When the baker called at the village he would sound his horn, and people would congregate to buy bread and exchange news. After one such occasion, when Bertha returned with the loaves, she said that an old man who had gone out looking for mushrooms

had failed to return. Villagers and police formed search parties, but so far in vain.

Not long before my departure, I developed an annoying cough and the doctor came to prescribe something to suppress it during my journey. He was young, informally dressed, full of laughter. He told us that his wife was English, and that he often visited her home county of Cornwall. I wished that I could have stayed longer in the microcosm of Aumessas. I had come to know some of my family better, with their problems and their pleasures. I had also begun to know a little about the surrounding community and to feel at home there.

A year later, I am sad to learn that the old man, lost while seeking mushrooms, was never found, and I am sharply grieved to learn that the young doctor has died of cancer. Holidays are not necessarily an escape.

Savoie Fare

Now 59, Ian Marshall has been confined to a wheelchair with paraplegia since the age of 31, and a visual handicap makes it impossible for him to drive. He visited the Savoie in 1988 with his wife, Judith.

Lying in the east of France on the slopes of the Alps, just below the southwest corner of Switzerland, the Savoie is an area of mountain scenery and lakes. It is familiar to the winter sports enthusiast, but it has much to offer the summer visitor too, as has the journey there.

The region now comprises two departments – Savoie and Haute Savoie – but it is a shadow of its former self, for in its heyday it covered parts of

modern Italy and Switzerland as well as France, spreading from Nice to Bern, and from Turin to Lyons. As it only became part of France in 1860, its towns look and feel quite different from those in other parts of the country. In July 1988 we visited the spa town Aix-les-Bains, stopping on the way at Vichy – another spa town but also famous for its World War II role as the seat of Marshall Pétain's government.

We took the night ferry (*Brittany Ferries*) to Caen and had a good night's sleep in the specially adapted cabin which was easily accessible for a wheelchair user, though the "up-and-over" entrance to the *en suite* facilities was not easy to negotiate. Arriving early in the morning, we took the opportunity to visit Bayeux, a few miles along the coast.

The famous tapestry is now housed in a specially designed building (the Centre Guillaume le Conquérant), which is accessible to wheelchairs via a back entrance (some of the staff do not appear to be aware of this fact and you may have to be persistent, but it is well worth the effort). As the hour was still early, even after our first French breakfast of the trip, we had time to kill before we could get in to see the tapestry. We gingerly tried the door of the cathedral, half expecting it to be locked, only to find a coach party of German tourists sitting in the pews, being lectured even at that hour of the morning.

This early activity gave us a full day for travelling, and we set off, picking our way through the area of Suisse Normande, promising ourselves a more leisurely visit one day. The town of Vichy was disappointing but its setting, in a natural bowl in the foothills of the Massif Central, was not. The River Allier has been used to form a lake, flanked by the Parc d'Allier and the Parc des Sources, which make up the spa's social centre. Wandering beneath the plane and chestnut trees along wheelchair-friendly asphalt paths, some protected from hot sun or rain by ornamental roofing, we realised just how seriously the French view spa treatments – the park was filled with people carrying small lidded baskets which held their cups for "taking the waters".

"I just wondered if the comparatively plain fare offered by the hotel restaurant had any connection with the nature of the spa's speciality"

Each spa specialises in alleviating a particular malady – digestive disorders in the case of Vichy. The four main springs are housed in the Pavillon des Sources, a splendid nineteenth-century edifice, now joined by a modern hotel to the Grand Etablissement Thermal –

the largest treatment centre of its kind in Europe – and the Bains Caillou not far away. The whole place has an atmosphere evoking the *belle époque*, with horse-drawn carriages for hire, a bandstand still used in the evenings and small cafés serving English afternoon tea and cake (and one does order cake, not gâteau) to groups of devotees sitting on the innumerable chairs scattered throughout the park. I could imagine some of the more famous *curistes* from the past – Louis XV's daughters, Napoléon's mother – enjoying the balmy air.

Perhaps incongruous in this setting, the air conditioning in our modern hotel (the *Thermalia Novotel*) afforded welcome relief from the more than balmy temperature on our arrival in the late afternoon. There is flat access to the hotel and environs, and one of the two lifts is large enough for a wheelchair. I've stayed in different rooms and the bathrooms have always been accessible. I just wondered if the comparatively plain fare offered by the hotel restaurant had any connection with the nature of the spa's speciality.

Leaving Vichy, we travelled mainly east to Roanne, enjoying the drive through forests flanking the upper reaches of the Saône, to Villefranche in Beaujolais country, where we should have paused to taste and perhaps buy. Instead we pressed on through Nantua to our destination, the small town of Rumilly. We had chosen to stay in a quiet, family-run hotel (the *Relais du Clergeon*) outside the town. Situated on the side of a hill, the ground floor of the hotel housed the public rooms and some bedrooms; the rest were built below as the ground sloped away at the back, giving a wonderful view over the valley from the balconies. The hotel was not adapted in any way (there were no hand-rails, for example) but it was just what we wanted because each of the places that interested us could be visited in a day – even Chamonix, at the foot of Mont Blanc.

We preferred to take the slower, more scenic route to Chamonix, via Chambéry, Albertville, Ugine, Mégève and St Gervais, saving the more direct route for the return journey. The first tourists arrived in Chamonix in 1741 and they were English, but the first ascent of Mont Blanc (4870m) was made by two Frenchmen – Balmat and Picard – in 1786. Depending on the weather, time available, your pocket, your mobility and your nerves, many walks and excursions can be made from the town. The Mont Blanc Carousel takes you over the mountain range by the highest cable car and back through the new 11.6-kilometre tunnel. Other cable cars go up to the belvederes at Brevent and Flégère.

Most people's favourite town hereabouts is Annecy, and there is much to see and do there, but Aix-les-Bains, on the neighbouring Lac du Bourget, is ours. The lake is the greatest expanse of water in France, some 17 by 3km and up to 100m deep. There is plenty of room to park under the trees and from there we strolled by the side of the lake, watching the hilarious antics of the children learning to sail in flotillas of dinghies, supervised by frantic instructors shouting, whistling and tearing about in motorboats. There is a lido for swimming in the lake, and opportunities to sail or windsurf. We crossed the lake by launch to the Abbaye Hautecombe, where the royal princes of the House of Savoie are buried and services are still sung in Gregorian chant.

The town has many fine buildings, including two casinos, one incorporating the opera house, and gardens, in which I was surprised to find a bust of Queen Victoria, who spent a summer here. There are museums housing a range of exhibits, from Roman remains to works by Rodin. The spa speciality is rheumatism. There are two sulphur springs used in therapy, and two sources used for mineral water.

Before returning to base that day we climbed the 20km winding road up Mont Revard (1491m) and parked at the summit to admire the panoramic view laid out before us – including the Mont Blanc range. We ate a late lunch in the summit restaurant, where the *patron* joined us and chatted in English about his time in Bristol.

"My undoing was the speciality of the house – vacherin – full of calories and cholesterol"

We returned to Chambéry to explore this one-time capital of the sovereign state, still the capital of the department of Savoie and seat of the Archbishop. With few other tourists about we enjoyed wandering down the old city centre's narrow streets, and the wide boulevards where the city walls once stood. About a quarter of the city buildings, towards the station, were lost in World War II, but these have mostly been replaced or restored. The castle was the ancient residence of the Counts and Dukes, and occasionally the Kings of Sardinia.

We found more tourists on our visit to Annecy, only 43km away from Geneva, where we enjoyed Sunday lunch at one of the many outdoor restaurants, choosing one which served good live jazz with good Savoie fare. We finished off our visit with a leisurely drive around the lake.

It was time to return home. Knowing that I had eaten too much, as usual in France (my undoing was the speciality of the house – *vacherin* – full of calories and cholesterol), and coming across my E111, I wondered if it would cover a visit to the treatment rooms at Vichy.

The Dordogne

In 1989, for the first time, Ian (who is paraplegic) and Judith Marshall were able to go abroad in May – Ian's favourite month. They had the use of a cottage in the Dordogne designed and built, not simply adapted, for wheelchair users.

We'd both recently retired, so with more time to spare we decided to spend a night en route, rather than tear down there in about seven hours of non-stop driving from the north coast. We chose to stay at Laval, where there is a modern hotel with at least one of its ground-floor rooms fitted with an adapted *en suite* bathroom. This had been confirmed the previous year, when we inspected the hotel, having learnt by experience that the wheelchair symbol in guidebooks cannot always be relied on.

Next morning we travelled south through Château-Gontier, following the valley of the Mayenne to cross the Loire at Angers. The wide and almost empty road system carried us speedily across the Loire, avoiding the city, into the vineyards of Saumur and on to Poitiers. Again a bypass took us on our way to Angoulême along another *route nationale* which offered three picnic areas; the one we happened to choose sported a disabled loo. Angoulême has not the luxury of a bypass but a one-way system, which is hardly a substitute. As this is the gateway to the Dordogne, and the French respect parking places for the disabled, we returned later to give the place our full sightseeing attention.

From Angoulême we travelled through Cognac country by minor roads, which are well maintained these days and wide enough to take large pieces of agricultural equipment; they are a joy to use as they carry very little traffic. The countryside is sparsely populated because the young people are leaving to find work in the cities and further north. Our hamlet (Gresignac) consisted of a few farms, a ruined church, and cottages – some empty – spread over a large area but with not a single shop. It is still rated as a commune (the smallest unit of local government), with a mayor and elected council, despite the electorate having fallen to barely more than a hundred.

It was a pleasure to move into accommodation which had been so thoughtfully designed and actually built by a young English couple in the old farmhouse next door. Our spare bedroom (the only upstairs room) was soon in use when our daughter and son-in-law arrived later that evening. They used the fly-drive service from Heathrow to Bordeaux (both *Air France* and *British Airways* operate this service); if your time is limited, or you do not fancy the long drive, this method is worth considering – the airport is a two-hour drive away and wheelchair users are regularly carried.

"Wherever we went, I could indulge my romantic notions of the past and my love of wine"

The next day was Sunday and Judith's birthday – what better excuse for trying the excellent food of the region? We turned to the visitors' book in the cottage, in which previous occupants had made recommendations, and chose Brantôme, which nestles in a curve of the Dronne, a tributary of the Isle. We entered the town by a peculiarly angled old bridge and found it bustling with activity – canoe racing on the river, a travelling fair in full swing and the fire brigade turning out. There was a choice of restaurants and we did justice to the occasion (eating in the evening presents the French with no problem, unlike the British Sunday). Returning home should have been a simple matter but in attempting to take a short cut across a river on a pontoon-type bridge we acquired a puncture. If you have to change a wheel of a foreign rented car in the dark, start feeling for the tools under the bonnet.

The region is compact enough to make it unnecessary to travel far to places of interest. If you like prehistory there are the caves at Lascaux and Les Eyzies (the Lascaux cave has been closed since 1963 because of the deterioration resulting from the heat and humidity generated by armies of visitors; you have to be satisfied with a replica and a museum). If you are more interested in the French meaning of *cave*, some of the finest wine tasting can be had between Périgueux and Bordeaux.

Wherever we went, I could indulge my romantic notions of the past and my love of wine. Bergerac lies on the Dordogne at the point where the ancient route from Lyons to Bordeaux crosses that from Paris to Lourdes. The town was captured by the Earl of Derby in 1345 at the start of the Hundred Years' War; the war ended in 1453, downstream from Bergerac at Castillon-la-Bataille. Near Castillon you can see the study – all that remains of the château – where Montaigne wrote his essays (which caused me to give up French at school).

The centre of Bergerac is pedestrianised, so that getting around in the wheelchair and viewing all the sights was relatively simple. The town is surrounded by vineyards, including the famous Château de Monbazillac, 6km to the south. The old wharfs in Bergerac are still intact, and it was from here that the wine went downstream to be loaded onto ocean-going vessels at Libourne. There is a small wine and boating museum at place de la Myrpe.

I used to believe that châteaux had to mean the Loire, but the Dordogne is estimated to contain over a thousand, many of them lived in and some open to visitors. A village near the cottage boasted a beautiful example, and I asked the owner of the local bar how the tiny village came to have such an edifice. He explained that up to the revolution the local vineyard (long since gone) supplied much of the wine to the royal court. He seemed in a sad mood sitting on the kerb outside in the dark. Women and children, he said, had started to come with their menfolk for their aperitifs, and he couldn't stand the noise!

"It seemed that the tourists had not yet arrived, but we met a few of the ex-pats"

Days of outings were interspersed with days of exploring the immediate locality – perfect for bird-watching or trying to recognise wild flowers. We were shown a small valley full of unusual orchids, one variety of which not even a professional Dutch grower could identify. The weather was dry for the time of year, but cold at night – one day a farmer near Thiviers told me that there had been a frost the night before which damaged his strawberries and some of his vines.

One cannot think about France, and particularly this area, without mentioning food. Perigord is famous for the quality of its goose fare (*confit d'oie*, *pâté de foie gras*) and its truffles, not to mention 101 things that they do with the walnut. New to us was eating at a *ferme auberge*, where we booked in advance and where the half-dozen diners had the undivided attention of the young farmer and his wife as we slowly ate our way through six courses of home produce from the grapefruit or walnut aperitifs to the liqueurs.

It seemed that the tourists had not yet arrived, but we met a few of the ex-pats, one a retired architect living in a 200-year-old farmhouse which had been empty for fourteen years. I asked him why so many buildings incorporated turrets in their design. It seems these were dovecotes, the birds being kept for their droppings, which provided the only form of fertiliser at one time. We found a teacher from our local school who had taken over a ten-bedroom hotel, and in his bar met an ex-Spitfire pilot living in the vicinity.

I enjoyed the holiday more than I expected and I am not sure why. Perhaps because there is more than appears on the surface and I enjoy probing gently.

A Strange Phenomenon

Since contracting rheumatoid arthritis in 1982, Alison Walsh has matched the progression of her disease with various modes of transport, starting with a bicycle, moving on to a moped when her knees complained, and retreating to the relative safety, warmth and comfort of a car when a few months of moped riding in central London ended in a crash. The effects of constant gear changing on arthritic ankles dictated the purchase of another vehicle, and she now relies heavily on a car with automatic transmission. She took it to Paris in December 1989 and May 1990.

Driving in Paris is a doddle (and that includes parking) – good news for people who are unable to use buses or the Métro. If you cannot grapple with high steps and impatient bus drivers, or endless underground corridors, awkward doors and yawning gaps between train and platform, try exploring Paris by car. This is not to say that I feel good about adding to the four million noisy, noxious cars which already threaten to swamp a beautiful city: if my feet were what they used to be I'd tramp the streets all day – the best way to discover any city – but those of us who are incapable of that must look for an alternative. In the absence of accessible public transport, for which Dial-a-Ride schemes are no

substitute, this has to be the private car; we can only hope for a cleaner, quieter version in the future.

Driving *to* Paris is also a doddle. Based on the recognition that for people with mobility problems their car is a necessity rather than a luxury, some car ferry companies carry disabled drivers' cars free of charge or at reduced rates (contact the *Disabled Drivers' Motor Club*). I have a personal preference for *P&O* boats, and always receive polite and efficient service from their staff. In December our ferry was delayed because of fog, but in May we left on time and sat in brilliant sunshine, eating bacon sandwiches in a sheltered corner of the nearly deserted deck.

The route from Calais to Paris couldn't be simpler; it's well signposted and the road is fast – you'll be there in three to four hours . . . unless you choose a foggy day. Spinning along under a scorching sun in May, with the windscreen steadily collecting a splattering of dead flies, windows down and the roar of wind and lorries preventing conversation, I found it difficult to recall the tortuous journey in December, when maximum speed was 20 or 30mph and all that broke the white monotony was the sudden looming of red brake-lights ahead.

The fog had cleared by the time we reached Paris, and the next day we were able to sit on the open top-deck of a *Bateau-Mouche*, enjoying the sun, ignoring the multilingual commentary which is punctuated by irritating electronic chimes, and instead listening to my brother's latest gossip and his own commentary on the sights. My visits are a mixture of catching up with Steve, discovering Paris – slowly – and meeting designers and fabric buyers in the fashion houses (my travelling companion sells silk to the likes of Yves Saint Laurent and Agnés b).

Bateaux-Mouches run from the Right Bank, between the Pont de l'Alma and the Pont des Invalides. There is parking at the point of embarkation and accompanied wheelchair users should have no problems boarding and sitting on the lower (enclosed) deck; the upper deck on our boat was reached by a spiral staircase. It's a touristy thing to do, and the boats are unbelievably ugly, but you can chat for an hour or so whilst drifting past such landmarks as the floating, eighteenth-century Deligny swimming pool, the Obélisque in the place de la Concorde, the twin clock towers of the Musée d'Orsay, the Jardin des Tuileries and the Louvre. Rounding the Ile de la Cité and the Ile St Louis, you catch the best view of Notre-Dame and, at the other end of the island, slip under the oldest Parisian bridge, Pont Neuf.

"A common excuse for bad access to museums (and other buildings for that matter) is the age of the building"

Although the December days were bright and sunny, there was a nip in the air and it was a good time of year for museums. Paris has a mind-boggling choice, and many are accessible: consult your copy of *Touristes quand même!* (Tourists just the same), be prepared to nose around for the wheelchair entrance, and if you want to leave nothing to chance phone ahead to double check.

Forget the Louvre: it's vast, confusing and intimidating; we spent a lot of time shuttling up and down in lifts which wouldn't stop at the floors we wanted (or thought we wanted) and I couldn't help thinking that it was all part of a nightmarish school trip, in which I had to view every one of the more than 300,000 works of art before I was allowed to see the few I'd set out to see.

The Musée d'Orsay, on the other hand, is a delight and worth more than one visit. It is accessible (toilets too), well laid out, well lit, with plenty of space and a manageable collection. There are fine views through the clock faces, across the Seine and up towards Sacré-Coeur. If you can negotiate a flight of eleven steps at the entrance, and squeeze into a slimline lift, the Musée Marmottan (rue Louis-Boilly, 16e) will reward you with a sumptuous basement selection of Monets. The few people there spoke in reverential whispers, the carpet deadened their footsteps, and there is comfortable seating for those who wish to ponder, admire, and catch their breath. I found the *Nymphéas* (Waterlilies) here more pleasing than those in the oval rooms at the Orangerie des Tuileries (place de la Concorde) which does, however, house some much loved works by other Impressionists. The Orangerie is accessible to accompanied wheelchair users.

A common excuse for bad access to museums (and other buildings for that matter) is the age of the building. The Institut du Monde Arabe (23 quai St-Bernard) doesn't have this problem: it's new and accessible, a mass of glass and polished metal. The "winking wall" on the south side is made up of thousands of contracting and expanding light filters, and is supposed to resemble the lattice-like pierced screens so common in Arab architecture. Inside, every aspect of Arab life is covered, with special exhibitions as well as the permanent displays. We saw a fascinating presentation of the art of carpet making, *Tapis present de l'Orient à l'Orient*, and many superb examples of this painstaking craft.

At the Petit Palais (entrance for wheelchairs on av Dutuit) we happened on an exhibition entitled *L'art de Cartier*

– a dazzling array of jewellery and clocks, beautifully lit and accompanied by the design sketches, with a few bejewelled ceremonial swords thrown in. There were many famous pieces, mostly made for the famous, including the panther brooch – diamonds and sapphires on platinum – made in 1949 for the Duchess of Windsor. From a wheelchair it was a struggle to see many of the exhibits, mounted on pedestals in glass cases, but half the fun of it was in listening to the excited exclamations of the well-heeled *Parisiennes* as they pored over each work of art.

"The Jardin du Luxembourg is the ideal resting place for weary explorers of St-Germain"

In the May 1990 heatwave we were more interested in outdoor activities. Sunday May 6 was Paris Marathon day, and we watched the gasping stragglers weave along the av du President Kennedy. In search of less energetic pursuits, we wandered in the dense shade of blossom-laden chestnut trees on the Allée des Cygnes, a sliver of land connecting two bridges across the Seine. At the Pont de Bir-Hakeim you can gaze up at the Tour Eiffel, and at the other tip of the sliver, just past Pont de Grenelle, is the Statue de la Liberté and good sunbathing territory. There are steps down to the Allée from both bridges, but there are plenty of seats and it's a peaceful spot, away from the more famous islands upstream.

For greenery and flowers, the visitor to Paris is again spoilt for choice, with a life-saving range of *parcs*, *jardins* and *squares* in which to walk off a triple-scoop sorbet, or to sit and eat it. The majority of these carefully tended areas are fully accessible and perfect for picnics.

With the marathon out of the way, we risked venturing into the Bois de Boulogne, for a late lunch in the Parc de Bagatelle (accessible toilets here, plus wheelchairs for visitors' use) amongst a multicoloured display of tulips, irises and peacocks. There are wilder parts to the Bois, and lakes to sit beside or boat on, and parking is easy.

Just beyond the southeastern tip of the Bois are the *Serres* (greenhouses) *de la Ville de Paris*, workshops of the municipal florist, with an accessible entrance and parking on av Gordon Bennett. Quite apart from the almost iridescent white tulips, the sea of blue pansies, and a beautiful deep pink rose named Ulrich Brunner, the greenhouses themselves made an interesting sight, clearly places of great industry but also built to look good – a sort of small-scale Kew, except for the group of men playing *boules* outside the main hothouse.

Back in the centre of things, the Jardin du Luxembourg is the ideal resting place for weary explorers of Saint-Germain, on the Left Bank. You can rest under the chestnut trees, eavesdrop on student tutorials, and potter amongst the blackcurrant bushes and espaliered pear trees in the southwest corner. These *parcs* and *jardins* provide exercise areas for many of the city's children, and their games are an established act in the world of park entertainment. In the Jardin du Ranelagh (16e) we stopped to watch an old-fashioned merry-go-round, cranked by a substantial, no-nonsense nanny, carrying a serious cargo of boys and girls. Foreheads furrowed in concentration, they aimed small batons through rings arranged just outside the sweep of the merry-go-round.

"Some of the Christmas window displays are pure fairy-tale fodder"

Light years away from this is the hi-tech scientific playground, Parc de la Villette (19e). There is underground parking here, or you can leave your car on the quai de l'Oise, cross the bridge over the Canal de l'Ourcq and sit in the park for a while before tackling the Cité des Sciences et de l'Industrie – a vast steel and glass laboratory for "hands-on" experience of the wonders of science. Kids, of course, love it, and the Géode – a giant steel ball housing the largest projection screen in the world. It was all too exciting for us; we escaped to the Parc des Buttes-Chaumont and sprawled on the grass which grows over what was, until the 1860s, an old quarry site used as a rubbish dump.

What's called the Jardin du Forum des Halles is not really a garden, but underneath is one of life's necessities for me – not the shops, which are unexciting here, but the swimming pool (*Piscine Suzanne Berlioz*, place de la Rotonde), which is fully accessible (with hoist), large (50m x 20m) and well organised so that swimmers don't tangle with splashers. Take the lift from Parking Berger; there are accessible loos in the Forum.

Early December is ideal for the shopper, window or the real thing, and some of the Christmas window displays are pure fairy-tale fodder. Go to Galeries Lafayette or Printemps (both on bd Haussmann) for a huge range of designer clothes and perfumes (and *Galeries Lafayette* for money changing on Saturdays); just trying on a few way-out hats on the ground floor is great fun, but the lifts are big enough for wheelchairs if you want to investigate further. There are many shops which are tricky for the less agile shopper, such as *Tati* (rock-bottom prices, pickpockets and football-fan crowds) or some of the smaller boutiques, but there is still plenty of scope for consuming.

If eating is the type of consuming you're after, head for the markets. The stalls heave with a luxuriant array of goodies – fruit and vegetables, fish, meat, cheese, flowers, chocolates. Self-catering is a pleasure in Paris, but eating out won't break the bank. Likewise staying in a hotel. Unlike central London, it *is* possible to find a reasonably priced and clean hotel room; the holidaymaker on a budget is much better catered for in Paris.

"You will be financially penalised for needing a large room"

However, the holidaymaker in a wheelchair on a budget is not. In general, you will be financially penalised for needing a large room for manoeuvring, an accessible bathroom and a wheelchair-sized lift. The hotels at the cheaper end of the range more than likely have no lift and no ground-floor bedrooms, tiny loos and bathrooms, and steps up to the entrance. Beware of wheelchair symbols in the guides: they often ignore steps up to lifts, split-level reception areas, narrow doors or steps at the entrance. The only way to be sure is to inspect it yourself: book your first night in a known accessible hotel, blow the expense; then select a few cheaper possibilities, hop into the car and research them; we had no problems booking rooms on the day.

Arm yourself with a good map for this exercise. The *Michelin Paris Plan No. 10, Sens uniques*, with street directory, shows the one-way systems and is indispensable. Buy it in Paris for half the price that the *AA* shop at Dover docks charges. Baron Haussmann completely restructured the capital in the second half of the nineteenth century, and as a self-navigating driver in a foreign city I am eternally grateful. The wide boulevards are a joy to travel along, the side streets can be used with relative ease to skip past trouble spots, and the sheer logic of the layout makes getting lost almost impossible. As for the supposedly volatile French drivers, I like them! What riles them is dithering – don't do it and you'll be spared the barrage of horns. After all, it doesn't matter if you take a wrong turn, or find yourself in the wrong lane – you're on holiday, and can take time to correct your route.

Perhaps I've been lucky, but I've never been thwarted in my search for a parking space; be prepared to take a couple of turns around the block, or the *place* (square), and keep your eyes peeled. Disabled badge holders are exempt from street parking charges (areas marked *PAYANT* in the road) and obtain a 75 percent reduction in car parks. The traffic wardens and police are tolerant of sensible, unobtrusive parking.

We always managed to park within easy walking distance of our target. Just as well when visiting the fashion houses, dragging a suitcase full of silk samples. At one big-shot's studio we were met by an elf called Sophy, in green and brown spotted shirt, brown mini, and black and white striped leggings; she toned in with the decor, which was muddy green and cream, steel and glass again, with bolts and rivets and pipes – we could have been on board a ship. Club music played in the background, there was much chattering amongst the workers, and far from feeling intimidated by these dictators of fashion I was pleased to see many pairs of feet in Doc Marten's boots. I have two pairs – standard black ones, and for summer a pair of green "leisure boots" – and I recommend them to anyone with walking difficulties; as important to me as my painkillers, they give adequate ankle support, they are light and flexible, and unlike some well-known brands of "training shoe" they do not require you to take out a second mortgage.

The phenomenon of two confirmed country bumpkins returning again and again to a city, not simply on business but also for pleasure, takes some explaining. My hairdresser says that I "like a bit of *chic* now and then, darling" but it's more than that. Everything about central Paris appeals to me: the architecture, the coffee, the pleasing vistas at every turn, the museums, the trees, the wrought-iron balconies; all this is mine with only a trace of the horrors of big cities, and with a luxurious freedom of movement. On each visit we are struck above all by the *élégance* – retained in the face of all the usual pressures on a modern capital. We'll be going back soon for another fix.

Independent Living in Nancy

In 1985 Sian Williams began studying French and European literature at university. She soon realised that she must spend some time in France, although as a wheelchair user the problems she envisaged seemed insurmountable. Towards the end of 1986 Sian started writing letters, with the aim of tracking down a suitable place in which to spend a year in France. By March 1987 her initial enthusiasm and optimism had turned to disillusionment, but then the letter she'd been waiting for arrived.

Back in the Sixties a group of physically disabled students in France recognised that great social change was necessary if they were ever to lead an independent life and realise their academic and social potential. Their determination to bring about this change led to the creation of *Groupement pour l'Insertion des Handicapés Physiques* (*GIHP*), whose aim was to improve integration of people with disabilities in all spheres of society and increase their independence.

GIHP has grown into a national organisation, with regional branches throughout the country. *GIHP Lorraine* is at Vandoeuvre, near Nancy, and it provides several services for disabled people in the area. There is an architectural bureau which aims to increase accessibility in the region, and an agency through which auxiliaries can be employed by those needing daily attention. There are ten adapted minibuses and the twelve drivers provide a similar service to *London Transport*'s Dial-a-Ride. Although at certain times it is quite expensive and delays do occur, it is on the whole an efficient service and gives a considerable degree of independence to many people living in Nancy. On any given day you can be sure of seeing a *GIHP* minibus on the horizon!

To enable students with disabilities to follow university courses, *GIHP* has created an accessible and well-adapted residential centre (the *foyer*) in Vandoeuvre. Each student has an individual bedroom and meals are provided, as well as physiotherapy and transport to and from the university buildings. When I received details about this centre I knew it was just what I'd been looking for. I made an application and in October 1987, loaded with far too much luggage, I arrived in Nancy.

Living in a French-speaking environment was initially an exhausting experience. Despite having studied the language for nearly ten years, it came as a shock to hear the speed at which conversations were conducted. And, not content with speaking quickly, everyone also used argot – French slang which never appeared in our school textbooks! However, as a result of total immersion in the French language, both my ability to speak it and my understanding of it improved dramatically.

I enrolled on French courses for foreign students. The subjects varied from geography to literature, from French grammar to history of art. Difficulties that I encountered, such as note taking, were overcome with the help of students and staff, and my efforts were rewarded with two diplomas in French Studies. It was a stimulating experience to mix with people from many different cultures. I met some wonderful people but the problems of getting about meant that I was unable to socialise with them as much as I'd have liked. By the end of the year, they all knew that people who rely on Dial-a-Ride cannot do anything without advance warning!

"Meeting them was an experience that I'll never forget"

During my stay, *GIHP Lorraine* launched a regional campaign to set up the first *Agence Pour Une Vie Autonome* in France. This campaign was inspired by the American *CILs* (*Centers for Independent Living*), which aim to improve the quality of life of people with disabilities and increase their independence. There are now nearly four hundred *CILs* in the USA and over fifty percent of the staff in each agency are disabled. The *CIL* gathers in one place all the information and advice that a disabled person is likely to need, such as details of benefits, legal rights and job opportunities.

As a means of gaining publicity for their campaign, *GIHP Lorraine* invited Ed Roberts, President of the American organisation, World Institute on Disability, to Nancy. Ed was severely disabled at the age of fourteen by polio but this has not prevented him from becoming a leading figure in the movement for disabled people in the USA. Not only was he the first severely disabled American to successfully pursue his university studies, but he also went on to help create the first *CIL* in Berkeley. He showed an incredible warmth towards everyone living at the *foyer* and his successes were an inspiration to us all. Judith Heumann, his partner at the World Institute on Disability, came to Nancy a few months later to continue the work that Ed had begun; her positive outlook and encouragement in the fight to improve facilities at the university were greatly missed when she left. Meeting them was an experience that I'll never forget.

"The family's hospitality knew no bounds – who says the French are cold ?!"

Luck was on my side because, as an English speaker living at the *foyer*, I was soon invited to help out with interpretation during Ed's stay. The week included filming for TV, and interviews with the press, with the aim of publicising *GIHP* and attracting financial support for the *Agence* from local industry. There were many lively debates on subjects such as the *CIL*'s role in the USA. Ed explained that the *CIL* network sees disability-related issues in a social and political context, rather than a medical one, believing that it is society, not the disability, which hinders an individual from achieving an independent lifestyle and fulfilling his or her potential.

In many countries the improvement of facilities in order to cater for the needs of people with disabilities is something which is generally accepted as desirable but is rarely compulsory. Ed emphasised that legislation is the way forward. After our own difficulties regarding accessibility at the local university, we were amazed to hear, for example, that in certain American states not only is it illegal for a university student to be prevented on the grounds of disability from following the course of his or her own choice, but it is also illegal for any class to be held in a room that is inaccessible for a student following that course.

As this was my first long stay in a foreign country, the race was on to visit as many different places as possible before I left! Although parts of Nancy

(the capital of Lorraine) are less picturesque than neighbouring cities Metz and Strasbourg, what remains of the original town (*la vieille ville*) is particularly attractive. Its narrow cobbled streets have been made into pedestrian zones, lined with small restaurants and antique shops. The city is dominated by place Stanislas, a spectacular square dating from the eighteenth century, its gilded wrought-iron gates and railings an impressive sight, especially when illuminated at night. The Museum of Fine Arts (Musée des Beaux Arts) is here, and there are a number of other museums worth seeing, including the Ducal Palace (Musée Lorrain), which now displays the history of the region, and the Musée de l'Ecole de Nancy, which houses an interesting Art Nouveau collection.

Just behind place Stanislas is the Parc de la Pépinière, where the annual jazz festival takes place in the autumn. If you're not afraid of heights, you can enjoy wonderful aerial views of the city when the fair pays its yearly visit to place Carnot. Every two years in spring the World Theatre Festival is held in Nancy. There are several cinemas and theatres in the city but access is sometimes a problem. However, Saint-Sébastien is a huge shopping centre which does cater for the wheelchair user (toilets excepted!).

I spent several long weekends at a friend's home in a tiny village of about a hundred inhabitants, near the small town of Mirecourt. In the past, while Lorraine played a leading role in the steel industry of France, Mirecourt was famous for its violin-making. It was like entering a different world as we drove over narrow stony tracks, collecting the milk on the way, to an old house built of sand-coloured stone. The family's hospitality knew no bounds – who says the French are cold?!

My visits to the village coincided with some special events. In December we watched the St Nicolas celebrations: processions through the streets of

Mirecourt, throwing sweets to the crowds, while in the village some children acted out Snow White and the Seven Dwarfs and then waited eagerly for Saint Nicolas to distribute his presents! Several months later, the atmosphere was rather more serious, with the presidential elections in full swing. We watched as the mayor of the village counted the votes and, that evening when Mitterand's success was announced, my friend's Dad showed his approval by firing three rifle shots into the air – some of the neighbours were not amused!

I stayed with another French family high up in the Vosges mountains. Their home is even more isolated, surrounded by pine forests and with its own fresh water source. It's not surprising that the Vosges attract many tourists. Gérardmer is very scenic, situated beside a lake and encircled by mountains. Further up, there are two more lakes, Retournemer and Longemer, and higher still, there are skiing resorts that supply snow even in April. Like most regions in France, Lorraine is renowned for its cuisine and the specialities that I enjoyed here included *quiche lorraine*, *madeleines* (small cakes) and *tarte aux mirabelles* (a tart filled with sweet plums, produced in the region).

Strasbourg is not far from Nancy, in the neighbouring region of Alsace. From the train the Germanic influence is evident, gradually creeping in to the style of housing. Saverne, situated between these two cities, deserves a visit. It has a beautiful town centre, with an eighteenth-century château and very ornate buildings, such as the Maison Katz, which dates back to 1605 and has an intricately decorated wooden facade. As well as being an important centre for European politics, Strasbourg has an old quarter called La Petite France, which is full of exquisitely designed sixteenth- and seventeenth-century houses.

I also visited Paris, and travelled by train to Brussels several times. (Although I found the French train system very reliable, this particular route was rather hair-raising: at Luxembourg the train divides in two, one half going to Belgium while the other shoots off to Holland. Need I say more? On one of my journeys a very quick dash was called for!) After nearly a year of planning and organising, then finding myself alone in a country whose language I could barely converse in, the ensuing nine months were packed with valuable experiences which more than compensated for the months of preparation. In this case, perseverance paid off!

Half a Loaf

Mairene Gordon has suffered from rheumatoid arthritis for over fifty years. She used crutches for fifteen years but now has artificial knees and hips. Of her travels in Italy, Spain, France, Greece and the UK, Mairene reckons that her holiday in the Dordogne caused most difficulties.

Foolhardy, I suppose, one could call my decision to take a coach trip to the Dordogne. Lacking a companion, I thought that travel with a small group was the answer. The biggest snag was that I couldn't manage to board the coach unaided, but I was promised help by the tour operator (*Francophiles*).

I travelled by sleeper from Fife down to London, where, with the help of a beaming porter (who refused a tip), I had a buffet breakfast and found a taxi.

The pick-up point was by the Shell building in the midst of London's ceaseless traffic. The coach was late, having tangled with the Chelsea Flower Show traffic, but eventually I was comfortably ensconced and speeding towards the coast. The Channel crossing was smooth and the coach was parked close to a lift which whisked me to the upper decks.

After a couple of hours' driving in northern France, we stopped for the night at a pleasant hotel in Beuvry. Dinner was good, and I began to get to know some of my travelling companions. The oldest was 88, a spry retired doctor who was accompanied by an elegant cousin a few years younger. Professional couples and retired teachers made up the bulk of the group.

Next day, we left for Tours, stopping for lunch at Chartres, where we were given time for sightseeing. The Cathédrale Notre Dame stands high above the old town and can be seen from miles away, floating above the roofs and trees like a vision between heaven and earth. The original Romanesque cathedral was burned down in 1194 and only one of the great towers at the west end (Le Clocher Vieux) survived intact. In 1506 the other tower was rebuilt in ornate Gothic by Jehan de Beauce, and is slightly higher than the old one.

As I entered from the bright sunlight, the cathedral seemed very dark, but this made it easier to study the glowing stained-glass windows with their vibrant blues and reds. A series of thirteenth-century windows present a panorama of medieval life: kings, princes and great ladies in ermine and gold cloth mingle with knights and priests; peasants work in their seasonal occupations; artisans sculpt stone, fashion wood, and weave. Other windows depict biblical scenes from the Old and New Testaments: early Church leaders, saints and martyrs. How keen they were on the suffering and death of saints!

But what impressed me most were the stone sculptures in the choir screen, begun by de Beauce in 1514 and worked on until his death in 1529. There are forty-one scenes – the work of various artists – which took two centuries to complete. They begin and end with the life of Mary, and in between are scenes from the life of Christ. The strength, delicacy and grace of these works held me spellbound. One which I found particularly charming was of a youthful Mary, in an embroidered robe, sitting sewing. Of course, many hours or even days could be spent viewing this magnificent cathedral, but I felt thrilled by what I had been able to see. At least in a cathedral or church there is always somewhere to sit and rest and meditate.

"I would walk as far as I could, then literally collapse at a convenient café"

At Tours, the bed in my room was too low, so an additional mattress had to be conjured up. Then I discovered that I'd left my "helping hand" (light tongs, essential for picking things up and assisting me when dressing) at the first hotel. However, my long-handled shoe-lift had a curved, hook-like end, so I wasn't altogether stuck. When I sat down to a meal of asparagus in butter, followed by trout with almonds, my difficulties receded into the background, but an injudicious bite at a chunk of French bread dislodged a crowned front tooth! After the initial dismay, I decided to put up with the gap until I returned home.

Towards the evening on the third day, we arrived at Saint-Céré, where we were to spend a week. The hotel was charming, with a terrace bright with flowers and greenery, and a resident mole-coloured cat with gorgeous green eyes. Alas, the short flight of stairs which I'd said I could cope with turned out to be a spiral staircase. However, the staff were very good at assisting me whenever they saw me making for the stair. My room was French provincial, with an old-fashioned bed, slightly on the low side, which meant a struggle to get out every morning. The shower taps were too stiff for me to turn on, and the loo was too low, but I am used to that. Otherwise, everything was fine. The dining room had family tables, so that I did not feel isolated but had a chance to make friends with my travelling companions.

Most days, we were taken by coach to surrounding places of interest. The countryside was lush and verdant, with old stone farmhouses, fields of sunflowers, vineyards, rivers, woods and deep gorges. One morning was spent exploring interesting villages along the banks of the Dordogne, including La Roque-Gageac, a picturesque place on the curve of the river. The old stone houses are squeezed between the water and the great cliffs behind. It seemed as though the cliff could topple at any moment – in fact, a few years ago a huge slab of rock did crash down on the houses beneath. But, as with people living beneath volcanoes, the villagers cling to their homes.

Another trip was to Domme, an enchanting hill-top town opposite La Roque-Gageac. We entered by one of the original gateways. An inscription on the oldest house (now the *Hôtel de la Monnaie*) told us that the town was built around 1280 on the orders of Philip the Bold. A steep narrow main street, flanked by lovely old houses of warm-coloured stone, climbs to an upper square with a church on one corner and the Maison du Gouverneur on the other. On the north side, beyond a fringe of umbrella-shaped pines, a stone parapet guards a sheer drop of hundreds of feet to the valley floor. The view is spectacular: the Dordogne snakes leisurely between fields of maize and tobacco, and beyond are the wooded hills of the Périgord Noir, broken here and there by ochre cliffs.

We visited Rocamadour, strung out along, and built into, sheer cliff, with shops and cafés at street level and, above, churches and chapels reached by a pilgrims' stairway of 216 steps. Pilgrims used to make the climb on their knees to reach the chapel of Our Lady of Rocamadour (Chapelle Miraculeuse) with its Black Madonna, but I could only gaze up from street level.

We spent some hours in Sarlat, the capital of the Périgord Noir. Beyond the main streets with their smart shops lies an entrancing medieval quarter, with cobbled streets and narrow alleyways, and fine stone buildings dating from the twelfth to the seventeenth centuries. The cathedral was built on the site of a twelfth-century Benedictine abbey church and the town grew up around it. A rather Italianate Episcopal Palace adjoins the cathedral, and opposite stands a beautiful Renaissance house with intricate stone carvings – the Maison de La Béotie. This was the birthplace of La Béotie, renowned poet and friend of Montaigne. In 1563, when La Béotie died, Montaigne was at his bedside, and afterwards wrote the famous essay *On Friendship* in his memory.

"I was simply too tired to enter and view the interior, knowing that I had to walk back to the coach"

My strategy was everywhere the same: I would walk as far as I could, then literally collapse at a convenient café, order coffee or lemon tea, and watch the world go by. What I was able to see was always dependent on where the coach parked. I did not attempt to see the prehistoric paintings at Font de Gaume, or join the descent at Padirac to take the underground river trip through the caverns. I bought postcards instead.

I did manage to see the ground floor of a Renaissance château at Montal, but on our return journey I saw only the facade of Fontainebleau. The grand entrance drive had to be negotiated and I was simply too tired to enter and view the interior, knowing that I had to walk back to the coach. I did at least see the "Horseshoe" staircase, down which, on April 20, 1814, Napoléon walked to bid farewell to the Old Guard as he was taken off to exile on Elba. With an able-bodied companion and a light, collapsible wheelchair, I could have seen much more and in greater comfort. But then, my considered philosophy is simple: "half a loaf is better than none".

Wintering in Roussillon

During the summer of 1981, Enid Fisher celebrated her seventieth birthday and to mark the occasion decided to follow it up by driving alone to the South of France, staying there from the New Year until Easter, to avoid the worst of the English winter.

Overweight and physically handicapped by multiple arthritis, I was able to walk only a very short distance, even with the aid of a stick, and I relied heavily on my electric wheelchair and my little car for mobility and independence. By way of preparation, I formulated a programme to reduce my weight, which might improve movement in my stiffening joints. I also had to acquire the necessary funds, part of which were raised by the sale of a few household treasures. I purchased a small trailer with ramps, so that I could load my wheelchair and tow it behind the car. This enabled me to see a little more of the countryside than would have been possible from behind the wheel of my car. On the positive side, I had an adequate knowledge of French and past experience of driving on the right.

I travelled overnight on the Portsmouth–St Malo car ferry. Informed by the office that there was a lift from the car deck to the cabins, I found on arrival that the way to the lift was blocked by heavy chains securing lorries to the deck. Help came from a large sailor who carried both my overnight bag and my handbag while I struggled up the stairs. My cabin was very comfortable and I persuaded a kindly stewardess to bring me coffee and a sandwich as the restaurant was up a further flight of stairs. The sea was choppy and I slept little, slipping and sliding on my couchette.

We arrived at St Malo in the early hours; I could find no one to help me, so I sat and waited, occasionally asking a passing crew member to send me a stewardess. Then I heard my car number being called over the loud-speakers. It was obstructing the lorries and they wanted it moved. No use! I could not carry my bags or get down-stairs without help, so I stayed where I was. Eventually help arrived and I descended to find my car and trailer alone on the car deck.

I drove out into total darkness and, after losing my way in a maze of one-way streets, enlisted a schoolboy on a bicycle to lead me to the road to Rennes. This turned out to be a night-mare: miles of massive road works, red triangles, diversions, traffic lights, mud and potholes. But at last dawn came. I was thrilled to see the sky becoming lighter and stopped at a bar for coffee. No croissants, no bread, but "would Madame like a madeleine?" Yes, please.

Two postmen having their morning glass of beer at the counter were joined by another man who remarked that St Brieuc was snowbound. In the increasing daylight I found that my trailer had acquired some dents and scratches, also that its electrical connection to the car was detached. I had driven along that busy and obstructed road with no rear or indicator lights on my trailer. However, I managed to attach it and everything worked.

"I began to ponder how to ask for a bed at the nearest house"

At Rennes it began to snow, lightly at first and blowing clear of the road, then more heavily, with deep ruts forming. The rivers were in flood; I crossed a wide stone bridge below which the water was only about a foot lower than the parapet. I began to ponder how to ask for a bed at the nearest house. But I reached Ancenis, and the *Hôtel de la Val de Loire*, without further problems.

Ancenis is an ancient frontier market town between Anjou and Brittany. The hotel was excellent and I thoroughly recommend it to any handicapped person. I stayed for three days in a ground-floor bedroom with *en suite* bathroom; there were no steps to negotiate and the food was delicious. The snow disappeared by the morning after my arrival, but the floods remained and the Loire and surrounding inundated countryside were an awe-inspiring sight. One of my outings was to the church of St Florent le Vieil, on the south bank of the Loire. Full of tombs and memorials, one inscription caught my eye – that of a Royalist leader who, on his deathbed, ordered the release of Republicans imprisoned in the church. His black marble sepulchre had been carved and erected by a Republican sculptor.

Soon after I left the hotel, on a Monday morning, disaster struck: the trailer became detached on the outskirts of a town, flew off and buried itself in a heap of rubbish on the roadside. I tried to move it but had to give up and drive into town in search of a garage. A mechanic, who must have been afraid to venture in a car with such a crazed elderly lady, followed me and easily hitched up the trailer. Monday turned out to be a bad day for driving – heavy vehicles are not allowed on French roads at the weekend, so Monday is busy. It was tiring to follow these lorries – it is always difficult to overtake with a right-hand drive and no passenger, and my trailer problems had made me apprehensive.

I travelled south to Roussillon in easy stages. Freezing weather prevented exploration of Châtelaillon-Plage, where I stayed for two nights in a comfortable, warm room in the *Hôtel St Victor* with a wide view of the rocky coastline. At Montguyon I stayed at the *Hôtel de la Poste*, in the town centre, with a lift and level parking.

"I slept in a bed with carved head- and foot-boards upholstered in yellow velvet"

At Agen (famous for its plums), on the main Bordeaux–Toulouse road, I left behind the traffic, filling stations and garish advertising, and turned off along a country road to Astaffort, where I found the *Hôtel de la Tour* – an old house, with many outbuildings full of antiques and interesting *objets*. There were magnificent views from the two windows in my bedroom, and I slept in a bed with carved head- and foot-boards upholstered in yellow velvet. On the walls were watercolours of Naples, where Madame's uncle had spent his winter months, as well as a painting of the boats on the Seine in Paris that were used as wash houses in the nineteenth century. A level garden was full of tiny cyclamen.

While staying at the *Hôtel de la Tour* I visited the thirteenth-century Prieuré de Moirax. A mimosa tree was in full bloom near the doorway. A notice on the collecting box said "Be honest, you may deceive M. le Curé but you will not deceive the Good Lord". On my departure, Monsieur, who was the chef, presented me with a bottle of his own *Prunes d'Agen*, plus an enormous picnic lunch for the journey.

> *"Mimosa bloomed abundantly and when I opened my shutters in the morning the fresh scented air of the garrigue was invigorating"*

After a stopover at Salies de Salat I continued through mountain scenery until I arrived in Quillan, a picturesque and ancient town on the Aude river. *Hôtel Pierre Lys* is on level ground and I stayed in a first-floor bedroom for a few days. This is Cathar country, scene of the fighting that led eventually to the annihilation of this religious sect which was persecuted by the established church. I visited the ruined abbey at Alet-les-Bains, which was destroyed by the Cathars. The village looked deserted and decrepit.

From Quillan I set off along the narrow Defilé de Pierre-Lys, a rocky gorge with astounding views, but I had to concentrate on keeping the car on the road. I descended through vines and olives into sunshine and lunch at Thuir, in a large restaurant with an all-male clientele. Everyone sat at long tables with bottles of wine from which they helped themselves. No one took the slightest notice of me and the meal was good and cheap.

Eventually I reached the valley of the Tech, which spreads out in a wide plain to the north of the Eastern Pyrenees. Here the weather is dry and sunny even in winter, although it is cold at night and often very windy. When I reached Argelès-sur-Mer, the *tramontaine* was blowing like a hurricane and there were olive branches scattered on the roads.

I was lucky enough to find a centrally heated flat belonging to a French couple from the north who had built a house (Les Sorbiers) divided into two flats as a retirement home. It is situated on the lower slopes of the Pyrenees about 6km inland from the Mediterranean. No one could have been more kind and helpful, and we quickly became friends. The owners live upstairs and I had the ground floor, which was completely separate with its own front door. Two acres of level garden gave me as much exercise as I could manage, and it was often warm enough to sit out in the sunshine. Mimosa bloomed abundantly and when I opened my shutters in the morning the fresh scented air of the garrigue was invigorating.

I used my car to shop in the mountain village about 2km inland. I joined the local library, did a little sightseeing, visited the Golden Age Club and made quite a few friends. Mostly I cooked my own meals, as two weeks in French hotels had added several kilos to my weight. But how pleased I felt that I had made it, especially when I saw my home town on French TV in a blizzard of snow – I had escaped a hard winter.

The months passed in a manner similar to my life in England but with the added bonus of new and stimulating surroundings, fresh acquaintances and lots of sunshine. I returned to the same flat for the two subsequent winters, but a slight stroke, with the attendant problem of being sent home by air, leaving my car with friends in Roussillon, put an end to my voyages south.

FRANCE: TRAVEL NOTES

Sources of information

French Government Tourist Office, 178 Piccadilly, London W1V 0AL; ☎071/491 7622. Might attempt to answer queries, but apart from a page of notes produced in 1988 they supply no information for disabled visitors, and tend to refer enquirers to other sources, in France. On the whole, you'll need to read French in order to make full use of the following organisations and their literature.

Association des Paralysés de France (*APF*), 17–21 bd Auguste Blanqui, 75013 Paris; ☎1/45.80.82.40. A national organisation, with many regional branches, set up to deal with the welfare of disabled people. *APF* publishes a guide to accessible accommodation all over France called *Où ferons-nous étape?* but this is of limited value, with too much white space and heavy use of symbols. However, departmental branches of *APF* can provide helpful information and lists of new, accessible accommodation as it becomes available.

Comité National Française de Liaison pour la Réadaptation des Handicapés (*CNFLRH*), 30–32 quai de la Loire, 75019 Paris; ☎1/45.48.90.13. Provides an information service for disabled visitors, including details of accessible accommodation, holiday centres adapted for disabled people, access at tourist sights, transport and sports facilities. *CNFLRH* also distributes three guides for disabled travellers (see *Books*).

Groupement pour l'Insertion des Handicapés Physiques (*GIHP*), 98 rue de la Porte Jaune, 92210 St Cloud. They run an accessible transport service in Paris, similar to *London Transport*'s Dial-a-Ride (☎1/47.21.74.90). Certain regional *GIHP*s organise a similar service, and it's always worth enquiring at the Mairie (town hall) because many towns in France operate some form of specialist transport for disabled people.

Association pour Adultes et Jeunes Handicapés (*APAJH*), 26 rue du Chemin-Vert, 75011 Paris; ☎1/48.07.25.88. An organisation for disabled adults and young people which can provide useful information such as addresses of French associations for all types of disabilities and of sports organisations for disabled people.

Ligue Française pour les Auberges de la Jeunesse, 38 bd Raspail, 75007 Paris; ☎1/45.48.69.84. The French Youth Hostel Association publishes a guide indicating those hostels which – in theory – are accessible.

Centre d'Information et de Documentation Jeunesse (*CIDH*), 101 quai Branly, 75015 Paris. Provides an information service for young disabled people and could supply details of courses offered at French universities.

Tour operators

Most of our contributors made their own travel arrangements, but there are scores of operators to choose from if you want a package deal, and a wide range of activities, including city breaks (try *Thomson Citybreaks* or *Time Off*), wine tours, art appreciation, language courses, camping (try *Keycamp Holidays* and ask Tim Smith at the *Holiday Care Service* for advice), boating (try *Hoseasons Holidays*) and many others.

A number of companies claim to cater for disabled clients but be sceptical, obtain confirmation in writing that special requests will be granted, and ask lots of questions. Mairene Gordon was promised help by *Francophiles*, and she did indeed receive advice about her hotels, but it was not absolutely accurate – a short flight of stairs is not the same as a spiral staircase, and the two present very different problems to someone with impaired mobility.

Another coach operator, *Shearings*, was praised by a deaf contributor, John Myall, who noted that a blind lady on the tour (in 1990) was also well catered for, that the company will advise which tours stop at hotels with easy access for wheelchair users, and that the booking form has a slot for stating any disabilities and special requirements.

Getting there

P&O European Ferries, *Sealink Stena Line* and *Brittany Ferries* offer concessions to disabled motorists (contact the *Disabled Drivers' Motor Club* or *Disabled Drivers' Association*) and accessible facilities on board their ships. *P&O* recommend the Calais and Le Havre crossings

FRANCE: TRAVEL NOTES

for passengers with limited mobility. *Sealink Stena Line*'s new vessels, *Fiesta* and *Fantasia*, are highly accessible — no storm sills on the main passenger deck, spacious toilets with grab-rails, plenty of room in the restaurant area. The only steps are to the duty free shop, and there is a ramped side entrance.

For information and bookings on **motorail** services, contact *French Railways* (*SNCF*, 179 Piccadilly, London W1V 0BA; 24-hour brochure hotline, ☎071/499 1075; bookings, ☎071/409 3518). Blind travellers can take a companion free of charge. If travelling by rail without a car, write to the *International Rail Centre* (Victoria Station, London SW1 1JU) to arrange assistance as far as the French coast. *SNCF* are responsible for the rest of the trip.

Flying to northern France seems an unnecessary expense unless you are pressed for time. Arrangements for boarding and disembarking at regional airports may be fairly primitive (see p.151).

Transport

Sian Williams judges the French **railway** system (*SNCF*) to be overall superior to *British Rail*, but similar in terms of accessibility. Some stations have ramps to enable wheelchairs to board and descend from the trains, but often it is up to the guards to carry the chairs. Most big stations carry free copies of a guide for disabled passengers (*Supplément au guide pratique du voyageur, à l'intention des personnes à mobilité réduite*).

The easiest way to get about France is by **car**; facilities at motorway service stations are generally excellent (see *Guide des Autoroutes à l'usage des Personnes à Mobilité Réduite*) but finding accessible toilets off the autoroutes is sometimes difficult. Parking is not a problem, even in Paris where there are generous concessions to disabled drivers (p.164).

Accommodation

Ian Marshall stayed at the following hotels: *Thermalia Novotel* (1 av Thermale, 03200 Vichy; ☎70.31.04.39); *Hotel Ibis* (Route de Mayenne, 53000 Laval; ☎43.53.81.82) – ask for room 13. He also recommends two campsites,

which he used when exploring the canals around Decize and Clamecy. There were no special facilities but the shower/toilet blocks were accessible and the entrance to each site was level: *Pont Picot* (*Office de Tourisme*, rue Grand-Marche, Clamecy, 58500 Nievre); *Camping Municipal des Halles* (*Office de Tourisme*, Hotel de Ville, Decize, 58300 Nievre).

The ground-floor flat which Enid Fisher stayed in can be rented from M. and Mme Fissier (*Les Sorbiers*, Route de Sorède, 66700 Argelès-sur-Mer; ☎68.81.13.34, no English spoken). On her way down to Roussillon, Enid asked her hosts at the various stopovers to phone ahead and book her next accommodation, which they were happy to do.

Enquiries and bookings for the accessible cottage in the Dordogne should be addressed to David Marsden (Gresignac, 24320 Verteillac; ☎53.91.04.41). Polly Higgins describes the layout:

"The kitchen was small and compact, so that one could stand or sit at the work surface and reach everything; the sitting and dining area was spacious and light, and easily heated by a wood stove. French windows opened from this room onto the walled patio with its barbecue and attractive greenery.

The ground-floor bedroom with its handsome limestone fireplace overlooked the walled garden still dotted with pansies in November. This bedroom gave onto the bathroom, designed so that wheelchair users have easy access to washbasin, toilet and shower. Upstairs was another double bedroom with views over fields and hills and the graceful ruins of an ancient chapel. Everywhere I looked, both in and around the cottage, there was something to delight the eye and I loved it all immediately."

Of the **hotel chains** that offer wheelchair-accessible rooms and *en suite* facilities, those that present the lowest bills include the following: *Les Balladins* (95 one-star hotels; 20 rue du Pont des Halles, 94656 Rungis; ☎1/49.78.24.00); *Campanile* (over 200 hotels; 31 avenue Jean Moulin, Marne La Vallée, 77200 Torcy; ☎1/64.62.46.62); *Climat de France* (138 two-star hotels; *Voyages Vacances*, 197 Knightsbridge, London SW7 1RB; ☎071/589

FRANCE: TRAVEL NOTES

6769); *Fimotel* (53 two-star hotels; 5 av de la Porte de Clichy, 75017 Paris; ☎1/40.25.50.50); *Ibis/Ubris* (240 two-star hotels, including 12 in central Paris; *Resinter*, c/o *Novotel*, Shortlands, London W6 8DR; ☎071/724 1000); *Neotel Transeurope Hotels* (66 hotels including 19 in Paris; *Consort Hotels* Ryedale Building, Piccadilly, York YO1 1PN; ☎0904/643151).

The above addresses provide a central reservation service; if you wish to confirm the suitability of the accommodation you (or your travel agent) should ask the reservations staff to contact the hotel direct. Consult the *RADAR* holiday guide and the *Holiday Care Service* for more ideas. *Access in Paris* (see *Books*) contains an updated (1991) supplement on accommodation. The research team for this guide found that the wheelchair symbol used in the official Paris tourist board hotel guide is unreliable.

Access and facilities

The minister appointed to oversee disability issues is himself disabled, a step in the right direction. However, Sian Williams found that the employment quotas are not adhered to, and the benefits that disabled people can claim are not sufficient for those who require a considerable amount of care; as in Britain, they are forced to rely on family and friends to help out.

Some parts of Paris and many of the small provincial towns are old and do not cater for wheelchairs. In Nancy, although an architectural bureau monitors all new buildings to ensure that they are accessible, there are still breaches of the regulations. Modern shopping centres and *hypermarchés* have good access, but restaurants, theatres and cinemas often pose problems.

Entrance to **university** in France is open to anyone with the *baccalauréat* (equivalent to A levels), whatever grade. There are several independent residential centres for students with disabilities, and those cities with such centres (for example, Nancy, Bordeaux, Montpellier) attract all the disabled students. At Nancy the accommodation is not equipped for severely disabled students. Access to the university buildings there is variable: a lift has been recently installed in the arts faculty to enable access to certain lecture rooms, but even the library for one faculty is not accessible. As in Britain, lack of finance is blamed.

Books

Access in Paris, written by Gordon Couch and compiled by the *Pauline Hephaistos Survey Projects* (*PHSP*, 39 Bradley Gardens, London W13 8HE), was published in 1985 but an updated accommodation supplement is available. Order from *RADAR* or *PHSP*.

French Farm and Holiday Guide (Farm Holiday Guides, £4.95) contains an illustrated selection of over a thousand *gîtes* (reasonably priced, rural self-catering accommodation — small cottage, village house, apartment, perhaps part of a farm). There is a section on "super *gîtes*" and *gîtes* for the disabled.

French Federation of Camping and Caravanning Guide (£7.95 from *FFCC Guide*, Springdene, Shepherd's Way, Fairlight, East Sussex TN35 4BB) details 11,300 touring sites and indicates which have special facilities for disabled people.

The Michelin Green Guide – Camping/Caravanning France (from bookshops, the *AA* or the *RAC*) indicates sites with facilities for disabled people.

The two volumes of *Touristes quand même!* (one for France, one for Paris, available from *CNFLRH* and from local *Offices de Tourisme* or *Syndicats d'Initiative*), although somewhat dated (1987), are clearly laid out and contain many useful addresses as well as notes on access to museums, galleries and parks. Symbols are explained in English.

Guide des Autoroutes à l'usage des Personnes à Mobilité Réduite can also be obtained from *CNFLRH*, and lists facilities on French motorways. Again, symbols are explained in English. The *AA Guide for the Disabled Traveller* uses this information in its section on "The Disabled Traveller Abroad".

Plainpied (10 rue Georges de Porto-Riche, 75014 Paris; ☎1/45.41.40.43) is not a book but a quarterly magazine (20F), worth getting hold of if you can read French and are interested in finding out more about "disability issues" in France.

Switzerland

A Long Love Affair

Ian Marshall first fell in love with Switzerland in 1947. Apart from a sight problem, he was not disabled, but a "grubby grammar school boy" of fifteen. The school trip made such a lasting impression that Ian was determined to return. By the time he achieved this, he was married with two small girls, and paraplegic to boot.

For our first holiday we chose to take a rented apartment in the canton of Wallis. I asked a Swiss friend, who had recommended the area, to have a look at the apartment on our behalf to check for accessibility. Things are much better these days in this respect and I feel more confident when booking. It is well worth shopping around as prices vary enormously. Accommodation is spotlessly clean and well appointed (even down to the atomic shelter).

My favourite route across the Channel is by hovercraft because it is quick and easy, although not cheap. If you choose a ferry crossing, then the shorter the better: anything over four hours, I think, requires reserving a cabin, and that can present its own problems. Modern vessels have lifts up from the car deck, and a good loading officer will place you exactly opposite the lift door. Without a lift it is necessary to muster four crew members and persuade them to carry you up several flights of stairs. Trying to explain in French that I should be carried up backwards, and the chair should be

tilted back rather than forwards, needed a little preparation and practice before boarding a French boat.

We decided to make journeying across France part of the holiday, rather than tearing along motorways. Each time we go we choose a slightly different route, and when we later took to camping and caravanning we took even longer as there is so much to discover and there are hundreds of sites to choose from. When not camping, two of our favourite hotel stops are Dijon, if entering Switzerland via Pontalier, and Gérardmer in the Vosges if making for Basel to join the Swiss motorway system. Payment of a flat fee (SFr30) allows you to use this network for the whole year and is well worth the expense. The disabled loos in motorway service stations are some of the finest I have found anywhere. The ordinary roads are determined by topography, so that they are twisting and time-consuming, but the best way to see the country if time permits.

We have found camping and caravanning in Switzerland most enjoyable but the sites are more crowded than those in France, and it is essential to book in peak season. As the Swiss keep their caravans on sites, rather than at home, you may find unoccupied vans taking up valuable space. The provision of facilities for disabled campers is increasing all the time.

One simple piece of luggage, with which I equip myself whether using a caravan, hotel, or rented accommodation, is a sturdy wooden stool, of the type found in a hospital gym. With the seat padded and universal castors attached to the legs, it enables me to move around inside a caravan and in other tight spots where a wheelchair would be far too large.

It is wise to carry warm and waterproof clothing because at high altitude the hottest day can give way to a cold night, and spectacular thunderstorms, a feature of late summer, can drench you in seconds. I find that struggling into a two-piece plastic rain suit will keep me bone dry, and this act alone often keeps the rain at bay! To find the warmest weather, try the Italian-speaking canton of Tessin, south of the Alps, with its famous lakes. Otherwise, Interlaken in the Bernese Oberland, with its many sites and attractions, is hard to beat as a tourist centre.

Nearby, overlooking the Thunnersee, I found almost the ideal hotel for wheelchair users. From parking in the village square, or the rear hotel yard, there is not a single kerb or step to negotiate to enter the hotel. A lift gives access to all floors. I say "almost" because the bathroom door was narrow and I would have been in trouble without my stool. But now there is an excellent publication, obtainable from the Swiss National Tourist Office (SNTO), entitled *Swiss Hotel Guide for the Disabled*, which not only makes sure of bathroom door widths but also details lift accessibility and provides other essential information which enables the disabled person to travel with confidence. This is not always the case with guidebooks displaying the wheelchair symbol, as I have found to my cost.

Where a wheelchair can be a positive asset is on the waterborne part of the integrated transport network. The lake steamers run like clockwork up, down and across the lakes, and provide an ideal means of visiting many of the lakeside towns and villages. Or, as the aforementioned guidebook puts it, "The boats on the lakes invite to discover lovely shores".

Boarding is by a simple gangway from the landing-stage. Waiting passengers hang about nonchalantly, but do not be fooled. At the last moment, panic sets in and they all insist on embarking first. The chair affords good protection as the crowd, six or eight abreast, squeezes onto a gangway designed for two. If you are lucky enough to have three companions, form up in good time with the two brawniest as vanguard, the third as pusher behind, and be ready to surge forward like a cohort of the Swiss Guard when the "off" is given.

> *"The Swiss sometimes have difficulty in reconciling the interests of disabled people with their national traits of tidiness and conformity"*

For some of the excursions by road our camper was not the ideal vehicle because of its width. In many of the smaller valleys, special passing places are necessary. Even so, we twice nearly came to grief, once when edging around a huge parked timber low-loader, when our wheels just clung to the crumbling edge of the mountain road, and again when squeezing past an on-coming postbus, which naturally had right of way.

To give the driver a rest, and relief from potential heart attacks, there are many coach excursions from the main tourist centres. If you cannot manage coach travel, there is usually a local taxi which will offer an excellent full day's outing at a cost per head of little more than that charged by the coach operator. We made a memorable trip to the Rhone glacier by this means. Zurich and some other major towns run specially adapted taxis which take wheelchairs. Trains are an easier option, particularly the intercity services, which even have disabled loos on board and are geared up to help. Ask at the station for the travellers' help service, and look for the SOS logo.

Despite all this, I believe that the Swiss sometimes have difficulty in reconciling the interests of disabled people with their national traits of tidiness and conformity. Such conflict may account for the problems that we experienced as pedestrians in one of their largest cities, where there was no provision made for wheelchairs to cross the road at a busy intersection. Pedestrians were forbidden to cross except by foot tunnel – useless to me because it had steps at both ends. Drivers seemed to accelerate on seeing us making a dash for it. In the event, all

that was dented was their reputation. Perhaps this was an exceptional example: in general, "walking" is both possible and rewarding – in cities, towns and villages on well-maintained pavements and roads, and even in rural areas and high valleys.

Some of the Swiss I've met have difficulty also in reconciling a sense of pride in their modern technological nation and a collective conscience about their environment plus a folksy peasant image of the past. In the tourist areas they make full use of the latter, especially on their national day, August 1. If you are drawn to yodelling, flag-throwing, shooting, alpenhorn blowing or fireworks, not to mention the village band playing their version of "Tiger Rag", August 1 is your day.

With its almost unbelievable landscapes, Switzerland may seem a most unsuitable country for the disabled visitor, but most of it can be reached and experienced. I am constantly drawn back to the place by the magical spell which fell upon me more than forty years ago, and crossing its frontier always feels like going home.

The Eiger on my Doorstep

At the age of 68, Beryl Bristow made her fifth trip to Grindelwald, in the Swiss Alps. She was partially sighted and in need of a new knee and pair of hips.

My three passions are photography, painting and studying Alpine flowers. This may sound somewhat bizarre, considering my poor vision, but I am able to enjoy these hobbies with the help of a close-up lens and strong

magnifying glasses. I originally chose to stay in Grindelwald to be near the Alpine flowers. I wrote to the local information bureau and received not only a mass of leaflets, but also a well written letter in English enclosing a pressed cowslip! In Grindelwald I had what I needed most – good transport in every direction – and I found a delightful hotel, the *Gydisdorf*, whose owners looked after every guest with great care. I felt happy and safe there, so in June 1987 returned for another stay.

I was taken to Torquay station in a Red Cross ambulance and my escorts saw me into my reserved seat – one for disabled passengers – with extra leg room and luggage racks nearby. *Swiss Travel* are the best operator for Switzerland, but I now travel independently, finding it cheaper. The journey is straightforward, providing I travel at weekends, which avoids a change of train at Basel. I already had a railcard, so I bought a Eurocard which gave me half fare on the Swiss main lines and Interlaken lake steamers, as well as concessions on most of the other lines. I booked lower bunk couchettes, reserved seats where possible and asked for a wheelchair at Dover.

A Red Cross escort met me at Paddington and I was soon speeding to Victoria to catch the boat train. At Victoria a porter heaved my trolley and shoulder bag onto the train and I looked for my seat. There were hoots of laughter as I quoted the seat number – I was the sixth person to lay claim to it. However, another seat was empty and its rightful owner, standing behind me, let me take it and settled himself further down the train.

Finding it difficult to get up and down for my ground-level close-up photography on this holiday, I concentrated on my painting. This was evident from my trolley! The pointed feet of my easel stuck out menacingly; my folding chair was tied onto the handle; my oil paints, bottles of medium, brushes and cloths were in a plastic box at the bottom, with a carrier bag of spare clothes and painting boards stuffed in at the top; every spare corner was filled. My shoulder bag held a large thermos of hot water and tea bags – a necessity as the train would have no refreshments on board and it was a twelve-hour journey from Calais to Interlaken. Cameras, tape recorder and a selection from my medicine cupboard were crammed into the bag's pockets. I had only a small amount of money in my handbag, but under my jumper I wore a child's satchel, in which I carried my keys, large sterling notes, cheque and credit cards and, most

important, the numbers of my Swiss travellers' cheques. Men wear a money belt but the satchel is better for ladies, particularly if they are plump like me!

Helping hands at Dover soon had me and my luggage off the train, and I sailed in my wheelchair through the passport office, along the quay and up the gangway onto the *Sealink* ferry. I found myself a seat next to the Purser's office and went to the cafeteria while the ship was stationary. After an excellent meal I asked the Purser to radio Calais and request a *chaise roulande* for me.

"A full moon, rising behind a forest, was reflected in a wide river running alongside the track"

At Calais I was lowered into a huge old wheelchair with copious blankets tucked around me. Piled on my lap was everything except the trolley – heavy shoulder bag, duty frees rattling in their carriers, a bag of yoghurts and milk shakes, and my handbag slung round my neck. We formed a small procession, an old man pushing me and a younger one following with my trolley. The station platform was full of small craters and we had to cross a number of railway tracks; the younger man assisted my porter in heaving me over these, and at last we reached the right train and my compartment.

I woke in the night and pushed up the blind: a full moon, rising behind a forest, was reflected in a wide river running alongside the track. Soon the river widened into a large lake and the moon cleared the trees, its silvery beam shining brightly on the water – a beautiful sight. Soon after 4am, the train slowed and stopped at Metz. I love this stop. I pushed the window right down, delighting in the fresh air after a night in the small compartment. There was little activity on the platform but I listened intently and was soon rewarded with the dawn chorus, right on cue!

From then on my excitement grew with every mile we travelled. After stops at Basel, Berne and Spitz, we approached Interlaken, and I could see that spring had arrived. There were bushes of purple lilac and pinky white clouds of apple blossom everywhere. As we neared the town I spotted the Jungfrau with its snowy crest.

Fellow travellers helped me to transfer to the local train. It's a 25-minute journey to Grindelwald and interesting all the way. Waterfalls of melting snow cascaded down the rocky cliffs to join the river rushing through the fields. The first hay was being cut and stacked on spiky sticks. The Eiger towered above us, then the valley widened out and we drew into the station. The taxi was waiting, as arranged, and we drove up into the village. After a couple of minutes we turned sharp left and I saw the Wetterhorn and then *Hotel Gydisdorf* – the lovely 100-year-old chalet which is the home of two sisters, Hanni and Marie Zimmermann. Their guests share the chalet, and Marie's flower-filled garden.

"In spring the flowers grow knee high and as thick as grass"

My room by the garden door was ready, and breakfast was brought into the lounge so that I could enjoy my favourite view of the Wetterhorn with my coffee, black cherry jam and rolls. The chalet is built on three levels: the lower floor has double rooms with facilities, the lounges are on the main central floor where there are also some single rooms and a double. Upstairs are the remaining bedrooms. The kitchen is Hanni's territory and her cooking is superb. The sisters and their staff obviously enjoy looking after their guests, and many return year after year. It wasn't long before I recognised a voice and saw a familiar face. Hanni and Marie take guests through *Swiss Travel*, whose rep calls regularly, or one can book privately.

Grindelwald lies at the head of a valley, at 1020m, and the swollen river which flows towards the lakes at Interlaken is fed by two glaciers and numerous waterfalls. The lower meadows are therefore lush, and in spring the flowers grow knee high and as thick as grass. The village became popular as a climbing centre in the mid-nineteenth century, and is famous for its guides and mountaineers: a more recent addition is a sports centre with large indoor pool and skating rink, tennis courts and gym.

I woke at 4.30am the next morning, opened my window and grabbed my cameras. I crept into the lounge and looked out at the Eiger in the pink glow of sunrise. Opening the window wide, I leaned out and framed the peak with a branch of apple blossom from the old tree below. At last I had the early-morning shots I wanted! Sunday proper began as it should, the church bells ringing with that resonant tone peculiar to the Alps, and the resident blackbird singing near her nest. I put my tape recorder on the window-sill and switched on; I start each holiday tape with that music. In the same morning, in between sketching in the crevices and filling in the vivid blue sky for a painting of the Wetterhorn, I also recorded cow bells echoing loudly in the narrow street below, and then six hundred young brass band players marching in a village competition.

I had dreaded my first ride in the chair lift, but on my fifth visit it was irresistible. From the *Gydisdorf* the lift (called the "First" because it takes you up to the Grindelwald "First", at 2168m) is only a couple of yards and a few steps to climb. The attendant sees you into one of the two-seaters and fastens you in, wrapping you in a vast waterproof if he thinks it wise. I recommend getting off at the second stop, Bort, where I found many varieties of orchid on my first trip. One year the slopes dazzled with a mass of bright yellow hawkweed, the following year there were sweeps of white Alpine buttercups and patches of purple cranesbill amongst the yellow. I have not seen the orchids again, but I always find gentians and bright-eyed primroses, pale mauve and shades of pink. In 1987 spring was later than usual, so I saw new vistas of colour – golden marsh marigolds on the higher slopes, cowslips on the lower – and I spotted my favourite flowers, *Sol danella* (snowbells).

"The mountains were now coated with thick new snow and the tops shone golden"

The chair lift stops beside the restaurant and the views are breathtaking. I walked up my favourite path to the waterfall and crossed over a new bridge, which I was glad to see. I took some close-ups of a fine gentian, and a portrait of a silky white goat who disturbed me from behind as I focused, bent double over the flower. It began to rain so I made my way to the restaurant and found a seat with three Japanese and four Swiss, who tried to persuade me to share their sausages and chips.

The clouds were closing in and I decided to return. Soon the clatter of the chair lift approached and I was amazed to see a lady sat on one seat with a large Alsatian dog on the seat next to her. When I told Hanni about it she replied, "Oh yes, it's a neighbour. She always takes him on the chair lift when they go for a walk." As I floated down, the rain turned to snow and the fir trees were sprinkled with a fine coating, like caster sugar.

It continued damp until after dinner the next evening, when the clouds suddenly parted and cleared over the Wetterhorn and the whole valley. Everywhere the mountains were now coated with thick new snow and the tops shone golden, then pink in the sunset glow.

I had never seen the glacier sparkle so brightly. I took the bus up to the *Wetterhorn Hotel* and walked down the path through the woods. It is an easy walk, and folk of all ages go as far as the bridge across the river of melting ice. It is an awesome sight, all the more so through a zoom lens. I saw that it was different this year – much wider and bigger than before. Although beautiful, the glacier is really a moving monster, travelling at the rate of one foot a year. The ground was too slippery for me to venture further than the bridge. It was clear that I couldn't reach the higher paths, so the other guests brought back some flowers for me and we spent a few happy hours in the evenings trying to identify specimens.

Because of avalanches I was unable to make my usual trip on the Pfingstegg cable car. On previous visits I found dozens of Alpines that were new to me. The first time I'd been advised to "take the path to the hut and the goats, and carry on to the glacier". I later had to admit that I'd seen neither hut nor goats, not even the glacier. What I did see was a great variety of flowers – I used two 36-print films in about a hundred yards! This was heaven on earth for me, much better than the Alpine Flower Garden at Schynige Platte (2075m), near Wilderswil, which was too formal for my taste.

"You don't have to be agile to sit in a café and simply take in the views"

I used my Eurocard for some rail trips. Numerous excursions can be planned with the help of the information bureau booking clerks at Grindelwald station. It's wise to plan in advance, using the freely available timetables, and to take a taxi, if not for the outward journey then for the trip back up the hill from the station after a long day out. Mürren, Wengen or Kleine Scheidegg are easily reached for spectacular views of the Jungfrau. The views between Kleine Scheidegg and Wengen are the best you'll ever see!

I went to Alpiglen on the side of the Eiger – just a few buildings, a hotel, and marvellous panoramic views. I loved the place. It had an atmosphere, an aura about it. Later, I read in *The White Spider* (by Heinrich Harper) that climbers had stayed in those buildings before attempting the North Face . . . no wonder it felt like hallowed ground.

The outings requiring the least exertion must be on the lake steamers and the "gondola" (like a car without wheels, operated as a cable car) to the Mannlichen (2310m). The steamers start from a spot near one of the rail stations in Interlaken. I like to get off at Brienz for a while and sit on the seats under the trees by the lakeside. This is the birthplace of the woodcarving industry and there are wonderful old pieces to be seen here, such as The Last Supper, carved from one piece of wood in the fifteenth to sixteenth century.

The gondola station is a short walk from Grund rail station. If you can manage to climb into the gondola this is a relaxing way to admire the scenery as you glide upward for about half an hour. With binoculars you may see the delightful marmots put on a friendly boxing bout, or perhaps some other examples of the elusive Alpine wildlife.

Grindelwald was one of the first Swiss villages to be developed as a winter resort, but there are many summer attractions which can be enjoyed by the less mobile tourist. The excellent transport network and the well-maintained paths enable those of us who are physically handicapped to reach at least some of the dizzy heights that are conquered by the knickerbocker-clad hiker and the climber with his crampons. And you don't have to be agile to sit in a café and simply take in the views.

SWITZERLAND: TRAVEL NOTES

Sources of information

Swiss National Tourist Office (*SNTO*), Swiss Centre, New Coventry Street, London W1V 8EE; ☎071/734 1291. A mine of beautiful brochures and maps, the SNTO also distributes the *Swiss Hotel Guide for the Disabled* (they ask for a £1 donation towards postage costs). Their head office (Bellariastrasse 38, 8027 Zurich; ☎1/288 1111) produces many publications, among them the *Swiss Youth Hostel Federation Guide*, giving accessible hostels and travel information including details of reduced fares.

Mobility International Switzerland (*MI Schweiz*), Hard 4, 8408 Winterthur; ☎52/256825. Can supply a newsletter containing tips and information for disabled travellers. .

The eleven **regional tourist offices** (list of addresses in the *Swiss Hotel Guide for the Disabled*) and the local information bureaux are recommended by Beryl Bristow as the best source of information: they will supply hotel and town guides in English, some with reference to disabled people. She also wrote to **Pro Infirmis** (Hohlstrasse 52, 8000 Zurich; ☎1/241 4411) who were obliging, if slow to respond.

According to *Pro Infirmis*, the Swiss are very slow to provide facilities, perhaps because there has been no war there for 200 years and there are no victims of war to cater for. In addition, each of the 3000 communities in the different cantons is a law unto itself, and some are progressive in their approach to providing for disabled people, others less so.

Tour operators

Although she now makes her own arrangements, Beryl Bristow recommends the *Swiss Travel Service Ltd* (Bridge House, Ware, Herts

SG12 9DE; ☎0920/5021). Before booking it is "absolutely essential" to contact one of three members of staff (named in the brochure) who will discuss your requirements. The brochure points out that the Scenic Tours are not suitable for disabled people.

Thomson Holidays should be able to advise on the suitability of their winter holidays, using their *Factfile* (see "Booking", *Practicalities*).

Getting there

Many travellers prefer to **drive**, taking their car at reduced rate on the cross-Channel ferries (see *Practicalities*, "By Sea"), as this gives greatest freedom of movement once in Switzerland. Making the journey by **train** might appeal if tackling narrow mountain roads and hairpin bends is not your idea of a relaxing holiday. Write to the *International Rail Centre* (Victoria Station, London SW1 1JU) to arrange assistance as far as the other side of the Channel. *Swiss Federal Railways* (same address as *SNTO*) take over after that.

If you **fly**, you'll be in good hands with *Swissair* (see *Practicalities*, "By Air") and have the comfort of knowing that Zurich airport boasts some of the most luxurious accessible toilets in the world – with adjustable seats and padded armrests! There are also good facilities at Geneva and Basel.

Transport

From the *SNTO* obtain the pamphlet *Swiss Travel System*, which gives details of the **Swiss Pass**: this allows travel by rail, boat and postbus, plus trams and buses in over twenty towns, as well as a discount on mountain railways. In addition you can take advantage of the Swiss Flexi Pass, Regional Pass, Swiss Card or Swiss Boat Pass.

Only fifteen minutes' notice is required at the booking office when asking for assistance on a train journey. Ian Marshall reports good wheelchair accessibility on trains – particularly intercity services, which have a special first-class compartment and loos for disabled passengers – and no problems on boats. On older trains you may have to travel in the baggage van if you wish to remain in your wheelchair.

Ask *MI Schweiz* for a list of adapted taxi services, which are available in several cities. Daily hire of a standard taxi is a good alternative to excursions by coach, and comparable in price, if you can transfer to a car seat but cannot cope with the steps on a coach.

Orange Badge holders are allowed to park for two hours where **parking** is prohibited or in red zones, and for four hours within blue zones or where time limits normally apply. Ask at the local police station about payment at parking meters. A summary of the various cantonal parking regulations for disabled drivers is available from the *SNTO* in London.

Accommodation

Although Ian Marshall recommends the *Swiss Hotel Guide for the Disabled* mentioned earlier, a cautionary note is sounded by Percy Biggs, who is confined to a wheelchair and travelled to Locarno in 1989:

"The guide listed the *Hotel Muralto* (four star) as a Category A hotel – accessible to wheelchair users. I booked a fortnight in September, with *Kuoni* (a Swiss company), requesting a "superior" room with balcony and lake view. As a precaution I added that the entrance to the bedroom, bathroom and lift needed to be adequate to take a wheelchair approximately 75cm wide. We then discovered (thanks to the travel agency, *Travel Care*) that the hotel had only one room suitable for a wheelchair user, on the fifth floor at the back of the hotel – no view of lake – and the charge was the same as for a superior room. No other rooms in the hotel were suitable. I complained to both the *SNTO* and the hotel owners (then *Best Western*, but no longer listed in their brochure) and received apologies; the tourist board promised in the future to give a more precise description of hotels in Category A."

Percy then tried the *Esplanade Hotel* in Locarno, also listed as Category A. On arrival at the hotel he discovered that it had absolutely no facilities for wheelchair users and no access to swimming pool, garden or bar. The manageress did make an effort to provide access to the pool, by having two steep ramps installed. Percy lodged a complaint with *Kuoni*, whose services, from booking the holiday through to

SWITZERLAND: TRAVEL NOTES

the return journey, "left much to be desired". *Kuoni* disclaimed all responsibility.

The most recent edition of the guide at the time of writing was published in 1987, so take note of the following, printed under the explanation of the hotel categories: "It is advisable to have the indications certified, regarding the accessibility for wheelchairs, when making the reservation." Also worth noting is the fact that Category A is well qualified, with a list of "less favourably accessible installations", including door widths of bathrooms between 65 and 69cm, any of which may make your Category A choice unsuitable – study the guide carefully *and* double check through your travel agent or with the hotel direct.

If you can manage a few steps and a short slope up to the entrance, *Hotel Gydisdorf* (3818 Grindelwald; ☎36/53 1303) is recommended. Children are made very welcome.

The *RADAR* holiday guide lists some other possibilities. Facilities on campsites are generally good, with provision for disabled people becoming ever more widespread; it's advisable to book ahead in high season.

Access and facilities

Switzerland is primarily a country to enjoy **outdoors**, so the main requirements of disabled tourists are likely to be some good surfaces for walking/wheeling along in the mountains as well as the cities, and reasonable access to some of the local modes of transport – lake steamers, cable cars, chair lifts – and to the best viewpoints.

On the whole, these requirements are met, with well-maintained roads, pavements and walking trails, even in remote villages. The spectacular scenery can be easily admired from a wheelchair at most vantage points, and where a restaurant or café is provided access is usually good. Toilet facilities are generally adequate, and those at motorway service stations excellent.

Of course there are exceptions (see p.178), and variations in provision for disabled people between cantons, as pointed out by *Pro Infirmis*, but there is much scope for enjoyable, if rather expensive, holidaymaking in Switzerland.

Health and insurance

Check the **altitude** of your destination and the places you want to visit, and confirm with your GP that it's safe for you to go. The **sun** is very strong at high altitudes; you should take a hat, high-protection suntan lotion and a sun block for nose and lips. An alpenstock is ideal on hills for those unsteady on their feet, and a shooting-stick is useful.

Remember that Switzerland is not a member of the EC, so there is no reciprocal **health service**. It is essential to have good insurance cover (see *Practicalities*).

There are over twenty different mineral springs in Switzerland for treatment of various conditions. A guide to Swiss **spas**, including hotels, is available from the *SNTO*. There is also a brochure giving details of homes and hotels specialising in convalescence.

Austria

Setting out for Mars

Eric Leary, a physiotherapist in private practice, travelled to Austria on the Orient Express, returning by Concorde. Eric is blind, but wrote his account with the help of his wife, Geraldine, who described everything to him throughout the trip.

When mulling over the things we would love to do, trips on Concorde and the Orient Express seemed to come top of the list, although we believed that cost would probably rule them out. I asked a travel agent for further information and received details of holidays entitled "Flights of Fantasy", in which our desiderata were included in one package. This was quite irresistible. We gasped at the cost, but it was quite evident to each of us that the other had made a decision.

Departure was a month ahead. Excitement seized us, and we talked it over from all angles. Who else would be likely to indulge in such a venture? What would the other passengers be like? A thousand such questions. We felt young again, and our tread became lighter.

At last the great day arrived, and we assembled in the *Grosvenor Hotel* at Victoria Station on a Sunday morning in May 1989. We all had coffee together, stiff and polite. Our heavy luggage was taken from us, not to be seen again until we reached Salzburg, and we made our way through several tunnels to the train.

There it stood, elegant, shining and inviting. Immaculate waiters were at the doors to receive us, relieve us of any small packages and hand luggage, and show us to our tables. The thrill of the occasion gripped us and we revelled in our surroundings: the table and wall lights of beautiful brass (brass is my passion), glorious matching table-ware, spacious armchairs and luxurious drapes. Champagne was served, closely followed by a fine hot lunch, served with care and attention to detail.

At Folkestone we embarked on the ferry, well directed by our couriers, who offered discreet assistance where required. Two passengers in wheel-chairs had no difficulty in reaching the private saloon reserved for our party. (However, anyone totally confined to a wheelchair would not be able to cope on the trains, as wheelchairs cannot be used in either the English or the Continental carriages.)

We walked a short distance at Boulogne to join the train for the next leg of the journey. We were allowed to cross the rails and inspect the train from all angles, cameras at the ready. I touched the polished brass of the doorhandles and the raised brass numbers and names of the carriages – ours was *Perseus*; it had formed part of Sir Winston Churchill's funeral train and was used to carry royalty and visiting heads of state.

Climbing aboard, we were greeted in perfect English by our personal steward, a young man named Albert. He showed us to our compartment and furnished us with all the details necessary for our comfort. Dinner would be served in one hour, allowing time to settle in and tidy up. We were expected to dress for dinner. It was at this point that Geraldine was desolate to find that she had forgotten to pack my dress shirts! A short depression followed, until she realised that the shirt I was already wearing would just about pass. A strong gin and tonic, which I had remembered to pack, soon put things right.

"At 7.30am, Albert appeared with a large pot of steaming coffee, copious fruit juices and some delicious croissants and rolls"

Having dressed, we had time to examine our compartment in more detail. There was a comfortable long seat to the left, which converted to two bunks. Below the window was a small table, secured to the wall and covered with literature. To the right of the door was a semicircular cupboard containing a washbasin and all the necessary toiletries, including soaps, toothbrushes and towels. The walls of the compartment were of the most beautiful woods, panelled throughout and illuminated by subdued lighting. Pleasant music was piped throughout the train, emanating, we discovered later, from a live pianist at the bar.

We made our way to the restaurant car, where Geraldine – in a reverie – did her best to describe the glittering tableware, crisp white cloths, noble cutlery and glassware, shaded brass lamps, perfectly turned-out waiters, and the walls which were decorated with exotic woods and Lalique glass panels. Most passengers were in evening dress, and several ladies wore elegant creations from the Twenties and Thirties.

I could devote the rest of this account to the meal. In addition to the appropriate wines, there were innumerable delicacies, including courgette flowers with scampi filling, lamb filled with truffle sauce, vanilla and bitter chocolate mousse – this was the *nouvelle cuisine* I'd dreamt of, five courses leaving us utterly content, as opposed to penniless and famished, which is often the case in England. We shared a table with a charming couple; the lady sitting next to me quickly observed the way Geraldine assisted me with certain dishes (such as the plaited potatoes) and immediately, without embarrassment, helped me throughout the meal. She took to the task as though she'd been a friend for years.

We returned to our cabin to find that Albert had made it ready for sleep. He suggested that breakfast should be taken early, as lunch would be served at 11.30am in order to disembark at 1pm. The train rumbled on into the night, along the edge of Lake Konstanz and into the mountains, past silent wayside stations.

Next morning, at 7.30am, Albert appeared with a large pot of steaming coffee, copious fruit juices and some delicious croissants and rolls. We were still proceeding through beautiful mountain country, which compensated for what we'd missed in the darkness. We packed and moved about a lot, endeavouring to work up an appetite for lunch, another delicious meal.

Leaving many passengers to continue the journey to Venice, we left the train at Innsbruck, where the chefs and stewards lined up beside the train to be photographed. Coaches awaited us outside the station and we enjoyed a panoramic drive to Salzburg, listening to our guide and to the strains of what

was to become the theme of our stay –
"The Sound of Music".

"Prices in Salzburg are in keeping with the surrounding mountains"

Reaching Salzburg at 4pm we were immediately taken to the suburb of Leopoldskron, to see the film's eighteenth-century von Trapp family villa. The next stop was our hotel, a five-star *Sheraton* and most grand. We were left to ourselves that evening, so we had a walk and a light meal before bed.

Amply breakfasted the following morning, we were taken to the Old Town by coach and conducted on a tour by a very well-informed guide. Salzburg certainly deserves its reputation as one of the most beautiful cities in the world, and the views of the Alps from the city are spectacular. The wheelchair users in our party found the Old Town reasonably flat, and easy to explore in spite of the cobbled streets. We moved through many gracious squares, were shown splendid churches and municipal buildings, and paid homage in front of Number 9, Getreidegasse – Mozart's birthplace and now a museum. We visited the seventeenth-century Schloss Hellbrunn, famed for its *trompe-l'oeil* ceiling, its fountains and the joke played by its original owner on his guests with the aid of clever engineering and some hidden water jets in the grounds. This is a very tactile experience for the visually handicapped!

We returned by coach for lunch at the hotel, but not before our lady guide had conducted Geraldine and me to a reasonably priced shop where we could remedy my lack of an evening shirt. This gesture was much appreciated, as prices in Salzburg are in keeping with the surrounding mountains.

In the afternoon we walked through the Mirabell Gardens, a lovely parkland area behind the hotel, beyond which

lay glorious mountains. We reached the Old Town and searched the squares. The market stalls were most fascinating, their glistening white cloths garlanded with flowers, and the doors of the houses behind them surrounded by posies. The bakery stalls pleased us most, with their great variety of breads, cakes and puddings, including *Mozart Kugel* and *Salzburger Nockerl*.

The Salzburg churches are magnificent, with solid marble altars and figures covered with gold leaf, gorgeous stained-glass windows and intricate woodcarvings. Marble is everywhere, partly because of the proximity of Italy, but also because a pink marble is quarried in the nearby mountains. Even the pathways are frequently made of marble chips, so plentiful is the supply. We sought out the small church and cemetery where the von Trapp children are said to have hidden. The cemetery is remarkable for the intricately carved monuments above most of the graves.

We visited the Mozardeum – the famous academy of music – and the Hohensalzburg castle which is the largest medieval fortress in Central Europe. We were particularly impressed by the townspeople's friendly attitude towards tourists, and one of our wheelchair users commented on the kind help she had received. Salzburg is far lovelier than we had expected, and we promised ourselves a longer holiday there.

"A string of ponies and traps awaited"

That evening we went to the Residenz Palace for a banquet and a classical concert. Mounting the imposing staircase on a red carpet, we were greeted by three horn-players from the Mozardeum playing a specially composed piece to welcome us. More players from the Mozardeum were assembled in the large hall and they performed a Mozart symphony. It was a stimulating performance, with youthful enthusiasm shining through, and at the end the hall rang with loud and prolonged applause.

In another elegant room we were given a champagne reception, after which a meal of the usual high standard was presented, the only difference being that there were six instead of five courses. We were entertained by a mountain band, composed of members of a farming family, who gave us a continuous selection of lively Austrian music. At the end of the evening we were shown down to the square where a string of ponies and traps awaited; thus we clip-clopped our way back to the hotel in the warm night air.

After a free morning and then lunch, we were due to leave. During the last few days the Austrian authorities had announced that Concorde produced noise above their newly prescribed level, so hurried international negotiations took place, resulting in our having to fly home from Linz instead of Salzburg.

"We had to shout, and we felt our systems rocking with the thrill of it all"

As we approached the airport the traffic grew heavier and heavier – the word had got around that Concorde was to fly from Linz for the first time, and the crowds had gathered. Police had been called to enable our coach to get through. There were people everywhere, on roofs, up trees, crowding the perimeter fence, all waving and cheering, obviously thrilled.

Leaving the coach we broke all the rules and circulated around the wonderful machine, taking photographs, until finally we were ushered on board. There was provision for the less mobile here: those in wheelchairs were transferred to a carrying chair and taken up the double flight of steps to the door of the plane. The crowds cheered and clapped as we taxied down the runway, and we, caught up in the excitement, responded with shouts and applause. On the last run, the pilot dropped the nose of the plane in salute and then, when just about everything went mad, we took off!

Champagne and lunch were served almost immediately, and for about thirty minutes we learned of Concorde's achievements from one of the crew. The fact which amazed me most was that when it goes supersonic, the plane expands by about 20cm, so that what was a continuous surface on the flight deck opens up to form a gulley on each side. On the aircraft's bulkheads were mounted several meters, providing such statistics as external temperature, speed and altitude. The external temperature was well below zero but friction against the side of the plane made the windows quite warm to the touch.

The captain invited us to the flight deck, pointing out that as the trip was so short and there were over a hundred of us, we would have to come up in pairs and spend only a minute or so with him. We all went, however, and I had to bend double – the plane is quite narrow and the flight deck even narrower, with the three crew members cramped together, allowing two of us just to squeeze into the entrance. I was advised by the captain to keep my arms well to my sides – just in case.

Since we could not go supersonic over land, we crossed the coast at Rotterdam, went for a short flip up to Edinburgh and then down to Clacton. At the point of crossing the coast, the burners were switched on. There was a powerful thrust; one sensed the forces operating. Concorde assumed a new dimension: up went the nose, and we had the feeling of setting out for Mars, as the aircraft was lying at a very steep angle. We had to shout, and we felt our systems rocking with the thrill of it all.

This cloud of elation lasted for about twenty minutes and then we levelled off, the burners subsiding. The excitement was exhausting, and we gasped a sigh of relief. We were down to a mere 600mph. In no time we were at Heathrow and making a faultless landing. We bade each other farewell, still somewhat numb and overawed. Would we do it again? Most assuredly, if we could find a sponsor!

An Improbable Ski Party

Ron Cottrell participated in the Uphill Ski Club (USC) trip to Kirchdorf, Austria, in January 1989. In his account he offers both praise and criticism of the organisation and the holiday.

I first heard of the *USC* on a BBC documentary in 1988. The idea of disabled people on skis seemed interesting and I decided to find out more about this little known charity. Some months later I received the brochures for their 1989 holidays and I set about raising the necessary funds (by commercial sponsorship).

Having secured a place on the January holiday for beginners, I travelled from my home in Rochester, Kent, to The Spastics Society Assessment Centre in Fitzroy Square, London. I found myself in a group which included people with cerebral palsy (CP), Down's syndrome, spina bifida, and handicaps resulting from head injuries: a wide range of abilities, both physical and intellectual.

We travelled in a very large, six-wheeled coach, fitted with all mod cons including toilet, video, and hot and cold drinks supplies. The seats were quite comfortable and each had an overhead reading lamp.

After struggling through Friday evening rush-hour traffic we headed for Dover and the 7.30pm *P&O* ferry to Calais. The *P&O* staff certainly knew their business with regard to handling disabled passengers: our coach was parked adjacent to the lifts, which took us straight up to the restaurant where we were served immediately with a meal.

At Calais it was the same efficient service and with minimal fuss we started on the overnight trip through France and Germany. There was a brief stop at Baden-Baden for continental breakfast at a roadside service station, and another one later for lunch. And so into Austria and the mountains, finally arriving at our destination at about 2.30pm on Saturday. I was absolutely exhausted and very anxious to retreat to my room and sort myself out.

Rooms and helpers allocated (one helper to each two disabled – a very good ratio), we set about unpacking and arranging our equipment for the week. Dinner that evening was served early, followed by a short lecture from the chief ski instructor on the activities for the week. On a *USC* holiday you are obviously expected to ski, and this rule is rigidly enforced; only if "grounded" by the party doctor are you excused from classes.

We were expected to be ready to leave for classes almost immediately after breakfast (8am), in order to be on the slopes by 9am at the latest. Help was constantly on hand and each participant was given equal tuition time by the instructors (three of whom came with us on the coach). However, those who needed extra help were given it, and those who simply couldn't physically cope on skis were given a sledge to use instead. No one was pushed beyond his or her capabilities, and as a total beginner I was given plenty of encouragement and a very fair proportion of my instructor's time. Skiers who made progress throughout the week were shifted to different groups further up the slopes.

"On no occasion did I experience help in a patronising way"

Although morning sessions were compulsory, most afternoons a choice of activities was available, including shopping, swimming and more skiing. From a purely personal point of view, the skiing was not entirely successful. After two days I had developed a severe blister on my left foot which made walking extremely painful. Daily medication was required, in the form of dressings and padding, but in spite of this, by Thursday I was unable to wear ski boots. My sincere thanks go to my helper (Jasper) for his kindness in lending me his soft Moon Boots for outside wear. I was by no means excused from classes, and on the final day I took part in the sledge race, which turned out well, as I won it!

In some ways the social activities outshone the skiing. They included a sleigh ride, a fondue evening, ski films and tobogganing, all of which I joined in except for the tobogganing. I felt that this was too dangerous for someone with a back problem (apart from my CP), a view that was reinforced by the previous evening's activity.

Simon, our chief instructor, told everyone after our evening meal to dress in ski clothing, excluding boots, for a "surprise" activity on the slopes. My instructor, Moky, assisted me in the long trek across the snow in the fading light, and I quipped that perhaps the *USC* had decided to perform a reconstruction of the "Malmedy Massacre", as seen in the Sixties film,

Battle of the Bulge. We dissolved in laughter as an imaginary headline came to mind: "Twenty Spastics Massacred in Austria".

On arriving at the scene of our "surprise" activity, we were handed a small paper cup of the local "fire water", not really my thing as I don't drink alcohol. Then came the Activity: we were given some kind of plastic tray to slide under our rear ends and skate down the slope on. Rather than be a spoilsport, I gave it a try, but one slide was enough and I retired with a sore back.

I also had reservations about the fondue evening. The food was good, but I felt that placing a pot of boiling oil in the middle of the table, and expecting people with coordination problems to cope with spearing pieces of meat on forks and immersing them in the oil, was a somewhat risky form of entertainment. Indeed a few near misses did ensue.

These reservations aside, I liked the *après-ski* atmosphere. It was fun, and although I didn't actually take part I was aware that a few "late-night binges" were being enjoyed by some of the party.

On no occasion did I experience help in a patronising way. Out on the slopes, anyone who fell over and was able to get up again without assistance was left to do so. Jasper definitely had the right attitude: if I needed help he was there; if I could cope on my own he didn't interfere.

Each helper was given a half-day to spend as he or she wanted. I saw this as good organisation, allowing the helpers time to themselves which was well deserved, especially since they had not only given up their own time for this holiday, but also mostly paid their own way.

The journey home was very tiring, but went smoothly, with a high standard of service again from *P&O*. Despite the fact that I did not achieve as much as I would have liked to achieve on the ski slopes, the holiday was an enjoyable and worthwhile venture. The organisation and assistance throughout the trip were superb and I found very little fault with either.

One point about which I do feel strongly is the mixing of mentally and physically disabled people in one group. In my opinion this simply did not work, and I know that if I were to join another *USC* holiday group I would not wish mentally handicapped people to be in the party. Of course, I am aware that some may feel likewise about me . . .

And for the Non-skier

Joy Without Skis is reprinted with permission of The Sunday Times. Margaret Hides was given the brief to find out if a complete non-skier could enjoy a holiday in a ski resort.

At the ski jump I soar fearlessly into the void, body correctly angled, almost lying against my skis, landing a world record away. In international slalom I hold back; it seems churlish to relegate great champions to second place. If ever I take up ice-dance, Olympic title holders will have to look out: my soul dances the pairs competitions single-handed.

Only the fact that disability – congenital, not the result of a flamboyant skiing accident – leaves me with no hip movement and sticks to walk with, prevents the flesh joining in. But, like thousands of people who do not participate in winter sports, I love the vitality and the visual impact of the sun-and-snow scene brought to our TV screens.

Well, hallelujah, there has been dawning awareness of the existence of non-skiers as a revenue source over recent years. Much of the attention we have been getting so far, however, misses the point. We are not in the market for left-overs when the day's skiing is finished. All too often the amenities that are said to have the non-skier in mind are the *après-ski* kind – the disco, the fondue party, the wood-choppers' ball.

The genuine non-skier is not like the holidaymaker who has gone intending to ski and after a couple of days become fed up with the exertion and dropped out – although a surprisingly high proportion do just that. We are the people who for some reason cannot join in all the athletic pursuits, people who nevertheless value the invigorating winter life and perhaps would like to accompany family members on a winter sports holiday. The ambulatory disabled may be prepared to take gentle country walks. All of us enjoy something to watch: children practising on nursery slopes, curling, a skating rink. Everyone appreciates a café, and a bright inn with unrestricted access.

"Better to sacrifice romantic dreams of a beautiful tucked-away valley"

Touring Austria, Lichtenstein and Italy, looking at resorts and hotels in winter, I discovered that the answer to these needs is not simply to be found in taking advantage of a skiers' package deal, especially of the lower-priced kind which usually take holidaymakers to one unsophisticated little village centred almost entirely on skiing.

For us to choose a resort geared to one activity and go with the intention of opting out is bad economics. You get charming guesthouses, looking like cigarette boxes, run on the assumption that people will be out all day on the slopes, returning only for *après-ski*. No one there finds need to provide a comfortable chair to put on your wooden balcony overlooking the fun of the snow scene. A compact lounge is frequently part of a general complex of bar, pocket-hankerchief dance floor, and disco – not a place to relax with a book.

But persevere. There is unexpected enchantment for those of us new to this world. There is the sight of a frozen waterfall looking like pale blue wax congealed on the sides of a candlestick. There are deep crisscrossed ski tracks glittering in the sun on empty white slopes between avenues of grey-green firs. The clean icy touch of mountain air brushes your cheeks, and the smell of hot spiced *gluhwein* welcomes you in from the cold. There is the caress of featherdown as you snuggle, naked and glowing, under a duvet, with the windows thrown open in night temperatures below zero.

Better to sacrifice romantic dreams (I had them) of a beautiful tucked-away valley. It will be full of happy skiers with nowhere for you to go. Choose the bigger, popular resorts; the main objection to holidaying in a town (traffic noise) is hardly valid because most people go about on foot, skis slung over their shoulders. Do not choose a hotel up a side street, and if necessary be prepared to pay a little extra for a well-positioned room from which you can watch all that is going on. Make sure that there is somewhere to sit in your room other than a hard, high-backed chair.

Seefeld, the largest place I visited, was the one which gave me most pleasure. While companions were out on the slopes I was browsing among the bookshops, or sipping lemon tea, or carrying out exhaustive research into Austrian cream cakes. A town like this is big enough to have a little of everything going on around the centre, and to offer rides in horse-drawn sleighs. Snug under a great weight of furs, feeling like a princess from a Russian fairy tale, I went over the snows into still, deep forests of tall conifers . . . sleigh-bells jingling . . . the pungent smell of horse . . . our breath visibly hanging on the frost . . . walkers saying "Grüsse Gott" as I passed by. (But note: there is a limit to this costly pastime.)

Perhaps I have not yet found the ultimate in resorts and hotels, but I do believe that the Tyrol offers outstanding choices. If I have set you looking, and if you discover answers before I do, let me know!

AUSTRIA: TRAVEL NOTES

Sources of information

Austrian National Tourist Office, 30 St George Street, London W1R 0AL; ☎071/629 0461. The tourist office produces a few notes for the disabled traveller, a rather basic leaflet (*Mobil Spezial*) on accessibility of the sights in Vienna, and a list of hotels and pensions in Vienna which was compiled by the Austrian Round Table and requires great concentration from the non-German speaker. A request for £1 donation towards postage costs comes with the leaflets. However, the *ANTO* will help with specific enquiries concerning accommodation (see opposite page).

Other information is thin on the ground in the UK.

AUSTRIA: TRAVEL NOTES

Tour operators

If a "Flight of Fantasy", or the full return trip to Budapest, is out of your price range, you might be able to experience the *British Pullman* carriages (which take passengers to Folkestone on the first leg) by joining a day excursion (to Salisbury, Bristol, Bath or Kent) or one of the special journeys that run throughout the year (to the races, or to celebrate Valentine's Day, Midsummer Night, Mother's Day and other such occasions). For the full range of holidays, contact *Venice Simplon-Orient-Express Ltd* (Suite 200, Hudson's Place, Victoria Station, London SW1V 1JL; ☎071/928 6000).

The *Uphill Ski Club* (*USC*, 12 Park Crescent, London W1N 4EQ; ☎071/636 1989) is a charity committed to offering participation in winter sports to disabled people. Every year the club takes over 130 disabled people on winter sports holidays. It is also in the process of establishing local groups in Britain for year-round dry skiing.

In answer to Ron Cottrell's criticism, the *USC* brochure clearly states that a mix of physically and mentally handicapped skiers are amongst their membership, and all skiers are invited to a pre-holiday meeting so that they can get to know their party and discuss any problems. Furthermore, the organisers feel that one of the advantages of a mixed group is that people with different disabilities can help each other: for example, a mentally handicapped member might carry a physically handicapped member's skis. This does seem to be more in the spirit of "integration", that much sought-after goal, and since there is a waiting list to join these trips it seems to be a successful formula.

Another organiser of ski holidays (in the Alps and Norway) and dry-slope training is the *British Ski Club for the Disabled* (c/o Hubert Sturges, Springmount, Berwick St John, Shaftesbury, Dorset SP7 0HQ; ☎0747/88515).

Transport

Flying, driving or travelling by train should present few problems, although driving probably requires the least advance planning. There are accessible toilets, restaurant and coffee shop at Vienna airport. See *Practicalities* for advice on choosing Channel crossings and airlines.

Austrian Federal Railways (*OBB*, same address as the tourist office) use lightweight wheelchairs to lift disabled passengers onto the **train** and these are narrow enough to be used inside the carriages. This facility must be booked three days in advance, at any Austrian station or by phoning the disabled services unit (☎1/5800 35800). The *OBB*-appointed travel agents, for example *DER Travel Service* (18 Conduit Street, London W1R 0TD; ☎071/408 0111), can make arrangements but will charge for the service.

Accommodation

The *ANTO* will supply a selective hotel list for a particular province or major holiday resort, giving addresses of hotels in that area deemed suitable for disabled people. The cities of Vienna, Salzburg, Innsbruck and Graz publish their own guidebooks, containing access information and special hotel lists for the disabled visitor; these are distributed by the local city tourist boards and the use of symbols makes them useful to non-German speakers.

Access and facilities

Contributors with limited mobility, including those using wheelchairs and crutches, report that Salzburg, Vienna and Innsbruck are relatively easy to explore, in spite of the cobbled streets. The well-maintained roads and pavements are appreciated by the "pushers" and, in the countryside, walks are often clearly signposted with an indication of distance, time and difficulty.

It is encouraging to see that people with all sorts of disabilities can enjoy the facilities for winter sports, and that there is scope in the winter resorts for the non-skier as well as the skier.

More information from the London tourist office – a stock of the access guides that are available, and the inclusion of access details (suitably verified) in all accommodation guides along with some information on transport accessibility – would be appreciated.

Belgium

There is Nothing like a Nun

Jane Nyman uses a scooter wheelchair and has no qualms about travelling alone unless she is entrusted to British Rail, who despite warnings in advance always leave her stranded. For many years Jane has visited the city of Bruges, staying as a guest in the English Convent, and she is probably their only guest to have been banned from the chapel, not on account of bad behaviour but for her own safety. She had a bad fall on the stone floor; she did not know at the time that she was developing Parkinson's disease.

Some of my most hilarious holidays have been spent in convents; I have always found them to be full of laughter, perhaps because a good sense of humour is essential in order to cope with community life! The English Convent in Bruges was founded by a relative of Sir Thomas More, and at one time was a school. The nuns now run a guesthouse and have successfully converted the building to accommodate both handicapped and able-bodied guests. The accommodation is plain but pleasant, with both single and double rooms. There is a spacious lift, and toilets and shower which are accessible to wheelchairs. Portable ramps allow access to every part of the guesthouse.

The nuns accept groups of handicapped people, such as those organised by *The Across Trust* who bring their own helpers (and their "Jumbulance"), or individual guests provided that they are independent, or with someone who will help them. The food is plain but good, and the very reasonable prices include morning and afternoon coffee, so that it is possible to avoid spending money on snacks. On Sundays or feast days the nuns produce delicious flaky pastries and wine. Light Belgian beer is served with the main meals – I was faintly shocked to see respectable elderly ladies drinking beer, but tried it myself and found it very enjoyable.

The convent has a lovely garden; the guests can take chairs outside and it is very peaceful. I used to be puzzled in the early days to notice that when bad weather threatened, the Guest Mistress, normally a dignified soul, would run through the cloisters, plastic bag clutched in her hand. I later discovered that the nuns had planted a young magnolia, and the Guest Mistress was dashing out to put a plastic hat over its blossom to protect it from the rain!

There is a carillon in the city centre, and if you are energetic and can cope with a steep and slippery staircase you can climb up to see the bells, each bearing the name of the man who cast it and the date. This is a city of bells, and from a seat in the convent garden you can hear not only the carillon but also many other church bells; there is a continual background murmur of soft chimes.

One of the sisters is always on duty at the reception desk, ready to sell postcards and deal with any queries. I have learnt over the years that there is no finer "fixer" than a Roman Catholic nun. They beat the Mafia any time, and if they do not know the answers they'll find someone who does. I once travelled back to England with a 92-year-old nun, and I wanted to do some last-minute shopping on the way at the airport. She insisted on writing down all the prices, in case she needed the information at a later date!

What to buy? Every time I go to Bruges I buy chocolate. The Belgians make a delicious dark chocolate in bars which are reasonable in price. However, if you want something really special, ask for *fruits de mer* and you will receive beautiful green, white and brown chocolates in the shape of seashells.

Bruges, or Brugge, to give it its Flemish name, is one of the loveliest cities in Europe. It was built by the Count of Flanders in the ninth century as a defence against the Norse invaders. Standing on the Reie river, the city rapidly established itself as a centre for trade. In the thirteenth century it became very prosperous, and was famous for its weaving and manufacture of cloth. Its annual fair was the most important in Flanders. The banking community thrived and import businesses flourished: fabrics from the East, furs from Russia and the Balkans, metals from Hungary, Poland and Bohemia, wool, coal and cheese from Britain, fruit from Spain and Egypt, Arabian spices and Rhenish wines.

The city attracted famous artists, such as Jan Memling and Jan van Eyck, and produced fabulous tapestries. The canny burghers invested their money in buildings and solidly built houses, which they decorated with beautiful paintings. Town planning regulations are very strict in Bruges, and the buildings have been preserved or reconstructed perfectly. No modern buildings or industries exist within the boundaries of the city. The inhabitants are rightly proud of their city, and it is a common experience to see householders scrubbing the pavements outside their houses. Each house has immaculate white net curtains, drawn slightly back to display some treasure or potted plant. There are flowers everywhere.

Bruges is also renowned for its lace, and some of the houses carry small glass plaques depicting a woman making lace, to show that the craft is still practised there. In the area called the Beguinage, which is a collection of old almshouses, where respectable spinsters received sheltered accommodation in the past, there is a cluster of shops selling lace. When the weather is fine you can watch the lacemakers sitting outside, with their bobbins flying at breakneck speed.

"The important thing is that everybody tries to communicate"

Within 200m of the convent is an interesting lace school, the Kantcentrum, where there are superb examples of lace designs from the past and where the techniques of both traditional and modern lacemaking are taught. Still within the 200-metre radius is my favourite church, St Annekirche. Most of the churches in Bruges contain great paintings or other works of art, but their architecture is a hotchpotch of styles. The St Annekirche is the second church to be built on its site – the first was destroyed by fire. The result is a perfect example of the Baroque style, which contains the most beautiful woodcarvings.

Other museums further afield include the Groeninge (Museum of Fine Arts), Memling and Brangwijn museums. The Groeninge and Memling museums are wheelchair accessible. The Gruuthusemuseum does not have access for handicapped visitors – no wheelchairs in the fifteenth century! It is a burgher's palace containing a display of lace, woodcarving, old furniture and tapestry, as well as collections of musical instruments and flat and goffering irons, used to produce the perfectly starched lace collars and frills seen in the paintings of this period.

If your taste is for sitting and watching the world go by, there are plenty of seats on the canal towpath, also very close to the convent. The main canal is used for the transport of commercial goods, and the barges occasionally tie up to the bank, offering a fascinating glimpse of life for the family on board. There are lines of washing fluttering in the breeze and often a row of potted geraniums; the household pets are given an outing, and the children let loose to play.

For a different perspective of Bruges, take one of the canal trips from the centre, starting off with half an hour on the quiet backwaters before joining up with the main canal which encircles the city (if you are susceptible to mosquito bites, arm yourself with plenty of repellent). It is unlikely that you will be able to take a wheelchair on board because the boats have to be very small in order to pass under some of the bridges in the backwaters. I recommend abandoning the chair and requesting help with boarding. The Belgians are an eminently practical race, and never miss a chance to earn some money!

The city centre is called the Markt, and once a week there is a large, busy market, selling everything from food to clothes. Just a few yards away are the traditional and very colourful fish and flower markets, and down by the Beguinage a weekly market selling china, books, brass and bric-à-brac. Markets have been part of the way of life for the inhabitants of Bruges for centuries. Also in the Markt is a tourist office, where they speak a number of languages and dish out brochures and information on every conceivable subject with typical Belgian efficiency.

"The cobbles, though picturesque, make it hard to push wheelchairs"

Although Catholic, the English Convent accepts guests of any faith. Flemish is spoken in this area of Belgium, but the nuns are trilingual and speak English, French and Flemish. Because visitors come from all over Europe, some from outside Europe, the Masses are said in more than one language. It is not in the least unusual to find the priest preaching a sermon which begins in one language and ends in another. The Easter Vigil Mass – when I became a Catholic – was in French, Flemish and English, and I was so bemused that I forgot that my responses were supposed to be in English, and dried up. In typically practical fashion, an English nun came to my rescue. As I had not been able to decide who should be my sponsor from the many nuns I knew, it was agreed that one nun should represent the whole community, so I ended up with 36 godmothers, which beats the royal family!

At the dining table you are likely to hear at least four languages being spoken, but the important thing is that everybody tries to communicate, and even if you can only manage a "good morning" in French your efforts will be applauded. The nuns are of various nationalities and will always translate if you are having difficulty. It is sad that the same tolerance for language does not exist outside the convent.

How to get there? I have tried a number of routes. You can take a train from Victoria (always very crowded) which connects with the Channel ferry to Ostend. If you tire easily, book a cabin. The station is only yards away from the dock in Ostend, there are frequent trains to Bruges, and the complete journey takes about four hours. The station in Bruges is outside the city, so you will need a taxi. Other possibilities are to fly Gatwick–Ostend, then taxi to Bruges, or to fly to Brussels and take a train from there.

When travelling alone you can arrange for the Red Cross (helpful, but I find them pricey) to meet you and put you on the right boat, train or plane; you must arrange this well in advance, stating the exact nature of your disability and what kind of help you require. My experience of the Belgian Red Cross was that they were very pleasant and efficient, and I would use them again. If you travel by car, remember that Belgium did not introduce compulsory driving tests until quite recently, and driving can be hair-raising!

Bruges is a compact city: with the aid of a map you can cross it within an hour. It was not designed with the handicapped person in mind – the cobbles, though picturesque, make it hard to push wheelchairs – but there is an easy path following the main canal round the city, past windmills and the historic city gates. It is best to visit in the spring or early summer, when the blossom is out. Later in the season the city becomes very crowded, particularly in the centre, as coaches decant tourists from all over Europe, and the schools make it a focus for educational trips.

BELGIUM: TRAVEL NOTES

Sources of information

Belgian Tourist Office, 2 Gayton Road, Harrow, Middlesex HA1 2XU; ☎081/861 3300. Distributes a hotel guide which uses the wheelchair symbol to denote those suitable for handicapped guests, but there is no explanation of the criteria that must be satisfied in order to be awarded this symbol. The **provincial and city tourist offices** also use the wheelchair symbol in their brochures, so it's worth making these your first port of call. The *City Tourist Office* in Bruges (*Dienst voor Toerisme*, Burg 11, B-8000 Brugge; ☎50/44 86 86), for example, indicates accessible hotels and restaurants, in its brochure, *Brugge 1991* (again, no criteria given); toilets for the disabled are marked on the city map. The art gallery and museum guide for the West Flanders region (in four languages, including English) classifies buildings as inaccessible, partially accessible and fully accessible to wheelchair users.

Belgian Red Cross (*Croix Rouge de Belgique*, rue Joseph Stallaert 1 – Bte 8, B-1060 Brussels; ☎2/647 1010) gives general advice, gleaned from a number of access guides, and offers the usual escort service.

Mobility International Flanders (*MI Vlaanderen*), Douglaslaan 20, B-2190 Essen; ☎3/667 4025. In the process of building up a databank of information on accessible holidays in Belgium and the rest of Europe which should be a useful source; they would also be pleased to receive access information for the databank. As well as exchange of information, a house-exchange project for disabled people is in the embryo stage (more contacts needed).

Transport

North Sea Ferries operate from Hull into Zeebrugge and have adapted cabins on each of their ships. *P&O*, generally well equipped for wheelchair passengers, sail the Dover–Ostend and Dover/Felixstowe–Zeebrugge routes; there

BELGIUM: TRAVEL NOTES

are no accessible toilets on ships sailing between Dover and Ostend (see *Practicalities*), but there are facilities at all ports. *P&O* offer passenger-only fares for disabled drivers (*DDMC* or *DDA* members) in adapted or automatic cars; *North Sea Ferries* give a fifty percent discount on car rates.

The **train** journey from London to Bruges, via Dover and Ostend, is swift and assistance at ports or stations can be arranged. *Belgian National Railways* (*SNCB*, 177 Regent Street, London W1R 7FB; ☎071/233 0360) can supply a list of Belgian stations and are happy to arrange assistance at the ones you want to use. Most trains have wide doors and lowered steps, and wheelchairs are available at many stations.

Full facilities at main **airports** and short journey times make flying an attractive option, but it's not cheap, and a car is useful for getting around once there.

Reserved **parking** places for disabled drivers are indicated by the usual blue and white "P" sign with additional wheelchair symbol. Usually you won't have to pay at meters. Orange Badge holders can park without time limit in restricted-time parking zones. Contact the *RAC de Belgique* (rue d'Arlon 53, B-1040 Brussels; ☎2/230 08 10) for more information about driving in Belgium.

Accommodation

For general information try the tourist office publications, and consult the *RADAR* holiday guide. Jane Nyman recommends The English Convent (Carmersstraat 85, B-8000 Brugge; ☎50/33 24 24): write to the Guest Mistress for information and bookings.

Access and facilities

There seems to be a lively access movement in Belgium, but similar problems to those still to be overcome in the UK: limited access to public transport, narrow choice of accessible accommodation in the lower price brackets, generally poor provision of access in eating places.

Access to tourist attractions is reasonably good, and although there is an air of defeatism where older buildings are concerned (if it was built in the fifteenth century it's not wheelchair accessible and that's that), it's heartening to see the use of the wheelchair symbol in so many tourist brochures, and to see the release of a new, free guide (see *Books*), produced with input from the *Action Group for a Better Accessibility for Handicapped People*.

Books

Guide Touristique et des Loisirs à l'usage des personnes à mobilité réduite (free from Ministère de la Communauté française, Direction générale des Affaires sociales, Manhattan Centre, rue des Croisades, 3-1210 Brussels) lists hotels, restaurants and tourist attractions throughout Belgium, and uses symbols to indicate accessibility. It classifies properties as accessible to wheelchair users with or without assistance, or to those who can walk but with difficulty; it also covers parking, access to lifts and toilets, facilities for visually handicapped and hearing-impaired visitors.

The Michelin Guide to Benelux indicates accessible accommodation in Belgium, the Netherlands and Luxembourg.

The Netherlands

Put your Money on a Good Hotel

Philippa Thomas is wheelchair bound, although she can manage on crutches for short distances. She also has a less visible disability – epilepsy. In February 1989 she took her first break, a long weekend in Amsterdam.

She's on the phone – Tamsin, my daughter – cheering me up as usual, encouraging me to come out into the world after this long time imprisoned by my immobile body (well, immobile legs). In fact, since November 1988 I've been peripatetic – I borrowed the money and bought a bike, a "booster-type scooter wheelchair".

"Nice to see you out and about: it must be lovely to do your own shopping; glad you're feeling better."

Bloody liars, I think, smiling: don't they realise I'm not, and not going to be better. Smile again, Philippa, you might need their help. "I know, it's absolutely wonderful to be able to do my shopping." May the ground open and swallow me up.

So, she's on the phone again: "Mother, book the tickets, Amsterdam, half term" (she's a teacher), "write it down, February 16th to 19th, home Monday, *book the tickets*." Money and Larkin come to mind:

> *Quarterly, is it, money reproaches me:*
> *Why do you let me lie here wastefully?*
> *I am all you never had ...*
> (Philip Larkin: "Money")

It's a major feat arriving at *Lewes Travel*, perched as it is at the top of Station Street, not to mention negotiating my way on crutches to the counter. Never booked a holiday in my life: we used to get in the car and go somewhere, before the illness, before the divorce. Leave the bike where the girl can see it, good for the image.

First decision: don't mention the epilepsy. "Amsterdam, long weekend, cheap as possible, me and my daughter." She looks at me – a pretty girl, with youth in her eyes – and smiles and selects some leaflets. "Put all your money on a good hotel," she advises. "If it's central you'll save, be able to walk everywhere ... well, ride, I mean ... and there's the fire risk you know ... wheelchair symbol." She smiles again and looks down, then picks up the phone.

Back home, safe and warm; Christ, what am I doing, how the hell do I get to London, let alone Amsterdam? Slowly the pieces fit together: bike to the station, ramp to the train, Carelink from Victoria to Liverpool Street, Tamsin will meet me . . .

And there she is, smiling, and here I am on the bike, knapsack and battery charger in the basket, mohair rug strapped behind me – off to Harwich surrounded by rush-hour London. We've booked second-class seats, but *British Rail* put us in first class so that I can transfer easily from luggage van to seat. The train gains speed and the journey begins.

"I transfer to my seat: it's going to be bloody uncomfortable despite the reclining positions"

Sealink meet us at Harwich – takes a bit of time because naturally they were looking for us where we'd booked and not where we'd been put. Suddenly Tamsin's gone, and strange men guide me across the wharf to the boat. It's so huge, and in the dark the smell of diesel oil and the black glistening ropes are a magic world. The air is wet and windy and I feel like a child again – "Little Tim and the Brave Sea Captain", and images of herrings and the northern sea. I drive on board where the lorries are loaded and a lift takes me to the deck. Our reclining seats are booked and through the window I can see shining stars. Above the bustle of the ship I hear the sound of waves.

Tamsin arrives with our passports, and checks emergency exits. I transfer to my seat: it's going to be bloody uncomfortable despite the reclining positions. I realise that somehow I am going to have to sleep on the floor, the problem being how to get there. Eventually, after pain-killers and sleeping tablets, I manage.

In the morning, the *Sealink* staff arrive to collect us and the ramp, to be loaded on the Dutch train heading for Amsterdam. The train, similar to our underground trains, is crowded and the bike takes up a lot of room. Still, everyone smiles and is nice, but I'm glad I've got my money belt and passport well hidden. I should have mugged up basic Dutch "Help" words and written them on cards. The train loos look pretty impossible too.

We arrive in Amsterdam just after 9am. It's raining, Lewes is somewhere in the past and Amsterdam is not what I'd expected; it's small, and there are trams and canals everywhere. We stroll the short distance to the hotel and pass through automatic plate glass doors onto the poshest, plushest carpets, in a foyer spangled with jewellery display cases containing diamonds, exotic plants and an amazing clock showing the time in London, Zurich, San Francisco and here. On the reception desk is a gigantic brandy glass filled with squares of chocolate for the taking, and no one, absolutely no one, minds me.

We are shown immediately to the lift and to our room, which is soft silvery blue and white with a veritable wall of louvred cupboards, a secret mini-bar and fridge, comfortable chairs, TV and writing desk. Then the bathroom: a wall of mirrored dressing table, piles of fluffy white towels, and the goodies – shower cap, bath gel, soap, mending kit. You name it, they've got it, and room service can supply anything else. Prefer a duvet? Naturally. Non-slip bath mat? In an instant, and with everything delightful squares of chocolate.

We plug the bike in to recharge, have hot showers and a rapid sleep, after which I am strong enough to face the rain and a canal trip. It is *so* pretty – the tall narrow houses, the shape of the gabled roofs against the skyline, and the soft romantic colours. Negotiating my way onto the covered barge was difficult, admittedly, and the thought that I cannot swim did cross my mind, but the trip is lovely. My daughter, who teaches art, is already sketching details of bridges and waterways; it *is* romantic.

That night we slept well, and after a traditional Dutch breakfast we visited the Rijksmuseum. The early Flemish paintings are enchanting, but best of all, amongst the fourteenth-century majolica, I find a plate depicting an absolutely furious Madonna scowling at the Christ Child who holds an apple in his hand.

On the way home we discover the flower market, just a street by a canal. The stalls contained not the boxed hothouse flowers I had imagined, but interesting structural forms: huge bunches of magnolia in bud, and branches of alder and birch. Because it is Amsterdam and February, we fill the basket of the bike with white tulips to bring home – plastic but very traditional!

On Sunday it's raining and we are going to meet Gary, Tamsin's boyfriend. The itinerary is Van Gogh, with the added bonus of a special Millet exhibition. I focus on Van Gogh's use of colour and see the reflection of his growing madness. Gary and his students join us, with terrible tales of their hotel: burst pipes, double bookings and inadequate heating. We were obviously well advised. Soon we are back in our hotel in time to pack, recharge the bike and rest before leaving.

On the spur of the moment, we both say "Diamonds!" and the porter arranges a taxi to one of the diamond factories where we can see them cut and polished. On the way we see the Jewish synagogue and a page of a diary with spidery writing in blue-black ink,

indecipherable – Anne Frank – a pressed flower, a violet, floats into my mind. I look at my daughter: "We shall have to come back again." She smiles, knows my identifications, and we go on to the factory, which is full of wealthy Japanese tourists.

We are treated as if we too are wealthy. In a locked room we are shown diamonds of incredible value and taught the difference between carat and colours. Shut in the strongroom with only the jeweller, watching him talk to my daughter of stones and settings and gems, I think of that other daughter and her writing, glimpsed and remembered, and how she and I would have shared a star, though of different colours.

Time to go home, time to go home, and the boat looms out of the darkness. *Sealink* are there to meet us, me on my bike and loaded with tulips. Tamsin goes through customs, then the man from *Sealink* smiles and shows us to a cabin: "Compliments of the Captain". My heart is warmed by the kindness.

Harwich, Liverpool Street, Victoria, Lewes and home. The castle is still here, the cats have been fed and the papers are waiting; no chocolate though. Next day, I meet someone I haven't seen for ages. "This is wonderful," she says, looking at my bike. "It must be lovely to do your own shopping again."

"Super," I say, with a ring of sincerity, "couldn't be without it."

Falling for the Countryside

Barry Atkinson has been to the Netherlands three times, the visits spanning a time of coping with a relentlessly progressive disease. In 1983, although using a wheelchair a lot, he was able to walk a little with crutches; by 1990 he was wheelchair-bound and, although able to transfer to toilet, bed and car, his balance had become very bad.

I first went to the Kingdom of Netherlands simply because it was there, close at hand and an unknown quantity. There was no burning ambition to visit the country, just a mild interest. Yet now I have been three times and expect to go again. I remain undecided as to the exact nature of its appeal, and find myself confused by a conflict of good and bad points.

The Netherlands are busy, full of life and colour, often beautiful in an unadventurous sort of way. The people are refreshingly matter-of-fact and extremely hospitable. But, at the same time, I find that their affluence leads to an unattractive smugness. There is also a disconcerting air of insularity which, although understandable in a small land, is not always easy to tolerate.

My introduction to the lowlands was in 1983, on a brief trip with my mother to see the tulip fields. Then, in July 1985, I spent three weeks under canvas at Ockenburgh in Den Haag with a Dutch work-camp. I went through the International Voluntary Service and was the only disabled participant. We travelled each day through Den Haag by bus and tram to Scheveningen, where we worked at Sparring, a day centre for disabled people. My return during the heatwave of 1990 was to revisit Sparring and to stay with friends.

"Even the disabled often thought they were receiving too much"

I can only claim to have any knowledge of the Netherlands south of Amsterdam, mainly Den Haag, Rijswijk and the seaside resort of Scheveningen. It is the industry and commerce of the small, overpopulated country (over 14,300,000 in less than 34,000 square kilometres) that has usually surrounded me, but this was least apparent when with Erik and Tonny at Rijswijk. The town is situated on the southeast of Den Haag and their flat is on the southern edge. When I had a night free of the work-camp in 1985 I stayed with them; at that time their

balcony overlooked peaceful, flat fields where horses grazed. By 1990 another line of houses had been built; the fields are still behind these, but my friends' balcony now stares at a busy road and at other people trying to lead private lives. It's a common enough story today, but none the easier to cope with for that.

Erik suffers from multiple sclerosis. The well-adapted flat made life much easier for me and, together with facts gleaned at Sparring, gave me an insight into the benefits available to disabled people in the Netherlands. In 1990 I noticed a change: 1985 was rich bonanza time – even the disabled often thought they were receiving too much! Monetary benefits were high and relatively easy to procure. Adapted cars were free and readily available. But by 1990, with much of the world finding finance tighter, I found the Dutch disabled less happy. They are "feeling the pinch", like everyone else.

However, unlike the English, they are given powered wheelchairs for outdoor use, usually of the most expensive type and extremely comfortable. That said, bureaucracy causes problems in the Netherlands as everywhere else: an aquaintance of mine had moved house, and the much-needed work on his necessary power-chair was not being done because the paperwork was not right.

Erik and I went into the fields at Rijswijk, he often pushing my self-propelled chair (I have a motorised wheelchair but it's not so easy to transport on the plane) from his sleek power-chair. There are bicycle paths (*fietspaden*) beside the roads in any busy area, and of course the country is mostly flat, so the going is relatively easy.

We left the houses and took a quiet, brick lane past the crematorium to a little bridge, crossing the gentle waterway which runs to nearby Delft. Cyclists rattled across the timbers of the bridge, heading up and down the lane which passed through the flat, open meadows and between glass-houses full of tomato plants. We could see the church of Wateringen between lines of poplars. We sat there for a while. The sun was warm and a herd of fly-bothered cows stood under the bridge. A soft breeze swayed the reeds and willow-herb. The water was still, with patches of duckweed and white flowering water lilies. We followed the waterway towpath for a while, passing a renovated windmill. It was the Netherlands at their best, pleasing to the eye and the opposite side of the coin to the world of modern business.

"The towns and villages are too clean and perfect for my taste"

About this time, I was also taken to Friesland, the northern part of the country which, rather like Scotland, sees itself as individual and independent, with some justification. From Amsterdam we drove into West Friesland and took the road across Ijsselmeer to the main body of Friesland. The crossing of the water-way is spectacular. To our left, hidden by the rise of the dike, lay the North Sea (more exactly, the Waddenzee, which stands between the mainland and the Frisian Islands). To the right was the broad expanse of the freshwater *meer*. Wildfowl swam at the edge, hard to identify from a speeding car but I saw mute swan, coot and grebe aplenty, and thought I saw pochard and scaup. Small boats sailed and fishing nets stretched across poles. At the end of the dike was a busy canal for the boats to pass between salt and fresh water.

We came to Sneek, in its lush agri-cultural setting, the countryside far less built up than the south and with even more waterways. With its perhaps too studied atmosphere of gaiety, Sneek is justly famed as a boating centre. It is also well known for its sports facilities for handicapped people. We visited the house of my companion's friend to

drink coffee. Like all the Dutch houses I have been in, it was compact, pristine and overflowing with plants, cut flowers and great cacti. It is as though every-one agrees that the country will be extended by a national effort of nurture! But, attractive and original though they undoubtedly are, the towns and villages are too clean and perfect for my taste. It was the exposed, uncluttered landscape which appealed to me.

Our return to the south was via the reclaimed fields of the Noord-Oost Polder and Flevoland. A livid sunset bordered the black clouds of an approaching storm. We drove through Amsterdam in torrential rain, the normally busy Dam cowed and deserted. The built-up south was decid-edly unwelcoming.

I spent ten days of my 1990 stay alone in a Den Haag apartment. A worker at Sparring had offered me the use of his home while he was away. Pleased to avoid the expense of a hotel, and preferring to be alone anyway, I gladly accepted. It was, however, not all easy. There were no steps, but lips at every doorway forced me to enter every room backwards. The owner had thoughtfully placed little ramps on the steeper lips, but it was the narrow corri-dors, just wide enough for a wheel-chair, that almost defeated me. These ran from the front door to the living room and from there to the bedroom. I had to travel the latter corridor back-wards, and I was not entirely successful in my efforts to avoid scraping the walls. I could not get into the shower, and the toilet was difficult.

There were, of course, good points. On four days I was collected by the Sparring transport and taken to spend the day with them. Erik and Tonny came to see me. Ans (from Sparring) took me shopping and generally kept in touch to see that all was well. She also watered the many plants! The apart-ment was situated on the fairly gentle Loosduinsekade which, despite the passing of trams and traffic, and a motorcycle shop next door, had many a quiet lull. I used to sit on the wide pavement in front of the *fietspad*, or in the tiny back garden in the shade of a sycamore tree. It would not have been possible for too long, nor without the help around me (more truthfully, it would not have been worth the effort), but I decided to stay put. I either showered at Sparring or washed at the kitchen sink.

On my next visit I hope to stay at the fully adapted *Hotel Restaurant Vredebest*, 200m from the sea at Wemeldinge (listed in the *RADAR* guide). The uniform flatness of the terrain, together with slightly better facilities and greater awareness than in England, make the Netherlands one of the easiest countries in Europe for a disabled visitor.

THE NETHERLANDS: TRAVEL NOTES

Much of the information included here was supplied by Jeanette Huber, who offers this opinion: "Because of its almost fanatical nationwide organisation, its outstanding facilities for the handicapped, and the generally good-natured and caring people, the Netherlands must be the most welcoming country for the disabled visitor." Another contributor, James Franey, says of Amsterdam, "Very civilised. Where else could one find a disabled driver's parking space unoccupied even in Damrak – Amsterdam's version of Oxford Street."

Sources of information

Netherlands Board of Tourism, 25–28 Buckingham Gate, London SW1E 6LD; ☎071/630 0451. Their booklet, *The Handicapped*, lists accessible accommodation (including campsites and caravans), restaurants, petrol stations, tourist attractions, animal parks, museums and pleasure boats. Many of these have been awarded the wheelchair symbol by *De Gehandicaptenraad* (The Handicapped Organization, 3500 AD Utrecht; ☎30/313454), indicating that they are accessible to unaccompanied wheelchair users; those without the symbol have adapted toilets, lifts or other facilities which render them suitable for accompanied wheelchair users or slightly more mobile travellers. There is, as ever, the rider that handicapped visitors are advised to confirm that facilities meet their own specific requirements by letter or phone call. But the booklet is nicely laid out, easy to use and free.

Getting there

KLM Royal Dutch Airlines get some bad press from John Bignell, who flew with them via Schiphol airport (Amsterdam) on his way to Africa (see p.277), but Schiphol otherwise has a good reputation, and Barry Atkinson recommends **flying** in general. Rotterdam airport is small and ideal for a wheelchair user. He took a forty-minute flight from Heathrow to Rotterdam (£89 return), preferring it to the seven-hour *Sealink Stena Line* **ferry crossing** from Harwich to The Hook (£26 each way for a stay of more than five days), even though he could have booked a fully adapted double cabin, with *en suite* toilet, for £15. According to Philippa Thomas (who received charming service from *Sealink*), a cabin is pretty well essential for any degree of comfort on the ferry.

Olau-Line sail from Sheerness to Vlissingen (Flushing) in eight hours; *North Sea Ferries* take ten hours from Hull to Rotterdam. Both offer fully accessible ships and specially adapted cabins (on *North Sea Ferries* that includes drop-down seat in the shower, low-level washbasin and alarm button as well as the usual wide doors and adapted toilet) which should be reserved well in advance. *Olau* give free passage to cars, *North Sea* offer fifty percent discount to disabled passengers (see *Practicalities*, "By Sea"). There are wheelchair-accessible toilets at Harwich, Hull, Sheerness, Rotterdam and Vlissingen, but not The Hook.

Transport

By using the **bike paths** a motorised wheelchair user could, if well protected from the weather, travel all over the country, preferably accompanied by a friend on a bike (or in another wheelchair). But check with the ANWB (see below) for local restrictions. You should always be prepared for dour weather: most of the bike paths are tree-lined or in some way protected from crosswinds, but winter winds can be very cold; check the weather forecast before venturing far from town. Seven railway stations rent out **tandem bicycles** for use by the handicapped traveller with escort.

If you can use **public transport** it is efficient, clean and cheap; a taxi will only be necessary in truly remote areas. In Barry Atkinson's experience, taxi drivers and staff on public transport are extremely helpful. Assistance at railway stations is made available if notice is given before noon on the day before travelling (☎30/331253, Mon–Fri 8am–4pm). *Nederlandse Spoorwegen* (*Dutch Railways*) publishes a timetable in Braille, and special booklets for the disabled traveller: *Gehandicapten op reis met de trein* and *Fiets en spoor*. These and other information on rail travel for handicapped passengers are available from *Nederlandse Spoorwegen* (Dienst van Exploitatie, Afdeling 3, Assisentieverlening Gehandicapten, Postbus 2025, 3500 HA Utrecht).

John Bignell describes his attempt to travel by train from Schiphol airport to the centre of Amsterdam in 1988:

"There is a lift from ground level down to the platform. The train had sliding doors but with a central pillar. This meant that my chair had to be collapsed to get it onto the train. The other passengers were most helpful but they had great problems with the chair. It is much easier to show people how to deal with the chair and then to get on the train, rather than get on first and then give instructions!

There is a steep ramp at the Dam Square exit, Centraal Station. Here I discovered the significance of my chair's tendency to turn to the right despite an even application of power to both wheels. Every time I took a run at the ramp, I got halfway up, then the chair slewed to the right. The incline took over and I swung right round to point downhill. After a couple of attempts I gave up. I hailed the first fit-looking person I saw and, with a cheery grin, he soon had me at the top."

The tourist board booklet, *The Handicapped*, states that the Amsterdam metro is accessible to wheelchair users with normal arm function, but since most of the metro stations are in the suburbs this is not much help for exploring central Amsterdam. The trams and buses are inaccessible, so the alternatives are motorised chair, taxi, boat trips on the canals, or hired car.

Disabled drivers may **park** indefinitely in blue zones or places with time restrictions, in special reserved spaces, and for two hours in no-waiting zones if there are no parking facilities nearby.

The **ANWB** (*Algemene Nederlandse Wielrijdersbond*) is the *Royal Dutch Touring Association* (Postbus 93200, 2509 BA Den Haag; ☎70/3147147), similar to the British *AA*, but offering more than just mechanical assistance with your car. Membership may not be necessary in order to fulfil your needs. Maps, information and special parking permits, as well as an outstanding emergency rescue service, make the ANWB an essential contact for anyone travelling by car (or using the cycle routes). Help is also offered for trips to neighbouring countries. Every town of any size has an ANWB office, but the larger offices in Amsterdam, Den Haag, Rotterdam, Utrecht or Maastricht carry information on the surrounding areas. You will find the listing in the telephone book under ANWB.

Accommodation

Hotels may pose problems. Many Dutch inns and hotels are old, narrow, town houses without lifts. However, every village in the Netherlands is represented by an information office, or **VVV** (pronounced "vey, vey, vey" – which stands for *Vereniging voor Vreemdelingenverkeer*), and most of these have hotel lists and should be able to help you find (and reserve) accessible accommodation. You

THE NETHERLANDS: TRAVEL NOTES

will find telephone numbers of these offices in all local telephone books: look for *VVV*. Most offices have English-speaking helpers. They will cheerfully give you all kinds of information – maps, museum guides, opening times, restaurant guides, where to get a wheel repaired, anything! *VVV* offices in Amsterdam are outside Centraal Station and at Leidsestraat 106; both are accessible.

Philippa Thomas recommends the peaceful *Ascot Hotel* (Damstraat 95–98, 1012 LP Amsterdam; ☎20/260066), which she booked through *Time Off Ltd*. There is a disabled person's room with wheelchair-accessible shower room and adjoining single room suitable for carer (or parents plus child). The staff were extremely courteous, and there were no problems with lift access or with leaving the scooter wheelchair in the breakfast room!

Many **campsites** have special features to tempt the *rolstoelgebruiker* (wheelchair user). Information can be obtained from *Stichting Nederlandse Jeugdherberg Centrale* (Prof Tulpplein 4, 118 GX Amsterdam). See also the tourist board booklet *The Handicapped* for the address to write to for the hire of an adapted camper van and folding trailer-vans.

Access and facilities

Jeanette Huber found that only the interiors of windmills and some castles were inaccessible. Most museums welcome and do not charge for visitors in wheelchairs, and some museums and castles have separate entrances and special routes inside for wheelchairs. In the northeastern province of Drenthe lies a perfect example of the accessible tourist attraction. The **museum village of Orvelte** (run by the Orvelte Foundation, Dorpsstraat 3, 9441 PD Orvelte; ☎5934/335), won the *European Year of Tourism 1990* award for providing the best tourism facilities for disabled people in Europe. The village shows rural life of the 1800s, and there are demonstrations of old trades and

customs throughout the year. The buildings include a working mill, sweet shop, smithy, clog workshop, sawmill and cheese factory: all are wheelchair accessible, and stairlifts have been installed in the few buildings that need them. There are wheelchairs available at the entrance, and a cassette tape, plus signposts with raised numbers and Braille marking, for visually handicapped visitors. Orvelte gives employment to many disabled people, including those with learning difficulties and mental handicaps.

Theatres make arrangements when notified in advance; for example, if requested a day ahead, or when tickets are booked, the Muziektheater in Amsterdam offers free use of a wheelchair which will be brought by an attendant to the car park upon your arrival.

The Dutch pioneered the use of **sheltered workshops**, and there are more than 200 scattered throughout the country. In an area called *Het Dorp* (the village), near Arnhem, most of the residents are severely handicapped and confined to wheelchairs. The village was built using funds raised during a 24-hour TV show, and has become an international showplace. The main street is heated and covered by glass. The residents administer the village. They are often seen riding their wheelchairs along the country roads surrounding the nearby Openluchtmuseum, a park covering almost a hundred acres showing how agricultural workers have lived over the centuries.

Books

The Michelin Guide to Benelux uses the wheelchair symbol to indicate accessible accommodation in the Netherlands, Belgium and Luxembourg.

A Travellers' Handbook for Persons with Epilepsy is available from the *International Bureau for Epilepsy* (PO Box 21, 2100 AA Heemstede; ☎23/339 060) and supplies information on over fifty countries.

Scandinavia

Sweden under Scrutiny

Charlotte Billington, who has cerebral palsy, took part in a Project Phoenix Trust Study Tour, a fact-finding trip to Sweden, in August 1984. The group set out to observe the country's much admired state welfare system, particularly in relation to its services for the disabled population, and to tackle a self-catering holiday in a specially adapted chalet-style farmhouse.

Our group was made up of thirteen able-bodied and ten disabled people, all confined to wheelchairs, with various disabilities including multiple sclerosis, cerebral palsy and spina bifida. Nearly all members provided their own funding but *Project Phoenix* does supply a small donation in cases of extreme hardship.

I chose to travel this way because, having been on a couple of these tours in the past, I knew that I would end up with more than just a collection of blurred snapshots and I would enjoy sharing and discussing our experiences with the rest of the group. Disadvantages are that you cannot expect to have much time to yourself, and that a gruelling timetable has to be maintained if all the goals of the holiday are to be achieved. A fair degree of physical stamina is required, as the general rule is demanding: very late to bed and up very early the next morning. Anyone requiring a great deal of nursing, or injections on a regular basis, would not find these trips suitable.

However, great care is taken to ensure that the people chosen for the trip are fit enough to cope with the strains of travelling. The Trust's board of directors also do their utmost to avoid personality clashes in each group, but everyone is expected to take the rough with the smooth. However well planned and streamlined things may look on paper, no one can predict the minor hiccups which inevitably occur.

We travelled from London to Sweden in a "Jumbulance", loaned to us by *The Across Trust*. It had eight berths, sixteen seats, a small galley where simple drinks and meals were prepared, and a chemical toilet. A rota was worked out to ensure that all the disabled members of the group had a six-hour rest period while the helpers had three hours wherever possible, but inevitably plans do go awry. None of us got much sleep on that 26-hour journey, so we were all shattered by the time we arrived outside the farmhouse near Falkenberg, a small fishing port on the southwest coast of Sweden.

Sunday, our first full day, brought the local media out. They wrote up the piece with great enthusiasm – it seemed that taking groups of disabled people abroad on holiday was new to them. We were local celebrities, and Falkenberg even ran up the Union Jack in our honour. We were taken on a guided tour of the town, with its tiny cobbled streets and quaint fishermen's cottages. The most interesting aspect was the Lutheran church, which was very plain and simple but had a fishing boat suspended from the middle of the ceiling.

"A spectacular four-hour lunch which included cold fresh salmon among its many courses"

We ended the day with a visit to an example of *Fokus* (cluster housing), which aims to enable disabled people in the area to live an independent life within the community. It was very impressive, with all the latest facilities, and the residents had their own apartments and were free to come and go as they pleased. But we detected overtones of a "ghetto" mentality in both residents and staff, which we came across again later in our stay, at another residential centre on the outskirts of Lund and at the largest leisure and holiday resort in Sweden, in Malmö. Although admirable in many ways, the resort appeared to be no more than a luxurious ghetto for the disabled, and the thought of a holiday there made most of us shudder.

In the light of these visits, I felt that the Swedes, for all their talk of freedom and rights for everyone, only want integration on the able-bodied majority's terms. We saw another example of their "caring" policy being dished out a little too efficiently for comfort when our Swedish hosts presented a slide show of a young girl called Maria. She was ten years old, very severely disabled by cerebral palsy, and had to rely on 24-hour care. A photographic record was being kept of her progress throughout her life. Every conceivable picture had been taken from every possible angle to chronicle her life from infancy to early puberty, including school and leisure activities. As we watched, the images blurred and the poor girl was reduced to the level of a performing animal in a cage. All this was to demonstrate the thorough workings of the welfare system.

On the plus side, a powerful political lobby of disabled people ensures that disability issues are not ignored in the Swedish parliament. A disabled child is sent to a mainstream school if he or she can manage it, and is provided with all the necessary aids. Otherwise, the special schools supply first-class education and exercise routines, as well as training in social skills for adult life. No employer is allowed to discriminate on the basis of disability, so that everyone gets a fair crack of the whip when applying for a job. The average able-bodied Swede treats his or her disabled counterpart as just another member of society and we encountered no prejudice during our stay.

We visited the equipment centre in Halmstad, Falkenberg's nearest large town, and spoke to the therapists and technicians about the aids and facilities that they provide for disabled clients in the area. We were so impressed by the fantastic electric wheelchairs and the bathroom and kitchen gadgetry (all supplied free) that we stayed longer than we had anticipated. After a picnic lunch and some shopping we drove to Hyltbruk for a barbecue laid on by one of the Swedish organisers of the trip at her lakeside farm. In the middle of a clearing in a pine forest stood a palatial chalet; a private beach, fishing boat and well-stocked lake were part of the estate. While some of the non-swimmers stayed at the chalet to help prepare the food for the barbecue, most of the group trundled down in their wheelchairs through the thicket to the edge of the lake, where some dabbled their toes and those who could walk paddled about in the cool, clear water.

"He treated us like visiting heads of state"

Southeast Småland is known locally as *Glasriket* (Glass Kingdom), and we were up early in order to reach the Kosta Boda glassworks by midday. Venetian craftsmen came to Sweden in the sixteenth century, but the glass industry was established by German immigrants in the eighteenth century. Surrounded by thick forests (providing fuel), the glassworks attract thousands of visitors each year. We watched the craftsmen at work and then picked up some remarkable bargains among the "seconds" in the large shops nearby.

In Gothenberg we inspected another well-equipped centre for the disabled, then visited the famous Liseburg Park – the biggest amusement park in Scandinavia. Here, amongst the beautifully kept gardens, you can find all the fun of the fair if that is your wish. It wasn't mine, so my helper and I went in search of a reasonably priced meal in one of the numerous cafés dotted about the fairground.

The longest and perhaps most tiring day of the trip began with breakfast on the Jumbulance at 8am, the beautiful scenery of Skåne rushing by as we munched our cornflakes. We arrived at an old monastery in time for a spectacular four-hour lunch which included cold fresh salmon among its many courses. There were speeches from our hosts and from various members of our group, after which there was just time for a quick stroll around the grounds, taking in a magnificent view of the nearby lake, before driving to our next port of call – a millionaire's stud farm.

Our host for this next stop was a jolly man in his seventies who has donated a substantial part of his fortune to cancer research, and used another sizeable chunk to purchase some of the finest Arab stallions in the world of which he was justifiably proud. He treated us like visiting heads of state: a row of chairs had been set out in front of the yard, and while we watched these superb creatures being put through their paces we were served ice cream and Campari and sodas by a band of waiters and waitresses who silently materialised at our sides. Now we know what it must be like for royalty – heaven! Our host insisted that we see the latest new-born foals, which meant some nifty manoeuvring of the Jumbulance down a narrow lane to another part of the estate, but it was worth the hassle – they were adorable!

From the stud farm we travelled to Lund, a medieval cathedral and university town, for dinner at the residential centre for the disabled. We were running an hour late, and our hosts had become a little agitated by our lack of punctuality (Swedes are sticklers for protocol and thoroughness). Although they were eager to get us into the dining room, a couple of people in our group managed to take advantage of the centre's swimming pool before dinner. Soon we were all seated around the pool, chatting about the day's events, and we arrived back at our farmhouse well after midnight.

"The fact that we had to clean up, pack and leave on the next day did not stop us carrying on into the small hours"

Our last day in Sweden gave us the opportunity for shopping in Halmstad, but before we were let loose to buy souvenirs and food for our Last Night Party, we visited the ambulance depot, and a few of us went on to visit the local hospital. Shopping spree over, we returned to the farmhouse to prepare our farewell feast, a token of thanks to our hosts for their generosity and kindness in making our first self-catering holiday such a success. There was enough food to feed the population of southern Sweden and much of it unfortunately went to waste, but apart from that everyone seemed to have a good time. The outside of the farmhouse was tricked out with coloured streamers and flags, making a festive backdrop for the group of folk dancers who came to entertain us. The fact that we had to clean up, pack and leave on the next day did not stop us carrying on into the small hours.

The aims of the trip were achieved with only a few minor hitches – mainly timing; an overnight stay would be incorporated on the next visit, as the journeys there and back proved too tiring to be completed in a day. Both sides were given food for thought: the Swedes might think more positively about organising group holidays abroad; we would take home some of their general attitudes towards disabled people, concerning education and employment. And we all learned a little more about integration.

High Mountains, High Prices

Confined to a wheelchair for the last seven years as a result of multiple sclerosis, Dorothea Boulton travels regularly. In 1986 she and her husband accepted an invitation to visit friends in Oslo and combined this with a trip to the west coast. Travelling in their own car cut down the expense and enabled them to take both electric and self-propelled wheelchairs.

After consultation with our Norwegian friends and with the Norwegian Tourist Board, we chose to travel with *Fred Olsen Lines* from Harwich to Oslo. Their Goat Trail Tour provided us with vouchers for ten nights in hotels, to be used as we wished. Information supplied included suggested tours and details of hotels, as well as an excellent book, *Motoring in Norway*. The crossing took two nights – a mini-cruise – and was an experience in itself.

We reserved a specially adapted cabin with shower and toilet *en suite*

(fine as long as your companion is fit and able to climb onto the top bunk!) and we found that we could reach most parts of the ship with my wheelchair. We enjoyed the entertainment provided, we sat on the deck in the sunshine, and when the ferry called at Hirtshals in northern Denmark we saw the most memorable sunset.

At rush hour on a Monday morning, with a public transport strike, Oslo was hair-raising. Fortunately we were heading west, out of the city, guided by our friends who accompanied us to our first hotel, high in the mountains at Geilo. Midway between Oslo and Bergen, Geilo is predominantly a winter sports resort. In early June most of the skiing had finished, though we could still see the ski runs. The town was quiet as the summer walkers and anglers had not yet arrived.

Early next morning we waved goodbye to our friends. We were on our own. The road became narrower and more winding as we headed still higher into the mountains. We passed a sign saying that the pass up ahead had been opened only the day before, and the weather was deteriorating! We had left Geilo in beautiful sunshine but now the mist was descending.

After the first day we soon adapted to the differing climatic conditions as we dropped from the mountains to sheltered green valleys, and then climbed up again. Driving between walls of snow ten feet high was no exception. Most of the driving was exciting but the most heart-stopping section was a descent through dense fog on route 7 to Hardangerfjord. We had expected to see the Voringfossen, Norway's most admired waterfall with a drop of 145m, but instead experienced the eerie sensation of hearing the tremendous roar but seeing nothing from the observation platform.

Our base for exploring the Hardangerfjord was the *Kinsarvikfjord Hotel* in the village of Kinsarvik. My most abiding memory of this area is the apple blossom around Lofthus. Norwegians travel for miles to see the blossom, enhanced as it is by the exceptionally beautiful setting – the blue water of the fjord backed by snow-capped mountains that seem to rise directly from the water, numerous waterfalls tumbling down their steep sides, and all bathed in glorious spring sunshine.

We travelled from Hardangerfjord to Sognefjord along routes 68 and 13 from Kvanndal and Voss. The road climbing into the Vikafjell range appeared vertical as we approached, and we could make out the four hairpin bends which have a road width of 5m and a gradient of 1:12. It was a relief to arrive safely at the top, where we stopped for coffee and admired the views of Lake Myrkdalsratn and its delta, home to nearly eighty species of bird. Our destination in the Sognefjord region was Balestrand, a small resort which we reached by ferry. We enjoyed three restful days at *Kvikne's Hotel*, situated on the side of the fjord, and explored the village and surrounding mountains.

To do the fjords justice it is necessary to use the ferries, which add a new perspective to the holiday. We never had difficulty in boarding them and they always ran to time. Only one of our journeys was made in bad weather (rain and low mist); otherwise we had marvellous views.

"We had coffee and Norwegian pastries beside a roaring log fire"

We left Balestrand on what promised to be the most spectacular of our ferry trips. Unfortunately this was the day it rained! While staying in Balestrand we learned that a new road tunnel under the Jostedalsbreen glacier had been opened the previous week. This meant that we could travel by ferry up Fjaerlandfjord to Fjaerland and then by road to Skei, thus avoiding a long drive with a detour to see the glacier. Despite the rain the scenery was dramatic and we were able to drive to an arm of the glacier called Supphellebreen, where we had coffee and Norwegian pastries beside a roaring log fire. From this café my husband went on to examine the edge of the glacier – I stayed by the fire! The drive under the glacier, with the ice shining blue-green, was out of this world.

This was our last day by the fjords and we headed northeast, eventually working our way south to Oslo. Again our route took us across snow-covered mountain plateaux and through warm green valleys, one of which (Skjak) is the driest part of Norway, with a rainfall similar to that in the Sahara desert. We stayed at the ski hotels in Grotli and Beitostolen, and although it was June we caught the atmosphere of winter sports at Grotli where the Finnish national ski team were practising. We stopped many times to view waterfalls and to eat at isolated log-cabin cafés which invariably commanded the most exciting views. We saw many old houses with grass growing on the roofs for warmth, and examples of the stave churches found in most villages.

Our return to Oslo completed the circle and our trip. We spent two days visiting some of the many tourist attractions, including the Holmenkollen ski jump which stands high above the city and gives excellent views across it. The jump was built for the 1952 Olympic Games and attracts visitors all the year round. In summer the ski basin is a lake on which floodlit concerts are held, the orchestra playing on a floating platform.

The Vigeland Sculpture Park should not be missed. In beautiful landscaped parkland all the works of Gastar Vigeland are displayed. His sculptures cover all aspects of human life from birth to old age, the centrepiece being composed of 121 intertwined human figures – a humbling sight.

"We arrived at the hotel to find that 'one step' was in fact 'one flight' of twelve steps"

Oslo has many museums: I found the Norwegian Folk Museum, the Viking Ship Museum and the Kon-Tiki Museum most fascinating. The first reconstructs the interiors of town and country homes from recent centuries, and brings together over 150 buildings from all over Norway in an outdoor exhibition, arranged to demonstrate regional variations in rural architecture. The Viking Ship Museum houses three restored Viking ships, built for the pagan ship burials practised by the Vikings. The decorative items carried on board and now on display include jewellery, cloth and ceremonial sleighs for use in the afterlife. The Kon-Tiki Museum commemorates the voyages of the Norwegian adventurer, Thor Heyerdahl: the first on a balsawood raft (*Kon-Tiki*) from Peru to Polynesia; the second on a papyrus raft (*Ra II*) across the Atlantic.

We found the Norwegians kind and welcoming wherever we went. They seem to be generally very much aware of the needs of disabled people. Communication was reasonably easy as most Norwegians speak English (they are taught it in school from the age of six). Even so, we had the occasional hitch as a result of translation difficulties. When booking our hotel at Grotli, my husband enquired about access and was told that there was one step – fine, we could cope with that. We arrived at the hotel to find that "one step" was in fact "one flight" of twelve steps.

Throughout our holiday we enjoyed the Norwegian cold table (*koldtbord*) and other typical food. Breakfast was always a very large meal – smoked salmon and scrambled eggs, cold meats and cheese. In the larger hotels, hot breakfasts were also available. For touring it is wise to be equipped for lunchtime picnics, as cafés are few and far between. Hotels will fill thermos flasks – but at a price. When eating out you will be reminded that Norway is an expensive country. The state has a monopoly on the supply of alcohol; wine, beer and spirits for private consumption can only be bought at state-run shops, and that which is served in restaurants and hotels is far from cheap. Wine with our evening meal was our luxury treat – but one bottle of a modest rosé at £16 had to last us three evenings!

Despite the expense we fell in love with Norway, and jumped at the chance to go again in 1989, this time to a wedding. It came as an unpleasant shock to find that prices were even higher than we'd remembered. But a visit to this beautiful country is well worth saving for. Probably one of the cheaper ways to do it is to shop around for an inclusive package, preferably including hotel vouchers or giving discount rates at hotels of your choice so that you can plan your own itinerary. We paid about £250 per person in 1986, for ferry and hotel vouchers (including breakfast); this did not include other meals or any meals on the ferry. It was possible to reclaim the cost of any unused hotel vouchers on return to England.

SCANDINAVIA: TRAVEL NOTES

Sources of information

Norwegian Tourist Board, Charles House, 5 Lower Regent Street, London SW1Y 4LR; ☎071/839 6255. They produce an accommodation guide that uses the wheelchair symbol and may still have a few copies of the *Travel Guide for the Disabled*, which was compiled in 1982 by the Norwegian Association of the Disabled and covers accommodation, transport and tourist attractions. The intention to update every two years is stated in the Preface, but this doesn't seem to have come off – a shame because it's difficult to rely on ten-year-old information.

Swedish National Tourist Office, 29/31 Oxford Street, London W1R 1RE; ☎071/437 5816. Well ahead with preparations for tourism in the Nineties. In 1990, the European Year of Tourism, Sweden launched a major campaign to improve the lot of the handicapped tourist, which should produce results in the areas of transport, accommodation and facilities at tourist sights. As part of the campaign the tourist board launched a new edition of the excellent *Holiday Guide for the Disabled* in English and German. It is a sizeable book, packed with information for tourists with mobility problems; allergy sufferers and people with visual or hearing handicaps are also catered for. No charge is made for this guide.

Danish Tourist Board, Sceptre House, 169–173 Regent Street, London W1R 8PY; ☎071/734 2637. In conjunction with the Committee for Housing, Transportation and Technical Aids, and with plenty of input from organisations of disabled people, the Danish Tourist Board publishes a refreshingly honest guide for disabled visitors, *Access in Denmark – A Tourist Guide for the Disabled*, with information on accommodation, transport, loos, restaurants and places of interest. The latest edition was printed in January 1989 and stocks ran out by the middle of 1990, but the tourist board will send you a clear photocopy of all 100 pages.

Finnish Tourist Office, Queens House, 66–68 Haymarket, London SW1Y 4RF; ☎071/839 4048. Produces no special handbook for disabled visitors. Some hotels are marked with the wheelchair symbol in the accommodation guide, but you'll need a strong magnifying glass – a battery of minute symbols makes it heavy going.

Tour operators

Fred Olsen Lines' North Sea routes have been taken over by *Color Line* (formerly *Norway Line*, see *Practicalities*, "Getting There"). *M/S Venus* sails from Newcastle to Bergen and Stavanger, and the brochure offers a selection of cruises, mini-cruises (see p.496), chalet stays, escorted tours and "go as you please" motoring holidays.

The *P&O Cruises* 1991 brochure includes voyages aboard the *Canberra* (see p.493) and *Sea Princess* to Norway and the Baltic.

Getting there

At international **airport** terminals, boarding and disembarking is usually direct via an airbridge. At regional airports passengers are more often carried up a short flight of steps from the runway. Facilities at major airports in Denmark are described in detail in the tourist board access guide. The Norway guide covers air travel but is out of date. For Finland, deal direct with the airline; there is no literature on the subject. Sweden's Arlanda airport is small and friendly. The Swedish airports allow disabled passengers their independence before boarding: check in your baggage, spend a minute registering at the service desk, then drift off and do as you please until about ten minutes before the other passengers are due to board when you report back to the service desk for pre-boarding.

For details of the North Sea ferry services and facilities at ports, see *Practicalities*. If you're planning a grand tour it's worth noting that *Color Line* operate sailings to Norway from the Netherlands, Germany and Denmark as well as Newcastle.

Transport

In general, it seems that **air travel** within the Scandinavian countries is the best bet for wheelchair users without their own cars. Certainly in Sweden it is surprisingly inexpensive, and even at the smaller airports the staff are smooth and efficient in their handling of passengers with disabilities.

SCANDINAVIA: TRAVEL NOTES

Rail travel is, on the whole, difficult, with adapted trains still in the experimental stage and only on major routes. Denmark's trial trains and Sweden's new type of second-class carriage enable passengers to remain in their wheelchairs throughout some intercity journeys. Full details are given in the tourist board guides for disabled visitors. Some of the intercity trains in Norway are equipped with a special carriage which has a hydraulic lifting platform and an adapted compartment for wheelchair users. No printed information is available for rail travel in Finland, but it is heartening to know that Helsinki now has an accessible Underground system as a result of a blockade by disabled inhabitants of the city.

Hire of adapted **cars** is also difficult, if not impossible, but if you take your own, driving in these generally underpopulated countries can be a joy, and in Sweden the provision of adapted toilet facilities at rest areas is becoming more widespread. The incidence of adapted toilets at petrol stations, motels and hotels is reasonably high and those along main roads are listed in the Swedish Tourist Board's holiday guide. The Danish Tourist Board's guide lists facilities on motorways and main roads. This is an unfortunate omission in the Norway guide.

Orange Badge holders can take advantage of reciprocal **parking** arrangements in Sweden, Denmark and Finland, and there are concessions in Norway although no formal regulations. Write to the Department of Transport (address in *Practicalities*) for details.

Accommodation

The Swedish Tourist Board's holiday guide includes impressive listings of suitable accommodation in hotels, chalet villages and campsites. The Norway guide does too, but be wary of the 1982 publication date; access details need checking. Accommodation is well covered in the Danish guide. Dorothea Boulton comments on the hotels she used (the hotel guide referred to is the Norwegian Tourist Board accommodation guide):

Geilo Hotel, Geilo. Wheelchair symbol in the hotel guide but step at entrance and four steps to ground-floor bedroom corridor. Neither bedroom nor bathroom specially adapted.

Kinsarvikfjord Hotel, Kinsarvik. No wheelchair symbol in guide but access good. Level entrance with no steps; lift; adequate bedroom but bathroom only accessible with help.

Kvikne's Hotel, Balestrand. Wheelchair symbol in guide. Extensive range of facilities; specially adapted bedroom and bathroom; lifts; easy access at entrance (no steps).

Grotli Hoyfjells Hotel, Grotli. No wheelchair symbol in guide. Entrance difficult (impossible without strong assistant); bedrooms not adapted and bathroom difficult.

Beito Hoyfjells Hotel, Beitostolen. Wheelchair symbol in guide. No steps at entrance; specially adapted ground-floor bedroom and bathroom; lifts; large indoor swimming pool but no hoist or ramp.

Nye Helsfyr Hotel, Oslo (just outside the city centre). Wheelchair symbol in guide. Good access, level entrance; lifts; excellent adapted bathroom and large twin-bedded room. Typical business hotel prices but weekend breaks are reasonable.

Access and facilities

As noted in Charlotte Billington's account, **Sweden** has been held up as an example to all of us regarding provision of facilities for its own disabled people, and not without good reason – the Swedes enjoy generous disability benefits and pensions, free aids and appliances, grants for housing alterations and car purchase, employment quotas and more. **Denmark** has a similar reputation.

But of course it's not all roses. Employment quotas sound good, but in Denmark disabled people live comfortably on their benefits; there are mutterings amongst employers that it is impossible to employ disabled people because they do not apply for jobs – they have no incentive to work. This level of aid for disabled people is extremely expensive; the Danish government is attempting to reduce personal taxation rates and a large balance of payments deficit by taking the responsibility for funding and administering social services from central to local government and by moves towards privatisation. Residential centres are out of favour and the trend now is

SCANDINAVIA: TRAVEL NOTES

towards individual, adapted apartments or shared houses.

Similarly, in Sweden there is a move away from the cluster housing (*Fokus*) of the Sixties towards *Boendeservice* (housing with service) apartments, in which residents do not share common bathing, laundry, kitchen and dining facilities. During the last few years some residents have negotiated for their own personal attendants to manage the entire morning routine, after which they rely on workers from the central *Boendeservice* staff (see *Independent living and attendant care in Sweden: a consumer perspective*, by Adolf Ratzka; *World Rehabilitation Fund*, New York).

The attitudes encountered in 1984 by the Phoenix Trust study group have changed enormously. There is decisive rejection of "resorts" or "centres" for disabled people; the emphasis has shifted to integration in the true sense of the word. In spite of these developments, it's interesting to note that both Danish and Swedish finalists in the European Year of Tourism competition to find the best facilities for disabled tourists in Europe were owned and run by disability organisations: the Hotel Årevidden in central Sweden is part of a group of four hotels owned by the *Swedish Federation of Disabled Persons* (*DHR*). Dronningens Ferieby holiday village, near Grenaa in Jutland, was built by the *Danish Multiple Sclerosis Society* (*Scleroseforeningen*).

There is clearly some way to go before commercial operators learn from these beautifully designed and fully accessible — both inside and out — properties, and act on the principles of tourism for all. But it is good to see that such accommodation is open to disabled tourists and their families or friends. The Swedes and Danes are keen to make the facilities which they have long provided for their countrymen and women available to, and known to, disabled tourists. In Sweden, where sport and appreciation of the countryside figure highly, a wide range of facilities have been and are being installed to enable disabled people to take part in all manner of leisure activities: fishing, shooting, skiing, canoeing, swimming, hiking the forest trails, looking for mushrooms . . . the great outdoors is being opened up in a big way and this is good news for disabled visitors to Sweden.

The forests, lakes (by the thousand), coastline and nature reserves are perhaps Sweden's greatest attraction, and the importance of making these accessible to *all* visitors has been recognised by one of Europe's more enlightened tourist boards. What's more, their boardwalks, asphalt paths and accessible toilets all fit in, so that wheelchair users feel part of the environment rather than passive observers. They can lean over and pick mushrooms or berries, can scramble (in their chairs) across the rocks to the sea's edge and feel the spray on their faces. This, more than any number of adapted hotel rooms or ramps at museum entrances, puts Sweden in a class of its own.

Useful addresses

Danish Multiple Sclerosis Society (*Scleroseforeningen*), 15 Mosedalvej, DK-2500 Valby; ☎31 17 04 66.

Swedish Federation of Disabled Persons (*DHR*), Katrinebergsvägen 6, S-117 43 Stockholm; ☎8/18 91 00.

Books

Dorothea Boulton recommends *Motoring in Norway* (£8.50, inc. p&p), which is one of many Norwegian Tourist Board publications available from BAS Overseas Publications Ltd (Unit 1C, 159 Mortlake Road, Kew TW9 4AW).

Germany

The End of East and West in Berlin

James Franey contracted poliomyelitis some years ago, and as a result uses crutches all the time. He visited Berlin before the Wall came down.

The Berlin Wall was erected in 1961, when East Berlin was pronounced the capital of the new German Democratic Republic. West Berlin became an island of capitalism and democracy inside East Germany. Only designated roads through East Germany could be used to reach Berlin, and there were three air corridors, all barred to *Lufthansa*, the German national airline.

In West Berlin, Kurfürstendamm (or Ku'damm, as it is colloquially called) became the main shopping street, full of glossy department stores and BMW showrooms. Prior to dismantling of the Wall, Ku'damm carried many tourists but little traffic for such a major city centre. At the top is the ruin of the Kaiser Wilhelm church, left as a monument after World War II, and beside it a modern bell tower.

At night Ku'damm comes to life, with tourists and locals alike sitting at street cafés, and buskers or bands playing impromptu concerts in the road. The atmosphere is laid-back and friendly. Nightlife elsewhere in West Berlin, however, ranges from the extraordinary to the downright dubious.

Away from the bright lights and glitter is the area of Kreuzberg, which the guidebooks generally point out as being

full of the black flags of anarchy and alternative lifestyles. Because of its special status and position in the midst of East Germany, the West German government gave tax concessions to people willing to live in West Berlin and exempted potential conscripts from service if they chose to live there. As a result, many radicals and fringe groups came to West Berlin and most settled in Kreuzberg. But with the demise of radicalism in the mid-Seventies it seems to have lost some of its gloss – visitors now find a run-down, inner city area.

The general picture, though, is one of a well-kept, wealthy city with parks, art galleries, theatres, museums, excellent food and good public transport. Most people speak English and are friendly. The Dahlem-Dorf Museum contains many fine paintings, including works by Rembrandt and Rubens. It is in the suburbs and easy to reach on the efficient, clean and accessible U'bahn underground system. Also worth a look is the Charlottenberg Palace which lies to the north of the city.

But there is another side to Berlin and, before the Wall came down, there was another city to travel to. Entry to East Berlin from West Berlin was, for Western tourists, by one of two means – either by train through Friedrichstrasse Station, or by sightseeing coach.

I first took the S'bahn (the suburban train) from Zoo Station, near Ku'damm, to Friedrichstrasse. The train was old, with wooden bench-seats, and it was crowded with West Berliners taking much-needed provisions to relatives and friends in East Berlin. The journey took only a few minutes and we passed through the Wall and No-Man's Land.

At Friedrichstrasse passengers left the train and made their way to the transit hall, which was straight out of a John le Carré novel. Shabby, with beige paint peeling in places, it was heavily guarded by East German militia. As always, there was a great queue to the booths where parcels were examined and day visas (a sheet of paper with a map of East Berlin on the reverse side) were issued.

The attitude of the East German authorities varied widely. Once, while I was standing at the back of a long queue, a militia man came over to me, looked at my crutches and said, "Ein dag?", to which I replied with almost the only German word I knew, "Ja". I was quickly escorted to the front of the queue, which saved me a wait of 45 minutes. This act of consideration was not matched by the militia man's counterpart in the glass booth. I was instructed to put my hair behind my ears to reflect my image in my passport. After much glancing between the passport photograph and myself, the man in the booth gave me a visa and I walked to the currency counter where I exchanged the mandatory 25DM for 25 Ost Marks.

Leaving the building and entering Friedrichstrasse itself, I was met by nuns in full habit collecting money for the church, and by East Berlin policemen escorting a large group of football fans away from the railway station. It was only a short walk, past a house where Engels once stayed, down to Unter den Linden, the famous road which leads down to the Brandenberg Gate and the Wall.

Most of the main buildings in East Berlin lie in Unter den Linden, including the Arsenal Museum, St Hedwig's cathedral and the Humboldt University. Nearby, at the Tomb of the Unknown Warrior, the East German Guard was changed in goose-stepping style reminiscent of a pre-1939 newsreel.

In the Arsenal Museum, which had no passenger lift, I was escorted (without asking) to the service lift by an official wearing a crew-neck sweater. He told me in broken English that I would be most interested in exhibits on the second floor which covered World War II. The service lift was obviously used for taking away the refuse.

"Here was the heart of East Berlin, and it was akin to Corby on a bad day"

On arrival at the second floor I was told to ask one of the other attendants to lead me back to the lift when I had finished. However, during my inspection of the exhibits I became aware of being followed – one of the attendants had decided to ensure that I wouldn't miss the return lift. As for the exhibits, there was a strong Soviet bias – which has been changed since the events of November 1989.

When I was ready to leave, my escort took me back to the lift and out through the main doors. I thanked him for his kindness and complimented him on his English. He told me that he spoke Russian better than he spoke English, and then added, mordantly, "the chiefs are American, the chiefs are Russian".

On leaving the Arsenal Museum I went by bus to Alexander Platz. Everyone was very kind on the buses and trains in Berlin, and I always received many offers of a seat. After getting off the bus I became aware that here was the heart of East Berlin, and it was akin to Corby on a bad day. The architecture was of the Stalinist variety – heavy, designed by someone who trained using Lego, and poorly built. In the centre of Alexander Platz was what the guidebooks proudly called "the world clock". Why one would want to know the time in Caracas whilst standing in the middle of Berlin was beyond me.

"It is possible to detect just a tinge of regret"

The food, too, was of amazingly poor quality. In the snack bars it was bad luncheon meat or ghastly sausage, served on stale bread. In contrast, the beer was excellent. A short walk to an ice cream vendor supplied me with ice cream which tasted like lard and had to be thrown away. A box of chocolates also had to be discarded.

In short, there was nothing on which to spend my 25 Ost Marks. A visit to the *Zentrum* department store was also disappointing. The goods on sale were shoddy, but cheap. I saw the wives of British servicemen buying lampshades; the sight of British servicemen in full uniform in East Berlin was even more bizarre.

People on the whole looked poor and badly fed. A visit to the housing estates brought to mind Thamesmead in London, or Hulme in Manchester. Rather incongruous, then, were the expensive hotels near Friedrichstrasse Station, all serving drinks at exorbitant prices and clearly not aiming for local clientele.

The vehicles in East Berlin were all Trabants and Wartburgs. Road signs indicated Warsaw, Prague and all points east. For me, exit back to the West was on the U'bahn. The train slowed down as we passed through lit but unused stations, manned only by East German guards, before we arrived in West Berlin.

For my second trip into East Berlin I joined a sightseeing coach. We went through Checkpoint Charlie and an East German tourist guide came onto the coach once we had crossed the border. It was worth travelling this way not only to reduce the amount of walking and for the convenience, but also to witness the sight of young East Berliners making rude gestures at relatively wealthy Western tourists.

Our coach took the party (largely consisting of Americans and Japanese) to the Soviet War Memorial, a number of sarcophagi commemorating those who died in World War II. Again, it was a reflection of the Soviet influence and their view of the war. As a party from the Soviet Union were standing to have their photograph taken, the younger Japanese in my group cavorted over the stones, laughing and giggling.

On board the coach we were told how rich East Germany was in all fields, and how such was the shortage of labour that a number of "guest workers" – from Mozambique, Vietnam and all over Eastern Europe – had come to swell the workforce. Nowadays, accounts of racism in East Germany are commonplace, and the "guest workers" find themselves strangers in a strange land.

We visited the Pergamon Museum, which stands on Museum Island and is a wonderful example of classical architecture. The Pergamon altar stands proudly aloft inside and, like the Elgin marbles, its return is demanded by its original owners.

On the way back an East German border guard searched the coach for dissident East Germans trying to flee to the West. He checked the toilet and used mirrors to scan the undercarriage.

The journey back to the West struck home the differences between the two sides of Berlin. The cars were invariably Volkswagens, Mercedes and BMWs; the people were sleek and well dressed.

Of course, what split the city was the Wall. Near Checkpoint Charlie there were viewing platforms, from which it was possible to read the graffiti. There was a heavy covering of slogans such as "the Wall must fall", as well as the usual obscenities. I went to inspect the Wall near Schlesisches Tor in Kreuzberg. On leaving the U'bahn station I walked down the road for about half a mile, until my way was blocked by concrete, stark and unmarked, running across a major thoroughfare and splitting families, streets

and communities. The buses had to do a U-turn in order to retrace their route.

Now the Wall is no more and Berlin is again the capital of a united Germany. Already there is an architectural competition for the redevelopment of Potsdammer Platz (once No-Man's Land), which was effectively the crossroads of Europe. Trabant have been taken over by Volkswagen, and massive aid will go to the East.

In West Berlin, the sense of being an island has gone. Ironically, West Berliners complain about the worsening traffic conditions and crowding on the underground system. It is possible to detect just a tinge of regret concerning the passage of East and West Berlin into history.

GERMANY: TRAVEL NOTES

Sources of information

German National Tourist Office, Nightingale House, 65 Curzon Street, London W1Y 7PE; ☎071/495 3990. Several German towns and cities publish access guides, and the tourist office can supply the addresses from which to order these. The office also provides a free leaflet, *Disabled Visitors to Germany*, which lists a number of sources of accommodation guides in Germany, plus addresses to write to for information on transport. An information request coupon is attached to the leaflet; and intending visitors can send it (with SAE and International Reply Coupon) to an organisation in Germany (*BAG der Clubs Behinderter und ihrer Freunde e.v.*, Eupener Strasse 5, D-6500 Mainz; ☎6131/225514) that has a database containing over 6000 accommodation (all types) addresses worldwide.

The **Touristik Union International** (TUI), Postfach 610280, 3000 Hannover 61 (☎0511/5670) has a centralised information bank on many German (and Berlin) hotels and pensions

that cater to the needs of disabled travellers or those with specific dietary requirements – not in specially designed and separate establishments, but within the mainstream of tourist facilities. The *TUI* can book you on to a package tour or organise rooms according to individual itineraries, taking into account each customer's needs, which are gauged from a questionnaire filled out before booking arrangements commence. Their services also include such details as providing suitable wheelchairs for train travel, the transportation of travellers' own wheelchairs, and the provision of transport at airports and stations.

Deutscher Paritätischer Wohlfahrtsverband, Brandenburgische Str. 80, 1/41, Berlin (☎30/86 00 10). Local advice on choosing hotels and wheelchair rental.

Landesbeauftragter für Behinderte, Sächsische Str. 30, 1/31 (☎30/867 6445). Local umbrella group of disabled and self help organisations, useful for finding addresses of more specific groups.

GERMANY: TRAVEL NOTES

From early 1991, enquiries about travel anywhere in Germany, East or West, will theoretically be dealt with from this tourist office. At the time of writing there is no information for disabled travellers in what was East Germany.

Tour operators

Madge Davidson and her husband joined a *KD German Rhine Line* (28 South Street, Epsom, Surrey KT18 7PF; ☎03727/42033) cruise on the Rhine in May 1988. She uses a wheelchair and was particularly impressed with the crew, who were extremely helpful: "they never made me feel any different to the other passengers". One of the *KD* boats, the *Italia*, is equipped with a stairlift for wheelchairs; otherwise, you'll have to manage a flight of steps between decks. There are no special cabins or wheelchair-accessible loos, but disabled passengers are frequently carried on these cruises. *KD* will organise a wheelchair at the airports on outward and return journeys.

Getting there

Lufthansa German Airlines (23–26 Piccadilly, London W1V 0EJ, ☎071/408 0442) produce a booklet, *Hints for Disabled Passengers*, and have been recommended by some seasoned wheelchair travellers. If driving, it's probably better to avoid the long Harwich–Hamburg crossing on the none-too-accessible *Scandinavian Seaways* ferry, *MS Hamburg*. Go instead for a shorter one, such as Harwich–Hook of Holland with *Sealink* and drive east through the Netherlands.

Transport

Deutsche Bundesbahn (*German Rail*) publish a booklet, mostly in German, listing services and facilities at stations; it's available at most ticket counters in Germany and from the UK office (Suite 118, Hudson's Place, Victoria Station, London SW1V 1JL; ☎071/233 6558). *German Rail* will arrange assistance at stations and tickets can be purchased through rail-appointed travel agents such as *DER Travel Service* (18 Conduit Street, London W1R 9TD; ☎071/499 0577). Assistance is provided by the "welfare

centre" at each station; they must be notified a few days in advance. Nearly all Eurocity and Intercity trains are wheelchair accessible, with adapted toilets on the newer rolling stock.

There is a list of motorway service stations with facilities for disabled people, *Autobahn Service für Behinderte*, available from *Gesellschaft für Nebenbetriebe der Bundesautobahnen* (Poppelsdorfer Allee 24, D-5300 Bonn); send an International Reply Coupon. Orange Badge holders may **park** in spaces reserved for disabled motorists, for three hours where no waiting is permitted, beyond the stated time in limited zones, and without charge at parking meters.

Accommodation

There are several regional **hotel lists**, available from addresses in Germany (see tourist board leaflet), that use the wheelchair symbol. The large, modern hotels are generally accessible.

The *German Automobile Club* (*ADAC*, Am Westpark 8, D-8000 München) publishes a **camping** guide (*ADAC Campingführer I + II*) which lists nearly 300 sites that are declared suitable for disabled people. The small number of contributors with experience of camping in Germany seem to bear out this optimism: Michael Turner, for example, comments favourably on German sites (p.487) and Jean Dyke, who is confined to a wheelchair and travels around Europe in an adapted camper van, found the "best campsite" in southern Germany, near Berchtesgarden – fully accessible facilities, with shower for the disabled in the same private room as the loo.

In Berlin, one **hostel** has been specially adapted for the handicapped: **Gästehaus der Fürst-Donnersmarck-Stiftung**, Wildkanelweg 28, 1/28 (☎30/40 20 12). It's essential to book well in advance.

Access and facilities

The profusion of access and accommodation guides covering what used to be West Germany suggests that general awareness is good and that provision of information for disabled travellers is taken seriously. (At least for

GERMANY: TRAVEL NOTES

German-speaking disabled travellers – many of the publications are available only in German.) Tourists exploring the country by car and making as much use of these guides as their linguistic abilities allow are unlikely to encounter insurmountable difficulties.

In Berlin, facilities in the western area are better than those in the east. Most of the major western museum have wheelchair access, as do many other public buildings. The full colour U- and S-Bahn map also indicates which stations are accessible by wheelchair.

But all the familiar problems – of only partially accessible public transport and public buildings, of high unemployment among disabled citizens (in spite of employment quotas and fines for employers who discriminate), of only half-hearted commitment to true integration of disabled persons into the community – are alive and well in Germany, and positively flourishing in the old East German territory.

The hope for improvement in these areas lies in large part with the independent living centres, which are located in a number of German towns. These organisations not only provide support, information and advice to local disabled people, but also act as a mouthpiece, pressing for change.

Books

According to James Franey, the best book on East Berlin is *Zoo Station*, by Ian Walker (Abacus); Berlin: coming in from the Cold by Ken Smith (Hamish Hamilton) is also good and the best guidebook is *The Rough Guide to Berlin*.

Poland

A Survival Guide for Poland

A sharp contrast to Annie Delin's Irish holiday (see p.98) was her trip to Poland in December 1989. Annie is just over one metre tall, and uses a wheelchair (a Major Buggy) when travelling.

On the list of places suitable for holidays for disabled people, Poland should come a long way down. This is not to imply that there are countries of the world where disabled people mustn't venture, but it's worth knowing that if you decide to sample the culture, history and political upheaval of this particular Eastern Bloc destination you should be ready for a hard time.

We travelled to Poland when the euphoria of a new democracy was sweeping Eastern Europe. The Berlin Wall had just fallen, Czechoslovakia was swept by the fervour of revolution, Poland had elected Solidarity representatives to government.

Yet there was no party atmosphere in Poland – far from it. The Poles were grappling with forty percent per month inflation, food shortages and gluts, galloping pollution from the iron and steel works in Silesia . . . and no repressive regime to blame any of the problems on. These, added to the historical problems – the after-effects of Nazi occupation and wartime devastation, and insufficient investment in development since the war – make

Poland one of the more depressed and depressing countries of Europe.

Two immediate difficulties face travellers with disabilities. One is that people in service positions (waiters, hotel staff, station porters, travel agents) are demoralised, undermotivated and completely without any desire to do their jobs properly. Try, for example, booking a rail ticket or requesting room service in scanty Polish – you are very unlikely to receive a sympathetic response.

The second problem is a purely logistical one. The condition of the roads and pavements does not make life easy for anyone in a wheelchair. On one occasion, when trying to cross a road at a zebra crossing, we came up against chasms up to 20cm across where the tram tracks had dislodged huge areas of cobbled road surface and they had never been repaired. Lucky for us that the driver of the oncoming tram decided to stop and wait for us to finish struggling across.

Against all of this, twelve days spent in Poland at this particular crossroads in history made up probably the most educational trip I'd ever undertaken. I learnt about the impact of great political upheaval on ordinary people, the realities of food and money shortages on a grand scale – even, on a trivial level, what it's like to be *really* cold.

I could not have absorbed the significance of the events plastered all over our papers during the past few months, as Eastern Europe changed its political structure, if I had not had the chance to meet people from both Poland and Czechoslovakia, with their very different accounts of what the changes meant.

"It was hard to imagine how things could be made harder than they already were for the Polish people"

For the Czechs, this was an exciting time. Strikes organised by students were actually having an impact, not just on people in the street but on the shape of government. Some of those I spoke to gave accounts of the spirit of cooperation and order within the university buildings during the strikes and sit-ins. There was a general feeling that we stood on the brink of a brave new era of freedom and enlightenment.

In Poland, without the safety net of government restrictions, food supply, working conditions and money had gone haywire. Just days after we left the country, the new government announced that Poles would have to put up with a cut in wages of twenty percent in real terms. It was hard to imagine how things could be made harder than they already were for the Polish people.

The word "inflation" took on a new meaning. When you've been in a country in which you are completely unable to spend all your money while those around you desperately save for the things you ignore, 2p on the price of a pint of milk at home seems pretty insig-

nificant. (In most of the hotels we stayed in, milk was unobtainable.)

When we arrived in Kraków, at an airport the size of some people's front rooms, we had our first "experience". Our plane was due to fly on to Warsaw and so, we discovered in the nick of time, was our luggage. Thanks to *British Airways*, our bags had been labelled "Warsaw" in spite of the fact that our tickets said "Kraków". As a result, my sister was required to climb into the hold of the plane and search out her own bags, while, below her, soldiers stood around smoking cigarettes.

Our three-night, off-season package (at £28 each) gave us no choice of hotel but, in fact, the *Hotel Wanda* came well up to scratch. It couldn't have been much less central – well out in the seedy suburbs – but with taxi fares generally less than 50p we could have sailed in and out of town all day without making much of a dent in our spending money.

Kraków city centre was once a gracious hub composed of medieval churches, a fine old market square, university buildings, monasteries and the magnificent Wawel castle, where for ten years a certain Karol Wojtyła was bishop before moving on to better things in the Vatican. The graciousness which was Kraków, however, is now faded and scarred by decay. Acid rain is washing the faces off the stone saints; smog removes the painted facades of old buildings; the bugle call which traditionally greets visitors every hour from St Mary's cathedral floats across a market square caked in grime.

In Kraków, we sampled for the first time the quality of service of *Orbis* – "Europe's oldest and most experienced travel agents, with sixty years' experience of service". There are *Orbis* offices everywhere, and they supply not only tourists but also Polish residents with rail, bus and airline tickets.

The first *Orbis* office we called at told us that they didn't sell rail tickets, and directed us to a main office which was closed all day Saturday and Sunday. (We had to travel on Monday, and rail tickets must be reserved 24 hours in advance.) Not daunted, we actually went to the railway station and managed to buy our own tickets at the third office we queued in. Later experiences of *Orbis* service included a 45-minute queue, duff information about a suitable hotel, inability to provide any map of the city centre, and being sent round the corner to a TV and radio shop when we tried to change money at the exchange desk.

The central part of our holiday in Poland was attendance at a conference hosted by the University of Silesia in Szczyrk – a tiny mountain village close to the border with Czechoslovakia. This was our second visit to the Tatra mountains. Our first was a day trip from Kraków to the little wooden town of Zakopane, where we were charmed by the intricate carvings on the houses, took a ride on a one-horse open sleigh, and envied the kids with their sledge-runner "prams" – so much more practical than wheels when the snow is 45cm deep and all the roads are ice-runs!

"We religiously followed wheelchair signs with arrows which plunged us into a dank, subterranean maze of urine-scented passages under the station"

In Szczyrk we stayed in a triangular lodge built and run by the state for the miners of Katowice, for their relaxation and health – just as well when you consider the disgusting air of Katowice. Szczyrk is a truly beautiful location for a skiing holiday, not commercialised or noisy, still a home for wildlife, and intersected by paths cut out of the snow, along which you can ski, sledge or walk with ease. Once again, fitting runners to the wheels of your wheelchair would make life a lot smoother, but our hotel reception staff did lend us a sledge!

From Szczyrk I spent one day visiting the Museum of Martyrdom at Auschwitz (Oświęcim on the Polish map). From Katowice, Kraków or Szczyrk it is sensible for a group to take a taxi, even though there are trains and buses. The taxi cost $80 between four of us; thus for just over £15 each we had door-to-door service on a visit which included two hours' travel and nearly six hours in the museum. Auschwitz is, for some people, an important feature of a trip to Silesia – certainly for me it was something of a pilgrimage. On the practical side, the guides are well used to helping people with disabilities, although nothing can overcome the fundamental discomforts of the buildings where the many exhibitions are housed. You will get cold and tired at practically any time of year.

When we returned to Katowice after the conference, we had to travel on to Wrocław by train. A very switched-on taxi driver took us to the disabled persons and baggage entrance to the station. We religiously followed wheelchair signs with arrows which plunged us into a dank, subterranean maze of urine-scented passages under the station. There was no signposting of any kind, and were it not for the appearance of a baggage handler on an electric truck we would be there still. Charitably, we must suppose that the sign we couldn't read in Polish said "Disabled people should be accompanied by a member of the station staff".

A little more cautious about signs with wheelchairs on them, we found our own way out of Wrocław station – using the stairs. Our hotel, however, greeted us with a reassuring sign: "Hotel attends to inmates physically not fully proficient".

It seemed in general that Poland does make an effort to accommodate the needs of disabled people, with reserved parking spaces, a ramped route into some of the museums we visited, and station access routes. Still,

we couldn't help noticing the reluc-
tance of taxi drivers approached by my
sister pushing me in a wheelchair, and
the evident relief when I sprang out of
the chair and it folded away to almost
nothing before their eyes. We also
asked ourselves what use it might be
getting into an art gallery by ramps and
then finding that only the scanty
ground-floor gallery was accessible
because of internal staircases. Then
again, is it always so much better in
Britain?

On our last day we had reached
Warsaw, where we fell into the arms of
an unofficial mafia of station porters,
taxi drivers and hotel staff, all demanding tips in dollars or sterling. Our taxi
driver attempted to charge twenty
times the metered rate for the journey
to the hotel (I am taking into account
the fact that the fare for any trip should
have been fifty times what the meter
read, because of inflation).

A survival guide to any such visit to
Poland should advise as follows. Do not
expect your polite attempts to speak
Polish to open any doors – a firm
demand and a cool "thank you" will
stand you in equally good stead. Accept
the help of any member of the public,
whilst resorting to station porters and
the like only if you have to – they expect
substantial financial reward. If you have
vegetarian dietary requirements, get
someone to write down the Polish for "I
do not eat meat" before you travel, and
place it in front of every waiter and waitress. Learn some German before you go
– it is more widely spoken and understood than English. Take small bars of
soap, chocolate and coffee sachets – for
yourself and to give to receptionists and
cleaners in hotels.

And when you meet someone who
wants to make friends and have a
conversation, fall upon them with cries
of joy. They will give you an insight into
the country that you cannot get as a
tourist, and they'll defend you against
the waiters, the taxi drivers, the
porters.

Czechoslovakia

An Empty Hillside

Joyce Benson's disabilities confine her to a wheelchair and although she is able to drive her own car she requires help to get in and out of it. Perhaps such phrases as "behind the Iron Curtain" and "the freedom of the West" sound dated now, but this account of a visit to Prague over twelve years ago is included because it aims to encourage other travellers to search out unusual destinations, even if greater risk and uncertainty are involved.

When my brother-in-law fell ill in Teheran on the return leg of an overland journey to Afghanistan, all hopes of the "holiday adventure of a lifetime" were dashed. The plan had been to drive across Europe with my sister to meet him in Istanbul and drive home in convoy together – not a great adventure for many, but being disabled as a result of polio I saw it as a holiday with a challenge.

In spite of this setback, I was mentally geared up for a trip and began to consider alternatives. My decision was soon made: Shirley, a friend for many years, a great extrovert and an experienced traveller, readily agreed to a trip behind the Iron Curtain, although after our return she did say, "Never ask me to go there again!"

The reason for choosing Prague was a book I had recently read which had made a lasting impression on me. *Seven Men at Daybreak*, by Alan

Burgess, the film version of which is called *Operation Daybreak*, tells the story of a small group of very brave men who, during World War II, returned to their native Czechoslovakia to assassinate Heydrich, the Nazi general who was at the time running the country. These men had lived and trained for the operation at a camp in the small village of Ightfield, near Whitchurch in Shropshire, only 24km from my home. The story of how the men prepared for and carried out their mission, for which they eventually paid with their lives, was simply and very movingly told. The grim photographs of the church where they died, and of the village of Lidice which was wiped out in revenge, inspired in me a desire to visit the town of Prague and see these places for myself.

We obtained visas from the Czech embassy and the necessary accommodation was booked through *Čedok*, the Czech travel agency. Entry and exit from the country were permitted only on the day and at the border crossing mentioned in the visas – an early indication of the lack of free movement in Czechoslovakia.

Our route by car to Prague took us through some of the wealthiest places in Europe. Nights spent in Arosa, Switzerland, then St Anton and Vienna in Austria – including a visit to the opera in Vienna to hear Joseph Krips conducting a performance of *Don Giovanni* – only served to highlight the enormous difference in living standards between East and West that we were soon to experience.

"I sat alone for half an hour, glancing at the watchtowers and listening to the baying of the guard dogs"

Leaving Vienna shortly before midday, we drove north towards the Czech border. We reached the frontier and passed the Austrian border guards. Crossing no-man's land we entered Czech territory and were immediately brought to a halt by a barrier across the road. Another barrier was lowered behind us and two heavily armed guards approached the car. They signalled that we should get out. Shirley did so, opened the boot and showed them the wheelchair, pointing at me; they seemed to understand. One guard took Shirley into a nearby building while the other took up his position beside the car. I sat alone for half an hour, glancing at the watchtowers and listening to the baying of the guard dogs, and wondered what foolishness had brought me to such a place.

An unusually quiet Shirley eventually emerged, the barrier was lifted and we drove away. The road to Prague ran through mile after mile of flat, deserted countryside. Occasionally we passed through small villages, almost empty of inhabitants, except perhaps for an elderly woman, in a headscarf and with an apron over her ankle-length skirt, driving a flock of geese. It was an eerie journey, a stark contrast to the busy country villages of England.

It was early autumn and the days were already shortening. As we entered the outskirts of Prague it was getting dark, and steady rain added to our navigating difficulties in the unlit streets. Shirley suggested making our way to the centre, asking the way to our hotel as we went – a good idea in theory, but not so easy when none of the people we asked spoke any English or German, and the lack of street lighting made it impossible to read any street names or road signs. The town plan supplied by *Čedok* was inadequate and after an hour of driving round a gloomy city we were becoming increasingly uneasy in what seemed a sinister and unfriendly place.

"Which way shall I turn now?" I asked Shirley, who was navigating.

"I have no idea," she replied, in a tone which implied that she was beyond caring.

For some reason I turned right, and found myself going the wrong way along a wide, poorly lit, main road. Seconds later, we were stopped by the police. Our first real contact with the Czech people, apart from the border guards, was heart-warming. Far from booking us, the police explained, in German, exactly where the hotel was; they stopped the traffic and sent us on our way.

"We quickly decided that the less time spent in the en suite bathroom the better"

We soon found the unlit square in which, the police had told us, the hotel was situated. I parked the car and Shirley went to look for it on foot. When she eventually returned her news was reassuring: "The hotel is just across the square, they speak English and are very friendly, and we can park outside the door."

Hotel Paris, the hotel to which we'd been assigned by *Čedok*, resembled a large, old-fashioned *British Rail* hotel.

After booking in and being asked to leave our passports at the desk, we were taken to our room, which was large, rather dark and full of heavy furniture. We quickly decided that the less time spent in the *en suite* bathroom the better – they appeared to be having trouble with the drains, a problem not confined to our hotel, as we discovered later!

On our first evening we sampled what the waiter told us was a typical Czech meal – roast duck with dumplings, preceded by a thin soup with a raw egg floating in it. We pondered how, in our brief stay, we could learn a little about Prague and the people who lived there. In the past I've found that visiting famous buildings and going to the theatre or opera, along with shopping for the almost obligatory souvenirs and presents, can tell you a great deal about a city and its inhabitants.

In the china department of the *Tuzex* shop, where tourists do their shopping, an elderly lady came to serve us. She spoke fluent English but when I remarked on this and asked if she had been to England, she said, very quietly, "No, that is not allowed." The sadness and resignation in her face still haunt me. The shop was empty, so we talked with her for a while. She went to endless trouble to help us find gifts which would remind us of her country. Apart from glassware, for which Czechoslovakia is famous, there is fine porcelain; a black china peacock bought in this shop is a treasured possession. A bottle of *Slivovice*, a fiery plum brandy and the national drink, was not a total success with the family and can be recommended only for hardened drinkers!

The Charles Bridge and Hradčany Castle are two of Prague's most famous landmarks. They are within walking distance of each other and also within walking (and pushing) distance of the *Hotel Paris*. Our way there took us through the Staroměstské Square, with its impressive turreted buildings,

including the old Town Hall and the Kinský Palace, so typical of Czech architecture.

Hradčany Castle is built on a small hill in the northwest of the city. At the time of our visit it was not open to the public but the reward for anyone who cares to climb the long slope up to the castle, as we did, is a panoramic view over the entire city, with the River Vltava flowing through it and the towers, domes and spires stretching away into the distance. Army wagons were much in evidence on the cobbled streets in and around the castle, and this rather restricted photography – since we had been warned never to take pictures of military equipment, care had to be exercised when using a camera.

"We saw no special facilities for the disabled, nor indeed any other disabled people"

The Charles Bridge told us more about Prague as it was then. A beautiful structure, famous for the life-size statues which line the parapets on each side, the bridge was black with grime. It was just one of the sadder features of the city – crumbling buildings, peeling paint, air polluted by the stench of petrol and open drains. Prague was a neglected city with an air of hopelessness. (More recently, I am told, major rebuilding projects and an improved general standard of living have given the city a more "cared-for" appearance.)

An evening at the opera reminded us of the economic gulf between East and West. The drab, faded auditorium of the Opera House was matched by the plain, almost shabbily dressed audience, and there were many empty seats. It was a far cry from Vienna – none of the glittering chandeliers, none of the elegantly dressed women adorned with expensive jewellery and well-groomed escorts. But the friendliness of the people compensated – the policeman who lifted me into my seat, and the usherette who spoke a few words of English and insisted on sitting with us throughout the performance and translating the programme. This was typical of the great kindness with which we were treated during our stay, and although we saw no special facilities for the disabled, nor indeed any other disabled people, we found that help was always willingly given if required.

We put aside a day to visit Resslova Street, where those few brave men had finally been cornered in the church, and Lidice, the village destroyed in revenge. Both were marked on the map, for which we were grateful – we were not sure how enquiries about them would be received.

On the way a short detour took us to Wenceslas Square, scene of so much activity during the 1989 uprising, and really a wide boulevard, at one end of which is the National Museum with a statue of St Wenceslas in front of it.

Resslova Street runs down to the river, and my memories are of a gloomy, empty, cobbled road lined with grim, forbidding buildings. The church was locked but we saw the memorial on the wall above the ventilation shaft – still pockmarked by bullets – and, underneath, a jam jar containing a few faded flowers. We felt an urge to drive away as quickly as possible.

Lidice lies a few miles northwest of Prague and we found it with no difficulty. The bare hillside, where once the village stood, is imprinted on my mind. Only a handful of stones remain of Horak's Farm, together with a cross crowned by a circle of thorns. The new village of Lidice is close by. Its little red houses look down on the empty hillside as if standing guard over the memories of its unhappy past.

We left Prague on a bright and sunny morning and drove west to the border town of Rozvadov on the West German border. As we drove into West Germany the sky darkened and the first few drops of rain began to fall, but we felt as if we'd emerged from a dark tunnel into brilliant sunlight.

Soviet Union

Russian Cruise

As a result of polio at an early age Biddy Haines has weak legs. At the age of sixty, osteoarthritis of neck and shoulders added to her problems, but good general health and plenty of energy enable her to take advantage of most types of holiday, as long as her luggage can be taken care of – it is difficult to manage suitcases when using walking sticks. She goes on these holidays not expecting to be able to take part in all the excursions and activities, but always finds more than enough to occupy and interest her. In July 1981 Biddy joined a cruise along the Volga and the Don.

My long-planned holiday had just been cancelled at a month's notice. I had booked a place on a series of coach and boat trips along the Rhine, but was told a month before departure that there would be no one to help with my luggage – this despite having received assurances over the past six months that there would be no problem. Then my neighbour happened to bring round a brochure containing details of the Russian cruise. The first step, as always, was to ring the airline (*Aeroflot*) to check whether a wheelchair would be available at Gatwick and Moscow; I was told that there would be.

There was a *Saga* courier on the plane, but I soon realised that she was so scared about the prospect of taking a group to Russia that her mental processes had seized up and she was in

no state to cope with special needs. As we approached Moscow I checked with the stewardess that a wheelchair would meet the plane but she looked blank and shook her head.

On arrival I stood in the passage from the plane with my hand luggage. Eventually a charming hostess took my bags, gave me an arm, led me to the front of the first queue and then gently faded away. (I soon discovered that this "Cheshire cat" procedure was often used as a way out of a problem.) I followed a sign to a desk where English was spoken and asked for a porter. One was found and I joined the other passengers. Although I am interested in architecture, statues and memorials usually leave me cold. However, on the drive from the airport we saw the modern tributes to the astronauts and space flights, and these were breathtaking. We drove through the suburbs of Moscow to a modern and luxurious hotel which had been completed in time for the Olympic Games, its vast concourse providing shops and other services for tourists.

Normally, I insist on a single room, but as the holiday captivated me I agreed to share, thinking that I could always rest when I returned home. The other passenger with whom I shared the very spacious room was a late-nighter, determined to enjoy every minute of a break from caring for a difficult invalid mother; I am an early bird, satisfied with the day's activities. She must have been appalled to find she was sharing with someone with white hair and wobbly legs. We would have got on, but when we eventually arrived at the cruise boat we found there were empty cabins and we were allowed to have one each.

Three nights in this amazing hotel allowed two full days for sightseeing. I did not join a visit to the circus or a tour of the city centre because there would have been too much walking. The weather was perfect and I was able to enjoy the view from our balcony of a large park and leisure area with sports facilities. I watched the families walking in the park and the youngsters heading for the sports arenas. Equally absorbing was the hotel's enormous vestibule, where I sat while visitors from all over the world circulated around me.

On the second day I treated myself to a taxi tour of the main points of interest, with a driver who soon became an enthusiastic guide. He spoke no English but between us we worked out such words as library, theatre and, of course, Bolshoi. The taxi could not enter Red Square but stopped at a good vantage point. Although the buildings are surrounded by huge, red granite walls, there is no sense of claustrophobia because the square is so vast.

The next morning we were to fly direct from Moscow to Rostov, on the Don, but because of weather conditions we were diverted to Donetsk, where our plane landed in the middle of a vast open space, with the airport building almost out of sight. The sun was beating down and there was no minibus or wheelchair. By this time I had discussed the problem with the *Intourist* guide, who spoke excellent English. The idea of using a wheel-chair, unless one was very ill, was completely new. In lieu of a chair, I was assigned a river boat captain to help me across what seemed like the Sahara desert. He normally operated on the Danube and was on our trip on some sort of training course. His English was not fluent and he was pleased to practise it.

The tourists on the aircraft were provided with lunch in a spotless restaurant. I don't think the locals fared so well. They seemed used to the delay, with little information about what was happening; internal flights cover the great distances between towns much as our bus network covers the UK. Finally we were able to reboard the plane and flew to Rostov. We drove along a tree-lined boulevard to our cruise boat, where all the other passengers were waiting for us somewhat hungrily, as the meal was not served until we were all aboard.

"The sing-song went on long after I retired to bed, which says much for Russian tolerance"

The following day we toured Rostov, now a flourishing regional capital. It is said to have grown from a small customs house, established in the eighteenth century to handle the growing trade between East and West. The Cossacks came from this area, and later we drove to Novocherkassk to visit a museum of Cossack history. I was impressed by the care taken with the collection of uniforms and equipment displayed on the ground floor. I decided not to attempt the stairs to other sections. It was a blazingly hot afternoon, and I sat on the main entrance steps, keeping an eye on the coach in case it moved off to collect the rest of the group from another entrance.

One day the boat was moored to an island for passengers to enjoy a picnic and a swim. Our cruise coincided with the wedding of the Prince of Wales, and I was surprised that the British passengers felt that there had to be some celebration, particularly on the ship of another country. However, one of the lounges was made available for an evening sing-song, and we found bottles of champagne on the dinner tables with the compliments of the captain for us to drink a toast to the royal couple. The sing-song went on long after I retired to bed, which says much for Russian tolerance. What the Germans sleeping on the deck below made of it I do not know.

"Chewing gum, chocolate and ballpoint pens were all in short supply and made useful "thank you" presents"

After cruising along the Don, through the Tsimlyansk reservoir and the thirteen locks along the canal linking the Don and the Volga, we reached Volgograd (Stalingrad). I did not go ashore because of the number of steps, but was happy to laze on deck in the sun and view the activity on the water, and the huge memorial dominating the city, through my binoculars. There were passenger ferries, vegetable market boats, cargo boats and pleasure craft bustling around me. It was difficult to imagine the river frozen over, as it is for several months of the year.

We cruised for two days along the Volga, passing small villages and huge hydroelectric schemes. At Zhiguli the river winds round the Zhiguli mountains and the banks are lined with forests, holiday homes and beaches. Many people were enjoying their summer holidays, fishing, sailing, rowing and swimming. We moored at a small landing stage in apparently rural surroundings. A short path through a wood led to a coach with a blue-eyed woman guide, who took us to Togliatti.

A modern town and the centre of the car industry, Togliatti (Tolyatti) was named in honour of the Italians who helped to establish the industry. The average age of the inhabitants was 27, so no grandmothers – or, as one passenger put it, no mothers-in-law. The sports fields and indoor skating rinks were full of children. Our guide had a young family, so I gave her some chewing gum for the children; chewing gum, chocolate and ballpoint pens were all in short supply and made useful "thank you" presents.

On board again, we cruised along day and night. The *Intourist* guide held classes to try to teach some Russian to those who cared to attend. A young university lecturer and an older medical consultant organised discussions in English and most of the British passengers joined in. We were encouraged to ask questions and not to avoid controversial subjects. I am reminded of some of these sessions when reading the international news today.

We were told that the presence of the Russian army in Afghanistan was to support the government there in trying to release the population from serfdom, so that there was wider ownership of land and means of earning a living. From answers about Poland we gleaned that the Russians were rather fed up with the Poles because they had given Poland financial support years ago, only to see it spent on expensive imported machinery to make goods for export – the Poles should have used this aid, which the Russians could ill afford, to produce goods for home consumption. On the subject of arms control we were told that the Soviet Union had sacrificed twenty million lives to "free the world from fascism" and that although they had no desire for war they had no intention of being overrun again; hence they must defend themselves, and hence the phrase which we heard repeated many times: "Never again".

On another day we visited Ulyanosk, the birthplace of Lenin. Founded in the seventeenth century as Simbirsk, a frontier fortress, it became the administrative centre for the Volga region in the eighteenth century. Lenin (real name, Vladimir Ilyich Ulyanov) was born and grew up here, and in 1924 the place was renamed in his honour. We visited the spacious city with its parks, gracious buildings and tree-lined avenues, all beautifully cared for. In the inner courtyard of the Lenin Memorial complex is the cottage where he was born, and other houses in which the family lived have been restored and used as museums or for archives.

At that point on our cruise we had flown south from Moscow to Rostov, sailed east to Volgograd and then northeast to Zhiguli and Ulyanovsk. Finally we arrived at Kazan, some 400 miles east of Moscow. In the early morning light the romantic buildings made a wonderful skyline as we approached. This was the first time we seemed to be at the centre of a rural community, with produce being brought in by old lorries and carts, the odd item of national dress and a few Tartar features on the faces of the inhabitants. The city was founded on the fifteenth-century cultural centre of the Tartars, and in the Middle Ages was the capital of a Muslim state. This history is reflected in the mosques and the Kazan Kremlin.

"All attempts to get out of the chair failed, so I hung on to the armrests and leaned back, accepting the inevitable"

While the rest of the party walked out from the central cobbled square for a closer view, I indulged in a favourite occupation – sitting in the square, watching the comings and goings of the local population. The city was spotlessly clean. My river captain helper, who had spent a few weeks in London on a course, said that he could not understand how a nation as caring as the British could tolerate the dirtiness and litter on our streets.

The next morning we set off by coach for Kazan airport. We flew to Moscow where the *Intourist* guide was clearly determined to show what could be done, after all my enquiries about facilities for disabled people. I was deposited in a wheelchair, in sight of Customs and Passport Control desks. Beyond these I saw a little man looking at me somewhat apprehensively. When chair and I got through the barriers, the little man and I agreed that we were meant for each other, without speaking a word, and we proceeded to a large waiting area for a long wait. There were no food kiosks, and a packet of Polo mints was all I had. I offered one to my pusher but he shied off as though it were poison.

Eventually, large metal doors opened at the end of the waiting area and I was pushed towards them. I realised with horror that immediately beyond was a steep flight of concrete steps, and I tried to convey to my helper that I would walk down them. I tried to get out of the chair – I was certain that the pusher had no experience of manhandling a wheelchair and that he did what he was told, in this instance delivering me to the minibus waiting to take us to the plane. All attempts to get out of the chair failed, so I hung on to the armrests and leaned back, accepting the inevitable.

The little man and the chair parted company immediately. I remained in the chair, banging the back of my head on the edge of each step until we crashed on the half-landing. Two large passengers picked me up and carried me to the minibus, by which time a doctor had arrived. He inspected the damage, took my pulse, gave me a couple of tablets and escorted me, walking, up the steps to the plane.

Gatwick's usual efficient transport and my friends with a car were a welcome sight. My arm movement had recovered but there was a lump as big as a hen's egg as evidence of my experience. When I wrote to the airline agent at Gatwick, referring to the advice received before my trip, he replied that I had been misinformed, as there was nothing for the disabled passenger at Moscow. No doubt it is all very different now – worth checking because it was a lovely cruise and the best value for money of all my holidays.

I am now eighty years old and my muscular strength has lessened considerably. I use a battery scooter and a car to get about locally but still possess the drive and enthusiasm to travel, and I am grateful for those tour companies that provide holidays for the less active. I am off to Canada with *Carefree* as I finish this account, and I have been on a number of other holidays where help was included as part of the package. If I book with a company that does not set out to provide special facilities or assistance to disabled holidaymakers, then I do not expect to receive help, nor do I ask for it (except for carrying my luggage): where steps, or walking distance, or walking speed of the rest of the party defeat me, I accept that I must miss out on some parts of the trip. It is not the duty of couriers or fellow passengers to assist me or to slow down to my pace.

Art Appreciation in Moscow and Leningrad

In December 1988, Joy Schwabe travelled with three friends to Russia for a five-day tour. She is a "little person", just one metre tall, a coeliac and at the time of the holiday had cataracts in both eyes.

The gluten-free diet was comparatively easy to cope with. Food is not of prime importance to me and, besides, the range of foods that I am allowed is quite comprehensive and I took special biscuits with me. I can walk only a limited distance, so I travel with a child's pushchair. I can manage a few steps if they are shallow. My friends knew of and understood my limitations; it required two people to overcome some of these, such as carrying me and my "pusher" up flights of steps.

We flew from Gatwick airport, a group of 29 plus tour manager and guest lecturer – the prime reason for the trip was to see art and architectural treasures. No special provisions had been asked for at the airport, and they proved unnecessary. I found the flight rather uncomfortable as I have a respiratory difficulty which worsens when I am sitting in a restricted position. But the air hostess was kind and attentive, providing two extra pillows which were a great help.

The passage through Moscow airport was slow. There were few trolleys and no porters, and we had no offers of help. However, no complaints – we had not asked for any special treatment. Our bus was waiting for us at the airport, and we were taken on a brief tour of Moscow before going to a hotel for a meal, prior to taking the overnight train to Leningrad.

First-class sleeping compartments had been booked for us and with two to a compartment we were very comfortable. A fully made-up bed was provided, together with tea and piped music. The heating was very efficient so we thoroughly enjoyed this part of the journey.

The view from the train was enchanting. It was almost unreal, straight out of *Doctor Zhivago* – brilliant moonlight sparkling on the snow, the silver birches and larches making wonderful groupings and patterns. I suppose it is a rare sight that absolutely matches up to one's preconceived ideas, but this scenery certainly did.

Our hotel in Leningrad was comfortable, with a lift to all floors. I could not operate this by myself, so I was obliged to go about with one or other of my friends. I had to share a room because I am unable to manage most light switches and some door handles; if there is no stool or chair available I cannot even use the washbasin. We took a golf ball with us, as we'd been told that sometimes there are no plugs; in the event, our bath had a plug but the washbasin did not.

The hotel was well heated, as indeed were all the buildings we visited. In the public buildings, including museums and theatres, it is customary to leave one's outer clothes in the cloakroom. In the cloakroom of the Hermitage Museum I obviously brought out the attendant's motherly, or even grandmotherly, instincts – she gave me a sweetie and patted me on the head (I am over seventy years old).

I am very interested in art, and had for many years wanted to visit the Hermitage. It was built by Catherine the Great as a private palace where she could go to escape the formality of court life. A very acquisitive lady, she began to collect works of art of many kinds. When she really got going, and was buying up as many European art collections as she could afford (of course, she had enormous wealth), the palace was enlarged.

The pictures which Catherine bought from the Walpole collection were of particular interest to me because the Walpole family house, Houghton Hall, is in Norfolk, not far

from where I live. Among more than a hundred pictures purchased at that time from the Walpoles were two Rubens, four Van Dycks and no less than nine Rembrandts. I do not know if the removal of any of these was responsible for the especially large silhouette of darker wallpaper in one of the Houghton rooms, but that's the sort of thing which fires my imagination. If I couldn't see the picture in Norfolk, I'd have to travel to Russia.

The Hermitage not only houses pictures from earlier centuries but also offers a huge collection of modern art, with some of the very best works of the artists represented. Some of Matisse's most famous pictures are on show, as well as a comprehensive Picasso collection, Monet, Gaugin, Van Gogh and many, many more – no wonder I couldn't wait to get there.

"I found myself hoisted aloft in my "pusher" and solemnly carried upstairs by two large men"

We were allowed to take my "pusher" into the building, but this was because it was a comparatively quiet time, out of season. What the ruling is about wheelchairs I don't know. There were no wheelchair users there when we visited, and no chairs on view at the entrance, awaiting the casual visitor as one might expect in our museums or galleries. There are no lifts in the Hermitage, and it is a strange sight to see enormous and priceless works of art being manhandled all over the building by the museum attendants; their experience worked in my favour, however, because when it came to negotiating the imposing staircase I found myself hoisted aloft in my "pusher" and solemnly carried upstairs by two large men.

The pictures were beautifully hung and the lighting was good. Of course, I was at a disadvantage, viewing from my peculiar angle and with cataracts, but if anyone had tried to describe the pictures to me I'd have bitten their ankles. It was somewhat unnerving for the person who was pushing me about, as I did occasionally stand on the seat of my pushchair without warning.

We decided to have lunch and continue viewing later. There is a choice of cafeteria or restaurant. The stools were too high for me in the cafeteria but we were allowed to eat our cafeteria meal in the restaurant. There are no packaged foods; fruit juices came in glasses and food was served straight onto plates, which we returned at the end of the meal; not a crisp packet in sight.

"We only scratched the surface, and I think we all felt some sadness when we considered all the things left unseen"

Among my lasting impressions of the Soviet Union is the monstrous scale of the place – more noticeable than usual, for me! Red Square is huge, the colours of its buildings made more vibrant by the contrast with dazzling white snow. After seeing that we passed through vast, snowy wastes on our train journey, and then came Leningrad, the great Winter Palace and the Hermitage Museum. When visiting the Winter Palace we had to wear giant felt boots to protect the beautiful marble and marquetry floors. As these are made to fit over the largest size of boots, you can imagine what I looked like!

Although there was always a solution to the problems we encountered, such as the staircase and high stools in the Hermitage, we saw no wheelchairs and no facilities for wheelchair users – no adapted lavatories, for example. We

couldn't see the kerbs for snow, so I don't know if these are lowered anywhere. The deep snow was no deterrent to us, as we were taken to our various destinations by bus. The entrance porch of one building was wet ice, so to prevent me falling (I was walking at the time) one of my friends put her bright woollen gloves on my feet.

We visited the Kirov ballet while in Leningrad and saw an evening performance of *The Nutcracker* by what seemed to be a young company. The colours of the interior of the theatre are glorious – pale turquoise, gilt and cream, like a scene from *Sleeping Beauty*. The Imperial Box is still there, no doubt used by state and visiting dignitaries. The theatre has kept one tradition, that of promenading in the corridor during the interval – all miraculously going the same way round.

Of course, we only scratched the surface, and I think we all felt some sadness when we considered all the things left unseen. On the other hand we were well satisfied with what we had experienced, and not one of the sights was a disappointment to me.

Our return to Moscow was by plane, not nearly as romantic as the train journey. At Moscow airport we had a rather distressing wait in near darkness on some stairs, and the flight behind us was called first, with the result that we were badly jostled. The flight to London was comfortable enough and at Gatwick one of my friends and I were picked up by a buggy. We sailed past the other passengers, including our two friends, leaving them to battle with the luggage. There have to be *some* advantages to being "different".

EASTERN EUROPE & THE SOVIET UNION: TRAVEL NOTES

Sources of information

Danube Travel, 6 Conduit Street, London W1R 9TG; ☎071/493 0263. The British agent for the Hungarian National Tourist Office, they provide the only official literature for these countries in which any wheelchair symbols can be seen.

Tourist offices for Poland, Czechoslovakia and the Soviet Union supply no specific information for disabled tourists, although staff at the Soviet office (*Intourist Moscow Ltd*, 219 Marsh Wall, Isle of Dogs, London E14 9FJ; ☎071/538 8600) were able to answer specific questions about access to museums and galleries. Wheelchairs are now available at Moscow airport, also at Polish and Hungarian airports.

Reliable information concerning transport, accommodation and other facilities are difficult to obtain, and will only emerge as more disabled tourists explore these countries.

Access and facilities

Although one visually handicapped contributor waxed lyrical about the caring attitudes towards disabled people in Hungary, and the ease of using public transport in Budapest, the general picture is pretty grim for the disabled Eastern European: scant regard to access by architects of public buildings, and little public agitation on this matter; tortuous procedures for acquiring special aids and appliances – most have to be imported; wheelchairs and work very hard to come by; general preference for segregation rather than integration of disabled people into the community; in Romania the treatment of disabled citizens has only recently come to light, and is summed up by one word – neglect.

In **Czechoslovakia** under communism, private charities were banned, with the intention that the state would provide for any ill or handicapped citizens. But the state had neither sufficient funds nor the drive to do this. Disabled people became social outcasts, the facilities in their institutions inadequate and antiquated.

There is hope for change in the wake of the recent political upheavals. Olga Havel, the wife of the Czech president, has set up a "Goodwill Committee", whose aims include the revival of charities and the eradication of the fear and ignorance which has resulted in society's rejection of the disabled. With the help of TV programmes and public meetings the committee has raised awareness, put disabled groups in touch with each other and initiated fund-raising projects. Progress is painfully slow, but in spite of the country's desperate economic situation the donations are rolling in, and Olga Havel's efforts abroad have brought in foreign currency which is vital for the purchase of medicines and equipment.

In the **Soviet Union**, disabled people have been kept under wraps for years. There is a chronic shortage of wheelchairs and other basic equipment. Disabled people receive tiny allowances and pensions and most cannot find employment. Since Mikhail Gorbachev's arrival on the scene, charities have been allowed to operate and all disabled people can form societies (in the past, only blind and deaf people could do this). The president of *APPAREL* (*Association of Young Disabled People KMO*, 7/8 Bogdan Khmelnitsky Street, 101846 Moscow; ☎095/2068 542), Alexei Kupriyanov, has become a new committee member of *Mobility International*, and the spring 1990 issue of *Mobility International News* records that letters arrive almost daily from new organisations in the Soviet Union. But conditions for disabled people living there remain harsh.

Life is no easier in **Poland**. Annie Delin's account gives some hints for surviving as a disabled visitor, but Poles with handicaps need more than a survival guide. Again, state benefits are low and obtaining work is difficult; medicines and appliances are scarce; the list goes on.

To become involved in **exchange visits** and discussion of common problems with disabled people in Poland, contact Conrad Packwood or Martyn Allen (Wellington Centre, 52 Chevalier Street, Ipswich, Suffolk IP1 2PB; ☎0473/226950), and to keep up with developments in Eastern Europe (as well as other parts of the world), subscribe to *Disability Now* (12 Park Crescent, London W1E 3HU; ☎071/636 5020) and *Mobility International News* (228 Borough High Street, London SE1 1JX; ☎071/403 5688).

PART THREE

NEAR AND MIDDLE EAST

Introduction

A t the time of writing, the aftermath of the **war in the Gulf** casts a shadow over all hopes of travel to the Middle East. Most flights have been cancelled or diverted; tour companies are shuffling resorts and temporarily suspending their operations. Many ancient sites have been destroyed, wildlife and habitats devastated. The inhabitants of the region face great danger as well as disruption of everyday life.

It's difficult to see beyond all this and envisage any sort of long-term recovery and stability. But, assuming eventual return to some semblance of normality, this part of the world will continue to attract many tourists: to visit sites of religious significance or the remains of early civilisations; to learn something of the feuds and struggles that punctuate the history of the Arab Emirates; to experience the stunning landscapes of the desert and the famed hospitality of the desert peoples; to float down the Nile in a felucca or shop in the souks.

For the disabled tourist the main problems are finding accessible accommodation at less than four-star prices, gaining access to sights, making do (almost everywhere) without any form of accessible transport, and tracking down a loo that doesn't require either the removal of the door or a delicate balancing act in order to use it. These are not insurmountable problems, but it would be cheering to see more widespread efforts to remove them.

Israel has seen most progress in all these areas, probably as a result of the organisations of disabled people, such as the *Israel Rehabilitation Society* (18 David Elazar Street, Hakirya, Tel Aviv 61909; ☎3/217043) which, through conferences and meetings, attempts to make changes on a variety of fronts, including access to buildings and awareness of disabled people's requirements.

Some **legislation** has been pushed through concerning hotel facilities (see Israel *Travel Notes*), but either this has failed to make an impact at the cheaper end of the market, or there has been a failure in communication. Perhaps the smaller hotels have made improvements, widened doorways, adapted bathrooms, but the promotion of this new-found accessibility has not been effective – there is certainly nothing in the tourist board brochures.

A recent issue of *Mobility International News* reports that the USA-based; non-profit organisation *Chazon Hagalil* (6589 Racquet Club Drive, Lauderhill, Florida 33319; ☎305/739-5332), established to encourage handicapped tourists (and families) to visit Israel, aims to develop a network of **"barrier-free, recreational resorts"** in Israel, starting in northern Galilee. The resorts are to have extensive ramping to beaches and fishing piers, and employees sensitive to the needs of guests with sensory as well as mobility impairments. Let's hope the accommodation in these havens of accessibility will be realistically priced.

Another of *Chazon Hagalil*'s aims is to initiate a work/study programme to run in conjunction with the hotel management curriculum offered at Israeli universities. This is getting to the root of the problem, and likely to be more effective than any amount of legislation.

Increasing **awareness** of the (often minor) modifications needed to make accommodation and sights accessible to those with limited mobility is of prime importance in countries where a wheelchair is a rare sight and there is an alarming lack of comprehension of the problems of those with limited mobility. Barry Atkinson comments on being directed to impossible places by a customs official on the border between Israel and Egypt; the officer clearly had no experience of wheelchairs.

The scarcity of accessible transport does not prevent tourists in wheelchairs from joining **organised tours**, given a tour company with the right approach. Guides are usually helpful and willing to push chairs or assist with boarding and disembarking; taxi drivers are also helpful. In Egypt there is a company that specialises in tours for disabled people, using an accessible, albeit basically equipped, vehicle. But the introduction of hydraulic lifts on at least half of tour buses would be a great step forward, as would the availability of hand-controlled hire cars and minibuses with tail-lifts.

In many countries the money is there, the flashy hotels, the shops, the hospitals, the highways, the modern airports. But the forces that fired the independent living movements, the pressures that brought about the necessary environmental changes in other parts of the world are largely absent – or only just beginning.

Israel

The View from Masada

Barry Atkinson spent three weeks in Israel, in January 1989, including a trip into Egypt's Sinai desert. He is virtually confined to a wheelchair but has strong arms and is well used to travelling alone.

It was not the entry to the country that I had imagined. I was alone and in a wheelchair, riding an Airbus to Ovda, instead of tramping wearily to some kibbutz near Jerusalem. But, let's face it, I was extremely lucky to be where I was. The tight security at Gatwick, the two-hour delay when customs officers refused a couple entry, the five-hour flight, all added to my anticipation.

Rather against my natural inclinations, I had chosen a hotel in the tourist area of Eilat, on the Red Sea, and a package agent, *Intasun*. The usual bank loan had paved my way; the hotel had the wheelchair symbol in the *Best Western* guide (which I had always found very satisfactory); I had a pocket full of travellers' cheques and felt safe. True, because of media coverage and the possibility of terrorist attacks on planes, many people had advised me not to go, but I had quite a bit of travel experience, and my interest in the conflicts between Islam and Christianity, plus the aura of desert lands, held sway. It was one of the best decisions I have ever made.

The Airbus landed in the dark at Ovda, in the Negev desert. I was

carried off the plane (there is no high-lift vehicle at present) and the *Intasun* coach drove to Eilat along the Egyptian border. My hotel, although living up to the luxury of its four-star status, did not, to my mind, deserve the wheelchair symbol. The steps to the dining room were soon overcome because I was given special service in an accessible coffee room. But, even with the door taken off, I could not get my wheelchair from the bedroom into the bathroom.

The *Intasun* rep advised me to move to the *Sport Hotel*, which has adapted rooms, but I liked where I was and did not want to pay the extra money to stay at the *Sport*. Instead, I obtained a second wheelchair from the local hospital and left it in the bathroom; I could then transfer from my own chair to that one when I wanted to use the bathroom. Problem solved! But I had to pay £175 returnable deposit to the hospital, which meant money tied up that I could ill afford (I used the credit card instead). This incident illustrates the advantage of having a tour company rep on the spot – she arranged the wheelchair loan for me. (I have since complained to *Best Western*, who sent a standard "sorry" reply and said that they had sent my letter to their branch in Israel. I have heard nothing more.)

My first trip was a two-day tour to Jerusalem, Bethlehem, the Dead Sea and Jericho – biblical names to conjure with! Via the *Intasun* rep, I had explained the position to the tour company and they had agreed to cope with the wheelchair and my lack of mobility. Later, after a marvellous two days, I paid the guide and driver a big tip. The same tour company refused to take me, unless accompanied, on a five-day trip to Cairo. Fair enough! I was in no position to argue and, judging by comments from those that went, perhaps they were right. I wheeled myself to a local restaurant and had a red-hot meal and bottle of wine instead.

One of the aspects of disability that I find difficult is coping with an early start. When travelling, especially alone, this is unavoidable and has to be accepted; often it is the only way to achieve anything. The trip to Jerusalem meant rising at 4am, but it was worth it. During the day, Eilat, although windy, was basking in hot sunshine at 75–80° F. It was early when we started but as we drove north amid the scree and rocky wastes of the Negev desert, the temperatures dropped. Forlorn acacia trees clung everywhere to the loose, gritty surface. As the sun rose, a collection of strange shadows appeared on either side of the road.

As the light grew we became aware of unexpected green areas, as kibbutzim broke from the desolate landscape.

Israel has watered itself from north to south by a National Water Carrier pipe which keeps even the deep south of Eilat (with an average annual rainfall of 25mm) fertile. The Sea of Galilee, fed by the River Jordan, is its main reservoir. The water-line, together with the intensive agriculture of the kibbutzim, are vital to Israel's survival.

When we came to the Dead Sea (actually two shrinking lakes) the sky was blue but the temperature cool, so few floated in the mineral waters. Instead we watched the rapidly changing salt deposits, which bloom across the sea like eaten mushrooms or lines of battered coral. The factory complex which is built on the site of ancient Sodom bursts with economic vitality 24 hours a day, using the minerals formed here.

"'Jerusalem has no heavy industry – only religion.' The immediate impression is one of graves"

Next we went to Masada where, in 73 AD, the Jews made a last desperate stand against the Romans, eventually committing a grisly mass suicide. Today the Zealots' action is revered, and I have seen pictures which show that the archaeological site is both carefully preserved and deeply interesting. But there was no way that my wheelchair could reach it. Masada rises 396 gaunt metres from the Dead Sea, and the ruins are on a plateau at the top. A cable car takes you halfway up, from where the view is magnificent, but a multitude of steps continue.

Sitting on the cable car platform, staring across the miniaturised desert and Dead Sea, I tried to put my frustration into perspective. There was a lot of life in front of me: the Jordanian border running through the centre of the Dead Sea, and nearby Qumran, now an unearthed Essene settlement, where the priceless Dead Sea Scrolls were discovered; and there was the Judean desert, barely disturbed by mankind.

In the manner of coach tours, Jericho – a peaceful city of date palms to the northeast of Jerusalem – was a rushed visit which left me with a feeling of attraction that only a return visit can confirm. Like Bethlehem, Jericho is an Arab town. Throughout the ages the city, which has been rebuilt many times, has remained close to Elisha's Spring. A site known as Tel es-Sultan has been excavated at intervals since 1868, and evidence of a colony as early as 8000 BC has been found. The falling of the city walls to Joshua's famed trumpets, whatever the real cause, happened about 1250 BC. We listened to the tour guide's patter, bought citrus fruit at a local market, and drove on to Jerusalem.

There was no disputing the guide's next statement: "Jerusalem has no heavy industry – only religion." The immediate impression is one of graves. The tombs lie on all the slopes of the walled, ancient city because the Jews are still awaiting the arrival of the Messiah, who will enter the Temple Courts through the now blocked Golden Gate. The dead buried here will be the first to rise.

"I was humbled at simply feeling the mortar, ancient and pitted, beneath my fingers"

Israel has a total population of over four million: over three million are Jews, 525,000 Muslims, 95,000 Christians and 53,000 Druze. Jerusalem is a holy city for all; despite the external conflict, the atmosphere is one of religious freedom. The followers of Christ move along the Via Dolorosa, with its fourteen stations of the cross, and worship in the Church of the Holy Sepulchre. Muslims visit their third holy city after the hadj (pilgrimage to Mecca; their second holy city is Medina).

A portion of the Koran speaks of a night journey made by Muhammed, accompanied by an angel. This journey is believed to have ended at Solomon's Temple, where the Dome of the Rock was built. Muslims visit this and the nearby El-Aqsa mosque. To the Jews, the Temple Mount – home to Islam's Dome of the Rock – is Mount Moriah, where Abraham bound his son Isaac for sacrifice. The hillcrest was also the site of David's altar, over which Solomon built the Temple, eventually replaced by Herod's edifice.

Today, only Herod's western wall (the famous "Wailing Wall") remains and has become a symbol of the unwavering faith and devotion of Judaism. After being vetted by the armed guards, we arrived at the Wailing Wall and found it very much alive, constantly visited by Jews who pray and rock in anguish before it. I rolled up to the men's section in my wheelchair and put my hand on the rough surface. Beside me a young orthodox Jew, black suited and with plaited hair falling beneath his dark, wide-brimmed hat, seemed to play out his nation's grief, his hand clutching the Torah. On my other side a rabbi talked with the male members of the family of a bar mitzvah boy; out of my sight the women gave vent to the poignant trill of eastern, female emotion. I was humbled at simply feeling the mortar, ancient and pitted, beneath my fingers.

Perhaps Jewish hotel bathrooms are all the same because, once again, I could not get my wheelchair through the door. Luckily, I could just get to the toilet and washbasins by using the basins as grab rails and swinging round. It was only for one night, and somehow the basins took my weight, but it was not the best of situations!

The morning saw us off to Bethlehem and the Church of the Nativity, which is shared by the Armenians, the Greek Orthodox Church and the Latins. We passed the little synagogue built on the spot of Jacob's burial of his young wife, Rachel. Bethlehem was disappointing in that, unlike much of the Holy Land, it has a totally commercial, "tripperish" feel. The gaudy tourist shops in the square by the church disperse all reverence. My wheelchair kept me out of the Grotto of the Nativity, and perhaps actually being in the place of Jesus' birth would have restored some of the emotion, but I was happy to leave and return to the Mount of Olives with its fantastic view of old Jerusalem. Here, despite the Arabs offering rides on their stolid, gaily bedecked camels, or pestering us to buy trinkets, there was no distraction. Below us was the ancient, walled city in all its splendour, fronted by the bright gold of the Dome of the Rock and the silvered rotunda of El-Aqsa mosque.

We returned to warmer Eilat, some 300km away, where, knowing my illness and aware of the need to pace myself, I spent a few quiet days sunbathing by the pool or slowly wheeling myself along the promenade. With friends I had made on the Jerusalem trip, I went to Coral World, nearby on the Red Sea. The underwater observatory was inaccessible to me but there was a marvellous aquarium. Red Sea marine life is unbelievably varied and colourful; the fish make a brilliant display, swimming amid the delicate lace-work of the coral. Apart from the observatory, Coral World is ramped and access easy; I paid reduced admission because of the observatory. For those who are able, the Red Sea is justly renowned for sub-aqua diving.

After some lazy days I decided on another trip. As before, I arranged this with the *Intasun* rep and a local company. I was to go into Egypt, to St Catherine's Monastery in the Sinai desert. I already had a visa, although I learnt when booking the trip that you can visit the monastery without one. As usual, the start was early; indeed, the dawn did not break until we were in Egypt, waiting outside the wretched frontier huts for a second coach to pick us up.

An Israeli coach had brought us to Taba (a tiny stretch of land then in dispute, now handed over to Egypt), and we had walked across the border. The guide pushed me and helped happily throughout. My experience of travelling in Arab lands has been that the ways of dealing with a wheelchair are often simply not understood, the problems of steps not considered. Here, the lethargic customs officials ushered me to impossible places, and were nonplussed when I could not go; only the common sense of the guide saved an awkward situation. But my excitement at being on the edge of such a famed desert could not be damp-ened, even if, watched by the tired eyes of the customs officers, we had to wait for ninety minutes for our second coach.

"My shouts of pain and panic were ignored; my legs trailed beneath the chair, waiting to break"

The early cloud departed and our transport arrived. At first we drove past hills of red and green rocks, alternating with regions of flat scree. Then came the higher ground, and layers of sand that hinted at Africa's Sahara, now so near. Sometimes a lone camel wandered past, sometimes a bedouin, protected and hidden beneath his robes. Where was he going? To the coast? To an isolated nomadic camp?

St Catherine's Monastery is run by Greek Orthodoxy, not by the Coptic Church as is wrongly stated in the tour-ist brochure. Named after the finding of St Catherine nearby, it still maintains the (disappointing) burning bush, and it overlooks Mount Moses. Not so long ago the only entry into the monastery was by basket, hauled up the walls. Today there is a door, but so narrow that a wheelchair has no chance. Besides, I could glimpse flights of steps inside, so I decided to wait outside with the sleepy bedouin "servants" to the monks.

However, two Egyptian guides were now in charge of us and, ignoring my protests, they carried me through the door, deposited me awkwardly on the ground and returned for the folded wheelchair. Somehow I clambered aboard and, panting, was inside the monastery. In fact there was little to see except the ornate grandeur of the incense-soaked church, and the burning bush which is almost hidden behind thick walls.

Trouble came, as I had foreseen, with the steps. The Egyptian happily pushed me along but when we came to the steps he simply carried on as though they did not exist. My shouts of pain and panic were ignored; my legs trailed beneath the chair, waiting to break, while I clutched uselessly at the armrests. Luckily, a member of the party saw what was happening and forced the bewildered guide to stop. Highly relieved, I was carried the rest of the way down.

Once outside, we visited the piles of bones of all the dead monks in the charnel house, then boarded the coach again. The mishaps in the monastery were soon forgotten amid the evocative spaces of the desert. A desert landscape is not only different, it is special. One's mind, attempting to deal with the empty spaces, is forced into strange, almost spiritual regions. If I ever get to the Sahara it surely cannot affect me as much as this, my first time in Sinai.

ISRAEL: TRAVEL NOTES

Sources of information

Israel Government Tourist Office, 18 Great Marlborough Street, London W1V 1AF; ☎071/434 3651. Much the best equipped in the region to deal with enquiries from disabled travellers, with copies of *Access in Israel* (see *Books*) to distribute.

Tour operators

Although he usually travels independently, Barry Atkinson booked an *Intasun* package in Israel and was glad to have a rep on the spot to deal with such matters as arranging wheelchair hire from a local hospital, and explaining his mobility limitations to the guide when fixing up trips with Israeli tour companies. *Thomson* offer a number of holidays in Israel.

If you fancy approaching by sea, and your budget is fairly unrestrained, *P&O* offer a number of cruises on the *Canberra* and the *Sea Princess* that take in the Holy Land, the pyramids and other "cradles of civilisation".

Getting there

El Al is one of the few airlines to place no limitation on the number of wheelchair passengers carried per aircraft. Although they do not carry aisle wheelchairs, passengers can bring on board their own collapsible, flight-approved chairs. One toilet aboard each 757 or 767 has been designed for use by on-board wheelchairs. Disabled passengers (individuals or groups) are pre-boarded.

El Al and *BA* flights land at Ben Gurion **airport**, where there are adapted toilets, low tables in the cafeteria and low-level public telephones. The "ELALIFT" will disembark or board up to ten wheelchairs at a time, and blind or disabled passengers may also use this service. Allow plenty of time if making a connecting flight because other airlines make use of the lift and there may be some delay before disembarking.

If you are flying on from here you may have to transfer to Sde Dov airport – it's about a thirty-minute taxi ride. There are unlikely to be

ISRAEL: TRAVEL NOTES

lifting vehicles at the regional airports, but check with *Arkia Israel Airlines* (Sde Dov Airport, P.O.B. 39301, Tel Aviv 61392; ☎3/422777), the domestic operator. Barry Atkinson flew direct to Ovda with *Dan Air*, and was carried off the plane.

There are regular **ferry** sailings from Greece, Cyprus and Italy to the Israeli ports of Haifa and Ashdod.

Transport

Although road conditions are pretty good, self-drive motoring is not recommended in the desert – put yourself in the hands of an experienced guide and driver, either as part of a group or by hiring a taxi by the day (negotiate the price before setting off). Taxis are usually large and probably the best mode of transport in the region, certainly for individual sightseeing or for getting about the cities.

Cars with hand controls can be hired from *All Tours Ltd* (14 Gaza Street, P.O.B. 4249, Jerusalem; ☎2/667676), and an adapted vehicle with tail-lift can be hired for transfers from *Yad Sarah* (Society for Loaning Medical Equipment, 43 Hanevieim Street, P.O.B. 6992, Jerusalem 91069; ☎2/244242).

Buses and trains are generally difficult – high steps, narrow doorways, and a stampede when the time comes to board. Don't plan to use them without a companion or two. On tour coaches the guides are usually helpful, but be sure to discuss your capabilities before booking and don't be surprised if some tours are simply not practical unless you are accompanied.

Accommodation

The law requiring all new hotels to provide facilities for guests in wheelchairs, before they are given an operating licence, has not been strictly enforced, and although the *Access in Israel* team set out to find three-star or cheaper hotels with good access, they found that there were nearly always some obstacles – mainly steps and narrow doorways. As ever, the more expensive hotels are more likely to suit. Nevertheless, there are some active disability organisations, and with pressure from disabled war veterans it may be that the situation has improved since this research was carried out.

There are some alternatives to the luxury hotels – *Access in Israel* lists a few accessible Christian hospices (up-to-date list from the tourist office or the Israel Pilgrimage Committee, P.O.B. 1018, Jerusalem 91009) and one youth hostel; kibbutz hotels are mostly three-star establishments and some of these have sympathetic owners, adapted rooms and good access.

A problem reported by our contributors, as well as by the researchers for *Access in Israel* and the *RADAR* holiday guide (1990), is the prevalence of narrow doorways, particularly to *en suite* facilities, and lack of turning and sideways-transfer space in rooms. The Israeli tourist board guide to Eilat states that the *Neptune* has ten rooms for disabled guests, but this hotel was visited by a *RADAR* inspector who found no turning space and no room for lateral transfer in the bathrooms. Barry Atkinson was unable to get his wheelchair through to the bathroom, even after taking the door off, at the *Caesar Hotel* in Eilat (no longer a *Best Western* property). The *Sport Hotel* (North Beach, P.O.B. 82, Eilat; ☎59/33333) does have adapted rooms but Barry found it too expensive.

Best Western now list five of their Israeli hotels as having "facilities for disabled persons": *Red Rock Hotel* (Eilat sea shore, Eilat 88107; ☎59/73171); *Sea View Hotel* (P.O.B. 27, Rosh Pina 12000, North Galilee; ☎6/937013); *Ganei Hamat Hotel* (Habanim Street, Tiberias 14100; ☎6/792890); *Grand Beach Hotel* (250 Hayarkon Street, Tel Aviv 63113; ☎3/5466555); and *Kfar Maccabiah Hotel* (Bernstein Street, Ramat Gan 52109; ☎3/715715).

Camping is also a possibility – for site locations, and some idea of the facilities, contact the tourist office and the *Israel Camping Union* (P.O.B. 53, Nahariyya 22100); organised sites are well equipped and offer accommodation in cabins, chalets or static caravans as well as space for private tents.

Access and facilities

Travellers with mobility problems are likely to need help in Israel, whether it comes from a companion, guide or taxi driver. More often than not, two pairs of hands will be required. Barry Atkinson's experiences suggest that will-

ISRAEL: TRAVEL NOTES

ing hands sometimes need guidance, simply because the ways of the wheelchair are not understood (p.246). But if ancient sites, tombs and churches are not always the easiest places to get to, at least local attitudes are in the main positive.

Away from the resorts and hotels, **toilet** facilities can be a problem, especially as regulating fluid intake is not an option – it's essential to drink plenty of water in these **temperatures**. If your disability prevents normal sweating, you'll need a different cooling system, such as liberal use of a spray-gun. Remember your limitations if joining organised tours: very early starts and stifling heat can be exhausting.

Books

Access in Israel (1988) was written by Gordon Couch and researched by *Pauline Hephaistos Survey Projects* (*PHSP*), and is up to the series' usual high standard (see "Books", *Practicalities*).

Egypt

Ups and Downs

Stephen Hunt's muscles have been progressively wasting since childhood, but getting a wheelchair rekindled his love of travel. In 1989 he went to Egypt.

I'd long dreamed of going to Egypt but the cost and logistics of the usual tour seemed beyond me, until I heard that Luxor had opened up to direct charter flights from Britain. This meant that I could just afford a two-week, "stay-put" package for myself and a friend/helper, and also be within my comfort limit for air travel. Luxor, once Thebes, lies between Cairo and Aswan, accessible to most of Egypt's ancient history.

My preparations are minimal. Too much anticipation and I'll start worrying if it'll work out. After all, a three- or four-star hotel is bound to have a lift and decent-sized bedrooms, with bathrooms a wheelchair can more or less get in and out of. No point in letting the hotel anticipate too much either; that's a superstition of mine.

Anyway, we get the best room in the place, our balcony overlooking the Nile towards the distant mountains guarding the Valley of the Kings. The friendly *Etap Luxor* is in the centre of town, five minutes' walk from the magical Temple of Luxor, built to the golden section several thousand years before its time. A short taxi ride in the other direction is mighty Karnak, Temple of Amun, featuring a history-and-histrionics light show

where I keep banging into things and nearly end up in the sacrificial lake.

I've never liked being with organised groups; independence is best. With some bedtime reading before going site-seeing, I can let my imagination be my guide. Travelling around by car is much more convenient than a group minibus, often cheaper, and, for me, always more sociable. It gives me a stronger sense of place – driving along in Gemal's dusty Peugeot, Egyptian music on his cassette player, stopping at the kind of cafés he likes.

Gemal is our regular driver. We find him on the taxi-rank outside the hotel among the other rogues. "I give you reasonable price!" means an exorbitant fare which you must finally reduce to about a third and then walk away, waiting to be called back. Unlike most, though, Gemal seems to realise that we could be a regular earner over the following two weeks, and so resists the temptation to go for the jackpot straight off and blow his chances. I also like his style – the fancy stitching on his jellaba, the car-phone cigarette lighter, the jaunty Father Christmas bobbing in the windscreen. "They're only after your money," cynics say. But it's just a game, a survival game, and I can appreciate that. Besides, I've always got along well with the people on this side of the Mediterranean. They accept me, it is the will of God. Gemal takes us to everywhere that's reachable on both sides of the Nile.

We start at Dendera, only 60km away, a short day's excursion. The temple is one of the more recent, only a couple of thousand years old. It's a real blockbuster, a Hollywood epic of a place, complete with extras – wearing white trainers and sunhats and carrying their own cameras. The problem isn't the crevassed stone floor, the sand or the boulders; it's keeping the tourists from under my wheels. I detour briefly to irrigate the desert and, on return, they've all gone, the last coach just leaving the car park in a cloud of dust. In the vast, gloomy emptiness of the temple we're alone with the ghost of Hathor, and a squeaky wheelchair.

> **"I've got nothing to prove; I already know how wonderful I am, and how marvellous it is, the way I get around"**

Next, to Edfu and Esna, going south, a more ambitious day out, provisioned with bread, cheese and fruit from the _Etap_'s resplendent breakfast table. To economise further we share the ride with a couple we've met in the bar. The temple is dedicated to the god Horus, the just avenger, a fierce-looking falcon wearing a sort of archdeacon's hat. It's a huge, rococo building, breathing dignity and power. The man who owns the papyrus shop in Luxor, where we drink tea every day, used to be the station master at Edfu railway station. Now that's what I call kudos!

Esna, for some reason, is not on. Gemal, for the first and only time,

dissents. "It's down, down," he repeats emphatically. Does that mean down-river? But Edfu was all right. "Edfu is up, up!" I don't understand. I insist he takes us to Esna. We just drive round the town, nice in its way, ramshackle, lively, and I eventually realise that the temple has a lot of steps – down. It's getting late, so we all agree not to press the matter. He was only trying to help.

We make several trips across to the left bank of Luxor on the car ferry. Unlike most tourists, on their "Wonders of Egypt" all-inclusive packages, we have time to explore the Valleys of the Kings and Queens at our own pace. We buy a comprehensive ticket and take pot luck. Some of the nobles' tombs will be too "up" and some of the kings' too "down". Tutankhamen's, for instance, is like a garden shed at the bottom of a fire escape, and crowded, too. I've taken on improbabilities before, but not if the disruption I'd cause would spoil the pleasure of others. After all, I've got nothing to prove; I already know how wonderful I am, and how marvellous it is, the way I get around. Of course, everyone takes John for granted. He's just the friend who's been heaving and hauling me around the temples and tombs, tipping me in and out of bed, handing me my toothbrush, and the rest of it; that's all.

Anyway, there are more than enough attractions on the west bank. The ultimate is Queen Hatshepsut's Temple, a massive Nash terrace of honey-coloured stone set into the face of a granite cliff. It's approached along a noble avenue of sphinxes and souvenir stalls leading to a sloping causeway where, according to the "God was an astronaut" theory, Pharaohs launched their rocket-planes. Finally, that glorious colonnade filled with picture-walls, and crowds of jostling punters. So powerful is the ancient ambience, though, that I effortlessly feel it as it really was.

Our shortest ride is to the airport, for the 644-kilometre flight to Cairo. "No trip to Egypt is complete without seeing the pyramids," the brochure says; that's what has been foolishly nagging me. So, by noon, we've haggled our way to Giza where I perambulate amongst the awesome trio for an hour and a half. Then it's a dash to the *Nile Hilton* for a quick browse around the bargain buffet, a romp through the Egyptian Museum, where I catch up with Tutankhamen, and we just make it back to the airport for the last flight to Luxor. That night I'm tossed in a tangled web of impressions and wake up feeling hung-over on adrenalin, wondering if it was all worth it. Well, at least we covered the same itinerary as the organised group at about half the cost.

We deserve a rest, a relaxing note to finish on. How delightful, then, the prospect of cruising in a felucca down the Nile! It's Gemal's cousin, of course, who owns one of these traditional sailing boats. He and his toothless crewman get helpfully in the way as the wheelchair plonks down on the deck. then we're away, gliding smoothly downstream, past the crumbling glory of the Temple of Luxor, the brash, rising *Club Med*, and on between fields tilled in the same way since before any of it.

Our destination, it turns out, is Banana Island, a well-known stopoff for tourists and, while John goes ashore to be exploited, I stretch out luxuriously on embroidered cushions. The Nile slaps softly around me, clumps of water lily drifting by. The sky is clear, azure blue fading into the far haze of the mountains. From the stern of the boat come the musical mutterings of the old boatman's afternoon prayers. Is it a dream? Is it really me here? John comes back, stamping his feet. He gave some baksheesh to an old beggar poised arthritically at the roadside and, on returning to the café to buy me a can of 7-Up, found him fully reclined under a tree having a fag! What's more, he had the cheek to put out his hand again. I almost fall off the cushions laughing.

"A furious altercation breaks out, trigger fingers twitch, they grapple with our boat"

On our way back, the river police make us pull into the shore as some big VIP boat is due to pass. But time means money in tourists' pockets for our sharp young Captain Moussa in his brightly painted Nile felucca. As soon as they've gone, recklessly urged on by us, he hoists the sail again. All goes well; we're beating along, hugging the shore, almost opposite the point where we left when, out of the blue, the police inflatable roars back around the bend and catches us in the act.

A furious altercation breaks out, trigger fingers twitch, they grapple with our boat. Suddenly I get a flash of inspiration and start waving my arms around and groaning loudly. As if on cue, with barely a pause, Moussa turns and gestures dramatically towards me: "This man is sick! I must take him to a doctor!" he's telling them. Whatever, it has just the right effect and the police veer off, muttering, leaving us to continue on our way. My old friend on Banana Island would have been proud of me; maybe I'll come back and do a summer season with him next year.

Sand, Flies and Holes in the Ground

Apart from hobbling a few steps with the aid of a crutch and helper, Maxine Smith is wheelchair-bound and cannot bend her legs. With her mother, Dorrie, she spent six days in Egypt, in November 1988; it was an expensive disaster.

Dorrie and I have holidayed abroad annually for twenty years. We have used several different travel agents, tour companies and airlines, but no matter how much preparation is made we have yet to experience a trouble-free holiday. We thought we'd found it when we discovered a company specialising in holidays for disabled people, set up by a travel agent after he became wheelchair-bound. Attracted by the brochure's claims of "hand-picked hotels, helpful staff, spacious bedrooms, assistance at airports, trouble-free holidays", Dorrie and I eagerly booked for a group tour of Egypt, seven nights half-board for £790 each. Father declined to join us, grunting, "I had enough of sand, flies and hole-in-the-ground loos when I was stationed there during the war."

Suspicions that it was not going to be as "carefree" as the brochure claimed surfaced three weeks before departure, when the travel company (*Threshold Travel*, Manchester) informed us that they had changed the Egyptian hotel and we would be unescorted as the group leader was ill. Four days before departure we were anxiously ringing them for flight tickets.

The journey from home began well as I sat, for the first time, in a real train compartment – much more pleasant than among the parcels and pigeons in a filthy guard's van. The short distance from Kings Cross to Heathrow took longer to cover than that from Cleveland to Kings Cross: we had been misinformed, and advised to take the Carelink bus to Victoria, then Airbus 1 to the airport; a short walk to Euston station for Airbus 2 would have been easier and quicker. So much for all the phone calls and correspondence (we asked *London Transport*, Kings Cross Stationmaster, *Threshold Travel* and their airport representative) to find the best way! My sister, convinced that there must be an easier way, had spent two days phoning transport and social service offices, as well as organisations for the disabled in London, but the only people who knew the facts (and were extremely helpful) were the Airbus drivers.

We have always used local airports, Teeside or Newcastle, to avoid such arduous train or taxi journeys, but on this trip we had no choice, so arranged to stay overnight in the *Skyways Hotel*. The courtesy coach driver refused to transport me to the hotel but the Airbus driver kindly did so when he saw our predicament. The hotel was accessible in that the entrance was level and had automatic doors, the corridors were spacious, restaurant, bars and some rooms were on the ground floor, and we were allocated a large, ground-floor bedroom and bathroom, so no lifts to worry about. However, I think it was accessible by chance rather than by design – there was no wheelchair symbol beside this hotel in the *ABC* brochure.

"More trouble at Cairo airport: our luggage was missing"

The following morning we took a taxi to Heathrow, waited in the coffee lounge while the *Threshold* rep checked our luggage in and booked our seats. And we waited. Thirty minutes before take-off, no sign of the rep, so Dorrie had her paged while I anxiously watched people going through to the departure lounge. The rep appeared with our tickets ten minutes before take-off, by which time the other passengers had already boarded, some not too happy at being knocked as I was carried in, or at having to change seats. Although I had given explicit instructions several times to *Threshold* and to the rep, we were allocated unsuitable seats – no space for my stiff legs, not near a toilet, in the non-smoking section – and, as usual, the stewardesses had not been informed of my requirements.

More trouble at Cairo airport: our luggage was missing. We arrived at the *Siag Pyramids Hotel* late at night, shattered after two gruelling days, but at least there was no unpacking – only the warm winter clothes we were wearing and a spare pair of panties from the previous day. The hotel was ramped at the entrance and had two large lifts, but very small bedrooms and we could not get the wheelchair into the bathroom without taking the door off. It was manageable, but I would not recommend it.

An excellent Egyptian company (*ETAMS Tours*) provided the trips and transport, but not for us the luxury of a hydraulic lift on the coach, only a simple, two-piece, portable wooden ramp, so long that it often obstructed the pavement or road and required two men to run a wheelchair up it. No clamps or safety straps, so the three wheelchairs in the group occasionally collided together on bumpy roads. On all the tours we were accompanied by a courier and a guide, both Egyptian, friendly and very helpful. The guide made the tours extremely interesting by giving running commentaries which explained the history of ancient Egypt, the lives of the Pharaohs and goddesses, and some of the local customs.

These trips were superb, the saving grace of an otherwise dreadful holiday, and some we could never have managed on our own. One in particular stands out vividly in my memory, the one most people would associate with Egypt – our excursion to the pyramids. Only a few miles away from bustling Cairo the coach began to snake through the vast Lybian desert. It is difficult to describe the feeling of isolation and tranquillity – no noise, no movement, except when a bedouin occasionally galloped by, kicking up clouds of dust.

"Cairo is a beautiful city but it's not very accessible"

After a short stop for camel rides, which I politely declined after watching one brave disabled lady almost topple off a spitting, mangy-looking beast, we drove around Sakkara and Giza. I was amazed at the size of the pyramids – 135m high, 225m along each side – and at their state of preservation. The courier and guide helped to drag and lift each wheelchair over sand and rough stony paths round King Zoser's pyramid, through a walled temple and courtyard which were in the process of painstaking renovation.

Next we were helped into Princess Idut's tomb, the walls covered with hieroglyphs depicting ancient rituals and everyday life, painted in 2000 BC, but the colours still bright. They were simplistic, as though drawn by small children – figures all faced front, no perspective, background objects painted above rather than behind the foreground objects. Hand-painted copies can be purchased in the papyrus factory, which we visited another day. The cheaper versions for sale in Cairo are not on genuine papyrus, but as the difference is imperceptible unless side-by-side they make ideal presents.

Egypt was not as barren as we had imagined. We were surprised to see exotic flowers and trees flourishing in Cairo, along the banks of canals, and in the desert at the El Fayuum oasis there are fields of fruit and vegetables. The population has increased rapidly over the last few years, resulting in mass unemployment, poverty and homelessness. We were sad to see people living among the mausoleums in Cairo's "City of the Dead", and families squatting by the roadside, their only possessions a couple of pans.

The Egyptians are very enterprising in the face of these hardships, and they charge tourists wherever they can – to take a camera into the Egyptian Museum, for cloth "booties" to put over your shoes before entering the mosques, for the loan of a blanket at the Sound and Light Spectacle at the pyramids (very cold, so wrap up well; Dorrie was too concerned about the strange creatures scampering about in the darkness to enjoy it).

"We looked like idiots with our woolly trousers rolled up to the knees"

Cairo is a beautiful city, with its colourful flowers and trees, and many ornate mosques, but it's not very accessible. There are high ridges on the edges of pavements and down the centre of roads – difficult for wheelchairs; parts of the city are quite hilly, and all of it is thronged with people and very noisy. Many roads have six lanes, but lane discipline and signalling are unheard of. During a hair-raising car ride we jokingly asked the courier if Egyptians take a driving test. "Yes, I passed first time," he proudly replied. "I had to drive straight for five minutes and then turn left!"

Important buildings were pointed out by the guide as we drove around Cairo, being deposited at places of interest. The Egyptian Museum displays statues and artefacts excavated from the tombs; those from Tutankhamen's tomb cover a whole floor (there is a lift). At the Khan-el-Khalili bazaar we were escorted through a maze of dark, narrow, bumpy alleys, every few yards engulfed by an overpowering aroma of spices and perfumes. Colourfully robed shopkeepers, all men, squatted outside tiny stores among piles of exotic souvenirs and other goods, cheerfully encouraging the tourists to buy.

In spite of the fascinating trips and guided tours, by the fourth day we were as sick as the proverbial custard slice. The hotel was awful (unhelpful staff, inefficient waiters, monotonous food, no choice, lounge in a draughty foyer so nowhere to sit in the evenings, bedroom and bathroom too small, disco too crowded) and our case was still missing. All that preparation to squeeze everything into one case had been a waste of time and effort; in the case were lovely cool clothes, sandals, half my painkillers, incontinence pads and pants bought specially, knowing there might be few accessible toilets.

With temperatures in the eighties we were hot, sticky and smelly, still wearing the warm clothes we'd travelled in: we looked like idiots with our woolly trousers rolled up to the knees, and the only things we'd managed to buy so far – tatty, gaudy T-shirts emblazoned with camels and Pharaohs' heads. Dorrie's heavy walking shoes were killing her; we both had "Pharaoh's curse"; I was in pain, eking out my painkillers (refused the guide's offer of substitutes after swallowing suppositories by mistake on earlier holidays). And, of course, I was desperate as usual – the only opportunity for toilets on tour days was at the lunch-stop.

Some toilet visits were traumatic, although we can laugh about them now. At the first stop we were relieved in more ways than one to find a "proper" toilet, but it was a painful experience: we hadn't noticed a large "meat hook" sticking up inside the bowl (perhaps to prevent long Egyptian garments falling in the water?). I tipped a small girl who'd helped us; suddenly a gang of children appeared from nowhere, rubbed their tummies, pointed at their mouths and tried to grab my handbag – very distressing and frightening.

At one café the guide said the toilets were dirty, so she directed us to "more hygienic ones". Yes, a hole in the ground and what a performance! With my feet on what looked like a cattle-grid, Dorrie gripped me tightly, stood me up and leaned me back so that I wouldn't wet my trousers but my feet kept sliding. After several attempts we gave up, and remained desperate until an hour later.

"On their own the problems we experienced might sound trivial, but together they turned our dream holiday into a nightmare"

More problems on the journey home. Our missing suitcase reappeared at Heathrow airport, and Dorrie had great difficulty pushing me and carrying two cases (we bought one in Cairo for essential clothes and toiletries). We had no assistance from the *Threshold* rep – we were outside at the Airbus stop when she eventually arrived. Travelling to Cleveland we encountered more mishaps: the train stopped briefly at our local station, then carried on, with us still on board! The waiting porters had looked in the reserved compartment and found it empty – we'd been put in the wrong one at Kings Cross. We arrived back an hour later, expecting to find my sister waiting to drive us home; instead there was a taxi, meter ticking away, as my sister was ill.

On their own the problems we experienced might sound trivial, but together they turned our dream holiday into a nightmare from beginning to end. One expects a few difficulties on package holidays but at least they are cheap. This "carefree" holiday was worse than a package but twice the price, which we had willingly paid on the understanding that we would enjoy the specialised services advertised in the brochure. Admittedly, some of the problems were not the fault of the travel company, but we sought an apology for those that were. Receiving nothing but excuses over a four-month period, I was determined that others should not suffer the same ordeal; I reported them to ABTA, only to be told that *Threshold Travel* had ceased trading. We are not surprised.

EGYPT: TRAVEL NOTES

Sources of information

Egyptian State Tourist Office, 168 Piccadilly, London W1V 9DE; ☎071/493 5282. Offers a brief fact sheet, *Special Services for the Aged and Disabled*, which recommends the services of *ETAMS Tours* (see below), lists five hotels with facilities for the disabled, and notes that the Egyptian Museum has now introduced a lift.

Tour operators

After some conflict with *Sovereign* over a penalty payment (due to an unavoidable change of helper), Stephen Hunt would choose *Thomson*, who offer a number of holidays in Egypt and Israel (see *Worldwide* and *Winter Sun* brochures).

Maxine Smith suggests booking your own flight and letting *ETAMS Tours* (*Egyptian Tourism and Medical Services*, 99 Ramsis Street, Cairo; ☎2/745721) arrange the rest. They supply a wheelchair-accessible vehicle for transfers to and from Cairo airport, as well as for sightseeing trips. Their guides and couriers are friendly and very helpful. But be prepared for a bumpy ride, with no tie-down facilities for securing the wheelchairs, and rather primitive boarding via a couple of planks.

EGYPT: TRAVEL NOTES

P&O offer a number of cruises on the *Canberra* and the *Sea Princess* that take in the pyramids, the Holy Land and other "cradles of civilisation".

Transport

Egypt Air (☎071/580 5477) have no aisle chairs on their aircraft. There are toilet and fork-lift (or similar) facilities at Cairo and Luxor airports.

There are regular **ferries** from Greece, Cyprus and Italy to the Egyptian ports of Alexandria, Port Said and Suez. Details can be obtained from the national tourist offices.

In Egypt, transport is not that easy: driving in the desert is potentially hazardous if you don't know what you're doing, buses and trains extremely crowded with high steps and narrow doorways. You're better off entrusting yourself to an experienced guide and driver, either as part of a group in a bus or coach (especially the "converted" one used by *ETAMS*) or by hiring a taxi by the day. Taxis are usually large and reasonably priced (negotiate the price before setting off), ideal for individual sightseeing or for getting about the cities.

Accommodation

Hotels that offer rooms for handicapped guests in Egypt are usually of four- or five-star standard with prices to match, and the tourist board and tour operators that do offer some guidance with finding accessible accommodation show little imagination or inclination to search out cheaper options. Try the *Holiday Care Service* fact sheet on Egypt

Maxine Smith was able to have her bathroom door removed at the *Siag Pyramids* (Sakkara Road, El Haram, Giza; ☎2/856022) but there was little room for manoeuvre, in bedroom or bathroom; on top of that, Maxine was unimpressed by food, service and other facilities. Stephen Hunt stayed at the *Etap Luxor*, a *Pullman Azur* hotel (Cornich El Nil, El Bahr Street, Luxor; ☎95/749177) – and liked it. The hotels recommended by the Egyptian tourist board are all five-star, except for the *Novotel Cairo* which is four-star (but no rooms for disabled guests mentioned in the *Novotel* 1990/1991 directory).

Access and facilities

The things that draw the crowds in this part of the world – pyramids, tombs, monasteries, forts, ruined cities, excavations – are, to say the least, difficult to reach in a wheelchair. A perfect example is Stephen Hunt's description of Tutankhamen's tomb – viewed from a wheelchair, it's a "garden shed at the bottom of a fire escape". The only course of action is to enjoy what can be reached, and adopt a philosophical attitude to the rest.

To see anything much, you're likely to need help, whether it comes from a companion, guide or taxi driver – preferably more than one of them. But Stephen Hunt found that attitudes to his disability this side of the Mediterranean were very easy to live with – the will of God and to be accepted without comment or discrimination.

Toilet facilities outside the big hotels are minimal, and holes in the ground require agility; those who are unable to support themselves on their legs may be in for a miserable time, particularly if planning to join sightseeing tours, visiting desert villages and so on. Until more wheelchair-accessible toilets are provided, disabled tourists who cannot cope with squatting over a hole must use incontinence pads, condom and drainage bags, or indwelling catheter, or – the least exciting prospect – never stray far from a hotel. Regulating fluid intake is not an option – it's essential to drink plenty of water in these temperatures. (If your disability prevents normal sweating, you'll need a different cooling system, such as liberal use of a spray-gun.) Remember your limitations if joining organised tours: very early starts and stifling heat will exhaust most people, so take plenty of rest days. Sightseeing by taxi allows you to set the pace.

Oman & the UAE

Boiling Oil and Velcro

Betty and John Layton visited the United Arab Emirates and Oman on a Kuoni tour in February 1989. Betty is an amputee.

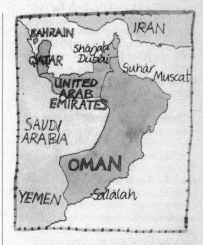

We flew to Dubai overnight by *British Airways* from Gatwick: as usual the wheelchair service and pre-boarding were excellent, with John dashing alongside carrying the hand-baggage – including the spare leg! *Kuoni* used *Orient Tours* of Sharjah as their agents and a rep took us from the airport to the *Dubai Inter-Continental*. Our room (near the lift as previously requested) was ready, although it was only 7am. We used *Inter-Continental* hotels throughout our travels and we were pleased with all of them; the staff were most friendly and helpful.

There are seven Arab Emirates and we only had time to visit three – Dubai, Abu Dhabi and Sharjah. Their histories are fascinating, with troubles and family feuds only a few years (and in some cases, months!) in the past. Our first walk along the creek which divides Dubai transported us to another world. The huge wooden dhows were lined three or four deep along the creek, advertising their sailing times and ports of call, and offering transport to all manner of cargo. *Abras* (water-taxis) dash across the creek, loaded with passengers going to work in the shops and offices of the new town. Near the end of our tour, Theresa treated us to a

ride in an *abra* so that we could see the hustle and bustle of the town and quayside from the creek. The crewman (and others) helped me on board.

The morning our tour proper was to start, we gathered in the hotel foyer, luggage at the ready. There were twelve of us, plus driver (an Omani called Sultan) and guide (Theresa, a German girl from *Orient Tours* who had lived and worked in Sharjah for eight years). Theresa knew the Emirates and Oman and their history well – no question defeated her, and her English was excellent. We twelve were a mixed bag: a group of three ladies; a pharmacist and his wife; a retired university lecturer; a lone lady, much travelled; a banker and his wife; and Kenneth Kendall, the retired newsreader.

We had an air-conditioned minibus for the trip. The luggage was stowed away in the back and there were plenty of spare seats; I was able to select one where my artificial leg would be most comfortable. Setting off south to Abu Dhabi, we obtained our first glimpse of real desert from well-maintained highways. There was high wire fencing to keep the camels from wandering on to the roads, and in some places, camel underpasses have been built for their safe crossing. Photo stops were made where the winds had blown the sands into spectacular ridges. I found it very uncomfortable, plunging unevenly into the hot, dry sand, and had to be content to watch my companions scramble about.

"Both mother and baby seemed amazed at what had happened"

Abu Dhabi, like Dubai, is a clean, bright, modern city which has risen from the desert in just 25 years. A drive along the corniche by day or night is quite splendid, with views of the sea, beautiful gardens and magnificent fountains to admire. The desert has truly been made to "bloom", and we were shown films of the Arabs' achievements in the petroleum industry, in agriculture and market gardening. Some native crafts are still practised in Abu Dhabi; at the boatyard in Bateen we watched dhows being built and renovated exactly as they have been for hundreds of years.

Further from the city limits the women are usually veiled and not many are seen on the streets. When we asked Theresa if the women were still treated as chattels she was highly amused and told us that they have a marvellous life: the men do all the work, bring the money home and do all the shopping for provisions while the women rule the house with a rod of iron – with help from the servants! They would not have life any other way, she assured us.

Most of Theresa's "lectures" were delivered in the comfort of the bus, thus avoiding the need to stand around too long – something I appreciated. All the public loos on the tour were holes in the ground; with an artificial leg one adapts, of necessity, to the required balancing act.

We drove inland through arid desert to the city of Al Ain, from which the Omani mountains can be seen in the distance. We visited a camel market where the sellers and buyers were doing their bargaining under the few scrubby trees, with the camels tethered and hobbled, well fed on green leaves and branches. We missed witnessing a birth by a few minutes; both mother and baby seemed amazed at what had happened!

In each area we went to the local souks – selling vegetables, fruit (dates!), fish and meat – and were impressed with how clean and tidy they were. The "litter laws" are frighteningly strict and it shows. In addition, any dogs found wandering around loose are shot; the only ones which seem to be kept are guard dogs.

The Buraimi oasis gave us a welcome cool walk through palm-shaded groves. This town until recently had a turbulent history – it has been fought over by Oman, Saudi Arabia and Abu Dhabi. Even now the inhabitants are suspicious of foreigners and keep their doors, with huge iron studs and bolts, firmly shut against prying eyes.

"Wind towers with sea breezes coming through open windows from the Indian Ocean"

Our entry to Oman was through the border post a few miles from Al Ain in the Hajar mountains. Our cases were hauled from the bus and each one opened and searched thoroughly. Any bottles were carefully sniffed at in case we were smuggling in hard liquor which, we had been warned, was absolutely forbidden (although alcohol is readily available to tourists in the hotels in Oman). Our "No Objection" certificates, passports and luggage were in order and we were waved on our way after over an hour in the hot sun. According to Theresa that was a quick and uneventful entry!

We went straight to Suhar, the main port of the Batinah which is the long, sweeping coastal plain, stretching from the Emirates border down to Muscat. The fish market beside the beach afforded a little shade – a roof over waist-high concrete slabs, on which cross-legged sellers sat, furiously bargaining with the buyers. On to a splendid fortress in Suhar, for which we needed permission to enter from the Wali's office across the road. The fort proved to be another cool haven, with thick mud and sand walls, and wind towers with sea breezes coming through open windows from the Indian Ocean. I seldom climbed to the highest level in the forts, but even the mid-level views were spectacular.

We drove down the coast, calling at Sahm where we saw shallow reed boats still used for fishing. After a long day we finally arrived at Muscat's magnificent *Al Bustan Palace Hotel*, built within the last five years for a meeting of the Gulf Cooperation Council. A fishing village was demolished and rocks blasted from the mountains behind the beach to make way for the hotel. The villagers were simply moved two miles down the coast and new houses built. In our bedraggled, travel-weary state we felt somewhat overawed by the hotel's opulence, the vast entrance hall with fountains playing – "a spacious atrium reflecting the so colours of its aqua blue tile and gold trim", says the brochure.

When Sultan Qaboos Bin Said, who was educated in England, finally managed to oust his father in 1970, he began to spend Oman's enormous oil wealth on housing, schools, clinics, hospitals, universities, roads and industrial investment. Before this change of ruler there had been no education for girls, only three boys' schools in Muscat and only tent

schools (again for boys) in the interior. Now everyone is given an education and in the evenings the mothers too can go to school. Women are encouraged to enter the professions, and at the airports we were greeted by women security officers.

"A lush, green coastal plain, with coconut groves and banana plantations"

Tourism is being cautiously encouraged but the rules are strict and until recently only visitors who were married and over 35 were allowed the "No Objection" certificate essential for obtaining a visa. We had some wonderful tours in Muscat, exploring the old town, a natural history museum, an aquarium and the harbour where generations of British sailors have scrambled ashore to paint the names of their ships in large white letters on the encircling rocks.

Westward from Muscat is Matrah, with its grand harbour and rambling souk of dark, shady alleys. Stalls selling clothing, spices, coffee, gold and silver are guarded by fierce-looking Arabs in traditional dress, with large daggers at their waists which one imagines are not only for decoration.

Late one afternoon, we flew 800km south to Salalah on the Arabian Sea. There was no wheelchair service or pre-boarding on internal flights in Oman, but the walks to the aircraft were quite short and at Salalah a coach took us to the airport building. Salalah is situated on a lush, green coastal plain, with coconut groves and banana plantations sprawling along a glorious sandy beach, the Dhufar mountains providing a backdrop.

From Salalah we drove east to Taqah, a fishing village where camels roam down to the beach. We saw the remains of old, wooden, "stitched" boats, their planks stitched together with leather thongs and the gaps and cracks filled with camel dung. While we were watching a group of fishermen selling their catch, a man from a small shop across the road begged us to have a cool drink from his large refrigerator. He wouldn't let us pay, so some of us picked up a few items from his store to buy, in recompense, whereupon he insisted that they also were gifts! The renowned hospitality of the Omani Arabs is undiminished by the encroachment of modern ways.

On to Khor Ruri and Sumhurum Bay, the old frankincense port and the remains of one of the legendary palaces of the Queen of Sheba. Here I felt daunted by the terrain – the prospect of clambering among the steep ruins did not appeal. But Theresa insisted, "You *can* do it!" and she hauled me through gaps and over walls, determined to get me to see the superb views and the wall inscriptions. It was well worth it.

"We were on the outskirts of Dubai just in time to see the start of a camel race"

The other way along the coast, westward from Salalah, took us to Mughsayl, within about 30km of the Yemeni border. The mountains are high and in some places sheer cliff drops down to the ocean. Inland, we went to Nabi Ayoub – Job's tomb – which is set in an elaborate garden and well guarded (no photographs!); we had to take shoes off to enter, which is impossible for me – I just looked through the doorway.

Back in Muscat our party divided, six to remain in the luxury of the *Al Bustan Palace Hotel* before flying home, and six to continue our travels –

even more room in the bus! We went to the interior of Oman, through the Sumail gap in the Hajar mountains, to Nazwa, one of Oman's ancient capitals and now the economic and provincial centre of the interior. Here the women are in purdah; tethered goats and camels are traded under a large tree in the town centre, and the souk is a dimly lit jumble of shops with the merchants sitting around in disorder.

After leaving Nazwa we visited an eerie ruined village, then stopped at Jabrin to examine a castle which is being restored. The ceiling paintings and decorations were very fine. The joy of our visits to the many forts and castles was their peace and quiet and cooling breezes. Of course there were also the grim reminders of their original purpose, that of repelling enemies – secret rooms and staircases, dungeons, spy-holes and the openings to the outside through which the defending forces poured the traditional boiling oil!

We arrived at the border at Jebel Hafit for our re-entry to the Emirates, and stopped overnight at Al Ain before driving back to Dubai through the desert. We were on the outskirts of Dubai just in time to see the start of a camel race. It took quite a while to get the forty or so camels lined up with their tiny jockeys (nine- or ten-year-old boys) firmly attached to their saddles with Velcro! They were finally off, some camels going the wrong way and being thoroughly whipped for doing so. We didn't stay to the finish as the course is about 10km long, but it was an exhilarating last memory of a wonderful and exciting holiday.

Sources of information

Raitt Orr & Associates, 35 Buckingham Palace Road, London SW1W 0RE; ☎071/828 5961. If you contact the information unit of the **United Arab Emirates Embassy** (☎071/581 1281) they will refer you here or to the national airline (*Emirates*). Raitt Orr, the UK representatives of the **Dubai Commerce and Tourism Promotion Board** (PO Box 594, Dubai; ☎4/511600), are helpful and will contact head office if unable to answer your questions.

Emirates, PO Box 686, Dubai; ☎4/228151. The Dubai office of the airline will be able to help with questions about airport facilities, but staff on the *Emirates* desk at Gatwick are also well informed (☎0293/502607).

Oman Directorate of Tourism, c/o Ministry of Trade and Industry, PO Box 550, Muscat; ☎794206). Tourism is a relatively new business in Oman and there is no tourist office in London, but the main office may have some useful information

Tour operators

Betty Layton was pleased with *Kuoni*'s arrangements, but this company may not be a good choice for non-ambulant disabled travellers (see p.282 and p.312). *Orient Tours* (P.O. Box 772, Sharjah, UAE; ☎6/549333) did a good job: as well as offering encouragement and assistance, the guide ensured that Betty sat in her preferred seat on the minibus and that "lectures" were given while sitting in the minibus.

Transport

There are toilet and fork-lift (or similar) facilities at the major **airports**, and *Emirates* carry aisle chairs on their A310 and A300 aircraft (which are used on all London routes) – these will fit into the specially adapted toilets for disabled passengers. The major *Emirates*

service is Gatwick to Dubai, but they also fly to Egypt and Saudi Arabia. Wheelchair passengers are disembarked by high-lift at Dubai, and there are accessible toilets in the terminal; wheelchairs are available.

Betty Layton found no wheelchair service or pre-boarding procedures for disabled passengers at Oman's airports; she either walked the short distance to the terminal or was taken by coach.

Once there, you are likely to have to take **tours** for any long-distance sightseeing: driving in the desert requires preparation, and distances are vast, though the roads are well maintained. In the cities, taxis are easily available and usually spacious.

The problems of high temperatures, which mean drinking plenty of fluids, and lack of toilet facilities occur again here – see Egypt and Israel. And again, watch out for exhaustion from trying to do too much.

Accommodation

In this part of the world you have little alternative to luxury hotels. Betty Layton used *Inter-Continental* hotels: *Dubai I-C* (Bin Yass Street, PO Box 476, Dubai, UAE; ☎4/227171); *Abu Dhabi I-C* (PO Box 4171, Abu Dhabi, UAE; ☎2/666888); *Al Ain I-C* (PO Box 16031, Al Ain, Abu Dhabi, UAE; ☎3/654654); *Al Bustan Palace Hotel* (PO Box 8998, Muttrah, Muscat, Oman; ☎740200). All gave friendly service but, as with Israel and Egypt, this is accessible accommodation at the top of the price range.

More moderately priced accommodation can be found at a handful of Mid-East *Holiday Inns* which advertise special rooms for handicapped guests: *Muscat* (CPO Box 2185 Seeb, Muscat, Oman; ☎697123); *Al Jubail* (Tareeg 101, Madinat Al Jubail Al Sinaiyah, PO Box 10167, Jubail, Saudi Arabia; ☎3/3417000); and *Jeddah* (PO Box 10924, Jeddah, Saudi Arabia; ☎2/6611000).

PART FOUR

AFRICA

Introduction

While famine, widespread malnourishment and indescribable poverty exist in the African continent, and wheelchairs are unheard of, talk of installing ramps and walkways, or providing accessible toilets, is premature. The point is brought home by John Bignell when he describes sitting in his NHS chair, gazing down from his hotel window at a demonstration of the local design of wheelchair – a plank on four castors.

In Sierra Leone, one of the world's poorest countries, and neighbour to some of the world's most appalling violence in Liberia, disabled people have no hope of owning a wheelchair, or any other aid – they must, in Kate Margrie's words, "make the best use of what mobility they have", with no prospect of any physiotherapy or other essential medical treatment. Government money is too often swallowed up in civil wars or by corrupt leaders, instead of being used to finance **public health and welfare programmes**.

Even with a wheelchair, the chance of greater independence and freedom of movement for people in the poorer countries would be remote. The infrastructure is non-existent, or creaking under the strain of age and lack of maintenance. The terrain is as rough as you'll find anywhere. Public transport is overcrowded and dangerous as well as uncomfortable – decrepit buses or trucks overflowing with people and animals. A smooth ride is impossible, even in the safari Land Rovers and Volkswagen vans.

For the visitor, whether disabled or not, the major obstacle is **getting around** – in comfort and without too many delays. Internal strife in several African countries presents another negative image to the tourist, and the Gulf conflict – with media reports of anti-Bush/Thatcher demonstrations in the North African countries – has taken its toll on the industry. Stephen Hunt, who writes elsewhere about Rome and Egypt, travelled to Morocco and the Sahara in February 1991, and found deserted hotels, empty swimming pools and puzzled, friendly locals, deprived of their usual form of income and longing to swing into action in their taxis, shops and hotels.

Most tourist boards and operators report that they receive very few enquiries from disabled people hoping to travel to Africa. But, as so often in other parts of the world, for some disabled travellers the attractions far outweigh the challenges. The excitement of **wildlife** observation seems to make a more lasting impression than the hazards of travel in safari vehicles. One contributor delights in the opportunity to get to know people who could almost be living on another planet, their outlook and way of life are so utterly different to her own; another finds the locals mysterious and impenetrable. The beauty of the scenery, the seediness of some of the cities, the thrill simply of being in Africa – all have an appeal, and can be experienced with a little preparation.

Outside the more developed and more aware countries – Kenya and South Africa, perhaps also the Gambia and Togo – Africa should be approached with caution; but it can be approached, whatever the more pessimistic tour operators have to say. Be honest and don't gloss over the less appetising aspects: the **climate** can drain the energy from a strong, fit, able body; insect bites can bring a range of nasty diseases; food and water may carry other diseases; a simple journey can take hours longer than planned; medical facilities will be few and basic.

The only concessions made to disabled travellers will come from the people you meet – but, with luck and if you take good advice before leaving, this may be all you need. When Stephen Hunt took a two-berth couchette on the overnight train from Nairobi to Mombasa, he found no widened doorways, no extra space for wheelchairs; in fact there was barely room to stand (supported from behind) at the wash-basin, and regular bouts of exercise and massage were necessary throughout the night to prevent cramp. But he was bombarded with offers of assistance on the platform: for the equivalent of £1 you can hire an extra holiday helper at stations, ailrports, tourist attractions – wherever there are steps, awkward entrances or pot-holes.

It is important that travellers (not tour operators) make the final decision on whether or not Africa is a suitable destination; if disabled travellers who have their eyes open to the problems find it a desirable destination then every effort should be made to accommodate them within mainstream tourist operations, and independent travellers should be given every assistance from the tourist boards when researching their trip, whether to find accessible accommodation or to ascertain facilities at airports. Then, as the numbers of disabled visitors grow, we might expect a few more ramps, some more wheelchairs (with hard tyres) at airports, the odd grab-rail or two in hotel bathrooms, perhaps even some provision for wheelchair users to join standard safari tours.

Because the information is patchy, because we received information on countries not covered by specific accounts, and because much of the general advice can be applied throughout the continent, the *Travel Notes* for this part of the book have been combined into a single section at the end. Hopefully future editions of this book will have a lot more to say.

Morocco

A Meeting in the Desert

Ivy Geach is in her late seventies, has arthritic knees, and walks with the aid of two sticks. In January 1988 she travelled, with a friend, to Morocco for a week's holiday.

Evelyn, though a few years younger than me, suffers from a painful back, so neither of us is very mobile. But that hadn't stopped us having a good time in Tangier in 1987; we enjoyed North Africa so much that we decided to pay another visit, this time to Marrakesh. We booked with *AA Travel* who were very helpful.

We had to make carrying our luggage as easy as possible, so we each bought a medium-sized suitcase, lightweight and with four wheels and a handy strap to pull it along. (One drawback was that in a hurry it tended to fall sideways.) We packed non-iron clothes suitable for an English summer, including woollies of course, in preparation for temperatures between 65 and 70°F.

An electric buggy was available at Gatwick to transport us and our luggage to a minibus, the driver of which helped us onto the plane. The flight was smooth and we found no fault with the airline's (*Dan Air*) service. At Agadir a coach was waiting to take us to Marrakesh. The airport is small, so a porter is unnecessary if you can manage a short distance with your luggage to the coach which waits outside the arrival hall.

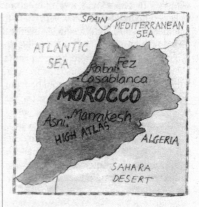

The four-hour drive to Marrakesh was tiring but so full of interest that it didn't seem too long. To someone used to desert scenery it might have been monotonous, but I found the changing light on the sand dunes hypnotic. I occasionally glimpsed a long-robed, hooded figure walking across the barren wastes; there was no sign of habitation – where had he come from and where was he going? I asked the courier about the mysterious figures but he smiled, shook his head and shrugged as if to say, "If I told you, you wouldn't understand." He was probably right. We stopped at a wayside café for coffee or mint tea and a visit to the loo – a square hole in a tiled floor. Avoiding splashes was difficult but it was warm so we dried quickly!

Hotel Kenza was splendid, exactly as described in the *Enterprise* brochure, the bedrooms *en suite* with lifts to each floor and everywhere immaculate. There was one drawback for anyone using a wheelchair – three steps leading to the dining room – but that could be easily overcome with the willing help of some strong-armed staff. The other guests were mostly French or Spanish, so the few Britons tended to stay together. We ranged in age from teenagers to a lively eighty-year-old gentleman who wore boxer shorts and a tartan bobble-cap, and we all got on splendidly. The teenagers couldn't have been more helpful, offering to fetch and carry for us and lending us their somewhat lurid novels.

Moroccan food is delicious and there is such a variety of dishes that any special diet shouldn't be a problem. The waiters were always polite and smiling, even when my heavy metal walking stick slipped from the back of my chair onto their feet – a not infrequent occurrence.

Marrakesh, much loved by Winston Churchill, is fascinating. According to legend, a date-carrying tribe from beyond the Atlas mountains besieged the early settlement, which was a crossroads for caravan trails going south. Date stones fell to the ground, germinated and so produced the famous palm grove, today the largest in the world. Under Ali Ben Youssef, Marrakesh became a fortified city, with underground irrigation canals to provide water for the palmery; these are still used to supply water to the beautiful gardens in the city. The old quarter, Medina, is enclosed by a 16-kilometre wall. Outside is Gueliz, the modern part, well laid out, with buildings of a delightful pink ochre colour.

"There was a peace and rightness about this scene which is hard to convey"

Marrakesh is a strange mix of the sophisticated and the primitive. The contrast between wealth and heart-breaking poverty is shocking. Expensive cars next to shabby carts, pulled by even shabbier donkeys, fill the roads, which have no traffic lights or street crossings. But the wide, tree-lines avenues are flat, so it's easy walking for disabled pedestrians, although the litter on the pavements can be a hazard.

Drinking coffee or tea outside one of the many cafés was quite an experience. We took to heart the words inscribed in Arabic on one of the many fountains: translated, they mean "Drink and contemplate". One morning I remember in particular. The sun was hot, the jacaranda trees in bloom, and we were sitting beneath an ornamental orange tree, watching the world go by. A haunting voice rang out from the minaret calling people to prayer. A jellaba-clad gentleman passing by suddenly stopped, unrolled the little prayer mat he was carrying and laid it on the pavement. Unmindful of us, he removed his shoes and knelt in prayer. A donkey trotted by, carrying a woman enveloped in long, dark robes, only her eyes exposed. There was a peace and rightness about this scene which is hard to convey.

The next day we visited the Djemaa El Fna – the famous square of Marrakesh, and entertainment in itself. The centrepiece of the town, it has everything: shops, fast food, snake charmers, fortune tellers – and beggars. The thronging crowds make it a riot of colour but the beggars, mostly children, tend to be a nuisance. It is impossible to give to all, so a friendly smile and a shake of the head will send them darting off to other tourists.

Around the square are shops and beyond the shops to the north are the souks, a maze of alleyways and open-fronted shops selling wares of every description. A helpful Frenchman joined us and showed us how to haggle, for haggle you must, even if it goes against the grain. We asked the price of some lovely caftans, looked aghast, offered a third, then ended up paying half the asking price. The beaming shopkeeper not only shook our hands but also gave each of us a small silk scarf to show that we were worthy opponents! He raised his hands in blessing as we left and we felt we'd made a friend for life. If you don't buy, there is no hard feeling on the side of the seller; if there is nothing that pleases you and he cannot make a sale, no matter – it is the will of Allah.

The spice shops were a joy: every conceivable spice displayed in big glass jars; powdered saffron sold by weight, an ounce of saffron for about fifty pence. For a couple of pence we bought small, roughly made clay dishes, which when dampened and rubbed produce a scarlet dye used by Berber women as a cosmetic.

"I wandered up and down the labyrinth of streets, eyed by hooded men"

The teenagers went with Evelyn and Mr Bobble-Cap up one alley looking for leather and jewellery. Being so slow, I lagged behind and got lost. I wandered up and down the labyrinth of streets, eyed by hooded men who sat cross-legged and motionless outside their shops. (The Moroccans are great ones for sitting: they sit beneath trees, against walls and on the edge of pavements.) I was about to ask, in my atrocious French, the way to the square, when a smiling little Arab boy came to the rescue. Without a word he took my hand and led me through the maze to the waiting coach. A cheer went up as I limped along with my ragged escort, who went away ecstatic, clutching a bar of chocolate and a handful of sweets.

One day we went on a coach tour to the Valley of Ourika, a complete contrast to the sandy roads we'd travelled to reach it. The valley is long, lush and green, cutting deep into the High Atlas. The steep sides are studded with trees and slashed by waterfalls, and streams snake across the valley floor. It's a perfect place to escape the oppressive heat of Marrakesh, and many people camp and hike in the area.

On the way back we passed a Berber village of beige, flat-roofed, clay dwellings, set well back from the road and enclosed by a high wall. Hassan, the guide, told us that the women were only allowed out of the compound on one day a week. That was to take their laundry to a nearby river where they could meet and chat to other Berber women also on their day out.

"Big deal!" I heard one teenager murmur to her friend, a remark fortunately not heard by Hassan. Morocco is very much male dominated. Although we experienced only polite, helpful men, we could not escape the feeling that they don't approve of female freedom. I tried several times to have a conversation with some of the Berber ladies, without success. They simply covered their faces more fully, smiled with their eyes and walked gracefully away – and how I admired that walk!

It was so hot the next day that I stayed alone in the the hotel while the others travelled to see the olive groves of Menara. I wished I had a sunhat, so I strolled along to a nearby café, hoping to buy one there as it stocked a variety of goods. No luck, but knowing there were more shops further on I asked whether or not they sold hats, thinking I'd save myself a walk in the heat. The café owner didn't understand English, even though I patted the top of my head to illustrate my request, so I tried French. He shook his head, looking more mystified than ever. He must have wondered why an elderly foreign woman, evidently a tourist, wanted to buy a horse. Well, it's not easy to recall schoolgirl French, and *cheval* and *chapeau* aren't too dissimilar.

The next coach trip was to a donkey market and to the Valley of Asni, famous for its minerals and semi-precious stones. The weekly donkey market was not only a place for selling or exchanging, it was also a lively get-together for the Berbers who came in from the desert to sell their wares and meet their friends. The sellers spread their goods in any available space between pits and boulders, and we had some difficulty weaving our way around tethered animals and squatting figures, some selling beautifully hand-embroidered caps. Long-robed Berbers blocked the way as they chatted excitedly to each other; as usual, no women were to be seen.

"For just over £1 I bought a chunk of roughly hewn amethyst weighing about 170g"

I think we were all glad to leave the smells and the obstacle course, and travel to the Valley of Asni, which was beautiful. We stopped at a village – just a café, a few clay houses and a shop – and the view from there was spectacular, the snow-covered Atlas mountains in the distance, looking so unreal in the shimmering heat that they could have been a backdrop in an old film. The shop had a variety of minerals and semiprecious stones on display, all quite cheap. For just over £1 I bought a chunk of roughly hewn amethyst weighing about 170g, a treasured reminder of the Atlas mountains.

On our final day we set off before dawn for Agadir, stopping again at the little café we'd visited before. I left the others there while I walked down the lonely road. It was cold but the sun was beginning to show, bathing everything in a pinkish, misty glow. Not thinking of anything in particular, I suddenly became aware of a dark figure standing motionless at the foot of a sandhill.

She was some metres back from the road and I wondered what she was doing there. Except for the café there was no sign of any habitation. Had she come in from the desert? We stared at each other, and I felt a surge of empathy towards the still figure. What she felt I don't know, but she slowly nodded her head and raised a hand. Before I could respond she disappeared into the mist.

They were calling me from the coach and as I was helped in I looked back down the road, searching for the mystery figure. There was only the empty landscape. It was one more strange memory of a remarkable holiday.

Sierra Leone

Nor Touch Arata

In spring 1989 Kate Margrie, who is paraplegic, travelled to Sierra Leone, attracted by a Health Education Project. She spent two months working with youngsters in the Eastern Province.

The four-month sabbatical which I took from work left me with two months' preparation time. I got my visa, my jabs, my travellers' cheques and my air ticket (via Moscow with *Aeroflot*). I had thought sanitation would be a problem, so paid a visit to my urologist; I didn't want to be carting around loads of catheters and pads. In the event there was always somewhere to go to the loo, even if it was just a hole in the ground, and supplied with washable pads I ended up being healthier during my two months away than I ever am in England.

A friend, Cath, had set up a youth workshop attached to the Lassa Fever and AIDS Research Project based in Segbwema, in the Eastern Province. This project was the brainchild of an American doctor, Jo McKormac, who established it in the Seventies in an attempt to control and understand the disease. It is now funded by the Center for Disease Control in the States. For this reason an American is always appointed as director of the project, which causes its own problems – coming in from the outside, the director may not be familiar with or understand local working methods, customs or needs – but does mean that the

Lassa team receive a higher than average wage by Sierra Leone standards.

The Lassa Project has a laboratory, where tests are carried out on the blood of affected people, and their own ward in the Nixon Memorial Methodist Hospital, where – unlike all other treatment – patients are treated free of charge. Education has always been a high priority for the project as Lassa fever is preventable. This gave rise to the VSO-funded post of Youth Workshop Coordinator, which is where Cath came in. She spent a year in Segbwema, initiating some spectacular events, culminating in the grand LASSARAMA which drew together nationally and locally known musicians who composed songs especially for it. The resulting tape is now played in every nightclub in the land, and people still talk about that wild night. However, since Cath's departure nothing really happened on the youth education side.

Nine months later, I arrived. I had already decided that I wanted to be based in one place and that I wanted to share my skills in community drama. I did a lot of research on youth education and AIDS, I tried learning some Krio and Mende (the two languages spoken in the Eastern Province), and I made a video with one of our Youth Theatres to begin an exchange with young people in Sierra Leone.

I arrived at Heathrow with a home-made rucksack, designed to hang off the back of my chair, my concertina and a car-load of friends to see me on my way. Then the trouble began. *Aeroflot* wouldn't let me on the plane without an escort, for "insurance purposes". Of course I could travel on that flight but only if I paid for an extra seat (£500) to allow one of their staff to accompany me! They claimed to have had no information from the travel agent, despite my insistence when booking that it be made clear to the airline.

"Moscow airport at night is not a very welcoming place"

There was no way that I was going to miss that flight, so I lied. "Yes, I can walk up steps. No, I won't ask for any assistance. Well, of course I could get out quickly in the event of an emergency" (as if it would make any difference!). I knew that once I was on the runway they'd simply have to help me on. It worked, but it did mean being carried by an air steward whenever I wanted to leave my seat, causing many eyes to turn. And that was only the beginning.

Moscow airport at night is not a very welcoming place. There is no lift to the restaurant, where I had to wait for eight hours, nor were any of the airport officials prepared to carry me down again. In the end, I asked some friendly passengers to help; I'd got this far and would never forgive myself if I missed the connecting flight! Many hours and

a beautiful sunrise later we touched down at Lungi airport, Sierra Leone. Getting through customs could have been a very harrowing experience if Abdul had not been there to whisk me through. (Abdul is the cousin of a friend and just happens to be the Chief Security Officer.) I had arrived, disoriented by the hustle and bustle, and hypnotised by the brilliant colours all around me. I had no idea what the next two months would hold.

My first night was spent in Abdul's house on the airport compound. We sat on the porch as the sun went down and the electric lights came on in the military compound opposite. I learned something of the corruption, the links between the President and the army, and the rocketing inflation (which tripled while I was there). Sierra Leone is considered one of the poorest countries in the world; the majority of the people hover between survival and starvation. Yet its land is agriculturally fertile and holds many minerals, including diamonds, and its waters hold a rich stock of fish. So what went wrong?

From 1961 to 1971 a very shaky, multi-party democracy operated, following on from British rule. But in 1971 Doctor Siaka Stevens became Executive President and from then on Sierra Leone has been a one-party republic. While I was there, an Asterix-style cartoon book was on sale, following Stevens' rise to power, expounding his virtues and providing an easy-to-read, colourful piece of propaganda. In 1985 Major General Joseph Momoh took over as President, after an "election" riddled with ballot rigging and petty bribery. Momoh was the only candidate. He was previously head of the armed forces, and while everyone expected him to reform the oppressive sanctions practised by his predecessor, nothing changed.

Soldiers now receive even greater perks, such as very cheap rice and electricity in their compounds. The people living in the country are becoming increasingly disillusioned as the economy goes haywire and Momoh has to honour his deal with the IMF by floating the leone (le). People are depressed and becoming more willing to speak out against the regime. Every single person I met wanted to leave Sierra Leone and never come back.

"I spent many an evening out on the porch trying to dispel a few myths about England"

No one really mentioned my disability, which I thought strange at first, particularly in comparison with the fuss made at the European end, until I realised what was going on. As a white woman (*poumie*) I was odd enough anyway, so the fact that I was sitting down, wheeling myself around, did not make a lot of difference. Sierra Leone is not an easy place to trundle about – the terrain is very rough – so I relied on people pushing, which practically at least was no problem. But there was a fine line between what I saw as my needs as a disabled woman, and what they saw as the needs of a white colonial, there to be served. Sierra Leone only gained its independence from Britain in 1961, and the "white is good" ethic remains. I spent many an evening out on the porch trying to dispel a few myths about England.

The Lassa Project is based in the Methodist hospital and nearby are a few ex-colonial houses. I was lodged in the bungalow; spacious, flat and an ideal venue for crèches, parties and rehearsing puppet shows. There was a mango tree outside and at 5am we collected the fallen mangoes to take for the kids in the education workshop. Every child I worked with was malnourished, and when the mangoes are ripe that's all they eat. Who can afford rice at 3000-le a sack, when the average monthly wage is between 500 and 1000-le.

With a few ramps installed, my base was accessible. But I'm not that skilled at oil-lamp maintenance, at building and cooking on fires, or drawing water from the well. I needed help, and the only way I could attempt to even this out was by giving in other ways . . . Every morning at 8am Soloman picked me up in one of the Lassa Project trucks to go down to the workshop. All along the red-dust track, women make their way to the town to sell their produce from laden baskets balanced skilfully on their heads. The Limba men – palm wine collectors – pass by with a gourd in one hand and a long, sharp knife in the other; using a rope they scale the never-ending heights of the palm trees to gather the alcoholic juice amassed in yesterday's gourd.

At the workshop several boys would be waiting, eager to sweep the floor, open the shutters or play on the drums. Word spread fast and soon dozens of kids were passing through our tiny workshop each day. I made badges with them, belts, hats, headbands and, once we'd got used to each other, puppets. I wanted to introduce something that they could spend time making and use, even after I had left.

With brown paper, local fabrics and many hours of sticking and sewing (girls and boys alike), the characters for our puppet show, *Nor Touch Arata* (Don't Touch Rats), were born. Lassa is spread by a certain type of rat and our story told of a young boy who caught the fever from eating food already touched by rats. The puppets were loosely based on several local characters, including the Lassa doctor, and there was always banter between the fascinated audience and the puppets. The response was amazing wherever we went: we piled into the truck, drove for hours to a tiny village where we were met by adults and children keen to watch, listen, ask questions and hopefully learn a little, too.

As might be expected, several of the people I worked with had physical disabilities. One boy with no speech was picked on by his peers as mercilessly as he would have been in Britain. One of the teachers in the local secondary school had his own wheelchair, which amazed me at first, then he told me that a doctor had sent it from England in 1988. During my stay I also visited a residential home for children with disabilities in Freetown, the capital. It is supposed to be a *Cheshire Home* but receives no financial assistance from the charity. Based in another ex-colonial house, the atmosphere is wonderful but the buildings are in a terrible state of disrepair. The girls' dormitory is upstairs and only a few lucky children have calipers.

With no training facilities for physio-therapists in Sierra Leone, disabled people just have to make the best use of what mobility they have, without much hope of ever acquiring aids such as wheelchairs. Nobody I came across owned a car, and public transport is a case of squeezing as many people as possible into a camionette. Mr Koli, the schoolteacher, had to pay extra to take his wheelchair on board. It was not unusual to pass an overturned truck on the highway, with all its passengers trying to flag down the next one to come along.

"I ended up staying in a Catholic nunnery due to lack of cheap, accessible accommodation"

The workers on the Lassa team are lucky: they have two well-used, never-reliable trucks which are continually taken to bits by the four drivers; travel-ling in them was a lot of fun, our jour-neys always ending in laughter. Apart from my daily trip to the workshop and excursions to surrounding villages, I actually travelled very little. But Wednesday nights are for nightclub-bing and even during Ramadan (the drivers are Muslim) we piled into one of the trucks, ready to boogie!

The nightclub reopened the day I arrived (good timing!). From the outside it looks like a wooden ranch hut, with a few tables and chairs on the balcony. Inside it's a different story. All round the walls are crudely painted portraits of Madonna, Michael Jackson, Stevie Wonder and Bob Marley. In the middle is the checked dance floor and the inevitable disco lights which flash in time to the music. The DJ hides away in a room no bigger than a box and turns up the decibels to make everyone from miles around think it's all happening at the club. It was good to see men dancing with men, and women dancing with women, and to hear every now and then the familiar heavy bass of "Lassa Fever No Gud-o", one of the project songs.

Perhaps I have made it all sound easy. It wasn't. Many times I felt very frustrated, for example on my visit to Freetown, where I ended up staying in a Catholic nunnery due to lack of cheap, accessible accommodation. The hotels are extremely expensive and very international, so if you're looking for somewhere to stay, the YMCA is cheap, clean and wheelchair accessible, but you do have to book in advance. Freetown is an incongruous mixture of solid office buildings, enormous hotels, banks with tinted windows and foreign embassies, rubbing shoulders with one-room shacks squashed together next to open sewers. Washing hangs between the shacks and the women cook as the children play.

The capital got its name from the freedmen (emancipated slaves) who were shipped over from America. The huge cotton tree, which isn't really but its fruit look like cotton wool, remains in the centre of the city as a reminder of those not-so-far-off days when slaves were bought and sold here. Sierra Leone was an unexplored land at that time, so someone had the idea of using it as a dumping ground for unwanted, "free" black men, women and children, many of whom had never been to Africa before. This naturally caused friction between tribes and even now many Creoles (descendants of the freedmen) consider themselves one up from the indigenous tribal people. It's a colonial history which we should be ashamed of.

"A tiny shack with an enormous sound system which seemed to be holding up the walls"

One of the songs which was played on every radio, in every bar, was "King Jimmy Bonga" and I wanted a tape of it as a memento. So we made our way through bumpy back streets, dodging kids, hens and rubbish, to a tiny shack with an enormous sound system which seemed to be holding up the walls. With a bit of cash, a nudge and a wink, we struck a deal and next day the transaction was completed. Another day the Lassa truck needed some spare parts so we drove out to what can only be described as the district of the second-hand car dealers. Bamboo structures house hub caps, alternators, wheel exhausts . . . every imaginable part piled high behind their seller, who sits patiently listening to a small transistor. "King Jimmy Bonga" keeps him company.

There is another side to Freetown. On its outskirts are the luxury apartments and vast, foliaged compounds with lush green plants and swimming pools. This is where the expats and bank managers live, in bright white buildings to match the bright white bodies. These places are "protected" by a high white wall, decorated threateningly with pieces of jagged glass. The Sierra Leonian watchman is on duty day and night, and earns less in a

month than the occupants spend in a day. There's a harshness about Freetown, and the glimpse I had of its other side was enough to make me yearn for the mango trees I'd left behind in Segbwema.

Being dependent on others was quite hard work, in sharp contrast with the lifestyle I'm used to. It meant that I didn't get to see the sights of Sierra Leone, but that wasn't what I was particularly interested in. On the other hand, it was wonderful to have more time than I've ever had to talk with people, to listen, and to learn those essential Mende words for "star", "moon" and "How many scorpions have you killed?" – these were the good times, whiling away the evening with old Pa Bocharie (the night watchman) and his wife, Matu, drinking palm wine by their fire under the stars.

"Do you have a moon in London?" Pa Bocharie asked me one night towards the end of my stay. How many moons apart our two worlds appeared then. And so I waved goodbye to newly made friends and all their warmth, to the rich soil, the corruption and the sunshine. Another tourist passing through. I will always remember the first showing of "Nor Touch Arata", performed in the middle of Segbwema with hundreds of people gathered round – the good times. But people are still dying of Lassa fever; despite all the research in America there is still no antidote; there is even doubt as to whether, once discovered, the inoculation will be made available to the Sierra Leonians because it will be so expensive. Fine for the American tourists visiting West Africa, though.

Tanzania

I Felt Like a King

**John Bignell has multiple sclerosis,
diagnosed in 1983, and is now unable
to walk more than a few steps out of
doors. He uses a standard, hand-
propelled, NHS wheelchair, which he
regards not as a prison but as his
passport to the world. In June 1988 he
was invited to present a paper to a
workshop on phosphates, organised
by the Commonwealth Science
Council at Arusha in northern
Tanzania.**

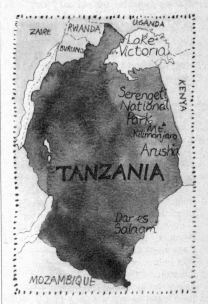

When I booked my flights – Heathrow
to Kilimanjaro via Amsterdam and back
– I informed the airline (*KLM*) of my
disabilities and that I would be unaccompanied. I requested wheelchair
assistance at all airports: no problem, I
was assured. I packed all my luggage in
a small suitcase which I could suspend
over the handles of my wheelchair with
two elastic grips, so that I could move
myself and all my gear about quite
easily.

I arrived at Heathrow one Saturday
evening to learn that the Amsterdam
flight was on time but the Tanzania
flight was delayed by technical trouble
for eighteen hours! I transferred to an
airport chair and was wheeled rapidly,
by a very pleasant gentleman, through
the customs and security checks and
eventually to the aircraft door.

At Schiphol, Amsterdam's airport, I
was met at the door by one of the cabin
crew with my own chair, and wheeled
straight through the formalities to the

airport *Hilton* for my enforced overnight stop. The design of my chair was
much admired by the *KLM* staff. After a
Sunday morning spent travelling by
train in and out of the city centre and
trying to discover where the disabled
could embark for a canal trip (by the
time I had established this, there was
no time for the trip!), I was taken in the
hotel courtesy bus back to the airport.

I checked my luggage and wheelchair in and was transferred to an
airport chair. I then began to understand why my chair had been so much
admired. The airport chair had four
small wheels, making it virtually impossible for the occupant to move it, and
with no cushion it was very
uncomfortable.

Because of the delay, instead of a magnificent midday view of Kilimanjaro to welcome me to Tanzania, I arrived at 4am, bleary eyed and in the dark. At the foot of the aircraft steps I was met by a wheelchair with very flat tyres. For once I had to wait my turn to be processed by immigration, health and currency officials, but at least I was sitting down! In the baggage hall I reclaimed my chair but not my case. At the missing bags counter I met some colleagues also attending the workshop who, unbeknown to me, had travelled on the same flight. Out of four of us, three had lost their bags.

"He drove like the proverbial bat out of hell"

We were taken to the hotel where I could unpack my camera bag, and then on to the Arusha International Conference Centre. The centre had not been designed with the disabled in mind. The nearest car-parking spot was some way from the door with a kerb to negotiate. Even on the ground floor there were steps all over the place. Fortunately, whenever I approached any steps, without being asked, four pairs of hands would grab the chair and hoist it and me into the air and up or down.

My presentation was in the afternoon, and the following morning we all left on a two-day field trip, giving no one time to buy new clothes. So, in clothes borrowed from other members of our group, I set off to visit the local geological sights. Out of the city, the roads, where they existed, were not well maintained. The driver of the Land Rover was very skilful but he drove like the proverbial bat out of hell. This resulted in a fast and bumpy ride. So bumpy that I managed to put my shoulder through the Land Rover's side window towards the end of day one. I spent the rest of the trip trying to hold my chair cushion between myself and the broken window to avoid being cut to ribbons.

We drove from the lush green of the Arusha area, pleasantly cool at about 1200m, down to the hot, arid and dusty surrounds of Lakes Manyara and Natron. Like many sufferers from multiple sclerosis my disabilities get worse when the temperature rises, so I relied on helpers to push me in my chair when I wanted to move more than a few feet from the car. I have a most unflattering photograph of me in my chair perched on the lip of a spectacular extinct volcano crater, to illustrate the sort of places I was taken to. This was reached after several hours of hard, dusty driving through an apparently deserted wilderness of powdery volcanic ash. The dust had barely settled when two Masai ladies appeared from nowhere to sell their colourful bead necklaces. When we stopped a few miles further on, we were surrounded by children, and the bartering currency of the moment was ball-point pens.

The one thing missing was wildlife. We saw only a few baboons, giraffe and zebra at close quarters. In the distance we did see a pink colouration on Lake Manyara, which, we were assured, was produced by thousands upon thousands of flamingoes. We also spotted a few vultures, hideous at close range but magnificent in flight.

"I had only to trundle through the restaurant door for food to arrive"

The *Novotel Mount Meru* (Arusha) was simple but clean and comfortable. It was three storeys high and had one small lift which could just accommodate me in my chair, but there was no room to turn. As the doors closed automatically after only a few seconds, as soon as I reached my floor I had to back out fast and hope all was clear behind me. Breakfast was always a buffet, mostly fresh fruit. As I cannot carry food and move, the hotel staff plied me with food at the table. They quickly cottoned on to what I liked, so I had only to trundle through the restaurant door for food to arrive.

The workshop talks continued to the end of the week, and on Friday at noon our suitcases arrived (via Brussels) and borrowed clothes could at last be returned. It was a good job the hotel had an efficient and fast laundry service.

One morning, when I looked out of the hotel window, I saw how the local disabled fared. A man was seated on a wooden plank, fitted with what looked at a distance like chair castors. He propelled himself by pushing on the ground with his hands. Seated in my NHS chair, I felt like a king.

I was taken by one of the workshop participants, a Dutchman on secondment to Tanzania from a Canadian university, to see Kilimanjaro. Or, rather, to see a bit of it. The top 3900m was always hidden by cloud. Ballpoint pens were acceptable in this part of the country too.

Sunday was the final day in Tanzania. The hotel desk were sure that there was a suitable service at the cathedral at 10.30am. They were wrong. I arrived by taxi at 10.15am, part way through a eucharist being taken by the bishop – in Swahili. Although I arrived late, knew no one and didn't understand a word, I felt very welcome and part of the congregation. At the end of the service I was greeted by the bishop and his fellow clergy like a long-lost brother. A charming young American woman appeared and gaily announced that taxis were hard to get in this part of town but she would try to fix me up with a lift back to the hotel. She disappeared and reappeared a couple of minutes later at the wheel of a car – the bishop's car. Incidentally, she was the only person I met on my trip who knew how to collapse my chair without first being told.

I returned to the hotel to find it in the midst of a power cut, so the lift was out of action. The current had not been restored some four hours later, when it was time to leave. One of the staff retrieved my case, which fortunately I had packed before I went to church. I went to the airport with the Dutchman; on the way, the clouds parted a little to reveal the snowcapped summit of Kilimanjaro, but at a range of about 50km it was not spectacularly clear – I had to inspect my photographs closely to convince myself that I really had seen the summit.

The airport was in chaos: they had also been affected by the power cut. With the help of some local knowledge and the cheek of my Dutch friend I soon found myself sitting in the departure lounge in the airport chair, still with the very flat tyres. Because the control tower had been without power our plane had been rerouted and our departure was delayed by four hours. This meant that a meal was served, upstairs of course. As there was no lift, my meal was brought down.

> **"A man was seated on a wooden plank, fitted with what looked like chair castors"**

At Amsterdam I was asked, as is customary, to sit in my seat until all the other passengers had disembarked. After everyone else had gone, the crew looked outside for the expected wheelchair. It wasn't there. Hasty recourse to the radio, followed by "Just a minute, sir, it will be here soon." After a few minutes there were more enquiries by radio, and the cabin crew were beginning to get agitated.

"Could I walk along the ramps to waiting trolley?"

"No."

"You may have to wait twenty minutes."

I had nothing better to do, as long as I made my connection. The ground-crew arrived to clean out the cabin, but the chair didn't. The only member of the cabin crew left on board was going frantic, talking into his radio. After about half an hour something had to be done or I would miss the connecting flight. On the arm of a well-built and charming ground stewardess, I walked along a seemingly endless ramp and through the arrival lounge to a waiting trolley. I was then driven to the departure lounge and had to struggle along another ramp to the next plane.

Back at Heathrow, I was met at the cabin door by another friendly face who sympathised over my experience at Schiphol. "You should have gone by *BA*." (He worked for *British Airways* and had only been loaned to *KLM* for my benefit.) I was whipped through immigration, one of the few advantages of travelling in a wheelchair, and into the baggage hall. My case was quickly found but my wheelchair was eventually located in Amsterdam. I was loaned an airport chair to see me home, and my chair was specially delivered to my house later the same day.

I wrote to *KLM*, complaining of my experiences, particularly the lack of wheelchair at Schiphol. After six weeks I had received no reply so I wrote again, asking specific questions about wheelchair availability at Schiphol. Their reply crossed in the post. It apologised for the misplacements and blamed a new baggage handling system. The reason for the delay in replying was that they were awaiting the results of an investigation. No findings were disclosed but they hoped

that the "generous" gift of a *KLM* marked ballpoint pen would compensate for the inconvenience. (It might have been of some use in Tanzania.) The second letter elicited nothing more than that *KLM* were surprised that I was not satisfied by their response. Still no explanations.

I tried contacting the Dutch Embassy in London, asking whom I could write to. They suggested their Ombudsman. His office replied that it was not their responsibility; they added that the embassy should have known better than to involve them. I also wrote to the Dutch Multiple Sclerosis Society. Their reply, far from being helpful, suggested to me that they were rather pained at me for querying the efficiency of their national airport and airline.

Finally, *KLM* admitted that they were having trouble with their new baggage handling system and that all available staff had been sidetracked to try to sort things out, thus no wheelchair help could be provided at Schiphol. This was hardly news, but surely prior commitments should be honoured, particularly since *KLM* staff had to be on hand anyway – all that was missing was the chair!

The attitude of *KLM* leaves something to be desired, although the staff I met were all splendid and as frustrated as I was by the problems encountered on my trip.

Zimbabwe

Silent Zimbabwe

For fourteen years John Myall has suffered from Ménière's disease, a condition that can cause severe attacks of giddiness and nausea, often without warning and lasting for several hours; at the same time it destroys the hearing. John's attacks have now lessened, enabling him to enjoy his passion for wildlife and wilderness areas, but the deafness remains. In June 1989 he travelled alone to Zimbabwe, to stay with friends and photograph wildlife.

The Land Rover edged its way along the track which was still unrepaired after the previous season's rains. The sun was well up and we were able to start shedding pullovers. It was mid-winter in Zimbabwe, an ideal time for travel in this part of the world. Although the nights are distinctly chilly, the day temperatures are more akin to those of a pleasant English summer, and – the biggest blessing – the insect life is mostly inactive.

We were hoping for a sight of a black rhinoceros; his tracks had been spotted the day before and he was the first one to wander into this area for many years. As our Land Rover reached the brow of the hill, the driver stopped. Some 275m ahead lay a thicker area of bush and, above, vultures were circling. Something was either dead or dying, and we had to investigate.

The Land Rover was parked off the track and four of us proceeded on foot.

At our approach the birds reluctantly withdrew; they had started to feast on three dead impala, each one with a wire snare cutting into its neck. The snares had been wired to trees, so that the harder these graceful antelope had struggled, the more quickly they had strangled themselves.

Sten (the guide) and I stayed put, not wishing to disturb anything as the two Shona trackers cast about for any evidence of the identity of the poachers. Only one set of tracks was found, made by well-worn soles with a distinctive chip out of the left heel. The man was almost certainly a local herdsman from the nearby village, out to obtain some meat to sell. He must have been delayed in checking his snares as the giveaway birds were making good use of his handiwork.

We checked out the remaining area and retrieved another ten wires, then the Shona pointed to a movement in the dry grass about 70m away – yet another impala with the deadly choking wire. He had struggled hard and the branch which the wire was attached to had snapped off. Although still alive he was beyond saving. As Sten went off to collect the Land Rover, so that we could load up and take away the carcasses, he handed me his rifle. He knew that I had had plenty of experience of African wildlife and firearms. Moving into close range, I worked the bolt to feed a cartridge from the magazine into the breech, aimed and fired. The impala jerked and then lay still. I barely heard the shot as I am now almost completely deaf.

The 36,422-hectare cattle ranch (not particularly large by Zimbabwean standards) is situated along the banks of the Chiredzi river, which is home for a fair number of crocodiles and hippos. George and Madeleine, friends of long standing, had invited me some time back to pay them a visit as soon as I felt up to travelling. In addition to ranching, they arrange photographic and hunting safaris. As a result of well-managed conservation policies, there is a good surplus of game which can be hunted without fear of endangering any species.

"A family of warthogs, led by an old fellow with some very impressive tusks, broke cover and took off"

Accommodation for clients is the typical African safari camp, with roomy sleeping tents (all fitted with insect screens and snake-proof zippers), toilets, showers, mess tent and, of course, the traditional log fire to sit around in the evening, drinking, exchanging stories and – for those who can – listening to the sounds of the animals in the bush. Dotted around the perimeter are the bits that make the whole thing work: cookhouse, stores, vehicle servicing area, and tents for the camp workers.

The flight from London to Harare caused me no major problems, although airport check-ins (like hotel receptions) can be a bit tedious if questions have to be written down for me. I was met at Harare by an air charter pilot who ferried me through customs at great speed, after which it was a short hop in a light plane to the ranch's private airstrip. This spared me an arduous nine-hour road journey.

Wherever I go, I make a point on arrival of putting the news about that I am deaf and a hopeless lip-reader, indicating my ever-present pencil and notebook (for those who can write in English). However, on the first day out with Sten and his two trackers, after a lengthy hike without seeing much, the party stopped suddenly and ducked down. Sten pointed and whispered to me. I saw and heard nothing, and was bewildered as to what I was supposed to be looking for. To my confusion, he whispered again, no doubt louder, when a family of warthogs, led by an old fellow with some very impressive tusks, broke cover and took off. They had heard the voice. It was here that we stopped to refine our system of communication.

A pencil and paper is not always ideal for bush use, and Sten was a slow writer, so it had to be a series of hand signals to identify the various animals. The most graphic was undoubtedly the scratching of the armpit to represent the baboon! In fact, Sten was quite an expert, as he had done all this before. As a professional hunter he had led many of the big safaris in Tanganika (now Tanzania) and Kenya, as well as working with the lions for the film, "Born Free". Some of his clients did not speak English (or his native Swedish), so hand signals became the common language when out on the hunt where quietness is absolutely necessary. Although I was armed with nothing heavier than a selection of cameras, the same rules apply; game must be stalked silently for a good shot.

A deaf person moving through the bush is presented with another problem. It is easy to presume that because you hear yourself making little or no noise, you are moving quietly. Not so! You may well only feel the dry twig snap, or your boot scuff on a rock, or the numerous thorns raking across your clothing, but the noise will be clearly audible to the nearby animal life. One morning I thought I had done particularly well as we approached a mixed herd of wildebeest and zebra. This was in spite of the fact that Sten had given me several reproachful looks. Idly thinking that all my old skills from years back had not deserted me, I had been lulled into a false sense of security – in fact, my hearing aid battery had gone flat.

"Behind a clump of bushes a mere 40m away – my planned destination – lay a lioness with the remains of her dinner"

A trip further afield, well clear of the main ranching area, hammered home the need for careful observation to make up for my lack of hearing. I had a dose of the "East African Quickstep" and signalled for the Land Rover to stop and let me run for it. A pair of strong hands grasped my shoulders and kept me firmly in my seat. Behind a clump of bushes a mere 40m away – my planned destination – lay a lioness with the remains of her dinner. She had roared, which had alerted the others; when I knew where to look and what to look for I could make out her outline. We moved on and I found another bush; after all, she was there first.

The other clients at the camp were an American honeymoon couple and a German hunter; six is about the maximum number of clients at any one time. Each person or small group can go out by day or night to do their own thing. The Americans spent several nights waiting up in a blind to watch the leopard feed. A blind is a ready-prepared hiding place, made of bushes and grass, for two or three people. It provides a clear view of the feeding animal while the watchers remain unseen. But the leopard's sense of hearing is acute, so any "unnatural" noise alerts him instantly and he disappears in one blurred movement. I tend to fidget, then fall asleep under such circumstances, so I gave the blind a miss. Gone is the boundless energy of my youth!

The odd afternoon sitting in the sun on the "beach" is a little more in my line these days. Just a small clearing on the river bank, the beach was about 70m from our tents. Small, brightly coloured birds darted about and monkeys chattered in the trees. One afternoon I got through three chapters of my book whilst being watched by a curious hippo who remained motionless in mid-river, with only the top of his head above the surface. I learned that he was a regular visitor, known as Fred. Although not renowned as a vicious animal, the hippo's huge mouth does inspire a sense of awe. Several species of African animal are capable of biting a human in half, but only the hippo can bite one into three! Fred and I made a pact: he stayed in the river and I stayed on the beach.

It was a holiday I am sure to repeat, and the photos (some at least!) were almost professional. Before leaving, I photographed as many of the African camp staff as I could with my polaroid camera and gave them the prints. On the last evening we had a farewell party around the campfire. Apart from the fact that it was time to say goodbye, I felt a tinge of sadness for another reason: the party emphasised the handicaps that deafness causes. In the flickering light of the fire any form of lipreading is next to impossible, likewise writing things down; even sign language gets lost in the dancing shadows.

AFRICA: TRAVEL NOTES

Sources of information

Few African tourist offices keep much information for disabled travellers, but some are happy to research it on behalf of individual enquirers. The tourist offices of Morocco, Tanzania and Sierra Leone supply no relevant information and have no plans to produce it. The *Kenya National Tourist Office* cops out and refers enquirers to *Pollmans Tours and Safaris* (see below).

Travel to South Africa will remain controversial until apartheid is unambiguously abolished, and we cannot recommend a visit. However, the combination of the country's relative wealth and its desire to promote tourism in the face of the travel boycott means that its infrastructure for disabled travellers is the best on the continent.

Zimbabwe Tourist Office, 429 The Strand, London WC2R 0SA; ☎071/836 7755. Will help with requests for information where possible.

South African Tourist Board, 6 Alt Grove, off St George's Road, London SW19 4BZ; ☎081/944 6646. Will obtain answers to specific queries from their head office in Pretoria and will contact hotel chains to ascertain the accessibility of particular hotels. The Pretoria office is in the process of compiling some printed information for disabled visitors, which should be available from the London office some time in 1991.

Tour operators

Ivy Geach had a successful holiday with *Enterprise* in Morocco and was pleased with their accurate description of the hotel.

Ian Piercy, of *Zambesi Hunters Ltd* (PO Box 139, Ruwa, Zimbabwe; ☎73/2567) handles bookings for George and Madeleine's ranch. *Zambesi Hunters* use several areas for their safari camps, depending on what type of scenery and animals the clients are interested in.

Safari Interlink (27–31 Jerdan Place, London SW6 1BE; ☎071/381 5229) made arrangements for a mixed-disabilities group of youngsters to travel through Zimbabwe and Botswana in 1990 (see "Booking", *Practicalities*), so they have some solid experience to draw on. They are fully aware of the difficulties – tourism in Zimbabwe is not yet the smooth operation that it is in Kenya, and awareness of disabled tourists'

needs is low – and insist on tailor-made tours, a private guide to accompany the disabled client in rural areas, and medical cover for evacuation by light aircraft in an emergency. Camps and hotels are chosen for accessibility, and all operators are notified in writing of travellers' requirements. A typical 18-day tour would cost about £2000–2500 per person, including flights, safaris, meals on safari, B&B elsewhere.

Stephen Hunt recommends *Thomson* – their *Winter Sun* brochure offers holidays in Morocco, Tunisia, Kenya and the Gambia; the *Worldwide* brochure features Kenya; all the resorts are covered by *Factfile* (see "Booking", *Practicalities*). *Horizon* are also plugged into *Factfile* and their African destinations include Tunisia and Kenya.

Kuoni operate on the principle that holidays that involve driving along dusty, potholed tracks, staying in accommodation without special facilities, are just not suitable for disabled people. This opinion seems to be shared by their reps: Jean Hamilton reports that although the Nairobi rep was good, his Mombasa counterpart was conspicuous by his absence and when he did turn up it transpired that he had booked one less on the safari, assuming that the wheelchair user would not be going.

Of course, tour operators can decide which clients to accept, and make decisions based on their knowledge of conditions "in the field", but from Jean's point of view the safari was the best part of her holiday – she felt equal to the rest of her group because no one was allowed off the minibus except at designated rest-stops, when the driver was happy to help her down, and she coped well with the accommodation.

The refusal to accept clients with wheelchairs on scheduled-departure safaris (which are much cheaper than the tailor-made excursions) is apparently a common policy amongst tour operators, the explanation being that luggage space is very limited on the safari vehicles. The *Pollmans Tours and Safaris* (52 Grosvenor Gardens, London SW1W 0NP; ☎071/730 3585) line is, "If you can possibly manage without your chair, and be helped on and off the vehicle (and to your accommodation if it's a safari of more than a day), then you can join a scheduled-departure safari."

AFRICA: TRAVEL NOTES

This is outrageous – in the words of a well-travelled paraplegic, "Always stay in your own wheelchair whenever you can, or keep it close by you. It is as personal as your trousers or bra, and more important in an emergency." Why not ask the able-bodied members of the party to cut down on their non-essential luggage?

Roger Elliott visited **South Africa**, and was delighted with the itinerary and arrangements made by *Tempo Travel* (Brunswick House, 91 Brunswick Crescent, London N11 1DG; ☎081/ 361 1131). Their ground handling agents, *Welcome Tours* (PO Box 306, Hout Bay 7872, Cape Province; ☎21/434-3890), organised all tours and transfers within South Africa and gave "excellent service".

It is worth bearing in mind, though, that any tour arranged in South Africa is likely studiously to avoid exposing travellers to those parts of the country where the agony of apartheid is still in evidence (as Roger's tour did).

Evette Johnson ot *Titch Travel* (15 Banksia Road, Rosebank, Cape Town 770; ☎73/2567) specialises in tailor-made tours for deaf or blind travellers, and can arrange tours for wheelchair users given sufficient time.

Getting there

If you avoid *Aeroflot's* flight via Moscow, there should be few problems on the major **airlines** that operate services to African countries – apart from the usual uncomfortable seating and cramped toilet facilities. *KLM* insist that all is running smoothly again now that their new baggage handling system is fully operational, but their aircraft do not carry aisle chairs.

Roger Elliott reports good service from *South African Airways* (251–259 Regent Street, London W1R 7AD; ☎071/734 9841) who carry aisle chairs (one accessible toilet per aircraft) and provide "passenger aid units" at all major airports. A *British Airways* flight is the safe option for flights to Tanzania, Sierra Leone and Zimbabwe: the aircraft are equipped with aisle chairs which can squeeze into two of the toilets.

It is at the African **airports** that difficulties may arise; often their only good point is a relatively small terminal building, so that the distance from aircraft to taxi rank (or coach pick-up point) is short – as at Agadir, Morocco.

Facilities vary enormously. In South Africa there are toilets and lifts and passenger aid units at major airports. In Tanzania (Kilimanjaro airport) John Bignell was transferred in a wheelchair with flat tyres, and the terminal building had no lift, with restaurant facilities on the first floor. Freetown's Lungi airport is a shambles, and getting into town can take as long as three hours, depending on the state of the ferry across the Sierra Leone River; the alternative is a five-hour taxi ride.

On her flight to Kenya in 1988, Jean Hamilton twice asked the crew to radio ahead for a wheelchair but on arrival at Nairobi there was no chair waiting for her. One hour after the other passengers had disembarked, a chair (plus irate stewardess) appeared. Jean was taken round the back of the terminal and dumped at lost property. Also in Nairobi, the parts of Stephen Hunt's wheelchair arrived at ten-minute intervals on the luggage carousel – standards of baggage handling leave something to be desired.

For travellers with no time constraints, aiming for northern parts such as Morocco and Tunisia (or even further – see p.474), the **drive** through France and Spain (or ferry to Santander to cut out the French section) makes an interesting alternative to flying. Ferries or hydrofoils from Spain to Morocco should be booked well in advance in high season (see *The Rough Guide to Morocco* for details).

Transport

Most Moroccan towns are small enough to explore by foot (or wheel), especially if you manage to find a central hotel. For getting about larger towns, such as Arusha in Tanzania and Nairobi in Kenya, **taxis** are generally cheap and drivers helpful. Local **buses** come in a variety of shapes and forms; most are overloaded and all inaccessible without assistance.

For cross-country journeys, **trains** may be usable with a companion, and **air travel** is a (rather expensive) possibility if you can put up with the poor facilities at many airports. In South Africa, efficient passenger aid units at airports make domestic flights a good way to get around. Travel by **car** is – in many parts of Africa – for the adventurous and mechanically minded only. The only country in which hand-controlled hire cars are available (from *Avis*) is South Africa.

If booking a place on a **safari**, or on tours using rented minibuses or Land Rovers, be warned that the road surfaces are usually appalling, and passenger comfort is not a priority when drivers are working to tight schedules – travelling at speed over rough ground is no joke.

Accommodation

There is accessible accommodation in many African countries: in the cities of the poorer ones it is restricted to a few, often overpriced, big-name hotels; in wealthier countries there are more possibilities in the moderate price bracket. Off the beaten track and in rural areas you'll find more single-storey buildings, which offer better prospects to the wheelchair user. You'll also be swamped with willing assistants, all ready to improvise – with ramps and other aids to accessibility – in buildings which at first glance seem devoid of facilities and totally unsuited to anyone in a wheelchair.

Bearing this in mind, it's probably not essential to go to great lengths to determine facilities, door widths or other details before departure. Accommodation is likely to present the smallest problems in Africa – terrain and transport are the main stumbling blocks. That said, some research is a good idea, the amount depending on the country to be visited.

Kenyan hotels with some facilities for the disabled include the *Nairobi Hilton* (PO Box 30624, Nairobi; ☎2/334000), the *New Stanley Hotel* (PO Box 30680, Nairobi; ☎2/333233), the *680 Hotel* (PO Box 43436, Nairobi; ☎2/332680), the *Castle Hotel* (PO Box 84231, Mombasa; ☎11/23403), the *Jadini Beach Hotel* (PO Box 84616, Mombasa; ☎01261/2021) and the *Diani Reef Hotel* (PO Box 35, Ukunda; ☎01261/2062), none of which could be described as budget accommodation.

Refer to *The Rough Guide to Kenya* for less expensive places to stay – cheap does not always mean inaccessible. While staying at the *Castle Hotel* for £50 a night, Stephen Hunt discovered similar amenities a short walk down Msanifu Kombo Street at the *Hotel Splendid*

(PO Box 84851, Nairobi; ☎11/20967), for less than half the price.

Information on **Zimbabwean hotels and safari lodges** is difficult to obtain. *Safari Interlink* suggest that *Spurwing Island Safari Lodge* (Private Bag 101, Kariba; ☎61/2466) would be reasonably accessible to most disabled people. *Zimbabwe Sun Hotels* (86 East Lane, Wembley, Middlesex; ☎081/908 3348) have about fifteen properties, some of which are accessible to wheelchair users. *Sikumi Tree Lodge* (Hwange National Park, Private Bag 5779, Dete; ☎18/2105) has one chalet designed for disabled guests, built closer to the ground with a ramped entrance. The *Hwange Safari Lodge* (Private Bag DT 5792, Dete; ☎18/331) has two modified rooms with wider doorways and grab-rails around toilet and bath; ramps are used throughout the hotel. The *Victoria Falls Hotel* (PO Box 10, Victoria Falls; ☎13/4203) has several ramps and all doors and rooms are large enough for wheelchairs. The *Monomatapa* (54 Park Lane, PO Box 12245, Harare; ☎4/704501) would also be manageable with prior notification.

In **Morocco**, the *Hotel Kenza* (Marrakesh; ☎4/448330) is recommended for ambulant disabled guests; wheelchair users would have to find a way round the three steps to the dining room. Make use of the *Thomson Factfile* if considering Moroccan or Tunisian hotels in the *Thomson* or *Horizon* brochures. The *Holiday Care Service* publishes a fact sheet in Morocco and Tunisia.

Cheap, accessible accommodation is hard to find in Freetown, **Sierra Leone**. Kate Margrie recommends the *YMCA* (Fort Street, P.O. Box 243; ☎22/23608) which is clean, accessible and cheap but often full: book in advance.

The *Holiday Inn* directory indicates that there are special rooms for handicapped guests at five African hotels: in **Morocco**, the *Holiday Inn Crowne Plaza Casablanca* (☎2294949); in **Zimbabwe**, the *Holiday Inn Harare* (PO Box 7; ☎4/795611); in **South Africa**, the *Holiday Inn Bloemfontein* (PO Box 1851, Bloemfontein 9300; ☎51/30-1111), the *Holiday Inn Durban* (PO Box 10809, Marine Parade 4056; ☎31/37-3341) and the *Holiday Inn Sandton*, Johannesburg (PO Box 781743, Sandton 2146; ☎11/783-5262).

AFRICA: TRAVEL NOTES

The UK sales office for *Holiday Inn* recommends the *Holiday Inn Cape Town* (PO Box 2979, Cape Town 8000; ☎21/47-4060) and is convinced that all hotels in this chain have at least one room with facilities for disabled guests, but it seems strange that the worldwide directory does not apply the wheelchair symbol to every hotel.

The *Downtown Inn* (formerly *The Landdrost*) in Johannesburg, is owned and run by *Holiday Inn*, but a questionnaire completed by the hotel in 1990 reveals that the toilet doors are only 63cm wide, there is no space beside the toilet for sideways transfer and it is impossible to wheel into the shower.

When booking hotels that are known to possess special accommodation for disabled guests in **South Africa**, request the "paraplegic room" and insist on written confirmation of the booking – take the letter with you.

The most satisfactory accommodation on Roger Elliott's South African tour was the fully accessible *Hazyview Protea Hotel* (PO Box 105, Hazyview, Eastern Transvaal; ☎13/1242, then ask operator for 51 or 115). *Protea Hotels*, however, say that in general their properties are not particularly well suited for disabled guests. Roger was told that there are some accessible huts at one of the rest camps inside the park. His experiences were less good at the *De Waal Sun* (PO Box 2793, Cape Town 8000; ☎21/45-1311), but this hotel, part of the *Southern Sun* chain, does in theory have a well-equipped room for disabled guests (80cm bathroom door width, about 100cm either side of the toilet, 185cm next to the bath but no "drive-in" shower).

The following *Novotel* hotels advertise rooms for handicapped guests: the *Bujumbura* (BP 1015, Bujumbura, **Burundi**; ☎2/22600); the *Sawa Douala* (B.P. 2345, Douala, **Cameroon**; ☎420866); the *Accra* (PO Box 12720, Accra North, **Ghana**; ☎21/667546); the *Abidjan* (BP 3718, Abidjan, **Côte d'Ivoire**; 320457); the *Dar el Barka* (BP 1366, Nouakchott, **Mauritania**; ☎253526). Although not advertised as suitable for handicapped guests, the *Novotel Mount Meru* (Moshi Road, PO Box 877, Arusha, **Tanzania**; ☎57/2711) is also reported to be wheelchair accessible in spite of the small lift.

Access and facilities

Having found an accessible hotel, wheelchair users travelling alone will probably find that they are imprisoned within its grounds – high pavements, potholes, ruts and boulders make many African streets impassable without help. Kate Margrie describes how the terrain made her totally dependent on others for mobility in sharp contrast to her life at home.

But the picture is not all gloom. General awareness is probably best in Kenya and South Africa. Stephen Hunt found ramped ramparts and wheelchairs at the entrance of Fort Jesus in Mombasa – disabled tourists are expected in some places. Roger Elliott found several facilities for disabled visitors at the Kirstenbosch Botanical Gardens in South Africa, and he was impressed to find most of the attractions of Gold Reef City accessible. And all contributors report that whenever they struggled, helpers came forward without prompting.

Health and insurance

It is important to take good advice on inoculations and other precautionary measures. Consult Richard Dawood's *Travellers' Health* (see "Books", *Practicalities*) as well as a reliable travel guide, and carry a first-aid/medical handbook with you. Although it's not good to pore over details of gruesome symptoms every time you feel a little off-colour, a brief check may enable you to take speedy action if you have the early signs of something unpleasant.

Check out the flying doctor service in the country you plan to visit; if there is none, make sure your medical insurance covers the cost of being taken by light aircraft to the nearest major hospital. For example, in Kenya the service is good and reasonably priced; patients are flown to Nairobi for treatment or repatriation. In Zimbabwe there is no such service (although there is a talk of a company setting one up), and to hire a small plane costs a bomb; you could be stuck at Victoria Falls, or at your safari camp, for 24 hours before being airlifted to Harare.

Books

The Rough Guides – West Africa, Kenya, Zimbabwe & Botswana, Morocco, Tunisia.

PART FIVE

ASIA

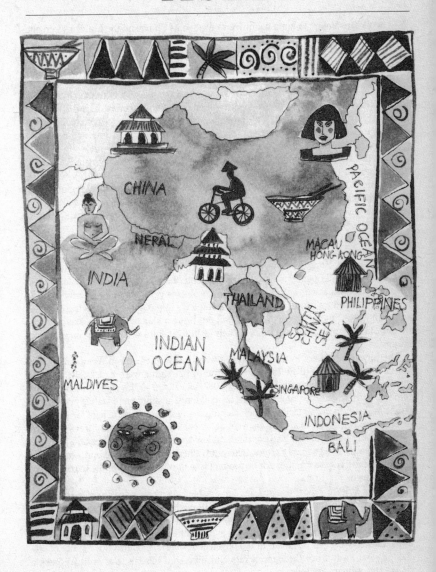

Introduction

|t is perhaps unjust to lump countries as diverse as China and the Maldives into one section, but one feature of travel to this area is the popularity of two- or multi-centre holidays – it is a long way to fly, and many travellers feel that to make it worthwhile they should take in more than one country, hopping from Singapore to Thailand, or covering Hong Kong, Macau and China in one trip.

Attitudes towards providing facilities for disabled people vary enormously and this can only be a brief survey of the countries visited by our contributors. At one end of the scale, in Singapore, Hong Kong and the Philippines, the authorities, egged on by voluntary organisations, are making some progress in their efforts to improve access to public buildings and public spaces.

Little has been attempted in the field of accessible **public transport** in Singapore, and the authors of *Access Singapore* (p.340) admit that there have been too few initiatives to reach the goal of a barrier-free environment, but there are encouraging signs, including increasing provision of ramps and wheelchair-accessible public toilets. The Singapore government announced in its 1989 budget that it will allow tax deductions to businesses for expenditure on features that improve accessibility.

Hong Kong's obvious disadvantage for the disabled visitor is the **lack of space** – tall buildings, crammed together, many with steps at the entrance. The most frequent complaint in the Hong Kong guide for handicapped visitors is the narrow doorways and lack of space in public toilet cubicles and hotel bathrooms. Sue Kelley found her accommodation spacious and experienced no problems getting around the city in 1988, but since the visitors' guide has not been updated it's impossible to assess the changes since 1987. We can only hope that 1997 will not bring a shift towards the stance taken by the Chinese, who appear to react to their lack of facilities with nothing more than a shrug.

The physical barriers in the Philippines were many when Alfred Azzopardi visited the country in 1984. But he found that some of the sights were accessible, and the introduction of the **Accessibility Law** in 1987 was a step in the right direction. This requires owners and operators of "certain buildings, institutions, establishments and public utilities" to install facilities such as ramps, wide entrances, railings for guidance of blind people, large lifts with controls at wheelchair height, public transport that considers the needs of disabled commuters, low-level public telephones and reserved parking spaces for disabled drivers. There are fines and threats of imprisonment for violators of the law, so it might not be too much to hope that some of the barriers have been removed.

There is little to report on facilities for disabled nationals or visitors in India, the Maldives, Bali, Thailand, Macau and China, although there is some impressive work going on with handicapped people in institutions such as the schools run by the *Indian Spastics Society*. Where access is gained it is more often by accident than by design. In India, bureaucracy can be added to the physical obstacles, in China the rigidity of officialdom, but away from the bureaucrats and blinkered officials, the ordinary people show extraordinary kindness.

Many contributors report warm welcomes and cheerful assistance: Alfred Azzopardi was treated like royalty in the Philippines; Hong Kong shop assistants hurried forward to open doors for Sue Kelley; the people of Bangkok rushed to help with Barbara Horrocks' chair, always smiling from ear to ear; Susan Preston was also impressed by the Thai readiness to assist; Daphne Pagnamenta was rescued from a crowded street by a young Indian boy.

If there is one area in the world where you are guaranteed a helping hand this is it, so that – if you can accept the drop in your accustomed level of independence – it's just possible to travel alone. In India certainly, and perhaps other places too, a tip might be expected, but this is hardly surprising where wealthy tourists are often the only source of income.

As in Africa and South America, the fact that you can rely on an army of assistants, either paid or voluntary, means that if UK operators are reluctant to accept you on organised tours, or insist that you are accompanied, there is an alternative. Outside China, where foreigners are marched from one party-approved site to the next, making your own arrangements can be far more satisfying and kinder on the wallet. The problems of **individual travel** encountered in some countries (India, for example) result not from a lack of facilities for disabled visitors, but from lack of good communications and fair, reliable booking procedures. If you have the time and the patience, and perhaps enlist the help of local agents who know all the wrinkles, independent travel in Asia is ultimately made possible by the friendly people.

Whether travelling independently or leaving the logistics to a tour operator, all the contributors writing in this section describe experiences that astonish, inspire, delight or revolt – holidays in these parts are an assault on all the senses, at times an enormous culture shock, and no amount of reading or research will prepare you for the sights, smells and sounds of the East. Next to this barrage, the search for an accessible toilet or hotel room will seem trivial to many travellers.

The *Travel Notes* in this section have been arranged in two parts: India and the Maldives, and the Far East.

India

India at Last

Daphne Pagnamenta was involved with the Riding for the Disabled Association for many years, responsible for their holiday organisation, and in 1978 was awarded a Churchill Fellowship to study outdoor facilities for the disabled in North America. In February 1989, coping with an artificial leg and a new hip, she spent ten days in India.

From the age of ten I had wanted to go to India, probably because for two years I was at school with a group of children whose fathers were all in the Indian Army and Civil Service. I studied their faded photographs of "Daddy's polo ponies" and "my ayah with her family", and listened with envy to their descriptions of Raj life and voyages home by *P&O* through the Suez Canal, impressed by their certainty that when school was over they would be going back.

I lost touch with my school friends, but my interest in India continued. I buried myself in the Jungle Books and *Kim*. I tried to understand the troubles of the Thirties, and was electrified by an enlightened history teacher who announced, "Mr Gandhi is not all bad, whatever your parents may say". World War II made it all more distant and after that I was fully occupied with a busy life and bringing up a family. During middle age a good deal of travel came my way, but India remained a distant dream.

In 1965 I lost a leg, but learned to live on good terms with my artificial

one, which did not slow me down too badly. However, arthritis in the other hip gradually worsened, difficulties increased and I returned to crutches and wheelchair, with the future looking black. In 1988, after several disappointments, the doctors managed a complete hip replacement. The immediate pain relief was like a miracle; I could expect to have one reasonably good leg again to help the tin one along. Two days after the operation I sat up in bed and said firmly, "Next year I am going to India."

I started off with ambitious plans: I must see the Himalayas and something of the south, as well as the more obvious Taj Mahal and the Ganges. I wanted to get to a game reserve in search of tigers, and wondered if I could fit in Calcutta and Mother Theresa. Very soon I realised that neither my stamina nor my purse would stand all this, and I must cut my plans down to size. I had to face up to my disability and my age. At seventy, my staying power was not as good as it used to be, and a very new hip, tin leg and rather dodgy back would pose problems. It was no good overestimating my ability, and I must be content with just a bit of India instead of the grand tour. The obvious bit is Moghul India – the "Golden Triangle" of Delhi, Agra and Jaipur – which is well served by package tours. Unless you are young and robust, or have reliable local contacts who know the ropes, it would be rash to try to go it alone.

I contacted the Government of India Tourist Office and a great many tour operators and studied a vast amount of literature. I found enormous variation in prices, according to whether private cars and luxury hotels, or buses and tourist hotels, were used. When I mentioned my walking limitations, operators immediately became cautious. One who appeared to run a suitable tour refused even to consider me, saying that they found the disabled a "worry".

Eventually, I landed with *Bales* – an established family firm – and discussed my problem with their overseas manager who was extremely helpful. Having convinced her that I was unlikely to be a liability and produced the requested doctor's certificate, I was booked in and promised all possible assistance. They gave excellent value and I never regretted my choice.

Before reaching this point I had had to solve the problem of a travelling companion. At first I insisted that in an escorted party I could manage on my own, but in my heart I knew that I needed someone with me. Any troubles would be more difficult to cope with than in a Western country, and it is not fair to trade on the kindness of strangers. To my delight a daughter proved willing to abandon job and family, provided that we would not be away for more than ten days, so ten days it had to be. When I looked at it realistically, ten days for two, in comfort but not luxury, was just about what I could afford. The grandchildren cooperated and were tickled pink at the idea of Mummy taking Grannie to India in a bus. Mummy was to discover a travel lust that she did not know she had.

"We dozed through an uncomfortable night and landed in the pink glow of a Delhi dawn"

I had four months for preparation, none too long. I went into training to get my new hip working as well as possible, plugging away at the physiotherapist's exercises and systematically increasing my walking distance by a few yards each day. I wanted to get the best out of my tour and my reading list was formidable: I learned a little about India's many ancient civilisations and caught up with her modern history; I became intimate with the great Moghul emperors and tried to sort out what Hinduism is all about.

The great day of departure came at the end of February – a good time for northern India, when temperatures are 70–80° F and the chance of rain is remote. Security was high at Heathrow where, as usual, the metal detector was excited by my tin leg. *British Airways* looked after me well while boarding, but the flight was an endurance test – a Jumbo packed with Indian family parties, wandering children and mountains of cabin luggage.

We dozed through an uncomfortable night and landed in the pink glow of a Delhi dawn. A surly carousel eventually spat out our suitcases (how glad I was not to be on my own) and we sat in a corner of the airport arrivals hall waiting for the *Bales* party to assemble. I could hardly believe I was in India at last. My daughter ventured through a door marked "Toilets", only to return hastily after finding herself in a narrow alley where the door to the Ladies was blocked by a row of elderly beggars sitting on the ground. We were certainly in India, and any further doubts were dispelled by the cows and swarming crowds in the streets, even at this early hour, on the way to the *Oberoi Maidens* hotel.

"How can you refuse to give in the face of such poverty?"

The hotel was a surprise and delight – a gracious, white, colonial building, sheltered from the busy street by a belt of trees, with a Raj atmosphere and a lovely garden full of handsome bougainvillaea and green parakeets. After a very necessary rest and toasted cheese sandwiches (less good value than the inexpensive Indian vegetarian dishes, we discovered later) we felt ready to face Delhi. The hotels we were to use at Agra and Jaipur were less special but perfectly adequate, medium grade and purpose-built with Indian touches – peacock feathers on the walls, some eccentricities as regards electricity and plumbing. Always there was kindly and willing service.

Our bus, to which we became absurdly attached, was a robust vehicle, as it needed to be. *Bales* had warned apologetically that Indian buses were different from Western buses, perhaps hoping to discourage unsuitable travellers at an early stage. In fact I found it more comfortable than expected, and I suffered no hardship, even on long journeys. The steps were a bit steep, but the splendid small boy who travelled with us as bus guard and general stooge always made it his business to help me up and down, and I was grateful to be allocated a seat near the front with good legroom. I took care not to hold others up on entry and exit – I wanted to avoid being a nuisance in a party with an able-bodied majority.

Most important, our driver was excellent and it says a lot for him that in often chaotic traffic conditions he never gave us a bad moment.

Firmly in charge of our pleasant party of 27 was our young Indian tour manager. He had an endless fund of information, as well as knowing the tricks of every trade. He assessed me and my limited walking ability very quickly and we came to an understanding. Where an extra long walk or an obstacle such as steep stairs lay ahead, he would warn me and suggest that I stay in an appointed place to be picked up by the party on its way back, leaving the final decision to me. In this way I ran no risk of holding everyone else up or of reaching a disastrous point of no return.

I had to miss a few things I should like to have seen, but managed about ninety percent of the sightseeing. I was glad I had not attempted to take a wheelchair with me: there would have been no room for it in the bus locker, and it would have been of little use on uneven and potholed pavements. I used two sticks and had crutches in reserve, although I never needed them. What was invaluable was a light, folding camp-stool – a must for anyone of limited walking or standing power. I used this while guides talked and while waiting on my own, and quite enjoyed my solitary sojourns, watching the life of India go by. Only once was I anxious, in the teeming Red Fort at Delhi, before I had become acclimatised, when our party seemed to take a long time returning and I wondered how on earth I should find a taxi to take me to the hotel if I had indeed been abandoned.

Travellers in India must be prepared for hassle at the tourist sites, which can be alarming at first. As soon as you climb down from the bus you will be pursued by pedlars selling junk of every kind, some of it attractive. It takes ruthless determination to get past them to the sanctuary of the site itself.

They are waiting for you when you emerge, even more persistent, and the best course of action is to return to the bus, the door of which is well guarded by the boy, and conduct any bargaining through the window. If you have hands fully occupied by sticks it is very difficult to ward off the items pressed on you and to struggle with cash, and there is extra persecution in the form of offers to "help you".

The sight of beggars in various stages of decay, of handicapped children pulled on crude trolleys, and of lepers holding out stumps of hands shocks and distresses. How can you refuse to give in the face of such poverty? Begging is officially very much discouraged, but if you cannot resist some pitiable figure give your small sum from the safety of the bus as it leaves; news travels fast and otherwise you will soon be surrounded. It is perhaps better to soothe your conscience by sending a donation to one of the overseas aid charities as soon as you get home. I also found the animal suffering very upsetting, and had to screw myself up to face the sight of overladen, worn out, ancient horses on the roads, and miserable sick cows that may not be put down.

"In India, splendour and poverty lie close together"

The sightseeing was very concentrated – this was not a take-it-easy tour. In Old Delhi we struggled shoeless, as required, up the many steps to India's largest mosque, the Jama Masjid, and looked down on the maze of streets below. We were charmed by a modern cream and pink Hindu temple, full of flowers, and sensed the reverence at Gandhi's cremation place. We drove round the elegant avenues of government buildings in New Delhi and wondered at Qutb Minar Tower, built in the twelfth century "to spread the shadow of God over East and West".

Approaching Agra we visited the great Emperor Akbar's tomb, later seeing the memorial to his favourite elephant at Fatehpur Sikri, the great city which he built in the sixteenth century. Of course, the Taj Mahal was the high spot of the round and even more magnificent than expected. We were given plenty of time to take in its ethereal beauty. I had to summon up all my staying power for the long walk through the gardens, but am so thankful that I just managed it and could see the marvellous inlaid work; a wheelchair would have been an asset there.

Jaipur held many treasures, especially in the City Palace complex, now a museum but built as a home for Jai Singh II. Elaborate blue and green gateways contrast with the pink walls, and within the complex is the Hawa Mahal (Palace of the Winds) where the royal ladies in purdah were able to look out on the wide streets from behind screened windows. But, as always in India, splendour and poverty lie close together: in a back street we visited a workshop where fine carpets were woven by hand; they made an impressive display as they hung in the sun to dry after washing. Among the workers were little girls of six or seven years old who were paid a few rupees for a full day's work, winding the wool and knotting the fringes with their tiny fingers.

At Amber, the fortress city and old capital of Rajasthan, a few miles to the northeast of Jaipur, we rode elephants up the steep approach. Yet another exquisite palace stretched along the crest of the hill, but the walking distance defeated me and I had to content myself with soaking up the view of the rugged Rajasthan ranges and watching the steady procession of elephants into the courtyard. I had a mild confrontation with one of the resident monkeys, who told me in no uncertain terms that I had pinched his favourite spot on the ramparts. He had already snatched someone's handbag so I did not argue with him.

It was not all buildings and works of art. From the windows of our bus we had an ever-changing view of the rural scene between cities. We saw the amazing difference between irrigated and arid land, the women working in the fields in their bright saris, droves of donkeys carrying fodder and bricks in panniers, and camels as we entered Rajasthan; the long journeys were never boring. We spent several hours at Bharatpur, once the scene of the Maharajah's great duck shoots but now one of India's most important bird sanctuaries.

"Although I delighted in seeing marvellous buildings and craftmanship, it was in the end the people who were most important"

There was one more excitement for me on the long road back to Delhi, in the form of a camel ride. I met the camel sitting in the garden of a rest house where we stopped for tea, and I could not resist the temptation. The mounting system is so simple: a dignified step on board, two violent heaves, and you are up and away – another test for the new hip and good for Grannie's morale.

We had the final day in Delhi to ourselves and spent about £5 on a splendid taxi which took us all over the place and waited at each stop. Most important was the President's Garden where, under conditions of strict security, we joined hundreds of Indians in best clothes and on best behaviour in procession round the magnificent garden, Moghul in design but full of English flowers. We felt that with them we were paying homage to their country, and it was a fitting end to a memorable trip.

It only remained to get to the airport at 3am for an even more exhausting flight home, with a long delay in Kuwait. Some people continued on tours to Madras and Nepal, and of course I had regrets that circumstances did not allow us to go on, making the most of the long-distance air fare, but I had stretched myself and was very tired and battered; I doubt that I could have managed more travelling without a week's rest first.

India for the disabled? It is a developing country with organised tourism still comparatively new, so expect no concessions or special arrangements. I never saw a wheelchair, a ramp or an adapted toilet, and anyone who walks with difficulty is very vulnerable. Crossing the street is a hazard; pavements disappear into potholes and piles of rubble; crowds jostle, and "Delhi belly" is apt to strike even those who eat and drink carefully. You need to be well prepared and robust enough in body and spirit to survive and to enjoy, and not feel threatened by the tremendous impact of a totally different culture.

When I look back I realise that although I delighted in seeing marvellous buildings and craftmanship, it was in the end the people who were most important. Amid poverty and squalor that makes our own urban deprivation seem trivial, a zest for living and a capacity for enjoyment shines through and defies definition. There is a welcome and a warmth, and much kindness which is very moving.

I cherish in particular the memory of a packed market where things went wrong for us. I failed to keep up with the party and the police had forced the bus to move on. The two of us could not find a square yard on which to plant my camp-stool except by an open drain where the smell was unbearable. A boy of about sixteen saw our plight and gently offered his help in rather formal English. He took us back to his brother's shop to rest and drink slightly curious tea until our bus reappeared, while a smaller boy gave us crumpled, faded rosebuds from a market stall. We bought spices, the least we could do, but there was no sales pressure and it was a bit of real hospitality.

Getting around India

Robin Reeley has multiple sclerosis (MS), diagnosed in 1985, and for many years had wanted to travel in India. When he sought advice from his GP and neurologist he was told, "We don't advise people with MS to visit hot countries and your mild condition could be affected by the heat. However, your condition is such that we would not insist that you cancel your plans. Your decision will be your own . . ."

Ashley and Jane Butterfield, of Yorkshire, charter a "second-class tourist car" railway carriage every autumn and run a number of four-week tours covering all of India. The "Bogie" is home, travelling between towns in a series of overnight trains. Two sitting/sleeping rooms for up to 26 passengers, dining room/library, toilets and showers are provided in this carriage. Most breakfasts and some evening meals are prepared by Jane and Ashley in the on-board kitchen, other meals being eaten out. Hotels are used for some parts of the tour.

I reserved a place on a tour starting in February 1987, and booked a return flight to Delhi (this is not arranged with the railway tour but left to the choice of individual passengers). Wheelchairs were provided for me at both Heathrow and Delhi airports, saving me from the fatigue of standing in queues, and easing the effects of the high temperature in Delhi.

A coach tour of Delhi was laid on, and we stayed two nights in a hotel before proceeding to New Delhi station and boarding the Bogie. As we headed south, the daytime temperature exceeded 90°F and I became steadily more tired, more often. I thought the increase in my disability was slight

until one evening in a cinema I tried to stand up and stumbled. I was alarmed to find that I could not stand. Two friends carried me, shoulder high, back to the hotel, where I had an uncomfortable night and wondered, is this it? Have I pushed myself too far, goodbye India and future travel plans?

The next day I readied myself for the worst. Carefully, I climbed out of bed. I could stand – just – and was able to walk slowly to breakfast. I shared an "auto" (motor tricycle rickshaw) to the bus station, from where a crowded vehicle took us to Mysore. I was beginning to feel better; we stayed in a hotel and were free to tour alone.

The widespread availability of rickshaws – combined with reasonably comprehensive information supplied by Ashley and Jane – gave me confidence to tour towns by myself. This fits in with the idiosyncrasies of my medical condition: at some times during the day I walk faster than most people, but I often have to walk more slowly. I carried my walking stick, not only for support but also to say "I'm ill, not drunk".

"Overnight bus travel in India is not very comfortable"

When we reached Cochin, only 210km from the southernmost tip of India, we were allotted six days of individual travel to reach Madras, some 600km distant. My chosen route covered about 1100km and went via the peaceful "canals" of Kerala, the beautiful forests of Tamil Nadu, then Kanniyakumari, Madurai and Kodaikanal. The "canals" are actually coastal lagoons, used for transport of freight (in traditional motorboats) and passengers (on ferries). The boats ply between larger towns, calling at many halts en route. Alleppey and Changanacheri are small towns with both railway and backwater connections, a morning being sufficient for the tranquil backwater journey between the two. The waterways are surrounded by pine forests and fields.

Kanniyakumari is the Land's End of India, where the Bay of Bengal meets the Indian Ocean: you can watch the sun rise over one and set over the other. The town is a popular pilgrimage destination for Hindus and centre for Indian holidaymakers, but the beaches are not very good. There are many comfortable, inexpensive hotels. A regular ferry service operates from the mainland to the Sri Vivekanada Memorial, located on two rocky islands about 200m from the shore. Built in 1970, the memorial commemorates a visit by the crusading Indian philosopher, Swami Vivekananda, in 1892.

Kodaikanal is acclaimed as the most beautiful hill station in the south of India. On the southern crest of the Palani hills, the town lies 120km northwest of Madurai. The altitude is 2133m and the views are spectacular, over thickly wooded slopes and precipitous rocky outcrops. The bus from Madurai follows a very scenic route and takes about four hours. I was very happy to meet a variety of travellers at the youth hostel in Kodaikanal, including a mountaineer from the USA, a young Australian couple and an Israeli girl who helped me down the steps to the hostel and persuaded the warden to let me stay, although there were no beds left that night.

I returned by bus to Madurai and had intended to take an overnight train to Madras. I was told that there were no seats – trains had been cancelled. I could not find out why, so I booked a seat on the overnight bus which was more than full on departure. Overnight bus travel in India is not very comfortable, but I arrived safely the next morning, having slept fairly well on my seat; some people had to sleep on the floor. I learned the reason for "no trains" – a terrorist bombing at Tiruchchirappalli had killed nearly thirty Indians and destroyed a bridge.

Madras is India's fourth largest city and the capital of Tamil Nadu. The city is relaxed and public transport efficient: buses are not overcrowded and urban commuter trains provide a convenient service. A long seafront on the Bay of Bengal ensures a supply of fresh sea air and a pleasant location for walks. There are several fine churches and temples.

The village of Mahabalipuram (Seven Pagodas) is a short bus ride from Madras: here there are fine beaches but the tide is very strong. Mahabalipuram is famous for its shore temples, which date from the seventh to eighth century. These temples have an appealing freshness and simplicity, in contrast with the more grandiose monuments seen later on the tour, in Agra.

In Madras I met up with the other Bogie passengers for a long train journey – one night and one day – to Bombay, some 1020km away. Then on to Agra, Delhi and the flight home.

In March 1988 I was back again, this time on a tour of northern and eastern India.

Our chartered carriage left Delhi for the 1500-kilometre journey to Howrah Station, Calcutta, a two-day trip with many short stops, we were sustained by plenty of *chai* (tea plus milk plus sugar, boiled together) from platform stalls, and Western-style meals cooked by Jane and Ashley. We arrived in Calcutta and were directed towards the trams, which travel through some of the oldest and narrowest streets in the city.

"I was walking with difficulty – heat and exhaustion had taken their toll"

Calcutta is the largest city in India, the capital of West Bengal, with an enormous population of very poor people. The slums at Anand Nagar (made famous in *City of Joy*, by Dominique Lapierre) have been razed to make way for the Underground, which runs between the city centre and the business area of Tollygung. Often described as an ugly and desperate place, Calcutta to many people sums up the worst of India, yet it is also one of the more fascinating cities and has some scenes of rare beauty – flower sellers beside the misty, ethereal Hoogly river, the superb collection exhibited in the Indian Museum.

Partition affected Calcutta more than any other Indian city. The jute-producing and export centre of India, Calcutta became a city without a hinterland, while across the border in East Pakistan (now Bangladesh) jute was grown without anywhere to process or export it. West Bengal and Calcutta were disrupted by tens of thousands of refugees fleeing from East Bengal, although without the communal violence and bloodshed that partition brought to the Punjab. Calcutta has been a troubled city, but it is a city with a soul.

I travelled on the Underground, and later in the day I sought directions from a helpful Indian man who both directed and supported me, since I was walking with difficulty – heat and exhaustion had taken their toll. We went a short distance in a rickshaw pulled by a man. There are many thousands of these in Calcutta, and a corresponding number of very poor people depending on them as a source of income. My return to Howrah and the Bogie was by local bus – an adventure, since I had to stand out in the street to catch it.

We continued from Calcutta to several towns of interest further south (thus hotter). I could get around OK by day, walking short distances and using cycle rickshaws. The majority decision of other passengers on the Bogie was to shut the wooden blinds at night, in order to keep out the mosquitoes. Mozzies don't like me, so no risk of being bitten at night for me, but it was very hot with the blinds shut. I woke one night and tried to turn over. My legs didn't respond and I fell to the floor. Not only were my legs as good as

paralysed, but also my voice was not fully operative. I was able to utter a few garbled noises, but could not make my cries for help understood. In the end, arm strength, driven by determination, got me back on the bench, there to sleep without moving.

"Never mind an illness having affected your handwriting, sir, the signatures don't match"

India is a dusty country, and I developed a cough. I asked a cycle rickshaw driver if he could take me to a chemist's shop for some cough sweets, but he didn't speak any English. Sign language was of no avail, so I forced a cough and the driver seemed to understand. I climbed into the rickshaw, and off we went to the local hospital! Eventually I found a doctor who spoke good English and I was able to explain my quest. He noticed that I was staggering and I explained why. MS is a very rare illnes in hot places like India; the doctor had read of the condition but had never seen a real live MS person. Investigations of my balance, sensitivity, reflexes and arm strength followed before at last the doctor gave me some cough mixture and sweets.

We returned via Rajasthan to Delhi, where I visited the *Indian Airlines* office to pay for my domestic air tickets. The problem came when I signed a travellers' cheque to make payment: "Never mind an illness having affected your handwriting, sir, the signatures don't match – you'll have to go to the bank." Two kilometres and two hours later, I returned with a fistful of rupees and paid for my tickets. That evening we went for a group meal in a Tibetan restaurant, leaving Old Delhi station on the night train for Kalka.

At Kalka we left the Bogie to travel on the narrow-gauge railway to Simla, the most important hill station in the days of British rule – in the hot season it was the "summer capital" of India.

The former Viceroy's palace (Rashtrapti Bhawan) is now a college of further education. For many years Simla (at 2130m) was isolated from the lowlands except by mountain trail. The railway was constructed in 1903, and roads came later. Today the town of Simla is anything but restful, being visited by many people, but the mountainous landscape is beautiful and the air fresh and cool.

"Kashmiri chicken, with a good selection of spices and plenty of rice"

From Simla I travelled alone by bus to Chandigarh for my first *Indian Airlines* flight to Srinagar, the capital of the state of Jammu and Kashmir, famous for its canals, houseboats and Moghul gardens. Now what? Four days relaxing on a sumptuous houseboat on Nagin or Dal lake? Not me. I wanted to go trekking: there are numerous beautiful treks in and around the Kashmir valley, varying from short day walks using the hill stations as starting points, through longer walks in the valley and across the surrounding ranges, to hard treks out of the Kashmir region to Zanskar or Ladakh. My illness would not permit me to walk very far, so when I visited the tourist information centre I asked, "How about pony trekking?"

My guide, Siddiq, asked me whether I would prefer to visit mountains or rivers and lakes: I chose the mountains. We gathered food, blankets, stove and fuel before making our way by autorickshaw towards the Srinagar bus depot. The roads in Srinagar are narrow and the drivers pushy: a local bus going the other way scrunched one side of the rickshaw, forcing it back a short way and removing the turn light.

The rickshaw driver stopped to assess the damage to his vehicle; the bus driver did not stop. Siddiq and I picked up our things and walked to the bus depot. The bus for the hill resort of

Pahalgam was just leaving: in desperation I stood on the rear ladder and prepared to climb up to the roof box, only to be dissuaded by Siddiq.

We caught a bus to Anantnag, a small town known chiefly for the curative properties of its sulphur springs, and from there went by tonga to visit Siddiq's friend in the village of Kaymu. Siddiq bought some chickens for supper; they were alive – just – to keep them fresh in the absence of refrigerators. Kashmiri chicken, with a good selection of spices and plenty of rice, made a delicious meal and I felt honoured to be eating in a village home. We watched some Indian and some Pakistani TV, keeping candles at the ready – three brief power cuts occurred during the evening.

Siddiq and I returned to Anantnag the next day, continuing by bus to Pahalgam. Two ponies and a ponyman were hired – one pony for me, one to carry the food (including a chicken) and other items. We walked together down the main street and along the mountain track towards Aru, which lies on a grassy plateau, surrounded by pine forests and mountains.

The 12-kilometre journey took about three hours. The mountain valley trail is a road in summer but covered by snow in winter. There was no snow in Pahalgam but an increasing amount as we trekked nearer Aru. My pony walked very close to the outside of the path. "He is a good walker," Siddiq assured me – just as well, since there would have been nothing to stop us sliding 20m down a steep hillside into the river if the pony had stumbled. We kept mostly to the path, taking one short-cut across a field where the snow was about 25cm deep, and fording several streams. Ponies don't like crossing streams, especially when the water cascades down a rockface nearby; my pony was reluctant but obedient.

We met Siddiq's young friend, Fayaz, in Aru and stayed in his "tourist bungalow"; the ponies and ponyman returned to Pahalgam. The power-line had collapsed several months previously, so no electric light. There were no washing or toilet facilities and little furniture, but it suited me fine. There was plenty of water, and cardamom or cinnamon *chai* to drink, and the chicken – cooked by Siddiq and Fayaz – tasted nearly as good as the one in Kaymu.

Fayaz and his father joined Siddiq and me for the return trek to Pahalgam, after which I travelled with Siddiq by bus to Srinagar and then by plane to the mountain town of Leh, the capital of Ladakh. There were many soldiers and no other white people on the *Indian Airlines* flight to Leh. My water flask caused suspicion at the check-in desk: "*Pani*" (water), I explained, and drank some to prove it.

The road between Srinagar and Leh is closed by snow for most of the year, so flying is the only way in before June. The runway at Leh is short and the surrounding mountains loom very close. The town stands at 3505m and the area is largely barren with little grass and few trees. The air is rarefied and visitors should spend time at an intermediate altitude (Srinagar, for example) rather than fly direct from Delhi or other low-lying areas.

The old town of Leh is clustered at the bottom of a hill beneath the old palace of the kings. Few western travellers visit this Buddhist centre, which is culturally closer to Tibet than to India. Along the banks of the Indus, close to Leh, lie several interesting buildings, including Shey – once the summer palace of the kings of Ladakh – and, further south, the Tikse Gompa, a 500-year-old monastery currently used by the largest contingent of monks in Ladakh. The most important word in the Ladakh language is *jullar* (hello); people are very friendly and the children are especially inquisitive towards western visitors.

I spent two days in and near Leh before flying back to Delhi. The railway tour had been good and Leh interesting, but pony trekking was, for me, the most wonderful experience. This is an ideal activity for disabled people who can walk, but not very far. I kept in touch with Fayaz and in October 1988 I made another pony trek in Kashmir with him and his Uncle Hassan. My inspiration is Dame Freya Stark, a remarkable traveller who used riding and pack animals to reach distant parts of the subcontinent when she could not walk by herself – a perfect example for the less mobile adventurer!

Visit India

Alison Walsh has rheumatoid arthritis. In January 1990 she travelled to India for the first time, with a companion who has visited the country six times in ten years and covered everything from tigers in the jungle to film stars in Bombay. The trip was planned as part business, part pleasure but turned out to be a five-week endurance test.

Not expecting anything in the way of facilities for the disabled in India, I landed in Delhi on a cold morning in January and was pleased to find a wheelchair waiting. My surprise at spotting a door marked "HANDICAP" next to the ladies' toilets at the airport quickly turned to disgust when I finally managed to heave the door open: plenty of room to manoeuvre a wheelchair inside, grab-rails too, but the bowl overflowed with excrement.

Hoping to see more of the country-side than aerial views, we purchased Indrail passes – over £100 each (first-class, non air-conditioned), valid for thirty days. These must be paid for in foreign currency and the story is that they give you priority when booking seats on the hopelessly overcrowded trains. Not so: priority is given to those who pay back-handers to the booking clerks, and even this much-loved system falters under the sheer weight of numbers clamouring for seats.

Train travel is ludicrously cheap and is used by millions, not only to get to work but also to attend every family event including births, deaths and marriages, not to mention all the relig-ious festivals. You would have to spend the whole thirty days on the train to notch up the equivalent of a hundred pounds' worth of journeys: better to book well ahead, just for the journeys you want to make; better still, avoid the trains altogether.

In Jodhpur, no amount of persuasion could find us a seat on the train to Udaipur and we finally agreed to take a "deluxe" bus, setting off at 5.30am. I realised then that my idea of deluxe and the Indian understanding of the word were poles apart. The road was, from beginning to end, appalling – a bumpy, narrow strip of tarmac, full of potholes and in many places deteriorat-ing into a gravel track. The bus rattled – every joint and every window shook violently until our heads seemed filled with the noise. None of the windows shut properly (it's very cold in the desert at night).

A combination of vibration and cold is not the best therapy for arthritic joints. The final straw was having to tie my legs in knots after the first stop, when a crowd of pushy Indian men filled the front of the bus, squatting, standing and slouching, covering every inch of space including my leg room. At every subsequent stop we were jostled and shoved, by men and women, when getting on and off the bus.

After two *chai* stops, when the hot sweet tea brought temporary relief, we honked our way through a busy market, scraping stalls stacked high with produce, and shuddered to a halt outside a workshop. Much hammering and welding in the region of the front axle, then more swaying down narrow streets until we left the town and headed towards the Aravalli mountains, gears crashing in anticipation of the struggle to come. We did make it to Udaipur, but in no state to appreciate anything except a long sleep and a dose of antibiotics from the hotel doctor – we were both, by this stage, suffering from sinus infections.

"An astonishing medley of farts, belches, snores, incessant high-pitched chatter, reverberating nasal snorts, throat clearing and spitting"

After we had checked out of our hotel in Udaipur and arrived at the station at 5.30pm we were met by our man from *TCI* (*Travel Corporation India*) who told us that he could not get us a seat in first class; would we be prepared to pay our way into the second-class sleeper car? We had no choice – we had arranged to meet someone in Jaipur at 6am the next day, he was to meet us on the train. Never mind, smiled the *TCI* man, at the first major stop the guard will move you into a first-class sleeper.

When we eventually found the guard during the Chittaugarh stop he was drunk and abusive. We returned to second class and lay down on the narrow three-tier bunks and shivered through the next nine hours, surrounded by an astonishing medley of farts, belches, snores, incessant high-pitched chatter, reverberating nasal snorts, throat clearing and spitting.

This tale is not a reflection of *TCI*'s incompetence: we used the agency to book all our accommodation and train journeys, and valiant efforts were made on our behalf at their Delhi, Agra, Jaipur, Jodhpur and Udaipur offices. But at each office we gleaned something of the difficulties they face: the struggle to obtain one telephone (can you imagine a travel agent working without a telephone?), the lack of a coherent policy on tourism, the lack of funds for preservation of the sights. The manager of one office said despairingly, "India is crumbling".

It did not surprise me to discover that none of our Indian hosts used the railways. They fly the state-owned *Indian Airlines,* who have the monopoly and are universally criticised by Indians and foreigners alike. Internal flights are a nightmare, known for their excruciating delays, blatantly rude staff, heavy overbooking and frequent disruption of reservations by travelling "VIPs" (government officials or army officers).

How *should* one travel then? Hire a car and driver? Expensive and not worth the aggro with drivers who want a tip every time they change gear. Nor did the Indian idea of a "deluxe" car (like the "deluxe" bus) coincide with mine – good suspension is a high priority in this country (particularly for a disabled person) and it is quickly destroyed by the crippling road surfaces. An old college friend, a journalist in Bombay, told me that she never moved from Bombay unless absolutely necessary and that I was *mad* to travel in her country!

The joys of domestic travel made a ten-day tour from Delhi a trial of strength, both mental and physical. The physical hardships are easy to imagine, the mental stresses difficult to convey. First, of course, the human and animal suffering leaves you reeling, however well prepared for it. Tiny children with rampant diarrhoea drag their red-raw bottoms along the side of the road; a mean-eyed man hurls bricks at a donkey's head because it has sunk to the ground, unable to carry its load up a steep slope.

Next to that, your constant battles to carry out the simplest task, from booking a railway ticket to buying a box of tampons, are hardly worth mentioning. But when your resistance is lowered by unrelenting noise and pressing crowds, you cannot fail to be rattled by widespread dishonesty and lack of courtesy, or by the fifth argument of the day with a rickshaw driver who insists on taking you to look at his brother-in-law's cousin's carpets when you want to go somewhere else – *anywhere* else as long as it's quiet.

The sight of the Taj Mahal did nothing to compensate for the misery. Agra struck me as a dirty, grasping little town which does not deserve the beautiful Taj. Agra Fort is reached across a deep moat that has become an open sewer. The buildings are neglected and overrun by monkeys; every darkened room we explored stank of urine. Fatehpur Sikri, 37km from Agra, was full of hawkers and persistent little men and boys constantly hovering and offering their services as "official guides".

"Open drains and piles of rotting rubbish combine with the fumes to produce a clinging, sickly smell all over the city"

Jaipur is no longer "The Pink City", more a grubby orange-brown, choked by hordes of ancient vehicles churning out noxious black fumes, their engines clattering and exploding, horns blaring. Open drains and piles of rotting rubbish combine with the fumes to produce a clinging, sickly smell all over the city; after a sightseeing trip by autorickshaw we would return to the hotel with blackened faces, stinging throats and clogged nostrils.

By maintaining a safe distance from the city centre we found Jodhpur more bearable: the views from the fort are spectacular and the museum well laid out, the guides informed and efficient. A tour of desert villages (arranged from the guesthouse *Ajit Bawan*) is a blessed relief from city squalor – you can eat lunch with the villagers in spotless huts built from cow dung and urine. The Maharaj will insist that as well as doing the standard camel ride you inspect the male camel's backward pointing penis and work out how he achieves copulation in spite of this apparent handicap (they do it sitting down). The bone-shaking jeep ride might be difficult for a disabled person and the desert presents problems for a wheelchair, but the silence is like manna from heaven.

"Monstrous old trucks driven by maniacs who would sooner squash you than alter their route or use their brakes"

None of the cities on this route could be easily negotiated in a wheelchair. Where there are pavements, for example in New Delhi, the kerbs are impossibly high, built for the monsoons; you would have to stick to the road, keeping a wary eye on the traffic. Although there are many human-drawn carts, bullock carts and cycle rickshaws, which travel slowly, the "Public Carriers" are monstrous old trucks driven by maniacs who would sooner squash you than alter their route or use their brakes. In the older parts of the cities the streets are rough, edged by open drains and crammed with animals, people and vehicles. There will be heaps of rubbish to steer around, as well as spreading puddles when the drains overflow.

It *is* possible to find accessible hotels because of the tendency to ramp flights of steps for the movement of luggage and equipment, but it is by accident rather than by design and you will have to stick to the luxury variety. The old palaces have bathrooms the size of tennis courts (no baths in the non-Westernised hotels, often no shower, simply a tap, a large bucket and a jug) but they may well have a step or two at the entrance – and wet stone or marble is *very* slippery, even for nimble feet. I found an accessible swimming pool at the *Shivniwas Palace* in Udaipur – some decorative marble steps to shuffle down – but usually there were steep ladders to negotiate, or else the pools were empty – it was winter, we were told.

The stunning architecture and air of past opulence in these hotels that were once palaces is something to savour, if you can afford to stay in them; it is a great shame that some are badly managed and the buildings poorly maintained. The *Narain Niwas Palace Hotel* in Jaipur is an example of both: cracked and disused swimming pool in neglected grounds, rooms dirty, staff unconcerned except when given a blast by our *TCI* man, food soon abandoned in favour of cup-a-soups and dry biscuits.

Leaving aside the deservedly admired Moghul architecture, I was unimpressed by more recent designs. I was directed to Chandigarh in the Punjab as an example of a "beautiful" modern city. Designed by Le Corbusier because the Punjab government convinced Nehru that no suitable Indian architect could be found, Chandigarh is a uniformly ugly series of concrete "sectors". Nek Chand's famous "Rock Garden" (sculptures made from everyday rubbish) provides the only relief from the monotony.

The tragedy is that Chandigarh is not an isolated case: the Indian architects of the post-1947 period were carried away by Le Corbusier's concrete mania and duplicated his work all over the country. India's architects are just beginning to look to their own culture for inspiration, and to design more "people-friendly" buildings. Perhaps the next stage will be to plan accessible as well as habitable structures, but it seems unlikely.

Towards the end of our trip, I visited Meena Verma, who has muscular dystrophy, is wheelchair-bound and lives in Ghaziabad, about 20km northeast of Delhi. Her mother explained that when she could no longer lift Meena (tiny though she is), an English friend had sent them a hoist. It took nine months to clear this essential piece of equipment through Indian customs.

"Those who do not fall under India's spell will suffer every time they leave their five-star hotel"

This is bureaucracy at its most absurd and an illustration of an attitude present at all levels in Indian society: in a population of more than 810 million, disability, both mental and physical, is common. It may be the result of disfigurement at birth, so that the child grows up as a money earner (through begging). It may be the result of disease, or genetic defect, in which case it is seen as punishment for evil committed in a past life or by one's ancestors. The handicapped must accept their lot and remain at home, cared for by that much cheaper alternative to the Welfare State – the Indian Family – or they should get down to the station on their chariots and demand their benefits from the train passengers.

Meena would love to travel and see something of her own country but she has been no further than Delhi because she cannot rely on receiving help along the way. She attracts a crowd of onlookers but her mother is left to struggle alone while lifting her out of the car and into her wheelchair. Then the problems multiply – unmade roads, lack of pavements, very limited access to buildings and scarcity of toilets.

In spite of the obstacles, Meena has chosen to remain in India – she runs a

kindergarten for twenty children in her house, she writes Urdu poetry and has a circle of good friends whom she will not leave. For the disabled visitor who falls in love with India, who delights in the noise, the colours and the smells, the problems will also be insignificant. But those who do not fall under India's spell will suffer every time they leave their five-star hotel.

India is an impoverished, Third World country in which the money for the building and maintenance of basic amenities too often simply does not reach the right department – it is siphoned off along the way by corrupt civil servants. The money for conservation of the Moghul masterpieces and other historic monuments has clearly gone astray. Yet the Indian government hopes to attract over two million foreign tourists in 1991, designated "Visit India" year.

Those involved with "Visit India", including UK tour operators, might consider whether the country can cope with the numbers already visiting before attempting to attract more. They might consider taking steps to safeguard the Indian population (and the wildlife) from the harsher effects of mass tourism – villagers around Goa have their water supply cut off for 23 hours out of 24 so that the beachside hotels receive a constant supply.

There is an urgent need to return to basics, to make improvements to the transport networks, the drainage systems, the hospitals, the standards of hygiene in restaurant kitchens – and a few public toilets wouldn't go amiss, particularly if they were wheelchair accessible.

The Valley of the Gods

In 1933, as a young and agile soldier serving in India, Hugh Chetwynd-Talbot visited the Kulu Valley, a hundred miles north of Simla in the Himalayas. In his diary he recorded that it was as near heaven as one could get, and in 1977, paralysed by polio from the hips down, he took his wife to see it.

Since the second century and probably earlier, the Kulu Valley has been one of the main routes between India and Central Asia. Manali, a village at the northern end of the valley, is at 1800m, and from there a track goes over the Rohtang Pass (4050m) into Lahoul and on to Leh, near the Tibetan border. From the top of the Rohtang Pass there is a fantastic panoramic view over massive peaks.

I saw it at dawn in 1933, and it had been my hope, until I became disabled, that my wife would see it too.

In 1976 we saw an advertisement for a package holiday under the patronage of the *RSPB* and the *RHS*, a birdwatching and botanical visit to Kashmir and the Kulu Valley. The itinerary involved a stay of six days on a houseboat on the Dal Lake near Srinagar, two days in a hotel in the mountain resort of Gulmarg, and eight days in the Kulu Valley based at Manali. I learned that since the Indo-Chinese War the Indian government had built strategic roads in the Himalayas so that, where I had walked along precarious mule tracks, a car could now be driven. Houseboat living might present difficulties, as might a gruelling itinerary and my calipered and bandaged legs in the heat, but there seemed no insurmountable obstacles. We decided to take the plunge.

At the end of May 1977, in a party of eighteen, we flew from Heathrow to Bombay where, after a hot wait of two hours, we flew on in an *Indian Airlines* plane to Delhi; another change took us to Srinagar. That final leg of the journey was hot but dramatic. The line of the Himalayas appeared low on our right soon after taking off, and the snow-covered peaks came closer as we flew almost parallel to them.

Srinagar is a military air base, and our arrival coincided with that of the Indian Minister of Health and the Commander-in-Chief of Kashmir. At that time India maintained a large garrison there against the threat of Pakistani invasion (a situation which has not changed). The coach drive from the airport took us through Srinagar and was stifling and bumpy, an exhausting end to some thirty hours of travelling during which we had had little sleep and the temperatures had been in the eighties and nineties.

We came to a stop on the shore of Dal Lake where *shikaras* (gondola-type boats) were waiting for us. Embarkation was a bit of a scramble for me, done mainly on my behind, but the cool, smooth progress across the still water of the lake, in its lovely setting surrounded by mountains, was a blessed relief. The houseboats are ranged along the far side of the lake; there are scores of them and they constitute one of the main attractions for visitors. Many of them have been in the ownership of the same Indian family for years, and some talk nostalgically of the good old days when British families spent the hot weather there.

The houseboats are mostly moored close to the shore and are boarded by a rather makeshift plank structure which I found perilous – the water below is far from pure! Each houseboat has three or four bedrooms, a sitting room, dining room, kitchen, shower and WC; the plumbing is inclined to be erratic, as is the electricity. Nabis and Bashir, the houseboat servants, gave us superb service and always seemed to be on hand when I needed help.

On the morning after our arrival we were woken about 5am by a cuckoo, and got up in time to see the sun light up the peaks, turning everything a pale rose with marvellous reflections in the lake. Later, during breakfast on the after-deck, we were interrupted by the arrival of a flower-seller, his *shikara* piled high with roses, syringa and all sorts of sweet-smelling, exotic flowers. He was closely followed by others, peddling carpets, carved trinkets and embroidered cloth, all very attractive but at prices which, we were warned, were exorbitant.

At about 10.30am we set off, a fleet of four *shikaras*, downriver to Srinagar. Two locks regulate the flow from Dal Lake into the rapidly flowing River Jehlum, and going downstream is easy. But the very strong current makes it hard work coming back and it takes two men, paddling with all their strength, to do so. The banks are lined with a native houseboat community, living an odd sort of semi-static life on the water. The conditions are incredibly squalid: drains, which all but made us ill as we passed them, run into the river just upstream of women washing clothes or cooking utensils; they in turn are just upstream of children bathing or women drawing water for cooking; the sequence repeats itself, with additional pollution from cattle that are stabled in many of the houseboats. Surprisingly, the river itself does not smell, and the scene is an artist's dreamland.

During the next day or two, nearly all our party succumbed to tummy trouble of varying intensity. The heat, the altitude, the diet and some fatigue no doubt contributed, but visitors can reduce the risks by ensuring that they drink water which has been boiled or purified, and by taking the usual precautions with food, in particular fruit and vegetables.

Getting about once ashore is not easy for a disabled person because of ditches and steps which have to be negotiated. I was lucky to be looked after by Nabis and Bashir. One evening they helped me all the way to a meeting in Ray's houseboat (Ray was the party leader), and they were waiting for me after the meeting ended at about 10pm. We had just completed the return journey when John (*RSPB* expert) came over and asked us to go back for a drink. We did, and when we left again, at 11.30pm, there were Nabis and Bashir waiting to see that I got back on board our houseboat without falling into noisome water on the way. I had told them not to wait.

The following days were spent by the rest of the party visiting the bird sanctuary, and various gardens and temples. I could take little part in that, so I explored the labyrinth of backwaters which surround Srinagar, and took a ninety-minute *shikara* trip, part of it through Kashmir's famous floating gardens, to the lovely Lake Nagin.

"A gallant chap lifted me off my steed and humped me, like a sack of coal, up the path to the hotel"

Soon the time came to say farewell to the faithful Nabis and Bashir, and to drive the 80km to Gulmarg, some 1200m higher than Srinagar. We passed through paddy fields and silkworm farms, then, as we climbed higher, through deodar (Himalayan cedar) forests. We emerged into a large, open, bowl-shaped area, around which are the houses and hotels of Gulmarg, and we came to a halt amid a crowd of porters and ponies. Our driver explained that no cars are permitted beyond that point; otherwise, the porters and pony-wallahs would be out of a job!

"Where's the hotel?" I asked, with a sinking feeling. He pointed to one on the far side of the bowl, standing at the top of a steep hillock and quite inaccessible to me. I explained this to the driver and an animated discussion ensued, involving about fifty Indians. They were fascinated by my calipers. Two of them advanced on me as I stood by the car and, before I knew what was happening, I found myself astride a pony, my stiffened calipers wedging me firmly, if uncomfortably, in the saddle.

We made good going and I felt almost regal as I saw the crowd escorting me. But the feeling did not last long. Within a short distance of the hotel but at the foot of the hillock, we came to a narrow gate. It was too narrow for my jutting-out legs to pass through and the procession came to a halt. An even larger crowd had gathered by then, and an even louder debate followed as to what should be done with me. Eventually it was settled by a gallant chap who lifted me off my steed and humped me, like a sack of coal, up the path to the hotel. He was pleased and tickled when I paid him double for being both a porter and a horse.

"Our bus cannot have been more than six inches from the edge of a thousand-foot drop"

The main attraction of Gulmarg is the profusion of alpine plants on the mountain slopes in the spring (*gul* means flower; *marg*, meadow) and, in winter, the excellent skiing. It now bears little resemblance to the flourishing resort it used to be, a large part of it having been, to use the Indian expression, "taken away for burning by the Pakistanis on the day of separation". While the rest of the party went up the mountains, botanising, I enjoyed a pleasant day admiring the lovely view from the hotel verandah and being chatted up by Indian fellow-guests.

Our flight back to Delhi was delayed for two days by low cloud over Srinagar, which prevented our plane from taking off. Delhi was very hot indeed, in the region of 100° F, with high humidity. We were only there for a few hours before going on by coach to Chandigarh, in the Punjab, where we spent a rather hot and uncomfortable night. We left next morning at dawn on the 300-kilometre drive to Manali, travelling this time in a bus instead of a coach. It had little in the way of springs and the seats were very hard.

The climb up from the plains was spectacular and we were soon some 900m up and in deliciously cool air. The road was new and well-graded but tortuous. Indian drivers blast their way everywhere with their horns, which we found somewhat trying, but that soon changed to a sense of relief when we outblasted the oncoming vehicles. Nevertheless, the twisting and turning and climbing, only to lose height again, made the journey most exhausting.

At noon we reached a mountain village called Mandi and it was decided that we should stop for a rest and lunch. I was delighted because it was there that, in 1933, on my return journey from Kulu, the road had been carried away by heavy rain, taking my bus with it, and I had been stranded for a week. I was finally able to walk out with my baggage on mules. It was interesting to see the place again after so many years.

The road onwards from Mandi is now much changed, running through the sheer, deep gorges at a higher level; we could see the old one far below. The new road is still narrow and twisting, and hair-raising episodes are common. There are few passing-bays, and drivers do not like reversing; they prefer to try to pass each other. At one such crisis, when we met an army lorry, the wheels of our bus cannot have been more than six inches from the edge of a thousand-foot drop to the River Beas. One of the party was heard to ask if she could get out and walk!

In the late afternoon we emerged with relief into the Kulu Valley, a widening expanse of green with the rushing, grey waters of the Beas running through it. Above the fields and the orchards there were heavily wooded hillsides and, ahead, snowcapped mountains. The valley is dotted with prosperous homesteads, each with its orchards of every imaginable fruit and its fields of corn. The villages of Kulu, Katrain, Nagar and Manali have developed into small tourist centres, and everywhere there are ancient Buddhist temples. No wonder it is called "The Valley of the Gods".

"As we lay on our backs in the sun we watched a pair of golden eagles"

Since the Indo-Chinese War there has been a considerable military presence in the valley, as well as camps of Tibetan refugees. Where, in 1933, I camped in isolation beside the river where I could catch my breakfast trout, there are houses and cultivated fields. Yet it remains idyllic, and although we had taken a gruelling ten hours to cover 300km the fatigue and discomfort seemed entirely worthwhile. The morning after our arrival in Manali, I looked out of the windows of John Baynon's Guest House, through an orchard of cherries and plums, down the valley to high peaks which looked like heaps of icing sugar in the morning sun.

A couple of days after our arrival, our companions left for a four-day bird-watching and botanising trek, which was quite out of the question for me. My wife and I hired a car and driver, and took on a cheerful lad called Preem who could cook for us. We set off in an attempt to get over the Rohtang Pass, staying nights in dak bungalows – travellers' rest-houses, which are spaced at intervals along main routes throughout India and are a legacy of the British Raj.

The road from Manali deteriorated to a single-track affair, hewn out of the mountainside. Climbing steadily, we soon left the green valley and the roaring river below us and were above the tree line. The only vegetation was coarse grass and scrub. We arrived at the *Khoti Dak Bungalow* (3750m) at 12.30pm. The *gusselkhanas* (lavatories) were arranged Indian-style, that is at ground level, which presented problems, but we were welcomed by an efficient *chowkidar* (caretaker) and the place was clean and well kept.

The bungalow had five bedrooms, each with its own *gusselkhana*, and a kitchen and servants' room at the rear. It was perched dramatically on a small, level area facing across the valley. As we lay on our backs in the sun we watched a pair of golden eagles working the mountainsides opposite us; the air was so clear that we felt we could almost reach out and touch them.

The next day we stopped 4km short of the top of the Rohtang Pass, brought up by a four-metre-high snowdrift. It had been a hair-raising drive as the road was officially closed and we were the first car to venture that far since the last snowfall. When the car came to a halt my wife insisted on continuing on foot. It was a stiff climb, especially at that altitude, and I was very pleased when both Preem and the driver decided to go with her.

My wife's diary describes the culmination of the climb: "At times we crossed what must have been the road but mostly it was snowfield to be traversed, falling now and then into water-holes invisible under the snow. The height and the steep ascent reduced my pace to forty steps forward and then a pause. The summit at last and a tremendous feeling of achievement overcame that of exhaustion. We sat in the brilliant sunshine, chewed biscuits, and watched through binoculars the magnificent snow peaks around us, and the endless panorama of range after range of the Himalayas."

They were gone for more than four hours and I was considerably relieved when I saw them returning. It only gradually emerged what a heroic climb my wife had performed and she did it, of course, largely for my benefit as I sat, frustrated, by the side of the road. It was no game for a granny and she did wonders to reach the top and add her flag to those on the Prayer Post which marks the summit. Thank goodness the weather was clear and she was rewarded by that wonderful view; apparently it came up to expectations.

The Maldives

Stuck in the Sand

In August 1989, despite misgivings from the tour operator over the suitability of the Maldives for a full-time wheelchair user, Sue Kelley, her husband Tony and their daughter Joanne took advantage of an offer for a three-for-the-price-of-two holiday in the islands.

Tony has often enthused about the Maldives, a group of coral islands off the southern tip of India. He had visited the island of Gan with the navy, and he painted a picture of real tropical islands, complete with swaying palm trees, white sandy beaches and crystal-clear lagoons. As we had travelled to a number of exotic destinations using the same tour operator (*Kuoni*), and we had overcome most problems on these trips, it was eventually agreed that as long as Tony and Joanne helped lift me on and off the boats, we should be able to manage a holiday in the Maldives.

The islands, covering an area of some 140,000 square kilometres, vary in size and character from mere sandbanks to lush tropical islands; they lie outside the cyclone belt and enjoy a warm, tropical climate throughout the year. It is thought that the first settlers were either South Indian travellers or Sri Lankans. The position of the Maldives on the sea routes from the Middle East to Malacca and China attracted the attention of Arab traders, whose contact converted the Maldivians to Islam in the twelfth century.

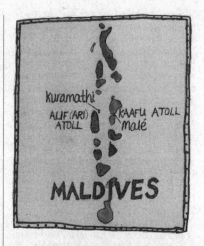

We were advised when packing to include umbrellas or waterproofs as it can rain heavily in the Maldives. Essential items included sunglasses, plastic shoes for swimming (to prevent nasty cuts from the coral) and an old T-shirt or pyjama jacket to wear whilst snorkelling. A basic first-aid kit, plus medicines for stomach upsets, sunburn and seasickness are advisable, as is a course of anti-malaria drugs.

We hired a car to take us to Gatwick, arriving at the South Terminal well before *Air Europe* opened their check-in desks. Finally we got our boarding passes and our luggage was taken. I was allowed to stay in my wheelchair until transferred to my seat on the plane, after which my chair was stowed in the hold. There wasn't much legroom, considering it was a long-haul flight.

We were delayed for an hour at Dubai because of an unaccounted-for passenger, but some four hours later we were descending over the Maldives. We could see large, green rings and horseshoe shapes, glinting like emeralds in the sun, and we could pick out those islands which were inhabited. We touched down on the runway at Malé airport with water either side, and I was assisted off, Tony and two others carrying me down the steps of the 757. In less than an hour we had cleared immigration, met the courier and were seated on the boat destined for our island, Kuramathi, a four-hour journey.

Getting onto the boat was easy: the stern was brought in tight to the jetty and we rolled the wheelchair straight on. To begin with I stayed in the wheelchair in the aisle between the seats, but as we left the protection of the coral reefs the sea became quite rough, so I transferred to a seat. Several of the passengers were seasick. Despite a sea breeze it was extremely hot.

Kuramathi looked quite large from the sea. It is the largest of a group of islands which form Ari atoll; the next two are Rasdhu (occupied by the fishing fleet and their families) and Treasure Island (uninhabited). Disembarking was as easy as boarding. A large number of men were waiting to carry our luggage, but at the end of the jetty there was a drop of about nine inches onto the sand – there were no paths, just sand! There was only one way of reaching the hotel: I had to be dragged, in my wheelchair, backwards across the beach.

We were met by the hotel manager and given the keys to our respective bungalows. The English contingent were accommodated in bungalows numbered in the eighties and nineties; because of the wheelchair we were allocated bungalow 26, amidst the Germans, situated near the sea, restaurant and coffee shop. Other facilities included a bar, disco and a small shop in the Kuramathi village.

From the outside the bungalow looked very much as expected – round,

with a thatched roof which overhung at the front to form a shady porch. Inside was very basic, with one double bed, one single, an electric fan, a small table, a flask of questionable drinking water, and an alcove with a rail for our clothes. The bathroom was only just wide enough for my wheelchair (which is small, only a 35.5cm seat width); it was tiled from ceiling to floor with white ceramic tiles, many of which were badly cracked.

"Our staple diet for two weeks was fish"

The courier had given us time to unpack and freshen up before meeting her in the bar. On entering the bathroom we found that there was no water, and our neighbours informed us that there was a fault and the supply should be back on later. I unpacked our clothes and Joanne hung them up; this proved to be a mistake, as the high humidity made everything feel very damp within hours – including our beds.

At the meeting we were told that it takes approximately thirty minutes to walk from end to end of the island, and that there are three resorts – ours, an Italian Village and the Blue Lagoon. Money was not required on a daily basis in any of the resorts: instead we signed for whatever we required and paid in full at the end of the week in US dollars. It is sensible to make a note of what you sign for, as many of us found that we were charged for facilities that we didn't use.

There was a diving school on the island; snorkelling and windsurfing lessons were also available, as well as fishing and island-hopping excursions. When visiting islands that are inhabited by the Maldivians, we had to observe rules on dress – no shorts or bare shoulders for women, no bare chests or short shorts for men. We were not allowed to take alcohol onto the islands (the islanders are Muslims) but it is for sale in the bars in the tourist resorts.

Kuramathi tourist resort is staffed by Maldivians, Indians and Sri Lankans. Their families are not permitted onto the island and the men were housed in dormitories. A mosque was provided amidst their living quarters and they were encouraged to participate in football, cricket and volleyball. Many didn't see their families for six months or more.

We were on half-board and our staple diet for two weeks was fish. Everything else is shipped in from India, Sri Lanka or Singapore; fruit and vegetables were few and far between, and meat was a rarity. The fish was well presented, in various forms: curried, fried, baked and barbecued. The Maldivians made their own bread and cakes, so those were fresh and plentiful. Joanne is a vegetarian and she was provided with cheese instead of fish when it was available.

Eventually the water came back on in our bungalow, and it turned out to be sea water. When it rained it was not unusual to see people standing outside washing their hair, in order to remove the salt deposits. Bottled water, like everything else on the island, was rather expensive.

The beach was covered with small pieces of coral. (It is forbidden to take home any coral, and your luggage will be searched to ensure that you don't.) Hermit crabs and small sand crabs were also in abundance; I found them very amusing to watch. The fish were another source of entertainment: I had only to place a piece of bread in the water and they came racing for it, even taking it from my fingers. They were all colours, from greys and browns to rainbow stripes, pink spots, blues and greens, yellow angel fish and small reef sharks.

Joanne and Tony can swim and snorkel well and they spent a lot of time in the water. I am not able to move in water, so Tony procured a large rubber ring, over the top of which I lay, wearing snorkel and mask. Tony pushed me out over the coral reef which encircles the island, where I could observe the beautiful underwater garden. The colours and shapes of the corals were breathtaking, as were the fish which ranged in size from those smaller than my little finger to some as large as my forearm. The most fascinating were the clown fish, diving in and out of the anemones. These daily trips were the highlight of my holiday.

As well as fish and crabs, the island played host to two herons and one of these birds became very crafty. When I fed the fish from the jetty, the heron walked down the steps and waited there patiently for the right fish to come and take the bread; then he dipped in his beak and made his catch without getting his feet wet! At about 4pm the fruit bats started to leave their roosts in the trees, and later they formed silhouettes against the moon – it was like the opening shots of a horror film.

"No paths or roads suitable for a wheelchair, and dragging one through sand puts a considerable strain on the puller and pusher"

Tony and Joanne took a couple of boat trips to the neighbouring island of Rasdhu, where they saw many coral and turtle-shell goods for sale despite the laws against export and import of these items. They purchased several T-shirts and brightly painted, wooden Indian masks. I didn't go with them because the terrain was similar to that on Kuramathi – no paths or roads suitable for a wheelchair, and dragging one through sand puts a considerable strain on the puller and pusher.

For anyone confined to a wheelchair, with limited or weak arm movement like myself, it is impossible to move anywhere on Kuramathi under one's own steam. When Tony and Joanne wandered off somewhere we made sure that I had everything I required and that I was placed where I would be in the shade for the duration of their absence; the sun was very hot and burnt very quickly. I also kept my raincover handy as the showers appeared suddenly and were often accompanied by an increase in windforce. The ground was soon inches deep in water after such showers, but it disappeared almost as quickly as the rain came.

"The helicopter arrived at 9.30am, kicking up an immense cloud of dust as it approached"

Joanne made plenty of friends of her own age, and they usually got together with a picnic lunch supplied from the restaurant, retreating to the far end of the island where they swam, listened to their "Walkmans" and played card games. They also did a lot of reading and exchanged books between themselves. Tony and I found many people to talk to, and we also got through several books. Resort workers and fellow tourists on the island were helpful and polite; we encountered no hostility regarding my disability.

Towards the end of our stay we were informed of the start of a new service: some British helicopter pilots had purchased a helicopter and were trying to persuade people to charter it for flights from islands like ours to Hulhule island, where the capital, Malé, is situated. We enquired about using it for the transfer to Malé airport, to avoid the four-hour boat trip. If we could muster twenty people at $94 each, we were told we could fly from Rasdhu (our island didn't have a clear area large enough on which to land the helicopter).

On the day of departure our suitcases were loaded onto the boat at 6.30am, along with those passengers not going by helicopter. We were taken to Rasdhu at 8.30am by boat; the sea was calm and the crew boarded and disembarked the wheelchair, with me

in it, without problem. We were escorted by the villagers, who appeared to have taken time off from their duties to observe the helicopter make its first landing on the island's football pitch.

The helicopter arrived at 9.30am, kicking up an immense cloud of dust as it approached the ground; luckily, we were safely assembled under the shade of a tree, away from this dust-bath. After a safety talk, Tony and the pilot carried me on board and then loaded the wheelchair once everyone was seated. The flight was probably the best way to see the islands and the atolls.

On alighting from the helicopter and paying our dues we were escorted to the terminal building to await the arrival of the boat with our baggage on board. After a cursory search by the customs officers we proceeded with boarding the plane. Getting on was a problem! The three of us were led away separately from the others by a young Maldivian, who then abandoned us at the bottom of the steps to the plane. I eventually had to climb them on my backside – a very tiring procedure. When I was almost at the top a flight engineer arrived and gave Tony a hand to lift me into my seat. The crew apologised and then complained to the airport staff for not providing assistance or informing them that I required help.

The four-hour flight to Dubai was interesting as it was so clear that we could make out the atolls and reefs, then the desert in Oman, with its dunes, rock formations and small settlements. Dubai was very hot and I stayed on board whilst everyone else went shopping.

I'm glad to have had the opportunity to see the Maldives (especially as they are destined to be the first land masses to disappear if the theories about the greenhouse effect are correct). It was a restful holiday, but marred slightly by the sand, which effectively made my wheelchair nothing more than an armchair. I don't suppose we will ever see the equal of the marine life we observed there, but I suspect it's not a holiday I'll repeat in the future. That said, there were many satisfied customers among our fellow travellers, particularly those who joined the diving school's expeditions.

INDIA & THE MALDIVES: TRAVEL NOTES

Sources of information

Government of India Tourist Office, 7 Cork Street, London W1X 2AB; ☎071/437 3677. Produce penty of leaflets, but nothing with any mention of disabled tourists.

Maldive Travel, 3 Esher House, 11 Edith Terrace, London SW10 0TH; ☎071/352 2246. Known amongst the islanders as "The Maldive Lady", Toni de Laroque of *Maldive Travel* is the British representative of the Maldives Ministry of Tourism. She has a refreshingly positive approach to disabled travellers.

Tour operators

Many operators are wary of taking a wheelchair user – or even someone with walking difficulties – to India, and reading the accounts here you can perhaps understand why; however, it is worth persevering. Once medical clearance had been obtained, and all the difficulties discussed honestly, *Bales Tours* (Bales House, Barrington Road, Dorking, Surrey RH4 3EJ; ☎0306/885991) offered Daphne Pagnamenta all possible assistance in India and she was pleased with their efforts.

Sue Kelley is a seasoned traveller and, accompanied by her husband and daughter, she has booked with *Kuoni* on a number of holidays – to Hong Kong, Macau and China and, most recently, to Kenya, as well as to the Maldives and India. The tour company therefore knows her well and will usually make the arrangements she asks for, although there was some hesitation over India and the Maldives. (Sue knows what she is capable of doing and is quick to explain her abilities to any operator who expresses doubts as to the suitability of the destination she chooses to visit; if necessary, she points out that she prefers not to be discriminated against on grounds of her disability.)

While recognising that the soft sand is a major poblem for wheelchair users, Toni de la Roque of *Maldive Travel* insists that disabled people should not be discouraged from visiting the islands, particularly if the holiday is intended to be restful: each island is tiny; there is not much scope for walking and the Maldives are essentially for lazy swims and lying in the sun, neither of which require great agility. She suggests aiming for resorts close to the capital, Malé. This avoids the need for long, uncomfortable journeys by boat to the more far-flung atolls. Kurumba and Laguna Beach are ideal; room number five at Laguna is virtually on the beach. She also points out that the warm water of the lagoons is perfect for swimming and the experience of feeding the fish whilst in the water, feeling them brushing against you, is not to be missed – something a blind person could also appreciate.

Thomson's *Worldwide* brochure includes several holidays in India, and their *Factfile* service (see "Booking", *Practicalities*) should be of use to disabled travellers wishing for more detailed information on the hotels and resorts shown in the brochure. *Thomas Cook*, who have basic hotel access information, and *Hayes and Jarvis*, who have a staff member with personal knowledge of all hotels, are also generally helpful.

Robin Reeley enjoyed a combination of organised and independent travel, using *Butterfield's Indian Railway Tours* (Burton Fleming, Driffield, East Yorkshire YO24 0PQ;

INDIA & THE MALDIVES: TRAVEL NOTES

☎02620/87230) and, for pony trekking (riding ponies, pack ponies, meals, tents and bedding provided as required), Fayaz Ahmad Milik (s/o Assdull Milik, r/o Aru, p/o Pahalgam, p/n no. 192126, Kashmir). Robin consulted *Trailfinders Travel Centre* (42–48 Earls Court Road, London W8 6EJ; ☎071/937 9631) for information and advice; they also booked his flights, both international and domestic.

Independent travel enables greater freedom and is often more rewarding (and cheaper) than either group tours or tailor-made packages. Searching out your own style of hotel and using local drivers and guides means that you make arrangements that suit you rather than the UK tour operator. But the aggravations – of making train or bus bookings, of negotiating with drivers and obtaining firm reservations with hotels – can be overwhelming for some; in which case arrangements might be best managed by *Travel Corporation India* (*TCI*) (N-49 Connaught Circus, New Delhi 110 001; ☎11/45181); the Delhi office is up two flights of steps but the Agra, Jaipur and Jodhpur offices are accessible. If possible, write in advance and tell them where you want to travel.

Getting there

Most direct **flights** are operated by *British Airways* or *Air India*, but numerous others call in on their way to the Far East or Australia – see the relevant *Travel Notes* for details. *British Airways* carry aisle wheelchairs and have at least one adapted toilet. *Air India* will not accept groups of disabled passengers, and their flights tend to be full to bursting point – every passenger has the equivalent in hand luggage of what most people send to the hold. In 1990 *Air India* sent Sue Kelley's wheelchair to Bombay while she went to Delhi. Sue was kept waiting nearly two hours before they acknowledged that the chair had gone missing. The next day the wheelchair was ready for collection at Delhi; Sue's husband wasted the best part of the day retrieving it.

Airport facilities at Delhi and Bombay are not too bad: the toilets should be given a wide berth, but wheelchairs are available, even if at Bombay you may be given a choice of a chair with flat tyres or one without footplates, and the airport attendants who push the chairs will ask for a tip before they have covered more than half a corridor; if they don't get it they'll abandon you. Malé in the Maldives is basic, but effective – you'll probably be carried off the plane.

Transport

In India, accessible **public transport** is virtually non-existent, and any method of travel is likely to be slow or uncomfortable or both. Where roads are more than tracks they are poorly maintained. Buses and cars are often pretty spartan; trains are difficult to get into, the seating less than luxurious and the toilets impossible. Domestic **flights** probably offer the best level of comfort and cut down journey times, but *Indian Airlines* are notoriously inefficient, with few facilities for boarding and disembarking, no toilets, often no wheelchair service, endless bureaucracy to cut through when booking a ticket – and you'll see nothing of the countryside.

Accommodation

In India the top-rate hotels are reasonably accessible – and reasonably priced by European standards – many of them have ramps and good-sized lifts. In the older buildings the style of the bathrooms lends itself to wheelchair-accessible showers – sloping floors, no lips or sills around the shower/tap, stool or chair readily supplied.

Robin Reeley recommends the *Hotel Ashok Yatri Niwas* (19 Ashok Road, New Delhi 110 001; ☎11/344511), Daphne Pagnamenta the *Oberoi Maidens* (7 Sham Nath Marg, Delhi 110 054; ☎11/2525464). Some of the rooms in the *Shivniwas Palace* (Udaipur 313 001; ☎294/28239) are accessible; the pool and courtyard provide a quiet haven but the food was poor. *Ajit Bhawan* (Near Circuit House, Jodhpur 342 006; ☎291/20409) has the songs-around-the-campfire atmosphere of an upmarket youth hostel, and its own cult following – guests return year after year for the desert trips. The food is delicious, the gardens restful; steps to the central courtyard (where meals are eaten) and in reception could be ramped.

INDIA & THE MALDIVES: TRAVEL NOTES

Access and facilities

In the cities, high kerbs, narrow, crowded pavements and dripping heat make getting around something of a trial; a companion is almost essential. The traffic can be heart-stopping, and litter – in the form of mounds of rotting rubbish – is a further obstacle. In rural areas the terrain can be formidable, with soft sand, rocky paths and dirt tracks to negotiate. Robin Reeley got around this in Kashmir by pony trekking, but for many the only way to see the countryside is from a vehicle: bus, train, taxi or even helicopter.

Access to sights even when you get there is too often only partial, which means that wheelchair users must sit and view the monument from outside, or be content with the exhibits on the museum's ground floor, and those with limited walking powers must see only half a Moghul palace.

Health and insurance

The main threats to good health in this part of the world come from contaminated food and water and, in some areas, disease-carrying mosquitoes. The effects of high temperatures and humidity should not be underestimated, and remember also that nights can be cold. But don't *over*estimate the dangers: with some simple precautions and common sense, plus advice from a good guidebook or from Richard Dawood's *Travellers' Health* (see "Books", *Practicalities*), you are unlikely to suffer more than a couple of days of "Delhi Belly".

If you don't have a strong stomach, it's worth taking a small travel kettle and some Cup-a-soups, or other foods that you know and love – when recovering from a bout of diarrhoea and faced with strange and spicy food, the comforting aroma of soup and a dry Cornish wafer will restore interest in the world around you.

Singapore

Looking for Excellence

Susan Preston has muscular dystrophy and uses a wheelchair outdoors; inside, she can walk a little, using a wall for support. In August 1987 Susan spent three weeks in Singapore, visiting a friend from her university days. The trip included a few days on Phuket Island, Thailand.

The ideal place to be in steamy Singapore is sitting in a wheelchair! The jungle of the island has gone and the tigers no longer roam wild, but the tropical climate remains, tempered by sea breezes that fan the warm air. I had just to sit back and think of all things oriental; my companions (my mother and Mary, a family friend) had to push, pull and tip my chair in the perspiring heat.

The reason for my trip was a friendship which began several years ago. Ah Mei studied with me at a British university, and after graduating had to return home to Singapore. Ah Mei is a conscientious organiser: her second-storey flat was inaccessible, so she trekked round the city-centre hotels to find one of reasonable cost with suitable facilities for me.

We were slightly surprised when she wrote to say that she had booked us into the YMCA! But she assured us that it was a hotel, not a male youth hostel. It proved to be excellent value for money, centrally situated at the beginning of Orchard Road, the mile-long shopping belt of the city.

On reflection, it was perhaps unwise for me to stay in an eighth-floor room – in the event of fire – but we had a splendid view of a small, green park below, the terraced, pastel-coloured Chinese houses, and the towering buildings of the modern city beyond. And from that height the flow of cars on the multi-laned, one-way system moved silently.

For my three weeks in Singapore, I was lazy: I barely had to walk at all. I had a bit of clambering to do, though, mainly in and out of taxis, but those taxis were a boon – there were droves of them! One guidebook estimated 10,000 in a city with a population of 2,500,000. Because they were so plentiful, cheap and anxious for custom, sightseeing was not a burden. All the taxis were large four-door saloons, and my chair fitted easily into the boot. Normally there was a dollar charge for each item of luggage, but window stickers in each taxi indicated that wheelchairs were carried free of charge. The reactions from the drivers were generally delightful, especially when they learned where we came from: "Scotlend! Cel-teek!"; "Scot-lend! Whis-kee!"; "Scot-lend! So far! I think you very brave!"

Singapore was in the midst of its National Day celebrations while we were there, commemorating its emergence as an independent republic in 1965. The pop song "We are Singapore" resounded from every loudspeaker; a giant rainbow, with the motto "Together . . . Excellence for Singapore", was constructed in the heart of Orchard Road; the TV propagandised the virtues of the nation and the unity of its people. From our lofty bedroom window we watched the annual parade of brightly lit floats, military contingents and dragon dancers, while jets soared overhead against the night sky. A percentage of the GDP is spent on this spectacle: during the recession of the early 1980s the floats had been few; this year, people told us, the celebration had regained its former glory.

"For our first few days there, part of me wanted to believe in the dream"

I had expected excellence from Singapore – an efficient, clean, tightly run, competitive society, a prosperous place. My first experiences confirmed this: Changi airport was beautiful, all brown, cream and chrome, with moving corridors and a fountain falling through three floors. A porter pushed me, and guided us through all the procedures (another advantage of being in a wheelchair – you jump queues!). Our "caretaker" was of Malaysian extraction, wore a brown uniform to match the decor, and was kind but took his responsibility very seriously: "Sit right back in the chair, please." Yes, sir.

The cleanness of the City of Singapore was immediately evident on the broad pavements of Orchard Road. Fines for dropping litter are enforced. As it is the shopping and hotel belt, you need money to be there, so the first people I saw were predominantly young, healthy and stylish. The TV, the radio, the posters, all told us that

Singapore strives for perfection and looks after its people. Given our first impressions of the island, we could not argue with the media.

I was physically shaken, then, as I waited to cross Orchard Road, to see a thin, unshaven man in his early fifties open the bin on the lamppost next to me, lift out a juice carton and suck up the dregs. I noticed that one of the letters strung out across the Orchard Road rainbow had fallen off. I saw bent, shrunken, old Chinese ladies sweeping the shop floors. And I heard a disturbed man shouting at no one in particular across the café tables.

Of course, all of these things I can see, probably to a greater extent, on British streets. But our TV and newspapers reflect this sadder side of life. In the midst of National Day celebrations the state-controlled Singaporean media projected a Utopian society and, for our first few days there, part of me wanted to believe in the dream. The broken rainbow over Orchard Road seemed symbolic of the reality.

What concern is there for the less able in Singapore? What of the "less perfect" members of society? Since my trip in 1987, I have been encouraged to learn from Ah Mei that the government has established a committee to improve provision and access for the disabled. Whilst there, I noticed that the newest shopping complex had special toilet facilities; one or two public buildings we visited had ramped entrances. The multistorey shopping centres which line both sides of Orchard Road are wheelchair friendly because of the large public lifts between floors. I met a group of young disabled people in one store: they spotted me first and came whizzing over in fashionable sports chairs to say hello. Their English was not good, but I gathered that they lived in a purpose-built complex.

Basic wheelchairs can be bought in the pharmacy departments; I saw one Singaporean gentleman being pushed in one by his wife. Deaf teenagers eagerly communicating in sign language were quite a common sight on Orchard Road. Pavement kerbs are by necessity very high because of the floods in the monsoon season; they are too great an obstacle for the lone wheelchair user.

"I learnt to avoid the gristly fish balls, and wasn't tempted by the pig's brain soup"

The government's liking for orderliness has its disappointing aspects. A picture of Singapore, circulated worldwide in the brochures, depicts the Chinese junks crowding Singapore River, enclosed by the old and new buildings of the city. I arrived at the spot with my camera, only to find the water bare. And the clutter of market stalls in the old town has also been tidied up: they are now unimaginatively contained within specially constructed concrete arcades.

But traditional ways of life are irrepressible. Singapore has its "Little India", its Chinatown, its Arab Quarter – the natural groupings of its people. Smells and cultures mingle: the stench of open drains in the Chinese street with a colonial name, Clyde Street; a tri-cart piled high with pineapple; the old Chinaman with his bare, concave chest, waiting to cross the road with me. A magnificent sultan mosque dominates Arab Street, where the cracked facades of the shuttered dwellings revealed warmth and homeliness inside. Fear of intrusion made me resist the temptation to photograph an old Arab in his blue jacket and white skirt, standing and eating from his bowl outside his pink and white house, a light burning within.

Ah Mei was keen that we sample authenticity, and with her we ate at the hawker centres. Originally, all kinds of food-sellers trundled their carts through the streets of Singapore. Today they are still called "hawkers" but are established at permanent centres throughout the island. The one on Ah Mei's housing estate was typical – a large, covered, outdoor café area with competing small food kitchens forming the perimeter and serving freshly cooked, inexpensive Chinese food. This is where the "ordinary people" congregate. I don't recommend bean cake, a violently coloured sweetmeat, green or pink on the outside, white, pasty and sickly on the inside. I learnt to avoid the gristly fish balls, too, and wasn't tempted by the pig's brain soup. But the other new tastes were sensational.

"I read and I forget. I see and I remember. I do and I understand." That is the philosophy of Singapore's Science Center, built in 1977. It was the forerunner of a new breed of science and technology museums, concentrating on the "hands-on" learning experience for visitors of all ages. There are over 400 exhibits to push, pull, crank and pedal. All aim to explain the world around us and what it is to be human. It is one of the liveliest museums I have ever visited; we spent hours there and had great fun.

Aerial photographs of the island show the skyscrapers but hide the leafiness of the city. As well as the generous sprinkling of rich green trees and flowering shrubs around the streets, there are several large, cultivated parks, usually outside the city centre. The oldest are the superb Botanic Gardens, founded in 1859. The gardens are famous for their collection of palm trees and for the Orchid Enclosure, but something new and more exciting for me was a walk through the designated Jungle Area – several acres left to grow wild. This was Singapore in its natural state, with strange, unknown bird and insect sounds emanating from the towering trees. The air was dank and heavy. It was a wonderful experience.

The Zoological Gardens are world class, with the emphasis on establishing natural habitats for the creatures, and Jurong Bird Park is said to be the finest in Asia. Tiger Balm Gardens have their own, horrible fascination, with larger-than-life, colourful, fibre glass models of mythical Chinese creatures in a hilly, open-air setting – a kind of Chinese Disneyland without the fun-rides!

"In this unlikely setting was a toilet for the disabled, albeit used as a broom cupboard"

Visitors to Singapore are not confined to the island. There are day-long bus tours across the border to Malaysia, and boat trips to the several small islands off Singapore's shore. The further away the island, the less developed and "touristy" it is. These islets with their sandy beaches are very popular with Singaporean families at weekends. Sentosa is the nearest (only five minutes by ferry or cable car) and the most commercialised, with monorail, musical fountain and roller-skating rink among the attractions. In contrast, on Kusu island, 45 minutes by ferry, there are only two small temples (one Chinese, one Muslim), palm trees and a tortoise sanctuary. Some of the islands are totally uninhabited. Lifting the wheelchair on and off the ferry posed no problems for the crew.

We also went further afield, to Phuket, an island off the western coast of Thailand. Our taxi driver to Changi airport was friendly, with firm views: as all roads lead to the airport, all faiths lead to God; he is a Singaporean – he does not need to sing the new song, he does not need the message of unity; he is loyal, this is his fatherland. We flew *Thai Airways*, who coped smoothly with me and my chair. The air hostesses were dressed in long, richly coloured silk national dress, and each female passenger was given an orchid. The flight was scheduled to take ninety minutes, but a monsoon was raging over Phuket. We circled the bumpy skies for forty minutes. I began to hope that we might be diverted to Bangkok, and we were.

In all, I boarded and disembarked from seven planes during the holiday, by a variety of means. Of course, in Bangkok, they had no advance warning of my arrival, but when we landed I was assigned a porter as before. This time, however, the poor fellow had to carry me down the steep flight of steps from the plane. He was trembling, I said a prayer, but Ah Mei's first words when we reached terra firma were, "Oh, I wish I had had my camera!"

We were guided through the empty, glittering new airport building to the original passenger lounge – rather old-fashioned, with its dark wood. In this unlikely setting was a toilet for the disabled, albeit used as a broom cupboard. For the first time on our trip to the East, we experienced the isolation of not being able to communicate with those around us; a feeling heightened by uncertainty over where we would be taken next. Our porter unexpectedly produced sandwiches and Coke for us, then without a word we were "portered" via a transit bus to the luxurious *Airport Hotel*, where we had a meal and spent the night courtesy of the airline. In the murky light of the next morning's dawn, on the way to the airport, we glimpsed the shanty dwellings on the fringes of Bangkok.

A nylon transit seat, or carrying chair, was a wise investment prior to our holiday. It has no rigid structure and rolls up when not in use. We did not have it "at the ready" when we were unexpectedly diverted to Bangkok, but we were better prepared when we landed at Phuket's small airstrip. And it was nice to see my own wheelchair waiting for me at the foot of the steps!

The monsoon had abated sufficiently for the plane to land, but I have never seen such heavy rain. The driven air was very warm. Our dinner that evening was eaten by the light of a small candle: a fallen coconut tree had brought down the power-line and the hotel's emergency generator had simultaneously exploded! We went to bed in clammy darkness, but awoke to a transformed scene. The waves were still quite high but the Indian Ocean glimmered a deep turquoise, crested with surf, and the white sand dazzled.

Singaporeans have a Western air of sophistication, an aloofness; the Thai were more open. None were kinder than the driver of the hotel minibus and the young lad who came along to help lift me, on our day trip round the island. By chance we had the bus to ourselves. I strapped myself into my transit seat and we soon established a quick procedure for transferring from bus to wheelchair, and vice versa.

"We went to bed in clammy darkness, but awoke to a transformed scene"

From my vantage point I saw the islanders living their lives: an old man in a sarong hoed his garden; two young boys boxed with red gloves; a young woman threw a pail of water over herself in the heat of the day; a middle-aged woman beat the dust out of her bed, and a young man sat on his doorstep, just watching. The landscape was detailed with wild, large-leafed banana trees and papaya, rubber plantations, ochre fields and green hills, bison-like cows, black and tan goats, white or pink Buddhist temples, and the occasional arched gateway leading nowhere. Corrugated iron, stone and palm-leaf dwellings were straddled along the wayside, with a few houses on stilts. Motorbikes were the means of transport for everyone: we saw an old lady on hers; schoolgirls in blue uniform rode three astride; one

man carried his dog perfectly balanced behind him on the passenger seat!

Before leaving Phuket, one balmy evening, we stumbled into a private party on the raised poolside area at our hotel, an event in honour of the Thai national football team who had reached the finals of the ASEAN games. Myriad coloured lights reflected in the pool and lit the young Thai dancers – girls of nine or ten in silk and gold traditional costume.

People applauded as the girls finished their routine and two of the troupe tripped daintily round the side of the pool to where the guests were seated. We watched admiringly too, then it dawned on us that they were coming in our direction. They bowed sweetly, took off their beautiful garlands of mauve orchids and slipped them over our heads! A brilliant spotlight dazzled us; glancing towards it, we noticed a TV camera recording the incident! The applause continued. We blushed with embarrassment but were utterly thrilled.

I haven't mentioned the sixteen-hour flights to and from Singapore, perhaps because next to the thrills and new experiences they fade into insignificance. If I have one plea to make, it is that the specially adapted toilets on board *British Airways* aircraft be made wide enough to accommodate the aisle wheelchair. A pamphlet of hints for the disabled traveller (there are several available – see the Department of Transport's guide, *Door to Door*), which I read prior to the holiday, advised drinking only the minimum necessary to avoid dehydration – too true! But I'd do it again, and gradually I hope to become a seasoned traveller, able to fall asleep at will and let time fly by.

Thailand

A Prayer to the Emerald Buddha

After spending eight weeks in Australia (see p.351) Barbara Horrocks and her husband Bill flew on to Thailand. Barbara has a congenital disease of the spine, of which she was not aware until well into her forties, when walking became very difficult and the pain unbearable. After two operations she is able to get about the house but has to use a wheelchair outside.

Bangkok is reputed to be the hottest city in the world. It must also rank as one of the most crowded and traffic congested. Despite these drawbacks it is a magical place, fascinating in its complexity, the mean hovels and magnificent temples jostling for position with hotels and shopping plazas.

We were caught up in a strike at Sydney airport, and consequently arrived in "The Land of Smiles" at 2.30am, expecting consolation by way of a rapid and traffic-free ride through a deserted city. How naive we were! The taxi ground to a halt in an enormous traffic jam, the pavements were thronged with people, and the mobile food vendors were doing a roaring trade.

A frantic traffic cop sorted out the jam and before long our taxi turned under an arch into a deserted back street. Although I am well past the first flush of youth and never go anywhere without my wheelchair, I was convinced that I was about to be kidnapped for the white slave trade! On better acquaintance I realised that many of Bangkok's best hotels are reached via this network of narrow streets, but for the moment I was relieved to see ours, every bit as swish as the brochures had pictured it. Our room was waiting, air-conditioned and welcoming with a basket of tropical fruit, and orchids on the pillows.

The following morning we break-fasted on what was surely the most sumptuous spread of our travels so far. Not the least of its attractions were the made-to-order-before-your-very-eyes, American-style pancakes with lashings of maple syrup. The memory still makes me drool and I have yet to lose their legacy from my waistline.

Our hotel, like so many in Bangkok, stood on the banks of the River Chao Phya (the River of Kings) and we were content to spend the next few hours on the terrace, watching the world sail by. The river is the lifeblood of Bangkok: many of her people live on it, and it teems with boats – ferries, shuttle boats (provided free by many of the hotels for their guests), fishing boats, private hire boats, floating food vendors and enormous barges consisting of one leading boat with maybe eight or ten others in tow, all loaded to the gunwales. To add to the congestion, great swathes of water hyacinth float downstream and threaten to clog the navigation channels.

A network of canals spread out from the river in both directions; these too are crowded, lined with humble dwellings – I hesitate to call them houses, although I was assured that they have all mains services, including electricity. Judging by the profusion of TV aerials sprouting from the roofs, it must be true. The Thai people use the waterways for bathing and doing the laundry, laughing and waving at passers-by.

Later in the day we used the shuttle boat – helped on and off with a smile – to visit River City, one of the many shopping plazas in Bangkok. They are cool and air-conditioned, with smooth marble floors that wheelchair users (and pushers) love, and they sell almost anything. But made-to-measure clothes, ready in 24 hours, are their speciality. The windows overflow with handmade Thai silk, in exotic patterns and colours to tempt the most reluctant purchaser. Bill was easily tempted, succumbing to the luxury of made-to-measure shirts in no time at all, but it was several days before I took the plunge.

That night we dined out of doors, sampling the delicious Thai food, a sort of cross between Indian and Chinese, with lots of noodles and very spicy, laced with red-hot chillies which the Thais eat with impunity. The wine was expensive, so we stuck to the local beer, a pleasant-tasting lager which was ideal in the hot, steamy climate.

The next day, recovered from our tiring journey, we joined an organised tour of the Grand Palace and the Emerald Buddha. The former is really a collection of palaces and temples, each one more fabulous than the last – a world of mythical beasts, covered with layers of gold leaf which glitter in the sun, to guard against evil spirits. The Chapel Royal contains the Emerald Buddha, the most sacred of all images. Unfortunately, a short flight of steps leads into the chapel, and wheelchairs are not allowed inside (I think they equate the tyres with shoes, which have to be removed). But if, like me, you are able to manage a few steps, it is impossible not to be overawed, or to say a prayer, whatever your religion.

"Coconuts served with the top sliced off and a spoon for scooping out the soft, sweet flesh"

After the tour we took the shuttle boat to River City again, so that Bill could have a fitting. We ate a delicious lunch in the plaza's restaurant for about £1.50 each, and watched an exhibition of Thai dancing in the flower-decked foyer before returning to the hotel to laze away the rest of the day.

Bangkok is not an easy city for the disabled. Like all cities on the monsoon trail, the kerbs are very high and we found no ramps. The pavements are crowded and often in a state of disrepair. The traffic makes London seem like a haven of peace and quiet.

Nevertheless, we were determined to see as much as possible, so the next morning we rose before it was light and joined a tour to the legendary Bridge on the River Kwai. Although the tour included a ride on The Death Railway and a visit to the beautifully maintained military cemetery, the day was not all gloom and doom. It was good to see rural Thailand. We lunched on board a floating restaurant on the River Kwai and stopped at a fruit market for an afternoon break. Here we bought juicy pomelos (huge grapefruit) which have a rich, refreshing taste, and the local coconuts which are served with the top sliced off and a spoon for scooping out the soft, sweet flesh.

Bill is a Normandy veteran, and one of our fellow passengers was an American lawyer who had been injured in Vietnam. They got on like a house on fire, assisted by great quantities of the local beer, and I will always remember the lawyer's soft, southern drawl, his politeness and his quiet way of offering assistance without making me feel in any way inadequate: "Let me help you, ma'am."

"The hot wind caught the spray from the fountains and showered us with cool water"

Needless to say, we had to keep asking the driver to stop, so that the men could rid themselves of one lot of beer, and buy more to counteract the heat. At every stop, curious, smiling children gathered round, just able to speak enough English to ask where we hailed from. When we told them (Liverpool) their smiles grew bigger and one of them invariably produced a football. Bill, who hasn't played football for longer than he'd care to remember, was prevailed upon to do a bit of coaching, on dusty petrol-station forecourts and strips of verges.

The next day we stayed closer to home, taking a ride in a *tuk-tuk*, a sort of motorised rickshaw, powered by a two-stroke engine and driven erratically and at great speed in and out of minute gaps in the Bangkok traffic. *Tuk-tuks* have a roof but no sides, so they are very cool, although it's impossible to avoid breathing in lungfuls of exhaust fumes. This kind of taxi is very cheap, whilst conventional taxis are not; you can cover quite long distances in a *tuk-tuk* for about £1 – less if you are clever

at bargaining! We found them convenient, with room to store the wheelchair, and great fun.

Very few *tuk-tuk* drivers speak English, but we were lucky and found one with slightly more than a spattering. We agreed a price for a couple of hours' sightseeing, and our first stop was the Gold Buddha – five and a half tons of solid gold, and quite a sight. Our driver took us in and out of narrow streets and back alleys, finding ways to avoid the more congested routes, stopping at temples, gem factories and silk emporiums, with a visit to Chinatown thrown in. We parted company at the gates to Lumpini Park, an oasis of greenery and peace laid out around a large lake, where we hired a boat, complete with shady canopy.

Despite the language difficulties, we were able to persuade the attendant at the ticket kiosk to look after my wheelchair, and while on the lake we had an interesting conversation in sign language with some Chinese tourists, swapping cameras to take photographs of each other and laughing in unison as the hot wind caught the spray from the fountains and showered us with cool water.

We felt able to face another early start the next day, and left the hotel in a private hire boat at 7am for a tour of the canals. It included a visit to a snake show, which I thought was repulsive, in a fascinating sort of way, but which Bill actually enjoyed, and one to the floating market. Here, women in straw peasant hats paddle their tiny sampans, filled with fruit, flowers and vegetables. The sight is a photographer's paradise, and if you can only manage one waterborne trip, this is the one to choose. Ensure that you are taken to the market at Damern Saduak; it is a long trip but worth it. The nearer floating market of Wat Sai is not much used any more, but the unscrupulous tour operator will try to palm you off with it. If your disability precludes boats it is possible to go by coach.

Our stay in Bangkok was flying past, and there was still so much to see: should it be another temple, a Thai boxing match, a trip to Khao Yai National Park? We settled for a coach trip to the Rose Gardens, a large park about 30km west of Bangkok, beautifully landscaped with roses and tropical plants. There are demonstrations of Thai crafts, plus a show including Thai boxing, a Thai wedding, the ordination of a monk, and traditional dancing.

We also saw a demonstration of elephants working logs. One of them became very curious about me, waving his trunk at my lap. Everyone except me was highly amused. Then Bill cottoned on, asking, "What have you got in your bag?" I realised that it wasn't me the elephant fancied, but the bananas intended for our lunch! Nervously I held them out. The elephant took them from me, as gentle as a kitten, and devoured them with relish.

The crowds were milling around, waiting for the show to begin. I was just wondering if we'd have to give it a miss, when I was tapped on the shoulder by a smiling Thai. He gestured for us to follow him, and we were guided round the back, through the stage door, and given good seats on the front row. My only complaint about the Rose Garden is that we'd booked a half-day tour, and realised too late that we needed a whole day to do it justice.

Bangkok *can* be explored by the disabled person; it takes a bit of spirit but is well worth the effort. Before we went, our travel agent said that everyone always wishes they'd had longer there. When we heard that we changed our plans and booked for eight days instead of four; even so, I wish we'd had longer. The Thai people may be diminutive (at five foot four I felt like a giant) but their smiles are enormous and ever present. They always helped with my chair, beaming from ear to ear when it was folded up, and positively splitting their sides when my folding walking stick disappeared into the depths of my handbag.

I'd like to see much more of Thailand, visit the beach resorts and the mountains, perhaps taking a trip into neighbouring Burma, political unrest permitting. Leaving aside (as we did) the red light district, the transvestite theatre, the bars and discos, there's a great deal of Bangkok still waiting to be explored. I hope the Emerald Buddha heard my prayer and that one day I'll get my chance to visit him again.

Bali

A Taste of Bali

Veronica Smith is 37 years old and confined to a wheelchair as a result of degeneration of the spine with neurological impairment. In March 1989 she travelled as a member of the Great Britain team to the World Rowing Championships for the Disabled in Perth. The championships had to be abandoned as they were hit by the tail-end of "Cyclone Dan", but Veronica went on to enjoy two weeks' holiday, spending a short time in Bali.

The Indonesian island of Bali is a place that I should dearly like to return to for a longer stay, not only for the climate and beaches, which are excellent, but for the atmosphere, the character of the countryside, the fascinatingly different culture and the natural charm and friendliness of the Balinese people. We stayed in the very comfortable, traditional chalet-style *Ramayana Hotel*, surrounded by tropical gardens, in Kuta which is one of the main tourist areas. It is on the coast, only 4km from the airport and 10km from the capital city of Denpasar.

The accommodation at the *Ramayana* is easily accessible, provided that one can cope with the occasional step in the gardens and on the paths leading to the chalets. The main entrance to the cottages is up three or four steps, so the wheelchair user needs someone to help with registering in the reception area. The easiest way to reach the chalets and gardens is

via the side entrance, which is on the level although rather rough. The chalets themselves are on one level and just big enough to manoeuvre a wheelchair inside. Each chalet has its own toilet and bathroom with level access. The spacious bar and restaurant are adjacent to the swimming pool and accessible via one small step.

Some visitors feel that Kuta is too "touristy" and too full of Australians who treat it as their Benidorm! This did not bother me and, even if it had, a short walk would have been enough to leave the majority of tourists behind. Kuta was vibrant from early in the morning, when the ground was strewn with individual, teaplate-sized offerings to the gods, made from palm leaves, petals and incense sticks, until late at night, when the street market and food stalls were still doing a brisk, noisy trade. I found it an intriguing place, best explored early or late in the day when it was cooler and rather less crowded.

The large street market in Kuta is well worth a visit, even if you are staying elsewhere. It runs the length of the main street and onto a wider, traffic-free area which leads to the beach. The market is obviously aimed at tourists but it is easy to find cheap, good-quality gifts and souvenirs. The best bargains are hand-tooled leather goods, beautiful batiks, and hand-carved and painted wooden items such as traditional masks. It is often possible to watch the craftsmen at work.

As well as these traditional-style gifts there are more evidently "touristy" ones; they do a particularly good line in astonishingly cheap T-shirts, shorts, and trousers known as Jakpacs which are cool and comfortable. The ones I bought cost about £3 per pair and are still going strong after 18 months of regular use. All stallholders expect their customers to bargain with them and they clearly enjoy the process; once I overcame my initial diffidence, so did I.

"Locally distilled arak resembles a lethal brew of turps and meths"

The most unhappy and thought-provoking aspect of the market is its beggar population. Bali is a poor country and many of its people live below the poverty line. The majority of the beggars are women with young children and babies: some may be out to exploit the tourists but many are in genuine need. I found it difficult to know how to cope with this: if I gave money to one I was at once swamped by others and pestered continually; on the other hand it seemed heartless to give nothing.

The market had the most atmosphere from about 7pm onwards and it was fun to wander around and mingle with the crowd. For serious shopping, rather than just looking, the evening was too crowded for a wheelchair user to shop easily. I found the best time was early morning, before breakfast, when there were only a few tourists about and

bargaining could be carried out in a pleasantly unhurried manner, amid the scent wafting from the incense sticks on the morning offerings to the gods.

"The simplicity of the setting has left a vivid memory"

Eating out in Kuta was a delight: the local Indonesian food was very good and reasonably priced; I especially enjoyed a Balinese dish of baked lobster. For the less adventurous there is plenty of familiar food, including the ubiquitous "fish and chippies"! The tap water in Bali is best avoided; bottled water is cheap and plentiful. The freshly squeezed fruit juices, particularly lemon, are delicious and refreshing, a glass of mixed fruit juice being a meal in itself and thick enough to support a straw upright. The same cannot be said of the locally distilled arak, which is made from the juice of the coconut palm or rice and molasses; it resembles a lethal brew of turps and meths.

All the restaurants and bars that I saw in Kuta were on one level with room inside for a wheelchair. As a precaution against flooding in the wet season, most buildings have one or sometimes two sizeable steps at the entrance. These would be a problem for an electric chair but are perfectly manageable in a manual chair if one has a friend to help when necessary; if not, the Balinese seemed quite happy to help.

On our first evening we hired a mini-bus and driver and were driven inland to Bone (pronounced Bona), a village near Gianyar where we watched an enthralling display of traditional dancing. The majority of Balinese people are followers of the Hindu Dharma religion, in which dancing plays an important part.

The first dance was a *kecak*, a unique Balinese dance which is accompanied not by a gamelan (orchestra) but by a choir of a hundred men. The *kecak* has its origins in an old ritual *sanghyang*, or trance dance, in which the dancer, in a state of trance, communicates with the deities or ancestors. Using the dancers as a medium, the deities or ancestors make their wishes known to the people. In the 1930s the old Indian epic, *Ramayana*, was incorporated into the dance. The atmosphere created by the sometimes restful, sometimes exciting rhythms chanted by the choir was powerful and compelling, unlike anything I have previously experienced. The sound complemented the dancing perfectly, alternately dreamy and dynamic.

The next two dances were also forms of *sanchyang* which developed from the religious function of maintaining a healthy and prosperous village by the driving away of evil spirits. The final performance was a fire dance, involving a man in a trance dancing repeatedly through and on burning coconut husks. The dignity and grace of the dancers, combined with the magnificence of the costumes and the simplicity of the setting – an earth-floored, barn-like building of bamboo and palm – has left a vivid memory.

Bali is not the easiest of places for wheelchair users to travel around. Many of the roads are rutted dirt-tracks; even the metalled ones tend to be full of potholes and badly driven motor scooters, bikes and minibuses (cars are rare). Many locals (and tourists) rely on "*bemos*", which are battered, canvas-topped jeeps, providing a very cheap, frequent public transport service. They are generally packed tight with locals, tourists and, sometimes, livestock! It is not unusual to see the Balinese hanging off the sides and back of the *bemo* if the inside is full. Great fun for the able-bodied but definitely inaccessible to wheelchairs!

Despite these difficulties, transport was not the problem I anticipated as minibus hire is cheap and efficient. It is possible to hire an air-conditioned minibus and driver for a whole day for a very moderate sum (about £10–15).

Keith and I decided to do this for our second day; the other two members of our group were more interested in soaking up the sun, so we left them by the hotel swimming pool.

We asked the driver to avoid the main tourist attractions and drive through the less well known areas. It was an excellent day: we travelled along narrow roads lined with bright, vigorous poinsettias five or six feet tall, passing villagers – even tiny children – carrying huge loads on their heads. We went through terraced rice fields, palm groves and villages, past ornately carved temples, and away into the mountains with their live volcanoes and vast, still lakes.

As we drove through the villages we frequently heard the distinctive music of the local gamelan. Many dances, festivals and ceremonies are accompanied by this orchestra, which consists of a two-string violin, a flute, gongs, drums and various combinations of unusual metal keyboard instruments suspended over bamboo resonating tubes, rather in the fashion of organ pipes. The music produced is strikingly beautiful, but difficult at first for ears accustomed to European music.

The Balinese are an artistic and creative people, fond of poetry, music, dancing and festivals; they are highly gifted in arts and crafts, especially woodcarving and silverwork. We drove slowly past numerous open-fronted workshops made of bamboo and palm, where men carved stone or wood and painted the finished sculptures. We saw women and girls constructing elaborate, tall temple offerings which were carried on the head to be placed in the temple courtyard.

So far, the Balinese have managed to retain a dignified individuality and maintain their unique culture. It would be a great loss if increased tourism, which is essential to the Balinese economy, were to erode these attributes. I hope that when I return I will find them intact.

The Philippines

No Concessions, no Prejudice

Alfred Azzopardi lives in northern Queensland, Australia, and has been quadriplegic since a road accident in 1965. On his first trip to the Philippines, in 1980, he wound up marrying his pen friend, Gina; they returned to the islands in 1984 with their first child.

The hustle and bustle of the vibrant marketplace, somewhere in Manila, capital city of the Philippines, is almost overwhelming. Countless stalls display almost every conceivable commodity, from antiques and woodcarvings to poultry and fish (dead or alive). A Filipino man sells pieces of pork, impaled and freshly roasted on bamboo sticks; another tows a cart selling ice creams. Vendors occasionally cool themselves with straw fans, and chase flies away with feather dusters. Shoppers stream everywhere and sounds of bargaining fill the air.

Children play, watch wide-eyed and sometimes tag along, fascinated and delighted by the sight of a foreigner in a chrome wheelchair. The heat is intense, the humidity stifling, and the sweet scent of oriental incense mingles with pungent wafts from market refuse. I move steadily onwards in my wheelchair, with my wife and the small group of my Filipino in-laws. I might be an unusual sight but I can tell that I am welcome here. An in-law usher leads the way, waving his hand for people to move aside, making me feel like some kind of dignitary.

We soon find what I am looking for – abundant tropical and exotic fruits, of astonishing variety (my hobby back home is rare-fruit growing). There are bright yellow, ripe mangoes, spiky, pungent durians, smooth, shiny, purple or green star-apples, enormous, knobbly jackfruit and hairy rambutans. I tell Gina and my in-laws which ones I want, and leave them to do the buying, not because I am in a wheelchair but because they are better at bargaining than a foreign *turista*.

When I arrived in Manila, the first thing which struck me was the cascade of colour and noise. The endless traffic, making its way through congested intersections, without traffic lights, has to be seen to be believed. The horns, sirens and shrills are incessant. Security guards, in starched uniforms with shining badges, seem to stand at every corner. Street workers in red shirts wear handkerchiefs tied over their faces to protect them from the traffic fumes.

The colourful "jeepneys" are a tourist attraction in themselves. Vivid graffiti, in keeping with the latest fads and fashions, decorate these vehicles, and their blaring stereo systems belt out the latest hit songs. Jeepneys are descendants of leftover US war jeeps, converted by imaginative Filipinos into flamboyant buses, carrying a dozen or so passengers. My standard-size wheelchair just fits between the two bench seats, and I have to bend my neck to avoid the ceiling, but the experience of riding in a jeepney, wheelchair and all, is worth any discomfort.

The best way for the traveller in a wheelchair to get around Philippine cities is by taxi, but taxi drivers are apt to forget to switch meters on for foreign visitors, disabled or not! The foreigner is very popular, as are his dollars. In a country of low wages, high unemployment, and no unemployment benefits or welfare system, money really does talk. Tourists will naturally be charged more than locals, but travellers from the richer countries can, nevertheless, holiday in the Philippines at much lower cost than in most other parts of the world.

As darkness falls, closed doors on ordinary downtown streets explode into an orgy of colour, music and entertainment – and, of course, there are girls. In a beer-house, bar girls dance to music on a mirrored stage which confuses the tired eye. Foreigners and Filipinos alike drink San Miguel beer and inexpensive drinks at wooden tables, and the cigarette smoke is too much for the air conditioners to handle.

We retire to a quiet restaurant with fine service, very cheap by Australian standards. The menu is mind-boggling. Philippine cuisine is an exotic, spicy blend of native, Southeast Asian, Chinese and Spanish influences. Dishes are elaborate, spiced with tangy flavours and tempered with rice. Traditional *lechon*, pig roasted on a spit over hot charcoal, is popular. *Halu-halo* is a favourite dessert – a rich concoction of several Philippine fruits, sweetened beans and other sweets, piled in a glass, topped by crushed ice and laced with milk.

"Strawberries thrive in the mountain climate, and a dollar will buy a basketful"

Manila is very twentieth-century, with modern skyscrapers, fine tourist accommodation, hurried pace, fashionably dressed youth and, unfortunately, slum districts and pollution. Lunetta Park, on Manila Bay, offers some escape. A path runs beside a neat line of young coconut trees, stretching for several kilometres along the bay, and often paced by joggers, particularly Americans. People picnic on the thin lawns under the trees, overflowing in places into the burning sunshine.

In the ruins of Fort Santiago, hundreds of years of Spanish rule come to mind. The stone walls, eroded now, are surrounded by well-kept gardens. People walk silently and respectfully through the relics, noticing the plaque, painting and tributes to national hero, José Rizal, whose writings and subsequent execution by the Spanish in 1896 fostered the cause of Philippine nationalism and independence.

To escape the clatter of the city we make the trip up the mountains to Baguio, the former summer capital and "city of pines". It is about six hours' drive from Manila. The transition from urban to rural scene is almost instantaneous: behind us the city is hazy, blurred and distorted by the smog and oily heat. Along bumpy roads we meet modern Japanese cars, old rusting buses, overloaded trucks, tricycles, bicycles, carts and jeepneys. I'm happy not to be driving.

We pass multitudes of roadside stalls and ramshackle *sari-sari* stores. The chequered pattern of green rice fields predominates, with patches of sugar cane, tobacco, corn and other vegetables reflecting the fertility of the densely settled lowlands. Bananas and sweet potato vines seem to grow everywhere in the Philippine countryside. Occasionally there's a *carabao* (water buffalo) at work in the fields.

The road becomes narrow and hazardous as it winds upwards into the cool mountains, skirting picturesque gorges and streams. Craggy mountains glare yellow and green-brown in the sun. Around a corner we meet a huge, weathered lion's head, carved out of rock and perched alone by the roadside, high above a tree-clad ravine. Recently painted eyes, as large as archery targets, and fangs the size of a child, must have required quite a climbing feat. Later we stop at a park with ornamental and pine trees, and lunch on preboiled rice, sweet bread, pork, chicken, vegetables, cobs of corn, boiled peanuts, pineapple and soft drinks.

In the Baguio markets, fine craftwork sells at much lower prices than in Manila. Strawberries thrive in the mountain climate, and a dollar will buy a basketful. Jams are dirt cheap and we load up with them. We buy necklaces of the exquisitely perfumed sampagita national flower from a young Igorot (mountain people) girl with a charming smile.

As we journey back to Manila the sticky heat greets us; it seems to get hotter every few kilometres. We cannot wait to get out of it again, to explore other rural areas. Our travels take us to Laguna province, with its large, freshwater lake where we watch a man walking out along rickety planks to feed his fish, farmed in cages of bamboo sticks, nets and wire.

If nothing else makes an impact on the visitor to Laguna, or indeed to most other provinces, the vast coconut plantations should. The land around the lake is covered with a forest of coconut trees, almost as far as the eye can see. Everything else seems secondary, huts and dwellings blending into the green-yellow environment. We stop and buy a drink at a roadside stall; a grinning boy slices the tops off each green coconut with one or two nimble strokes of his *bolo* (a type of machete). Nearby, in the shade (not of a coconut tree – people have been killed by falling nuts), two young men study their chess game.

Not only is the coconut a source of food and drink, but it also provides income-producing copra (dried kernels) and coconut oil. Stacks of stripped and plaited leaves are used for thatch, craftware, hats, mats, fans . . . the possibilities are endless. Souvenirs and utensils are made from the shells. The fibrous husks are turned into rope and matting or used for fuel. Even the tree sap is used, fermented into a powerful liquor.

Beaches, within a few hours' drive from Manila, are idyllic: sun-bleached, creamy sand and inviting, turquoise sea against an evergreen, tropical backdrop where butterflies chase one another among the gold or pink and white, sweet-scented frangipani blooms. I am only slightly taken aback when we have to stop and pay for these privileges at a toll-gate along the road leading to the beach.

"I suddenly realise that this is dangerous – I cannot move because of the crowd and confusion around me"

Almost everywhere outside the commercial areas I see poultry, in particular slim roosters which look like hens because their red combs and wattles have been removed, streamlining the birds for the notorious *sabong* (cockfighting). The gamecocks are secured in safe, shady spots by string attached to a leg, or are held, stroked and fussed over, by their masters. Cockfighting, though the brochures won't mention it, is the most popular indigenous sport.

One Sunday morning I am taken to a cockpit arena somewhere in the hills near Quezon City. In a large, grassy clearing among towering trees and dilapidated sheds, the cocks and their owners gather. The stench of droppings is overpowering and the crowing continuous. I am carried, wheelchair and all, by several men (they are all men here) eager to lend a hand, and placed within metres of two speckled cocks which are held back by their owners. A razor-sharp gaff, several centimetres long, is tied to a leg of each cock. Hundreds of boisterous onlookers clamour for action.

"Be prepared to see some sights which the tourist board won't advertise"

The cocks, fighting with beak and spur, come my way and I suddenly realise that this is dangerous – I cannot move because of the crowd and confusion around me. For seconds that seem like eternity the cocks deliver their death-blows right beside my chair. I am out of the arena before the next fight.

Access can be difficult for people with substantial physical disabilities in the Philippines, mainly as a result of the sheer weight of numbers of other human beings, but also because of the lack of smoothly paved footpaths and the absence of any special concessions – no special buses or taxis, no specially designed toilets. The lot of disabled Philippine people is a tough one: there are no disability benefits, and aids such as wheelchairs are expensive and hard to come by. Poor beggars in rags with obvious disabilities are sure to be encountered – be prepared to see some sights which the tourist board won't advertise.

But the disabled tourist's problems are not insurmountable; I saw and experienced as much as the average able-bodied visitor to the Philippines. I had the advantage of living with a Filipino family, although this was important more for learning about the country than for overcoming obstacles as a severely disabled person. Foreigners, including disabled ones, are given an inexplicable film-star status, so you can forget problems of disability-induced prejudice. Philippine people told me: "We look at what a person is like inside rather than outside." Disability never seemed so irrelevant. I was received everywhere with unselfish hospitality, smiles, genuine concern and a courteous desire to please which helped me to forget any aches and pains, and to feel comfortably free of self-consciousness.

Hong Kong & Macau

The Pied Piper of Fushan

Sue Kelley is disabled by an MS-type virus, and uses a wheelchair. She has travelled a good deal, with the help of her husband, Tony, and daughter, Joanne. In 1988 they booked places on Kuoni's "Asian Adventure Holiday", and here Sue describes their experiences in Hong Kong, Macau and China.

Descending into Hong Kong airport was quite a nerve-racking experience. The plane sank down amidst the roof-tops of Kowloon, past washing hung on poles protruding from windows, and landed on a runway built on reclaimed land which projects into the harbour (Hong Kong is Chinese for "Fragrant Harbour"). The airport itself held no problems for the wheelchair: once we had been whisked through customs and immigration the *Kuoni* courier escorted us to a waiting bus for the journey to our hotel.

An array of shops flashed by the bus windows, their neon signs coming alive as darkness drew in. Much of Hong Kong is vertical, so the few areas of flat land are crammed with buildings which seem to reach endlessly into the sky. Our hotel was in the busy Kowloon peninsula, surrounded by other hotels, nightclubs, bars and shops. The room allocated to us was extremely large and accommodated the three of us adequately.

Beyond Kowloon are the New Territories which extend to the frontiers of mainland China; here the colony changes character from industrial complexes and new suburbs to duck farms and banana plantations. By far the best-known region, and containing a quarter of the total population, is Hong Kong Island.

The most interesting and cheapest way to get from Kowloon to Hong Kong Island is by *Star Ferry*, which has excellent, clearly marked access for wheelchairs on the second-class deck. The mass of buildings as we approached the Island made a spectacular urban vista, and the cacophony of the busy harbour was thrilling.

Our main aim in Hong Kong was to enjoy the hustle and bustle of shopping. Taxis were very cheap and the drivers most courteous; they never objected to putting the wheelchair in the boot. In the shops, assistants rushed to open doors, which saved a lot of trapped fingers when manoeuvring through the entrance. Ramps were frequently provided and we often gained access via dropped kerbs, designed to allow movement of goods trolleys in and out of the shops.

We did try public transport on one occasion, boarding a free bus to the *Peak Tram* funicular railway which climbs straight up the mountainside to Victoria Peak (on Hong Kong Island). The driver assisted us on and off the bus, and at the railway station we were boarded in a special compartment equipped to carry wheelchair-bound passengers. The train ride was rapid and at the summit we alighted into a shopping area from which elevators took us up to the viewing platform. We could see all over Hong Kong. It was very windy on the platform, so we descended to the shops area, bought ourselves jumpers and then returned to watch darkness fall and the neon lights spring into action on the skyline.

We took the hydrofoil from Hong Kong to Macau, the last bastion of Portugal's sixteenth-century empire. Access to the hydrofoil was ramped, and once aboard I was able to sit with Tony and Joanne whilst my chair was stowed beside the seats. The journey took about an hour; we were met by a courier and taken by bus to our hotel for lunch before an afternoon tour of the island.

Macau is famous for its casinos, open 24 hours a day, and handily surrounded by pawn shops. As the bus wound through the streets we could not help being impressed by the elegance of the houses we passed. On Macau's highest point is the Penha Roman Catholic church, and from this vantage point we looked down over the island, the harbour and the bridge – some 2.4km long – which connects Macau with the island of Taipa. In the harbour an ornate dragon boat lies alongside the maritime museum; access for wheelchairs is limited to the ground floor in the museum but it is well worth a visit.

We were taken to view the Buddhist temple in the harbour known as "Matock the Goddess of Ama", where we learnt the origins of the name Macau: Ama is the goddess of fisher-folk, and *cau* means "bay" in Portuguese; the island was originally called Amacau, the "A" being dropped later. This mixture of Eastern and Western culture, epitomised by the ruins of St Paul's church, with its facade of saints, Chinese dragons and Portuguese *caravela,* can be observed throughout the island.

We returned to the hotel for our evening meal, after which the three of us decided to take a stroll around the town centre. The streets are cobbled and quite steep, so it was hard work for Tony who was pushing the wheelchair, but we did find some ramps. Tourist shops mingled with the local hardware, herbalist and noodle stalls.

Seventeen fellow tourists joined us in the hotel foyer the next day for our trip into China. The bus took us to the Barrier Gate, erected more than a century ago, which separates Macau from The People's Republic of China. We had to alight with all our luggage and we were each given a numbered badge; these numbers were stuck on the fronts of our passports. Particular attention was paid to the number of cameras carried by each tourist and on return they made sure that we brought out the same number.

"I got out and sat on the floor whilst the children took turns to sit in the chair"

After passing through the gate we were met by three Chinese tour reps: Yen and Kathy – our guides – and the bus driver. The bus was large and comfortable, housing two refrigerators which we could use to keep drinks or edibles cool. Tony helped me into the front seat of the bus alongside Joanne, while the driver placed the wheelchair in front of the seat opposite for easy access. Everyone was helpful to us on entering and leaving the bus – not once were we left to struggle on our own.

Despite the fact that there are no privately owned motor vehicles in

China (all belong to the state or to large corporations), the roads were quite congested. We passed through a countryside of duck farms, paddy fields and fruit plantations, stopping in the village of Yongmai to see how the people live and work in a farming commune. The home of one of the farm leaders was quite spartan compared to Western homes, stone built with a tiled roof, with no washing machine or other labour-saving appliances. Cooking was on an open fire and the lounge contained wooden benches along one wall. I was unable to go upstairs but those who did reported clean but bare rooms.

We saw the workers in the fields, one lady with a baby strapped to her back as she hoed. Moving on to the village school for children aged three to seven years, we were surprised to see that they did not wear school uniform. They were playing games in the playground but stopped to stare at us, regarding me in particular as though I had arrived from outer space. Kathy told me that I was the first wheelchair-bound person she had brought on this tour and that the children were not used to seeing disabled people out and about. I got out and sat on the floor whilst the children took turns to sit in the chair, but they would not be pushed in it.

Our next stop was the memorial house of Doctor Sun Yat-Sen, the founder of the Chinese Republic. Referred to by the Chinese as the "Father of China", he is credited with freeing the people from feudalism. Photographs and documents tell the story of this physician who trained in the USA and became a revolutionary statesman. It was interesting to learn that his medical knowledge helped to change traditional practices such as the binding of girls' feet. Once again I was restricted to the ground floor but as most of the information was here I did not miss much.

Lunch was served in the *Zongshan International Hotel*. The dining room was elegantly furnished and the meal consisted of seven courses accompanied by beer or orange juice, followed by Chinese tea. Fushan – a city famous for its silk and porcelain – was to be our next stop for the night, and here the dinner consisted of yet another seven courses. The food is not my best memory of this holiday – I often wished I'd brought some supplies with me, along with some cutlery, as my limited hand movements turned eating with chopsticks into a major feat.

"On looking up from my writing I was astonished to find myself surrounded by a sea of smiling faces"

After dinner Yen and Kathy took us on a walk to the village store where they sold food on the ground floor, fancy goods upstairs. The stairs were very steep, so I opted to stay put amongst some floral displays and write my postcards while the others went to browse. On looking up from my writing I was astonished to find myself surrounded by a sea of smiling faces.

My first thought was that I must look very odd writing with a pen stuffed inside a foam bicycle-handle grip, but once joined by Kathy and Yen I learned that it was the wheelchair again attracting attention. The crowd numbered well over a hundred, and as the store closed and I was reunited with the rest of the group we were amazed to find these Chinese people falling in behind us, more adding to their number as we walked back to the hotel. Several of our group took photographs of the scene, which must have resembled the Pied Piper in a wheelchair.

After leaving the hotel around 9am we stopped at Fushan's art and craft workshop, where we observed the workers making lanterns and paper sculptures, and painting scrolls; the finished products were available for purchase. The silk factory was next, its antiquated appearance and work methods reminiscent of conditions in English mills in the late 1800s. The silk was on sale for approximately £2 a metre.

"In China the drive to separate the visitor from his foreign currency was much in evidence"

We arrived in Canton, or Guangzhou as it's locally known, in time for lunch. The biggest city in Southern China, Canton straddles the Pearl River and teems with people and bicycles. At peak times the cyclists sit in silent traffic jams that make the jams in our cities look like minor hold-ups. After eating at the *Guangzhou Restaurant* we walked to the local market which sold fish for ornamental ponds, as well as food in the form of livestock (live being the operative word), including snakes, frogs, chickens, cats, dogs, ducks and what looked like maggots! Many of these items had featured on our tables at previous meals, and the more sentimental amongst us were pleased to clamber back on board our bus, heading for the zoo.

We had hoped to see the pandas at the zoo, but only one emerged briefly from his house. As compensation we did see some beautiful white peacocks. The zoo is situated on a hillside, which makes hard work for wheelchair pushers. Tony was fortunate that Yen took turns with him, enabling me to see more than might have been possible on our own.

It was late afternoon when we arrived at our hotel, *The White Swan*, which is a world showpiece. As we entered, a waterfall cascaded from the third floor down into an ornamental pool surrounded by jade statues and pagodas; a jade tree, about six feet tall with large peaches hanging from its branches, graced one side. After our evening meal Kathy and Yen walked us

to a local park for a cultural show, a form of opera with colourful costumes. On the way back to the hotel we watched the activity on the busy Pearl River.

The next morning our bus deposited us at the railway station, where checking of passports and baggage was slow but we eventually found ourselves aboard the train bound for Hong Kong. I was transferred to a reclining seat beside Tony and Joanne; the wheelchair was stowed behind us. The compartment was clean and smart, complete with a TV set.

The journey back to Kowloon gave us a final glimpse of China, and time for reflection on the diversities that we had observed during this brief visit. In China the drive to separate the visitor from his foreign currency was much in evidence and almost certainly accounts for the many stops in shops and factories on our tour, although the sales methods used were more subtle than the high-pressure techniques used in Hong Kong. We wondered whether the takeover in 1997 would affect the huge gulf between rich and poor in Hong Kong – our impression was that in China everyone shared life's basics, and whilst they were materially poor in our eyes we saw no evidence of abject poverty or starvation. Admittedly, however, the tour was designed so that we had little free time to wander, and those who did found that one of the couriers followed them and guided them back to the fold.

On re-entering high-tech Hong Kong we felt we had passed through a time-warp, leaving China's utilitarian state behind us. Our visit left us with much to ponder on, and a desire to return and perhaps consider the gains or losses made on either side – in terms of wealth, lifestyle and individual liberty – when the dust settles after 1997.

China

Fame at Last

For Betty Layton and her husband John, the festive season of 1987 was a Christmas with a difference: no slaving over a hot stove or facing mountains of washing-up; instead they went to China on a three-week Kuoni tour, from Peking (Beijing) in the freezing north to Canton (Guangzhou) in the subtropical south, with suitable clothing packed for the extremes of weather and Betty's spare artificial leg in the hand baggage.

We set off on a *British Airways* flight from Heathrow on December 19, leaving behind a bewildered family. The wheelchair service and pre-boarding were excellent as usual, and we enjoyed every moment of the flight. During our waking time we were visited by Julia, the young *Kuoni* rep who was kept busy seeking out and introducing herself to all 21 members of our group. Julia was superb – helpful, diplomatic, wise beyond her years and calm whenever disaster threatened.

Next day at noon, we arrived in Hong Kong where we stretched our leg(s) before taking off for Peking. Getting into China is a slow process. We all had a number stuck to the cover of our passports and had to line up strictly in order at immigration; this was the only identification recognisable by the very young soldiers who stared at our passports and at us, trying to match both with their visa lists. My

wheelchair had been sent to meet the wrong plane and there was – with a shrug of oriental shoulders – nothing to be done about it. I had to walk every inch of the way, and very long it was too, up and down stairs and slopes to the luggage carousel. John and I were numbers 3 and 4 in the group, so the immigration queue did not move until we arrived!

The drive from the airport to the hotel kept us awake. It was fascinating – bicycles by the thousand, most cyclists and pedestrians wearing mouth and nose masks. We arrived exhausted at our hotel at 5pm, only to be told to meet at 6pm for dinner. From this moment we were conditioned to early meals, early starts and not a minute wasted. We were met in the foyer and taken by coach to the *Sun Park Restaurant*. By this time it was dark and the bikes were still weaving about – no lights!

Our first dinner in Peking taught us that if hungry we had better learn the art of using chopsticks (take your own chopsticks, by the way – some wooden ones are very dubious). The Chinese called us the "Group of 21" and we always had two large tables, with a turntable in the centre. The food whizzed round and if we were lucky we managed to grab a passing morsel with our chopsticks. Small dishes of starters were ready on the turntable as we sat down; then the main meat, fish, shellfish and vegetable dishes arrived, followed by rice and then soup! Fruit or sweet cakes came next, and throughout the meal tea, soft drinks or beer were served. Each course was served and whipped away quite quickly, and a great pile of hot flannels were usually brought to the table for a clean-up half way through the meal.

"The tombs, regalia and artefacts were well worth the effort of climbing 91 steps"

On most tours, hotels are not known until arrival in a particular town. All ours were Westernised, with *en suite* facilities, and the only advice I can give is to ask for a room near a lift (some corridors seem very long at the end of a day's sightseeing). Perhaps fortunately, we did not stay in ordinary Chinese hotels or lodging houses. Apart from breakfast we rarely ate in our hotels; it seemed that we were to be shown as much as possible by having lunches and dinners in different places each day. We were often given a separate room in restaurants, which was a pity. There were large vacuum flasks of hot water and tea bags in our rooms, so we could make tea at all times. Drinking water was also provided.

The *CITS (China International Travel Service)* agents met us and took charge in each location, settling our programme with Julia. In Peking, two young girls, one of whom was a student guide practising her English, took us to the Ming Tombs. We approached them through the Sacred Way and the Avenue of the Animals, lined with massive statues of real and mythical beasts, along which the Ming Emperors were carried to their tombs. The visit was well within my capabilities, and the tombs, regalia and artefacts were well worth the effort of climbing 91 steps.

On to the Great Wall, special parts of whose enormous length are easily accessible. From here you can walk for miles in either direction, with extensive views over the hills. The slopes were difficult for me, and it was cold and windy, but I managed to get to the famous section where the Queen had had her photograph taken in the autumn of 1987.

Back in Peking, the Forbidden City was the site of a splendid tour which took two hours, yet we did not see all the temples, palaces and museums. The exhibitions of clothing, carriages and furniture were well set out and we were left to view at our own pace, then met and taken to the next venue. After this came the now-infamous Tiananmen Square, with the Great Hall of the People on one side. As we walked around, astonished at its vastness, we were being stared at, long and hard. We got used to this in time, but it was quite disconcerting at first. Many Chinese, especially those from the country districts, had never seen Westerners before and they think we are so ugly – large noses, protruding eyes and queer-shaped faces!

After a Peking Duck Banquet on our last night, we left very early the next day for Xian. We were to go by military plane but the fog came down and we were stranded in the spartan surroundings of the military airfield buildings. The authorities certainly did not lose face – they sent us to a brand new hotel nearby (it seemed to be for the exclusive use of the high ranking army and airforce personnel) and we were given the best meal of our stay in China.

The fog eventually lifted and we took off for Xian. Airport wheelchair service does not exist for internal flights in

China, nor does pre-boarding. However, we always managed to get to the plane before it left! On the flight we were given tea, orange juice, chocolate biscuits, a half-pound packet of wafers, a model aeroplane and an airways bag! We decided that the military personnel were trying to outdo the civilian airlines. On our journeys throughout China we were inundated with gifts – key-rings, brooches, postcards by the packet – and fruit, drinks, biscuits and chocolates were always available on boats, trains and aircraft.

The tour of the Terracotta Army site was the high spot of our visit to Xian. Once again we were left to wander round the huge building (about the size of a football pitch) which has been erected over the "army". One end is set out with the repaired army figures and horses in rows; across the middle are the sections they are working on – with a leg, an arm and the odd hand being painstakingly excavated from the mounds of soil and rock.

"Gin and tonic has never tasted so good out of plastic film cartons"

From Xian we were scheduled to fly to Nanjing, but the Chinese had "forgotten" to tell *Kuoni* that the flights did not operate in winter. The alternative was to travel overnight and most of the next day by train. The *CITS* agent vanished into thin air, leaving Julia to sort this out – no mean feat as they hadn't booked enough sleepers for us. There was quite a fight, with Julia holding her own against a barrage of objections from the sleeping car guardian, the cook, guards and all manner of officials. A delightful, English-speaking Chinese wife of a professor came to Julia's rescue and it was finally sorted out with Julia paying excess for the sleepers and for the meals that they "forgot" to book.

As it was Christmas Eve, the Group of 21 celebrated in the appropriate style once the battle was won. Glasses were at a premium, and gin and tonic has never tasted so good out of plastic film cartons. We were determined to make the cook work for the extra payment he had received, so we bravely faced his wobbly eggs and toast on Christmas morning. Getting on and off trains could be a problem, but there is always a "mounting block" and plenty of hand-rails and helping hands.

In Nanjing we went to Sun Yat-Sen's Mausoleum which I viewed from a distance (392 steps). The founder and first president of the Chinese Communist Republic, Doctor Sun Yat-Sen lived in several different cities and each *CITS* agent gave us a potted history of his life, showing us the houses he lived in and offering us a number of different dates for his death. We saw the two-tier road and rail bridge over the Yangtze and went up by lift to look down on the river's busy traffic. We took a short train trip to Wuxi, a delightful town.

While waiting for our trains we always found ourselves in the first-class waiting rooms with high ranking Chinese but no "ordinary travellers", of which there were hundreds. We were ushered out of the waiting room as the train approached and settled in a special coach. When we moved from place to place we put our luggage outside our hotel rooms and it appeared as if by magic at the next hotel. It received quite rough treat-ment, but nothing was lost apart from a few straps and handles.

In Wuxi, on Sunday morning, we were taken to a student college where the teenage students and their families were taking part in a song, dance and magic performance on a makeshift stage. The Chinese laugh hysterically and enjoy any performing act; they shuffled along the benches to make room for us to join in the fun. They all wanted to practise their English, and Julia was persuaded to ask us up onto the stage where we sang "Jingle Bells" – they were very polite and clapped enthusiastically. As we were leaving, they crowded round, eager to hear about Western housing, shopping, work, school – every conceivable aspect of life, in fact.

In the afternoon we embarked on a journey along the Grand Canal to Soochow. I worry about leaping aboard boats with my artificial leg, but from sampans to hovercraft the crews have always made light of my problems and been most helpful. From the canal we saw a real slice of Chinese life: old houses line the canal and the dwellers wash their clothes and fish in it; the barges, piled high with vegetables, reeds, bricks and other commodities, are skilfully steered in long "trains", missing bridges and other boats by inches. They simply push each other out of the way with long poles – us, too, when we were in their way.

"Crocodiles of very young children pointed at us in the coach and fell about laughing"

Soochow is another fascinating town. We visited landscaped classical gardens, all beautifully kept, with courtyards, little bridges, pools and gazebos, lovely trees, flowers and bonsai trees. They are very peaceful and have attractive names – The Humble Administrator's garden, the Lingering garden, the Fishermen's garden. We went on to a sandalwood fan factory and to the Institute of Embroidery where we saw exquisite work in progress, using minute stitches. No wonder nearly all the workers in the dimly lit rooms needed spectacles – or soon will.

Another train journey took us to Shanghai, a very different city, packed with twelve million people. A coach trip of two miles took us at least an hour, sometimes more, and the congestion on pavements, streets and bike lanes was accepted as normal by the Chinese. The traffic was either stationary or just creeping along, and this gave us wonderful opportunities to observe life in the city.

Washing was hanging from lines stretched from upper windows to trees on the roadside. The bicycles and carts (drawn by men and women) groaned under mountains of goods. The only people with cars are high ranking officials; there are lots of taxis and the government owns them too. Crocodiles of very young children pointed at us in the coach and fell about laughing; our progress was so slow that they passed us again and again, with renewed laughter each time.

We were taken to the Zhing Zua commune, just outside Shanghai, which has its own shops, schools, smallholdings and hospital. We were astonished to be shown the treatment rooms in the hospital – heaving with patients, lying head to toe on benches around the room, with needles in various parts of their anatomy. The camera fiends among us really got going! Doctors, nurses and patients all took our visit with bland equanimity. In the pharmacy small quantities of dried herbs, bugs and caterpillars were being weighed into brown paper packets, to be boiled up by patients into a sort of tisane – a truly different world.

From Shanghai we flew to Guilin, where Julia was delighted to find an old *CITS* friend and, unusually, another official from Canton. She never knew who was meeting us at each venue; they seemed to vary the agents for each tour – some were most cooperative, some a little awkward! It was New Year's Eve and we were handed invitations to a special dinner and official entertainment that evening in Guilin.

The day was spent on the Li river, admiring its extraordinary scenery – conical hills and mountains, riverside villages, bamboo rafts, water buffalo and cormorant fishermen. Lunch on board was Mongolian hotpot, which was quite hard work: we had to cook everything ourselves in a large dish of boiling water kept hot over charcoal – one pot to every half-dozen people. We cooked bits of chicken, fish, meat, greens and beans, and at the end drank the broth – it was a challenge and a change. (Which reminds me, some public loos in the East are only holes in the ground, and balancing can be very tricky with an artificial leg, but hotels, restaurants and, surprisingly, boats and many trains have Western-style loos.)

"We were on the telly, in the newspapers and were wined and dined until we were giddy"

We flew from Guilin to Canton on New Year's Day and began to realise why the Canton *CITS* agent had been dogging our steps. We were given numbered envelopes on the flight and told to remain on the plane until all the other passengers had left, then disembark in number order. Looking through the plane windows we could see a troupe of dancing girls with feather fans, a band and a group of officials. A large banner proclaimed that we were the "First Group to Arrive in Canton on New Year's Day in the Most Auspicious Year of the Dragon – 1988"!

On leaving the plane we felt like royalty. The band played, the girls danced, the TV cameras whirred and we were introduced one by one (in number order) to the city officials. Our envelopes contained invitations to various celebrations which went on during our two-day stay. We were on the telly, in the newspapers (they presented us with copies and photographs to take home) and were wined and dined until we were giddy.

We also found time for some interesting visits in Canton: a jade factory; the 5000-seat Sun Yat-Sen Memorial Hall; a granite sculpture of five goats, the city emblem of Canton (quite a climb); the Temple of the Six Banyan Trees which is the seat of the Buddhist Society of Canton, and the truly beautiful Chen Clan Classical Learning Academy gardens and temples, desecrated during the cultural revolution but now being restored.

Our last dinner was preceded by a cocktail party given by *Kuoni* in the Songbird Room (real birds) of the *White Swan Hotel*. The next day we boarded the train to Hong Kong and after a few days to recover from nearly 5000km of travel in China, flew home to London. Christmas and New Year will never be the same again.

Sources of information

Hong Kong Tourist Association, 125 Pall Mall, London SW1Y 5EA; ☎071/930 4775. May still have copies of *A Guide for Physically Handicapped Visitors to Hong Kong*, the latest edition of which was published in 1987. The guide is a joint venture of *The Canadian Club of Hong Kong* and *The Canadian Chamber of Commerce in Hong Kong*, and they wisely suggest in their Introduction that until the next update, "it will become an increasingly prudent precaution to telephone ahead and ensure assessments are still valid" – Hong Kong is a rapidly changing city.

Singapore Tourist Board, 1 Carrington House, 126 Regent Street, London W1R 5FE; ☎071/437 0033. Distributes *Access Singapore*, a project of the *Singapore Council of Social Service* (11 Penang Lane, Singapore 0923; ☎336-1544), which uses roughly the same clear layout as the Hong Kong guide, is more up to date (1989) and covers hotels, hospitals, places of interest, shops, libraries, cinemas – every sort of building you are likely to visit – but nothing on transport.

National Tourist Office of the Philippines, 199 Piccadilly, London W1V 9LE; ☎071/439 3481. Supplies a list of three hotels with facilities for disabled guests, as well as some notes on the activities of the *National Council for the Welfare of Disabled Persons* (2nd Floor, Philippine Sugar Center Annex Building, North Avenue, Diliman, Quezon City; ☎73/961165).

China National Tourist Office, 4 Glentworth Street, London NW1; ☎071/935 9427. No information for disabled visitors; staff advise that travel in China is very difficult for disabled people and there are no facilities for them. Even the general tourist information from this office appears curiously outdated.

Macau Tourist Information Bureau, 6 Sherlock Mews, Paddington Street, London W1M 3RH; ☎071/224 3390). General brochures only.

Tourism Authority of Thailand (TAT), 49 Albermarle Street, London W1X 3FE; ☎071/499 7679. They suggest contacting the TAT information counter on arrival at Bangkok airport.

Indonesian Express, 70/71 New Bond Street, London W1Y 9DE; ☎071/491 4469. There is no UK tourist office for Indonesia, only a specialist tour operator: they exhibit a fairly cautious attitude to the idea of taking on disabled clients and have no experience to draw on.

Tour operators

Depending on the destination (Singapore, Hong Kong and Bangkok cause least consternation), operators may balk at the prospect of accepting a wheelchair user, or even someone with limited walking capacity, into their tour group – they consider the obstacles too great, particularly for an elderly, inexperienced or unaccompanied traveller. But, with a bit of persuasion, some will take the plunge.

Betty Layton has had previous experience of travelling with *Kuoni*, and was delighted with their very capable rep on her Chinese tour. It seems that although first-time enquirers may receive a polite refusal from *Kuoni* for certain destinations, if you persist and build up a track record you might be treated to a more positive response (see Sue Kelley's experience, p.312).

Thomson's Worldwide brochure includes several holidays in the Far East, and their *Factfile* service (p."Booking", *Practicalities*) should be of use to disabled travellers wanting more detailed information on the hotels and resorts in the brochure.

Basic access information (terrain, steps at entrance and inside, accessibility of lift and public rooms) is kept on file at *Thomas Cook*, and this operator is happy to take accompanied disabled clients to destinations offered in the *Faraway* brochure (which include Thailand and the Far East). At *Hayes and Jarvis* one member of staff has first-hand knowledge of all the hotels used and can be consulted for advice on wheelchair accessibility.

The greater freedom of independent travel, however, can be more rewarding (and cheaper) than either group tours or tailor-made packages. Searching out your own style of hotel, using local drivers and guides means that you make arrangements that suit you rather than the UK tour operator. Whether the headaches outweigh the rewards is very much a matter of individual taste.

THE FAR EAST: TRAVEL NOTES

Getting there

It's well worth shopping around for the best prices (if you need help, ask *Trailfinders*; ☎071/938 3366), as most popular **airlines** can cope smoothly with wheelchair users or other disabled passengers. Those that carry aisle wheelchairs, and have at least one toilet adapted, include *British Airways*, *Emirates* and *Qantas*. *Cathay Pacific* will carry a "skychair" on request, and one toilet per aircraft has "facilities for invalids", although these do not include aisle chair accessibility. You can also expect good service (but no aisle chairs) from *Air Lanka*, *KLM*, *Lufthansa*, *Singapore Airlines* and *Thai Airways International*.

But flights are long (sixteen hours to Singapore), economy-class seating is cramped and even specially adapted toilets are not big enough for comfort. Prepare to wake up on your first morning in the Far East feeling stiff and very tired (p.319).

Avoid *Garuda (Indonesian) Airlines*, who assured Veronica Smith that aisle carry-chairs would be available on all flights, that seats had been reserved near the toilets, and that arrangements had been made to transfer her safely from one plane to the next. There were no carry-chairs, and Veronica and her companions had great difficulty obtaining seats near the toilets. Getting on and off the planes involved shuffling up flights of steps, being carried without a carry-chair or, on one occasion, entering the plane via a food conveyor belt which deposited them on the wet floor of a refrigerated food truck, where they waited until the truck was raised to the level of the aircraft door.

Airport facilities vary from basic but adequate (as at Denpasar in Bali) to good, with wheelchair-accessible toilets, lifts, ramps and reserved parking (as at Hong Kong International, Changi Singapore and Narita International Tokyo). At Seoul, in South Korea, scene of the 1988 Paralympics, the lifts are provided with buttons and information panels at wheelchair height and coded in Braille.

Disembarking from international flights is usually by airbridge or lifting vehicle, but be prepared to be carried off in Bali and if flying shorter hops such as Singapore to Bangkok (p.318).

Transport

Facilities for disabled passengers are confined to parts of the Hong Kong and Japanese **public transport** networks: a Dial-a-Ride service during off-peak hours and at weekends in Hong Kong; boarding and toilet facilities for disabled travellers on the Kowloon–Canton railway; special compartment for wheelchair passengers on the funicular train to Victoria Peak (Hong Kong Island); accessible second-class (lower) deck on the Hong Kong Island–Kowloon *Star Ferry*; ramped access to the Hong Kong–Macau hydrofoil; some facilities for disabled passengers on parts of Japan's rail network – including the installation of tiny cubicles in several carriages of the Japan Bullet Train, so that wheelchair users can sit in solitary depression, isolated from the general run of humanity.

In general, however, contributors have made excellent use of the available, **non-adapted transport**. Taxis are fine for exploring Singapore and Hong Kong, their drivers helpful. *Tuk-tuks* (if you can clamber in) or shuttle boats and ferries (with help from the crew) are the thing in Bangkok. It's even possible to ride a Philippine jeepney, wheelchair squashed between the two bench seats, head touching the roof (p.328). In Bali, an air-conditioned mini-bus can be hired quite cheaply for a day's sight-seeing (p.325) – with a roll-up transit chair and a couple of friends, getting in and out of the bus is an easy operation.

For cross-country journeys, any method of travel is likely to be slow or uncomfortable or both. Where roads are more than tracks they are poorly maintained. Buses and cars are often pretty spartan; trains are difficult to get into, the seating less than luxurious and the toilets impossible. Domestic **flights** probably offer the best level of comfort and cut down journey times, but expect no facilities for boarding and disembarking, no toilets, often no wheelchair service, endless bureaucracy to cut through when booking a ticket – and you'll see nothing of the countryside.

Accommodation

Hotel rates are generally lower than in Europe, so the fact that the more expensive hotels tend to be the ones with wheelchair access may be less of a problem here than in other parts of the world. Barbara Horrocks, for example, stayed in two of the very luxurious *Shangri-la* hotels (89 Soi Wat Suan Plu, New Road, Bangkok, ☎2/236-7777; 22 Orange Grove Road, Singapore 1025, ☎737-3644), both fully accessible, for prices that by oriental standards were high (upwards of £90 a night in 1991) but compared with London rates seemed reasonable.

If the *Access Singapore* guide is to be believed, the city of Singapore offers a wide choice of hotels with good facilities for disabled guests, including full acccess to bathrooms. The guide lists the metropolitan YMCA, which has ten steps at the entrance, but Susan Preston stayed at the central YMCA hotel (1 Orchard Road, Singapore 0923; ☎337-3444). She joined the YMCA for the purposes of her holiday, and paid a nightly rate of £7.70 per person, room only (1991 rates are about £20; book at least five weeks ahead). Sue's air-conditioned room contained three beds, colour TV, fridge, telephone and tea-making facilities, and the *en suite* shower room with toilet had plenty of space for manoeuvre in the wheelchair. The hotel has its own cafeteria and a *McDonald's* on the ground floor.

In Hong Kong there are wheelchair-accessible facilities at several hotels, but the 1987 guide for handicapped visitors indicates that bathroom doorways are usually too narrow to admit a wheelchair – check this when booking. Sue Kelley stayed in spacious accommodation at the *Park Hotel* (61/65 Chatham Road, Kowloon; ☎3661371), with easy access to the *en suite* facilities.

In Macau, Sue stayed at the accessible, five-star *Mandarin Oriental* (Avenida de Amizade; ☎567888). There are cheaper options amongst the *pousadas* and guesthouses, but you'd have to contact them direct to ascertain facilities for wheelchair guests. The *pousadas* are generally converted Portuguese churches, so access to these may be difficult.

In Bali, Veronica Smith stayed at the *Ramayana Hotel* (Jalan Bakungsari, Kuta, PO Box 333, Denpasar 80001; ☎361/88429), which was easily accessible apart from the odd step in the gardens.

The Philippine tourist office recommends the *Philippine Village Hotel* (Naia Avenue, Pasay City; ☎2/8338081), the *Manila Hotel* (Rizal Park, Manila; ☎2/470011) and the *Manila Peninsula Hotel* (Ayala/Makati Avenue, Makati, Manila; ☎2/8193456); the first two offer adapted transport.

Access and facilities

There are plenty of ramps in Hong Kong and an increasing number in the City of Singapore, as well as facilities for disabled people in several Japanese cities; in Nagoya, for example, all the pavements, kerbs and subways are marked with coded, ribbed strips to guide blind people.

But outside the air-conditioned, marble-floored shopping plazas that have become a feature of some Asian cities, the going gets tough for wheelchair users. High kerbs, narrow, crowded pavements and heat make getting around something of a trial; a companion is almost essential. Traffic and litter provide an added obstacle in a number of cities. Singapore, with its heavy and enforced fines for litter louts, is the shining exception to this.

The terrain in rural areas can be formidable, with soft sand, rocky paths and rough dirt tracks to negotiate: for many the only way to see the countryside is from the seat of a vehicle. Susan Preston explored Phuket island by minibus; Veronica Smith saw Bali the same way; others used coaches, trains, jeeps, boats – none of these adapted for disabled passengers but all manageable with help.

Access to sights, however, is too often only partial: wheelchair users must sit and view monuments from outside or be content with the exhibits on a museum's ground floor. There is good access to some outdoor attractions such as the Rose Gardens in Bangkok, or the Singapore Zoological Gardens, but the scope for introduction of ramps, lifts and wide doorways, not to mention some accessible public loos, is enormous.

Health and insurance

The main threats to good health in this part of the world come from contaminated food and water and, in some areas, disease-carrying mosquitoes. The effects of high temperatures

THE FAR EAST: TRAVEL NOTES

and humidity should not be underestimated, and remember also that nights can be cold. But, as a general rule, don't *over*estimate the dangers: with some simple precautions and common sense, plus advice from a good guidebook or from Richard Dawood's *Travellers' Health* (see "Books", *Practicalities*) you are unlikely to suffer more than a couple of days of "Delhi Belly".

If you don't have a strong stomach, it's worth taking a small travel kettle and some Cup-a-soups, or other foods that you know and love — when recovering from a bout of diarrhoea and faced with nothing but strange and spicy food, the comforting aroma of soup and a dry Cornish wafer will restore interest in the world around you.

PART SIX

AUSTRALIA AND NEW ZEALAND

Introduction

T here are wedding bells in more than one of the accounts in this section, and not a single trip which does not involve visiting relatives or old friends. But even without the cushioning effect of contacts down under, Australia and New Zealand are two of the world's more civilised destinations for the disabled traveller. The message of these accounts is that disabled people are expected and welcome visitors, rather than surprise guests, in accommodation, public buildings and at tourist attractions. Perhaps the exception is public transport – most types are inaccessible to lone wheelchair users.

General attitudes towards disability are good, Donald Crowther (p.360) being the only contributor to experience any unpleasantness. Most people report widespread friendliness and unfussy assistance whenever required. It is particularly refreshing to read of coach drivers and tour guides who are cheerfully willing to lift tourists in wheelchairs, in marked contrast to the more usual attitude that if you cannot manage yourself then you must be accompanied.

When considering a holiday in Australia or New Zealand the biggest turn-off is probably **getting there**. Most people break the journey at Singapore or Bangkok, but it is a long haul, and what may be minor irritations on a short hop to Greece are likely to cause misery on an eighteen-hour flight. The problem of visiting the aircraft toilets is magnified: it seems crazy for airlines to provide an "adapted" toilet which is only marginally bigger than the standard broom cupboards that pass for loos in the economy section. *Air New Zealand* make some effort to get round this by taking disabled passengers to the first-class loos if more space is required. In an ideal world the adapted toilet should be large enough to accommodate the aisle wheelchair and an assistant.

The best way to cover long distances within Australia and New Zealand is probably by air. *East West* are the cheapest **domestic airline** in Australia; *Australian* produce a comprehensive brochure for their disabled passengers; *Ansett* score highly as travel agents as well as for good all-round service on domestic flights in Australia. *Air New Zealand*, *Mount Cook Line* and *Ansett New Zealand* cope well with disabled travellers within New Zealand.

Access on Australian **interstate trains** and on New Zealand's *InterCity* services is generally poor: it's impossible to get a wheelchair along the corridor, never mind into the toilet. Rail travel is not out of the question – major stations have collapsible wheelchairs (these are available for use on board the *Indian Pacific* from Sydney to Perth) – but full-time wheelchair users will have to arrange assistance.

For overland travel a **hire car** or camper van allow greater independence. Although not widespread, vehicles with hand controls are available, and carrying your own set of controls will open up a wider choice of rental firms. Roger Elliott reports great kindness from other road users when he ran into trouble on a couple of occasions in remote areas.

Getting around the cities presents few problems, although Roger Elliott had to grapple with high kerbs and difficult access to shops and banks in northern Queensland. Sydney is equipped with the fully accessible Monorail, and taxi drivers are helpful everywhere. **Wheelchair-accessible taxis** can be booked in advance in almost every Australian (state) capital city. In New Zealand, the *Total Mobility* project, set up and coordinated by the *Disabled Persons Assembly*, provides an accessible, discounted taxi service for some 75 percent of New Zealanders with mobility problems. Visitors can take advantage of this form of transport through one of the organisations involved in the scheme (p.382).

All types of **accommodation** are covered in these accounts, from pre-booked, luxury hotels, through cheap motels found along the way, to rough and ready camp-sites. If facilities were not always perfect, they were always adaptable to suit individual needs, and the general awareness of the requirements of disabled people is said to be good in both countries. Perhaps the biggest plus is that travellers who need wheelchair access are not confined to the luxury hotels – there is a good spread of accessible options across the price range.

No single source lists all the accessible accommodation in Australia, but the numer-ous disabled support organisations in each state can help with enquiries and the experi-ences of our contributors suggest that it is not difficult to find suitable rooms en route. The scarcity of accommodation allowing independent access noted by David Gray in New Zealand in 1984 seems to have been improved upon if we are to believe the 1990–1991 edition of the access guide produced by the New Zealand Tourism Department – more reports are needed to confirm this.

Few **tourist attractions** or **recreational activities** are out of bounds for disabled visitors: David Gray found that it wasn't necessary to hike the mountain trails to appre-ciate the scenery in South Island; you don't have to be able to walk to enjoy swimming and diving amongst brilliant coral fish on the Great Barrier Reef. A practical and posi-tive approach from the crew make small boats and light aircraft accessible. Boardwalks and sealed-surface or compact-chip tracks enable wheelchair users to wander through rainforests and national parks. Barbara Horrocks' worries about access at Ayers Rock were swept away by a cheerful tour guide, and Sheila Murray found few problems in Perth, taking her disabled daughter everywhere – to the beach, the dolphinarium, the shops, even to dinner at the Yacht Club.

Easy access cannot be taken for granted: there is room for improvement in many areas (p.384), but overall the levels of awareness and the provision of facilities for disa-bled people are better than average. John Moore found that in some places toilet facili-ties for disabled people were not indicated by the usual wheelchair sign because it is assumed that accessible toilets are incorporated everywhere. And help is always at hand: the friendliness of both Aussies and Kiwis, their readiness to assist, is perhaps the strongest theme of these accounts. To find the two together – generally good access *and* willing helpers – is rare indeed.

Australia

Wheeling around Queensland

Andrew Healey is a Navy-trained helicopter pilot who broke his back in a flying accident in 1985. Now paraplegic, he is a public relations consultant and freelance aviation writer. As a result of the crash, Andrew was unable to attend his brother Nick's wedding in Queensland, but made it for their first anniversary, in January 1987, travelling with his wife, Linda.

We found a good deal on the tickets, applied for the visas, organised hotels, packed callipers and crutches into my ski bag and set off just after Christmas, flying first to Singapore for two days, then overnight to Brisbane for the meat of the trip and finally home from Sydney after four weeks away.

For the longer legs of the trip we booked with *British Airways*, mainly because at the time they were adapting their Boeing 747s to make one of the loos accessible to the aisle wheelchair. I am sure they have completed the conversions by now, but we flew to Singapore in an aircraft "yet to be modified".

If it happens to you, don't panic – your body dehydrates during a long flight and although I drank plenty of fluids like a sensible traveller should, I didn't need to empty the leg bag once. If you can manage a long-ish transfer from the aisle wheelchair you should be OK. I also stood up at times by hauling myself up on the headrest of the

seat in front (I recommend you introduce yourself to the occupant first).

At Brisbane airport we had to take a ten-minute taxi ride from the international to the domestic terminal. We flew north to Rocky (Rockhampton) in a very smart *Ansett Australia* Boeing, after which the airport at Rocky was a surprise – very small and utilitarian. I had to suffer the indignity of being fork-lifted down from the aircraft – hated that. Nick met us there, though, and we could start the serious holidaymaking.

We had only the weekend to get over the jet lag, acclimatise, and meet up with my uncle and aunt in Yeppoon (a small town on the "Capricorn Coast", to the east of Rocky) before Nick and his wife Jane drove north with us towards Cairns and the Barrier Reef. Nick had a Volkswagen camper van and the idea was to use the campsites along the coast, then find a chalet or something in Cairns.

The sites we came across during the four-day trip were surprisingly easy to deal with from a wheelchair. I could use the loos in each one, and because we took along a collapsible plastic stool I could shower every evening. We soft-bellied Poms were initially a little nervous of using the toilets after dark: every time the loo was flushed it set off a cacophony of croaks from the tree frogs living in the cistern above. And the possums are fearless – so accustomed to people that they wander arrogantly all over the campsites. One evening I heard a scrabbling noise and wheeled round with the torch. If someone had done that to me I'd have jumped a mile, but the possum – for it was he – just stared. We got used to all this wildlife as time went by.

After one leg of the journey we stopped for the night at a campsite at Eungela (inland a bit from Mackay), with spectacular views from the top of a ridge and one lovely hotel complete with pool – and launch ramp for hang-gliders! At the campsite there were signs inviting visitors to take a woodland trail through the tropical rainforest, so we set off. That was a mistake. What started off quite innocuously as a clear, swept path ended up as an assault course, from which we finally emerged, sweating and swearing (them sweating, me swearing) as night was falling. As a diversion, Nick then assured me that a nearby stream and pool were full of platypus, so I set up post with my camera and tripod. I have some great shots of bubbles and ripples if you're interested: good ploy, Nick.

Further up the coast, we caught a ferry from Townsville to Magnetic Island, hired a Moke and found a beach for the day. There was room for us all in the Moke if we each carried a bit of the wheelchair – thank God for lightweight chairs. The beach was delightful, straight out of the brochures and practically deserted, except for flocks of brightly coloured lorikeets (wild budgies!) and a bar and grill in the shade of the trees. They served Cokes and stubbies (bottles of beer – I was beginning to talk Strine by then), as well as toasted sandwiches – what more could a chap ask for?

"We left in a hurry after ten days, before the scratched and scored skirting boards were discovered"

On the beach we made rather imaginative (I thought) use of a sturdy lilo which we had bought in Yeppoon. Any time I felt like a swim, I left the wheelchair with the rest of the stuff, sat on the lilo and went for a drag down to the water's edge. We felt quite smug after that. Our day on Magnetic was great fun, so much so that we repeated the exercise on the way back south.

By the time we reached Cairns, the novelty of living out of suitcases in a camper van was beginning to wear thin for Linda and I, so we were keen to find somewhere a bit more permanent. We moved into a campsite chalet, while Nick and Jane – hardier types – pitched their tent nearby. Linda was so relieved at finally being able to unpack that she prowled round our new home like an expectant lioness.

The chalets were all raised above the ground with two steps up, so once inside I was there for the night. There wasn't a great deal of room for the wheelchair, but I managed. We shifted the bed against the wall so that I could manoeuvre the chair from the bed to the bathroom, and that was all that was required. The room wouldn't have suited if I'd been alone, but it was only a place to sleep, after all – we spent all day every day outside, either exploring or loafing around the pool. We left in a hurry after ten days, before the scratched and scored skirting boards were discovered.

The high point of the whole journey was, of course, the Great Barrier Reef. We took a day trip out there on a big catamaran and had a wonderful time. The boat from Cairns was no problem (the loo was, but then with the heat . . .) and if getting into the water meant a little bum-shuffling it was more than worth it to be able to snorkel around and take it all in. I could make it to the stern in my chair and shuffle onto the diving platform (almost at deck level) which was then lowered to the water.

"On the odd occasion when we needed outside help we encountered nothing but good-humoured willingness"

I saw plenty, most of which I couldn't identify. There were thousands of brilliantly coloured reef fish, like you see in the pictures, but I particularly remember enormous groupers and giant clams. Through my diving mask the groupers seemed to be between two and four feet long and almost as broad. They looked fearsome but were quite harmless, I was assured. The clams were dotted about the sea bed and we swam down to take a closer look. In reality they close up very slowly, so that the old myth of divers getting their feet caught is just that – a myth.

The only slight disappointment was my inability to scuba dive. Nick could, and he hired a tank to go exploring a bit lower down the reef. He saw a great deal more as a result, and I envied him that. But the inability was nothing to do with the disability: there was a piece in the local paper while we were there about a young American paraplegic who was doing the diving course. I could have done it too, but I didn't want to commit myself to the same place for most of our stay in Cairns. For the same reason we only went to the reef once; as a diver I could have done a proper exploration, so learning to dive is now a priority.

One of the side trips on the reef was to Green Island, where I was unable to get to the underwater observatory.

Together with a rock pool at Josephine Falls on the journey up, these were the only two things I couldn't take part in during the entire trip.

We did one other beach day while we were in Cairns, to the Northern Beaches. We had become throughly spoiled by then, so the idea of sharing a beach with over a dozen more people didn't impress, but we went for a drag and a swim, splashing around for a good half-hour. There were marked and netted areas for swimming because it was "stinger" season – enormous box jellyfish are found along the Queensland coast from late October to early May, and they have a reputation for injuring and sometimes killing those who brush against them. While swimming, we noticed a couple of blokes sticking notices in the sand, but since the wording was facing away from the sea we ignored them. It was only after we got back to our towels that we read, *"Danger: no swimming allowed – netted areas infested with box jellyfish"*. Thanks, chaps.

Northern Queensland is very hot in January. We made two trips inland to escape the heat, to an area called the Atherton Tablelands. It was still hot here, but less sticky. It's dairy country and, if you don't look too closely at the vegetation, not unlike England. We visited a marvellous freshwater lake called Lake Eacham. Although I have always been a little wary of swimming in "fresh" water (because it is usually anything but), I think this was the best swimming I had in Australia (barring the reef, perhaps). There were picnic tables in the shade of gum trees, a disabled loo (it's a shame to have to use the design of public toilets as a yardstick for a good day out), and to get into the water all I had to do was fall off the jetty! It was only about a two-foot drop, so getting a lift out was not too difficult. The water was cool and crystal clear, a pleasant change from the sea, which was so warm it often wasn't refreshing at all.

Cairns is a fast growing town with its own international airport and several swish hotels. It has lots of smart clothes shops, and restaurants of varying standards. I ate an interesting "Dundee Platter" (water buffalo, crocodile and venison fillet, I am now embarrassed to relate) in one, and a pretty tasteless Mexican meal in another.

After ten days in Cairns we made our way south again. From Rocky we flew to Sydney (upgraded to first class, which was nice) and after weeks of slumming it in camper van, tents and campsite chalets, we booked into the *Southern Cross*, a smart hotel in the city centre. They have some adapted rooms and I thoroughly recommend it, as long as you don't want to use the rooftop pool, which is inaccessible.

Sydney is a nice city (usually a contradiction in terms as far as I am concerned): airy, cosmopolitan and dead easy to get around. We caught the harbour ferry (all sloped access) across to Manly and also went to the top of Centrepoint tower. We ate in Chinatown and drank in some smart bars; I'd like to go back some day.

We flew straight home from Sydney, on a modified 747 this time, to the worst snowfall for years. I wouldn't fly direct again, but that is nothing to do with being disabled – it's just a boring flight. I also wouldn't dream of suggesting that the whole trip was a doddle: there were times when obstacles did present themselves, but with a little planning (plastic stool for showers, lilo for sand-dragging sort of planning), most of them can be overcome without the frustration which would spoil any trip. We were with friends, but on the odd occasion when we needed outside help we encountered nothing but good-humoured willingness – "She'll be right, mate." I wouldn't do a trip like that on my own, but then I wouldn't anyway (tried it once, years ago, and had a rotten time).

What would we do differently next time? Steer clear of the meat pies – still the Australian national dish and to be viewed with suspicion – and make sure the mosquito spray is in a different shaped tin to the athlete's foot spray. I covered myself liberally with the latter one sultry night at the Cairns drive-in.

Old Haunts, New Thrills

Barbara and Bill Horrocks used to live in Australia, and in November 1988 they returned for a holiday – a sentimental journey, a reunion with friends and relatives, and an exploration of places not seen first time round. Barbara is a wheelchair user but can walk a little.

Our *Qantas* plane touched down at Sydney and passengers had to disembark even if Melbourne was their final destination. Because I am disabled we were allowed to stay on board and we took the opportunity to have a wash and brush up. From Melbourne we were booked on a domestic flight to Launceston, Tasmania, where Bill's brother and his Australian wife were waiting to meet us.

At Melbourne we were escorted by a friendly Aussie, who chatted twenty to the dozen. "No worries," he kept repeating, in the broadest Strine, as we made our way through customs and immigration and down miles of corridors to the luggage collection point, where I was reunited with my wheelchair. Unfortunately, the same could not be said of my suitcase. It had been off-loaded at Sydney. This proved to be only a minor hiccup, as my medication was in my hand luggage, and the suitcase turned up the next day.

Tasmania is a lovely island, about the size of England but with only a fraction of the population (less than 500,000) – ideal, then, for those who seek peace and quiet. Like England it has four distinct seasons and a temperate, though warmer and more settled, climate. The scenery is beautiful, with a great deal of variation.

We spent some time recovering from jet lag, discovering Launceston and meeting friends and relations before hiring a car and driving south to Hobart, the island's capital. The "motor-way" between the two cities turned out to be nothing more than a two-lane highway, but the traffic was very light by our standards.

Hobart is quite small, with a nice, "solid" feel to it. We visited Battery Point, reckoned to be the most complete colonial village in Australia. Many of the houses, all of which are lived in, are as they were in the 1830s and 1840s, with picturesque wrought-iron railings to their verandahs, yet the high-rise casino (without which no self-respecting Australian city is complete) is within walking – and wheeling – distance. Nearby Salamanca Place is a restored dockland area, chock-a-block with craft shops and restaurants.

No worries with access to the revolving restaurant on the top floor of the casino: it is reached by a lift which goes from the ground floor and opens directly into it. My memories of that evening are of good food and excellent service, complemented by ever-changing views of majestic Mount Wellington, the pretty harbour and the city nestling close against it, the magnificent Tasman Bridge and the vast, blue Southern Ocean which stretches without interruption from Tasmania to the South Pole. We were particularly lucky to be there for the end of the Sydney to Hobart yacht race, and to witness the winner drop her sails and come gracefully to rest.

"But for the efforts of a friendly Ansett travel clerk, who managed to find us a serviced apartment, we would have tasted the joys of sleeping in the park"

The next day we drove to the old convict settlement of Port Arthur, situated on a long, narrow peninsula and joined to the mainland by an even narrower neck of land. The terrain is rugged, with deep inlets reminiscent of Scottish lochs, and densely wooded mountains. The convicts were not intended to escape, and none who tried were successful. Closed in 1877, after a decline in the number of convicts, Port Arthur lay derelict for many years, but it has been beautifully restored.

We stayed two days in Hobart before driving back to Launceston up the east coast, passing through little seaside towns with familiar names – Swansea, Falmouth and Beaumaris – and others more exotic, like Triabunna, Bicheno and Binalong Bay, where we picnicked on fresh crayfish, purchased from a roadside stall.

By this time, having passed through Singapore and Bangkok on the way to Australia, we were old hands at airport procedures: when the staff at the Launceston check-in desk tried to transfer me into yet another airport wheelchair, we declined the offer. We pointed out that my own chair was more comfortable, easily folded and light to handle. After a little persuasion, they agreed, and I was not separated from my chair until we were at the door of the aircraft. After that I was never parted from my own wheelchair one minute sooner than necessary, and by the time our holiday ended we had flown in eighteen different aeroplanes and been in every conceivable kind of lift.

(Once, when we flew out to the Barrier Reef in a battered eight-seater, I was heaved into the aircraft by the pilot himself! Aussies have no delusions of grandeur, and will turn a hand to anything – or anybody! My slimline wheelchair came into its own on this occasion because the "hold" was the space behind the back seat, and a conventional wheelchair would have caused problems.)

Our plans included a three-day visit to Canberra, and that's where we headed next. I thought Canberra a stunning city, with its purpose-built Courthouse, Library and superb Parliament Building, which has a garden on the roof where you may walk, or be pushed, because the architect believed that the people should be above parliament. All the public buildings have easy access for wheelchairs and the city is flat as a fluke, so "no worries" if you fancy going walkabout. Once on the move, however, it is difficult to pick up a taxi, so make sure that your pusher is up to the task.

There's much to see in Canberra, and most of it's worth the seeing (including Australia's War Museum, although that might put a damper on the holiday spirit), but in the end it all seemed a bit sterile – soulless, some-how – and I was quite ready for Sydney, the next stop on our itinerary.

As we soon discovered, Sydney is anything but soulless; bustling and vibrant, it was the one place where we almost came unstuck. Not wishing to be tied to time, we hadn't booked ahead, and soon realised that neither love nor money would buy us a hotel bed for the night. But for the efforts of a friendly *Ansett* travel clerk, who managed to find us a serviced apart-ment, we would have tasted the joys of sleeping in the park.

But, as so often happens, our lack of foresight turned out for the best. We thoroughly enjoyed the apartment, which was quite luxurious and very centrally situated. We sallied forth each morning to explore, and never needed to use buses or trains, although we did resort to the odd taxi. All the fresh air gave us a healthy tan, and Bill developed some fine leg muscles.

We stayed five days, taking in the shops, Darling Harbour, Circular Quay and its adjacent Rocks – yet another resurrected dockland area, full of atmosphere. I was wheeled through Chinatown, and we took a taxi (a touch of extravagance there) out to the famous, but rather tatty, Bondi Beach. We rode the Monorail and enjoyed a fascinating tour of the Opera House, both of which have special facilities for the disabled. We also took a Captain Cook tour of the harbour, and the ferry boat crew, like the Monorail and Opera House staff, were more than helpful. We ate out each night – Italian, Chinese, Spanish, even Korean – and once at an open-air restaurant on the Rocks, built to resemble a sailing ship, complete with masts and sails. Of course, we had to find places that had easy access, but that was no real problem.

"We hired a car for the week so that we could do the sentimental journey bit"

Our next stop was Brisbane, where we once lived for three years. I was younger then, and not in any way disabled; in my eagerness to pick up the threads, I had forgotten what a hilly place it is. *The Summit Central Apartments*, though within normal walking distance of the centre, are situated high above the city. Bill's arm muscles grew to match those in his legs as he struggled to stop me running away from him, and the return, uphill journey was no joke in the sticky heat.

We hired a car for the week so that we could do the sentimental journey bit. The suburbs had grown a lot in twenty years, but otherwise they were much as we remembered: a jumble of pastel-coloured wooden houses, resembling a fading patchwork quilt, with many of them built on stilts to catch the breeze and allow the floodwaters to run away. Lush gardens, bright with bougainvillaea, poinsettia and jacaranda, sweep down to the river where the well-to-do have their own private jetties. Altogether it is a pleasant, easygoing, subtropical city, but for the disabled tourist, without old haunts and old friends to look up, I reckon two or three days would be enough, especially taking those hills into consideration.

Our last evening in Brisbane we dined al fresco at a riverside restaurant, on lobster, crayfish and gigantic prawns, accompanied by a salad which was a work of art to look at and a delight to eat. After saying our sentimental farewells the next morning, we set off in the hire car for Mackay, nearly 1000km to the north, well and truly in the tropics, and the gateway to the Barrier Reef.

"We were slightly disconcerted to be greeted by a hostess who appeared to have stepped straight out of 'Hi-De-Hi'"

If you like fruit you will never starve in this part of Queensland. Mangoes, pineapples, melons, bananas, pawpaws, and more, grow in profusion. Huge self-service fruit stores abound, and at farm gateways carts piled high with produce tempt the traveller to stop and buy. The owner is usually asleep under a large umbrella, or else there is a notice inviting customers to help themselves and throw their money in a bucket!

Motoring makes one aware of the size of Australia: mile after mile of unremarkable scenery goes by, punctuated by towns that are smaller than English villages; we were struck by the sameness of the gum trees and the fruit plantations, by the relentless dust, and the "highway" which in reality is a narrow strip of rather bumpy tarmac. The fruit

plantations gave way to sugar cane and, as evening fell, we reached Mackay, a pleasant little town which is part resort, part sugar terminal. We stayed one night; I'd have liked to have stayed longer, but our flight to the Barrier Reef was already booked.

Our little jaunt to the Barrier Reef and a later one to Ayers Rock were the only bits of our holiday which were in any way "packaged". There are dozens of islands and as many choices of accommodation. You pays your money and takes your choice. We chose South Molle, under the impression that it was less commercialised than some. Even so, I was a little worried that I would be out of place amongst so many bronzed, athletic specimens of humanity. As a wheelchair user I was in the minority, but in fact it didn't matter a bit.

We were slightly disconcerted to be greeted at South Molle Island by a hostess who appeared to have stepped straight out of "Hi-De-Hi", and we soon realised that our island was more developed than we had been led to believe. However, after the initial introduction, we were left to our own devices.

We had a lovely cabin right on the beach, with palm trees that rustled in the evening breezes and the lapping of the Coral Sea to lull us to sleep. During the day I sunbathed and wallowed in the warm sea water, while Bill went for walks around the island, collecting coconuts and bits of coral from the beach. We breakfasted each morning by the Olympic-sized pool, where we could have had snorkelling lessons and played water polo if we'd been that way inclined, and later we watched the brightly coloured reef fish from the wooden jetty, as they came in search of leftover bread rolls. Our evenings were spent just enjoying the balmy temperatures and gazing at the stars. Faint strains of music reached us from the bar-lounge, but these only served to heighten the romantic atmosphere.

After three days we were well rested and ready to resume our travels. Water-taxi and plane took us to Townsville, where we collected another hire car and drove to Cairns. If I had to choose one place out of all Australia in which to spend a holiday, it would be Cairns. A town of wide, shady boulevards on the Queensland coast, with the Atherton Tablelands at its back, Cairns is renowned for its big game fishing. The boats belong in a Hollywood movie – we simply looked and dreamed.

From Cairns we toured the Tablelands, both by car and by bus. It is an area of rushing waterfalls and dense, hardwood forests which open out into rich dairy farming country, dotted with towns which appear to be locked in a 1920s time-warp. At the opposite end of the scale, we visited Port Douglas, with its ultra luxurious *Sheraton Mirage* holiday complex and what is reputed to be the biggest free-form swimming pool in the world. We rode on the Kuranda scenic train, sipping champagne as we marvelled both at the breathtaking scenery and at the ingenuity and bravery of the men who constructed the railway during the gold rush. (Access to the train is difficult if you cannot walk at all.) We pottered about the villages that lie along this stretch of coast, buying souvenirs and gifts, and we had fun devising a way of cracking open a coconut which we found lying on the beach.

Eight days were too few, and it was with mixed feelings that we relinquished the hire car and flew to Alice Springs, the jumping-off point for our tour of Ayers Rock and The Olgas. Transfer from the airport to the town was by bus and the driver greeted us cheerfully: "Good afternoon, folks; welcome to Alice Springs. You're very lucky – it's cooler today, only 40 degrees. Yesterday was a scorcher (did he mean 40°C wasn't it?) and tomorrow the forecast is 43 degrees."

No wonder I almost burnt a tender part of my anatomy when I sank into my wheelchair, for it had been standing in the sun, and I was scantily clad! A cool beer was called for, but we were dismayed to realise that we had been foolish enough to arrive in Alice at 4pm on a Sunday and the town is dry until 7pm on Sundays. They were the longest three hours!

"We had spent five weeks on the move and it wasn't long enough"

The next morning the luxury coach arrived at 6.45am to take us to Ayers Rock, a five-hour journey with a stop for morning tea and a short break at a camel station, where the more adventurous members of our party could ride on one of the beasts.

Nothing – film, book or TV programme – had prepared me for the impact of Ayers Rock. Despite the proliferation of Aborigine souvenirs and the busloads of tourists, the Rock maintains its air of mystery, and I came away deeply moved and impressed by the dignified Aborigines and by the sincerity of their beliefs concerning Uluru, the name by which they know Ayers Rock.

I went prepared to remain on the bus whilst the more able-bodied visitors explored, and I was more than a little concerned about the whole thing. In the event, I saw as much of Ayers Rock as most. With the help of the *Pioneer Trailways* guide, a burly, cheery individual, and other willing tourists, I was wheeled, somewhat bumpily, around the base of the rock, and lifted into the caves to see the paintings. And I certainly wasn't the only one not to attempt the steep climb to the summit – you have to be very fit for that. There's nothing wrong with my eyesight, and I was able to enjoy the changing face of the rock as the sun went down, camera clicking frantically, the same as everyone else.

Our tour-about was almost over. The next day we flew to Melbourne, en route for Tasmania and a last visit with our relations. We had spent five weeks on the move and it wasn't long enough. Australia is a vast continent, pretty well adapted to the needs of the disabled. We covered many thousands of miles by land and air, but we still had to miss a great deal.

Our path was smoothed before we went by *Travelbag* of Alton, experts in their field who made all our initial bookings, and within Australia by *Ansett*, who produce beautiful brochures and through whom we were able to obtain not only plane tickets, but also hotel rooms and our tours to the Barrier Reef and Ayers Rock. I am grateful to the staff of *Qantas* and *Ansett*, who were unfailingly courteous, and to all the Aussies who helped me on my way.

Honeymoon First

As a result of a gunshot wound sustained whilst serving with the army in Northern Ireland in 1981, John Moore is disabled and uses a wheelchair most of the time. In 1989 he and his fiancée, Stephanie, took a five-week holiday in Queensland.

We arrived in Brisbane, Queensland's capital, to be greeted by my aunt and uncle, with whom we were to stay for much of our holiday. The sky that evening was dark and cloudless, studded with bright stars. By day or night, the sky is an impressive feature in the southern hemisphere, more vivid and colourful than England's dull shades of grey.

The southern Queensland climate is subtropical, with warm or hot days in the summer, and sunny, cool days in the winter. In January and February, heavy showers develop and the temperature can reach 85° F or so. In March, whilst we were there, it rained heavily for three days but then the clouds gave way to perfect blue skies and the occasional clump of pure white cloud. In the winter months (June to August), the weather is ideal, with very little rain and plenty of warm sunshine, temperatures averaging 72° F. Many Australians living in the cooler states

holiday in Queensland at this time of year.

Some of our time was spent with my relatives, visiting their favourite haunts. The Sunshine Coast, named for obvious reasons, is only a thirty-minute drive from their home in Burpengary, near Brisbane. At the southern end of the Sunshine Coast are the mysterious Glasshouse Mountains, the result of volcanic activity millions of years ago. The mountains, with their trachyte peaks, present weird and wonderful shapes, especially at dusk and dawn.

The mountains are surrounded by well-wooded pastures and plantations of tropical fruit, stretching towards the coast. Mooloolaba, Caloundra and Noosa Heads are small towns on the Sunshine Coast offering miles of unspoilt beaches and total serenity. Poised on the edge of Laguna Bay is the resort of Noosa Heads, with its 430-hectare national park containing a network of walking tracks that wind through the rainforest and command wonderful ocean views. The park also houses an animal sanctuary, and coastal lakes which are inhabited by elegant black swans, pelicans and cranes.

Everywhere we travelled along the Sunshine Coast we noticed the provision for disabled people; most places were accessible to wheelchairs. One outstanding example, often billed as one of the world's tackiest tourist attractions, was "The Big Pineapple", some 100km north of Brisbane. This large fruit plantation is among the most popular sights in Queensland: the 16-metre-high, plastic pineapple has a top-floor observation deck overlooking the tropical fruit trees.

Access is excellent, allowing disabled people to all levels, and we were particularly impressed with the audio-visual displays, telling the story of the pineapple. We managed a short ride on a sugar-cane train through acres of mangoes, pineapples, sugar cane, nuts and spices. Toilet facilities and car parking spaces for disabled people were provided everywhere, making me feel very welcome.

My aunt had kindly pre-booked a hand-controlled car from *Budget Rent a Car*, outlining my disability so that they could provide suitable controls. We used *Budget* because we had been pleased with their service on our previous holiday in Australia. It is advisable to book a vehicle well in advance and confirm it in writing.

"The whole area alive with wild creatures, including possums, cockatoos, frogs and lizards"

Driving regulations in Australia are virtually the same as in the UK – drive on the left, don't drink and drive, and don't exceed the speed limit which is 100km/hr. We were made aware of the Queensland police force's tough stand on speeding one hot and humid day, when we were caught travelling at 114km/hr and fined A$40 on the spot.

The car we hired had ample room to store my wheelchair in the boot. As well as automatic transmission (standard on most cars), it had the essential air conditioning – an absolute must when coming from a cold UK winter. In all we travelled nearly 3000km in three weeks, including a memorable trip to Mackay, some 970km north of Brisbane, at the southern end of the Great Barrier Reef.

On the map, the distance to Mackay seemed quite short, and there appeared to be only a few places worth visiting on the way. How wrong we were. The Bruce Highway follows the coastline of Queensland from Brisbane to Cairns. Only 80km north of Brisbane the dual-carriageway peters out, and the further north one travels the more remote and lonely the road becomes, although it is well maintained, with no potholes and very few tight bends.

The surrounding countryside is magnificent, with tall gum trees scattered about and the whole area alive with wild creatures, including possums, cockatoos, frogs and lizards. Unfortunately, we did not see many live kangaroos – most were lying at the roadside, victims of fast-moving cars and trucks. Kangaroos rest in the shade during daylight hours and move about at dusk and dawn, often crossing roads to reach new pastures; this is when most fatalities occur. Some vehicles have "roo-bars" fitted on the front to prevent damage from large kangaroos.

After a full day on the road, we stayed at the *Gladstone Country Club Motor Inn* which had a small number of rooms for disabled people, with flat access, wide doors, level shower and, of course, air conditioning. The next day we arrived in Mackay, a lovely town boasting modern shopping facilities and fantastic beaches which were completely empty. During our four-day stay at the *Miners Lodge Motel* (again, well equipped to accommodate disabled guests) we achieved our ambition of seeing the Great Barrier Reef – or, at least, a small part of it.

Our first glimpse of a reef was from the air. We hired a small aircraft and pilot from the airport nearby and planned a short flight over the Whitsunday Islands, landing at a remote island called Brampton for lunch and a quick swim. What an adventure! We spent nearly an hour in the tiny aeroplane, gazing at the beauty below – the clear greens and blues of the tropical sea, dotted with small islands and darkened in places by banks of reefs – and nearly three hours on Brampton Island which is a perfect setting for its luxury hotel with two fine swimming pools and a miniature airstrip. Our brief stay (too brief) allowed us to take a cool dip in the sea and enjoy a wonderful fresh salad on the patio outside the hotel, admiring a view of the sort only usually seen on postcards: a calm bay, surrounded by lanky palm trees and lush vegetation, with a pale blue sea washing gently along a narrow white sandy beach – paradise!

"An entrepreneur with a spray-gun treating queues of bronzed sunbathers with suntan oil"

The following day we boarded a large sea cruiser with about a hundred other people for a trip to Credlin Reef. At first we were unimpressed by what we saw – just endless sea and sky. But as soon as we were persuaded to try snorkelling our mood changed dramatically. Although I am only an average swimmer, without much use of my legs, I found snorkelling quite easy. Stephanie, too, was eventually coaxed into the water, and she enjoyed every minute.

The warm sea with the strong sun filtering through it, and the vibrant colours of fish and coral made our two-hour swim an unforgettable pleasure. The coral makes an incredibly beautiful picture, a dazzling mixture of purple, pink, yellow, white and red, sculpted into spectacular shapes. There are over 340 varieties of identified coral; the most common ones we saw were the staghorns and mushroom corals. Spread among these were waving fields of soft coral, colourful anemones, sea urchins and sea slugs. Shellfish clung to the reef while shoals of fish, including red emperors, coral trout and demoiselles, darted around us. Finally, with the tide going out and threatening

to strand us all, we returned to Mackay.

Back in Burpengary, we visited Brisbane's new Botanical Gardens which are in the foothills of Mount Coot-tha. The tropical house, in the form of a futuristic dome, has a superb display of plants and full wheelchair access. The gardens also contain a lagoon and pond, a demonstration garden, ornamental trees and shrubs, and a large collection of Australian native plants. Whilst in the area we called in at the Lone Pine Koala Sanctuary by the Brisbane River. There is good access and the keepers allow visitors to "cuddle" a koala and have their photograph taken, for a small fee. The sanctuary houses about a hundred koalas, some tame kangaroos, lizards and native birds.

Possibly one of the most well-known parts of Australia is the Gold Coast, where the Aussies go on holiday. Only an hour's drive south of Brisbane, it has a reputation for possessing all the glitz and glamour of an international resort but at about half the pace. The "Coast" is a stunning stretch of white, sandy beach, washed by white-capped waves and lined by modern apartment blocks, hotels and restaurants. This is a sun- and fun-lovers' paradise, and for those who can resist the enormous temptation to lie on the beach all day there is a great deal of entertainment on offer.

Dreamworld is a Disney-type fantasy for all the family; Sea World is Australia's largest marine park, with dolphins, whales and sea-lions on display. We chose Surfers Paradise, a resort known for its large waves, and we found ourselves a small spot on the beach as soon as we'd checked in to a comfortable and reasonably priced motel (*Earls Court Motor Inn*). We watched an entrepreneur with a spray-gun treating queues of bronzed sunbathers with suntan oil – the Australians have a healthy respect for the power of the sun and the risk of skin cancer.

After a few hot hours on the beach we returned to the motel to use the swimming pool there (the sea was far too rough for me). Towards evening we took a two-hour trip on a river cruiser around the man-made waterways to see the magnificent homes of some of Australia's richest people – impressive, but a bit too perfect!

During our short stay on the Gold Coast we spent a day in the hinterland around the Tambourine Mountains and the stunning areas of rainforest which are only a forty-minute drive from the beaches. The day we chose to go the weather was poor, with low cloud and occasional showers, but even that could not mar the beauty of the towering mountains, luxuriant rainforest and delicate orchids. Stephanie even managed to push me along a rough track beneath giant trees and staghorn ferns to a cascading waterfall. The fast-flowing waters, though, were extremely cold and we didn't feel brave enough to take a dip.

Our final visit to Brisbane, two days before we returned to the UK, was for an important event – our marriage! We had fallen in love with Australia on our first holiday there and decided to marry in Queensland. So in our case the honeymoon came first! Whether it's marriage, a honeymoon or a holiday you're after, I recommend Australia, especially for disabled people – you'll be surprised at the excellent facilities and easy access to most places.

Tasmania to the Tropics

Donald Crowther lives in Hobart, Tasmania, separated from mainland Australia by Bass Strait. As a result of arachnoid cysts in his spine, Donald is paraplegic and confined to a wheelchair. In July 1988 he travelled with his wife to Cairns, North Queensland.

We booked our return flight from Hobart straight through to Cairns with *East West Airlines* about ten weeks before we intended to travel. There were two reasons for choosing this airline: it was the only one which allowed us to make the journey without changing planes, and it was cheaper than the larger operators, *Australian Airlines* and *Ansett Australia*.

A week before we were due to leave, our travel agent called to say that our return flight with *East West* had been cancelled, and arrangements made for an alternative flight with *Ansett*, leaving Cairns at 6am, changing at Brisbane and Sydney where there would be an hour's wait, then flying to Melbourne for a three-hour stopover before flying on to Hobart. We were not at all pleased with this development, so after much negotiation we were booked on a flight leaving Cairns around noon, with a change at Brisbane, then direct to Melbourne and only a short wait there for the flight to Hobart.

A couple of days before our departure my doctor called and fitted a catheter. This allowed me some time to get used to it before flying. At Hobart airport my wheelchair and I were put on a fork-lift truck and driven to the small Fokker where we were lifted to the aircraft door. I was carried to my seat while my chair was stowed in the hold.

During the six-hour flight the airline staff were very helpful; we landed at Devonport, Sydney, Coolangatta,

Brisbane, Townsville and, finally, Cairns. My wheelchair was waiting on the tarmac when the fork-lift lowered me from the aircraft, and I was wheeled to the reception lounge where our daughter, Jill, was waiting.

"The manageress was very hostile, and said that she would refuse to take disabled people in wheelchairs in future"

Jill had booked us into a self-catering unit at *City Gardens Hotel/Motel*. This consisted of a large living room, bedroom with two single beds, toilet and shower, a kitchen with stove, dish-washer and fridge, and a laundry with washing machine and dryer. Like most modern beds, ours were too low – OK to get into but too low to get out of – and this was the cause of the only unpleasantness we encountered on our trip.

My wife went to the reception desk and explained the problem, suggesting as a solution a brick placed under each leg. The manageress was very hostile, and said that she would refuse to take disabled people in wheelchairs in future. A young Swedish student, work-ing as a general porter, overheard this and came round to our room to apolo-gise for the rudeness of the reception-ist. He found two wooden beams which he placed under the bed, and this did the job to perfection.

Cairns is very flat and ideal for a wheelchair. It's in the tropics but all the buildings are air-conditioned. On our first day we booked a Calm Water Lunch Cruise, which started at the pier. I was pushed up the gangway onto the enclosed upper deck of the catamaran, *Terri-Two*.

We cast off and sailed into the harbour, with a running commentary from the skipper on the various vessels that we passed, including Jacques Cousteau's floating observatory with rotary paravane sails. Also pointed out were the old Customs House, now converted into a modern shopping arcade, the naval dockyard and the seaplane base where the Americans used to operate Catalinas in World War II.

A little further on we entered the mangroves, where we spotted blue cranes, white egrets and a giant sea eagle. Usually it is possible to see the odd crocodile sunning itself in the heat of the day, but not that day. We pulled into one of the little inlets for lunch, a pre-packed meal of chicken and prawn salad and various tropical fruits.

Starting back after lunch along another stream, we passed an old hulk, the story of which was related by our skipper. In the 1950s a man called Moodie came to Cairns. He was believed to be a Canadian and his inten-tion was to build a boat out of mangrove wood. Everyone laughed at this, as it is well known that mangrove timber doesn't float. Moodie's reply was that steel doesn't float, but they build ships out of it and they float!

After a spell in town, Moodie disap-peared into the swamp, appearing at times to buy supplies and fittings for what became known as "Moodie's Ark". When several weeks went by without his customary trips to Cairns for supplies, the police were called in. They went to Moodie's camp and found him dead. He died of a heart attack, and rumour has it that there is a fortune in a Cairns bank, waiting to be claimed by Moodie's next of kin. So far, despite enquiries in Canada and Ireland, no one has been found.

Another way to explore the mangrove swamp is the Board Walk, which is close to Cairns airport and accessible to wheelchairs. The walk is raised about two metres above the swamp and there is a choice of routes, one taking about twenty minutes, the other about an hour. A notice at the entrance advises visitors to smear themselves liberally with insect repel-lent, but we did not take this precaution and suffered no bites. The advantage of the Board Walk is that it enables the visitor to view the various types of mangrove growth at close quarters and, by remaining quiet for a short time, to see many of the swamp's inhabitants, including crabs and mud skippers, birds and butterflies.

Our next cruise was a full-day outing to Green Island, a coral outcrop of the Great Barrier Reef about 20km east of Cairns. It's a real "Robinson Crusoe" tropical island, with a good selection of white coral beaches, swaying coconut palms and thatched huts.

Once again the journey was by fast catamaran. To board it I went up the gangway to the top deck but at the island I was carried to the lower deck for unloading. The island is totally accessible and there is a large outdoor café/bar where you can eat under palm-thatched shelters. Among the many attractions on Green Island is the aquarium – with crocodile pens – and an exhibition of Aboriginal arts and Melanesian culture.

My special interest is agriculture, so the most fascinating visit of our holiday for me was on the mainland, to a fruit farm northwest of Mossman. The proprietors have planted an array of tropical fruit trees and shrubs, and a guide takes parties of about ten people around the trees, explaining where each one came from and describing the taste and use of the the fruit. Back in the reception area we were able to sample some of the dried fruits as well as those fresh fruits that were in season.

Innisfail, to the south of Cairns, is the heart of the sugar industry and on the Bruce Highway is the CSR Sugar Museum, very well laid out and readily accessible to the wheelchair-bound visitor. Displays chart the development of the early sugar plantations and describe how the Kanaks (South Sea Islanders) were brought in to work the fields. Later, the Italians started to dominate the industry in north Queensland. We saw the old locomo-

tives and lorries, as well as the equipment used in the harvesting and processing of cane sugar, and finished our visit with an interesting film.

Some 20km or so from Innisfail, on the Palmeston River, is the legendary Babinda. The story goes that two Aborigines fell in love but they were from different tribes so their love was forbidden. They ran away together but the elders of the tribes chased them. When cornered, the two lovers jumped into the deep waters of the gorge at Babinda and were drowned. The spirit of the girl remains and lures single young men to their death: every year there is some tragedy, when young men slip off the rocks into the freezing water. There are strong undercurrents, and the men are gone in moments. A plaque at the entrance reads "In loving memory of our beloved son, who came for a visit and stayed for ever".

"I would make the trip for this view alone"

We took a number of day trips during the remainder of our two-week holiday, including a few to some of the beautiful beaches in the area – Holloway Beach, Yorkeys Knob and Trinity Beach – and a spectacular train trip to Kuranda. Unfortunately, the wheelchair and occupant have to be lifted manually both onto and out of the train, but the journey is well worth the trouble.

The train follows the coastal plain, through fields of sugar cane, and then starts to climb the mountains. The track hugs the mountainside and crosses chasms on trestle bridges to pass in front of the breathtaking Barron Falls – I would make the trip for this view alone. There are steps out of the station at Kuranda, so we were unable to visit the town and its market, but we had a cup of tea and admired the station gardens before returning.

We drove to the Tablelands, following the zigzag road from the coastal plain, up through dense rainforest to fertile plateau and the small town of Atherton, centre of a thriving tobacco and groundnut industry. Our next stop was Lake Tinaroo, where the North Queensland Electricity Authority have built a dam and developed the lake into a recreational area, with café, boating and walks. We had lunch and went for a short stroll, meeting a cassowary along the way. One of Australia's comic birds, the cassowary is rather like an ostrich but with bright blue legs. Some visitors were feeding it but this bird can be dangerous and is best given a wide berth.

On the way to Mossman we stopped for a light lunch at the expensive *Sheraton Mirage Port Douglas*. It is completely accessible and its golf course, acres of tropical gardens and swimming pools are worth seeing, but only the very affluent will consider staying. We were disappointed that we could not travel to Cooktown – the roads are not good and the boats not accessible to wheelchair users.

But we did not miss very much, and finished our holiday with a slap-up dinner at the *Cairns Hilton* to celebrate Jill's birthday. The town is so level that we were able to walk – and wheel – to the hotel and back. In spite of the muddle over our return flight to Hobart, it went off without a hitch.

In my experience, travel for paraplegics in Australia is generally easy. I carry a fold-up toilet, which is accepted by airlines and takes up very little space in the car. If travelling by car it is advisable to stop at about 3.30pm and book your accommodation, especially in popular areas. Australian country motels are usually one storey and accessible. If booking a hotel in advance state the width of your wheelchair, as some bathroom doors are too narrow. One thing is certain: nothing is perfect for everyone. Beds may be too low, or even too high, and toilets may lack rails or grab-bars, or be tucked behind doors, but most facilities are usable or adaptable.

A Spirit of Adventure

Operation Raleigh takes young people all over the world to give them the opportunity to develop their self-confidence and leadership skills. The venturers come from a variety of countries and the projects they undertake involve scientific research, community tasks and adventure. In the summer of 1989, after a demanding selection process and hectic months of fund-raising to cover the cost of his place, Roger Elliott, who has spina bifida and is confined to a wheelchair, joined an expedition to Queensland as a member of staff.

On arrival in Cairns I found the temperature very warm and the airport staff very helpful, quickly taking me through all the formalities. Although Cairns is the newest international airport in Australia, there was only one disabled parking bay, which was hard to find; the door of the disabled toilet was difficult to open and the layout poor. I hope that the new terminal building, which was under construction, will provide better facilities.

The drive to Operation Raleigh's base at Herberton, southwest of Cairns, was eventful as we took the road which runs round the Gillies Range – there are 186 hairpin bends! It's a distance of not much over 100km but the drive takes about one and a half hours, especially at night when you have to watch out for cattle, kangaroos and other wildlife on the road. The area around Herberton is known as the Atherton Tablelands and comprises volcanic lakes set in virgin rainforest, rolling outback plains and rich red farmlands.

Our headquarters was a disused vehicle workshop which by its very nature had limited facilities. It became known as "Laurel's Shed", Laurel being the owner of the property. She lived nearby and became a good friend. Our living conditions were very basic: two electric rings for cooking (I never want to see pasta again!); the water was often cold and clothes had to be hand washed or taken to the launderette in Atherton. In October we had to call the fire brigade to burn off the undergrowth around Laurel's Shed because of an influx of poisonous snakes and tics which had hospitalised a local person and killed one of Laurel's cats.

My first job was to telephone the manager of the bank to be used by the expedition, as part of my duties related to the finances of the project. I found that access was going to be difficult as there was a flight of steps at the entrance to the bank. After some discussion it was agreed that we should meet in the staff rest-room at the rear of the bank which would be accessible with some help.

I discovered that both Herberton and Atherton had access problems. In order to enter many of the shops I required assistance and because of the hilly nature of the area and the high summer rainfall, high kerbs and storm gullies are needed to deal with the volume of water. However, I always found the locals ready and willing to assist me.

After two days in Australia I was driven to Cairns to collect my hire car from *Budget*, who had fitted hand controls to a four-door, two-litre automatic with power steering and air conditioning. A couple of slow trips around the block were enough to get used to the American-style hand controls. I tried the wheelchair in various positions in the back of the car, but finally had the front passenger seat removed, which provided a better storage area.

"I had been told in London that the expedition would be hard work and not a holiday"

Because of the distances between the towns and cities in Australia, it is necessary to plan journeys carefully, checking the types of road you will encounter, and to take a map, noting the names of the towns you will pass through. You must check oil, water, petrol, brakes and tyre pressures, and look under the vehicle for any leaks or loose parts. Spare cans of water and petrol should be carried, also chewing gum in case of damage to the fuel tank. You should take some food and drinking water, and stop regularly while on the road to refill the petrol tank and to drink.

The monotony of driving through mile after mile of outback is relieved by the sight of wheeling kites and eagles on the lookout for food and swooping on unsuspecting small mammals, birds and snakes. Other wildlife to be spotted include kangaroos, wallabies, emus, budgerigars and colourful parrots.

If you have a breakdown, you should stay with your vehicle and if it is very hot get into the shade underneath the car. However, when I had a puncture at night, while returning from a visit to some newly made friends, I waited for thirty minutes for a passing car without success. I got out my wheelchair and made my way back to a small town, where I found that the home of the garage proprietor was only accessible up a flight of steps. Having managed to attract attention, I was invited in to wait while the garage owner took my car keys and sorted out my problem, for which he made no charge.

I had been told in London that the expedition would be hard work and not a holiday. This certainly proved to be the case – no eight-hour days and five-day weeks! Apart from work on the accounts, I helped with public relations, talking to schools and other groups about the work of *Operation Raleigh*. The radio was manned by a staff member in order to keep in touch with the project sites, and I did this from time to time.

"There was so much to see, hear and smell that I simply let my senses take over"

There were two disabled people among the forty members of staff, and one disabled (deaf) venturer out of 109 youngsters from Australia, Italy, Japan, the UK and USA. The venturers were divided into groups and moved from site to site in order to involve them in as many projects as possible. Only six or eight staff remained at base at any one time; most were out on the sites, supervising the projects. Considering the range of ages and backgrounds among staff and venturers, the atmosphere was generally harmonious and a spirit of adventure and enthusiasm always evident.

I was able to visit some of the sites, most notably that at Cape Tribulation, where Captain Cook's ship, *Endeavour*, went aground in 1770. Here, where the rainforest literally meets the reef, the venturers assisted the Parks Service with the construction of a walking trail, incorporating signage, displays and viewing points. The only access to the national park is via the Daintree River ferry and a four-wheel drive vehicle, and it was a relief to find a level car park on arrival in the national park.

The trail included a 400-metre boardwalk which I was invited to try out in my wheelchair. Walking or pushing was easy, and there was so much to see, hear and smell that I simply let my senses take over. There are some eighty different types of trees towering above, creating a canopy through which shafts of sunlight pick up the hues of the multicoloured birds and butterflies. Below the lush undergrowth, insects scurry about, collecting and consuming fallen vegetation, and the brush-turkey and flightless southern cassowary peck busily at the ground. I found it all very exciting and it is good to know that the new boardwalk will enable disabled Australians and tourists to enjoy this experience.

I went to the Undarra lava tubes, a huge radial pattern of tunnels nearly 100km in length, formed by the movement of lava outwards from a series of now-extinct volcanoes. It is hoped that the area can be opened up to tourists; an airstrip has already been constructed and hotel accommodation is planned. The venturers checked to ensure that all existing caves were plotted accurately, numbered and tagged. They did a thorough survey of each cave and the vegetation around the entrances, finding some rare and unrecorded species of insects. The lumps of volcanic rock strewn over the area prevented access in my wheelchair, but with the help of the venturers I was carried up to the entrance of a couple of the caves. The trees and ferns are greener here because most of the caves contain water. An unpleasant smell greeted me, resulting from the bat droppings and the damp.

"The rains came and with them an invasion of cane toads, croaking in chorus"

I also visited the canoeing and rafting project on the Gregory River where, with some difficulty, I was able to do some canoeing. I saw the restoration work being carried out by the venturers on the old jailhouse and the railway station in Normanton and, because some of our other projects were delayed by a hold-up of equipment in the Melbourne dock strike, I arranged for the Bishop of Carpentaria's church at Forsayth to be completely refurbished. Due to the condition of the church, services were being held in the local pub but on November 23 the church was reconsecrated.

I joined in some of the activities of the area, attending the Tin Miners' Festival Ball, the Atherton Flower Show, theatrical performances and viewings of work by local artists. I was contacted by the Chairman of the Atherton Disabled Group and invited to meet them and talk about access and facilities for the disabled in the Greater London area. I helped them to start a survey for presentation to the local authority.

As summer started, the rains came and with them an invasion of cane toads, croaking in chorus. The smaller ones came in under the door of the shed to join the large spiders and a range of other insects that kept us company. Clothes had to be shaken and shoes checked every morning. More friendly, if noisy, visitors were the kookaburras who came to the shed daily in the hope of being fed. Their usual diet is insects, reptiles and small mammals but they eagerly accepted sausages and burgers, and some became so tame that they could be hand fed.

Although life was tough and the work hard, I did make the most of my free time. I did a 3000-kilometre drive, starting down the coast road which leads from Cairns to Townsville. I stopped at Cardwell, in sugar cane territory, where I stayed on the waterfront, in a guesthouse run by a very pleasant Australian family who provided excellent room-service meals. There are superb views over the Great Barrier Reef and Hinchinbrook Island, the world's largest island national park, with towering mountains, sometimes shrouded in cloud, waterfalls and thick vegetation. It is possible to take a boat trip around the clear waters of the Hinchinbrook Channel – 56km of enclosed waterways to view some of the 400 species of coral, 1500 varieties of tropical fish and many unique forms of marine bird life.

"At small airstrips it is not at all unusual to find cows or kangaroos creating a hazard"

From Townsville I took the main road which follows the line of the railway to Mount Isa. The capital of northwest Queensland, Mount Isa is built around a huge copper, silver, lead and zinc mine, attracting miners from all over the world. Underground excavations exceed 380km and there are 120km of underground railway lines. Tours of the mine, both below and above ground, are available and I was able to go a mile underground and watch the trains and special mining vehicles at work. I also went to the mining exhibition which opened in 1988 and is the only one of its kind in Australia.

Other stops on my journey were Pentland, Hughenden, Julia Creek and Cloncurry (home of the first flying doctor base). One night, having not found anywhere to stay, I pulled off the road and prepared to sleep in the car. This was fine for a while, but I was soon disturbed by kangaroos grazing nearby and passing road trains, so I decided to drive on. I was horrified to discover that the wheels were bogged down in loose shingle and I could not move the car.

I waited until a lorry approached in the opposite direction and flashed him down with my headlights. He stopped, climbed down from his cab, and I explained the problem. He fished out a tow rope and in minutes had me back on the road. His parting gesture was to hand me a copy of a map showing all the lorry parks on the

Flinders Highway, a kind thought and typical of the help I so often received in Australia.

In addition to a great deal of driving, I did some flying. Tourists can join the mail planes on their flights and I went to Normanton as well as several cattle stations. When landing at small airstrips it is not at all unusual to find cows or kangaroos creating a hazard. The pilot has to perform a low flyover, or sometimes two, to frighten them off.

I obviously wanted to see the Great Barrier Reef, so I took a flight on one of the seaplanes that fly over it. I chose the 43-year-old Grumman Widgeon with the apt registration VH-WET, and flew over the reef to Princess Charlotte Bay, home of the main prawn fishing fleet. I was also lucky to be invited to join privately chartered aircraft for a number of trips, including one to a tin mine at Kangaroo Creek and another to the biggest gold mine in Australia at Kidston (no samples allowed!). I even tried rounding up cattle in a helicopter (a Bell 47). We flew very low among the trees, rapidly changing direction and catching the branches with the helicopter's landing skis. I love flying but have never felt so vulnerable, and I was sure that we would crash. It was an experience I do not wish to repeat!

While taking a look at Mareeba airport, I accepted an invitation from a helicopter pilot to join him on a flight to check bush fires in the area. I was surprised by the loud retorts of exploding tree trunks, and the pungent smell of burning eucalyptus. By day, all one sees are large areas of smoke, but by night the red ribbon of fire is a dramatic sight. The fires can be started by electrical storms, careless picnickers or landowners clearing the area to encourage new growth of grass for cattle. Normally left to burn themselves out, the fires can get out of hand if a strong wind develops. Then the small fire brigades are joined by the local community to create fire-breaks in an attempt to stop the fire spreading.

I flew home to England in November, leaving behind a temperature of 85°F and arriving at a very chilly Heathrow. At Christmas I exchanged greetings cards and letters with some of the Operation Raleigh staff and venturers as well as some of the Australians I met. It is good to keep in touch and perhaps meet again sometime. I only saw a very small part of Australia and I hope to return. In the meantime I have had some interesting experiences, and retain many great memories and *hundreds* of photographs!

Family Matters in Sydney and Perth

Lorna Hooper has multiple sclerosis (MS), diagnosed in 1980, and she is now confined to a wheelchair. She travelled to Australia at the end of July 1989.

I was both excited and alarmed when my second son David brought his Australian fiancée home to meet the family and wanted us all to attend their wedding in Mudgee, northwest of Sydney. One of my problems is that I cannot stand heat and I know that Australia can be very hot. After my first reaction, which was to say, "Yes, we'll go", I got cold feet. But David and Raeleen decided that their wedding would take place in August, which is of course winter in the southern hemisphere, and remembering my son's words ("think positive, Mum") I resolved to make the trip, come what may.

It is absolutely vital for anybody as disabled as I am to undertake such a journey with a companion of the same sex. My daughter Catherine agreed to accompany me and to share with my husband Brian the problems involved in taking me to the loo. I suffer incontinence and my bowels frequently take me by surprise. In private places Brian could cope, but not all public conveniences have facilities for the disabled, and in these situations Catherine took over.

"If we had known then what we know now, we would have faced the trip with confidence"

A secretary in London and well used to making travel arrangements for her boss, Catherine undertook all the bookings. She found that by travelling with *Qantas* we could have a free internal flight; this proved useful as my brother and his family live in Perth and we wished to spend some time with them in Western Australia.

We chose to break the journey at Singapore to give me time to adjust to jet lag. Besides, the thought of such a long flight appalled me: I am restricted to sitting most of the time but it is vital that I exercise my limbs and move around a little as I would otherwise seize up. There is not much room in airline seats and there are no special seats for disabled passengers. Brian worried about the effect of the heat in Singapore on me but his fears were largely dispelled by the facts that I survived the hot English summer of 1989 better than expected, and that our hotel in Singapore would be fully air-conditioned.

I was at first refused a visa on medical grounds, but a report from my doctor, who said that I was fit to undertake the journey, soon did the trick. As the day of our departure approached we were filled with a mixture of excitement and apprehension. On reflection, if we had known then what we know now, we would have faced the trip with confidence. Our fears were mainly figments of our imaginations – visions of embarrassing ordeals and insurmountable barriers. As it turned out, all were unfounded.

When we arrived at the aircraft door the cabin crew brought a small aisle wheelchair, to which I was transferred. I was wheeled to my seat and lifted into it by my husband and one of the stewards. My own chair was loaded in the hold and transported free of charge. One of our worries was that it would be lost, or even parts of it lost, because it disassembles into five parts. But we labelled every part and suffered no losses.

One minor setback in all the aircraft was the lack of space in the loos for somebody like me who requires the assistance of a helper. Most of the aircraft we boarded had no special toilets for disabled passengers; the ones we did see had grab-rails either side of the seat but were only slightly larger. Brian and Catherine found it quicker and easier to manhandle me to the nearest toilet, where with some difficulty my daughter provided the necessary assistance.

The journey to Singapore consisted of a flight to Athens, a one-hour wait there and a further eleven and a half hours to Changi airport, Singapore. I managed to get away with only two visits to the toilet on the second leg. Catherine explained my predicament to passengers queuing for the toilets and they gave me priority. I found people very kind and considerate, willingly allowing me to jump the queue.

I did of course go equipped with incontinence pants and pads, and these frequently needed changing. However, to avoid real embarrassment we had prepared ourselves well: my doctor had arranged for me to have a supply of enemas, which could be self-administered, and I had one before each flight.

At two of the airports on our itinerary (Changi and Sydney) disabled passengers were boarded by "high lift" – a vehicle which operates hydraulically and looks rather like a large removals van but has a platform at the rear and over the front cabin. Its only drawback is the time it takes. When we arrived at Sydney the three of us in wheelchairs were last to disembark. By the time we claimed our luggage and were free to leave, all the other passengers had gone. Fortunately, David and Raeleen had the fortitude to hang on for a bit and we eventually met up – great relief all round. Mind you, we saw parts of airports that one is not normally permitted to see, and I greatly appreciated the efforts made by *Qantas* to accommodate me – I cannot praise them enough.

Although we loved the hustle and bustle of the City of Singapore, we found it to be a paradise for shoppers and gourmets rather than for wheelchairs and disabled people. The hotel staff were helpful and the taxi drivers very considerate, but being pushed around on the uneven pavements was most uncomfortable. Sydney, however, is a different world, where disabled people are well catered for.

Australian hotels and motels are required by law to provide facilities for disabled guests. There were plenty of adapted loos and these were always spotless. (The first thing we noticed about Australia was the lack of litter.) When we visited attractions such as zoos, gardens and marine parks I was allowed in free and my "pusher" at half price.

Our first few days in Sydney involved champagne breakfast at a beach café in Manly, a suburb of Sydney where David played most of his rugby. We toured the beach and promenade, and I bought a handmade stone replica of a duck-billed platypus. We sunbathed on Palm Beach and visited the zoo, which is known for its spectacular view over the city. A ride on a monorail also gave us a bird's-eye view of part of the city and the harbour.

After about a week we left Sydney and crossed the Blue Mountains, climbing well over 900m and then dropping down to the inland plateau where the town of Mudgee is situated, some 450m above sea level. The drive took four and a half hours – Australians always measure journeys in time rather than distance.

"I was above the guard rail, looking straight down – I've never been so scared in my life"

Mudgee is a renowned vineyard area and we stayed amongst the vines at a motel built and run by David's new parents-in-law. The motel (*Hithergreen Lodge*) had one room for disabled persons, with a large *en suite* washroom, toilet and shower complete with grab-rails. We were the first guests to test it out and I am pleased to say the room passed with flying colours.

The wedding was to take place in the Mudgee church and the reception at the motel. The day before the wedding my husband was taken fossicking (panning for gold), admittedly in a worked-out creek but he thoroughly enjoyed the experience. Meanwhile, I had a facial, my first ever, and I felt wonderful afterwards. I was also taken out by a lady friend of the family to look around Mudgee. I saw some beautiful, old colonial-style bungalows and some very fashionable new ones, with a multitude of different coloured roof tiles, so that no two roads looked alike. I was taken a few miles into the bush, where my guide's husband had grown up during the depression in a little cottage made from mud and wattle. The earthen floors were kept damp in the hot weather to keep it cool and lay the dust.

After the wedding, which went off very well, we all felt rather flat, so decided to go hot-air ballooning. I was lifted in by my other son Richard and placed on a stool, so that I could see over the top of the basket. David held on to me and then Richard got in, the idea being that two strapping helpers would be better than one. However, when the pilot got in, the balloon would not take off, so Richard had to get out and Raeleen took his place.

What a wonderful trip it was, so quiet and peaceful, and of course a completely different view of the landscape. I saw the Blue Mountains in the distance, giving off the deep blue haze from which they derive their name – this results from the scattering of light by dust and droplets of oil exuded from the leaves of the eucalyptus trees, a phenomenon found nowhere else in the world. The pilot gave me a perfect landing, but everyone else a bumpy one – I think he wanted to shock all the others but took pity on me.

In the evening we went out looking for kangaroos and saw about eight. They are very shy creatures and we were lucky to come upon them so close to the town. We were treated to another memorable glimpse of Australian wildlife the next day, in the Blue Mountains, where we saw some beautiful birds, mainly galahs (cockatoos), their plumage bright with lovely colours. We also saw and heard the famous kookaburra. The viewing points in the mountains were accessible to wheelchairs, a ramp being provided next to any steps.

One viewpoint we stopped at had a vertical drop of several hundred feet immediately below. I was sitting on a bench further back when Richard came over and said, "Mum, this you must see." He picked me up and carried me over to the edge; with him being so tall and me at chest level, I was above the guard rail, looking straight down – I've never been so scared in my life.

Back in Sydney, on one of our last days, we hired a launch, both families joining for a final celebration. No sooner were we under way than out came the champagne. Raeleen's father had been attached to the harbour

police earlier in his career and was able to point out all the landmarks – the famous "coat-hanger" bridge, the Opera House and Darling Harbour where all the tall ships moored during the bicentenary celebrations – and also the best place to buy fresh prawns and oysters for lunch.

The men took turns steering the launch and my husband was delighted that during his turn he piloted the boat back under the bridge – not many people can claim to have done that. We wound up a perfect day with dinner at the top of the Centrepoint tower, which has a revolving restaurant over a thousand feet above the city. The views over the city lights were magnificent.

"The wild flowers were just beginning to come out. I brought a few home, pressed them and put them amongst our photographs"

All good things come to an end, and we had to move on to the second part of our trip, visiting my brother, his wife and son in Perth. We hadn't met for 26 years and after all that time wondered how we would get on. We needn't have worried; in no time at all we were chattering like monkeys, recalling events from our early days and bringing each other up to date with our lives. He took a week off work and showed us round the city.

We liked Perth, with its old-style city centre, pedestrian precincts and first-floor shopping galleries. It was all so clean, and unspoilt by new blocks set amongst the old buildings. We wandered in Kings Park and gazed down at the Swan River. My husband, once a keen cricketer, insisted on visiting the WACA (for the uninitiated, this means West Australian Cricket Association) ground where he touched the sacred turf.

While in Perth we met old school friends who had retired to the area; it certainly seemed to be a popular place for people who had lived abroad most of their lives and did not fancy returning to the cold, damp UK. None of our friends had experienced any difficulty integrating into Australian society. We had heard before our trip that the British were not too popular in Australia but we found everybody most amicable and pleasant.

The temperature was considerably warmer than in Sydney, and the wild flowers were just beginning to come out. I brought a few home, pressed them and put them amongst our photographs in the album. They set it off beautifully. It was a memorable first visit to Australia and although I do not suppose we will ever go again I like to think that I could. Who knows? We might have to return to see our first grandchild.

An Outdoor Life

Sheila Murray is a single parent with a severely mentally and physically handicapped daughter, Thea. In November 1987, just before Thea's third birthday, Sheila took her to Australia for a holiday.

"And if you ever get the money together, do come and visit." I have friends, both nurses, who emigrated to Australia in 1981 and now live in semi-luxury in a suburb of Perth. How could I resist? We had the money – my savings from when I last worked – and we had the time. After making a few telephone calls, taking advice from friends and the medical world, the project seemed more and more attractive.

Thea is severely brain damaged as a result of meningitis. She cannot walk or talk but is a bright, happy child and a joy to be around. I owe it to her and myself to give her the best possible quality of life and that includes a taste of adventure! We finally boarded the jumbo jet after months of planning, careful checking of dates to ensure that we lost no benefits, and obtaining letters from doctors declaring her fitness to travel.

The flight was better than I expected, although Thea was awake for nearly twelve hours with excitement, and she lived on a diet of porridge and bananas for twice as long. We changed flights at Singapore, where we were shown great kindness by the Chinese airport staff; I doubt if any of them will forget the sight of me squatting in the crowded lounge in oppressive heat, trying to get some liquid into Thea.

After an ecstatic reunion, over a champagne and croissant breakfast, my friends and I began to plan the next four weeks. The feeling of freedom from doctors' appointments, physiotherapy and hospital visits was worth every penny – I was finally alone with my child. The most immediate problems were practical, and a trip to the shops for supplies was necessary that afternoon; forget jet lag – I was not going to miss a minute!

"She was in the swimming pool every day with the local children whether she was in agreement or not"

The Sunday markets in Australia are a treat – no licensing laws, so a whole week's shopping can be done, including exotic vegetables, fruits, seafood, meat, even clothes. Suitable nappies proved difficult – I could not find my favourite brand and many were tried before I eventually settled on a satisfactory alternative. A small slip-mat for the shower and a potty were the other basic essentials.

Staying with friends was a bonus as they had all the required sun blocks and fly repellents for Thea. She was lathered up each morning, and since we all spent so much time keeping her out of the sun it was a surprise to watch her turn a honey brown. Although visiting British passport holders can be treated in public hospitals under the reciprocal agreement between the NHS and Australia's public health care system (Medicare), my hosts had provided for us temporarily on their private health insurance policy. To be absolutely safe I had also taken out insurance to cover any medical expenses that might be incurred.

The two teenage daughters of the house readily and eagerly took over much of the physical caring for Thea – she was in the swimming pool every day with the local children whether she was in agreement or not. Thea loved the stimulation of a happy, noisy household. The hot climate seemed to encourage visiting, and the pool was always full of laughter.

A small capsule on the West Coast, Perth is an exciting, vibrant, skyscraper city with the emphasis on a modern experience rather than culture. There were few problems with wheelchair access, lifts in all stores and ramps in air-conditioned shopping malls. I am used to the stares of the general public when out with Thea but this was not much in evidence down under. In fact, people were friendly and more than once I was stopped by passers-by: "My sister's boy has cerebral palsy – his name is Tom, what's your little girl called?" Few inhibitions and a refreshing openness made shopping trips less of an ordeal and more of a day out (no problems with the language either, thanks to "Neighbours").

Australia is mostly a hedonistic society, with fancy cocktails, excellent restaurants, expensive designer clothes and a great deal of time spent on outdoor pursuits. They have the climate and amenities to convert restless energy into surfing, sailing and beach activities. The disabled are welcome and I had no difficulties in taking Thea to the beach (except on very hot days), the sailing marina, the dolphinarium . . . we even dined at the exclusive Perth Yacht Club.

"Eating in Australia was a revelation"

One of Thea's favourite outings was to the Dolphinarium and Aquatic Centre, just a few kilometres from Perth. Her face lit up as she listened to the barking sea-lion being fed, the splashing aquatic show with seals jumping through hoops, and a spectacular finale with my friend's daughter – "Princess for the day" – swimming with the dolphins in the pool as part of the Aztec theme show. It was wonderful.

Eating in Australia was a revelation. I had anticipated burgers, pizza and barbecue food, but I was pleasantly surprised to find a gastronomic experience which could hold its own anywhere in the world. I tasted some of the best Chinese food outside the Orient: butterfly prawns in honey and sesame seed, fresh fruit salad with textures and tastes I could not guess at. Cooking with fruit is an Australian speciality – triangles of rainbow trout gently fried and served on a bed of mango purée, wafer-thin escalope of pork in a hot plum sauce, and delicate baby chicken baked in lemon. Each day brought new delights in takeaway food – cheese sausage with crisp french fries, and irresistible flavours of ice cream. The weight piled on in leaps and bounds but it was worth it!

Set in the beauty of the Australian bush, 60km from Perth, is a Spanish villa complex with a wide range of activities for the whole family. The excitement of a chair lift was tempered by coping with a wriggling child, but with the view of Mount Bodeguero and the surrounding countryside as prize I was glad to have made the attempt. The highlight of the day was provided by the performing Andalusian horses which are trained for seven years before appearing in the ring. We all enjoyed a smorgasbord lunch (an Aussie favourite) before watching the horses in a memorable show set to Spanish marching music and involving difficult manoeuvres such as the capriole, Spanish walk, passage and levarde.

I had expected Australia to be similar to the USA, but I could not have been more wrong. Although both countries are vast in comparison to most European nations, their people's concept of travel differs widely. Internal flights in Australia were not as cheap as I had anticipated – the cost of a return fare from Perth to Sydney was the same as to Hong Kong or Singapore. A trip to Melbourne, Darwin or Canberra is what I had mentally planned before leaving England, but unlimited funds or time are necessary for this sort of travelling. There is a regular train service from Sydney to Perth which, I was reliably informed, would be an interesting journey and ideally suited to a disabled passenger who could see the countryside at a leisurely pace in the comfort of an air-conditioned carriage. However, as we had only four weeks, this was out of the question for us.

"Snakes, crocodiles and poisonous spiders are not found in every garden"

We found that whereas in America people think nothing of driving up to a hundred miles for a meal, this is not the case in Australia. Any venture outside the major towns or cities has to be treated with respect and caution; the bush is not a place to get lost or even to go for a stroll on a Sunday afternoon. Miles of featureless landscape have confused the best equipped explorers, the survival rate being lowest in high summer when temperatures are upwards of 105° F. We took our holiday from early November to December, when the average temperatures are between 74 and 96° F – comfortable for an adult and bearable for a small child in a wheelchair. The months of January, February or March are best avoided by the disabled traveller.

Contrary to popular myth, snakes, crocodiles and poisonous spiders are not found in every garden, but the wildlife, especially the birds, is rich. Parrots are constant visitors and the sound of the kookaburra is a delight. Pure white cockatoos cross the main highway and we even heard of a kangaroo in a nearby suburb, nonchalantly hopping down a busy street. Household pets are big business and most families have at least one cat or dog; many have more unusual animals. It was very amusing to hear the sound of two cats, a parrot screeching, guinea pigs squeaking, a canary singing and Thea shouting, in unison, with the kookaburra chipping in from outside, all wanting their breakfast at the same time.

But colour, rather than sound, is my most abiding memory of Perth, from the dazzling reds, pinks, yellows and greens of the young people's clothes in the city centre, through the many shades of the plants and foliage in the suburban gardens, to the deep blue ocean and creamy sand of the beach.

A visit to Perth would not be complete without experiencing Rottnest, a small island off the coast in the Indian Ocean. A short boat ride transported us to a tropical paradise used mainly by the locals as a holiday escape from the city. No cars are allowed and it was a joy to be able to push the wheelchair around undisturbed by traffic. The beaches, although crowded, were clean, the rock pools warm (yes, Thea was in again!) and the seafood was delicious.

Gentle kwokkas – small, furry animals unique to the island – roam about in safety, completely tame and loved by the visitors. I felt satisfyingly relaxed and could scarcely believe that a bustling city lay on the horizon. Apart from lazing on the beaches, voyages around the island are popular with the tourists. Seated in armchair comfort, passengers can view schools of brilliantly coloured fish, as well as hundred-year-old wrecks lying trapped by coral formations, from the glass-bottomed boats.

"As I enjoyed the warm sunshine for the last time I felt a supreme sense of achievement, even peace"

It would be easy to think of Australia as England with sunshine, but the differences emerge after a few weeks. Cultural stimulation is thin, and even the Australians admit that their TV schedules are probably the worst in the world! However, the outdoor life beckons and is enjoyed by all. When the time came for our departure I must admit to a sense of sadness, not only for leaving dear friends, but for saying goodbye to a nation whose main catch-phrase is "G'day". We had encountered a level of friendliness which will be hard to forget, and I should love to return.

On the morning of our departure the house was in chaos with last-minute packing, so I slipped away quietly for a final dip in the pool. The sun shimmered on the water as I swam and there was hardly a sound – unusual for an Aussie morning. I know what the future holds, caring for a handicapped child, but as I enjoyed the warm sunshine for the last time I felt a supreme sense of achievement, even peace, knowing that I had been capable of looking after my child without the backup of a well-meaning but occasionally intrusive medical service. At that point, I was ready to face anything or anyone.

We returned to a cold, wet December evening and Thea laughed and sparkled. Both our lives have been greatly enriched by experiences which coloured our activities for many months. There is still sand from the Indian Ocean at the bottom of the wheelchair – somehow I can't bear to brush it away.

New Zealand

Going for the Big One

Thirteen years ago David Gray broke his neck playing rugby. Although technically a tetraplegic, he did regain substantial power and control in his hands and arms. In 1984, not keen to rush from university to an office job, he purchased a round-the-world air ticket. David's account concentrates on his experiences in Australia and New Zealand.

I was reluctant to ask any but my closest friends if they'd like to come with me, for fear they might think I wanted and needed a carer (pig-headed independence is one of my faults). No one on the approachable list had the time, the money *and* the inclination to come along, so my choice was made for me – I would go alone.

Once the money was paid there was no backing out. Preparations were made months in advance: extensive exercise to get myself to peak fitness (a relative term), reading every guidebook with even a shred of information on access (for all my research, most such information related to the USA), fitting solid tyres to my wheelchair (the outback is not the place to get a puncture), and arranging supplies of every medication I might need. I even practised balancing my suitcase and travel bag on my lap, a skill which was to get plenty of use.

Finally, armed with an address book listing some relatives and "friends of

friends", I set off to London one January morning. My trip did not get quite the flying start I had hoped for. At my first stopover, Singapore, the cabin crew and airport staff contrived between them to overlook the fact that I needed assistance to disembark, and I eventually left the plane in an undignified manner with my arms hooked round the shoulders of two of the sturdiest stewards.

Jet lag did not encourage exploring, but the really intimidating fact was that I was *on my own*! If I was to see anything beyond the streets around my hotel, I had first to get in and out of a taxi (assuming one would stop for me) and next to take the risk that my destination would prove impractical for me in my wheelchair. Add potential language problems and it all seemed very daunting.

Nevertheless, I did make it to a few places, including *Raffles Hotel*, where some passing strangers were press-ganged into assisting me up the flight of steps at the entrance. Over one of the hotel's famous gin slings I made the acquaintance of an Australian businessman who has since become a regular pen pal and assured me of knowing at least one person in Australia.

The flight to Sydney was uneventful, although being sprayed on arrival (to prevent import of insect pests) was a novel experience. My wheelchair appeared without one footplate, which turned up later considerably bent, but several blows with a hammer provided an adequate repair job.

Arrival time was before 7am, so I had booked no accommodation, assuming it would be easier to locate when I wasn't several thousand miles away. The tourist information desk suggested a downtown hotel but I discovered that "flat access" actually meant five steps in the lobby, and "suitable rooms" meant that the bathroom doors were too narrow for my chair. After several fruitless telephone calls, I remembered the name of a brand new hotel, mentioned by my neighbour on the flight. My hunch turned out to be correct: the *Southern Cross* offered state-of-the-art accessible accommodation. The only drawback was the de luxe price, leaving me no alternative but to find another hotel as soon as possible.

A visit to the downtown tourist office (only twelve steps to negotiate) supplied the answer. They helped me to locate a great hotel with reasonable prices in the rather tame "red light" district. The *Crest*, used by *P&O* for their staff, subsequently became my base and provided a room with a stunning view of the Opera House and harbour bridge. There was flat access from the street to the lobby.

Early January in my home town of Belfast is more often than not wet, cold and windy; in Sydney the sun shone every day and the temperature was delightful. The Opera House was high on my list of places to visit and more than lived up to expectations. It has its critics but to my eye is an outstanding piece of architecture, complementing beautifully its setting in Sydney harbour. Nearby is the ferry terminal where there are numerous boats to be boarded (without difficulty) for sight-seeing or travel to other parts of the city. Ever seen a sail-board marathon? I did, and the sight of three thousand sails remains fixed in my memory.

The first floor of my hotel contained a number of shops, including a travel agency where discussions with the owner led to a trip to a local winery. He arranged for a few willing hands to lift me to the front seat of the coach when it stopped at the hotel, and similar help at each place of interest. The main attraction was the wine tasting and steak barbecue, preceded by demonstrations of sheep-dog handling, sheep shearing and boomerang throwing.

"For an angler like myself, the first stop had to be the Bay of Islands"

During my month in Australia I sampled life thousands of miles to the west, in Perth, where on several days the temperature reached 100° F but the relatively low humidity made this tolerable. Introductions from friends to some locals opened doors for me, and I was able to share the pleasures of more wine tasting, a cruise on the Swan River and a night at the races before heading back to Sydney and then eastward again to Auckland, New Zealand.

I had arranged for a hire car and, as promised, *Avis* provided one with hand controls. The steering knob I had specified was missing but fortunately I had taken the precaution of bringing one with me. The car proved invaluable over the following two weeks, as I wandered around North Island, although it took some getting used to (the hand controls were of an unfamiliar type) and was quite exhausting to drive since it was very large, had no power steering, and its four-door design required me to devise a totally new means of getting myself and, more importantly, my chair into the car unaided.

"I gave a lift to a hitchhiker, who in return helped me along a forest path to see the biggest kauri of them all"

For an angler like myself, the first stop had to be the Bay of Islands in the far north of North Island – the El Dorado for big-game fishermen. I headed over the Auckland harbour bridge (widened by the addition on each side of an extra prefabricated lane, constructed by the Japanese and known locally as the "Nippon clip-ons") and on to Paihia. On the journey my enthusiasm was whetted by radio bulletins reporting the progress of a struggle between a giant marlin and a fisherman who had hooked it the previous day! Victory went to the fish after 32 hours, when the line had to be cut as a storm threatened the boat.

I checked in to the modern *Paihia Sands Motel* which had a ramp to one of its apartments. Surprisingly, the architect had then spoiled his good work by installing a cabinet which blocked free access to the bathroom. However, I found I could manage by using an ordinary chair, placed immediately inside the doorway, and the friendly motel owners (Bill and Wanda) made up for any problems. They cheerfully cooked my catches and even took me out to dinner one evening.

Bill arranged for a coach tour to the North Cape and helped me get aboard. This turned out to be a day well spent: the driver's commentary was interesting; the area was rich in history and sights, including the Cape itself (where the Pacific Ocean and Tasman Sea meet) and we had a thrilling drive through the surf for part of the Ninety

Mile Beach (actually only fifty miles long).

The old whaling town of Russell, on the other side of the Bay of Islands, is also well worth seeing, and a cruise on the bay is a must, even for non-anglers. At Waitangi there is a Maori meeting house, complete with war canoe, at the site of the signing of the Waitangi Treaty between the Maoris and *pakehas* (white men) in 1840. My car developed a puncture on the way to Waitangi, on a fairly deserted road, but my luck held – while I sat and considered how to tackle it, a car drew up and two Dutch tourists had the situation sized up and the tyre changed in no time at all.

On the return journey to Auckland I chose the west side of the northern peninsula, famous for its forests of kauri, immense trees with straight trunks which live for centuries, if given the chance. I gave a lift to a hitchhiker, who in return helped me along a forest path to see the biggest kauri of them all, named "Tanemahuta", in the Waipoua Forest Sanctuary.

Some distance southeast of Auckland is Rotorua, the centre of the active thermal springs area of New Zealand (complete with power station driven by naturally produced steam) and also an important stronghold of the Maori people. Combined with the fascinating geological sights in the area, these springs make Rotorua one of the most popular holiday resorts in New Zealand, despite the sulphurous fumes from the many geysers.

While most geysers are difficult to approach closely, there is little problem in finding a viewpoint. A nearby cultural centre at Whakarewarewa gives exhibits on New Zealand's history, as well as talks and demonstrations of the Maoris' traditional skills, such as woodcarving; there is a reconstructed Maori village to examine at your leisure. The Agrodome makes an entertaining show out of educating visitors about everything to do with the country's major industry – sheep farming – and there are examples of most important breeds, plus displays of shearing and sheep-dog handling.

Next stop was for more fishing, this time for the legendary trout in Lake Taupo. Question was, where to try my hand? I spotted a boat being drawn out of the water by three men and decided to ask their advice. They showed me their catch – thirteen *huge* trout which were apparently considered only average in size! The fishermen confessed to being unsure where I could gain access to the lake shore, and asked me back to the boat owner's farm for a cup of tea while they discussed the problem.

Despite having guests staying with them they then insisted that I stayed the night. Once that was arrranged, they towed the boat back to the lake, launched it, arranged my licence and took me out for a few hours, during which I hooked and landed my prize trout. Dinner that evening was a grand affair, and the next day I ate trout before heading on my way.

My route took me southwards through Tongariro National Park, a spectacular area with several volcanoes which simmer for most of the time, and occasionally erupt. A fairly good road leads up to the permanent snow line, where there are chalets for winter skiers. Driving is at a leisurely pace since the main highway passes next through the Paraparas, a scenic area of hills which cause winding bends for some 50km before the road reaches the coast at Wanganui, where I stopped with relatives for a while and where financial constraints dictated the return of the hire car.

A local festival gave me an opportunity to meet people and savour the "Kiwi" lifestyle. The importance of farming was again apparent, with contests of both sheep shearing and log cutting. Food was produced from a *hangi*, a traditional oven created by putting embers in a hole in the ground, over which food is steamed in baskets. The results were edible, but it is definitely not a case of "the old ways are best"!

Wanganui offers pleasant parks, a good regional museum and jet-boat trips on New Zealand's second longest river, but it wasn't long before I was off again, this time sharing a trip around South Island with two cousins. We caught the ferry from Wellington on one of the days when the elements were living up to the local name for the town – "Windy Wellington". After an uncomfortable crossing of the Cook Strait (during which some enterprising schoolboys collected up all the bags provided for those feeling seasick, and then sold them to the desperate passengers!), we sailed into the calm waters of beautiful Queen Charlotte Sound and docked at Picton. A short drive in the waiting hire car brought us to Nelson for an overnight stop with friends.

"We enjoyed a celebration meal with fellow "survivors" in the park visitors' centre, while we waited for earth-moving vehicles to free our cars"

For the next few days we travelled down the west coast, calling at the odd-looking Pancake Rocks at Punakaiki, a natural glow-worm dell at Hokitika, and a seal colony at the unfairly named Cape Foulwind. The Southern Alps rise only a few miles inland, and with the moist air coming off the sea torrential rain is not uncommon in this area, but the sun shone for us the whole time. Before long, we reached Westland National Park, which features superb views of Mount Cook and the park's two glaciers, the Franz Josef and the Fox. It was here that the most dramatic incident of our trip occurred.

A narrow road wound along a steep-sided valley, providing the only access to the Fox Glacier. A rare thunderclap sent everyone dashing for their cars, but before we could leave, the valley's swollen streams brought rock slides crashing down across the road, blocking it to depths of about 6m and stranding nine cars. By sheer good fortune no one was hurt. While we assessed our position the forest rangers arrived and decided that a speedy withdrawal was called for. Several tourists helped to hoist me, in my wheelchair, over lots of mud and rock, after which we enjoyed a celebration meal with fellow "survivors" in the park visitors' centre, while we waited for earth-moving vehicles to free our cars.

"I succeeded in spinning the car off the road in a flurry of gravel"

Once reunited with our car, we drove through more and more breath-taking scenery – the Haast Pass, Lakeland, Queenstown, the Remarkables (a range of mountains), Te Anau and Fiordland National Park. The views of Milford Sound from one of the regular cruise boats are out of this world and not to be missed by any visitor to the area. Undoubtedly, the many hikers and walkers who head for the famous trails among the mountains gain most from this natural paradise but there is plenty enough to see from accessible venues too.

In contrast, accommodation designed for wheelchairs was quite scarce – to tour without booking ahead required flexibility and willingness to rely on help, at least to get in and out of the usual cabin-type motel rooms. If the situation hasn't changed and this isn't your style, some research will be needed in order to organise an itinerary around suitable stopping points. *New Zealand – Where to Stay* uses the wheelchair symbol, and there is now a separate access guide listing accessible accommodation – see *Travel Notes*.

Back on North Island I stayed for a few days at Palmerston North, with a family I had met in Paihia. After only a brief acquaintance they had invited me to visit them and they were most generous with their hospitality – another example of the friendly attitude I found to be the norm among New Zealanders. Perhaps it is a legacy from the days

when the early European pioneers relied on each other as they struggled to make a living in a new land, or maybe it stems from the fact that so many Kiwis have themselves been travellers, either as students or when emigrating from other parts of the world.

My ten-week stay was rounded off with another trip in an adapted hire car, this time to the Coromandel peninsula where I succeeded in spinning the car off the road in a flurry of gravel (unsealed roads are quite common), fortunately without causing too much damage. Again, the mountains, coastline and forests made marvellous scenery, and a couple of wild dolphin put on a show in Whitianga harbour.

A drink at a nearby bar reminded me that so far the really monster fish had eluded me, for above the door was the preserved head of a giant marlin, landed in Mercury Bay. So back I went to the Bay of Islands, stopping again with Bill and Wanda. One of their friends kindly took me fishing in his boat free of charge (professional boats can charge up to £200 per day). Despite my efforts nothing big came my way, but any sense of disappointment was minor given the beautiful weather and views.

Having stayed longer than intended in New Zealand, I skipped my intended visit to Fiji and flew on to Hawaii. From there I flew to the States, stopping off in San Francisco, San Antonio and New Orleans. Florida was to have been my final destination but, in truth, homesickness suddenly took hold and, combined with a dwindling supply of travellers' cheques, sent me flying home from Miami only a few hours after I arrived. I hadn't seen or done absolutely everything I had dreamed of, yet I'd savoured more than most people ever get the chance to experience. Many a time I'd received help, sometimes vital help, but for all that, my original concerns and fears disappeared in Singapore, to be replaced by a confidence which is perhaps one of the greatest rewards of travel.

Sources of information

Australia and New Zealand set a high standard for provision of information for disabled travellers – plenty of it, mostly up to date, and several organisations to turn to for more detail.

Australian Tourist Commission, Gemini House, 10–18 Putney Hill, London SW15 6AA; ☎081/780 2227. Can provide copies of *Travel in Australia for People with Disabilities* (July 1990), a useful twenty-page "fact sheet" produced by the commission after consultation with various Australian disability organisations. Copies are also available from the Senior Information Officer, Information Section, Australian Tourist Commission, 80 William Street, Woolloomooloo, NSW 2011 (☎2/3601111). The text is concise and frank, with sections on getting there, getting around, equipment hire, where to stay and what to see. Publications, support organisations, specialised services, tourist bureaux and tour operators are listed state by state; the only gripe here is that for many organisations only the phone number is supplied – the address would be useful. The intention is to update every two years.

There are eight specialist **tour operators** for disabled travellers in Australia, some of which act as information agencies; details are given in the tourist commission guide.

ACROD (*The Australian Council for the Rehabilitation of the Disabled*), PO Box 60, Curtin, ACT 2605, Canberra; ☎62/82 4333. Has a library and information service, holds copies of a large list of access guides and can tell enquirers where to obtain these.

New Zealand Tourism Office, New Zealand House, Haymarket, London SW1Y 4TQ; ☎071/973 0360. Has copies of *New Zealand Access: Guide for the Less Mobile Traveller* (1990–1991), a glossy accommodation brochure produced by the *New Zealand Tourism Department* in Wellington. The criteria for acceptance in the guide were supplied by the **New Zealand CCS** (formerly known as the *NZ Crippled Children Society*, 86–90 Vivian Street, PO Box 6349, Te Aro, Wellington ☎4/845677). The general tourist board guide, *New Zealand Where to Stay*, also specifies suitable accommodation ("paraplegic units") for disabled people, again using the *New Zealand CCS* specifications.

Disabled Persons Assembly (*DPA*), PO Box 27186, Wellington; ☎4/857 828. Involved in a number of different activities relating to their aim of "Full participation and equal opportunities for all people with disabilities in all aspects of New Zealand society". There are 35 regional *DPA* assemblies, and it's worth contacting them for local information; for example the Christchurch and Districts *DPA* has recently (1990) published an excellent 300-page book about the Canterbury region (price NZ$5, from *Disabled Persons Centre*, 314 Worcester Street, Linwood, PO Box 32074, Christchurch; ☎3/795636). Although the regional *DPA*s may not be able to answer all travel queries they'll put you in touch with someone who can.

New Zealand Disabilities Information Bureau, 840 Tremaine Avenue, Palmerston North; ☎63/62311. One of twelve members of the *NZ Federations of Disability Information Centres* (list of addresses available from *New Zealand CCS*), has some useful information on recreational opportunities for disabled people – skiing, camping, riding and other outdoor pursuits.

NZ Paraplegic and Physically Disabled Association, PO Box 610, Hamilton; ☎71/82207. Can supply information on sporting activities throughout New Zealand.

Tour operators

Barbara Horrocks recommends *Travelbag* (12 High Street, Alton, Hampshire GU34 1BN; ☎0420/87877), specialists in travel to Australia and New Zealand. They offer direct flights, stopovers and round-the-world trips. Barbara was also pleased with *Ansett Travel Service* (offices all over Australia) who made flight, accommodation and tour bookings while she was in Australia. *Pioneer Trailways* (now *Pioneer Express*; UK agent *Southern Cross Travel and Tourism*, 2 The Square, Riverhead, Sevenoaks, Kent TN13 2AA; ☎0732/740421) gave her a successful trip to Ayers Rock, the *Pioneer* guide making light of wheeling her over the bumps around the base of the rock.

AUSTRALIA & NEW ZEALAND: TRAVEL NOTES

John Moore recommends *Austravel* (20 Savile Row, London W1X 1AE, ☎071/734 7755; or 25 Trenchard Street, Bristol BS1 5AN, ☎0272/277425), another specialist, again covering everything from the cheapest (*Britannia*) charter flight to a round-the-world air cruise.

The organisers of Roger Elliott's expedition – not a tour company, of course – are at Operation Raleigh Headquarters (Alpha Place, Flood Street, London SW3 5SZ; ☎071/351 7541); there are some ten expeditions a year, each lasting about ten weeks.

Outward Bound Australia (PO Box 4213, Sydney, NSW 2001; ☎2/2612200) organise adventure holidays along similar lines. Their "Mixed Ability" programmes are designed to "bring disabled and able-bodied people together in a wilderness setting to participate in outdoor adventure holidays". *Outward Bound Trust of New Zealand* (PO Box 3158, Wellington; ☎4/723440) run special courses at the Cobham Outward Bound School near Picton.

There are many other operators worth investigating, including the airlines and cruise companies. A couple of *P&O* cruises on the *Canberra* (see p.493) call at Australia and New Zealand.

Getting there

Qantas (Qantas House, 395/403 King Street, London W6 9NJ; ☎081/846 0466, reservations ☎0345/747767) produce a whole series of passenger care leaflets, the relevant one for disabled passengers being *Travel Care – Air Travel for People with Disabilities or Special Medical Conditions*, which is obtained by phoning ☎0800/747767 (free). The Australian airline comes highly recommended, by several contributors, for efficient service, good facilities and willingness to treat each passenger as an individual.

Roger Elliott asked *Qantas* staff at the Heathrow check-in desk if his lightweight wheelchair could be stored on the flight deck rather than in the hold – no problem. He was transferred to the aisle wheelchair at the door of the aircraft and taken, without fuss, in this chair to the toilets whenever necessary during the flight. Roger comments that although the aisle chair was suitable for him (he is quite small, weighing only 57kg), larger passengers might have a struggle.

Andrew Healey used *British Airways* and flew back on a modified Boeing 747 with one loo just accessible to the aisle chair. He suggests avoiding direct flights, not because of difficulties with disability but because of the boredom factor. Most people seem to stop over in Singapore or Bangkok, and are glad of the break.

Air New Zealand (Elsinore House, 77 Fulham Palace Road, London W6 8JA; ☎081/741 2299) have a "skychair", for use aboard their aircraft. The footplates are reported to be somewhat high, which might be tricky for people with stiff hips or knees, but otherwise it is comfortable, with soft vinyl seat and removable armrests. Disabled passengers are given seats behind the crew rest, where there is adequate legroom but no fear of blocking the exits. Assistance is available in the loo, and passengers will be taken to the first-class facilities if more space is needed.

Cathay Pacific will carry an aisle wheelchair on request and offer good legroom (p.341). If an aisle chair is not the prime consideration the choice of major airlines operating regular scheduled flights widens to include *Thai Airways International*, *Singapore Airlines*, *Lufthansa* and *KLM*.

Veronica Smith's experience (see p.341) gives grounds for avoiding *Garuda* (*Indonesian*) *Airlines*, even though they are considerably cheaper than *Qantas* or *BA*. The Indonesian staff were polite, cheerful and well meaning, but that was the only positive comment made in Veronica's subsequent letter of complaint to *Garuda*'s head office in Jakarta. After a lengthy correspondence with Jakarta, the matter was dealt with more efficiently by the London office, and each member of Veronica's group received £100 in compensation.

Transport

The leading **domestic airlines** in Australia seem pretty well geared up for disabled passengers. Reservations are generally made through international carriers or travel agents, and special requirements should be stated at this time. Although internal flights may seem

AUSTRALIA & NEW ZEALAND: TRAVEL NOTES

expensive there are a number of discounts available to overseas visitors, details of which can be obtained from a travel agent or your international airline.

Australian Airlines (7 Swallow Street, London W1R 8DU; ☎071/434 3864) keep a few copies of a brochure for disabled passengers which contains ground plans of the major domstic airports; ask for a photocopy. *Ansett Australia*'s brochure is only available from their Melbourne office; this airline has a club, *Ansacare*, for regular disabled travellers – their details are kept on file and handling advice is unnecessary. *East West Airlines* offer a fifty percent reduction on the economy fare to a disabled passenger who has to travel with an escort (a letter from a disabled organisation must be produced when tickets are purchased).

New Zealand's three main domestic carriers are *Air New Zealand*, *Ansett New Zealand* and *Mount Cook Line*. Reservations on *Mount Cook Line* are made through *Air New Zealand*. Passenger care leaflets are available from *Air New Zealand* (Head Office, Private Bag, Auckland; ☎9/797515) and *Ansett New Zealand* (Head Office, PO Box 4168, Auckland; ☎9/396235) travel centres throughout New Zealand. The handling of disabled passengers is smooth, with the full range of services: wheelchairs at airports, folding aisle chairs, seat-belt extensions, quadriplegic harness, leg rests, oxygen equipment, incubators, carriage of guide dogs and electric wheelchairs, safety briefings for passengers with impaired hearing or vision.

Facilities at **airports** are usually adequate. Roger Elliott had problems with toilets and parking at Cairns before completion of the new terminal building, but most airports offer parking close to the terminal, accessible toilets and cafeterias, ramps, lifts and, in some cases, phones fitted with inductive couplers. Airbridges are used only at Sydney, Melbourne and Cairns; boarding is by fork-lift at other Australian airports. In New Zealand, disabled passengers disembark along with everyone else by airbridge at Wellington and Auckland; at Christchurch a fork-lift is used. If travelling by small aircraft you'll probably be carried on and off.

Roger Elliott made a number of flights in **light aircraft** with private charter companies such as *Hinterland Aviation* (☎70/559831). *Coral Wings* (☎70/518042) arranged his trip on the Grumman Widgeon flying boat over the Great Barrier Reef; *Cape York Air Service* (☎70/359399) run post office charter flights that take fare-paying passengers; *Sunbird Airlines* (☎70/359899) run charter and regular services all over Queensland. All these companies are based at Cairns airport.

Rail travel is possible with advance warning in both countries, but facilities are far from perfect. *Railways of Australia* (4–85 Queen Street, Melbourne, Vic 3000; ☎3/6080811) and New Zealand's *Intercity Services* (Head Office, PO Box 12440, Wellington; ☎4/712877) are represented in the UK by *Compass* (PO Box 113, Peterborough PE1 1LE; ☎0733/51780).

Ramps and special folding chairs are required to transfer wheelchair-bound passengers from platform to a seat on the train – a standard chair cannot be used on board. Perhaps for that reason, there are no wheelchair-accessible toilets on the trains. But there's good news for visually impaired travellers on New Zealand's *Intercity* rail services – a fifty percent discount on all fares – and for wheelchair users in Sydney, where a relatively new overhead rail system (Monorail) is fully accessible, with ramps and lifts at stations, and a special carriage for wheelchair passengers at the front of the train.

Intercity is New Zealand's largest passenger network, operating the trains, ferries and coaches. They control *The Interisland Line* **ferries** (Head Office, Wellington Railway Station, Private Bag, Wellington; ☎4/725599) that run between Picton (South Island) and Wellington (North Island). There are two wheelchair-accessible car ferries, *Arahura* and *Aratika*; the passenger ferries have ramps, and crew will assist where necessary; it's probably a good idea to phone ahead to make arrangements.

Travel on the launches, catamarans and other passenger boats that ply between the island resorts and mainland Queensland may involve some manhandling by the crew, either between decks or when boarding and disem-

AUSTRALIA & NEW ZEALAND: TRAVEL NOTES

barking; accessible loos are rarely, if ever, provided on board.

A few wheelchair-accessible coaches are available for group hire in Australia (contact *ACROD*) and New Zealand (see *New Zealand Access* and consult disability organisations). There are no **bus and coach** companies in either country that fit hydraulic lifts to their vehicles for general use, but on standard tours the drivers will assist with boarding, ensure disabled passengers sit nearest the door, and store wheelchairs or other equipment in the luggage compartment. Urban buses are generally inaccessible if you cannot manage the steps.

The UK offices of *Avis* and *Budget* (used by our contributors for **hire of adapted cars** in New Zealand and Australia respectively) insist that cars with hand controls are no longer available in either country. However, material produced by disability organisations in 1990 suggests that hand-controlled car rental can be arranged at certain offices in Australia or New Zealand.

In Australia, *Budget* do have a few vehicles equipped with hand controls (Roger Elliott hired his from *Budget Rent a Car*, Lake Street, Cairns, Qld; ☎70/519222), but a better option might be to take your own set of controls with you and have them fitted to a standard hire car on arrival – that way you can shop around for a good deal with a local firm. The *Paraplegic and Quadriplegic Association* (phone numbers of regional branches listed in the tourist commission guide) can help with the fitting of controls.

In New Zealand, *Avis Rent-a-Car* (Private Bag, Wellesley Street, Auckland; ☎9/5251982) can fit hand controls to some models. *Budget Rent a Car* (Oxford Terrace and Lichfield Street, Christchurch; ☎3/660072) have two hand-controlled cars which service the whole country, so they must be reserved well ahead of departure.

Horizon Holidays (530–544 Memorial Avenue, PO Box 14069, Christchurch Airport; ☎3/535600) has a "Paravan" (an adapted camper van) available for hire. It is fitted with an electric hoist, and the rear seat of the usual "twin cab" has been removed so that the wheelchair passenger can sit behind the front seat, secured by wheelchair clamps and with ample, padded headroom.

The major highways are mostly well maintained but be prepared for some rugged surfaces in wilder parts, and remember that distances on the map are deceptive; carry a fold-up toilet if the journey spans many hours between towns. Treat long drives as minor expeditions rather than Sunday jaunts (p.362).

Visitors to New Zealand can join the *Operation Mobility* **parking** concession scheme by filling out a short application form (from any branch of the *New Zealand CCS*) and obtaining a temporary Mobility Card. This allows a vehicle carrying a disabled driver or passenger to use any of the reserved parking spaces; it allows time concessions on metered spaces and restricted areas, as well as stopping to unload or pick up in restricted areas. There are specified parking spots for disabled drivers in Australian cities; see access guides or ask city councils for details.

Availability of **wheelchair-accessible taxis** is good but advance notice is required (at least 24 hours) in Australia, and pre-booking is advised in New Zealand, particularly around school start and finish times. *Qantas* can arrange for one to meet you at the airport on your arrival in Australia. There is a fleet in every Australian provincial capital except Hobart, and phone numbers for booking are supplied in the tourist commission guide.

In New Zealand, there are eighty odd "Maxi Taxis" (Toyota Hiace vans with hoists and tie-downs) operating throughout the country under the *Total Mobility Taxi Service*. The major disability organisations (*New Zealand CCS*, members of the *NZ Federation of Disability Information Centres, Arthritis Society, Multiple Sclerosis Society, NZ Association of the Deaf, Royal NZ Foundation for the Blind*, some hospitals) issue vouchers that entitle the holder to a discount: at present this varies, but the aim is to charge half fares everywhere eventually. Visitors can obtain vouchers through one of the issuing agencies.

Accommodation

You should be able to find something to suit any budget or access requirements, from camp-

AUSTRALIA & NEW ZEALAND: TRAVEL NOTES

sites through to five-star hotels, particularly those built after 1980. Motels and motor inns seem to provide the most accessible low-cost accommodation. If you travel without booking ahead, stop by mid-afternoon to allow plenty of time to look around. It might be a good idea to pre-book if planning to stay in the cities during high season. The following accommodation is recommended by our contributors.

If money's no object, the *Regent of Melbourne* (25 Collins Street, Melbourne, Vic 3000; ☎3/6530000) is, according to Barbara Horrocks, magnificent, the only niggle being that breakfast is served in a mezzanine restaurant (if not in your room), access to which is via a service lift.

The *Southern Cross* (Cnr Elizabeth & Goulburn Streets, Sydney, NSW 2000; ☎2/20987) is centrally situated and in the de luxe (five-star) price bracket. It has adapted rooms but the rooftop pool is inaccessible. David Gray suggests the *Crest* (111 Darlinghurst Road, Kings Cross, Sydney, NSW 2011; 2/3582755) as a much cheaper alternative, with flat access from street to lobby, and rooms with stunning views of the Opera House and the harbour bridge.

Hithergreen Lodge (Henry Lawson Drive, PO Box 169, Mudgee, NSW 2850; ☎63/721022) – "your home away from home in the vineyards" – is run by Peter and Robyn Burgess and has one well-equipped room for disabled guests, with spacious *en suite* bathroom.

Australian contributor Cathy O'Reilly, who is quadriplegic and lives in Adelaide, recommends *The Wheel Resort* (Lot 1, Broken Head Road, Byron Bay, NSW 2481; ☎66/856139), a small group of comfortable self-contained cabins, all specifically designed to accommodate wheelchair users and set in 2.5 hectares of natural coastal bushland and established gardens. There is a 15-metre, solar-heated pool with ramp and PVC wheelchair, and wide pathways through the bush. Byron Bay's beaches and facilities for a range of activities, including scuba-diving, windsurfing, horse-riding, fishing, are within easy reach. Disabled and able-bodied guests are equally welcome and rates are very reasonable.

Wrest Point Hotel Casino (410 Sandy Bay Road, Hobart, Tas 7000; ☎02/250112), also de luxe, has easy access and a lift to all floors; it's advisable to book ahead because this is a very popular hotel.

Sheraton Hobart (1 Davey Street, Hobart, Tas 7000; ☎02/354535) and *Sheraton Ayers Rock* (Yulara Drive, Yulara, NT 0872; ☎89/562200) are typical *Sheratons* – comfortable, good access, five-star prices. The *Sheraton Mirage Port Douglas* (Davidson Street, Port Douglas, Qld 4871; ☎70/995888) is fully accessible and worth visiting just for a drink if the room rates are out of your range.

The *Lakeside International Hotel* (London Circuit, Canberra, ACT 2601; ☎62/476244) is four-star, within walking distance of Lake Burley Griffin (ask for a room overlooking the lake), and easily accessible.

The Summit Central Apartments (Cnr Leichhardt & Allenby Streets, Brisbane, Qld 4000; ☎7/8397000) are accessible, with pleasant staff, but it's a steep climb from the city centre.

The four-star *Ramada Reef Resort* (Cnr Vievers Road & Williams Esplanade, Palm Cove, Qld 4879; ☎70/553999) is a low-set development with easy access, right on the beach and designed around a grove of ancient melaleuca and palm trees; the staff are friendly and helpful and there is a free shuttle bus into Cairns.

There is a variety of accommodation available on South Molle Island resort, which is reached by plane from Townsville to Hamilton Island, then water-taxi to South Molle – a bit awkward for wheelchair users, but Barbara Horrocks found everyone helpful. She stayed in a comfortable, chalet-style room on the ground floor of a "Whitsunday Unit", with views over the Whitsunday Passage. The price includes all food, and to feel that you've had your money's worth you'll need a huge appetite.

Consult the *Queensland Tourist and Travel Corporation* (Queensland House, 392 The Strand, London WC2R 0LZ; ☎071/836 7242) for a comparison of all the islands and resorts along the Great Barrier Reef; their brochure tells you how to get there, what you can do on each island, what's included in the cost.

AUSTRALIA & NEW ZEALAND: TRAVEL NOTES

There's even a mention of facilities for disabled visitors, with an address to write to for further information.

John Moore stayed at the *Gladstone Country Club Motor Inn* (Cnr Far Street & Dawson Highway, Gladstone, Qld 4680; ☎79/724322), the *Miners Lodge Motor Inn* (60–62 Nebo Road, Mackay, Qld 4740; ☎79/511944) and the *Earls Court Motor Inn* (131–133 Nerang Street, Southport, Qld 4215; ☎75/914144), all of which are wheelchair accessible.

Roger Elliott recommends the budget-priced *G'Day Tropical Village* (7–27 MacLachlan Street, Manunda, Cairns, Qld 4870; ☎70/537555).

The *NRMA Accommodation Directory 1990* (*National Roads Motorists Association*, 151 Clarence Street, Sydney, NSW 2000; ☎2/2609222) indicates establishments with "independent access" and "access with assistance" but the facilities do not have to satisfy any standard criteria and are not verified, so it can only act as a starting point.

By the end of 1991, the automobile associations in each state (addresses in the tourist commission brochure, *Australia: A Traveller's Guide*) hope to have completed a new survey of accommodation throughout Australia, using questionnaires supplied by *ACROD*. The access information should be consistent and reliable, and will be incorporated in their mainstream national tour books, using symbols to denote "independent access" and "partially accessible – enquire further".

New Zealand Access lists a wide selection of accessible accommodation. In addition, several youth hostels have been recently upgraded and made accessible; for details of these contact the *Youth Hostels Association of New Zealand* (PO Box 436, Christchurch). David Gray stayed at the *Paihia Sands Motel* (Paihia, Northland; ☎9/4027707), where he gained access to the bathroom using a chair placed just inside the doorway, but the friendly owners more than compensated for this design fault.

Access and facilities

The overall picture is rosy. There are scores of helpful publications, most of them reasonably up-to-date, and the tourist boards work well with disability organisations to ensure accuracy of information. It's pleasing to see some reference to disabled visitors in at least two general brochures (*Australia: A Traveller's Guide* and *Queensland*); the logical conclusion would be the incorporation of access information throughout all brochures, following the lead of the automobile associations and their tour books.

Access and facilities at tourist attractions are, by all accounts, enviably good. High kerbs may be a problem in the tropical and subtropical regions, but most cities are relatively easy to explore in a wheelchair (prepare for some tough gradients in Brisbane). Special facilities – ramps, wide entrances, lifts and so on – are generally provided at museums, zoos, theatres and public buildings, and accessible restaurants and toilets are widely available. And for the visitor there are plenty of access guides, "mobility maps", loo guides and lists of reserved parking spaces to consult.

But to get the best out of Australia and New Zealand, the great outdoors must be sampled, whether that means lying on the beach, donning a wet suit, wheeling through the rainforest or floating above the scenery in a hot-air balloon. Most contributors report that they were excluded from very few activities on their holidays, although even the Aussies have yet to come up with a solution to the problem of getting a wheelchair down the beach to the sea – perhaps more boardwalks?

Again, access guides have been produced, detailing the opportunities open to wheelchair users, and there are a number of sources of up-to-the-minute local information: regional departments of sport and recreation, environment and planning, conservation and land management, woods and forests (ask tourist offices for addresses), as well as the disability organisations and resource centres.

The guide to accessible walks and picnic areas in New Zealand, *Out and About*, was published in 1988 by the Department of Conservation (PO Box 10420, Wellington) and is now out of print but the *New Zealand CCS* have hopes of a revision or reprint soon.

This is not to say that Australia and New Zealand are "barrier-free". Disability groups are actively involved in encouraging greater public

AUSTRALIA & NEW ZEALAND: TRAVEL NOTES

awareness of the need to remove architectural barriers, to provide much greater access to public transport, to achieve equal employment opportunities and legal redress where discrimination occurs. All the familiar battles are going on, but for the visitor with disabilities both countries provide enough facilities to make them very accessible holiday destinations.

Health and insurance

No worries about standards of health care, and pharmacists will supply most drugs (you'll probably need a prescription from a resident doctor). Take a letter from your doctor or clearly written prescription for your usual drugs, particularly if you are carrying a large supply.

In Australia, insect repellents, sun blocks and a light folding wheelchair are likely to make the biggest contribution to comfort.

Mosquitoes will be a nuisance in many areas; it can be very hot and very humid – if excessive heat worsens your disability try to travel in November or December, avoiding January, February and March; a slimline wheelchair is invaluable for trips in light aircraft, small boats or overloaded cars and camper vans.

Apart from the dreaded jellyfish, the unfamiliar Australian wildlife is more likely to startle than injure – sharks, crocs and poisonous spiders do exist, but your chances of an encounter are extremely slim. The bush should be treated with respect but it can be explored, and, as Sheila Murray observes, the gardens are not *all* crawling with snakes and redbacks.

The only poisonous creature in New Zealand is the very rare katipo spider, and maximum summer temperatures are nothing more than pleasantly warm.

NORTH
AMERICA

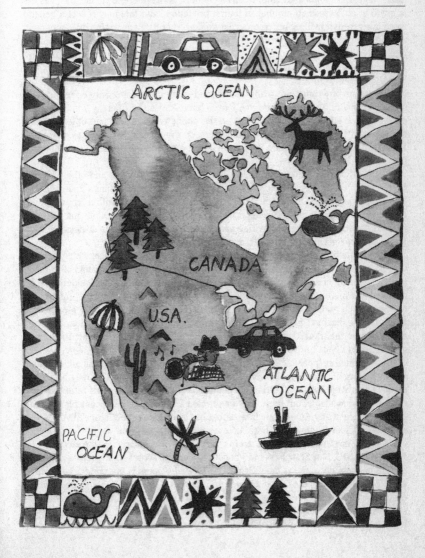

Introduction

E ach state (in the USA) or province (Canada) is responsible for its own arrangements for provision of access and facilities, so legislation, standards of facilities and information about them can vary widely. Some reference to disabled visitors is made in an increasing number of tourist brochures, and this may reflect a general trend away from providing separate access guides. There are plans, already in motion in at least one Canadian province, to gather reliable accessibility information and incorporate it in all mainstream tourist literature. If this operation could be extended to other provinces, and across the border into the USA, information for disabled visitors would be much easier to come by.

At the time of writing, not many access guides are up to date, and you might have difficulty obtaining copies before you leave. Once across the Atlantic, you'll find that tourism office staff are highly efficient on the phone or in person, and other sources, such as the *Canadian Paraplegic Association* or the *Society for the Advancement of Travel for the Handicapped*, are very helpful. But extracting information by letter may be a slow process.

This is OK if you don't need to pore over maps, access guides and other relevant brochures in order to make sense of the mind-boggling range of things to do and see. But as contributors point out, the USA and Canada are vast, and with a limited length of holiday and limited funds it is important to have at least some idea of what you want to visit, what transport to use (parking permits have to be arranged in advance in many states and provinces), where to stay, and what's accessible.

Perhaps the theory is that visitors do not need to research; they can simply assume that access is good wherever they are likely to go. The following accounts offer much supporting evidence for this, but many travellers appreciate and use guidebooks for disabled visitors, and there must be some who would benefit from easy and quick access to such guides, when planning their trip. Apart from that small niggle, there is much for the disabled traveller to admire throughout the USA and Canada. Although conditions on the transatlantic flight are no better than on any other plane, the ease of getting around North America should make it all worthwhile.

Most airlines responsible for **domestic flights** are happy to accommodate people with any form of disability, although seat reservation and pre-boarding may be problematic. For travellers who like the independence of personal transport, **adapted hire cars** are also available, but there may be problems with fitting hand controls and with luggage space: many American cars look big but are short on boot space; if you have a bulky wheelchair to stow, your best bet is a van or "station wagon".

Facilities are good on urban **trains**, as noted particularly in the accounts of Washington DC, San Francisco and Vancouver. *Amtrak* scores highly for its efforts on the US national network, as does Canada's *VIA Rail*. Access is not perfect but *Amtrak* and *VIA* are way ahead of many European networks. Travel on **buses** is not such an easy option. Although some cities operate accessible bus services, these are not always successful, and inter-city bus companies have so far failed to provide facilities for boarding wheelchair users on their vehicles – a recurring theme throughout this book.

Greyhound offer a discount which allows a disabled person to travel with a companion for the price of one ticket, but there are steep steps at the entrance and no hydraulic lift.

There are no problems reported with using **taxis**, apart from Christine Panton's unfortunate experience (p.414), which had nothing to do with disability. Wheelchair-accessible cabs are tested in Vancouver by Rod Semple (p.442), and Frieda Maguire recommends the limousine service in Toronto (p.445) – large, luxurious and cheap.

Many **boat** trips are described in these accounts, and wheelchair users managed them all. Special boarding procedures, well-designed vessels and willing crew members make possible a ride on the famous *Maid of the Mist* under the Niagara Falls, shooting rapids on the St Lawrence, and a whale-watching trip off Nova Scotia.

According to our contributors, good **access to public buildings and tourist attractions** is the norm. Carolyn Lucas found that even the caves in Frijoles Canyon, near Santa Fe, had ramped access. Visitors with disabilities can enjoy all the museums and galleries of the Smithsonian Institution in Washington DC, the casinos of Las Vegas, the scent of pine in the Canadian Rockies . . . the list is endless.

Although the praise far outweighs the criticism, however, it's not all roses. Carolyn Lucas comments on the bad road and pavement surfaces, high kerbs and patchy provision of ramps in New York City (p.390). Nic Fleming found that New York's accessible buses are unwilling to stop for wheelchair users (p.426). The majority of rides in Disneyworld, Florida, are accessible to disabled people, but facilities are not so good at the original Disneyland, in California, where it is impossible to get a wheelchair aboard any of the rides and the toilets are inadequate for wheelchair users.

The **toilet and bathroom facilities** in the States come under scrutiny from Arthur Goldthorpe (p.403), whose involvement with UK access committees enables him to compare designs of facilities on each side of the Atlantic. In Canada, Christine Swan (p.432) noted some problems with hotel bathroom design in 1983, although more recent visitors had better experiences.

Suitable **accommodation** seems easy to find, whatever your budget, partly thanks to the larger scale of buildings. Arthur Goldthorpe and Shirley Lihou (p.411) quickly located self-catering or motel accommodation once at their destinations. Those who booked ahead generally found good facilities in hotels and motels. The widespread availability of accessible accommodation is probably partly the result of the constant flow of meetings and conferences, often held at hotels, organised by the numerous **associations of disabled people**. Vigorous lobbying has forced progress in many areas, including access, housing, transport, employment, training and education.

The passing of the *Americans with Disabilities Act* in 1989 brought protection of the rights of disabled people to a national level in the USA. Although some provisions of the act are to be phased in very gradually, others, such as the requirement that all new public transport buses are equipped with lifts, are already in operation. Canadians are still working to introduce new federal legislation, but there is plenty of activity in the provinces working for full economic integration of disabled people.

USA

Drama on the East Coast

In June 1989, after months of preparation, Carolyn Lucas started a four-month trip to the USA, funded by the Winston Churchill Memorial Trust, to undertake a study entitled "The Training and Employment of Professional Actors with Disabilities in the USA". Her husband took sabbatical leave to accompany her and pursue courses of his own. This is the first of three accounts written on their return. Carolyn uses a wheelchair – she is capable of walking, but finds it too painful.

We were ambitious, perhaps overambitious. The plan was to spend June on the East Coast, visiting Washington DC, Boston and New York, passing through nine states and fitting in sightseeing as well as working on the project. We had a tough start, with an eleven-hour journey to Washington via New York, changing planes and negotiating customs and immigration at the frenetic John F. Kennedy (JFK) airport. One third of the aircraft's baggage, including our own, was accidentally left there. Once in Washington, it took us two hours, in a hired Buick, in the dark, to find our hosts' address – we had directions from the wrong airport.

A tip or two here: avoid flying via JFK – it's a huge airport, the staff are overworked and the heat in summer is a killer; and, if using an international

hire company, book your car in advance – it's cheaper from the UK. We ordered the smallest possible model, but in both Washington and Boston, when they saw me and the wheelchair plus four months' worth of luggage, they offered us a larger car. So we found ourselves swanning around in a limousine at no extra charge.

Washington DC was our base for most of the month, and the *Very Special Arts Festival* provided a focus for our stay. One of the Kennedy family started the *Very Special Arts* organisation and it now runs projects all over the world. It is based at the Kennedy Center, a prestigious flat-roofed structure by the Potomac river. Why flat-roofed? According to one commentary, presidents who die of natural causes are commemorated by domes and needles; those cut down in their prime, like Kennedy and Lincoln, are awarded flat roofs.

Dancers, artists, actors and musicians with disabilities come from countries all over the world to display their skills in this week-long festival, which also includes seminars, workshops and exhibitions. It's a huge enterprise with funds to match, and it introduced me to new contacts as well as affording me the opportunity to meet many of the people I would come across later in my travels.

A group of sight-impaired children from Clapham, London, represented the UK with a choreographed circus routine. *Access Theater*, from Santa Barbara in California, performed *Storm Readings*, by a severely disabled writer appearing with his brother and a signing actress. This play was presented in the Ford Theatre, where Abraham Lincoln was assassinated – the box in which he was shot is still draped in flags. One of the highlights of the festival was the performance of a play by a young writer based on her own experiences of living with muscular dystrophy. Produced by a well-known director, it was a very creditable first script which won the Henry Fonda Award.

Our first full day was the hottest June 1st ever recorded in Washington – 98°F with 100 percent humidity. We had our first experience of getting hopelessly lost in Washington's obsessively over-planned road system, something we repeated several times daily for the remainder of our stay. Traffic lights by the thousand, every traffic circle quite different in design from all the others, with a forest of speed and parking signs but no directions until you have overshot your junction – once in the wrong lane and swept across the Potomac river into Virginia, you can say goodbye to Washington for the next hour or two!

So, instead of driving in Washington, check out the marvellous Metrorail system – clean and efficient – and do the rest on foot (or wheel). My appointments tended to be at opposite ends of the city and, as the Metrorail network is not extensive, my use of it was limited. But you should have no problem in seeing the main sights if you use a combination of Metrorail and the accessible buses. It was very heartening to see two guys in wheelchairs on their way to work by Metrorail – unimaginable on the London Underground.

Of all the Washington monuments, the most affecting was the Vietnam War Memorial, a black marble wall engraved with the names of the 50,000 men who died in that terrible war. Set into a grass bank in a tapering V-shape, it begins with one name and rises to hundreds in each column. Relatives were "rubbing" the engraved names, and posies and tributes littered the base. The crowds were silent as they walked away.

"You are almost guaranteed access in every building you are likely to visit"

One thing I discovered early in my visit is that federal (national) funding to any organisation is contingent on the provision of full access for disabled persons to their premises. This has had such an impact on public consciousness that you are almost guaranteed access in every building you are likely to visit. Parking for disabled motorists is usually available too, with heavy penalties for those who abuse it. This commitment, enshrined in legislation, has been crucial in the fight for civil rights for disabled people. It should be taken as a model if the appalling lack of facilities and opportunities in the UK is to be addressed.

My study took me to Gallaudet Model Secondary School for the Deaf, which has an extensive theatre programme and sets some of its students off on a career in the performing arts. The course at Gallaudet is notable for the quality of the teaching and of the tutors. Well-known directors and teachers in the theatre are invited to conduct workshops. On my visit a mixed group of Russian and American deaf students were taking a movement class with a member of the *Merce Cunningham Dance Company* from New York. The Russians were accompanied by their director and his wife, and were taking part in the summer school. I was told with great excitement that plans were in motion to set up a theatre for the deaf in Moscow in a building recently donated by the government.

The deaf community in the USA seemed to me to be the best integrated and most successful and active in the disabled arts movement. Highly "vocal", and fighting their corner for the past twenty years, they have attained a high degree of respect in the theatre world, which in turn has had its effect on public consciousness and acceptance. American Sign Language lends itself to dramatic presentation: it is expressive and lyrical, and can create a kind of poetry in movement that would be hard to achieve with the more blunt and utilitarian British Sign Language.

"It was hard not to be shocked at the evidence of human degradation as we ran the gauntlet on 42nd Street"

Reasonably priced accommodation in **New York** is difficult to come by, but we were offered rooms at a centre for new playwrights, in a converted church on 44th Street, close to the theatre district on Broadway. At $30 a night, as opposed to $100 in a hotel, our two small, shabby rooms were much appreciated, even if it meant hobbling up two flights of stairs.

We discovered later that the area in which we were staying, around Times Square and the bus station, is known locally as "Hell's Kitchen" – not the most salubrious in Manhattan. The first afternoon we decided to orientate ourselves, and walked in the immediate vicinity, taking in Grand Central Station, the Empire State and Chrysler buildings and the Rockefeller Center.

Loud, fast, brash and steamy, New York is everything that I was ever told and, for those who live in it and love it, vital and exhilarating.

But it was hard not to be shocked at the evidence of human degradation as we ran the gauntlet on 42nd Street – junkies openly snorting coke, the homeless huddled in doorways, disturbed people of all ages turned out of mental institutions to survive on the streets. The destitute scavenge in trash bins, filling up bags and trolleys with empty cans and bottles, to be redeemed for cash at supermarkets.

On my arrival in New York, I was invited to a meeting of a *People with Disabilities Committee*, formed by the three entertainment unions. The meeting took place in a splendid 44th-floor suite on Times Square, overlooking the Hudson river. Everyone was very welcoming and many were anxious to tell me their own experiences of being a performer with a disability.

I was impressed by the businesslike manner in which the meeting was conducted and by the dedication of the union executives who had initiated the committee. Annual auditions are set up, open to all actors with disabilities, and casting agents and directors are invited. Screen Actors Guild, Equity and the American Federation of Television and Radio Artistes have appointed Affirmative Action officers, who work full-time at promoting the notion of minority groups – including the disabled – participating fully in TV work, advertising and the performing arts. The Screen Actors Guild officer, Elaine Brody, was very generous with her time and described to me how she travelled all over the States, convincing advertising agents and their clients of the need to represent *all* sections of society in their promotional material.

Our plans to take a car into Manhattan had been greeted as madness by everyone. We were told that the traffic is horrific and parking impossible. I suppose it depends on what you are used to; in our case it is central London, so the driving styles were familiar enough and the density of traffic was certainly no worse than at home. In fact, once you have worked out the one-way streets, the grid system makes it much easier to find your way than in London. Parking can be a problem, but armed with a temporary disabled parking permit, organised in advance, it is by no means impossible. Prepare to pay a lot for overnight parking, though – cars have to be off the streets for street cleaning.

Taxis are an alternative means of transport, if you can manage them, and since they comprise at least fifty percent of the traffic in Manhattan there is no shortage. But you will need nerves of steel: the driving is unpredictable and the road surfaces comparable to a lunar landscape. New York taxi drivers – short on knowledge of the city, I was told, and many of them unable to speak English – use their horns constantly as a means of communication.

In between appointments, we found time for short bursts of sightseeing: to the Statue of Liberty, taking in the view of the Manhattan skyline, to the World Trade Center's 107th-floor observation deck, and to the smart shops on Madison Avenue. The Trump Tower, with its expensive boutiques, is a masterpiece of vulgarity in salmon-pink marble, with glossy brass trimmings, and plants cascading into an atrium fountain.

A Jesuit, Brother Ricky Curry, runs the *National Theater Workshop of the Handicapped*, the only training establishment exclusively for disabled people in the country. The criteria for securing a place here are not physical ones, but students must have stamina, creativity and intelligence. Brother Curry is an ebullient and persuasive character who founded the centre in 1977. He has a disability himself and is aware, through personal experience, of the difficulties that talented people face in the performing arts. But he insists that, with professional training and high motivation, his students can achieve a successful career as actor, director or playwright.

"The city is all its reputation claims for it and more – manic, sweltering in summer, deafening and sometimes threatening"

New York can be daunting if you are not accustomed to inner city life – disabled or not. You'll need a tough helper if you use a wheelchair: kerbs are high, the provision of ramps is random and the roads are like roller-coasters and full of potholes. Prepare for your visit by deciding on your method of transport and contacting the appropriate organisation for advice (see *Travel Notes*). Access to buildings is nearly always provided.

The city is all its reputation claims for it and more – manic, sweltering in summer, deafening and sometimes threatening. But being disabled sometimes helps – I was wished well by junkies on occasion! Try to find somewhere to stay where you can get some sleep (the university campuses let rooms during the vacations). Garbage trucks, taxi horns, sirens, burglar alarms and general all-night mayhem conspire to prevent sleep – and you'll need every minute you can grab. New York is not for the faint-hearted, but visit it if you can, just for the experience.

Boston had a familiarity about it. British and Irish origins are immediately apparent in its architecture and layout – narrow streets, churches and a market square which claims more eating places per square yard than anywhere else in the nation. The skyline of towering skyscrapers, seen from a harbour cruiser, is now not so different from that of New York and, astonishingly, has only developed in the last ten years.

The trains on the Rapid Transport System, known as the "T", just miss out on being accessible. There are elevators at most stations, but the two steps onto the trains are steep and we did have to negotiate a turnstile once. The buses are accessible, I'm told, although I didn't use them. Parking and finding our way about presented the usual city problems. Some of the terrain was hilly, so take a strong companion, and ramps are only patchily supplied.

Boston is trying to revive its cultural centre – five new theatres are to open soon. As part of this revitalisation, we saw a production of a version of *The Bacchae* on Boston Common, with a chorus of lissom, sequinned, leotard-clad girls and young men, singing rock songs between the dramatic episodes. At least it was free.

Visits to the National Theater of the Deaf and to Yale University took us out of Boston, far into the Connecticut countryside. Chester, a small village tucked away into wooded hills halfway between Boston and New York, seemed an unlikely location for a professional company of deaf actors. Yale University, far from the rolling green campus I'd imagined, was disappointingly set in the drab port of Newhaven, and we suffered in the extreme heat there.

But Connecticut was redeemed for us by the town of Mystic, which provided an "experience" of seventeenth-century life in the way that Americans achieve best. The site has been set up with restored buildings, complete with working shipyard, forge, and a rope factory in a shed a quarter of a mile long. With the sun setting over the Mystic river, we could have been on a Devon estuary.

Making our way along the coast, we drove across Conanicut Island into our ninth state, Rhode Island. Newport is best known as a yachting centre and has a rather over-restored, touristy wharf. It also boasts the oldest (and very handsome) Episcopalian church in the USA. Out on the headland, Palladian mansions, on the grandest scale, sit alongside French châteaux and German Baroque castles. Many are open to the public.

Boston marked the end of the first part of our travels. Next stop, Los Angeles, a very different world and a blissfully relaxing one for those with mobility problems – and the weather is perfect, too!

Another America

From Los Angeles, on the second leg of her four-month tour of the USA, Carolyn Lucas travelled into New Mexico. As a wheelchair user, she found surprisingly few obstacles, even in the desert.

The journey to Santa Fe by train is probably the nearest I will ever get to feeling like an intrepid traveller, and was one of the highlights of our American trip. We had wanted to visit a different part of America, and decided on New Mexico. Flying would have meant missing the landscape; it was too far to drive, but *Amtrak* – usually an expensive way to travel – was offering a reduction on twenty percent of the tickets, to $94 for the 3220-kilometre round trip.

Relaxing in the comfort of an *Amtrak* coach is the way to survey the majesty and scale of the American landscape. Passing through the mountains from Los Angeles to the Mojave Desert, through Arizona and into the high desert of New Mexico, gives some idea of what the continent has to offer.

We pulled out of the Art Deco, Spanish-style Grand Union Station in Los Angeles at 8.30pm, in the vast, silver *South West Chief* locomotive. We could not but feel a thrill of anticipation for the seventeen-hour overnight journey (four days for those carrying on to New York), 1600km and one third of the way across America.

Collected from the station concourse by truck – for the halt, lame, blind and infirm – we and our luggage had been deposited in the "handicapped only" compartment, and settled in the spacious coach for only twelve people. Stretching out on the reclining seats, with pillow and footrest, we were welcomed by our attendant and told that we would be well looked after and our meals brought to us. One gentleman even plugged in his respirator.

By the time we rolled out of the station, it was dark. The train trundled slowly and soundlessly, except for the distinctive American loco hooting, through the Los Angeles suburbs of Pasadena and Pomona. The lights of the city were left behind at San Bernadino; we climbed through the mountains and down into the Mojave Desert.

Dark, distant mounds were silhouetted in the moonlight, sage brush and scrub lined the track and there was the occasional trail of head- and tail-lights as trucks headed across the desert in the darkness, or lined up in convoys to sleep the night away in lay-bys. We stopped at Barstow and Needles – ghost stations in the dead of night.

After a brief nap, we woke to dawn breaking over the Coconino Plateau in Arizona. The sun cast long shadows over the ponderosa pines, mesquite bushes and meadows of tall, yellow daisies. The conductor arrived with our breakfast, selected from an extensive menu, as we crossed the flat lands of the Navajo Reservation, with distant views of the buttes and mesas of the

Painted Desert. The blood red of the Little Colorado river trickled beside the track.

"A parched landscape of red sandstone, dried-up stream beds, and jagged, black lava fields – home to countless rattlesnakes"

At Gallup, "Indian Capital of the World" (the usual hamburger bars and tourist-trap craft shops), an Indian guide from the Laguna tribe boarded and gave us a commentary on the landscape and local people living in the ancient pueblos that we could see from the train. Traditional adobe houses sat alongside mobile homes; the more isolated dwellings had a truck rusting in the yard and maybe a horse. Sacred sites were pointed out to us, and the uranium mines owned and administered by the tribes.

We crossed the border into New Mexico, were told to change our watches to Mountain Time, and lost an hour. The terrain changed into a parched landscape of red sandstone, dried-up stream beds, and jagged, black lava fields – home to countless rattlesnakes.

Across the Continental Divide, mountain ranges appeared in the distance and we came to the valley of the Rio Grande. Not very grand here, but a pastoral and domestic picture of trees and green fields on the approach to Albuquerque. The train stopped for cleaning and servicing and we were invited to stretch our legs and look at the Indian craft work on display.

The legendary Santa Fe Railroad actually bypasses Santa Fe. Either the terrain was too difficult, or the locals were reluctant to find the cash to take the railroad into the town. Our hire car met us at Lamy, the nearest station, 25km away in the desert.

This is high desert. Santa Fe is at 2100m elevation and you can often see at least 80km in every direction – to ochre and red sandstone cliffs, rock faces, mountains and mesas. One million years ago, a volcanic eruption in the Jemez Mountains spewed lava over a 1000-square-kilometre area, 300m thick in places. The lava has eroded away into spectacular rock and cliff formations, leaving a labyrinth of canyons.

In Frijoles Canyon, part of the Bandolier National Monument, the Anasazi ancestors of the local Indians exploited the natural features of the soft rock and scoured out the Swiss-cheese holes to make homes for themselves, high on the canyon walls. They then added adobe extensions to enlarge their living quarters. The remains of the circular adobe village lie at the foot of the canyon. A steep ramp made even the caves wheelchair accessible, and there was very little that I could not get to in the area. The views are stunning, and plenty of picnic places are provided, with accessible loos in all public places.

We drove up the 3000-metre Sangre de Cristo mountains to sit, joined by chipmunks, among the aspens. We listened to La Traviata under the stars at the Santa Fe Opera, 16km into the desert, wheelchair space provided.

Taos, an old town and Indian pueblo, is the mecca for tourists, and we headed there along the mountain road. The famous multistoreyed pueblo and massive, walled adobe church of St Francis are a focus for all the artists of the area.

Until recently, the tiny Indian or Spanish villages were almost cut off, and they retain a remote and primitive air. Truchas church is like a Welsh hill-top chapel, albeit with vibrantly coloured, painted reredos, net curtains at the window and an ancient stove in the nave. Chimayo has the only healing shrine in the States, and a little room, stifling with heat from votive candles, is crammed with testimonies, the crutches of the healed and offerings of all sorts. Next door, an even smaller room contains the red healing dust in a hole in the floor, to be applied or dissolved in water and drunk. As we left, a party of Mexican ladies arrived, covering their heads and chanting as they entered the church.

Santa Fe has an interesting range of architecture, mostly wheelchair accessible, ranging from old and new adobe structures (including the local Safeway supermarket and car park!) to Spanish-inspired buildings and "Wild West" wooden arcades. It is an "arty" place – galleries abound and Indian art prolife-rates, produced by Indian artists or white Americans jumping on the band-wagon. Indian craftsmen and women, selling pots and silver and turquoise jewellery, sat under the arcades of the Palace of the Governors, which housed Spanish viceroys, then pueblo Indians and finally US government officials.

Antique Navajo rugs, Hopi *katchinas* and pueblo pots could be found in the galleries along the narrow, sun-soaked Canyon Road. It was a pleasant place to spend a bonus two hours, as our train from Chicago had been delayed by flash floods.

Our journey back was comfortable. Tourists from the Grand Canyon, loaded with rucksacks and bleary-eyed with sleep, boarded the train at Flagstaff, Arizona, in the early hours. Dawn came up over the Mojave Desert, silhouetting the Joshua trees and the shacks littering the sides of the track. The train hauled itself through the mountains and back into Los Angeles around 9am. The contrast between the open vistas of desert and mountains in New Mexico, and the urban sprawl and glistening skyscrapers of Downtown Los Angeles could not have been greater. We had certainly achieved our aim of catching a glimpse of another America.

Drama on the West Coast

After the East Coast cities of Washington DC, New York and Boston, then Los Angeles and New Mexico (described in the previous two accounts), Carolyn Lucas finished off her working holiday with a month in San Francisco.

When the early navigators, including Sir Francis Drake in 1579, passed down the Californian coast, they missed the gap at the Golden Gate. The existence of the inland sea of San Francisco Bay was not discovered for a further two hundred years.

Probably the most spectacularly situated city in the world, San Francisco is certainly America's most beautiful. This stretch of Northern California has much to offer – a dramatic coastline, redwood forests, historic Spanish missions, the Sierra Nevada mountain range, the wine country of the Napa Valley and the counties of Mendocino and Sonoma, and of course the city itself. San Francisco is tucked into the bay, joined to the other cities which ring the water by the 7.25-kilometre Bay Bridge, and to Marin County by the Golden Gate Bridge.

Our base for the final month of our trip was Sausalito, a short drive over the Golden Gate Bridge from San Francisco. One of our first outings was with an ex-forester who knew and loved the city and wanted to show it off to his English visitors. We must have looked a strange sight, with myself in a wheelchair, my husband, and a tall, elderly gentleman in stetson and cowboy boots. However, most things go in San Francisco!

The ferry from Sausalito took us across the bay (chair lift for wheelchair users on the boat, of course) and we wandered down Market Street and through the Embarcadero complex of homes, shops and offices, to the Bank of America. Not many tourists know about the cocktail bar in the Bank of America, the tallest building in San Francisco, towering above even the famous "Pyramid". The bar, on the 52nd floor, is open to all visitors, commanding panoramic views over the city, the bay, the docks, Alcatraz and other islands.

Angel Island, which we overlooked from our bedroom, is a popular weekend picnic venue, reached by boat from the city or from Tiburon. It is a nature reserve with an eight-kilometre, paved perimeter trail. Cloaked in mist when we went, the island is usually a good spot for lovely views of the bay.

San Francisco is built on forty hills, many of them practically vertical – residents negotiating them every day soon develop a distinct list! But a virtue of the city is that it is compact enough to get around on foot or wheel, without the use of a car, by using buses (*MUNI* – the *San Francisco Municipal Railroad* operates the transport system in the city), trains (*MUNI* or *BART* – the *Bay Area Rapid Transit* rail system runs into the city from the East Bay and outer suburbs) and the occasional cab. All public transport is accessible, and helpful information for disabled people is available. But it is hilly, so you need a strong pusher.

> **"She did not give anyone the opportunity to deny her the right to follow her chosen vocation"**

We took an exciting trip on a cable car (folding the chair). At one point, halfway up one of the hills, a car pulled out in front of us, necessitating an abrupt halt. It seemed that we were prevented from rolling back into the bay by nothing more than the brute force of the conductors hauling on the brakes. Accompanied by much bellowing and clanging of bells, we endured a hair-raising lurch back to the nearest level junction, before cranking up for a re-run at the hill.

Other attractions of San Francisco include the Japanese Tea Garden, complete with tea-house, pagodas and landscaped gardens, and several art museums in the Golden Gate Park. The Mexican Museum at Fort Mason has a shop crammed with enticing, inexpensive and colourful gifts. The Ghirardelli complex, on the site of the old chocolate factory, is a fun place to walk around, with shops and restaurants; Pier Nine with its vast range of seafood is nearby. San Francisco is a gourmet's delight – food of every nationality is available, and there is no finer Chinese food outside China.

"The disability movement in America really had its beginnings on the campus of Berkeley"

When you have exhausted the city, take the ferry across to Sausalito and visit the scale-model of San Francisco Bay. Though open to tourists, the model was constructed by the Army Corps of Engineers and is used primarily to study the impact of natural and artificial changes in the bay, tidal movements, salinity and the shifting of silt. I met a wheelchair-bound guide here, who had previously worked on Mount Tamalpais in Marin County. When I asked her if she had come across any resistance to her becoming a ranger, she replied that she did not give anyone the opportunity to deny her the right to follow her chosen vocation.

The Pacific coastline of Marin County, all of it National Park, is surprisingly varied. It ranges from precipitous cliffs to the calm, coastal marshes of Point Reyes, with its earthquake trail at the site of the epicentre of the devastating 1906 earthquake. A fence with a staggered six-metre gap has been retained to show how far the earth moved. This trail and others are accessible. Tomales Bay lies along the San Andreas Fault, protected from the coastal cloud, and has lovely silver sands like those of Hearts Desire

Beach. We called in for lunch at Bolinas, a quirky, creekside village of "alternative", Sixties-type inhabitants who regularly cut down all the signposts to the place.

Mount Tamalpais is the highest mountain in Marin. A long, twisty drive took us to the top where we could see, from the accessible trail at the summit, the tops of the San Francisco skyscrapers emerging above the plume of cloud pouring in through the Golden Gate. The views are extensive – to the end of the eighty-kilometre bay, south to the Big Sur mountains, and to the Farallon Islands out to sea. Sometimes, they claim, even the snow-crested Sierra Nevadas, over 300km away, can be seen.

Climatic conditions here are extraordinary. A pall of cloud often hangs over the coast and it finds escape routes through gaps in the mountains. Low cloud pours through the canyons at tremendous speed, like dry ice on a stage, disappearing into thin air when it reaches the brilliant sun and cloudless skies of San Francisco Bay.

The disability movement in America really had its beginnings on the campus of Berkeley, in the East Bay area, where the first Center for Independent Living was founded, so I took the opportunity to find out about it. I met Judy Heumann, of the World Institute on Disability, who told me about the Americans with Disabilities Act, which was passed by Congress during my stay. This federal act is seen as part of the civil rights legislation, outlawing discrimination of any sort toward disabled people with regard to employment, transport and accessibility. It is parallel to the legislation already adopted by most states in America, but acknowledges the rights of disabled people in national law.

I was invited to see the latest production of *Theater Unlimited*. The play, performed mostly by talented, mentally disabled youngsters, was based on research that uncovered the use and abuse of mentally handicapped conscripts in World War II. What was striking was that the material – evolved through improvisation by the group, with a professional writer to hand – in no way talked down to either performers or audience. It was a competent script and could have held its own on a professional stage.

A visit to a production company making educational films took us to Sacramento, California's capital. It is a pleasant, green city, despite its location in the heat of the San Joaquin Valley. The old town, down by the Sacramento River, has been lovingly restored in typical "Western" style: there are saloons, hotels and stores with flat-fronted, wooden arcades or decorated, plastered balustrades and raised boardwalks.

The Pacific Railroad ran through Sacramento on its way to San Francisco. The town is now the site of an excellent railroad museum which includes a simulated, moving Pullman coach, as well as massive locos that carried the early settlers across the forbidding Sierras.

"The offending vehicle was unceremoniously hauled away. If only that would happen at Sainsbury's"

One of the joys of driving in the States is the availability of parking spaces. You rarely find an able-bodied person in a space reserved for the disabled. There is far more respect for disabled drivers than in this country, although the penalties of being cited or towed might have something to do with it. The only parking transgression I witnessed was at a motor-racing circuit where we arrived to find the disabled spaces full. The tough lady in charge pointed to a sleek, red Firebird and said, "If they're disabled, I'm Queen Elizabeth!" She called a tow-truck and the offending vehicle was unceremoniously hauled away. If only that would happen at Sainsbury's.

The Sierra Nevadas, the highest mountain range in the USA, contain one of the most dramatic valleys in the world, at Yosemite. During the Ice Age, glaciers filled the valley formed by the Merced River. As they moved, they gouged out a great trough, deepening into a valley until eventually a lake formed. As the river slowly deposited silt, the lake vanished but streams continued to pour from the mountains into the valley, producing the legendary waterfalls.

Yosemite's popularity ensures that the campsites, cabins and hotel are full most of the year, and numbers of visitors are strictly limited. We had booked some weeks ahead and were lucky enough to be reserved a cabin with ramp and bathroom (not all have this facility). Disabled guests can also be accommodated at the *Ahwahnee Hotel*. Facilities for disabled people are excellent and, apart from one restaurant, all are accessible. Perhaps the nicest surprise is the number of paved trails, some steepish, but still manageable in a wheelchair.

The waterfalls are mostly dry in the autumn, but Bridal Veil, although wispy and blown around by the wind, sported a rainbow halfway down. My husband climbed high to see another fall, while I spent a magical morning sketching in a meadow ringed by pines and surrounded by mountains. Climbers on El Capitan, over half a mile high, on one of the sheerest rock faces in the world, were mere specks, even with binoculars. Their sleeping hammocks hung from hooks on the cliff like seaweed pods. We walked to Mirror Lake, now mostly dry and turning into meadow, and sat in the trees by the emerald pools of the river rimmed with golden sand.

A long drive took us to Glacier Point, high above our cabin, to see the magnificent views down the Yosemite Valley and over the High Sierras. We watched Half Dome turn red as the sun went down, and the moon rising, moving imperceptibly as if being pulled by a string from behind the distant peaks.

It's another lengthy drive to Mariposa Grove, home of the giant sequoias or redwoods. A truck tours the grove, stopping at the 2700-year-old Grizzly Giant – 90m high and nearly 9m in girth – and the tree through which a bus can be driven.

When the Spanish controlled California, Father Junipero Serra, a Franciscan missionary in Mexico, took on the task of founding a series of missions up the Californian coast. From San Diego in the south to Sonoma in the north there are 21 missions, built in the Spanish style and restored after their secularisation in the middle of the nineteenth century. Carmel, founded in 1770, south of Monterey, is one of the most beautiful – "the jewel of the missions". Set back from the ocean, in the Carmel Valley, the white walls are ablaze with bougainvillaea and hibiscus, and the gardens burgeon with shrubs, flowers and cacti. Inside, church and living quarters are brightly painted with Mexican designs.

"Four wines at a time are offered at each winery, and you really have to visit several to compare"

John Steinbeck lived in the Monterey area and made it the setting for much of his work, including _Cannery Row_ and _Tortilla Flat_. Its main claim to fame these days, though, is the Monterey Bay Aquarium. As if they are not rich enough, the residents of Pebble Beach charge tourists for the "Seventeen Mile Drive" along the coastal road. But it's worth paying the few dollars to drive through the pine trees lining the golf course to watch the Pacific breaking over the boulder-strewn beaches.

South of Carmel, the mountains of Big Sur plunge thousands of feet into the Pacific Ocean. The Pacific Coastal Highway clings perilously to the edge, and viewpoints are provided at regular intervals to survey the majestic coastline. At one such point, we could hear the honking of sea-lions, visible only through binoculars, basking on the rocks below.

In the 1860s it was discovered that the climate of Northern California is ideally suited to the cultivation of grapes. European immigrants soon set up wineries in the Napa Valley and on the slopes of Sonoma and Mendocino counties. The wineries are all very hospitable and open their vineyards for tours and wine tasting. In retrospect, it might have been wiser to take a tour, rather than drive. Four wines at a time are offered at each winery, and you really have to visit several to compare.

With visits to Calistoga (an early mining town, with hot springs and a spa), nearby Old Faithful (the geyser which spouts every forty minutes, on the dot) and the settlements along the Russian River in Sonoma County, we had come to the end of our four months of travel – not before time, as it happens. Two weeks after our departure, the 1989 earthquake struck. I had asked a few San Franciscans how it was that they were able to live with the prospect of a major disaster under their feet. The response was always the same: "Well, we've lived in Ohio (or Kansas or Iowa) and we suffered truly terrifying hurricanes regularly. San Francisco is such a beautiful place to live, we'll chance it!" I could see their point.

One of the Crowd

In Washington DC, Frances Hill found that wheelchair access to public buildings and public transport is no longer a dream but a reality. It is a city which has taken the needs of the handicapped into account.

"The Nation's Capital", as they say on American TV, is the home of the US government, the National Archives and the FBI. If you are lucky enough to fly in on one of the frequent clear days, the vast green areas and multitude of white buildings will leave a lasting impression.

We stayed at the *Days Inn Downtown* (1201 K Street, NW), which has several rooms adapted for handicapped people. These are very comfortable; in some an extra inch or two would have been welcome in the doorways, but it was possible to manoeuvre. Some rooms have queen-size beds, others two single (plus sofa bed). Fold-up cots are available for a small extra charge. Being senior citizens, my husband and I obtained a special rate; if you book two to three months in advance there is a substantial (nearly fifty percent) reduction.

Having rested, unpacked and "settled" to some extent, we sallied forth to explore. Washington is a well-designed city, divided into four quadrants, the northwest containing most of the places you'll want to visit. All the sidewalks (pavements) have "curb cuts" – areas at corners flush with the road: no jolting (good news for wheelchair riders who have pain); no struggle to lift the chair (good news for companions); no taking a run at it – just smooth sailing from sidewalk to road and back again. There are tactile markers for the visually handicapped.

It wasn't long before we noticed box-like structures resembling bus shelters at regular intervals along the sidewalks. Further investigation revealed that these contained lifts descending to the Metrorail, to the level where tickets are purchased. The fare system is simplicity itself – a single charge regardless of distance. We each bought a $5 magnetic strip ticket from a machine and found that the remaining balance was automatically printed each time we inserted the ticket at the barrier. After six trips the remaining twenty cents was recorded and added to our new ticket. All so easy – no lengthy queues for tickets before each journey.

Passing through the barrier, we came to the stairs, escalators and a lift with the wheelchair sign displayed (elderly people and mothers with push-chairs are also free to use it). Thus we descended to the level of our choice and boarded the train, the floor of which was flush with the platform (again, the edges were well marked for visually handicapped travellers). Spaces were provided on the train for safe and convenient positioning of my chair, and before arrival at each station the name was announced quite distinctly, giving passengers time to prepare for exit. The stations are wide, with many seats, high vaulted roofs and excellent lighting and ventilation – not a bit of litter or graffiti in sight (sadly, not so in the street lifts).

"I was utterly thrilled to be just like any other passenger"

I saw several handicapped passengers using the trains – alone, well dressed, carrying briefcases, obviously business people, as well as students on their way to school or college, chattering eagerly and "one of the crowd". I was utterly thrilled to be just like any other passenger and would have happily spent all day exercising my new-found freedom and independence. Of course, there was too much to do to spend hours on the subway, but we did use the trains every day and saw many parts of the city that we would never have found by car (Washington, like any big city, has its parking problems).

My main objective was to visit the National Art Gallery and as much of the Smithsonian Institution as possible. Since childhood I've loved the Impressionist painters and have seen many works in London, but "Woman with a Parasol" only in books and on postcards. To see the original close-up was a wonderful experience. I sat in front of it and gazed and gazed, feeling like a teenager meeting her pop star idol.

"While glad of any form of admission, I am always pleased not to be part of the 'Deliveries'"

The gallery has much to offer besides the pictures. There are many visual pleasures, including the architecture and layout of the display halls, and a lovely large restaurant and garden, with moderately priced service and cafeteria sections, the whole facing a glassed-in "waterfall wall" which is beautifully relaxing. The lifts, toilets, restaurant and gallery are all accessible.

Indeed, all the buildings of the Smithsonian are accessible. It is an amazing collection of museums and galleries, tastefully incorporated into their surroundings, with many parks and garden backgrounds, and an absolute minimum of litter (it is rare to see any around the city). The complex was the inspiration of James Smithson, an English scientist who in 1846 bequeathed half a million dollars to "found an establishment for the increase and diffusion of knowledge among men". It is now administered as a private foundation, funded mainly by Congress but also by a succession of large legacies over the years.

All buildings have front-door entrances for the handicapped; while glad of any form of admission, I am always pleased not to be part of the "Deliveries". There is so much to see that on a short stay you have to be selective. To name just a few of the options: the National History Museum; the African, Near Eastern and Asian Museum; the Botanical Gardens; the Freer Art Gallery, which was formerly a private collection containing the famous Whistler Blue Room (the guard who unlocked and showed us this was as pleased and proud as if he had painted it himself); the Hirshorn Museum and Garden of Sculpture; the Famous Explorers' Exhibition at the offices of the National Geographic magazine. Admission is free to everything except the J.F. Kennedy Center for Performing Arts.

We spent half a day touring the National Air and Space Museum, a must for my husband, who served in the RAF during World War II. The sight of V1s and V2s brought back some vivid memories. The museum charts the history of powered flight from the days of the Wright brothers' flimsy craft to the giants of space exploration. The static exhibits are wonderfully augmented by audiovisual information. We were particularly intrigued to enter a space module containing figures depicting life aboard the craft. We would have stayed longer but had to leave when a bomb scare closed the building!

For a change of pace we visited the National Zoological Gardens (easily reached on the subway) which are well laid out in undulating grounds with a clearly marked wheelchair route. I was pleased to see that the animals had plenty of room in which to live and roam. The big attraction was a disappointment – giant pandas are far less endearing than their toy counterparts. Surprisingly, we found access to the restaurant very difficult, eventually settling for entrance via the exit – there are plenty of takeaway kiosks throughout the grounds but most had long queues.

Apart from the Smithsonian, which deserves a holiday all to itself (don't be put off by so many museums – several have modern themes and there is something to suit everyone), there are the other tourist attractions of Washington: the White House, Senate Building, Grant's Tomb, Arlington Cemetery, the Lincoln Memorial – the latter is awe-inspiring when floodlit at night.

Originally called The President's House, the White House was painted white when rebuilt after the war of 1812. It was Theodore Roosevelt who authorised the adoption of the present name in 1902. There are free tours but you have to queue for tickets on a time and day of issue basis; be prepared to wait or even return on another day should the quota be filled. There are seats at frequent intervals along the route.

Viewing is somewhat limited for wheelchair users: the ground floor only is accessible, but the staircase is lovely and you can sit and let your imagination run riot as you wait for the return of your group. We learnt some interesting details about the history of this fine building (many people are unaware that the burning of the White House by British troops in 1812 was in retaliation for the burning of Fort York – now Toronto – in Canada by American

troops) and at least I can say "I've been there!"

A car is unnecessary in Washington but we did use one to drive out to the nearby 80,000-hectare Shenandoah Valley National Park, which is best seen in early to mid-October when the colours of the fall (autumn) leaves are truly spectacular. (September to October tends to be off season for visiting Washington; April to May is the time to see the War Commemorative cherry trees in bloom.) The "tourist route" to Shenandoah is along the 160-kilometre Skyline Drive, which provides breathtaking views of the valley itself and the Allegheny Mountains. The many well-equipped parking areas allowed us to stop and take in the scenery at our leisure.

Also worth a visit – and essential if you are a history buff – is Gettysburg, which has exhibits depicting scenes from the Civil War. There are many other battlegrounds nearby, a stark reminder to the carefree holidaymaker that not much more than a hundred years ago this young country almost tore itself apart in bloody battles which claimed over a million lives.

Bargain Breaks in Southern California

Arthur Goldthorpe makes regular visits to his son and daughter-in-law in California, accompanied by his wife, Nina, and his youngest son, David. Although in a wheelchair permanently, Arthur also wears callipers which enable him to stagger a few paces with support.

All our visits have been made around Easter for two reasons: to coincide with

David's school or university holidays, and to take advantage of the low-season rates and special package deals. In 1989, we booked with *American Airlines*, at the low-season rate, from Manchester to San Diego via Chicago. This necessitated a change of plane at Chicago; judging by our previous experiences of flight delays, time taken boarding and leaving aircraft, customs and immigration, and finding a wheelchair-accessible toilet, the hour allotted in the schedule for the transfer seemed pretty short – but we decided to risk it.

I rely on being able to "walk", with the aid of my callipers, down the aisle of the aircraft to a toilet at least once during a transatlantic crossing, using the backs of the seats for support. We had as usual reserved seats close to the toilets, but realised that my customary laborious excursion would be impossible because the seats and other handholds ran out before reaching the cubicle.

Necessity being the mother of invention (if you have to go, you have to go!), I summoned the chief stewardess and asked if I could use one of the food carts as a mobile support to bridge the gap. With her help edging the trolley forward, I was able to complete the journey to the toilet. On this aircraft the cubicle had a sloping roof, and the usual lack of handholds made standing up even more difficult than I had anticipated. It is not surprising that I was nearly exhausted when I finally fell back into my seat.

"It was only by hanging on grimly that I was able to prevent the transit chair from rolling around the cabin"

My heroics apparently did not go unnoticed. As we were waiting in the aircraft for ground staff to bring the narrow transit chair needed for my disembarkation, the chief stewardess approached and graciously presented me with a splendid box of *American Airlines* chocolates, adding, "Please accept these with our compliments, and thank you for travelling with *American Airlines*." David assures me that she added under her breath, "Have you thought of travelling back with *Pan Am*?" but I cannot confirm this!

Our flight itinerary suggested that we would land at O'Hare airport in Chicago and leave from the same terminal. In reality, we landed at a subsidiary terminal, and passengers had to transfer by bus to the main *American Airlines* terminal for customs and immigration. I remained on the aircraft, waiting for the paramedics to bring the transit chair, getting more fidgety as time passed.

By the time help arrived, my own wheelchair had been whisked off with the rest of the luggage, so that I had to remain strapped into the narrow lifting chair when transferred to the very dilapidated (uncharacteristic of America) transit vehicle. It was only by hanging on grimly to the sides of the vehicle that I was able to prevent the transit chair from rolling around the cabin during the short drive to join the rest of my family. If I had not been strong enough to do this, it would have been a dangerous journey.

To offload its passengers the vehicle had a tail-lift, which successfully unloaded the one other disabled passenger and was then returned to allow me to disembark. As the operator pressed the "down" control, the button fell off and we lost more precious minutes as a solution to the problem was sought. Just as a sharp piece of plastic was found to activate the circuit when pushed into the broken switch, Nina and David arrived with my own chair, having rescued it from the luggage carousel, cleared customs and immigration, and located the boarding gate for our next flight.

Then followed a mad rush down seemingly endless corridors, without any mechanical assistance from travelators – this in one of America's busiest airports. Stopping only for a toilet call, we raced straight to the boarding gate for immediate transfer into the waiting plane.

Whatever the frustrations and anxieties of the change-over, the flight itself soon made up for them. It was a perfect, cloudless sky as we left the Great Lakes and cruised over miles of completely flat terrain, divided into huge, neat farms by grids of roads. The land became gradually more undulating, the roads and farms more varied, as we approached the foothills of the southern end of the Rockies.

Flying westwards in the late afternoon in March, with long shadows cast by the dying sun, we could easily appreciate the contours of the ground below. Soon we were passing over mile after mile of snowcapped peaks of the Rockies. On the west side of the mountains the landscape became arid, a barren wilderness of deserts and mountain ridges.

"Sometimes extraordinary efforts are made to allow disabled people to enjoy leisure facilities"

The most moving experience, however, was flying over the Grand Canyon, marvelling at the scale and beauty of this gash in the earth's surface, as it lay bathed in evening light. This flight from Chicago to San Diego intensified one of the feelings aroused by my visits to California – humble admiration for the early pioneers who crossed this enormous, inhospitable wilderness in the centre of America, with primitive, horse-drawn vehicles, to reach the fertile west coast.

San Diego is a beautiful city, built around a large bay, naturally protected by the Point Loma peninsula, and home to the United States South Pacific fleet. The smaller Mission Bay is devoted to aquatic sports and has miles of beaches which make it an ideal holiday venue. The city claims to have the most equitable climate in the USA. Amongst its attractions are an exciting and extensive Sea World, the magnificent Balboa Park with its museums, the world-famous San Diego Zoo, and a well-preserved Old Town on the site of the first European settlement in California.

The first few days of our three-week holiday were spent living out of suitcases in my son Christopher's small apartment in the hills overlooking Mission Bay. This gave us time to look for suitable wheelchair-accessible accommodation. A visit to the *International Visitor Information Center* secured the last copy of an access guide to San Diego – very modest by UK standards – and a much more useful accommodation directory, which

indicated which hotels or self-catering units had an "HR", or handicapped room. Imagine our delight when we found from the directory that *Beach Cottages*, in a prime position on the promenade next to the beach, had an HR on the second floor with lift access, at a reasonable price within our budget.

We knew from our previous trips to America that although all new buildings have to provide facilities for disabled people, the standards vary considerably from those in the UK. Access into and around premises (including beaches) is generally very good; indeed sometimes extraordinary efforts are made to allow disabled people to enjoy leisure facilities; but suitable bathroom and toilet facilities for more severely disabled people can sometimes be hard to find.

The bathroom in our suite at *Beach Cottages* was typical of others that I have come across in the USA. There was plenty of circulation space, with good access to the washbasin, and a bath with shower unit inside. Unfortunately, two sliding glass panels, running along the edge of the bath as splash guards, meant that only half of the bath could be exposed at any one time, thus making it very difficult for anyone disabled to use either bath or shower.

The toilet in this room was adjacent to the bath, so that there was no support rail on that side; instead, there was a wall-mounted rail behind the toilet and a fixed "L" rail from wall to floor at what we would consider the transfer side. I found it possible to position my chair obliquely across the front of the pan and transfer from there, but this may not suit everyone. The message is – wherever possible – check out the bathroom before booking any accommodation.

In spite of the differences in design of facilities, it is still possible to tour the USA without detailed planning and pre-booking because there is so much accommodation readily available in all price brackets. Very reasonable accommodation can be booked either on a room-per-night basis (irrespective of the number of occupants), or as "efficiencies" (self-catering apartments). The latter have a small kitchen area which I have found useful for a quick wash if the bathroom required a heroic effort to enter. On several occasions, when my difficulties had been explained to the manager, we were offered an efficiency at the lower, room-per-night rate, on condition that we did not use the cooking facilities.

"A one-legged roller-skater propelling himself along at incredible speed with two elbow crutches"

The complex of *Beach Cottages* and the block containing our apartment led straight out to the promenade, a fairly narrow walkway which runs several miles up and down the foreshore. It seemed to be permanently frequented by a mobile mass of young, elegant Californians, ostentatiously keeping fit and displaying their charms in skimpy beachwear. Unlike our English resorts, which bristle with a profusion of "thou shalt not" signs in an attempt to keep footpaths for pedestrians, the promenade in San Diego offered a good-humoured challenge to dodge the cyclists, skateboards, roller-skaters and joggers speeding in both directions. Other vehicles included manual and powered wheelchairs, a motorcyclist, a huge, custom-built tricycle, and a one-legged roller-skater propelling himself along at incredible speed with two elbow crutches.

A major bonus of being in the centre of a holiday area is the profusion of restaurants and takeaways. Because of the competition there were many cost-saving inducements at various establishments. These discounts made substantial savings in our holiday budget and were freely advertised with the necessary vouchers in the local

weekend papers. At one restaurant, as senior citizens (over 55 in the USA), my wife and I could order allegedly smaller portions of the standard meals at a reduced cost, and still stagger from the table grossly overfed. Two meals for the price of one were widely available at slack times, and many takeaway (or home-delivery) establishments gave discounts on future purchases, or a free giant Coke with each order. For anyone really hungry, an omelette restaurant offered free meals to any person who could finish their 32-egg special!

Useful savings were also obtained in other ways – many of the larger hotel chains, for example, give a ten percent discount to senior citizens, but this has to be arranged when checking in. With senior citizen discounts for Nina and myself, and a bargain saver for David, the cost of a boat trip around the harbour in San Diego was reduced from $11 per person to $7. To board the boat it was necessary to descend a horrendously steep ramp, but before we could ask for help two burly sailors appeared and manhandled me down the slope to the lower level of the vessel. As I was unable to get on the upper deck to take photographs, I was positioned in my wheelchair with an open window to my right and within reaching distance of the small bar on my left.

The cruise covered most parts of the enormous natural harbour, with good views of the naval vessels, an airforce base and the downtown skyline of San Diego accompanied by a detailed commentary. A most impressive feature of the bay is the high-level Coronado Bridge linking mainland San Diego with the upmarket coastal suburb of Coronado. The white-clapperboard, red-roofed and turreted *Hotel del Coronado* has been used for location shots in many films, the most famous being *Some Like it Hot*.

Another bargain was a "Gamblers' Break", which enabled us to fly to Las

Vegas and have two nights at a first-rate hotel at very modest cost. This included a package of incentives, ranging from free prawn cocktails with a meal to reduced admission to shows, used to lure us into various casinos. The colour, bustle and vitality of "the Strip" at night is unique, and you need spend no money to enjoy wandering through the casinos, which are all freely open to the public and invariably wheelchair accessible.

San Diego is only 13km from the Mexican border, and we spent a memorable day in Tijuana, where the gloss put on for the tourists cannot hide the poverty evident only a block or so away from the colourful main shopping streets. Since the insurance rates for American cars crossing into Mexico are astronomical – a true reflection of the risks, as we discovered later – we left our car in a car park by the border, and crossed through customs with little formality.

"It became clear that driving here was only for the brave or foolhardy"

On entering Mexico we were immediately besieged by hordes of small boys, touting for customers to take a taxi the mile or so into the centre of Tijuana. Without meaning to, we found ourselves being guided to one of the mass of large, yellow "Tijuana taxis", parked haphazardly in the loading area. Our vehicle was a veteran classic "gas-guzzler", able to accommodate the four other members of the family comfortably across the back seat. This left me to transfer into the front seat over an "L"-shaped tear in the leather upholstery.

My wheelchair was tossed into the boot by our driver, whose build was in proportion to his taxi, and with a screech of tyres we shot off towards Tijuana. The car bounced over rough patches, scraping the exhaust noisily on the ground. As we plunged into an undisciplined traffic jam across a road

junction, where each inch of ground had to be stolen by nerve or guile, it became clear that driving here was only for the brave or foolhardy.

The main shopping street of Tijuana (Avenida Revolución) is a mixture of bazaar-type stores – full of colourful Mexican pottery, hats and other souvenirs – and very expensive shops containing exquisite leather goods, glassware and jewellery. On the pavements, every few paces would bring forth an invitation to purchase cheap beads and other goods from Mexican children; at intervals, sadly, poor families huddled together, begging with a plastic bowl. Being unsure of the standard of hygiene or the strength of the chilli, we took a safe option and went to *Woolworths de Mexico* where, but for the pricing of the goods, we could almost have been in a high-street store anywhere in the UK.

As one moves eastwards from the densely populated coastal strip of California, the hills become ranges of mountains and between them the flat plains become progressively more arid. Grass gives way to scrub and then desert, on a scale which only becomes apparent when driving through or flying over the states of California, Arizona, Utah and Nevada. Few people fail to be fascinated by the way in which different desert plants have adapted to their climate. This is typified by the symbiosis between the tall saguaro of the Arizona landscape and the foothill or yellow paloverdae.

The seeds of the saguaro need the shade of a bush to become established, and usually germinate beneath a paloverdae tree which, with its very deep root system, survives on the moisture which has seeped far into the ground. The saguaro, with its expansive root system just below the surface, does not compete with the host tree; it can quickly absorb water from any sudden rainstorms and is capable of storing up to six tons in its expandable trunk.

If you are fortunate enough to be in the desert in the few weeks in spring when the flowering season breaks, you will see this usually barren country briefly transformed into a breathtaking, gigantic rock garden, with a profusion of flowering shrubs, small cacti and other ground plants in yellow, white, red and pink.

Our 1989 holiday was blessed by a freak spring heatwave, with temperatures touching 96°F one April day. This is quite rare for San Diego, even in summer, and it enhanced further the image of "Sunny California", making us count the months, on our return, until our next visit to this beautiful and varied part of America.

It's OK to Scream in Orlando

In April 1987, Stephen Latham and five friends spent two weeks in Orlando, Florida. The group consisted of three tetraplegics (Stephen, Stuart and Dave) and two paraplegics (Bob and Ian), with an able-bodied friend (Austin) as nurse and escort.

As it was to be something of a working holiday for Austin, the remaining group members decided that it was only right that we should pay for his flight and accommodation – we drew the line at his bar bill! Austin deserves special mention as we could not have managed the holiday without him.

We chose Orlando as our destination for several reasons: I had been there before, and I recommended it; the weather is good; there are countless attractions and, most important, *everywhere* is accessible. We picked April as the best time to go because it would be easier to get around – easier for pushing the wheelchairs, as the weather is not unbearably hot (although temperatures reached the high eighties while we were there) and there are not the huge crowds that are found in the summer, especially at the major attractions.

We booked our holiday with *Jetsave* through our local travel agent, but we ensured that they were well acquainted with our requirements, particularly with regard to our hotel rooms. The choice of hotel and room can make or break a holiday for a disabled person – this point needs to be stressed to all who work in the travel business. We chose a *Holiday Inn* hotel because it has rooms for disabled guests, is well situated, with numerous bars, shops and eating places close at hand, and, again, I could recommend it.

"We were ready to hit the town, or, in our tired condition, at least to slap it gently"

The airline staff (*British Caledonian*, now *British Airways*) were helpful – no better, no worse than other airlines I've used. The *Jetsave* package was good value for money but we did land at Bangor, Maine, for refuelling. All passengers had to disembark here for customs but we were allowed to stay on the aircraft. I have since flown with *British Airways* and although the flight was more expensive we still landed at Bangor.

For the transfer from Orlando airport to the hotel, a coach was laid on. However, as this entailed being lifted onto the coach, and we had only one escort, we arranged with the tour rep to use taxis. We arrived at the hotel, found our rooms and were ready to hit the town, or, in our tired condition, at least to slap it gently.

The major attractions of Orlando are well known – Disneyworld, Epcot, Sea World, Kennedy Space Center, Wet 'n Wild, Boardwalk and Baseball, to name a few – and we were determined to visit as many as possible. The tour operators run trips to the main attractions but as these involved the use of coaches we decided to hire a car.

We had tried (through our travel agent in England) to hire a car with hand controls, but as a result of problems with the rental company (*Avis*) we had to take a car without them. (*Avis* also tried to overcharge us for several hundred miles which we had not covered, and this issue was not resolved until we were back in England.) We hired a large station wagon (rather like the *QE2* on wheels) which would accommodate us all, although it was rather cramped. Luckily we all had lightweight, folding wheelchairs with removable wheels, which could be stored in the back, leaving the inside of the car resembling a giant Meccano kit. An advantage of having the car was that we could make our own timetables, visiting what we liked, when we liked, and staying as long as we wished.

Despite the fact that you can overtake on both the inside and outside lanes, driving in the States is straightforward and all the big attractions are well signposted. The only problem we experienced was in having one driver and five "backseat drivers", all issuing instructions at the same time.

We used the car for one week, while the second, more leisurely week was spent around the hotel and at local attractions, to which we could push. It is best to space your activities out, visiting an attraction or two for a few days, then having a rest day. Attempting to visit something every day is extremely tiring – not only for disabled people. On one of our quiet days we went on a helicopter trip over Disneyworld, Epcot and Sea World. Although expensive, it was a good experience and well worth it. As with the coaches, you have to be lifted aboard the helicopter, so able-bodied friends are invaluable.

"It is not that they don't want to help, but their insurance laws, and the fear of litigation if anything goes wrong, deter them"

A three-day pass for Disneyworld and Epcot enabled us to spend a day in each attraction, finishing on the third morning with Disneyworld and travelling by monorail (only a five- to ten-minute trip) across to Epcot for the remainder of the day. Some of the highlights for us were a four-hour "quick visit" to the *Rose and Crown* English pub in Epcot, and watching some of the group attempting to board one of the rides while it was still moving (this was one of the few which could not be completely stopped for boarding).

All the shows and rides are good, but those which should not be missed include the Country Bear Jamboree, the Pirates of the Caribbean and the Haunted Mansion (all in Disneyworld), as well as the Living Seas in Epcot, and the Sea-Lion and Otter Show at Sea World.

There is so much to see and do in the theme parks that it is best to pick up the guidebooks or leaflets at the entrance and follow the route which takes you round the attractions that appeal most. There are special vantage points and viewing sections for the disabled at the shows, and often priority access is given in the theme parks. Able-bodied people do not abuse this system, and it is efficiently supervised by the venue's employees. At the Kennedy Space Center, special arrangements for disabled people are made for tours of the base.

One note of warning should be sounded concerning the theme-park rides. The majority of the rides are fine for disabled people, but the "white-knuckle" rides are a different matter. If you decide to go on one of these rides, you *must* have an able-bodied person with you, if only to cover your legs with theirs to keep yours in place. However, on this holiday I was persuaded to go on one of these rides alone – the general idea was that you spun round and round and finished the ride upside down. Thinking that gravity would hold my legs in place, I decided to ride in the car on my own.

Not recommended! My brain must have been back at the hotel when I made that decision. No sooner had the ride started than I realised that this was *not* my idea of a fun day out. While I was hanging on for grim death to keep my backside on the seat, my legs were doing a breakdancing exhibition, twirling above my head. Questions such as "have I written my will?" flashed through my mind, but I was too busy screaming to think of much else.

"The only drawback to Florida is that it can spoil other holiday destinations for you"

One of my friends noticed the trouble and managed to attract the ride operator's attention. She stopped the ride, there was no harm done, and we all had a good laugh. When I joined the ride, I had jokingly asked the girl if it was OK to scream . . .

Although the people of Florida are generally very friendly, they are not likely to help with lifting either disabled person or chair. This particularly applies to theme-park employees and coach or taxi drivers. It is not that they don't want to help, but their insurance laws, and the fear of litigation if anything goes wrong, deter them. If they injure you, they are afraid that you'll "sue the pants off them".

Nightlife is well catered for. We visited numerous bars and eating places (Chinese, seafood, Italian,

Japanese, fast-food, you name it), all close to the hotel. It was great to be pushing around at midnight, wearing only T-shirts and trousers, and it was strange to come out of cool, air-conditioned bars and restaurants into the warm air outside.

To reach the nightspots, we did our "chicken run", which entailed waiting for a break in the traffic and then pushing across a four-lane highway. Drivers usually let us cross, but it was hair-raising at times. On several evenings, entertainment was provided by the locals (mostly youngsters) in their cars, some of them spectacular models, cruising up and down the main street by our hotel. We simply sat on the sidewalk (pavement to you and me), drinking cans of beer, laughing and joking with them as they passed by.

Even the best laid plans can go wrong, and things went wrong for us, but the incidents made us laugh and provided entertaining holiday stories when we got home. On one trip, to a shopping mall, we made a bad choice of route and ended up having to push five miles back to our hotel, most of the way along a busy main road against the traffic (there was no sidewalk).

At the end of our night out at a local German *Bier Keller*, Austin followed us, after a couple of minutes, out of the bar and found a scene of pure chaos. I had unwittingly tried to push open a locked door with my footplates, been thrown off balance and was attempting to get back into the vertical position. Two of the group were definitely "under the influence" and one was being supported by the fourth member. The fifth man, having laughed so much at what was happening, had accidentally rolled backwards off a high step and fallen out of his wheelchair.

I wholeheartedly recommend Florida to disabled people. Most of our party have been back to Orlando, this time in a larger group of fourteen people (five disabled, five able-bodied wives or relatives, and four children), and again had a great time. The only drawback to Florida is that it can spoil other holiday destinations for you – they don't have the same appeal any more! Everyone needs a holiday now and again, and if you sit at home forever pondering the pros and cons you'll never get to shake hands with Mickey Mouse, will you?

Corinne's Choice

Shirley Lihou's daughter, Corinne, has Down's syndrome and at the age of 26 is literate and numerate to the level of a ten-year-old. When asked where she would like to go on holiday, Corinne replied, "Disneyworld – to see my friends".

Five years later, after much saving, we were whirring over the Atlantic on a *Monarch Airlines* Boeing 757, on a family holiday to Florida. It was the autumn of 1988 – hurricane season – and we caught the slipstream of Hurricane Gilbert, the one which so relentlessly battered Jamaica.

We had not pre-booked any accommodation, but after picking up a rented *Alamo* car (booked by our travel agent in England) we quickly came across a suitable motel. We were followed by an English couple whom we had met in the car rental offices. They had visited the area before and were very interested in Corinne. We discovered that the wife had been a geriatric nurse; it is often the case that those who have had contact with disabled people are able to approach Corinne without appearing awkward or embarrassed. By travelling around with Corinne we hope that the public will learn to accept "different" people more easily. We have always found English people on holiday very ready to chat, and pleasantly curious about our daughter, who is also keen to exchange words.

To keep the cost down we mostly used travel lodges or motels. As we were visiting in the off-peak season, we (three) had the use of a six-berth family apartment for the first four nights whilst we were visiting Disneyworld. The cost did not include utensils, so we had to venture forth to the local supermarket to stock up. We bought articles that we could take home, such as a handleless, dual-purpose, stainless-steel pan – one in which we could boil eggs there, and later use as drinking bowl for our dog back home!

We had been advised to allow four whole days in Disneyworld, which covers a huge area, but we were not convinced. We wished to see more than Disneyworld for our money. Equipped with flat shoes, picnic basket and the book, *What not to see in Disneyworld* (in other words, how to do the resort justice when time is short), we set off early every morning with a pre-arranged schedule. We did not admit to being tired until we returned to our motel!

Corinne's favourite rides were Jungle Cruise, 20,000 Leagues under the Sea, and "flying" aboard a pirate galleon with Peter Pan through the skies over London to Never-Never Land. Her visit to Mission Control, followed by "blast off" on moving seats for a journey to Mars, scored another hit – Corinne believed she was actually going there! The All-America parade, held every afternoon in Main Street in "The Land of Make-Believe – The Magic Kingdom" was another highlight. To be photographed with Pluto was sheer bliss, and as for those masks of Pluto, Mickey and Donald, even Mummy wore one – she was really in the spirit.

Of course, you can stay at the conveniently located accommodation within the Walt Disney World Resort, so that you can return to the attractions in the evening after a rest in your hotel. *Buena Vista Palace* has 870 rooms, eight restaurants, swimming pool, sauna and free tennis; the *Howard Johnson Resort Hotel* has 323 rooms plus penthouses. Unless you want a really upmarket holiday spent entirely in the Disneyworld village, however, it's an unecessary expense, especially if you have fortitude like us.

Moving on to another major attraction in the resort, Epcot, we found something which Corinne deemed "even better than The Magic Kingdom". At the Magic Eye Theatre we viewed a three-dimensional "musical motion picture space adventure film", starring Michael Jackson. There was never a dull moment in Epcot, and we returned to the car full of chatter about what we liked best.

The enormous, gleaming geosphere called Spaceship Earth, 56m high and dominating the whole of Epcot, is two worlds in one – Future World and World Showcase. The time machine took us from the distant past to a possible future, a fantastic experience. The process of loading and unloading visitors on and off the rail cars was very slick and the waiting time minimal.

If needed, a limited number of wheelchairs and motorised trikes are available at the stroller and wheelchair rental station at the base of the spaceship. Complimentary tape cassettes and portable recorders, intended to assist sight-impaired guests, can be obtained from the information centre (Earth Station). To encourage the use of dining facilities in Epcot, food and drink are not allowed into the centre, but we were ignorant of this fact beforehand and no-one seemed to notice. Food and drinks were rather expensive and the beer in

the "typical UK pub" within the World Showcase was £2 a pint.

Corinne was fascinated by The Living Seas, another Epcot attraction. We watched dolphins, sharks and groupers swimming lazily around us in gigantic tanks. The never-ending stream of visitors had no time to notice my daughter and I kneeling on the carpet with our noses glued to the sides of these tanks – we were hypnotised.

"A version of The Wizard of Oz, performed by 'Sea-Lions of the Silver Screen'"

Sea World, a major attraction situated off Interstate 4 and International Drive, is home to the four-ton killer whale, Shamu, and Baby Shamu who was born in captivity. Corinne's face was a picture when Shamu surged from the depths of the tank and dramatically swept a wet-suited lady about six metres into the air. How she applauded! At the Sea-Lion and Otter Stadium we witnessed a version of *The Wizard of Oz*, performed by "Sea-Lions of the Silver Screen". During the intervals a brilliant mime artist entertained the audience; Corinne was captivated and giggled throughout all his antics.

After the hectic pace in Orlando, we were glad to find a more peaceful resort for the remainder of our holiday. We weren't aware that Florida is so low-lying – only a metre above sea level in most places. As we motored west through Tampa we were surprised to discover the main highway flooded. We were diverted down to the Gulf of Mexico and, wishing to be near the sea but not to the tourist-weary towns of St Petersburg or Clearwater, we drove a little further south, opposite Sarasota and in manatee (sea-cow) country.

The journey was uneventful but the weather was sultry and we passed several "Evacuation Point" signs, which we later realised were to assist the population when the storms came and a hasty escape was necessary. We could appreciate their importance when Hurricane Gilbert hovered in the distance, turning the skies to shades of deep purple, blue and black, churning up the sea and whipping through the palms. We wondered, as we sipped our wine on the porch at the *Silver Beach Resort*, Longboat Key, where the porpoises and pelicans would take shelter from the relentless blast. Corinne was excited, not foreseeing the outcome if the hurricane turned its fearsome head inland. Thankfully, it did not, veering instead towards Texas, but I contemplated how quickly I could pack if the need arose.

We followed up a recommendation and visited *Moore's Stone Crab*, a restaurant founded in 1927 by Jack Moore who walked the flats in the bays, collecting stone crabs by hand. As his business grew, he started rowing a boat up and down the coast, sleeping on the beach at night. All traps used today are built by hand and crabs are brought in daily. The claws are carefully removed and the live crabs are returned to the waters to regenerate their claws. The Florida lobster (crawfish) is also trapped, and all other seafood is local, coming from the fishing village of Cortez or from the Florida Keys.

Corinne was determined to fish, so we purchased a small rod and reel from the Cortez harbour shop. She managed to bring in a flounder and a sheepshead along the estuary, but unhooking them was left to her father! I found a disused crab-pot in which to keep them for a while and photograph them; we later set them free.

Another must for Corinne was a "live" American football match. On the recommendation of a waiter serving in a nearby restaurant, her father took her to see a local high-school match. They set off one evening to the Balvanz stadium to see the Bayshore High School team (The Bruins) play the Tampa Bay Vo-Tech "Fighting Vulcans", complete with cheerleaders

and a marching band called The Honeybears. Corinne and her father returned at midnight. "It was brill!" exclaimed Corinne.

We satisfied our daughter's last request – to visit Spaceport USA – on the day before our departure from Orlando airport. A modern, air-conditioned, double-decker bus took us around the campus on a two-hour tour with taped commentary. There were many stopping points along the route.

The 56,656-hectare Kennedy Space Center reservation protects more endangered species of birds, mammals and reptiles than any other area of the USA. Sanctuaries were set up in 1963 and 1975, and alligators and herons can be viewed on the primitive Barrier Beach.

"Corinne still recalls the spectacular film, "The Dream is Alive", which was shot by NASA astronauts on their missions"

The terrain covered by the Kennedy Space Center was first mapped by Spanish explorers over four centuries ago. Cape Canaveral was selected as the launch site for testing long-range guided missiles after World War II. In 1964, NASA (National Aeronautics and Space Administration) was relocated to Merritt Island, which was chosen for the gigantic Apollo rocket, around which we were able to walk.

Corinne took many photographs, including one alongside Saturn 5, which dwarfed her. During the tour we saw a recreation of the first lunar landing. Corinne still recalls the spectacular film, "The Dream is Alive", which was shot by NASA astronauts on their missions. Watching the space shuttle lift off on the massive, five-storey screen is a thrilling experience – from countdown to touchdown we could believe we were there!

Our daughter's bedroom is bedecked with posters of her American experience and she still has a penchant for double-decker hamburgers. We had to get used to the fact that biscuits are cookies, chips are french fries, crisps are chips, a starter is an appetizer, a credit card is a charge card, a tip is a

gratuity and petrol is gas, but wherever we travelled we were *all* made to feel welcome, and at no time did we encounter prejudice. We would repeat the adventure without hesitation.

Whirlwind USA

At the age of 63 and after a 20-year lapse, Christine Panton had cancer again and required radiotherapy on a daily basis. Three months after she had finished the treatment she was weak and couldn't walk far without getting out of breath. She had been advised to eat a good protein meal at least three times a day; this caused her to put on 35 pounds, which exacerbated her arthritis in feet and hips. Christine's husband, Jim, is diabetic and needs insulin twice a day, but as long as he keeps his drugs cold and eats at regular intervals, the world is his oyster.

I felt frail and depressed, but the promise of a six-week holiday was as a carrot to a donkey. I just *had* to be well enough to go. First, I checked with my specialist (I'm afraid I didn't confess how extensively we were going to travel). Jim ordered an adequate supply of insulin and ensured that the details in his Medic-Alert bracelet were clear and correct. We consulted our travel agent regarding insurance, stating our medical problems, and obtained cover for all eventualities.

The next step was pure excitement. Every relevant brochure was studied and discussed. The American tourist office in London sent us information on temperatures, advice on clothing and eating out, even free tickets to tourist attractions. Many tour operators offer

tailor-made packages to the States, but *American Express* seemed the most flexible; it is available to non cardholders and can be booked through most travel agents.

America is an enormous place, each state like a separate country, and we wanted to see it all. Gradually, we sorted our priorities, and the finished package was everything we could have hoped for. It cost about £1700 per person in 1988, including the flights (seven in all), hotel rooms (not food), two-week coach trip, and villa rental in Florida. All our accommodation was excellent and my request for vegetarian meals on all flights was honoured, although not by very appetising ones. Our outward and return flights were with *British Airways*, our internal flights with *Continental Airlines* – all gave the usual civil service, cramped seating and mediocre meals.

First stop – JFK airport, New York. The courtesy bus took us through slum areas, miles of filth and graffiti, and deposited us outside beautiful Grand Central Station. Here we were tricked by a bogus taxi driver, who pocketed our fare and melted into the landscape. After this we caught a yellow cab and the driver, a huge black man, gave us a lesson on survival in New York: "Never trust anyone, and hang on to your money." Then he restored our faith in human nature by refusing any payment.

I shall never forget my first glimpse of the amazing Manhattan skyline – it was thrilling. But we were glad to reach our air-conditioned room, away from the 99 percent humidity outside. We were 21 floors up but could still hear the constant traffic noise and wailing of police and paramedic sirens. There was a pop concert on at Madison Square Gardens, exactly opposite our hotel. The road was filled with mounted police and excited fans. We watched from the hotel foyer and marvelled at this bustling, terrifying city.

"By the time I realised I'd been tricked, our other bag had gone"

Next day was spent walking the streets to Times Square, which was disappointingly seedy, awash with garbage and pathetic human derelicts. Later, we enjoyed a spectacular river trip to the Statue of Liberty, then returned to visit *Macy's*, which I found bewildering and too big for comfort.

On the following day we waited at the hotel for the bus to Newark airport. I guarded the luggage in the lobby while Jim kept watch in the street. Two swarthy men approached me: "Your bus is in and your fellow wants you." I picked up the nearest bag and staggered outside; by the time I realised I'd been tricked, our other bag had gone.

It's a common trick – a lookout man notes the position of a possible victim and telephones from the lobby to his waiting accomplices. We were fortunate that the bag I grabbed contained all our drugs and medication, together with money and passports. Wicked, dirty old New York – I wouldn't have missed you for the world.

After the robbery we were shocked and therefore negligent about eating properly. I arrived in Los Angeles exhausted, and Jim was totally confused, unable to find his baggage tickets or remember our destination. Once aware of our problems, the chap on the gate was instantly helpful, waiving the baggage-ticket check and showing me the way to phone for the hotel shuttle bus. A few sugar lumps and a Mars bar later, Jim was his old self

again! A comfortable night in the *Mayfair Hotel* gave us time to regain our equilibrium and we were up bright and early to meet our friends from Cherry Valley.

The next five days were spent in a whirl of wonder. We visited Universal Studios and Disneyland. We watched tumbleweeds blowing in the pretty streets of Palm Springs and sailed round a hotel lounge on a pleasure boat. Huge glass walls rose at our approach and we sailed majestically out of the hotel and round the golf course. We were only visitors to the hotel, and we only bought an iced tea, but we were made to feel as welcome as the most affluent guest.

We had intended to visit the *Spruce Goose* (flying boat) and the *Queen Mary*, both at Long Beach, but first we drove to a campsite 80km away and 2400m up Big Bear Mountain. Here I fell in love with the cheeky blue jays and the peaceful pine forests where they live. Seeing my rapture, our long-suffering friends offered to fetch their trailer-home, so that we might camp there for two nights. This could only happen in America, I thought, as we sped 80km down the mountain, stocked up at a shopping mall and struggled back just in time to go to bed.

"The pace of the trip is quite fast – we were required to rise at 6am on most mornings – and there is little time for relaxation"

The forest was a magical place by day, but breathtaking when a huge moon shone through the trees and the heat of the day gave way to the perishing cold of the night. The campsite was perfect, complete with fire-pit, barbecue and picnic table. We spent the next day in nearby Big Bear City, where an Octoberfest was in full swing. Everyone gave us a great welcome and there was singing, dancing and drinking, which ended in much hilarity and a rather hair-raising drive back to camp.

Saying a reluctant farewell to Pat and Leo, we returned to our hotel in Los Angeles and the following morning caught the *Greyhound* coach which was to take us on "The West Coast Wonderland Tour". This is offered as an escorted coach trip or an independent tour by self-drive car; departure is from Heathrow. The price includes several excursions, accommodation and a few (very good) meals. The pace of the trip is quite fast – we were required to rise at 6am on most mornings – and there is little time for relaxation if you take advantage of the extra excursions, which in my opinion were worth every penny of the £300 per person supplement.

The steps of the coach were steep but willing hands were always there to help. The coach was comfortable, air-conditioned and equipped with a toilet which we were asked not to use unless we were desperate. Normally, cold drinks are available on board, but it was late in the season (September) and we had to fend for ourselves. We stopped at least once each morning and afternoon for about half an hour, as well as stops for sightseeing and lunch.

We soon learned to stock up on canned drinks for the journey. It was difficult to find pure fruit juice – most drinks were of the sickly sweet, cola variety. To a diabetic person regular food is a necessity, so we were careful both to allow sufficient time to eat before embarking on the day's programme, and to carry sufficient snacks and drinks on the coach to cover the gaps between meals.

At the start of the coach trip I confided my medical problem to our courier and whenever we stopped I had the opportunity to choose between joining the others, or leaving my husband to explore while I sat inside the coach (where the air conditioning was left on for me) or outside where the courier often found me a seat or recommended a café.

We joined the tour on the fourth day – the rest of the group had been sightseeing in LA for three days. Our first stop was Sea World, where I marvelled at the rapport between the sea creatures, including dolphins and whales, and the humans with whom they performed. On to San Diego, where I purchased a large Mexican hat – how glad I was to have it during the following scorching ten days.

"We sat at candle-lit tables beneath the stars, listening to 'cowboys' singing"

A spectacular drive through the desert came next, and a pause to photograph giant cacti. I wandered happily in open-toed sandals until warned of rattlesnakes, black widow spiders and tarantulas. Thank goodness we saw nothing but a lizard. The scenery unfolded in never-ending grandeur, until we reached Rawhide where we sat at candle-lit tables beneath the stars, listening to "cowboys" singing. Smoke curled high from the barbecue where 1600 giant steaks are cooked each night. I don't eat steak but chicken was happily substituted.

The highlight of the tour was a helicopter trip over the Grand Canyon – I am desperately afraid of heights but I knew I *must* go. Flying low over the treetops, the pilot warned us to "prepare for a sudden drop beneath us". Nothing could have prepared me for the enormity of the void which suddenly replaced the land below. The canyon is, in places, over 40km wide, and stretches for some 1600m down to the tiny river glimmering in the distance. I clutched my husband as we flew between mountain ridges and deep clefts, wheeling and soaring amongst multicoloured rocks that are millions of years old. During the half-hour trip, the theme music to *Chariots of Fire* was softly played into our earphones. It was one of the few times when I have welcomed background music – it fitted the occasion exactly and each time I hear it I relive that awe-inspiring experience.

Ironically, this ride also gave me my worst moment of the holiday – trying to get into the helicopter. My husband had already been strapped in, and I just hadn't the strength to pull myself up. I suppose to the ground crew it was a hilarious sight – a fat lady dangling precariously and needing an undignified push. To me it was humiliating and exhausting. If I had asked for help in advance there would have been no problem, but once on the launching pad with all that noise it was impossible to make anyone understand. Nevertheless, I would do it again, dangle and all.

From brash Las Vegas, where we stayed at the opulent *Golden Nugget* and visited the incredible *Caesar's Palace*, we travelled on to Yosemite National Park. I sat in an amphitheatre while a ranger gave a talk on bears and forest fires, and cicadas "sang" in the pine trees. Yosemite is a rugged wilderness and we felt rather cheated that we were only given a few hours to enjoy it, when the itinerary had stated two days. These changes may be made if the driver or courier deem it necessary, perhaps because of weather conditions or other factors outside their control.

We fell in love with San Francisco, however, where we rode on a cable car and took a trip around the bay amidst noisy sea-lions and seals, then strolled around Fisherman's Wharf and sampled clam chowder. We travelled the Pacific Coast Drive on our last day, pausing for lunch at Carmel, where the pedestrian has right of way and cars stop whenever you cross the pretty, tree-lined streets.

Back in LA we parted from our coach companions, spent one more night there and took a 5am flight to New Orleans. We had chosen to stay in the French Quarter, which is the oldest part. Although some areas appear neglected and seedy, there are many beautiful buildings, their delicate, wrought-iron balconies hung with flowering baskets. Our hotel (*The Royal Sonesta*) was luxurious, built around a garden courtyard with heated swimming pool – much enjoyed in the early evenings – and large patio (with bar).

The days were hot and humid, but it is in the warm evenings and after dark that New Orleans comes to life. Jazz music spills out from every doorway and the streets are thronged with pedestrians wandering from bar to bar, enjoying the live bands and foot-tapping the night away. There are also many sex shops and girlie shows, invitations to orgies and other dubious delights – we stuck to the jazz.

"We watched the sun go down with such a flourish that as it slipped over the rim of the world everyone stood up and clapped"

Five heady days later we flew to Orlando where my old school friend of fifty years ago was there to meet us, having driven for eleven hours from North Carolina. We were to entertain Iris and her husband, Bill, in a rented villa about 50km north of Tampa airport, with easy access to Highway 19, in Port Richey on the west coast of Florida.

The comfortable, well-equipped bungalow on the edge of a lake had its own swimming pool (unheated) and came with a free car. There were three double bedrooms, two bathrooms, a large lounge-diner and a superb kitchen, all spotless. The patio furniture included sun-beds, table and chairs. The surrounding properties were all different, many in Spanish style and with delightful cactus gardens. The weather here, as in most places we visited, can be extremely hot and it is essential to check with your travel agent when you choose your dates.

Our problem with the heat was keeping the insulin cool! In Europe we have always found a refrigerated mini-bar in our room; we expected to find the same in America – not so. However, the *New York Penta Hotel* provided us with one as soon as we explained our predicament. A couple of the smaller hotels agreed to keep the insulin overnight in their kitchen fridge. Our greatest discovery was the ice machine – to be found on each floor of most large hotels. We only had to fill the plastic ice-bucket (provided in each room) and the drugs stayed cool in our air-conditioned rooms despite the heat and humidity outside. Jim also took a small "cool pack" which was frozen overnight and then kept, with his insulin, in a waterproof sponge-bag for daytime travel – this proved invaluable.

We thought the highways and scenery of Florida were rather bill-boarded and commercial. In Tarpon Springs, a sponge-diving centre almost entirely inhabited by Greeks, we took a boat trip and watched a sponge diver at work. Surprisingly, sponges are black and slimy when harvested – they don't look fit to go in the bath. The Greeks run many good restaurants and gift shops selling sponges, shells, lovely junk jewellery, summer clothes and other such tourist treasures.

Due to our late arrival the owner of the villa allowed us to stay an extra day – typical of the generosity and desire to please which we experienced all over the States. Our last evening was spent in an outdoor restaurant overlooking the Gulf of Mexico. Here we watched the sun go down with such a flourish that as it slipped over the rim of the world everyone stood up and clapped.

The four of us drove in leisurely fashion up the East Coast for ten more days with Iris and Bill in North Carolina. They had previously lived on the beach but, finding the hurricanes too lively, bought a bit of pine forest inland and had their home transported on the back of a lorry to its new site. Two men had to sit on the roof to push the overhead wires out of the way of the chimney, but Iris didn't even have to pack her china.

The house had been mounted high among the trees, with utility rooms and garages beneath. It was like living with the birds and quite delightful except for the water bugs – black, shiny creatures, inclined to scuttle across bathroom floors just as I was about to have a shower.

"Our greatest problem was that our disabilities didn't show. To the world, we looked like a man with a lazy, fat wife"

The natives of North Carolina have the most charming accent and everyone was friendly and hospitable. The countryside is almost English, and full of interesting sights. Many of the old plantations are now clubs and golf courses; the wayside cafés have toilets for "Men folk" and "Wimmin folk", and play background revivalist music.

It was in one of these cafés, with its red gingham tablecloths and jam-jar glasses, that I asked what "hush puppies" were. A passing waitress heard and, within minutes, brought a basket full of little cornbread rolls for me to try, and a pile of pretty paper place mats which had southern recipes printed on them. "Take them home to England," she said, "to remember us by." As if I needed anything to remind me of these warmhearted people.

We viewed the pretty town of Wilmington from a horse-drawn buggy, and chugged up the river in a beautiful paddle-steamer. The US battleship *North Carolina* is at anchor here; it is a fascinating museum, surrounded by notices saying, "Don't feed the crocodiles".

I attended the local church where, after a happy service and some wonderful singing from an all-female choir, I was surrounded by kind folks wishing me well. The local people hugged and kissed me on meeting, and when our stay ended, five of them turned out to wave, bearing gifts, and posies to pin on my suit.

From Wilmington airport, Jim and I flew to Raleigh, where we changed flights for the last leg of our trip, to Washington DC. The flight from Wilmington was in a small aircraft which held about twenty people sitting in bucket seats each side of a narrow aisle. There were wonderful views, as it did not fly very high. The baggage check at Wilmington is very slow because it is only a small airport, so allow plenty of time; transfer between planes was directly across the tarmac.

Washington looked from the air like a multicoloured carpet – it was "the fall" and the trees were a riot of autumn hues. On the ground, our overall impression was of beauty and poverty, side by side – clean, white buildings and men wrapped in sacks on park benches. Our last day was spent in the Smithsonian Institute, where I walked through a space rocket and performed a simulated landing on the moon!

Back to earth with a vengeance for our overnight return journey to dear old England. It was good to be home, but what a holiday. In retrospect, our greatest problem was that our disabilities didn't show. To the world, we looked like a man with a lazy, fat wife who both needed constant feeding! This only goes to show that you should never judge a sausage by its skin – I hated being fat, was sick to death of eating, and would have been delighted to walk around with the others.

If you are similarly placed, my advice is to notify in advance any needs you may have, whether it be on the plane, coach or at the hotel, and not be afraid to ask for help. You'll get it and served with a smile. Our overwhelming memory of America is the friendliness of its people and their willingness to please. "Enjoy" is a much-used word over there, and that's what we did.

USAir Go to Court

Angela Deakin is a teacher, foster carer and magistrate. During the past twenty years she has travelled extensively with her family, including many foster children. In August 1989 Angela and her husband, Robin, attended an International Foster Care Conference in Michigan, and around that they organised a holiday in the USA and Canada, taking their multiply handicapped foster child, Christopher, with them.

Robin made all the bookings – flights, hotels, car hire – before we left, mostly using free telephone numbers in the States. We obtained a great deal of helpful information from the book, *Discover North America*, published annually by Discovery Press Group.

Wardair (now *Canadian Airlines*) gave us a smooth flight to Canada and superb service to both able-bodied and handicapped travellers. On arrival in Toronto the disabled toilets were a revelation – separate male and female facilities in spacious and fully equipped rooms, a welcome relief from the cramped aircraft facilities. Outside the terminal there are specially designated vehicles to carry people in their wheelchairs.

Various companies in Toronto offer reasonably priced tours of the sights and, as long as they are given warning at the time of booking, a wheelchair poses no problems. We joined a minibus group for a day trip to Niagara Falls. It was a wonderful experience and Christopher, who is blind, loved the spray from the falls blowing in his face!

We joined the long queue waiting to get in to the CN Tower, only to discover at the entrance that we should have gone straight to the head of the queue, where staff escort wheelchairs through the ticket booths (disabled visitors do not pay). We were shown into the lift and told how to move between the various observation decks by use of the lifts. The able-bodied sightseer, once up the tower, has to use the stairs between floors.

"Everything tends to be bigger and wider, apart from disabled toilets"

It is impossible to reach the highest outside observation gallery in a wheelchair. However, after much discussion amongst tourists of many nationalities, some strong young men decided to carry an American girl, who had multiple sclerosis and was travelling alone, up the flight of stairs and round the gallery. She was delighted! The remainder of the tower is wheelchair accessible, although you may have to ask the security guards to open special locked doors in places.

Lunch in the revolving restaurant was brilliant – a seventy-minute, circular tour of Toronto – and our little lad slept right through it. We left Toronto with the feeling that the Canadians treat people with disabilities not as handicapped people, but as people with special needs. Every aspect of life and work seems geared to satisfying those special needs with the minimum of fuss.

The USA is vast and deserves all the many superlatives used to describe it. We read all we could and studied maps at length before making a selection of places to visit – this is important because there is so much to see and distances are so great that an enormous amount of time can be wasted. After spending a week near Detroit for the conference, we flew to California for a touring holiday which was to

include a special Disneyland trip for Christopher.

Disneyland in California is the original, and therefore not as accessible to wheelchairs as the Florida Disneyworld. We had been led to believe that we could get wheelchair and child on some of the rides, but this was impossible. However, Disneyland was light, bright, attractive and noisy. Mickey, Donald and Goofy were beautifully costumed, lovely for Christopher to touch. He thoroughly enjoyed his visits. The *Tahitian Restaurant* supplied wonderful food and an exuberant floor-show; the restaurant staff coped admirably with the wheelchair.

The only disappointment in Disneyland was our trip to the toilet facilities – no separate toilets for the disabled, only a cubicle in the Ladies or Gents. After waiting in the long queue and struggling through the milling masses to reach the end cubicle, I discovered that it was wider but no deeper than the standard cubicle, so I could not get the wheelchair in. I was able to carry Christopher and change his nappy in the loo, but it must be very awkward for older disabled people. My husband tells me that the layout was the same in the Gents.

We found this to be a common problem in the States; everything tends to be bigger and wider, apart from disabled toilets. Las Vegas supplied the exception to prove the rule: we could have thrown a party in the toilets there – very large and very clean, affording privacy for both disabled and attendants.

In the UK we had pre-booked a day tour of the Grand Canyon with *Scenic Airlines*, who did not blink at carrying a wheelchair and were kind and helpful throughout. The flight over the canyon was unbelievable, all orange, pink and mauve rocks and deep green trees and bushes. Deep in an almost inaccessible ravine, a tribe of Indians live what seems from the air an idyllic existence.

An excellent lunch was included in the price, and we had time for a walk along the rim, taking in some spectacular views. All facilities and gift shops were wheelchair accessible, bar one in a tiny old house.

The temperature was very high, well over 100° F. This posed problems on the return flight as the aircraft was not pressurised. Our son fainted and we had trouble getting him to regain consciousness. I asked the co-pilot for oxygen but they did not carry any. The pilot immediately took the aircraft down to treetop height and made an emergency landing at Las Vegas.

Christopher had come round by this time, but the police, paramedics and two ambulances were waiting at the airport – all very dramatic. *Scenic Airlines* staff were most concerned and ready to assist in any way they could. It is important to check carefully before booking if you think an unpressurised aircraft or lack of oxygen may endanger your health; there are other aircraft available.

"For the first time in our lives, Robin and I stood in the middle of a crowded aircraft, having a blazing row with the cabin crew"

We used internal flights a great deal to cope with the distances that had to be covered. Airlines in the USA are deregulated, so do not have the same standards of care and concern that we expect in Europe or Canada. We had problems with *USAir*, who did our internal flights. They issued boarding cards with seat numbers but changed the seats around by the time we reached the aircraft. This is particularly upsetting for disabled passengers who need someone with them. Our three seats together in non-smoking became three separated seats in the smoking section on two of the flights we undertook.

For the first time in our lives, Robin and I stood in the middle of a crowded aircraft, having a blazing row with the cabin crew. They saw no reason why our handicapped, blind and non-speaking child could not manage among total strangers in the smoking section. Eventually, we got three seats as designated on the boarding cards, but by this time the plane was late and no one was happy.

Some airlines are far more willing and able to carry and cater for disabled passengers. *Canadian Airlines, Northwest* and *Delta* all welcome disabled travellers and will often pre-book seat numbers to ensure maximum comfort for their passengers. *Wardair* (*Canadian Airlines*) gave us four bulkhead seats so that Christopher could sleep across two of the seats and we had plenty of room. Our luggage for this trip included a large quantity of special disposable nappies, plus 48 bottles of baby Ribena, medical supplies and a wheelchair, none of which was counted as part of our luggage by the airlines. They accepted it as special supplies for our child and there was no charge.

In the major American cities we used taxis for getting around; having got used to the doors being locked as soon as we were in (to stop muggers), we had some very interesting sightseeing tours. We hired a seven-seater van from *General Vehicle Rentals* for our journey between Los Angeles and San Francisco. American cars (limousines) are all bonnet and very little boot space, so be careful if you have wheelchair and luggage to carry. The vans are very practical, as they have windows all round and the back rear seat folds forward behind the next row of seats; this leaves a large space to accommodate a wheelchair and luggage, and there is still seating for at least four people. We found our van very comfortable for long journeys.

Wanting to see natural America, we toured the Sequoia and Yosemite national parks. On arrival, we asked the rangers for a disabled pass to attach to the windscreen; this enabled us to use the "disabled parking". In Yosemite the village car park was full and overflowing but parking for disabled was still available (very different from the UK). In the States, anyone parking in a space reserved for disabled drivers without a special pass on the windscreen is likely to be heavily fined, and cars illegally parked may be towed away and "crushed"! We were told that we should have applied to the Department of Transport in person and obtained a windscreen sticker to enable us to take advantage of all "disabled parking" anywhere in California.

The Lassen National Volcanic Park, in Northern California, deserves a visit but the shop and cafeteria were accessible only via a steep flight of steps. This was quickly solved by people helping to carry both child and wheelchair up the stairs. It was worth the effort – the view was impressive. Most sights around the park are accessible for wheelchairs but the sulphur smell is very strong!

Our accommodation throughout the holiday was excellent and all pre-booked from England. We used mostly well-known hotel or motel chains, such as *Best Western*, *Howard Johnson* and *Vagabond*, staying in the rooms for handicapped guests – generally large, with bathrooms on the same scale – which made life a great deal easier. Most hotels and motels have launderettes on their premises or nearby; these are cheap and efficient, so we had no problems with washing and drying clothes. We also took the opportunity when booking a room to rent a refrigerator, which proved very useful.

Hiring the van in Los Angeles and returning it to San Francisco gave us the freedom to travel where we wanted. Roadside diners and truck stops offered excellent value, but if you do not want sauce (often hot strawberry jam) poured over your eggs and bacon, be sure to tell them *before* you place your order. The same applies to hot jacket potatoes, into which they will pour anything, including ice cream! Food is generally cheap in the USA and just about every taste is catered for. Americans claim to be very health conscious and the salad bars are superb, often with a choice of thirty or more items from which to make your selection.

In conclusion, there is much to see and much that is accessible in Canada and the USA. The US cities have horrendous crime problems, of which eighty percent are drug related, but natural America is magnificent and well worth the journey. Transport, accommodation and eating present few problems, and with careful planning it is easy to get the best out of both countries.

Back in England, we claimed £1127.46 from *USAir*, to cover the cost of cancelled tickets and endless telephone calls to get flights reinstated after *USAir* had incorrectly cancelled them. This amount included £500 in compensation for the airline's total lack of concern, their rudeness and the harassment we suffered.

We received two cheques from them, reducing the amount owing to £837.64; we took them to our local County Court and sued them for the balance. They did not bother to defend the action and we were awarded judgement. We sued the UK office because we had made the original contract with them. To get the money we had to send in the County Court bailiffs.

All along, we claimed that *USAir* did not want to be bothered with adults or children with handicaps. In addition, we complained that the US airlines' policy regarding boarding works on the basis of "first on the aircraft, sit where you like". This causes tremendous problems for disabled people and passengers with families. It is a far cry from the orderly European system which ensures that a boarding card with number will secure your allocated seat. Finally, we were disappointed to discover that the US airline timetables are for guidance only and not intended to be relied upon.

USA: TRAVEL NOTES

Sources of information

United States Travel and Tourism Administration (USTTA), 22 Sackville Street, London W1X 2EA; ☎071/439 7433. Write – it's impossible to get through on the phone – for addresses of the state and major city or county tourism offices, and UK addresses of car hire, coach or rail companies, and domestic airlines. While *The United States Welcomes Handicapped Visitors* is out of date (1984) and out of print, and there is no sign of a new edition on the horizon, the USTTA is trying to obtain information from each state tourism office for its own files.

It is perhaps too much to ask one office to supply a comprehensive database for disabled visitors to such a vast country. Each state does things differently and provision of access information is no exception: about a third of the states include mention of facilities for handicapped visitors in their guides; some produce specific booklets on the subject. Your best bet is to turn up in person at the state, city or county tourism office; if you must plan ahead, write well in advance of departure to the states you think you'd like to visit: some are listed below, addresses of others from the USTTA.

Virginia Division of Tourism, 1021 East Cary Street, Richmond, VA 23219; ☎804/786-2051. Virginia produces the most detailed handbook, the result of a campaign launched in 1984 to encourage awareness of travel opportunities among the physically disabled. *The Virginia Travel Guide for the Disabled* (1989) is published by a charity, *The Opening Door* (Route 2, Box 1805, Woodford, VA 22580; ☎804/633 6752) and is distributed free of charge to disabled people. The 300-page guide is a mine of clear, detailed information – for travellers with mobility, visual or hearing impairment.

Washington DC Convention and Visitors Association, 1212 New York Avenue, NW, Washington DC 20005; ☎202/789-7000. Distributes a useful fact sheet and six-page "Feature Release" which should enable any visitor with a handicap to make the most of the attractions of the city. *Smithsonian: A Guide for Disabled Visitors* can be obtained (in print or Braille) by writing to the *Visitor Information*

Associates Reception Center (Smithsonian Institution Building, Smithsonian Institution, Washington DC 20560) or phoning ☎202/357 2700 (voice) or ☎202/357 1729 (TTY).

State of New York, 1515 Broadway, 51st Floor, New York, NY 10036; ☎212/827-6250. Their New York travel guide lists accessible campsites and uses an access code for attractions covering parking, steps at entrance, lifts and grab-rails in toilets, but there is no mention of facilities for visitors with sight or hearing impairment.

New Mexico Tourism and Travel Division, 1100 St Francis Drive, Santa Fe, NM 87503; ☎505/827-0291. Produce a brochure, *New Mexico Vacation Guide*, which uses the wheelchair symbol only on one page, to indicate facilities for disabled visitors in the state parks. Scant mention in the guides does not necessarily mean scant attention to provision of facilities for disabled people, though – Carolyn Lucas experienced few problems.

California Office of Tourism, 1121 L Street, Suite 103, Sacramento, CA 95814; ☎916/322-2881. Produces only general guides with no information for disabled visitors, but access in California is generally good, and city access guides (not always comprehensive or up to date) or fact sheets are often available at local tourism offices or information centres: the *San Francisco Convention & Visitors Bureau* (PO Box 6977, San Francisco, CA 94101-6977; ☎415/391-2000), for example, offers the *Guide to San Francisco for the Person who is Disabled* (1987).

Massachusetts Office of Travel and Tourism will put you in touch with Boston's *Information Center for Individuals with Disabilities* (20 Park Plaza, Room 330, Boston, MA 02116; ☎617/727-5540, voice; ☎617/727-5236, TTY) which will answer requests for information by phone or mail, or in person (the centre is open Mon–Fri 9am–5pm).

Society for the Advancement of Travel for the Handicapped (SATH), 26 Court Street, Brooklyn, NY 11242; ☎718/858-5483. A non-profit travel industry organisation whose members include travel agents, tour operators, hotel and airline management, and handicapped people. For advice on New York, or if

USA: TRAVEL NOTES

you have a specific enquiry about anywhere else in the States, *SATH* can refer you to the appropriate member, but they are hard up and busy, so send an International Reply Coupon and allow plenty of time for a response.

Mobility International USA, PO Box 3551, Eugene, Oregon 97403; ☎503/343-1248. Will answer transport queries and operates the usual *MI* exchange programme for disabled people and their friends (see *Practicalities*).

Tour operators

Many UK tour operators offer holidays in the USA; if they are unable to arrange a trouble-free stay for disabled clients in this generally very accessible country, there is something wrong with their understanding of "customer service". Christine Panton (p.414) was delighted with her trip, care of *American Express*, and Stephen Latham (p.408) judged his *Jetsave* package good value for money. (*Jetsave*, by the way, ask disabled clients to complete a form, signed by their doctor, giving details of the extent of disability; but they do make efforts to ensure that the type of holiday booked is suitable and that their rep in the States is well aware of all requirements.)

We have received no reports of holidays with the tour operators who specialise in catering for disabled travellers, such as *The Assistance Travel Service*, which claims expertise in arranging trips to Florida, or the joint venture between *Virgin Holidays* and *Threshold* which offers fly-drive packages to Florida and California (see *Practicalities*, "Booking").

If you have a special interest – perhaps a burning ambition to experience the "Wild West" or to visit the battlegrounds of the civil war – there is almost certainly an appropriate package, offered by one of the hundreds of US tour companies, many of whom can cater for disabled travellers or specialise in organising disabled group tours. These operators may be listed in the state tourism brochures, or you can ask for help from the *Handicapped Travel Division* of the *National Tour Association* (546 East Main Street, P O Box 3071, Lexington, Kentucky 40596; ☎606/253-1036), who will put you in touch with operators whose tours match your needs, interests, budget and holiday dates.

In Wyoming, for example, amongst the adventure package operators, you can choose from four companies which make provision for disabled people to join their tours. *Access Tours, Inc.* (3900 South Park Loop, PO Box 2985, Jackson, WY 83001; ☎307/733-6664) use mini-buses with wheelchair lifts for leisurely trips (up to eight days) through Jackson Hole, Grand Teton and Yellowstone National Park. *Antelope Outfitters* (350 North Main, Buffalo, WY 82834; ☎307/684-2225) offer the dubious pleasure of wheelchair hunts for deer and antelope. *4-Bear Outfitters* (137 Road 8VE, Powell, WY 82435; ☎307/645-3109) run programmes in winter (snowshoes, snowmobile, ski, sled, skates or camping) and summer (rodeos, rafting, museums, camping) and welcome "physically challenged" guests. *Trails West* (365 Main Street, South Pass City, WY 82520; ☎307/332-7801) offer short trips in a covered wagon or on horseback, sleeping in tepees, with all meals cooked over an open fire – ramps give easy access to the wagons.

Getting there

Most airlines flying the Atlantic seem pretty good. *Virgin* offer their disabled passengers priority check-in and the choice of making their own way to the aircraft door or being pushed by an airport attendant. All aircraft carry Newton skychairs (40.6cm wide), and on charter flights to Orlando "upper-class" seats, with more legroom and greater pitch, can be purchased for a nominal sum.

Most contributors report satisfactory service from the cabin crew and just-bearable seating arrangements. It's going to be cramped, and trips to the toilet will require heroic efforts – Arthur Goldthorpe used the food trolley as a prop on his *American Airlines* flight (p.404)! – but since there is not much to choose between the major airlines operating transatlantic flights, the main consideration is likely to be cost. Shop around, and use a reputable company, such as *Trailfinders* (☎071/938 3366), if you go for discounted airline tickets.

Aisle chairs on *British Airways* and *Virgin* flights will squeeze into at least one of the toilets, but the heroics don't end with getting into the cubicle. Sloping ceilings, no grab-rails

USA: TRAVEL NOTES

and absolutely no room for manoeuvre mean that for some people an alternative has to be found – something more effective than simply limiting liquid intake.

Transport

Most **domestic airlines** give discounted fares to residents of other countries, and many offer air passes which are useful if you plan to do a lot of flying. Contact the airlines at their UK addresses (ask USTTA for a list). *USAir* gets the thumbs down from Angela Deakin (p.421), *Scenic Airlines* the thumbs up (p.420); *Delta* or *Continental* should be safe options.

Facilities at the major **airports** are generally good, although Arthur Goldthorpe experienced some problems at Chicago (p.404). As in Britain, if you give advance notice at the time of booking, you should have a smooth flight, but ask about pre-boarding procedures – as Angela Deakin says, "First on board, sit where you like" is not ideal if you need extra legroom or proximity to the toilet, or if you must sit with your companion.

Long-distance **rail travel** facilities are very good and, as with air travel, there are some special discounts to look out for (p.394). The USTTA can supply addresses of the four UK agents for *Amtrak* (*National Railroad Passenger Corporation*, 60 Massachusetts Avenue, NE, Washington DC 20002; ☎202/383-3000). If you make bookings while in the States, give 24 hours' notice and either use a travel agent or call (toll free) ☎1-800 and ask for USA-RAIL, the Special Services Desk. Assistance can then be arranged according to your requirements. Hearing-impaired passengers should call ☎1-800/523-6590 (or 6591) for information and reservations.

Almost every *Amtrak* train includes one or more coaches and, when available, sleeping cars with accommodation specially designed for use by handicapped passengers, including accessible toilets. Guide dogs travel free and may accompany blind, deaf or disabled passengers in the carriage. Full details of the *Amtrak* service are available in the brochure, *Amtrak's America* (ask the UK agents or write to *Amtrak Distribution Center*, PO Box 7717, Itasca, IL 60143).

Greyhound **buses** (*Greyhound World Travel*, Sussex House, London Road, East Grinstead, West Sussex RH19 1LD; ☎0342/317317) form an extensive inter-city network, a cheap means of touring the country. Although not equipped with lifts for wheelchairs, these buses are not out of bounds to wheelchair users (see p.429); *Greyhound* staff will assist with boarding (inter-city carriers are required by law to do this), and the "Helping Hand" scheme offers two-for-the-price-of-one tickets to passengers unable to travel alone for medical reasons (doctor's certificate must be produced).

A handful of **car hire** companies offer cars with hand controls, given sufficient notice: *Avis* (Stephen Latham had trouble with this company, see p.409); *Europcar/National* (controls available in some states and cities; only on Class F, full-size cars; no extra charge and only three to seven days' notice required); *Hertz* (who declined to give details of hand-control availability in the States); *Lindo's Rent-a-Car* (available on any class of car; a local charge of $25 is made for fitting hand controls outside Florida and Georgia).

Arthur Goldthorpe suggests taking a car without hand controls, hired more cheaply from a local company, if you are travelling with an able-bodied companion. His decision was coloured by meeting two young disabled Americans in Florida who had ordered a car with hand controls to be available at Miami airport when they arrived. On landing they were told that the car was not ready as the fittings had only arrived that day. They had to travel 80km to Fort Lauderdale and return next day for their car.

By shopping around, using the Yellow Pages, it's possible to find good deals with local firms, including a fair rate for Collision Damage Waiver (which you must have). Many firms will bring the vehicle to your door and then allow you to drop it off in the airport car park when you leave.

Virgin/Threshold use *Lindo's Rent-a-Car* to provide adapted cars for their fly-drive packages, but it is worth doing your sums when considering any fly-drive deal, remembering that each person in a party will be paying an extra supplement for the use of a single car – if

USA: TRAVEL NOTES

there is an able-bodied driver in the party it will certainly be cheaper to rent a car from a local firm in the States.

A comfortable alternative worth considering is to hire a **van** or trailer home. Angela Deakin's seven-seater without adaptations gave ample space for wheelchair and luggage, but it is possible to hire fully adapted vehicles, with hand controls, lifts, clamps, raised roof and wide doors. Contact *SATH* or state tourist offices for some addresses. Angela found that child safety harnesses were not available in the states she visited.

The American Automobile Association (*AAA*, Traffic Safety Department, 1000 AAA Drive, Heathrow, FLA 32746-5063; ☎407/444-7000) produces information for disabled drivers in the form of the *Handicapped Driver's Mobility Guide*, currently out of stock and being revised. When reissued it can be ordered from Quantum-Precision Inc. (225 Broadway, Suite 3404, New York, NY 10007). There is a reciprocal arrangement with the *AAA* giving free breakdown cover for *RAC* or *AA* members.

Write in advance to each city or state for **parking permits**; you'll need a doctor's letter with your application. Rather than wait for the relevant department to post your permit, call in and collect it when you arrive. Americans are not good at answering correspondence, but are very efficient on the phone and in person.

For a New York permit write to *Department of Motor Vehicles*, Empire State Plaza, Albany, NY 12228 (☎518/474-0841) and collect it from *New York City Department of Transportation*, Office of Parking Control, 51 Chambers Street, Room 423, New York, NY 10007 (☎212/566-1317); parking is very restricted, and expensive overnight.

For Boston write to *Registry of Motor Vehicles*, 100 Nashua Street, Boston, MA 02114 (☎617/727-3703); parking is limited Downtown.

For the state of California, write to *Department of Motor Vehicles*, PO Box 932328, Sacramento, CA 94232 (☎916/732-7243). The Los Angelenos are wedded to their cars (seventy percent of the city's area is devoted to the car – roads, gas stations, parking lots), so don't have any expectations of the public transport system. Distances are so vast that you must have a car; rush hour on the so-called "freeways" lasts from about 5am to 7pm, but parking conditions are near perfect. In San Francisco, on the other hand, bus and train systems are accessible, so a car is unnecessary.

The Orange Badge is valid in some cities and states, including Washington DC and New Mexico. Washington, however, is a nightmare to drive in and public transport definitely recommended.

Taxis (cabs) are generally plentiful and large enough to accommodate a folded wheelchair in the boot (trunk). There are accessible **urban networks of trains and buses** in several towns and cities, although there are variations across the country. In Las Vegas, for example, Arthur Goldthorpe found that every other bus running up and down "the Strip" had a lift (accessible buses being identified by a blue wheelchair symbol on the front, and a hoist next to the side door), while in San Diego very few routes had accessible buses.

Carolyn Lucas reports accessible buses in San Francisco, Boston and New York. By the end of 1990 some 75 percent of New York buses were fitted with hydraulic lifts and wheelchair spaces. Visitors can apply (at least three weeks before their trip) for an identity card, enabling them to take advantage of the "Reduced-Fare Program for Senior Citizens and Disabled Persons". Card holders obtain roughly half-price travel on local buses, some longer journeys, and on the subway. Write to the *New York City Department of Transportation*, Reduced-Fare Program for Disabled Persons, 253 Broadway, 5th Floor, New York, NY 10007.

But don't get too excited – Nic Fleming has this to say of New York buses: "The lifts hardly ever work, and the drivers hate having to stop and get the seldom-used machinery into action. They usually refuse to stop for wheelchair passengers."

The Metrorail system in Washington DC is a dream for disabled visitors accustomed to London's Underground. Each station is equipped with a lift (with Braille number plates) to all platforms from street level. The driver makes station and on-board announcements of train destinations and stops. Hearing-impaired passengers are warned of an approaching train by pulsating lights along the edge of the platform.

For information about the availability of accessible public transport in the city you plan to visit, contact the *American Public Transit Association* (1201 New York Avenue, Suite 400, Washington DC 20005; ☎202/898 4000).

Accommodation

Thanks to the activities of the numerous organisations of and for disabled people in the USA, including regular meetings all over the country, those involved in the US hotel and motel trade are, in general, acutely aware of the needs of guests with handicaps. This is good news for disabled visitors to the States, who will mostly be spoilt for choice when looking for somewhere to stay – there is accessible accommodation in all price brackets, although it's wise to check the bathroom layout before booking (p.405).

The big hotel and motel chains have accessible rooms in many of their properties and often use the access symbol in their directories, although the facilities the symbol represents are usually unclear. *Best Western, Days Inns of America, Holiday Inns, Howard Johnson Motels* and *Vagabond* are recommended by contributors.

It's worth investigating the smaller establishments, in particular the huge array of self-catering units, if only to escape the "sameness" of the chains. Unless you are travelling to a very popular spot in the height of the season, you should not feel obliged to book from the UK. With some help from the local visitor information centre you are very unlikely to find yourself without a roof over your head and more than likely to save yourself a few bucks.

Christine Panton recommends the *Mayfair Hotel* (1256 W. 7th Street, Los Angeles, CA 90017; ☎213/484 9624), *Golden Nugget Hotel* (129 E. Fremont, Las Vegas, NV 89125; ☎702/385 7111), *Sir Francis Drake Hotel* (Powell and Sutter Streets, San Francisco, CA 94101; ☎415/392 7755), *Carmel Mission Inn* (Highway 1 at Rio Road, Carmel, CA 93922; ☎408/624 1841) and *The Royal Sonesta Hotel* (Bourbon Street, New Orleans, LA; ☎504/586 0300).

Reservations for a disabled unit among the "rustic tent cabins" in Curry Village, Yosemite National Park (recommended by Carolyn Lucas, p.399), can be made through the *Yosemite Park and Curry Company* (California 95389, ☎209/252-4848; for information ☎209/372-0264).

Access and facilities

The message in the US accounts is clear: **access to buildings, sporting activities and tourist attractions**, including national parks, beaches, forests, mountains or desert, is good. This is particularly true of public buildings such as museums, art galleries, historic houses or monuments which receive federal money. Buildings which are owned, leased or operated by the US government, and were designed, altered or constructed after 1970, must, by law, be accessible to all.

Access to the arts gives further cause for admiration. Carolyn Lucas describes the work of some gifted groups of disabled actors in States; facilities for disabled theatre-goers are equally impressive. At the John F. Kennedy Center for the Performing Arts in Washington DC, it goes without saying that all theatres are accessible to wheelchair users but in addition there are infrared listening systems in three of the six main theatres. With a set of headphones a hearing-impaired patron may "sit anywhere in the house, adjust the volume and enjoy"! For blind patrons there are recordings of scripts with detailed descriptions of sets and costumes in shows performed in the Opera House, Eisenhower and Terrace theatres.

Many theatres in major cities offer substantial discounts to handicapped patrons for certain performances. The National Theater, also in Washington DC, offers a limited number of half-priced tickets on Tuesday, Wednesday and Thursday evenings and Sunday afternoons. The National is unique in the USA in providing a permanent booth for a narrator to describe the performance scene by scene; this narration is available twice a month, transmitted by headphone to visually handicapped members of the audience.

Arthur Goldthorpe sounds a cautionary note regarding **toilet facilities**: although most places have toilets ostensibly for disabled

USA: TRAVEL NOTES

people, the layout may be different to those found in the UK, often failing to allow sufficient space for lateral transfer. A design frequently encountered in older buildings is an extended cubicle three feet wide with handrails attached each side. If you cannot transfer in these circumstances you may have to rely on toilets in the fast-food restaurants; on the West Coast, it seems, *McDonald's* provide better facilities than *Burger King*!

Cubicles for disabled people do not have integral washbasins, so that you may have to grapple with awkward taps and towels or hand-driers that are difficult to reach. The unisex toilet – necessary for those who rely on help from a spouse or companion of the opposite sex – is rare in the USA; in over four months of travelling Arthur Goldthorpe found only one toilet clearly marked as "Unisex". Anyone requiring this facility might be lucky in smaller shops and restaurants, where a single, unisex "washroom" often provides the space needed for a wheelchair.

Health and insurance

Costs of even minor medical treatment in the States will take your breath away, so don't skimp on insurance (see *Practicalities*, "Insurance"). If taking medical supplies of any sort you must have a copy prescription from your doctor; it's also a good idea to carry a doctor's letter stating your medical condition and treatment regime.

A word of warning about the climate of the East Coast, from Carolyn Lucas: "It can be extreme in summer and winter; the best time to go is spring or autumn. The humidity can be so enervating that you quickly run out of energy, especially if you or your companion are lugging a wheelchair around. Out of town, insects can be vicious and a doctor should see to their bites. My husband was affected and had to take a course of antibiotics as a precaution against possible development of rheumatoid arthritis."

Repair, sale and rental of **wheelchairs** are handled by medical supply companies, which can be found via the Yellow Pages. For tyre repair, try a bike shop.

If you need information regarding sale or repair of **hearing aids**, and sale or rental of TDD, contact *The National Association of the Deaf* (814 Thayer Avenue, Silver Spring, MD 20910; ☎301/587-1788). Hearing-aid dealers are listed in the Yellow Pages; they require a prescription from an audiologist in order to sell or repair hearing aids.

The National Federation of the Blind (1800 Johnson Street, Baltimore, MD 21230; ☎301/659-9314) can send white **canes** and other specialised equipment anywhere in the States, and will also issue identification cards certifying blindness – these may have to be produced for discounts on bus or train tickets.

Canada

Satisfied Customers

Travelling across North America by Greyhound bus, spending days and nights on board, might seem a little crazy and impractical for a full-time wheelchair user. But Dee Hopkins did it, in 1983, accompanied by her husband, Gerry.

Whatever the time of day or night, no matter how long or short the journey, travelling on a *Greyhound* bus is exciting. Thundering along the highways we had conflicting feelings – not wanting the journey to end, yet looking forward to reaching our destination, where we could begin a new adventure. The drivers made it even more enjoyable; they were friendly and helpful, and pointed out places of interest, especially to us, occupying the front seats which gave us splendid views of the passing countryside. Our fellow passengers seemed to feel the same sense of excitement, almost trepidation, as they boarded, and it didn't take long for a special kind of camaraderie to develop amongst us. We exchanged holiday experiences, discussed our plans, and took advice about our proposed destinations.

No one seemed to mind that we had to take our time getting on, or that we had to take the front seats. The only way I could get up the steps was to sit and push up with my arms until I reached the top, where Gerry lifted me and put me on the seat. Trousers are the most dignified clothing for this operation. The unusual method of ascent didn't worry me, especially since

twice a day the passengers are asked to leave the bus and it is taken away for a thorough cleaning, inside and out.

When booking, I had supplied a doctor's certificate, stating that I need help, so that we were able to take advantage of the Helping Hand scheme, whereby I bought a ticket and my companion travelled free. This was very important because money was our main problem; we had to work on a very tight budget because Gerry gave up work to look after me. The most difficult decision was choosing where to go; in the end, after a trip to the main library in Norwich to look up the *Greyhound* timetables (we photocopied the appropriate pages), we booked a ten-day trip, leaving midweek from Portsmouth, New Hampshire, and travelling through the Rockies, across Canada.

Travelling light was essential; trying to push a wheelchair overloaded with luggage as well as me would be almost impossible. So we restricted ourselves to a small suitcase of lightweight clothing which rested either on the arms of the wheelchair in front of me or on the footplates, between my knees. A flight-bag was hung from the handles at the back, and Gerry carried a holdall over his shoulder.

Thanks to the kind invitation of my pen friend in Maine, we were able to spend our first night with friends, who saw us on our way with plenty of provisions – meat in small tins and jars for sandwiches, coffee and dried milk, soft drinks in cartons, cheese and crackers, nuts and raisins, puddings in easy-to-open cartons, and many other items which saved us having to shop. We did treat ourselves to one hot meal a day, mainly takeaways which were so huge that we usually needed only one for both of us.

The first bus was to take us to Boston, Massachusetts, where we would change buses and carry on into Canada, via Syracuse, Albany, Buffalo and the Niagara Falls. We said farewell to our friends, who were a little worried about us – they gave us an envelope with some dollars in, to use in emergencies, but we were determined not to use it, and we returned it unopened when we finished our journey.

We slept on the bus that first night, partly to save money and partly because we wanted to arrive at Niagara Falls first thing in the morning. Sleeping on the buses is easy, especially if (as recommended) you take a small travel pillow, or have a shoulder to rest on – I had both. I also took a small cot blanket, as the air conditioning can be a little too efficient at night. However, I don't recommend sleeping consecutive nights on the bus; had money not been such an important consideration we would have spent every night in a motel.

The first thing we did on arrival at Niagara Falls was to find a much-needed hot breakfast, with coffee. Almost anywhere in America, once you've bought your first cup of coffee, you can have as many refills as you can drink, for no extra charge. After breakfast we made our way across the small town to the Tourist Information Office, where they supplied us with the name

and address of an inexpensive motel, and with all the information we needed about the area, including the times of a sightseeing tour, due to start later that morning.

We found the motel clean and comfortable, with colour TV and two queen-size beds, which we collapsed onto for a couple of hours. Later we climbed aboard Bessie bus for a very interesting tour, which we found surprisingly cheap – and it certainly saved us a lot of energy. We passed the falls and then followed the river. The fact that impressed me was that the falls started way downriver, thousands of years ago, and since then they have gradually cut back into the rock to reach their current position. The river was slowed down in recent years by a very long barrier which can control the flow; it is hoped that this will slow down the process of erosion.

We were taken down the cliffs to the rapids; the others had to climb down many stairs but I was able to descend in a small lift. My most vivid memory of the falls is the colour of the water – deep, deep green, almost like washing-up liquid – and the ferocity of it, cascading down with a deafening roar, so close to the road and only separated from us by a slim iron railing.

"The job of the front-seat occupants was to watch out for stray moose"

The next day we were back on the *Greyhound*, heading this time for Toronto. There we had a few hours to spare, so we left our bags in a locker and made our way out of the bus station, trying to remember our route for the return journey. The shopping area was fantastic, my favourite being the photographic shop, where customers could change into old-fashioned clothes and be photographed, the finished product developed in authentic sepia tones.

As usual, I had to find a "restroom" (toilet), and in 1983 the facilities for disabled people were nowhere near the level provided now in Canada and the USA; the awareness of disabled people's needs was not as high. Back at the bus station, I was getting desperate, so we sought out one of the many security guards who patrol the bus stations at night. We explained our predicament, and the fact that we had another hour to wait before catching our bus, and he escorted us to the Ladies. He stopped everyone going in, and when the last lady came out he waved my husband and I inside – now that is what I call service! What surprised us was that no one seemed to mind, and Toronto bus station is a very busy place, even at night.

At 1am we boarded the bus and headed out of the city. Our driver informed us that we were on Moose Patrol; we thought he was joking, but he told us that the job of the front-seat occupants was to watch out for stray moose that happen to roam onto the highway. If hit the moose can cause an accident, not to mention the damage to themselves.

It was still dark when we reached Lake Superior; we followed the lake for miles before we came to a smaller lake and beside it the little town of Wawa (meaning Goose), originally an Indian settlement, so called because the Canada geese call there when migrating, and the lake is covered with them. As the sun rose we left Wawa, after our rest stop, and we were able to see beautiful Lake Superior shimmering orange in the morning rays.

Our next stop was Thunder Bay, a compact and attractive town, renowned for its amethyst mines. As we travelled towards it we saw the purple seams in the rocks where the engineers had blasted through to build the highway. We had planned to stay one night before travelling on through the Rockies to Vancouver, but my legs had become so swollen that we decided to abandon our plans to see the Rockies, and stay put for three days.

We climbed off the bus, collected our bits together and made for the Tourist Information Office where, once again, we obtained a comprehensive list of motels, their facilities and prices. We found a cheap one with cooking facilities, colour TV, telephone and the regulation queen-size beds. The only problem we encountered at all in our accommodation was the showers – I couldn't stand up in them. We sorted this out by putting a towel on the floor under the shower; I then sat on the towel and showered, after which my husband lifted me onto my chair. All our motel rooms were very spacious, so I had no trouble manoeuvring the wheelchair once inside.

"We proved we could do it on a shoestring and still have a good time"

We enjoyed our stay in Thunder Bay. The weather was very hot, but not humid, and we walked everywhere (or my husband did). The streets were all straight, as if laid out on a grid, and very wide. The locals seemed amused to see us plodding along the streets – they all use cars. We found the people rather reserved and, although helpful, not very receptive to strangers. Perhaps this is because it is not really a tourist town, more a small industrial centre, with ships coming and going at the docks. There are few places of interest for the tourist, apart from the amethyst mines, where guided tours can be made (but not by wheelchair users), and the jewellery shops in town.

Late in the afternoon on the third day, we boarded the bus for our return journey. After a long ride in the darkness, we experienced another beautiful Canadian sunrise. The driver showed us where a tornado had passed, leaving a trail of destruction a couple of miles wide. We passed through the nickel-mining town of Sudbury, then arrived in Toronto. We had planned to spend the night in the city but as there was a big exhibition on, we couldn't find a room, so we had to head back to the bus.

At 12.30am the bus heaved its way tentatively onto the still-busy streets, back to the border and into the USA. A couple from our bus were held up at the border by customs officials, leaving us way behind schedule. We were worried about our connections at Buffalo and Boston, and several other passengers were affected, so the driver contacted Buffalo and asked them to hold up the bus for us. That driver in turn contacted Boston and we were able to continue to Portsmouth, and our friends.

No sooner had we arrived home than we were planning another trip. We don't know if we'll ever get to go again, but it will certainly be fun planning. There are a few things we would change, such as not sleeping so much on the bus, but shortage of money and time (we were only given seven days on our Canadian visas) gave us little choice on this trip. We proved we could do it on a shoestring and still have a good time, and at the end of our journey, despite a tinge of regret that we didn't reach the Rockies, our greatest emotion was satisfaction.

Canada: Second to None

Although confined to a wheelchair for the past 26 years with muscular dystrophy, Christine Swan is a fairly "active" disabled person, able to work full-time, to drive and to lead a very full life. In September 1983 she and a companion carried out an all-expenses-paid research trip on behalf of a tour company (Travelmarrs) to assess the facilities for the disabled traveller in Canada*. They covered some 32,200km across the country from east to west, starting in Toronto and finishing in Vancouver.

We arrived in Toronto in brilliant, mid-afternoon sunshine with temperatures

---

* The project which sponsored Christine's trip terminated in 1984 due to "lack of support and interest". Although *Travelmarrs* produce the well-known Handicare insurance policy for mentally and physically handicapped travellers, the company is no longer involved in holidays or travel arrangements for disabled people.

in the upper eighties. Our first few days were full of interesting sights, including Black Creek Settlers' Village and the CN Tower. Because of the nature of the village – early settlers' houses (many with steps), unmade roads – it would be difficult, without spoiling its authenticity, to make it entirely accessible to disabled visitors, and it was impossible to view many of the buildings internally. We gained access to the lower viewing area in the CN Tower by lift, but a wide heating-system grille around the revolving area prohibited wheelchair-bound visitors from fully appreciating the view.

But the highlight of our stay in Toronto has to be our visit to Niagara. After lunching – on scallops in champagne; veal in cheese and tomato sauce with vegetables; fudge cake with hot chocolate sauce; ice cream and double cream; coffee and hazelnut liqueur – in the Skylon Tower revolving restaurant, I was able to don the regulation hooded oilskin and sail in the *Maid of the Mist* to the foot of the falls, where our senses were overwhelmed by the mighty rush of water and the spray which engulfs the excited passengers.

We stayed in Toronto at the *Inn on the Park*, where breakfasts were taken beside the open-air swimming pool, served by attractive waitresses in skimpy shorts. Ramps were provided at intervals over three or four steps leading to the dining room and to the pool area but these, particularly the internal ramps, were very steep and I needed three attendants to negotiate them in my chair. In addition, my wheelchair, which is fairly narrow (63.5cm), would only just go through the bathroom doorway. The brochure did state that any bathroom door could be removed on request but this is not ideal when sharing a room. In all other respects, however, the hotel was very satisfactory.

"In the winter, this freezes over and thousands of office workers skate to work on it"

After four days, it was off by rail on a seven-hour journey to the beautiful capital, Ottawa. Canada's national rail company, *VIA Rail*, is to be commended on the thought and planning which it devotes to facilities for disabled passengers, and on the advice it gives to intending disabled travellers. The service and willingness of *VIA* personnel on our journey was first class. (See *Travel Notes* for more information.)

In Ottawa we were treated to a performance of *The Gondoliers* at the Arts Center, which has level access and helpful staff. The restaurant is accessible and the theatre has a gently sloping walkway in three sections to the upper-floor auditorium. The Ottawa Art Gallery also has level access and good facilities.

The following day we viewed Government House, the embassy buildings, each set in magnificent grounds, the Prime Minister's house, overlooking the Ottawa River, and the Training School for Mounties. We had a guided tour of the Senate buildings (special entrance for disabled visitors) which were completely accessible. There is virtually no industry in Ottawa – the majority of the residents are employed by the government – so it's a clean city, architecturally beautiful, with lovely parks in the centre. The Rideau Canal also runs through the centre; in the winter, this freezes over and thousands of office workers skate to work on it.

After Ottawa, we travelled back to Toronto for a three-hour flight to Saskatoon, Saskatchewan, where we flew into rain and cooler weather. One of the trips we enjoyed here was a visit to the Western Development Museum, a complete indoor village with sidewalks, and shops stocked as they were a hundred years ago. There are carriages and cars in the road, and a railway station with sound effects. We had no access problems apart from the double doors at the entrance, which were set too close together, allowing insufficient room to get the wheelchair through into the space before opening the inner doors.

We stayed at the *Holiday Inn*, where access to the dining room was level but, in common with most other hotels, the bathroom was too small for manoeuvring. Upon leaving, we were advised that this hotel did have a special room for the disabled guest but we had not been booked into it. We visited the *Saskatoon Inn*, a hotel and restaurant, very new at the time, designed with sloped walkways throughout from ground to first floor. It was a real showpiece, with indoor swimming pool and gardens.

From Saskatoon, we drove about 400km across the vast wheatfields of the Prairies to Regina, where our first port of call was the Royal Canadian Mounted Police Museum and Chapel. The museum is accessible; the guide advised us that a ramp was shortly to be provided for the three steps at the entrance to the chapel. The *Regina Inn* supplied our accommodation, and the facilities in both bedroom and bathroom were convenient; the dining room had level access.

Another flight took us 800km to Calgary – not, as I'd imagined, a small "cowboy town", but a large city with many skyscrapers where, like New York, the pavements downtown rarely see the sun. The only view I had of the Calgary Stampede Showground was from the revolving restaurant in the Calgary Tower (good access by lift) where we had breakfast one morning – sausage, bacon, pancakes and maple syrup, all on one plate at the same time!

There were several steps at the front entrance of *The Palliser Hotel*, but we obtained access through the rear entrance via the lift from the multistorey car park. The toilet was situated behind the bathroom door and we were unable to manoeuvre my wheelchair around. We were transferred to another room which was better. There was flat access to the dining rooms in this hotel and in the *Chateau Airport*, where we were booked into a suite for disabled guests. Here there was room to manoeuvre in the bathroom, a useful handrail on the wall next to the toilet and lever taps on the washbasin, but the basin was set too high – another common problem in the hotels we inspected. The bedroom was fine.

"There are pine-log cottages, each specially designed for the disabled, and paved trails through the forests"

From Calgary we took a two-day, 800-kilometre trip into the Rocky Mountains. Those were bright and sunny days; never have I been anywhere so beautiful. The lakes at the foot of the mountains are a rich, sapphire blue; there are perfectly shaped pine trees growing on the sides of the snowcapped mountains; the air is crystal clear; the silence is both calming and awe-inspiring. At every bend in

the road we were presented with a view more lovely than the last, not just for a few miles but for hundreds upon hundreds of miles.

Whilst in the Rockies we visited the *William Watson Lodge*, Kananaskis Country, which has been provided by the Canadian government for handicapped residents of the Province of Alberta. There are pine-log cottages, each specially designed for the disabled, and paved trails through the forests which lead to viewing areas overlooking the mountains and lakes. At each junction in the trails, the texture of the ground changes, so that a blind person can tell where the turnings are. We were shown around by Ross, who is blind but knew his way instinctively and was able to describe the breathtaking views to us. It was a real pleasure for me to go through the forests with the scent of pines heavy in the air – this is something that we wheelchair-bound folk are not often able to do.

On the first night of our Rockies trip we had a balcony room overlooking the lake at *Chateau Lake Louise*. It was dark when we arrived but it was a good start to the following day to wake up to the sun shining on snowcapped peaks and the blue lake just below our window. The bedroom and bathroom were adequate but again I had difficulty moving around the bathroom. We had to negotiate five or six steps to the dining room where we feasted on reindeer meat, but there is another dining room with level access – it was closed on the day of our visit.

We would have given anything to sit all day and take in the beauty of the surroundings at *Chateau Lake Louise*, but we had to move on, another 400km or so, to Jasper. Here we were booked into a suite for disabled guests in a superb hotel, *Chateau Jasper*, where the proprietor had obviously given much thought to the facilities. This was the only hotel with space next to the toilet for sideways transfer, although it was too close to the wall on the other side for my needs. There was a handrail beside the toilet, lever door handles and a sloping mirror towards the wash-basin. However, the basin was set much too high and the modern, pull-out mixer tap was difficult.

We took a cable car to the top of Whistler's Mountain which was concealed by cloud. There was no prob-lem with boarding or leaving the cable car but the sides of the car were a little too high to enable seated passengers to take in the view. The viewing area at the peak was accessible – we sat and shivered in pouring snow!

The next day we drove back to Calgary and flew on to our final city, Vancouver. It is easy to understand why so many people settle here: the lovely harbours, and beautiful Stanley Park (with totem poles, peaceful lakes and accessible aquarium) in the centre; the winters on this side of Canada are more like our own, with perhaps only one or two falls of snow; Glenmore (the revitalised dockside area) is interesting and attractive, as well as easily accessi-ble. Both the city and the island are places which I should like to visit again and spend more time in.

We stayed in the *Hyatt Regency*, which offered excellent facilities and well-planned rooms. The ferry to Vancouver Island was accessible, although the route to and from the ferry by lift for disabled passengers could have been better signposted, and there was a long walk to board the ferry from the departure lounge.

Of course, we were privileged on our trip. We were transported by car, driven in each province by a guide provided by the tourist boards, and we received VIP treatment, with visits to the mayors of several cities, press inter-views and TV appearances. But none of this detracts from the fact that we met many kind and helpful people during our stay, and it was clear that facilities for the disabled are kept very much in mind. There are dropped kerbs in every city, ramps where there is even just one step, and accessible lifts every-where. I was also very impressed by the fleets of Handy-Dart and Wheel-Trans buses, which transport disabled people on any trip that they wish to make.

"With careful planning and a sense of humour it is possible to achieve the impossible"

It is very difficult to ensure that *every* hotel room is suitable for *every* disabled person, or for every type of handicap. The two main problems which I encountered were the limited space around the toilet and the height of the washbasin: it is not necessary for the wheelchair to go under the basin, only up to it. Our bedrooms were generally satisfactory, with plenty of room to manoeuvre, but all the hotels we used were first class – I doubt that the facili-ties at the cheaper hotels would be so good.

The most trying part of travelling abroad, especially on long trips, remains the flights, where one's wheelchair is whisked away at the airport and loaded into the hold, to be produced again (if you're lucky) at the destination. More training should be given to airline staff regarding the correct method of lifting, and they should always be prepared to listen to the disabled person's requests and advice on this. The aircraft seats are particularly restricting and, of course, one is expected to be superman (or woman) as far as visiting the loo is concerned.

Even so, with careful planning and a sense of humour it is possible to achieve the impossible. I have spent many other happy holidays, before and after my trip to Canada, but only one approaches the high standard of hotels or scenery: a week in the glorious summer of 1989 with *Disaway* in the *Hydro Hotel* in Crieff, Scotland (see p.113), comes a very close second.

Large Marge Steals the Show

When he travelled to Canada in 1989, Steve Veness was 29 years old and had been a paraplegic for ten years.

"Yes, of course we'll come over and see you," my wife Judy and I had somewhat rashly promised when we heard that our friends were to be posted to Canada for three years.

After eighteen months, a large dose of guilt at our unfulfilled promise, coupled with a dash of adventurous spirit, saw us wandering aimlessly through Heathrow airport, trying to look as though we knew where we were going. Well, we did know that – Nova Scotia, Toronto, Niagara and the Rockies were all firmly on our itinerary; the big unknown was how we would fare en route.

We had booked our *Air Canada* flights through *Thomas Cook* who, they assured me, had told the airline that I would need full assistance with boarding and leaving (or deplaning, as the Canadians call it). Sure enough, *Air Canada* oozed confidence, and with an air of polite matter-of-factness swept me (and Judy) straight onto the 767 ahead of the crowds.

Although we did not know it at the time, we were already gaining the first of several advantages that we were to enjoy on our holiday as a result of my disability. This only dawned on us later, when we flew from Toronto to Calgary and had to rough it in the economy class – on all the other flights we were given business-class seats, although we had paid for economy throughout our trip.

At Halifax airport, after a smooth, civilised (business-class) journey, we were brought down to earth by our first flight of stairs, by a hire car with no hand controls and by the rain! The stairs, to be fair, did have a (very slow)

stair-lift, and the rain we were used to, but the lack of hand controls meant that Judy would have to drive the 118km across Nova Scotia to our hotel in the Annapolis Valley (she was not amused!). My admiration for the fact that *Hertz* were prepared to fit hand controls to each car we hired for no extra charge soon evaporated, to be replaced by tired cynicism amid the flurry of apologies. Two days later, hand controls fitted (to a larger car at no extra cost) and hire charges for the first two days waived, admiration returned and was to remain throughout three weeks of trouble-free motoring in four different cars.

Nova Scotia is a curious mixture of easy-going, rural provincialism and brash American influence. It is not a materially rich area, but it is dotted with small farming towns, the inhabitants of which seem to have a quality of life that cannot be measured in pounds or dollars. Despite severe winters, the long, warm summers allow the province to grow large quantities of apples, peaches, bilberries, wheat, sweetcorn and other vegetables. We were able to enjoy a wide range of fresh produce by visiting the cheap pick-your-own farms.

Religion is clearly important to the people of Nova Scotia: each town has several fine wooden churches, usually in pristine condition with a recent coat of white paint. Most of the churches had ramped access (uncommon in the UK); indeed, access to buildings throughout Nova Scotia – and the rest of Canada – was very good.

In contrast to the peaceful grace of Nova Scotia's churches, eating out was an American fast-food affair, with "Donut" shops and burger-bars very much in evidence. One favourable aspect of the fast-food restaurants is that many have toilets which are accessible to wheelchairs – no bad thing given the Canadian habit of never allowing you to empty your coffee cup. Another point in their favour (in my eyes) is that they serve enormous help-ings. One could easily manage on two meals a day – so I'm told. Prices, on average, were about half of what we would expect to pay in the UK, provided we avoided wine, which was usually very expensive.

Our flight to Toronto was another smooth one and this time a hand-controlled car was waiting for us at the airport, which was just as well, since we hit Toronto at 5pm on a Friday afternoon in a thunderstorm – Judy was definitely *not* going to drive! For anyone considering hiring a car with hand controls, they seem to be fitted on the left of the steering wheel in Canada – this takes a little getting used to if you are accustomed to controls on the right.

Toronto is a very clean city which exudes an air of confidence in the future. A large number of modern buildings were under construction or had just been completed. As well as the ubiquitous office blocks and shopping malls, recent buildings include the Skydome – a vast sports stadium which is home to the Toronto Blue Jays baseball team – and the CN Tower, which at over 540m is the world's largest free-standing, man-made structure. These two are sited close to one another and I strongly advise against trying to visit either on a day when the Blue Jays are playing at home!

We booked the *Bond Place Hotel* in Toronto through *Thomas Cook*, who indicated that it was suitable for wheelchairs. It was, provided you didn't want to go to the toilet – our room had an *en suite* bathroom with a door width of no more than 21 inches (53cm). Fortunately, I was able to transfer via a chair onto the toilet, and as we were only staying for two nights we made do.

For us, the real reason for stopping off at Toronto was to visit Niagara Falls, which appear on the map to be very close to Toronto. In fact, we drove about 200km from our hotel in the city centre to the falls – the size of the country was one aspect of Canada which we found difficult to come to terms with.

Having arrived before 9am to beat the Labour Day weekend crowds, we thought we would be able to head back to the hotel by early afternoon.

Things didn't go quite according to plan: we did everything, bar the barrel-ride, and we had to drag ourselves away at 10.30pm! Half expecting the falls to be an anticlimax, we soon realised that none of the guidebooks do them justice. Two factors were particularly pleasing: access to all the main tourist attractions was excellent (and we bypassed the long queues to the falls tunnels and to the truly exhilarating *Maid of the Mist* boat trip); in addition, we were pleasantly surprised not to be stung with exorbitant prices or poor quality in any of the attractions, including the excellent *Terrace Restaurant* where we had lunch. (I am sure that if the Niagara Falls were in the UK, it would be a different story.)

> *"We were able to see many species of wildlife, including mountain goats, bighorn sheep, mule deer, elk and coyote"*

After Toronto and Niagara, we headed west to the heart of the Rockies, in search of "the great outdoors". The area centred around Banff and Lake Louise presents a heady mixture of massive, snowcapped peaks, clear mountain air, tumbling rivers, snow, ice and plentiful wildlife. Although cross-country hikes are clearly out of the question for us, many of the most famous spots in the region are accessible by road or by short, well-laid paths from the road.

Not to be missed are Lake Louise (including brunch at *Chateau Lake Louise*, overlooking the lake), Moraine Lake and Takkakaw Falls (380m high and spectacular in a very different way to Niagara). As well as giving its name to a skiing village nearby, Lake Louise is a very popular tourist attraction. The green waters of the lake, hemmed in by lofty mountains on three sides, attract visitors by the hundred each day. To see it at its best, go there at sunrise, before the crowds arrive, and watch the pink mountains mirrored in the surface of the lake.

Also worthwhile is the drive along the Icefields Parkway to the Athabasca Glacier, stopping at the Peyto Lake viewpoint on the way. On that drive, and also on the way to Radium Hot Springs, we were able to see many species of wildlife, including mountain goats, bighorn sheep, mule deer, elk and coyote. In case this sounds like too much wilderness, the region does have centres of civilisation in the form of fine restaurants, such as that at the *Post Hotel* in the village of Lake Louise, and good shopping, especially in the centre of Banff.

We had an excellent (but expensive) meal at the *Post Hotel*; the staff were very friendly, access was good and the hotel had an aura of unpretentious luxury. If we ever get the chance to go to the Rockies again I hope we can afford to stay (and eat!) at the *Post Hotel*. In Banff, *Melissa's* is *the* place for breakfast – a six-ounce sirloin steak with eggs is one of the more popular offerings on the menu.

"Five magnificent humpback whales and many porpoises"

After our time in the Rockies we had planned a two-night stop back in Nova Scotia, to say goodbye to our friends before flying back to the UK. In the event, our last full day in Canada was a day which will live in our memories for a long time to come. Whilst we were "out West", our friends had booked a whale-watching trip from Brier Island on the westernmost tip of the Nova Scotia peninsula.

Rising early, and feeling slightly jet-lagged, we drove 330km down the peninsula, across two roll-on, roll-off ferries, to arrive at the tiny fishing port just in time for the trip. My slight anxieties about how I was going to get onto

the boat disappeared as four strong men easily lifted me – somewhat heavier after three weeks in Canada – together with wheelchair, on board. (In fact, I was not the only person in a wheelchair on that trip.)

Once we had left the harbour we motored out into the Bay of Fundy on a flat-calm sea. We were soon lucky enough to see the first of five magnificent humpback whales and many porpoises. The people running these trips are scientists engaged in whale research; they were therefore able to give an informed and enthusiastic commentary on the whales' behaviour. The scientists can recognise individual whales from their markings, and they were pleased when we sighted "Large Marge" together with her eight-month-old calf – a mere baby at 7.5m in length.

The whales did not seem to mind the boat and at times swam alongside and underneath (one actually went to sleep beside us!), but the calf was very inquisitive, not having seen the boat before. The organisers sight whales on 97 percent of the trips (and refund ticket money if none are seen) but we were especially lucky to see so many, and such a wide variety of behaviours, including breaching (jumping clear of the sea), feeding – and sleeping! In every sense it proved a fitting climax for our holiday.

Canada is not a country that we would have visited unprompted, but it left us with some lasting memories – of homely farming communities, busy city streets, awesome natural grandeur and vast open spaces untouched by human influence. When we think of Canada we think of Lake Louise at sunrise, Niagara Falls seen from *Maid of the Mist*, and a mother and calf swimming in unison. We also think of the people we met – friendly, generous and proud of their country – for whom my wheelchair never seemed to be a problem. Our trip not only gave us a feel for their land, but also made us realise how easy and worthwhile long-distance travel can be.

Proud to be a Montrealer

Dorothea Boulton is confined to a wheelchair. When in August 1988 her daughter, Jane, took up a research post at McGill University, Montreal, it seemed the ideal opportunity for Dorothea and her husband, Paul, to visit Canada.

We started planning our visit when Jane suggested that May or June were suitable months to consider; during the winter months it is extremely cold, with a lot of snow, while in July and August it is very hot and humid. We decided on May and, as our departure date drew closer, the weather in Montreal was cool and wet, presenting us with a packing dilemma – we knew that it would soon become quite warm. Indeed, we were to see for ourselves that spring comes quickly in Canada, and just as quickly turns to summer.

Jane collected as much information as she could and brought home various guidebooks at Christmas. In addition, we obtained advice and information on flights, fares and packages from *Wardair*, *British Airways* and *Air Canada*. We eventually selected four city-centre hotels which seemed to offer the special facilities that we needed (accessible entrance, rooms with an adapted bathroom, lifts large enough and doorways wide enough to accommodate a wheelchair). On her return to Montreal, Jane visited all four hotels and inspected them.

We chose to stay at the *Holiday Inn Crowne Plaza* in central (downtown) Montreal, although the facilities offered there were similar to those at the other three hotels, and indeed many other hotels outside the downtown area. Our room was large, and the well-adapted bathroom provided sufficient turning space for my wheelchair. There were bars around both bath and toilet; the washbasin was at a comfortable height; the only disadvantage was the lack of walk-in shower.

After we had booked our flights with *Air Canada* I had to complete a complicated medical form before the airline would confirm my ticket (not a problem we had experienced on our previous travels with *British Airways*). On arrival at Heathrow, the arrangements made on booking worked well and *Air Canada* staff met us at all the relevant places, finally lifting me to my seat on the plane.

We were settled in by the cabin staff and took off on time. The flight went smoothly and we even coped with emptying my catheter bag. (We carry a urine bottle in a suitable plastic bag which we use at the seat – easier and less embarrassing if side seats near the toilet are pre-booked, and most airlines will arrange this.)

After seven hours we landed on schedule during a downpour. Again, all the arrangements worked perfectly and we were soon in a taxi with Jane, enjoying the hour-long drive into the city. We had been warned about the standards of driving in Montreal but it still came as a shock when our taxi driver, realising that he was not allowed to turn right at a set of traffic lights, promptly turned left, stopped, then reversed the five hundred yards to our hotel against three lanes of traffic.

The facilities offered by the *Holiday Inn* were excellent and, after a good night's sleep to recover from the jet lag, we were ready to start exploring. Jane was working during the day, so we were on our own. We had decided not to hire a car, but to use taxis, which are reasonably cheap. Jane supplied us with city guides, including a very good one for the disabled visitor, *Montreal – Useful Information for the Handicapped*, which gave us some idea of what to see.

The weather started cool and showery, but after only two days the sun came out and it rapidly became hotter, resulting in temperatures in the nineties. As I have difficulty coping with heat we soon appreciated the air conditioning in the hotel and the shopping malls.

Modern Montreal is famous for its underground city, reached via one of the many fabulous shopping malls. I have never seen so many good quality clothes shops, but then the Montrealers are extremely smart and fashion conscious. Each mall has two or three levels above and below ground; on the lowest level there is always a large, open square filled with tables and chairs. At lunchtime these areas come alive as the small takeaway stalls around the perimeter open and offer food of almost every nationality.

It is said that eating out is the Montrealer's favourite hobby. At the end of their day's work, the city's inhabitants crowd into the hundreds of small restaurants which line many of the streets and small squares. During our ten days in the city we ate at many restaurants offering different cuisines at very fair prices. There is entertainment in the form of street theatre, there are craft stalls to browse amongst, and the atmosphere is wonderful.

The main shopping street, with yet more boutiques, department stores and restaurants, is St Catherine Street, which forms the backbone of the downtown commercial centre. Leading off it is Crescent Street, restored to its nineteenth-century elegance and housing more stylish boutiques and art galleries. In the evenings the bars, restaurants and trendy nightclubs come into their own.

The larger part of Montreal is situated on an island, in the centre of which is Mont Royal, a beautiful natural park known locally as the Mountain. We spent a lovely day exploring it, although Paul needed a long sleep in the sun to recover after pushing me to the top. About a third of the way up the Mountain is Beaver Lake, which in winter months is an outdoor skating rink. Also in winter the Mountain is crisscrossed by ski-trails, and on the steeper slopes there are downhill ski-runs. When we visited, the Montrealers were enjoying the first hot weather of the year by picnicking and strolling along the many paths.

"The beauty of the stained-glass windows, the colour and the carvings took our breath away"

Most of the city centre is very modern, with numerous skyscrapers, but in close proximity there is the old town to be explored. In 1960, Old Montreal (the original city) was a deserted collection of old buildings. During the first half of the twentieth century the population gradually moved away from the river and the port, towards the new commercial centre of the city. But in the early Sixties Old Montreal was declared an area of historic interest, and commercial activity slowly returned.

Much of the area has been restored and has become a major tourist attraction which one can tour by horse-drawn *calèche* (carriage) – I'm afraid this was one of those things which we didn't attempt. The centre of Old Montreal is place Jacques Cartier – a lovely square surrounded by outdoor cafés, restaurants and craft shops.

There are many historic buildings and museums to visit in the old town but, for us, the most outstanding is the Notre Dame Basilica, in the place d'Armes, the centre of religious and economic activity during the nineteenth century. The basilica is not an attractive church from the outside but, as we entered, the beauty of the stained-glass windows, the colour and the carvings took our breath away. We spent a long time quietly absorbing the artistic and architectural treasures in this church.

The entrance to the Vieux Port (old port) is from place Jacques Cartier. Montreal is one of the world's largest inland ports, situated on the St

Lawrence River but 1600km from the Atlantic Ocean. Pleasure cruises can be joined from the Vieux Port, and the great river is the scene of much summertime activity.

As it was very hot (even for May), Jane suggested that we might like to take a cruise, but my husband had other plans! He had noticed in the guidebook an entry with the wheelchair symbol next to it – "Shooting the Lachine rapids in a jet boat" – and duly made enquiries. Yes, they could manage a disabled person as long as I could "hold on" (I can – just). We were told to bring a change of clothing as we may "get a little wet".

We arrived at the wharf 45 minutes before noon. "Help!", I thought when I saw the boat, "What am I doing? I don't even like little boats." The shallow-draft jet boat could seat twenty people, and in it we were to mount and descend the rapids where the St Lawrence drops some fourteen metres in a series of steps.

Our party gathered – French Canadians, Mexicans and ourselves – and we were given our instructions and our protective clothing. Two men dressed me in a thick, woollen sweater, waterproof jacket, life jacket, waterproof trousers and Wellington boots. We were all given a waterproof poncho to put on when we arrived at the rapids.

When everyone was suitably dressed, my wheelchair was bounced down twelve steps onto the floating jetty alongside the boat, and I was lifted in. I sat in the centre of the boat and at this point one of the crew kindly took a photograph of us! The trip upriver to the rapids took about forty minutes and provided fine views of the city. I knew we had arrived when everyone else stood up and became very excited.

Then started one of the most exhilarating experiences of my life as the boat was driven up and down the rapids six times. We encountered whirlpools and giant waves, and endured soaking after soaking – from head to foot. It was

marvellous! Not once did I feel apprehensive, only a sense of loss when we set off back to the port.

We were all convinced that we were soaked through to the skin, but when we shed our protective clothing there was not a damp patch to be found. My sense of achievement was made all the greater when my husband said, "I'm proud of you – I really didn't think you'd make it when you first saw the boat." But I did, and it was one of the highlights of our trip.

"The panoramic view from the top, over Montreal, the surrounding region and the St Lawrence River, was worth the agony"

In 1976 Montreal hosted the Olympic Games; a visit to the Olympic Park, and to the Botanical Gardens which are situated nearby, makes a pleasant change to museums and shopping malls. The park is vast and includes the main stadium, the swimming pools, the velo drome and all the facilities of a major sporting venue. Towering above the stadium is the world's tallest inclined tower, rising to 167m above the ground, a height which is equivalent to a fifty-storey building. In the upper front section the angle of inclination is 45 degrees, which perhaps should be compared with that of the Leaning Tower of Pisa – only five degrees.

The top three stories of the tower form observation decks which are reached by way of an exterior cable car, the only one of its kind in the world. It travels up the backbone of the tower and has two level cabins which can accommodate ninety people. As I have difficulty with glass-fronted lifts, the thought of the cable car was daunting. Although I made it to the observation deck, I must admit that my eyes were tightly shut on both journeys. However, the panoramic view from the top, over Montreal, the surrounding region and the St Lawrence River, was worth the agony.

A shuttle train runs from the Olympic Park to the Botanical Gardens, on the other side of a busy highway. The gardens are the third largest in the world and we spent a pleasant day exploring the different layouts and the glasshouses. The latest addition is a Japanese Garden, still in the process of construction but already providing a beautiful and peaceful oasis away from the crowds.

This was our first holiday spent entirely in a city and we were pleasantly surprised. Montreal provided us with a wealth of things to do and see. Inevitably there is much that we missed, so the city is well up on our list of places to be revisited. Perhaps next time we will be able to visit during the colder months and see the winter sports, both in Montreal and in the nearby Laurentian mountains, as well as enjoy the many cultural events staged in the city.

Although Montreal is French-speaking, with a different accent to that of European French, most people speak English and there are few communication difficulties. We enjoyed meeting the Canadian people, finding them charming and very helpful. Montrealers are justly proud of their city and we were made welcome throughout our stay.

Transportation Issues in Vancouver

In July 1986, The Fourth International Conference on Mobility and Transport for Elderly and Disabled Persons was held in Vancouver as one of the "theme periods" of Expo 86. Rod Semple, a severely disabled (multiple sclerosis) English immigrant in Canada and a leading light in the fight for the improvement of conditions for the handicapped, attended the conference with his wife, Janet.

We arrived at Toronto's Lester B. Pearson airport in good time and, baggage and other formalities attended to, we were assisted aboard the *Air Canada* L10-11. Arriving at Vancouver airport four and a half hours later, we noticed a couple of Handy-Dart vans – the Vancouver equivalent of Toronto's Wheel-Trans. On learning that these vans wouldn't be able to take us (we hadn't made an application for a tempo-rary pass), Janet and I decided to try out one of the wheelchair-accessible cabs run by *Vancouver Taxi*.

We were to use this fleet of Checker Taxis and new Chrysler "Magic Vans", which have raised roofs and portable ramps, quite extensively during our week in Vancouver; although too expensive for everyday use, a small fleet of them could probably operate quite profitably in Toronto (they also carry non-handicapped passengers and, occasionally, small pieces of furniture!).

Our accommodation turned out to be something of a disappointment, the bathroom being not too accessible and the furniture old and chipped. We were very fortunate in that after a couple of days we were able to move to the *Georgian Court Hotel*, which is adjacent to Expo and is in the downtown area. It has two "handicapped suites" and we highly recommend it.

BC Transit had recently opened its computer-operated SkyTrain rapid transit system, which runs between the Vancouver Waterfront station and New Westminster. The entire system is wheelchair accessible; the stations have elevators and the trains have space for wheelchairs in the carriages. We often used the SkyTrain system to travel to and from New Westminster.

We also rode the wheelchair-accessible SeaBus ferry, which sails from the Waterfront station across Burrard Inlet to Lonsdale Quay in North Vancouver. The views from the ferry are spectacular – the Vancouver skyline, the North Shore mountains and the shipping in the inlet. This stretch of water is busy with yachts, smaller boats and floating petrol stations for the convenience of boats and seaplanes. There are landing strips for the seaplanes, with walkways to the shore for the island commuters. The planes fly in time after time in the morning, unloading the workers, then collect them all for the homeward journey from 4.30pm onwards. Many hotels look out over this scene, with the North Shore and Grouse Mountain (wrap up well – there's snow most of the year on the mountain, but a very pleasant restaurant at the top) in the background.

Following a "getting acquainted" reception at the University of British Columbia (UBC) on Sunday night, the conference started in earnest on Monday morning. The delegates (approximately five hundred people from around the world) took part in the opening ceremonies and the first debate – Compulsory versus Voluntary Compliance with Legislation – dealing with issues involved in setting up transportation systems for the disabled. After the opening session the delegates split up to attend the symposia of their choice.

As North York (Ontario) member of the *TTC Wheel Trans Community Committee*, and Chairman of the *North York Transportation Committee for the Physically Disabled*, I chose to attend the symposium on Municipal Specialised Transportation Services. We discussed the organisation of parallel transit systems for the disabled in the Canadian Western Provinces and London, England, as well as a subsidised taxi service in Quebec.

Other lectures I attended on Monday dealt with inter-city bus transportation (my own particular "bag"), using the Newfoundland Roadcruiser as an example of what can be done. One of the exhibits at the outdoor display at the conference was *Transport Canada*'s Accessobus, a new MCI 102A3 highway bus fitted with a centrally mounted elevator which can lift a person in a wheelchair to one of two tie-down locations on the bus.

> *"It is my fervent hope that inter-city bus companies will abandon their traditional apathy towards those of us who cannot climb the bus steps"*

The day's formal activities wound up with the showing of the *British Rail* film "Just like the rest of us", which showed the efforts that *BR* is making to provide access to its rail network. In the evening we headed over to a scenic spot behind the Museum of Anthropology, overlooking the ocean, for a salmon barbecue with Indian entertainment. We watched the sun set behind the mountains.

A trip to the Expo 86 site was scheduled for Tuesday afternoon as part of the conference events. I was lucky enough to be one of the two people in wheelchairs who rode the Accessobus from UBC to Expo – it was great! After Expo the bus was to be loaned to inter-city bus carriers across Canada for evaluation. It is my fervent hope that inter-city bus companies will abandon their traditional apathy towards those of us who cannot climb the bus steps. Is there any good reason why we should be denied access to what is supposed to be a public transportation system?

On arrival at Expo we were met by members of the A (for Access) Team, a group of young people who assisted the delegates in wheelchairs throughout the conference period and whose services were very much appreciated. With the help of Thomas, Janet and I spent the rest of the day looking at Expo, using the wheelchair-accessible monorail to visit parts of the site.

People in wheelchairs were given priority at most of the pavilions, which helped considerably since long queues seemed to be the norm. We visited the British, German, Italian and Ontario pavilions, took the SkyTrain shuttle to the Canada pavilion and returned to the main site by *Transport Canada* wheelchair-van. After a late supper in the Romanian pavilion it was time to head back to the hotel.

After the final and most interesting (as far as I was concerned) seminar, on coordination and privatisation of transit systems, the official closing ceremonies took place, and I then joined an optional tour of *BC Transit*'s Handy-Dart offices in New Westminster. The evening found us in Gastown, enjoying supper at *The Old Spaghetti Factory*.

Most restaurants in Vancouver are accessible and there is a wide variety of cuisines to choose from. Canadian-Chinese food is excellent and very reasonably priced. China Town is fun to explore, not as oriental or as captivating as its namesake in San Francisco, but certainly worth a visit.

On Thursday we took the SkyTrain to New Westminster to visit a temporary exhibition, Transporama 86, on the river front. It was an interesting collection of old autos, trucks, a street car, trolley bus and several old railway cars. After spending some time there we travelled back to Main Street station in Vancouver, where we took a look at the *VIA Rail* pavilion. A combination of large displays, mime actors and films are used to show the story of train travel in Canada. Also featured is a train of old, restored *Canadian Pacific Railroad* passenger cars, billed as "The Millionaires' Train". I could only see this from the outside but I understand that the interior is quite impressive.

Our final full day in the Vancouver area started with some uncertainty. We wanted to visit Victoria, on Vancouver Island, but were not sure how to get there with me in a wheelchair. In the end, we were able to set up a ride on Handy-Dart over 75 percent of the trip on land, *Vancouver Taxi* handling the rest. *BC Ferries* managed the waterborne section.

"Victoria has the reputation of being more British than the Brits themselves"

The cruise through the mountainous Gulf Islands was very pleasant if rather windy. To be fair, it's not always windy, and the views – landward to Vancouver and the north coast of British Columbia, or seaward to Vancouver Island and the other islands – are difficult to describe without sounding "over the top"; it's an experience which should not be missed and is easily within reach of any wheelchair user.

Travelling on a ship with elevators was a first for me, and we made good use of them. We met one young chap on the ferry who was making the journey from Vancouver to Seattle unaccompanied in an electric wheelchair. He was using a combination of para-transit systems and ferry boats, and he told us that he'd made the trip several times.

Victoria is a pretty seaside town with very attractive landscaped areas along the main roads, and a beautiful shoreline. It has the reputation of being more British than the Brits themselves. There is an interesting Marineland, built out into the sea. Visitors descend in a sort of glass lift to the sea bed where they can observe marine life where it should be observed. I wondered . . . do the fish gather daily to see what's new in the human tank?

Handy-Dart dropped us outside the famous *Empress Hotel* in Victoria. After the traditional English high tea we boarded a double-decker bus for a tour of Victoria – one can sometimes do surprising things in a wheelchair! We had time to do just a little shopping before taking the Handy-Dart back to the ferry at Swartz Bay, stopping en route at Butchart Gardens.

Originally a disused quarry and an ugly blot on the countryside, the owner's wife undertook to turn Butchart into a paradise for horticultural types and flower lovers. Hillside and valley paths wander amongst rare trees and gorgeous blooms, both common and exotic. Because of the sheltered location and the care lavished upon the gardens, all plants flourish in healthy profusion. One well-travelled man said that they were the loveliest gardens he'd seen – praise indeed from an English gardener!

Our flight back to Toronto went fine except for a bloody-minded *Air Canada* passenger rep who didn't feel inclined to exert his strapping, six-foot frame to assist another employee in transferring me to my own wheelchair at Toronto airport. He preferred instead to kick suitcases off the conveyor belt and stroll around trying to look important. After some thirty minutes the transfer was accomplished with someone else's more willing assistance. Too bad, *Air Canada*, up to this point you did well, but please improve your food! (Subsequently, *Air Canada* sent me a letter of apology and a cheque to cover the cost of the unsatisfactory food.)

It was a fascinating conference and a wonderful trip. Conference aside, Vancouver for the holidaymaker offers a great deal: good access, good food, wheelchair-friendly transport and masses to do. Scenically, it lacks for nothing. From almost all vantage points the views are incredible, from UBC across to the North Shore, from North Shore back over the city, from Grouse Mountain over everything. The best time to go is March to June, or September after Labour Day (first Monday in the month).

A Helper's View

In 1984 Frieda Maguire's brother, Des, was severely brain damaged in an accident. Now in a wheelchair, Des is pretty much back to normal mentally, although his powers of concentration and short-term memory are not up to writing an account of his travels. Frieda describes a journey to Canada which was marred by very poor service from their travel agent, *Chieftain Tours*, of Dublin.

The letter, with a Canadian stamp, dropped through our letterbox one dull February morning. A very dear nephew's wedding was to take place in mid-May 1988, in Burlington, Ontario, and we (my sister, brother and myself) were invited. The questions started almost immediately: could Des manage a transatlantic flight, how much would it cost? The list of initially insurmountable problems seemed endless.

While we were still at the "should we?", "could we?" stage, the phone rang – it was our sister (the bridegroom's mother) with two questions, "Are you going?" and "What are you going to wear?", the latter being by far the most important. After much burning of the midnight oil, the decision was made, and travel arrangements got under way.

It was a charter flight – the cheapest fare we could get – with *Air Canada* from Dublin via Shannon to Toronto.

My nephew, Greg (who could accommodate the remainder of the party on floors, under stairs and generally hanging from the rafters) booked Des, my sister and I into a hotel about five minutes away from his house.

A day or so from departure we got word from *Chieftain Tours* that there had been a change of plan, and that we would have to go down to Shannon by coach instead of plane – a journey of about three hours by road. Our immediate problem was how to get Des onto the coach, knowing that the doorway would be narrow and the steps steep. We couldn't contemplate it, even allowing for assistance up the steps, and we had no option but to take the car and stay overnight somewhere in the Shannon region.

"To say that our modest bungalow would fit easily into Des's room is no exaggeration"

Having decided that, another problem presented itself: the homeward flight ended at Dublin, and our car would be at Shannon. We contacted *Chieftain Tours* and they agreed that one of our nephews could travel down on the coach, pick up the car and drive it back to Dublin for us.

With everything organised (or so we thought!) we headed off for an overnight stay in the southwest. We were about to leave for Shannon airport the next day, when my sister phoned to tell us that, in fact, they were flying to Shannon after all, and *Chieftain Tours* had asked her if we could drive *back* to Dublin (170km) to catch the plane down! Our whole purpose in travelling down by car was to make the journey less tiring for Des.

We had been among the first to book the charter flight with *Chieftain Tours*, and I had specified from the outset that my brother was confined to a wheelchair and would require every consideration to make the long and arduous journey as comfortable as possible. I put the blame for this fiasco entirely on the travel agent.

At Shannon, when the first boarding call came, Des had to queue with the other 300 passengers, and absolutely no concession was made for him. The seats allocated were in the second row, near the exit door of the plane. The very narrow aisle was made even narrower by the curved bulkhead. There was no way an underweight contortionist could have clambered into the seat allocated to Des – it was quite, quite impossible, and embarrassing for him, too.

After much dissension amongst some able-bodied passengers, two seats were given to us at the front of the plane and a third seat further back. The whole episode was a terrible experience for Des, and I would not travel on a charter flight again if I could find an affordable scheduled flight. If you have no alternative, then I advise you to insist on *pre-boarding* as well as a roomy situation on the plane.

At Toronto, we were met by a limousine (ordered by Greg) which took us to the hotel. Des was installed in what I can only describe as an enormous armchair in the front, beside the driver. The cost was about £22, and considering the degree of comfort and the length of the journey (about an hour), this form of transport is to be recommended.

Our accommodation in the *Venture Inn*, Burlington, was on the flat, just off the main lobby. To say that our modest bungalow would fit easily into Des's room is no exaggeration. It contained two double beds, a large round table, comfy chairs, TV and telephone, yet we could easily have held a small reception in it. A bathroom with a wide door opened off the bedroom and was equipped with all the facilities a disabled person could wish for, bar one – a slip-mat. There was a small stool in the shower area, and Des missed his footing and fell one morning. I pointed out the need for a mat to the management, but we weren't supplied with one. So, being wise after the event, our advice is to ask for a rubber mat, or whatever else you need for your safety, before using the bathroom.

There was a connecting door from Des's room to ours, and we had our own bathroom. Linen and towels were changed daily, or more frequently if required. We brought Des's own pillow and some protective covering for the mattress, just in case of accidents.

A short walk down the corridor brought us into the lobby, where tea and coffee were available at all times. Breakfast, which was inclusive and self-service, was served in the lobby from 6am. We took a tray and brought three breakfasts – fruit juice, muffins, croissants, jams, tea or coffee – back to the room, where Des could eat in complete comfort, sitting at the round table and overlooking the lake and small park outside. The great advantage of this was that he didn't have to get dressed for breakfast, and we could go down to collect it wearing our housecoats.

Burlington is a charming, small community, situated on the shores of Lake Ontario, within sight of the bridge over to the Niagara Falls. The pace of life is relaxed and easy-going, the people polite and helpful. A square has been restored and paved, housing small shops and restaurants – a delightful place to meander, and perhaps sit at one of the outdoor cafés surrounded by trees, and tubs and window boxes overflowing with colourful flowers. It was an ideal spot to bring Des in his wheelchair, for a breath of fresh air in peaceful surroundings.

The wedding day dawned as perfectly as anyone could have wished. The tiny hamlet and church made an ideal setting for what was essentially a very small and quiet wedding. The church presented a small access problem, in that there were several steps up to the entrance, but a couple of able-bodied young men were on the scene to do some wheelchair lifting.

The reception was held at the holiday home of the bride's parents – a log cabin! Nothing for us could have been more Canadian. The front of the cabin was two-storey, the back three-storey, as it was built on a hillside. Four or five strong helpers were required to push Des in his wheelchair up the steep grassy slope to the reception. The return journey was somewhat speedier, if rather thin on safety!

As always, when you are on holiday, time is in short supply. We were in Canada in May, and there were trips just starting – including one around Toronto harbour on a tall ship, with assisted boarding for wheelchair users – which would have been lovely to take. But we didn't have the time. An excellent publication, *Toronto with Ease* (published in 1984 and now well out of date) gave us all sorts of useful information, especially regarding access.

"The dreaded sign 'This section closed' was slammed in front of me"

A word of advice for the able-bodied as well as the disabled traveller: after the transatlantic journey you will probably have to allow a few days (about five in our case) to recover normal sleeping and eating patterns. Our stay was only two weeks, and for the first five days we were all in various stages of slumber: any time we sat on a comfortable chair we were off into the land of nod. It was infuriating, as we really *wanted* to stay awake and savour all the new experiences. The perfect length for our trip would have been about three weeks.

Following the disastrous seating arrangements on the outward flight, I was determined to see that Des had a comfortable trip home. With this in mind, I phoned ahead of our departure date, in the hope of booking a suitable seat. I was told that I could book seats only if I got to the airport three hours before check-in time.

So, on the day of departure, I took all the luggage, ordered a large taxi to take me to the coach pick-up point, and away I went! If you have ever joined a long check-in queue, with three sets of luggage and just one pair of hands, you will get the picture at Toronto airport! Every time a passenger finished checking in ahead of me, I had to kick, carry or pull our over-stuffed bags a few feet forward.

With elbows finally about to rest on the check-in desk the dreaded sign "This section closed" was slammed in front of me, and the voice behind it asked us to join the end of the other queue. If Des had been at the airport at that stage, I'd have asked for a loan of his wheelchair! When I eventually checked in, the seats I wanted were not available.

On the homeward journey, my unfortunate brother had to be lifted over the heads of other passengers and placed in a very cramped seat next to my sister. I was somewhere else on the plane. In the face of all the discomforts, Des never once complained, but it is not in his nature to do so. He still frequently recalls his Canadian holiday, and doesn't seem to have been put off the idea of travelling long distances. My few suggestions for less troublesome trips are to travel in old, comfortable clothes, to do your homework, to use scheduled services, and to keep your luggage manageable – foreign countries have shops and launderettes too.

CANADA: TRAVEL NOTES

Sources of information

National Tourist Office of Canada, Canada House, Trafalgar Square, London SW1Y 5BJ; ☎071/930 8540. Canada is even larger than the USA, so that, again, one national tourist office cannot hope to cover the whole country. The national office, however, is good for general information and for providing the addresses of the ten provincial tourist administrations (five of which have offices in London). Each province produces its own literature, much of which contains some reference to disabled visitors.

Canadian Paraplegic Association (CPA), 1500 Don Mills Road, Suite 201, Don Mills, Ontario M3B 3K4; ☎416/391-0203). The provincial tourist offices in London are usually happy to refer specific enquiries to their head offices, but they may ask you to contact the provincial head offices of the *CPA*. The head office above should be able to supply local access guides, accommodation information, and details of accessible transport. A list of *CPA* provincial offices can be obtained from Canada House

(Canadian High Commission, Commercial/Economic Division, Tourism Section), or you can enquire at the appropriate provincial tourist office.

Canadian Rehabilitation Council for the Disabled, 1 Yonge Street, Box 2110, Toronto, Ontario M5E 1E5; ☎416/862-0340. Produces two quarterly magazines, *Access* and *Rehabilitation Digest*, as well as a resource book for disabled and elderly travellers, *Handi-Travel* (US$12.95 plus $3 postage). The most recent edition was published in 1987.

Travel Alberta, 1 Mount Street, London W1Y 5AA; ☎071/491 3430. Include a list of wheelchair-accessible hotels and motels in their accommodation guide, and mark accessible toilet and washing facilities in their campground guide. *Your Complete Guide to Fun Times in Edmonton* (!) uses three codes for accessibility to the city's attractions – limited, good and very good – and gives a contact number for additional information (☎403/428-8424). The Alberta Division of the *CPA* (Box 20, Weber Centre, 5555 Calgary Trail, Edmonton

CANADA: TRAVEL NOTES

T6H 5P9; ☎403/438-5046) is more down to earth, very helpful and can put you in touch with the four regional branches.

Tourism British Columbia, British Columbia House, 1 Regent Street, London SW1Y 5BJ; ☎071/930 6857. Produced a *Travel Guide for the Disabled* more than eight years ago but unfortunately have not updated it. The accommodation guide indicates accessible hotels, motels and campgrounds, with a clear list of criteria that the property has to satisfy in order to be classified wheelchair accessible. All other queries should be addressed to *CPA*, British Columbia Division, 780 SW Marine Drive, Vancouver V6P 5Y7 (☎604/324-3611).

Tourism Nova Scotia, 14 Pall Mall, London SW1Y 5JH; ☎071/930 6864. The *Nova Scotia Travel Guide* indicates hotels and motels that cater for guests with mobility, visual or hearing impairment (mainly the big chains – *Best Western, Holiday Inns, Sheraton* – but some independents), a few wheelchair-accessible campgrounds, and attractions that are at least partially wheelchair accessible. Readers are referred to the *Nova Scotia League for Equal Opportunities* (Box 8204, Halifax B3K 5L9; ☎902/422-4768) for details of transport services and access to recreational facilities, and to *CPA*, Nova Scotia Division (5599 Fenwick Street, Halifax B3H 1R2; ☎902/423-1277) for access guides, further information or assistance.

Tourism Ontario, 21 Knightsbridge, London SW1X 7LY; ☎071/245 1222. Their link to *Ontario Travel* head office in Toronto will be able to provide more detailed information about access to accommodation and activities in the province. Some booklets contain specific information about services for people with disabilities, including camping, horse-riding, tent, trailer and motor home rentals. The guide to provincial parks (produced by the Ministry of Natural Resources) shows that many parks have accessible toilets, showers, picnic areas or visitor centres, but only two advertise wheelchair-accessible "self-guided trails" and none of the parks list accessible boating facilities.

Ministry of Tourism and Recreation, 77 Bloor Street West, Toronto, Ontario M7A 2R9; ☎416/965-8208. The Ontario office of the ministry is masterminding – with great energy and enthusiasm – an impressive operation which aims to improve the quality of service and information available to disabled travellers. *Project Challenge*, now known as the *"Open for Business* Accessibility Program", is working on four fronts: standardising accessibility criteria; educating the tourism and recreation industry about the market and needs of disabled clients; improving the methods of collection of accessibility information from the industry, and improving dissemination of information to disabled customers.

Phase 2 of the project was launched in March 1991 and entails encouraging operators to make use of an education pack containing a training video, accessibility workbook, access survey, tape measure and pencil. Phase 3 will involve the integration of the results of access surveys of tourist establishments into ministry tourism information services and publications by 1992. The information will be updated yearly.

Until completion of phase 3, the staff of *Tourism Ontario* in London will refer any queries that they are unable to answer to the Ontario office. Once in Canada or the USA, you can call a toll-free number for advice: ☎1-800/ONTARIO (668-2746). Other sources include the Ontario division of the *CPA* (520 Sutherland Drive, Toronto M4G 3V9; ☎416/422-5644) and the *Office for Disabled Persons* (2nd Floor, 700 Bay Street, Toronto M5G 1Z6; ☎416/326-0111, voice or TDD).

Office of the Agent General for Québec, 59 Pall Mall, London SW1Y 5JH; ☎071/930-8314. The standard *Montréal Tourist Guide* lists accessible hotels, gives an indication of accessibility of attractions, and supplies a few useful addresses. If that is not enough, *Montréal – Useful Information for the Handicapped* is free from the *Greater Montréal Convention and Visitors Bureau* (1555 Peel Street, Suite 600, Montreal H3A 1X6; ☎514/871-1595). Quebec's version of the *CPA*, the *Association des Paraplégiques du Québec*, pass on all queries concerning travel to *Kéroul* (4545 ave Pierre-de-Coubertin, C.P. 1000, succ. M, Montreal H1V 3R2; ☎514/252-3104), an organi-

CANADA: TRAVEL NOTES

sation which specialises in travel for mobility-impaired people, and publishes the bilingual guides, *Accès Montréal* (free) and *Accès Tourisme* (CN$10).

Tour operators

Air Canada, Canadian Airlines and *British Airways* will provide information on packages, and there are scores of UK tour operators offering holidays in Canada, including *Jetsave* and *American Express Holidays* (see p.424).

A number of Canadian travel agencies specialise in tours and individual travel for handicapped people. Most of these are members of *Assist* (*Association for Specialised Services Involving Special Travellers*), and you can find out more by writing c/o ACTA (*Association of Canadian Travel Agents*), Suite 1106, 75 Albert Street, Ottawa, Ontario K1P 5E7 (☎613/238-1361).

Getting there

Air Canada is one of the best carriers for travellers with disabilities (see *Practicalities*, "By Air"), but Frieda Maguire's account (p.445) suggests that charter flights are best avoided. Take time to search out a good deal and book ahead on a scheduled flight. *Air Canada* aircraft are equipped with Wilshire aisle wheelchairs and better-than-average toilet facilities, and the airline is in the process of evaluating and upgrading its procedures for disabled passengers. Steve Veness (p.436) received outstanding service, although Dorothea Boulton (p.439) found their medical form rather offputting and notes that she is not required to complete one for *British Airways*.

Canadian Airlines (formerly *Wardair*) are praised by several contributors, not least for the high quality of their food! Staff are reported helpful and friendly, but although each aircraft carries an aisle chair it cannot be taken into the toilet cubicle.

Transport

Air Canada's Wilshire chair has no armrests and can therefore be used on the narrow-aisle aircraft that are operated by their six regional airlines responsible for **domestic flights**. In addition, on Boeing 727 and Airbus 320 aircraft at least one toilet is equipped to accommodate disabled passengers.

Facilities at **airports** are generally good, although John Bignell experienced some difficulties when flying between Toronto and Pittsburgh in 1988. On the outward journey, at Toronto airport, he had to transfer to a small Jetstream which was parked away from the ramp. Even in its lowest position, the ramp ended in mid-air, with a service stair down to the runway and an internal flight of stairs for passengers. Fortunately, John can manage a few steps, but there was a solid rail on the right and a lethal rope on the left, the exact opposite of what he requires, which is to hold his stick in his right hand and something solid in his left. John's comment: "I did not enjoy my ascent! Please can we have something solid on both sides."

On his return journey, the *USAir* (see also Angela Deakin's account of her experiences with this airline, p.419) flight from Pittsburgh landed at Terminal 2 and the onward flight to London left from Terminal 1. John was taken to the pick-up point for the airport bus and left to his own devices: "When the bus arrived, there was what may be described as a short game of American football without the ball. I was rescued from the melée by a Canadian couple. He looked after their case and my chair; she saw to their young baby and my case."

Over the last ten years or so, Canada's **national rail network**, *VIA Rail*, has improved access to its stations and trains for passengers in wheelchairs. In the next few years, conventional trains will be equipped with wheelchair tie-downs, narrow, folding wheelchairs, tools for reducing the width of some manual chairs, and accessible (to narrow chairs – door width 67.3cm) toilets. At present, a tie-down and accessible toilet are available only in LRC first-class cars (LRC – VIA 1) travelling the Quebec–Windsor Corridor.

VIA accepts manual wheelchairs, not exceeding 81cm in width and 182cm in all other dimensions, as checked baggage, and electric wheelchairs weighing no more than 114kg, provided that the departure and destination stations have the facilities to load and

CANADA: TRAVEL NOTES

unload them. This can be checked when booking. In the UK, bookings should be made through your travel agent, who will then inform the UK sales agent (*Compass*) of your requirements.

Those with speech or hearing impairment can obtain information and make reservations in Canada by telephone: in Toronto, ☎416/368-6406; elsewhere in Canada, ☎1-800/268-9503.

VIA require a minimum of 24 hours' notice for travel on the Quebec–Windsor Corridor, 48 hours on transcontinental and other routes. Your ticket will show that a Special Service Request (SSR) has been issued.

The services that are available with this advance notice include the following: boarding assistance at many stations; pre-boarding if you arrive an hour before departure; voltage regulators on certain trains for the use of respirators (48 hours' notice); non-allergenic pillows for passengers with allergies; stretcher service (48 hours' notice); meals served in sleeping compartments to passengers unable to use the restaurant facilities; special meals; a roomette at no extra charge for blind passengers who have reserved an upper berth and are travelling with a guide dog (dogs accompanying blind or deaf passengers may travel in any class); free travel for an escort if a passenger is unable to provide for his or her personal needs (eating, medical care or personal hygiene) – a medical certificate must be produced.

The National Timetable (available from *Compass* if your travel agent does not have a copy) indicates accessible stations (with parking, toilets and ramps) and stations where trains can be boarded from the platform by wheelchair lift or with assistance from *VIA* personnel. If you have any questions that your travel agent cannot answer, write to Customer Relations, *VIA Rail Canada*, PO Box 8116, Station A, Montreal, Quebec H3C 3N3.

Greyhound World Travel (Sussex House, London Road, East Grinstead, West Sussex RH19 1LD; ☎0342/317317) handle bookings for **inter-city bus travel**, a viable option for a wheelchair user with a strong companion who can travel free on the "Helping Hand" scheme (p.429) or for anyone unable to travel alone for medical reasons.

A wheelchair-accessible **coach** with hydraulic lift and on-board accessible toilet can be hired for groups (nine tie-down wheelchairs plus fifteen ambulatory passengers, or any combination) from *National Motor Coach Systems* (Box 3220, Station B, Calgary, Alberta T2M 4L7; ☎403/240-1992).

In general, however, inter-city bus services are inaccessible to wheelchair users without assistance. The only province to supply details of a standard bus service which has the capacity to take wheelchair users (two per coach) is Ontario (*Ministry of Transportation*, 1201 Wilson Avenue, Downsview M3M 1J8; ☎416/235-3983, voice; ☎416/235-4986, TDD), where Hamilton-based *Canada Coach Lines* (☎1-800/263-8582) cover the route from Kitchener to Buffalo airport via St Catherines, Niagara Falls and Buffalo four times a day.

Car hire with *Hertz* began badly for Steve Veness (p.436) but turned out well in the end. *Avis* also offer cars with hand controls in Canada. *Thrifty Car Rental* (10 Manitou Drive at Fairway, Kitchener, Ontario, ☎519/893-5210; or 160 Weber Street South, Waterloo, Ontario, ☎519/742-4411; for worldwide reservations call toll free ☎1-800/FOR-CARS) offer "The Magic Wagon", a Dodge caravan CV with ramp, two tie-down wheelchair positions and seating for three other passengers plus driver.

Fully accessible **motor homes** and trailers are available for sale or rent from *Ability Plus* (184 St David Street, Lindsay, Ontario K9V 4Z4; ☎1-705/324-3079). A motor home with hydraulic lift can be hired from *Motorhome Vacations Canada* (12563 Highway 50, Bolton, Ontario L7E 5R9; ☎416/857-2253).

Each province makes its own arrangements for disabled drivers' **parking**, and it may be necessary to contact the appropriate regional branch of the *CPA* on, or prior to, arrival. Drivers must complete the *CPA* form and produce a letter from their doctor stating their disability. Parking permits are processed immediately and cost about £3. The Orange Badge is valid in some areas, including the province of Ontario.

The *CPA* office will probably also be able to supply a list of companies providing accessible taxis, as well as details of the local special

CANADA: TRAVEL NOTES

transport services for disabled travellers. In Edmonton, for example, physically disabled visitors can obtain a temporary registration number (call ☎403/468-6025) and use the *DATS* (*Disabled Adult Transportation System*). Vancouver has Handy-Dart (☎604/264-5000), Toronto has Wheel-Trans (☎416/393-4111), both of which require an application for a temporary registration number. *Vancouver Taxi*'s fleet of wheelchair-accessible vehicles can be hired like any other taxi, but Rod Semple deems them rather expensive for everyday use (p.442).

If you can transfer to and from a car seat, you should have no need of adapted transport. Dorothea Boulton used the standard taxi service in Montreal, and Frieda Maguire was surprised by the standard of comfort and the reasonable price of the hired limousine service from Toronto airport.

The fact that there have to be alternative systems for travellers with disabilities implies that accessible public transport is lacking in some areas. But there is widespread awareness of the problem and the newer systems, such as *BC Transit*'s SkyTrain (p.442), are fully accessible. The *Transportation* section in the 1990 *Action Plan* produced by *The Premier's Council on the Status of Persons with Disabilities* (Alberta) will sound familiar to disabled residents of many other countries, including Britain:

"Society's response to the transportation needs of people with disabilities has been to develop costly parallel systems that only offer restricted service because of the cost . . . Neither the parallel nor the public systems adequately serve the needs of people who are disabled, especially those who have severe cognitive deficits, visual impairment, hearing impairment, or minor to moderate mobility impairments . . . Travel *between* municipalities for people with severe mobility impairments is restricted to use of a private car."

The document makes interesting reading and is available (in book or audio cassette form) from *The Premier's Council*, 250 Garneau Professional Centre, 11044 82nd Avenue, Edmonton, Alberta T6G 0T2 (☎403/422-1095, voice or TDD).

Accommodation

Finding suitable accommodation should not be too difficult for wheelchair users, but Steve Veness' experience with *Thomas Cook* (p.437) and the *Bond Place Hotel*, Toronto, and Christine Swan's comments on bathrooms, door widths and ramps (p.433) give weight to the argument for verifying facilities with the hotel before booking, and basing plans on information supplied by the tourism office or the *CPA* rather than a travel agent.

It is rare for the provincial accommodation guides to mention hotel facilities for people with handicaps other than restricted mobility. These travellers may find help from local branches of the Canadian associations of people with their disability, such as the *Canadian Hearing Society* (Head Office, 271 Spadina Road, Toronto, Ontario M5R 2V3; ☎416/964-9595) or the *Canadian National Institute for the Blind* (National Office, 1931 Bayview Avenue, Toronto, Ontario M4G 4C8; ☎416/480-7580).

Many hotel and motel chains have properties that cater for disabled guests: *Best Western, Days Inns, Hilton, Holiday Inns, Howard Johnson, Journey's End, Novotel, Quality Inns, Ramada, Relax Inns, Sheraton, Travelodge, Venture Inns, WelcomINNS*. Those that offer the full range of facilities for wheelchair users – parking, level entrances, ramps, spacious rooms for handicapped guests, access to all public rooms, wide doorways, large lifts and accessible public toilets – tend to be in the higher price brackets.

But you may not need the complete range, and there is so much accommodation to choose from that you are sure to find something to suit both your budget and your access requirements. The motels and smaller hotels are often cheaper and more likely to provide a room on the ground floor; one contributor found himself in a "handicapped suite" on the ninth floor of the Pittsburgh *Hilton* – not ideal in the event of a fire.

A number of hotels are recommended by our contributors. Dorothea Boulton stayed at the *Holiday Inn Crowne Plaza* (420 rue Sherbrooke Ouest, Montreal H3A 1B4; ☎514/842-6111), one of many accessible hotels in downtown

CANADA: TRAVEL NOTES

Montreal. Her daughter inspected three other properties (addresses in the *Montréal* accommodation guide) and found similar facilities at *Delta Montréal* (the guide now lists this as accessible only to an escorted wheelchair user), at *Hotel des Gouverneurs – Le Grand* and at *Le Méridien Montréal*.

Steve Veness made his choice from the Nova Scotia, Alberta and British Columbia accommodation guides. *Mid Valley Motel* (Middleton, Nova Scotia; ☎902/825-3433) is a cheap, cheerful and accessible motel. *Mountaineer Lodge* (Box 150, Lake Louise, Alberta T0L 1E0; ☎403/522-3844) is much smarter, ideally placed for touring the Rockies, easily accessible but quite expensive. *Sunset Motel* (Box 86, Radium Hot Springs, British Columbia V0A 1M0; ☎604/347-9863) is not so well placed for touring the Rockies but has spotless, good-value self-catering units (one to three bedrooms), good accessibility and very friendly, helpful owners. Steve also suggests that, if you can afford it, you stay at the *Post Hotel* (Box 69, Lake Louise, Alberta T0L 1E0; ☎403/522-3989).

Christine Swan recommends *Chateau Jasper* (Box 1418, Jasper, Alberta T0E 1E0; ☎403/852-5644) and the *Hyatt Regency* (655 Burrard Street, Vancouver V6C 2R7; ☎604/687-6543). Also in Vancouver, Rod Semple was very pleased with *The Georgian Court Hotel* (773 Beatty Street, V6B 2M4; ☎604/682-5555). Incidentally, an impressive 19 out of the 28 downtown Vancouver hotels/motels in the British Columbia *Accommodations* guide are listed wheelchair accessible, and several are reasonably priced.

Frieda Maguire found all the necessary facilities (except a slip-mat) and plenty of space at the *Venture Inn, Burlington* (2020 Lakeshore Road, Burlington, Ontario L7S 1Y2; ☎416/681-0762).

Access and facilities

The general reaction of most disabled visitors from Britain is that standards are high at the majority of tourist attractions, from Niagara Falls to Montréal's shopping malls; from a cruise around Vancouver's Gulf Islands to a performance at the Ottawa Arts Centre. Independent travel is easy – whether by plane, car, train or boat (buses not so easy) – and travel without an escort, even for someone more than slightly disabled, is certainly possible (p.444). Reports of assistance from Canadians, willingly and cheerfully given, are plentiful.

In a country with such a wealth of natural beauty and tremendous opportunity to enjoy outdoor pursuits, there is surprisingly little reference to the accessibility of these attractions in the tourist brochures. However, the *CPA* is under contract to assist the *Canadian Parks Service* in developing accessibility guidelines and implementation timetables, and assessing new technology for National Parks, Historic Canals and Historic Sites. All divisions of the *CPA* are involved in evaluating these sites.

The *CPA* is active in many other areas, including human rights, employment, income, housing, transportation and education. A copy of their quarterly magazine, *Caliper*, will give some insight into the concerns of many disabled Canadians. Perhaps the biggest issue for the Nineties is that of full economic integration of disabled persons, and the fight is on to persuade the federal government to take action on three broad fronts: federal legislation, improved accountability to ensure that recommendations are carried out, and greater federal-provincial cooperation.

Health and insurance

The same warnings about medical costs apply to Canada as to the States – obtain adequate insurance cover and carry a copy prescription in case you need fresh supplies of drugs.

Wheelchairs can usually be hired from hospital supply companies. UK tourist offices may be able to provide details of rental services in their own provinces.

PART EIGHT

SOUTH AMERICA

Introduction

t's hard to imagine a greater contrast in terms of access and facilities for disabled people than that between North and South America. Many South American governments fail to provide adequate living conditions for the majority of their peoples; they have not even begun to think of building an accessible environment. Neither precarious democracies nor harsh dictatorships create a climate in which disability organisations and pressure groups can flourish.

As far as the traveller is concerned, however, these are rich countries with some powerful **attractions**: the awe-inspiring Andes and Amazonian rainforest; spectacular wildlife and perfect beaches; fascinating temples and other relics of ancient civilisations; beautiful colonial architecture and smart boutiques in the modern cities. Whether to enjoy these, the many brands of South American music or to browse amongst the handicrafts, tourists are visiting the continent in growing numbers.

Naturally enough, the South Americans are keen to promote their assets and attract as many tourists (and their wallets) as possible. On the Venezuelan island of Margarita the rapid recent development of the main town, Porlamar, has included ramps at all entrances, and provision of first-class hotels with good access to all amenities. Maybe – just maybe – this is a result of the fact that a significant proportion of visitors come from the States, and wherever the North American tourist has been the chances of finding a mobile ramp or a grab-rail are increased.

But Margarita is very much the exception, and the sheer **physical difficulties** of travel in South America may explain why relatively few accounts of travel here were received in the first place. Meanwhile, the task of educating the governments, planners, designers and tourism operators has barely started. Removal of basic physical obstacles – on public transport, in accommodation and public buildings, at tourist attractions – is often an inexpensive and simple matter but for now, in most South American countries, it is not even considered, and action may still be years away.

At least two forms of **transport** – aircraft and taxis – are no less accessible than in many other parts of the world, and most disabled travellers will be able to use both. There are no special facilities on trains or at stations, but with assistance rail travel is possible. Perhaps most tricky are the many different types of boat: gentle gangways, lifts, widened doorways and adapted toilets are rare sights, and some acrobatics and several pairs of hands will be required when boarding and moving about on board.

Reliable information on **accessible accommodation** will be virtually impossible to find, so your best bet will be to follow Sue Kelley's example and simply turn up. Of course there are luxury hotels which, with their grand entrances·and spacious rooms, tend to be more accessible, but budget accommodation will throw up all the usual obstacles. Doorways in city hotels may be too small for wheelchairs; jungle lodges are often raised on stilts. It's necessary to compromise, adapt and ask for help.

The nature of many of South America's most spectacular tourist attractions makes exploration by wheelchair hard work, and **removal of barriers** is neither inexpensive nor simple – it entails reshaping the landscape. Trekking through rainforest, following the Inca Trail to Machu Picchu, or watching wildlife among the craggy

Galapagos Islands present formidable problems. It can be done, but not without strong companions.

The attitude and helpfulness of the ordinary citizens cannot be faulted: only good reports, of friendly assistance, often from people with no concern for their own comfort or safety, have been received; one wheelchair user found her progress along a busy pavement in Buenos Aires easier than in many European cities, pedestrians moving aside without fuss or hesitation, like the Red Sea in front of Moses.

The South American people, and a few enlightened tour operators, make possible some fairly **adventurous travel**, including bird-watching from a dugout canoe in the Ecuadorean rainforest and hiking across lava formations to spot flightless cormorants in the Galapagos islands. Flights in light aircraft above the Angel Falls and over the Andes, jeep rides and jungle walks – those who really want to can participate in most activities.

And, as more disabled travellers take the plunge and consider South America as a viable holiday option rather than an impossibility, the authorities will see that provision of facilities for them makes sound commercial sense. In time, if the battles against national debt, inflation and inhuman regimes can be won, the ensuing stability may allow the development of proper **financial support** for disabled South Americans and perhaps even the beginnings of an independent living movement. Conditions for disabled travellers might then improve dramatically.

In this section the *Travel Notes* are again gathered together after the accounts.

Venezuela

Success in South America

Sue Kelley, a wheelchair user, and her husband Tony spent the first half of July 1990 on the island of Margarita, off the north coast of Venezuela. They found excellent facilities for disabled people.

The name Margarita means "pearl" in Greek, and it was the lure of the pearl which led to the first Spanish settlement of this part of South America. Spanish is the native tongue of the islanders and the natural pearls found today are recovered by fishermen and sold to local jewellers.

The journey to Margarita with Venezuela's national airline, *Viasa*, was quite long, some fourteen hours in all, but service on board was good and we had ample legroom. We landed in Paris to take on more passengers, then took off for Caracas where we were taken by bus to another airport across town. There we boarded a smaller plane which flew first to Barcelona (in Venezuela), then on to Porlamar airport, Margarita.

The *Falcon* reps were waiting to greet us, once immigration formalities had been completed and we had retrieved our baggage. Only momentarily surprised and certainly not put off their stride when they spotted my wheelchair, they took us on another bus to our hotel, the *Margarita Concorde*. We were so tired that we just rolled into bed.

Once refreshed we took stock of our surroundings. The hotel had excellent facilities for someone in a wheelchair: it was ramped throughout, to all its amenities, including the pool and the beach. Situated on the beach was a large, wooden platform with a thatched roof and bar at one end; it was only a couple of feet from the water and was a good place to park myself and enjoy the sights and sounds of the sea, with its large population of pelicans.

Falcon took us on a bus tour on the first day, to get us acquainted with the eastern side of the island; visits to the western side should be made only in a four-wheel drive vehicle. Jeeps can be hired at very reasonable rates, or one can participate in an organised jeep safari. We took the former option, and discovered that Margarita could be mistaken for two islands.

The larger, eastern half is the most densely populated, with many villages of Spanish colonial-style buildings scattered along the coastline. Palm trees are predominant, along with an abundance of tropical flowers and fauna the like of which we only see in hothouses. Between the coast and its green, hilly backdrop lie valleys full of banana, mango, avocado, melon and pineapple plantations.

The western side is a largely uninhabited desert wilderness, with few roads and only the occasional fishing village. It looks like Arizona, with its bare cliffs and heavy concentration of cacti, some round like footballs, sprouting pink flowers, others as tall as trees. My most vivid memory is of the incongruous meeting-point of desert landscape and ocean, with the dramatic colours of a sunset lighting up the sky.

On the north coast of the island, approximately midway between west and east, lies La Restinga lagoon, a network of waterways surrounded by mangrove trees. We hired a boat and its driver at a cost of about £5, or 350 *bolivars* (petrol was very cheap, around 14p a gallon, but inflation was running at 100 percent). Whilst wandering through the channels of La Restinga, we were shown the beds of oysters growing amidst the roots of the mangroves. The pearls cultivated from these oysters are sold mainly to Japanese buyers – many find their way onto necklaces made by Mikimoto.

Margarita has many splendid beaches, and an efficient bus service to and from the hotel is provided for guests who wish to explore those further afield. The most tranquil waters are found on the southern shores, but working northwards along the east coast the waves become stronger and beaches here are popular with surfers. Since taxis are so cheap on the island, I didn't even try the bus service, but a couple of strong helpers would be necessary to negotiate the steps at the entrance. I have on past holidays gone up the steps of buses on my bottom – a little undignified but it works.

The main town of Margarita is Porlamar. We were surprised to find a well-planned town with a wide selection of designer shops. As a duty-free shopping zone, Porlamar sells many goods, from clothes and jewellery to alcohol and perfume. In the main streets are the designer shops but up the side roads one can browse in shops selling local crafts and handmade items. The centre of the town is quite modern, with pavements ramped at intervals. There are traffic lights to assist pedestrians crossing the busy four-lane roads, and we found the majority of drivers most courteous and patient, allowing us to cross at our leisure. Whilst wandering around the town we stopped to watch a game of basketball – a favourite sport, taken very seriously by the locals. There are many places to eat in Porlamar and we found the dishes on offer – not only in the town but also on the beaches and in the hotel – varied, well presented and very reasonably priced. A three-course meal for two cost around £4.

A statue of Simon Bolivar stands in the town centre. He is credited with winning Venezuela's independence from the Spanish, and many roads, as well as the currency, are named after him.

"We flew inland to the savannah, dotted with herds of cattle and a few horses, and crisscrossed by rivers"

A short taxi ride to the outskirts took us to a large textile market which required several hours to walk around. Traditional handicrafts made from local materials can be found all over the island. Each town has its own speciality: hammocks and furniture in Santa Anna; handbags or *mapires* from broom and hemp cord in Pedro Gonzalez; traditional and modern ceramics in El Cercado, to name but a few.

The Venezuelan government has not been slow to realise the potential financial rewards to be gained from tourism. It is funding the development of

Porlamar's centre, with new hotels planned and a shopping mall which is expected to generate some $14 million in additional business each year. A special dock is also planned for the many cruise ships that take millions of tourists annually to other ports in the Caribbean. These plans, added to the fact that Porlamar is only a short drive along excellent roads from the airport, mean that the town is destined to become a thriving tourist centre.

"Scarlet macaws, parakeets and toucans fly in and out of the trees"

It is my guess that the Venezuelans' strong commercial sense has played a part in persuading the architects of the facilities on Margarita to make the majority of amenities accessible to *all* tourists; we found ramps at entrances almost everywhere, making life easier not only for disabled visitors, but also for mums and their pushchairs.

Evenings are not my best time, but for those who like a bit of nightlife, the hotel had a number of venues: a vocal group in the lobby bar, a dance band in one of the restaurants and a disco on the top floor. There were also occasional barbecues by the pool, with steel bands providing the music. The younger members of our party often went to the discos in town and enjoyed them. At weekends many girls from the Venezuelan mainland joined the disco crowd – there are four girls to one boy in Caracas!

Flights from Porlamar to Caracas left every hour and cost $10 return. *Falcon* organised several tours and we decided to participate in one which included a flight over the Angel Falls – the tallest waterfall in the world. The Twin Otter would take three hours to reach the falls, stopping midway for refuelling.

From the ragged coastline, where streams rush through lush vegetation towards the sea, we flew inland to the savannah, dotted with herds of cattle and a few horses, and crisscrossed by

rivers, the largest of which is the Orinoco. Sir Walter Raleigh travelled up the Orinoco in his bid to find the lost city of El Dorado, over a century after Christopher Columbus had penetrated this hinterland and thought he'd found the Garden of Eden.

The pale green of the prairies started to roll into foothills, and we could pick out roads and the occasional mine (Venezuela is rich in minerals, oil, gold and diamonds). As the foothills were succeeded by mountains and dense jungle, we spotted many rivers, dropping sharply from one level to another as we neared the Angel Falls.

Some fifteen times higher than the Niagara Falls, but with a smaller volume of water, the Angel Falls cascade down from the Auyantepuy mesa, whose flat top is 72km in diameter. There seem to be hundreds of these sheer-sided, flat-topped mountains, and the isolated environments on top, in which unique plants flourish, are said to have inspired Conan Doyle's "Lost World". We flew around the falls four times in all before landing at an airstrip in the jungle called Kavac. Here Tony and I separated from the rest of the party, who were to proceed on a trek through the jungle, under waterfalls and upriver in a dugout canoe.

The two of us were taken by jeep to the Indian village of Canaima, situated on a lagoon into which three waterfalls plunge. There is a small beach, with a few sunbeds, and visitors can swim in the waters of the lagoon which are stained by minerals the colour of Coca-Cola; the Indians believe that the waters have healing properties. The village is neatly laid out and spotlessly clean. We were provided with a lunch of beef, vegetables and a corn-like potato, followed by fresh fruit. Whilst enjoying our lunch, sitting beside the lagoon under trees laden with ripe mangoes, we were able to watch the scarlet macaws, parakeets and toucans fly in and out of the trees, picking up food that had been left for them. It was wonderfully relaxing and we sat there until evening started to draw in.

We were taken back to the airstrip to join our now exhausted but happy party for the return flight. When we stopped for refuelling at Angosturi we were able to look over the plane which Jimmy Angel was flying when he discovered the Angel Falls in the late 1930s.

For the energetic visitor, *Falcon* offers a trek up the Amazon by horse and canoe, as well as a trek from Kavac through the jungle, over rivers and chasms, Indiana Jones style. The village of Canaima is also used as a base for trekking into the jungle, one possibility – only for good swimmers and the very fit – being a three-day trek following the river to the base of the Angel Falls. Other activities include Microlite flying, fishing trips, water-skiing, scuba diving and snorkelling.

This was a very successful holiday for us, and involved no long-term planning – we did not even enquire about accessible accommodation when booking. The *Falcon* reps, Grant and Toni, were not only friendly but also very helpful, full of energy, information and enthusiasm. In the first year that Margarita has been actively promoted to British tourists, we found that nothing had been forgotten as far as the provision of facilities is concerned.

Ecuador

A Golden Wedding Anniversary

Hugh Chetwynd-Talbot is paralysed from the hips down, and wears weight-bearing callipers on both legs. He was 76 years old in July 1985 when he and his wife, Cynthia, celebrated their golden wedding anniversary in a lodge in the upper Amazon jungle.

When I spotted a picture of the *Orellana Flotel* in a glossy travel brochure, we agreed that floating up or down the Amazon would be a pleasant way to spend our anniversary, and that our old friends Peter and Maria could probably have us to stay for a day or two in Quito, the capital of Ecuador.

"While you are about it," they wrote, "you might as well do the cruise round the Galapagos Islands." They made it all sound so easy.

I have found that, apart from giving the travel agent a clear idea of my disability, it is useless to ask whether particular hazards are likely to be insurmountable. Having committed myself, I feel that I must go through with it. Had I foreseen the hazards which lay ahead on this trip, I doubt that I should have undertaken it. Jane, of *Bath Travel* in Marlborough, entered wholeheartedly into the adventure and took great trouble over details and planning. To our joy, she arranged for us to link up with a *World Wildlife* package holiday in Quito. Our flight was with *Air France* via Paris and Guyana to Quito, taking some seventeen hours.

We flew over the rainforests of Guyana and then over the snow-covered peaks of the Andes as dawn was breaking. Quito is 2850m above sea level, in a valley between high Andean ranges which, with their many active volcanoes, rise in places to 5700m. The landing at Quito is dramatic: after weaving his way down a winding, narrow valley, the pilot appears to put the enormous plane down in a street – the runway is in the middle of the city.

In spite of the early hour, Peter was there to meet us and whisked us away to his bungalow a few miles outside Quito, approached up an avenue of avocados. Central Ecuador lies in a wide valley between two massive ridges of the Andes, each of them boasting snow-covered volcanoes, seven in all. Cotopaxi (5978m) is the highest volcano in the world. The sun setting on the white peaks is a very lovely sight.

Covering the valley as we did in Peter's Land Rover, over appallingly rough roads, I encountered no difficulties at all and became more and more confident.

Being on the Equator, there are no seasons as we know them, and the climate at about 1200m is very pleasant; the countryside is not unlike parts of northern England. Quito itself is delightful, too, but it has been ravaged so often by earthquakes that it is noticeably lacking in really old buildings. Nevertheless, the Spanish influence is much in evidence; Ecuador did not achieve independence from Spain until 1835.

About twenty percent of the population is of Spanish or European descent; eighty percent are impoverished but proudly independent Indians. The local village markets display their embroidery, silver and gold work, woodcarving and fascinating *objets d'art* carved out of bread which is specially treated for the purpose. The Indian villagers object most strongly to being photographed, and one of our party had his camera broken.

"The Ecuadorean guide surveyed me and my sticks with some gloom"

At the end of the week we left Peter and Maria and joined the *World Wildlife* party of twelve, with whom we were to fly down to the Amazon basin and board the *Orellana*. Doctor Derrick Green, the group leader, and Maurice, the Ecuadorean guide, surveyed me and my sticks with, I thought, some gloom. They had never had to cope with a disabled person before. I assured them that I should be quite happy to sit on deck with my powerful binoculars.

"You're not travelling five thousand miles just to do that," said Derrick.

A superb, if precarious, flight, past two of the snow-clad volcano peaks – Reventador and Cayambe – and down into the steamy heat of the rainforest, brought us to a tiny airstrip. Children

playing on it scattered as we made to land; a rickety bus took us to the river bank and the first difficult hurdle – a two-foot gap, between the shore and the "flotel", in which I could see fast-flowing, muddy water.

"An anaconda had been caught underneath it a few minutes before we arrived"

A scramble over that on all fours brought the second hurdle into view – nearly vertical ladders only eighteen inches wide led from deck to deck; food was on the lower one, our cabin (and loo) on the middle one, and the bar and observation deck were on the top. I need width in order to obtain a good handhold, so the narrow ladder looked insurmountable for me. However, with much help from my gallant wife, who took care of my feet, we managed the ladder, not only on that occasion but on several others.

The next day, our wedding anniversary, we took to dugout canoes – most exciting affairs, fashioned out of single cedar trees. Powered by two 30-kilowatt outboard motors, the canoes travel at about 50km/hr and require skilled operation by the steersman and a man sitting in the prow, as the river – about 1000m wide – is littered with uprooted trees, stuck on hidden sandbanks.

After an hour or so, and a visit to a missionary station, we turned off into a narrow creek where the dense jungle pressed down low over the banks, and there were wonderful creepers hanging from trees about 75m high. Some 5km up the creek we pulled into the bank.

"This is where we land to get to the jungle lodge," said Derrick. I looked aghast at the muddy bank and the rough, steep track beyond it.

"There's a tractor and trailer at the top," said Derrick, encouragingly.

"Can't be done," I said, half fearing, half hoping that I might be asked to return alone to the *Orellana*.

"You'll have to hump him," said Cynthia, and she showed Derrick and Maurice how to make a fireman's lift by linking their hands under my behind. Away we went, Cynthia leading the way with one of my heavy, calliper-weighted legs under each arm. The temperature was a very moist 102 degrees. As we walked down the aisle fifty years earlier, we could scarcely have foreseen such a way of celebrating its anniversary.

Limoncocha Jungle Lodge is a primitive affair of bamboo, built on stilts as a precaution against creepy-crawlies. An anaconda had been caught underneath it a few minutes before we arrived. Divided into four-berth cubicles, the lodge had a dining area with a bar in one corner.

After lunch, Derrick announced a bird-watching cruise in a punt on the large lake which we could see through a gap in the jungle. It was about a mile away and down 150 rather slippery wooden steps. Undaunted by their efforts during the approach to the lodge, the carrying team went into action again. The last few feet were particularly exciting for me as I could look down from my perch – past the narrow duckboard on which Derrick, Maurice and Cynthia were somehow keeping their feet – to where some shoals of fish were swimming in the clear, shallow water of the lake. "Piranha," said Maurice.

As we coasted round the lake, we had an excellent view of the virgin jungle surrounding it. Experts making this circuit have counted 463 species of birds and predators; we can name but one or two. There were brightly coloured macaws and members of the parrot family, as well as a very curious, large game bird called a hoatzin. Butterflies were everywhere, some of them the size of teacups. There were no signs of monkeys, and Derrick told us that the natives have almost eradicated them with their blowpipes which can kill at a range of 130m.

It was too early for the *caymans* (alligators), although we did see one as it emerged from the high grass to enter the water. The rest of the party returned after dark to photograph them by flashlight, including a baby which Derrick pulled into the boat for them to examine.

We returned to the lodge in time for dinner, but I was slower than the rest in cleaning myself up. By the time Cynthia and I reached the bar, the whisky had run out and we had to salute each other in fizzy lemonade. At the end of the dinner, Derrick produced an iced cake, which he had somehow nursed all the way from Quito, a charming gesture to bring a happy anniversary to an end. Derrick told us that we had scored a double first: the first disabled person to reach the lodge, and the first couple to use it for a golden wedding celebration.

"There is complete trust between the animal world and human beings"

Jungle walks followed, then a further night in the "flotel" and a hair-raising flight back over the Andes, in thick cloud with one engine hiccupping. We had been up at 5.30am most mornings, but in the luxury of a hotel in Quito we enjoyed a brief two days of doing virtually nothing before flying the 970km over the Pacific to the Galapagos Islands.

Our plane landed on a bleak, windswept, little island on which a wooden shed and some loos were the only buildings; the latter were firmly padlocked and we were told that had they been open we should not have enjoyed using them. A bus, even more rickety than the one at the Amazon airstrip, took us a couple of miles to a jetty where a *panga* (gig) awaited us. Maurice had been replaced by Mongo, who quickly adopted the "humping" technique for carrying me. He had to perform some quite remarkable and at times dangerous acrobatics, with me clinging like a limpet around his neck.

Mongo and Derrick manhandled me into the *panga*, then out of it at the foot of the gangway of the yacht, the *Santa Cruz*, which was to be our home for the next eight days. Ships of that size are fairly easy for me to negotiate, as good handholds are available in most places. The main hazards are the substantial storm-sills, about six inches high in main doorways.

The routine was for the *Santa Cruz* to move from one island to another during the night. A shore visit would leave the ship at 9.30am and return about noon, when we would "up anchor" and move on again to another island. There followed another shore visit during the afternoon, getting back on board about 6.30pm. Dinner at 7.30pm and a briefing at 9.30pm (about the flora and fauna to be seen the next day) left one ready for an early bed.

In this way the main points of interest in most of the islands were covered and were amplified by Derrick and Mongo, whose knowledge was profound. Derrick had spent seven years in the islands, studying the giant tortoises for his university thesis, and he referred to the archipelago as "my islands". His delight in them made him, I suspect, even more determined than myself that I should see all that I possibly could.

The sea was far from flat and the *Santa Cruz* was unable to get close inshore, so the daily disembarkation and boarding was often hazardous. It was comparatively easy to stand behind Mongo on the gangway and clasp him about the neck, ready for him to pick the right moment to jump into the *panga*. It was far more difficult for us to be propped upright in the bobbing *panga* and for Mongo then to jump out of the boat and onto the gangway. The *panga* was often moving up and down by three metres or more in relation to the foot of the gangway.

Having got me ashore, my helpers used the humping technique in order to take me to the most inaccessible places so that I could see items of special interest. Much of the flora and fauna is unique, not only to the Galapagos but also to an individual island. Everywhere, there is complete trust between the animal world and human beings: sea-lion colonies had to be invited to stop playing "I'm the king of the castle" while we landed on their rocks; a frigate bird sat, unmoved, on a nest with a chick under her while I took a photograph at a range of about two metres.

"The evening lights threw purple shadows over the volcanoes and the clouds seemed to reflect the rippling lava below"

The government of Ecuador exercises some control of the archipelago; in theory, only 25,000* people may visit the islands in any one year and the rules for doing so are very strict. Five Ecuadoreans, who broke one of the rules by bringing shells back to the yacht, were not allowed to go ashore for the next two days.

It is difficult to single out any particular landing out of about fifteen which Mongo and Derrick did with me, but our last one stands out in my memory. It was on Fernandina, by far the largest island in the archipelago, on which there are five active volcanoes. One of them erupted as recently as 1984 and we could see clearly how the lava, pouring down and cooling as it went, left great black ribs several feet high, with deep crevasses between them – rough going indeed for my intrepid team, but they never faltered.

They had to carry me for about 500m before we reached sand and they could

---

* According to the International Union for Conservation of Nature, the actual figure is nearer 42,000 visitors a year.

pause for a rest. As we pressed on to the far end of the island we saw the unique flightless cormorants, found only on Fernandina. These birds are so free from predators that the energy for flying would be wasted and their wings have become embryonic, useful only for balancing on land; they swim beautifully.

I had already made acquaintance with land iguanas; on Fernandina I met – at very close quarters indeed – their cousins, the marine iguanas. They live during the day in the sea, absorbing plankton. When they come ashore in the late afternoon, they lie on the rocks in a close mass, expelling a constant spray of salt water out of their system. It hangs over them like mist and can be seen from quite a distance. Both land and marine iguanas might be the inspiration for pictures of dragons, but they are quite harmless and I had them crawling over my feet as I watched them.

No account of the Galapagos Islands would be complete without mention of the ubiquitous frigate birds, with their extraordinary, scarlet-chested display – the biggest chest wins the bride. We saw blue, red and masked boobies with strikingly coloured feet, charming penguins, and a rather solitary pair of pelicans, each of which had lost an eye. Pelicans pair for life, and Derrick said they must have paired in sympathy for one another!

As we left Fernandina for the *Santa Cruz*, the evening lights threw purple shadows over the volcanoes and the clouds seemed to reflect the rippling lava below. As the ship headed for Baltra Island and our rendezvous the next morning with a Boeing 727, the sunset was the most beautiful one of our entire trip, putting the finishing touch to our mid-Pacific idyll.

I learnt a lesson from the Galapagos experience, which had never occurred to me before. Neither Mongo nor I could wear life jackets during our antics, and with my callipered legs I should have sunk like a stone, probably taking Mongo with me, if he had lost his footing. In my eagerness to get ashore I allowed Mongo to risk his life in helping me. On reflection I believe that we should be very careful regarding what we allow others to do for us. I have never encountered the least prejudice, and always received an almost embarrassing degree of generosity, kindness and understanding, both on the part of officials and fellow travellers – it would be wrong to abuse this.

Sources of information

The South American embassies and consulates might have a tourist desk – some have a quite sophisticated operation – but even the best can only send out a couple of leaflets and a list of tour operators: most will ask for a SAE first. There is no information for disabled visitors, and the best way to learn anything about these countries before departure is to do plenty of reading – guidebooks, travelogues and novels – and pick the brains of an experienced tour operator.

Tour operators

Full marks to *Falcon*'s reps in Venezuela, who received no advance warning of Sue Kelley's wheelchair but took it in their stride and made alternative arrangements for Sue when she could not manage the more strenuous parts of the organised trips.

Hugh Chetwynd-Talbot received conscientious service from his travel agent (*Bath Travel*, Malborough) and enthusiastic assistance from the leaders and guides on his *World Wildlife* tour.

Bales Tours (Bales House, Barrington Road, Dorking, Surrey; ☎0306/885991) contributed hours of planning and much valuable advice to the *Journey of a Lifetime Trust* (*JOLT*, see *Practicalities*, "Financial Help") tour in 1988: a group of eighteen disabled and disadvantaged youngsters and three adults were accompanied by one of *Bales*' tour managers on a month-long journey through Colombia, Ecuador, Peru, Bolivia, Paraguay and Brazil.

Journey Latin America (16 Devonshire Place, London W4 2HD; ☎081/747 3108) have a great deal of experience to draw on and have arranged holidays for disabled people in the past.

Getting there

There are **direct flights** from London to many South American cities with *British Airways*, and most South American airlines fly direct to their home cities, but on discounted tickets it's more than likely that your journey will involve a plane change: at Paris with *Air France*, Amsterdam with *KLM*, Madrid with *Iberia*,

Caracas with *Viasa*. This can push flight times up considerably, so stamina is the first requirement for a trip to South America.

Sue Kelley was pleased with service and legroom aboard her *Viasa* (*Venezuelan International Airways*, 19–20 Grosvenor Street, London W1X 9FD; ☎071/493 3630) aircraft. *Viasa* will seat disabled passengers near the toilets but do not carry aisle chairs. A wheelchair service is available at Caracas **airport**, and most other international airports should be reasonably well geared up.

Transport

Domestic **flights** are probably the smoothest way to cover any sort of distance; facilities at airports are minimal but at least there is plenty of help available, and the flight will be more comfortable and safer than travelling along rough and dusty roads.

Cross-continent, self-drive travel is not for the faint-hearted or the non-Spanish/ Portuguese speaker: mountains, rainforest, swamps, grasslands or parched plains offer a formidable choice of terrain. But **car** or jeep rental is good for exploring the coastal, more populated regions, as Sue Kelley discovered on the island of Margarita (p.458).

Traffic congestion in many South American cities is legendary, and it's wise to switch to **taxis** for getting around. They are cheap and wheelchairs are easily stowed in the boot. **Buses** are often used for airport transfers or organised tours; hydraulic lifts and tie-downs are unheard of, and most people with limited mobility will need assistance. Long-distance buses will almost invariably be crowded and uncomfortable, with few concessions to those who can't battle their way to a seat: but if you can manage them, they're very much part of the South American experience.

Rail travel is possible with help: the *JOLT* group travelled by Peruvian train from Machu Picchu to Cuzco, then a twelve-hour journey to Juliaca; a Swedish wheelchair user reports no problems with boarding the train in her chair and travelling from Argentina to Paraguay; but there will be no such luxuries as wheelchair-accessible toilets – at stations or on the trains.

Guard your belongings on trains, however: in Peru especially they're notorious for robberies.

Many forms of **waterborne transport** are available, from dugout canoes to sleek hydrofoils. Again there are no concessions to disabled passengers: muddy banks to scramble down, steep flights of stairs between decks, and delicate balancing acts required for boarding and disembarking are just a few of the hazards, but strong companions and willing crew members seem to make up for the deficiencies in accessibility.

Accommodation

The general lack of information for disabled travellers, combined with the difficulties of attempting to make independent reservations – let alone enquiries about steps and door widths – to any but the big international hotels, suggests that it might be best to adopt Nic Fleming's approach to finding accessible accommodation (see p.504): assume that all problems can be solved on the spot, and simply turn up armed with a positive attitude.

This certainly worked for Sue Kelley, who stayed at the *Hotel Margarita Concorde* (Avenida Raúl Leoni, Bahía El Morro, Porlamar, Nueva Esparta, Isla de Margarita; ☎95/613333), where all amenities, including the beach, were fully accessible.

In contrast, Hugh Chetwynd-Talbot's accommodation was far from ideal: food, cabin and bar each on separate decks on the *Orellana Flotel*, linked by nearly vertical ladders, and no gangway for boarding; *Limoncocha Jungle Lodge* built on stilts; six-inch storm-sills in the doorways on board the *Santa Cruz*.

If you want to be sure of a reasonably accessible room, or at least to have a couple of definite reservations around which to work a more casual itinerary, the *Hilton, Holiday Inn* and *Inter-Continental* chains have hotels in South America (Brazil, Colombia, Venezuela), Central America and the Caribbean, and a pretty good record on accessibility. Only the *Holiday Inn* directory uses the wheelchair symbol to indicate availability of rooms with facilities for handicapped guests. A good tour operator or travel agent should also be prepared to request access details from hotels on your behalf.

Access and facilities

Briefly, access to public buildings, tourist attractions and transport is poor and there are no special facilities for disabled people. That said, South America is a large continent and it is unjust to dismiss all of every country as inaccessible. The facilities encountered by Sue Kelley at her Venezuelan hotel were perfectly adequate, and both Sue and Hugh Chetwynd-Talbot (as well as the *JOLT* group) had memorable and successful holidays, lending weight to the view that anything is possible, given the right attitude, and plenty of help from passersby.

The fact remains that there is generally very little interest, at government level or among the tourist authorities, in providing access to all amenities, toilets for disabled people, parking for disabled drivers – or in compiling information on the subject. If Sue Kelley's theory is correct, and the Venezuelan authorities have recognised the economic sense of attracting *all* tourists to Porlamar's centre, then there may be hope for the rest of South America, particularly in countries that are struggling with crippling national debts and high inflation, where tourism promises prosperity.

The aims must be to allow disabled travellers greater independence, and to provide easy access not only to the shopping malls and city centres, but also to the wild places. This is the responsibility of tour operators as well as governments: when wheelchair users and deaf or blind people are positively encouraged to take part in cruises on the Amazon and treks in the jungle, there'll be cause for some celebration.

Health and insurance

The health worries in South America seem to be predominantly the effects of high altitude and the weird and wonderful insect life – as well, of course, as Montezuma's Revenge. But a bit of common sense, advice from Richard Dawood (see *Books*) and a good guidebook should dispel the myths and ensure adequate preparation.

Pregnant women and those with very high blood pressure, or with heart or respiratory

SOUTH AMERICA: TRAVEL NOTES

problems, should consult their doctors. For everyone else the best precaution is to ascend slowly, spending a few days at each level before moving on. At high-altitude locations you'll need suntan lotion, hat and efficent sunglasses during the day and warm clothes at night.

There are well-trained, English-speaking doctors in most countries, and good pharmacists in all big cities. Carry insect repellent and anti-diarrhoea treatment as well as your usual drugs.

Books

Travellers' Health, by Richard Dawood (OUP, £5.95) has a section on the effects of altitude.

In the Realms of Gold (Michael Joseph, £14.95) is written by wheelchair traveller and food critic, Quentin Crewe.

The Rough Guides to Brazil and Peru.

PART NINE

TOURS AND CRUISES

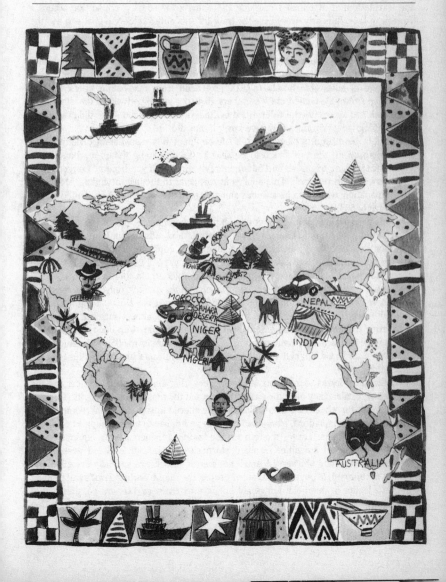

Introduction

On most of these trips the journey constitutes the holiday: in effect this is one big section on "Getting There", and these are, perhaps, experiences of travel in its purest form. For Jack Davidson the journey was a race along mountain roads; for David Bonnett it entailed crossing the Sahara; for some a cruise, for others a European tour. In nearly every case the traveller sets out to achieve a goal – to win the race, to arrive at the other side of the desert, to reach the polar icecap, to take the helm of a large sailing vessel . . .

The following accounts are, on the whole, success stories, usually as a result of a little bit of help along the way – some extra hands to put up the tent (p.487), some local knowledge of accessible hotels (p.482), protection from man-eating tigers (p.480), assistance from able-bodied crew members (p.492) – combined with a few strokes of good luck and an attitude best described by Roderick MacDonald – "we didn't go looking for things to go wrong, nor did we worry if they did".

Careful **planning** also plays a part: it can be fun, and is essential for expeditions in remote areas, but there is much to be said for leaving some things to chance; you should start a long trip fresh and full of energy – unlikely if you become bogged down in paperwork and research. This applies in particular to the task of finding accessible accommodation, which can be arduous and only partially successful if attempted before departure (p.504).

From a luxurious cabin on a cruise ship to a homemade tent in the desert, our contributors report no disasters with **accommodation**, although at times a change of itinerary was necessary because no suitable hotel could be found at the planned stopping point. But the advantage of touring is that stays of one or two nights are the norm, and most people can manage most access problems on a short-term basis.

Another bonus is that apparently rugged conditions can not only be survived but also prove far more memorable than a suite in an accessible *Hilton*: a night under a mosquito net in Australia's Northern Territory seemed almost magical to Frankie Armstrong (p.502); a trip to an uninhabited island, armed only with bed-roll, notebooks and first-aid kit, formed a lasting impression on Nic Fleming (p.505); an evening with Arab guests in David Bonnett's thorn-bush encampment was a highlight of his Saharan expedition (p.476).

Of the many forms of transport used when covering long distances, the car and the ship seem popular; they offer the easiest access and the most comfortable ride (barring seasickness) for wheelchair users. **Cars** can be altered to suit individual requirements with a range of adaptations, from hand controls and hoists to lumbar support cushions and swivelling seats. Large, modern **cruise ships** are increasingly equipped with spacious lifts to all amenities, ramped storm-sills, cabins for disabled passengers, accessible toilets and showers. A small number of vessels are specially designed and built to accommodate physically disabled people: the *Jubilee Sailing Trust*'s sail training ship is a leader in this field. Long-haul holidays by **train or bus** are possible with a companion or two, but probably not the easiest options for wheelchair travellers. Dee Hopkins managed a journey on *Greyhound* buses across North America (p.429), but found the going pretty tough and had to stop short of her goal for an enforced rest. If you have no helper and have to rely on assistance at stations, the prospect of arranging it all before departure, which is what most rail companies demand, will be unappealing. Even after meticulous planning and advance warnings, the promised assistance may well fail to materialise.

For travellers with visual impairment an **aircraft** feels safer than a train – it's impossible to step out on the wrong side, and airlines in general are more geared up to handling disabled passengers. But a ship is probably ideal, even for unaccompanied visually handicapped passengers – there's space to wander and crew or fellow passengers on hand to look out for obstacles.

The traveller who covers a lot of ground, crosses many frontiers and passes through remote areas, cannot expect to find good standards of accessibility and facilities for disabled people everywhere. But, according to the following accounts, it somehow doesn't seem to matter in the way that it might on a two-week holiday spent in one resort.

Drawn on by the sense of rising to a challenge, perhaps hoping to achieve their "Personal Everest" (p.478), some of these writers took on long and difficult journeys. In describing them they talk mostly of the thrill of extraordinary experiences, of total departure from their normal lives, of adventures that would be dismissed by the majority of tour operators as "unsuitable" for disabled people. The rewards are obvious.

Expeditions

Sand in my Callipers

The idea came in 1969, when David Bonnett, who is disabled by polio, and some student friends coaxed a disintegrating Ford Anglia across the Atlas mountains in Morocco. From the mountains they saw the desert and they resolved to drive across the Sahara one day . . .

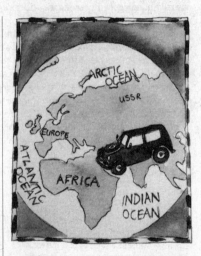

Seven years later, poring over my school atlas, so old that it still has the Empire marked in pink, we planned a route passing through France, Spain, Morocco and on to Algeria, from there across the desert to Niger and finally to Lagos in Nigeria. Whether then to turn right or left would depend upon the location of the most recent military coup, but from Lagos we would loop north, homeward bound.

My three fellow armchair dreamers were old student friends, wiser now and conscious of being drawn into an unwelcome world of careers and mortgages; this was to be a last petulant kick before settling down. We had travelled together as a group before and were reasonably aware of our respective strengths and weaknesses. As the only disabled member of the group I was fairly confident of support in difficult moments.

We found a thirteen-year-old, longwheelbase Land Rover, and an *RAC* inspection confirmed our feeling that this was a sound vehicle. The next problem was the selection of hand controls. I had decided that a bellowstype vacuum clutch unit was essential

in order to avoid the effects of sand on moving parts. Quotes from specialist firms proved numbingly expensive, and inept attempts at attracting sponsorship were politely rebuffed.

Fortunately, Terry Willett of the *Paraplegic Olympic Committee* came to the rescue and the conversion was carried out with servo-assisted brakes and spares for everything. He will remember my test drive with horror; I remember his pale face with some amusement. But here was a lesson for the future: the controls were installed down to a price and subsequently proved unreliable and a major source of frustration to me.

Preparations continued with what seemed like endless paperwork; no one should underestimate the amount involved, including calculations of distances, journey times, fuel consumption and capacity, and – most difficult of all – obtaining visas. Medical and other insurances were mostly arranged through the *AA*, as were the various driving documents; the *AA* were consistently helpful and practical with their advice.

There were regular deletions and additions to our huge list of requirements, but shopping finally began: tinned foods, dried foods, camping gear, motor parts, binoculars, compasses, maps and water containers, not forgetting two thousand tea bags and eighty toilet rolls (yes, we used all of them). Using *Disabled Drivers' Motor Club* concessionary ferry tickets, *Townsend-Thorensen* patiently altered their paperwork to suit my panic phone calls, swapping dates and times. But, at last, travellers' cheques and passports in hands, we sailed for France.

Being October, the time of the wine harvest in Charente, southern France, I had rashly agreed to earn extra money with the others by picking grapes for a fortnight. Adopting the motto of the three Musketeers – all for one and one for all – somehow seemed appropriate, but two weeks in rain-soaked French furrows almost broke my spirit. I still wince at the memory of my rusting callipers and sodden surgical boots.

Nevertheless, this time did allow us to work together under some pressure and survive with a good deal of humour. A further week remained in our rented cottage, enabling us to complete sewing our mosquito-proof tents (don't be fooled, no such thing exists), a vehicle service (my job) and carefully planned loading of the Land Rover. Reeking of oil, Gauloises and garlic, we set off for Spain. The autumn weather showed no mercy for our trial run at camping, and three damp, cold days later we arrived at Algeciras.

Ferry tickets were cheap and, clutching our picnic lunches and bottles of beer, we happily settled into our deck chairs like all good English holidaymakers. The juddering boat skirted

Gibraltar and about an hour later we bumped gently into our African berth. Jostled by cloaked men and veiled women along palm-shaded streets, we purchased cheap wines and spirits in anticipation of scarcity further south. Loaded thus, we drove through Moroccan customs conveniently oblivious of the fact that these should have been declared.

We detoured first to Chechaouen, where we and our illicit alcohol were warmly received by an old friend. The presence of a band of European travellers quickly came to the notice of both pedlars of "heaven" and the local police. Our subtle interrogation by a detective inspector wearing a fez made us unwilling celebrities; the scene had all the charm of a film clip from *Casablanca* but, unlike Bogy, we didn't stay. Instead we packed our bags and fled over the Rif mountains, back to the coastal scenery we had left just a week before. Despite the southern latitude, our climb to 900m took us through a blizzard all the way to Ketama; thank goodness I had taken my Shetland woolly.

"I realised with a sinking feeling that we were lost"

After a few days in Algiers, we headed south to the desert. The 1300km from the coast to In Salah were straightforward for us in our reliable Land Rover; even the steep and twisting route across the Atlas mountains to Laghouat was not too difficult. Climate changed slowly but topography dramatically, from the lofty peaks to the seemingly endless plateaux. The distant horizon, shimmering in the heat, was at times flat in every direction, and the unerringly straight road became almost hypnotic. Pulling over to the side to allow the occasional oncoming lorry to pass was the only relief. Confusing mirages frequently played tricks on us under the increasingly hot sun, and we arrived at In Salah desperate for some shade but feeling that we were at last getting somewhere – this was where the road ended.

In Salah was breathtaking and came up to all my picture-book expectations of an oasis town. Its ancient walls rose straight out of the sand; they had resisted intrusion for centuries but the town opened its gates casually to the modern, motorised traveller. Inside was the welcome shade of fig trees, sculptured mud houses and narrow alleys in deep shade. It was hot and silent; the market would not open again until after dark.

Several other expeditions were in the central area of the town; they too were preparing for the drive south. After hand-pumping 190 litres of petrol into our tanks and our ten jerrycans, and taking on 75 litres of water, we scurried off alone. This was not bravado, but to avoid the embarrassment of an audience when we surely got stuck in all that sand. Within just a few kilometres calamity struck and our hitherto unused shovels were brought into action as the rear wheels sank into the soft desert sand – a regular feature of the ensuing 2250km. In such situations the benefits of being a disabled driver became clear – at least I was spared all that dreadful digging and pushing. My contribution was to remain at the wheel.

"Out of the impenetrable blackness, two cloaked Arabs appeared, perhaps guided by our fire"

The liberal sprinkling of abandoned wrecks across the desert sometimes took the humorous edge off our struggles. At one point, while following the piste (the broad track formed by heavy desert lorries), I was bewildered by the route passing either side of a large dune. The guiding oil drums, weighted with sand and made more visible with a tall pole, were suddenly no longer to be seen. After travelling along what seemed to be the obvious route for some time, I realised with a sinking feeling that we were lost. In tense silence and feeling very alone, we backtracked, a difficult process with little to mark our way. With someone posted on the roof rack, desperately straining eyes through binoculars, an oil drum was finally spotted. Allah, for the moment at least, was still smiling on us.

The Sahara is unrelentingly hot and emphatically silent, the tranquillity disturbed only by us or a greedy gerbil foraging around the campfire. Choosing a campsite was sometimes impossible; the beautiful sunsets quickly gave way to total darkness, after which we simply had to stop where we were. In the light there was a compelling need to identify something – a large rock or a thorn bush, anything, as a reason for stopping precisely "there". Shelter from the wind could be another deciding factor, for although our tent was attached to the Land Rover it felt frail in a strong desert wind. Even long tent pegs are of little use in sand, and we usually collected rocks as anchors.

Camping in the marginal shelter of a solitary thorn bush one night, we had some surprising visitors. Out of the impenetrable blackness, two cloaked Arabs appeared, perhaps guided by our fire. How they later returned from whence they came still puzzles me. An amusing evening was spent with our guests, attempting to converse in sign language while sipping sweet coffee. This was what we had come for, and we were not disappointed.

The last Algerian town that we visited was Tamanarasset, a dusty collecting ground for travellers and those who feed off them. It was an obligatory stopping place where papers and passports were checked. Once in, we were warned that it would take several days to get out, and the town was full of anxious people, kicking their heels until they could move on. We decided to accept the delay: after submitting our papers we drove back north for a short distance to the beautiful Hoggar mountains where we camped for a few days. We found a deep pool of water in the mountainside, fed from the 2740-metre-high peaks, and here we swam and rested in our private paradise until our papers were finally cleared.

"Camping for a few days on silver beaches where coconut trees drape their leaves in the water"

Some days later we crossed an invisible border at Assamaka into Niger. From the sands to the savannah, passing busy water holes and grass-hut villages, the fierce sun barely glimmered through a dust haze which extended for several hundred kilometres. At Dannet we were more than usually grateful to find chilled beer available; this was our first stopping place in Niger. Camped in our home-made tent, we were lulled to sleep by throbbing drums and chorus singing from a village nearby. The following evening we ventured into the village to see a play which took place in an open school playground. Despite our difficulties with the language, and the lack of props or backdrops, the story was clear, compelling and witty. The subject? The risks of adultery!

Halfway across Niger is Agadez, an orderly town with wide spaces and a large market, dominated by its mosque. Unlike Tamanarasset, here we felt like travellers, not tourists, and the people, whilst as curious about us as we were about them, just went on with their business. After a couple of days, loaded with some fresh vegetables, fuel and water, we pushed on, to the grasslands where the tracks were occasionally as tricky as anything we had experienced in the desert. Dried-up river beds of fine silt had to be crossed, and we seemed to be constantly in four-wheel drive. The local solution to these problems appeared to be to hurtle at great speed towards the obstacle, hoping that momentum would see the vehicle through. It did not always work.

Three days' driving brought us to Zinder, where we encountered metalled road after 2250km of bone-shaking tracks and soft sand. As the roads became better, so the driving became worse, judging by the number of crashed and upturned lorries that marked the route to Lagos. On one occasion I had to administer first aid to a stricken driver who beamed at me while I cleaned his open wound with neat TCP.

When we reached Lagos, our southernmost destination, I swore never to curse a London rush hour again. The bustle and intensity of the West African coastal cities was an unwelcome contrast to the solitude of the desert. Problems with obtaining papers from the Sudanese consulate in Lagos forced a decision to drive west along the Atlantic coast rather than east towards Ethiopia. We drove through the corridor of Benin to Togo, camping for a few days on silver beaches where coconut trees drape their leaves in the water, another African paradise.

But all was not well in our paradise. The frustration of creeping indecision had generated a tension between us. The hand controls on the Land Rover were playing up again, and dry leather calliper straps kept tearing. I was having to tack rubber sheeting to the soles of my boots in a clumsy attempt to repair them, and I had run out of walking-stick rubbers. We were travel weary, a situation not to be underestimated, and I was beginning to feel ill. We had been away from home for about four months, most nights spent in our tent for four. We were all yearning for privacy and the chance to make independent decisions.

That chance came sooner than expected. I had felt increasingly lethargic, and looking at myself in a wing-mirror one morning I saw that my eyes were yellow. Thumbing through my well-worn first-aid book, I remember my sick feeling of unwelcome comprehension – I had yellow jaundice. Ten days later, after hospital quarantine in Accra and, for some reason, a diet of poached eggs, I was ignominiously flown home. Heathrow airport had just been released from the clutches of a porters' strike and was engulfed in a January snowstorm. It was nice to be back.

Perhaps next time I'll take two vehicles and several friends, and try to get the balance right between pressing on and remaining in romantic places, between the value of being together as a group and the importance of occasional independence. Did I say next time? Quick, back to the armchair.

Personal Everest

Jack Davidson had polio as a child; Mike Jackson lost his arm in a car accident when a teenager. This is the story of their participation in the Eighth and Ninth Himalayan Rallies in India, in 1987 and 1988.

My biggest problem is my height (1.5m). The seats in most rally cars are bolted down or welded to the floor, and my feet often don't reach the pedals. I need to be relatively close to the steering wheel, as do most rally drivers to gain leverage, but I also need to have my shoulders hard against the seat to help me operate the clutch with my left foot, the one affected by polio.

I grew up with my disability, and it hasn't hindered me too much, but for Mike, losing a limb whilst still a teenager was a shattering blow. However, after a rehabilitation period he once again took up the sport he had just begun to enjoy. Mike began co-driving on navigational road rallies, but it wasn't long before he felt he could do better behind the wheel. In fact, he proved that not only could he control the car with his left hand, using his artificial right arm to steady the wheel, he could also win championships.

In 1985, the engine of Mike's Ford Escort blew up in spectacular fashion and destroyed the steering. With the

car approaching something like 160km per hour, an accident was inevitable; two spectators were injured and this was the start, basically, of the problems with "disabled" drivers competing in motor sport. Despite the fact that Mike had nearly 25 years of experience, the *RAC Motor Sports Association*, the sport's governing body in the UK, banned him, and others like him, from participating in special stage rallies from January 1, 1987.

Although permission was given for Mike to enter road events, he wanted the thrill and excitement that only special stage rallying can bring. In 1987 he expanded his horizons and saw the Himalayan mountain range. With the help of the *Himalayan Rally Association*, Mike secured a sponsored flight on an *Air India* 747. He and co-driver, Howard Patterson, with their Opel Manta in the hold, flew to New Delhi via Geneva and Rome. I accompanied them as a sponsored photo-journalist.

Apart from the obvious problems in freighting the rally car – all the paperwork had to be completed in quadruplicate, individually signed, and bonds posted (to ensure that what you take into the country you take out, even if it's in hundreds of little pieces in dozens of plastic bags) – Mike's main difficulty, with his artificial arm, was in setting off the security alarms in each and every airport. Caused all sorts of panic, that did.

My problem was the length of the corridors between check-in desk and aircraft. I always get the furthest-away room in the hotel, too. I am slightly asthmatic, and often guilty of carrying too many cameras, lenses, film, as well as Jacobs cereal bars and Lucozade tablets, a tape recorder, pads and pencils, a bottle of whisky (a gift, you understand), so it got pretty tiring for my left leg.

It was around 90°F when we arrived in New Delhi, to be greeted (not personally, thank goodness) by two fakirs dressed only in a couple of loin cloths and holding hands. Our next introduction was to the roads and driving standards of the taxi drivers and the *Delhi Transportation Corporation* bus drivers.

Most of the time the drivers tend to keep to the left side of the road, but their vehicles have never been near an MOT testing station. Our taxi was a fairly modern Hindustan Ambassador (1958-type Morris Oxford), with three operational cylinders and a matching number of shock absorbers. Somehow, with one hand continually pressing the horn, the other on the gear lever, our driver found his way to the *Lodhi*, a grand looking but lizard-infested hotel. (Actually the lizards keep the mosquitoes at bay, so it wasn't that bad.)

Inside, the plumbing, which dates back to the early 1900s and hasn't changed since, is something else. When I turned on the bath tap, the lights went out; when I tried the shower the water seeped out of the pipes instead. And trying to write under one of those enormous helicopter rotor blades (they call them fans) required a great deal of self-discipline and paperweights . . .

After about three days, and a few hundred rupees, Mike managed to extract his Manta from the airport customs buildings in time for the rally. (That in itself was a miracle.) Mike was seeded at 17, just ahead of world championship drivers Andrea Zanussi and

Per Eklund. The Eighth Himalayan Rally started from the Jawaharlal Nehru Stadium in New Delhi, and ahead lay a course of 3220km, across hot, dusty plains, through dried-up river beds and the jungle of the Jim Corbett Tiger Reserve before a magical first glimpse of the Himalayan mountain range. At first, all we saw was a faint outline through the haze, and we wondered how anything could be so high. I'm used to Ben Nevis, at 1342m, and this lot looked gigantic.

Mike set off in his Manta; I was in a hired Ambassador with Yorkshire photographer Gavin Lodge, guide Vikram, and turban-charged driver Palsingh. We had two punctures on one of our old (and bald) cross-plies early on day one. "What have I let myself in for?" thought I. I'd already been sick through eating an omelette near the Taj Mahal; I had what is known as "Delhi-belly" and a stack of Jacobs cereal bars and Lucozade tablets to keep me going. And a supply of cement pills to stop me going!

"I lived on my cereal bars, Lucozade tablets and porridge for two whole weeks"

At the end of the first day we had climbed to 2000m in the mountains, to the old British army holiday resort of Nainital, nestling beside a tranquil lake. It looked good, but smelled awful. Only the rhododendrons gave the place a bit of colour and scent. One thing that did surprise me was the porridge – it really was good, almost as good as back home in Scotland. I lived on my cereal bars, Lucozade tablets and porridge for two whole weeks; I came back slimmer and fitter, and awfully glad to see a plate of my mother-in-law's mince.

From Nainital to Ranikhet we travelled up one mountain, down the other side, up another mountain, down the other side. The scenery was certainly spectacular, perhaps not as beautiful as the mountains and fjords of Norway, or indeed the west coast of Scotland – the deforestation of the Himalayas is quite noticeable – but it had a character all its own. The view of 8000-metre-high, snowcapped peaks from the _Savoy Hotel_ in Mussoorie was awe-inspiring.

Mike, by this time, had climbed to 3000m without oxygen and was in seventh place overall. But the rear axle threatened to break away from the bodywork, and only his vast experience kept him in the rally. He managed to tie it together with wire and rope, but the damage had been done and Mike was forced to retire at three-quarters distance. His first attempt at scaling the heights was over.

In 1988, Mike decided to have another go, with the same car, but converted to Group A specification and fuel injection, and with a new co-driver, Chris Fewlass. My good friend, Geoff Stone, and I hired a Group N Maruti Gypsy (an Indian-built Suzuki Jeep). Like Mike, we had delays upon delays in getting our vehicles out of customs; Gavin had summed it up nicely in 1987 when he said that the Indians make the Spaniards look quick!

"The old man lit a fire by the car to ward off the wild animals"

That said, the Indians were always extremely courteous, helpful and never said no. Unfortunately they said what they thought we wanted to hear, not what might actually be. They nod their heads from side to side: a severe nod means you've got a good chance of getting what you want; a mild shake means you haven't got a hope; something between the two could loosely be termed the norm. As if anything in India was the norm. I vividly remember seeing a man cutting the presidential lawns near India Gate – the lawn mower was being pulled by a sacred cow.

Other lasting memories of India are the passengers hanging from the roof, the doors, the windows of anything that

moved; wall to wall people; ear to ear noise; dawn to dusk sunshine. I made a trip to the Taj Mahal in an air-conditioned bus (that is, the windows were open), complete with a very noisy video; whenever you see a TV screen or hear a radio in India you are subjected to either a blinding headache or a cricket match.

At the start of the Ninth Himalayan Rally, Mike and Chris were at number 9, Geoff and I were at 24. Right away, Mike struck trouble. He stopped on the opening stage with fuel injector problems and fell to last place overall. We plodded on and finished the first leg in an amazing 18th place overall. From then on, as the route went uphill, we slipped back down the field. With rocky, unsurfaced mountain passes, full of hairpin bends and 3000m up, our knuckles turned a delicate shade of yellow through the sheer grip on the steering wheel.

On the second day Mike began to climb through the field, passing the elephants and the Marutis as though they were standing still. The twisty, metalled road up to Nainital, however, caused a repeat of the problems encountered in 1987, when the rear axle failed, and he retired on the spot. Chris thumbed a lift to summon help and Mike stayed with the car. Things happen slowly in India (as you may have gathered) and it was getting dark when an old Hindu appeared on the scene. He muttered away in Hindi, but Mike, of course, couldn't understand much – except the words "man-eating tiger". Mike leapt inside the car, closed the windows and locked the door, whilst the old man lit a fire by the car to ward off the wild animals. By morning, Chris had returned with help and eventually they got the car back to Nainital, where they found that Mike's bottle of whisky had leaked all over his clothes. He went to bed that night smelling happy, but perfectly sober!

Geoff and I were not without our problems: we had bounced off a tree in

Corbett Reserve and had someone throw a stone which smashed our non-laminated windscreen just prior to crossing the Ganges. If only the *Lodhi Hotel* could provide a shower like that. We also suffered a puncture but we battled on until the sixth and last day with our dreadfully slow Maruti. It got slower and slower, until the complete throttle pedal assembly fell off on the last, 22-kilometre, competitive section.

"Geoff changed gear for me as I steered with my left hand and operated the throttle with my right"

With political extremists throwing petrol bombs and stones, an immobile Jeep was the last thing we wanted. Geoff jumped out and rigged up a temporary throttle cable, a PVC-coated wire, from the carburettor linkage back through the driver's window (which was jammed after our earlier escapade with the tree), whereupon I managed to pull it and speed off down the track. The harder I pulled, the faster the Jeep went. In fact, it had never gone faster in the five previous days due to a faulty location on the bulkhead. Perhaps that was just as well, considering the white-knuckle country we'd driven through. Anyway, Geoff changed gear for me as I steered with my left hand and operated the throttle with my right.

With our Jeep well and truly wound up, we caught up on a Nissan Patrol Jongo (Jeep) before having a sideways "moment" and sensibly slacking off to ensure a finish on what must be the toughest road rally in the world. Geoff managed to effect repairs after the competitive section and only the run-in to New Delhi was left. Following a Jongo, with the crew hanging out of every window and waving aside all oncoming traffic, was very exciting. They waved off the road the overcrowded buses; they waved aside the overloaded lorries, the aged Royal Enfield motorbikes, scooters, the cyclists, the bullocks, the camels and the odd sacred cow. But they missed one Ambassador, on the outskirts of Delhi, heading straight for us. It was Geoff's turn behind the wheel, and somehow he succeeded in squeezing the Maruti between the insane Indian and the bridge parapet, while I managed to push the co-driver's horn button right through the dashboard!

We finished the rally in 42nd place overall, my best ever result on a big event and Geoff's first attempt at a rally. Mike deserved better. After all, to participate and to be competitive, negotiating all those hairpin bends, river crossings and sacred cows, took some doing. India isn't the easiest of places to get around; the facilities leave a lot to be desired, but it is a challenge. I hope that readers will take from this story a share of Mike Jackson's courage, and in return give him their good wishes for a third and successful attempt at his "Personal Everest" when he finds the funds and eventually returns.

Touring

A Giant Buffet

Roderick MacDonald is disabled by a form of muscular dystrophy which confines him to a wheelchair. In June 1984, accompanied by a friend, Neil, and Neil's son Scott, he travelled by car through eight European countries.

A brilliant sun dazzled our eyes on the morning we headed eastwards from Zeebrugge. The fatigue of a 640-kilometre journey from Scotland and a late night on the ferry soon evaporated on the drive through Belgium. The Datsun's boot was crammed with luggage and the wheelchair had to go on a roof rack. This proved to be an advantage when stops were made; it was quicker and easier to take the chair from the roof rather than shift everything around in the boot.

Saarbrücken in Germany was the intended destination that day, and we reached it following a long delay in Luxembourg, where armed police stopped all traffic to search for bank robbers. We couldn't find accessible accommodation in Saarbrücken and had to go on to Strasbourg.

After driving around the city in a fruitless search for a suitable hotel, Neil (a policeman) stopped at a police station. He explained our situation, showing his International Police Federation card. The French police led us through the busy streets of Strasbourg in a police car, lights flashing, stopping other cars as we sped towards a hotel some 3km away. They booked us in, made sure we left nothing of value in the car, and departed with best wishes for a successful holiday.

Neil was in the act of fixing up the wheelchair when a small man, perhaps in his late forties, emerged from the hotel. He lifted me out of the passenger seat, regardless of my 76kg weight, and plonked me in the wheelchair. Before we could gather our senses, he proceeded to pull me up a flight of stairs.

It transpired that this hotel was populated by ex-foreign legionnaires, mostly of German origin, who spent a few months of each year in France to fulfil a residential regulation for their pension. The rooms were inexpensive (about £5 per night each) but everything was clean and adequate.

After a short rest and a wash, we met the small man again. In a combination of English, French and a little German we learned that his name was Jean and he'd retired from the legion in 1969. He was as hard as nails but very amicable, showing us photos of places he'd visited in the South Pacific, and introducing us to Heinz, who'd been shot in the head when parachuting in French Cameroon. Though paralysed down his left side, Heinz had fought back to remarkable fitness. He insisted on taking us to a restaurant and despite his disabilities we found it difficult to keep up his marching pace.

Surrounded by more legionnaires we enjoyed an excellent meal with wine and it was quite late when we arrived back at the hotel. Nobody seemed to take any notice of my wheelchair, except when offering help. Our duty-free whisky appeared and with Heinz and Jean, and later *le patron*, who couldn't sleep because of our noise, we drank until the early hours of the morning.

The showers did not supply hot water – cold was the legionnaires' preference and it did have the effect of waking us up. Neil and I envied twelve-year-old Scott, bright and cheerful, who was of course too young to have developed bad habits. After breakfast, Heinz took us on a tour of the old part of Strasbourg. As you'd expect from a city housing the EEC Parliament, Strasbourg is modern and cosmopolitan, but it is dominated by the medieval Cathédrale de Notre-Dame and still retains its historical atmosphere.

By noon we were making our way through scorching heat into Germany, towards the Black Forest. Afer visiting the picturesque Rhine Falls, where we encountered a wedding and were showered with sweets, we spent the night in *Hotel Kirschen*, Lottsletten, in a small peninsula of Germany which juts into Switzerland. On through Zürich and along the southern shore of two lakes, Zürich See and Walen See, stopping for coffee in Vaduz, capital of Liechtenstein. We decided to make Innsbruck by

nightfall and made good speed until we reached the Arlberg pass. Ignoring the tunnel, we took the high road over the top. The road twisted and turned at acute angles with precipitous drops into rocky ravines only a mistake away. From a lay-by at 1800m we got out to take a few photos and the cold wind took our breath away.

In Innsbruck, finding an accessible hotel was difficult but we finally secured rooms at the *Wilder Mann Hotel*, which was all but full of senior citizens from Lancashire. We headed straight for the bar, where a large glass of beer went down very well after a long day travelling. Walking along Innsbruck's tidy streets late that night, after a magnificent dinner, breathing in the refreshing air, I was struck by the proximity of the mountains. When looking up at the jagged peaks silhouetted against the sky my neck was bent right back; when leaving the confines of the restaurant, or peering into shop windows, a glance upwards would transport me into another world.

"I insisted on frequent stops at the many beer gardens to avoid dehydration"

From Innsbruck we drove north, passing majestic mountains and crystal-clear lakes, to Munich. In Bavaria we saw the Wagner-inspired castles which the mad king, Ludwig II, had built at his country's expense. With a multitude of tourists swamping the area the castles were frankly a disappointment, and we pressed on to Munich, where we booked into a hotel opposite a brewery. Our unanimous decision after our two-day stay was that the beer in Munich was good – very good! Feeling sorry for Neil, who had to push me around the city under a cloudless sky, I insisted on frequent stops at the many beer gardens to avoid dehydration and exhaustion.

Munich is a twin city of my native Edinburgh, has excellent facilities and seemed to be full of friendly people (perhaps the beer had something to do with that). We walked the pedestrian precinct, beginning at the station and progressing through the fourteenth-century Karlstor gate (one of the three remaining gates of the original medieval city) which is situated beside a spectacular fountain – a tempting sight on a hot June day.

The precinct continues along Neuhauser, with its many and varied shops, then opens out into the Marienplatz, the square in the heart of the city. Here we rested in an outdoor café, looking up at the carillon on the New Town Hall (Rathaus), unfortunately fifteen minutes after the 11am performance. The Rathaus is not really new, built in 1909, but much newer than the nearby fifteenth-century Altes Rathaus which today houses a toy museum. To the left, towering over everything else, stands the twin-domed Frauenkirche, the symbol of Munich, dominating the city's skyline.

Using a wheelchair in Munich was very easy, and where help was required there was no shortage of volunteers. Time was not on our side on this holiday, and it is difficult to obtain an objective view of a land and its population during a brief visit, but the Bavarians did seem to me a pleasant and relaxed lot, out to live life rather than simply survive it. In the Englischer Garten, where we anticipated a beer, we encountered hundreds of people sunbathing naked – even if our climate was better, I somehow cannot imagine this going on in Edinburgh or Birmingham! Situated to the west of the River Isar, the Englischer Garten dates from the eighteenth century and is one of Europe's largest city parks. The leafy avenues by the river gave us welcome relief from the sun, and the whole effect is one of natural countryside rather than landscaped parkland.

We didn't use our cameras in the Englischer Garten, but many rolls of film were exposed during the holiday. Using a medium-format camera I captured some shots in the Olympic Stadium which I was able to sell to a photographic agency back home; from a wheelchair it is easy to obtain steady images without using a tripod, simply by resting the camera on your lap. The view from the top of the 150-metre Olympic tower was startling. The weather was clear, enabling us to see the entire city, with its domes and spires reflecting the light of the morning sun. Also visible was the pool where Mark Spitz won his seven gold medals, and the terraced buildings of the Olympic village where Arab terrorists stormed the Israeli quarters in 1972. The nine hostages taken were killed in a shoot-out at the airport, along with four of the Arabs and one policeman.

"As I rolled out of the chair I was conscious of the barrier at the bottom of the steps and the 1500-metre drop"

Of course, in Munich we had to visit a traditional Bavarian restaurant: mountains of food and litres of beer consumed in a vast hall, ringing to the sounds of music and dancing. We had difficulty moving from the table after our weisswurst, a tasty recipe of veal served with baked potatoes and salad. I again felt sorry for Neil when he had to haul himself and me out of the restaurant and back to the hotel. I was OK, sitting in the wheelchair! Neil never complained, and every obstacle was brushed aside with "No problem!", but he did collapse when we got back to the hotel that night.

Leaving Munich it was a relatively short drive, by our standards so far, across the Austrian border to Salzburg. We found an excellent hotel, *Gasthof Grunauer Hof*, in a village called Wals, a few kilometres from town. Our room had a balcony with a view of the Untersberg; this is "Sound of Music" country and though not great fans of the film we had to admit to spectacular scenery.

In the bar, watching the European Championship match between Spain and West Germany, we were surprised to hear local Austrians cheer loudly for the Spanish. As far as football was concerned, they explained, they would support anybody except their overbearing neighbours. Thinking of our own situation in Scotland, we recognised a similarity: we also take great delight at the defeat of England. A kind of empathy existed between the Austrians and ourselves, both having neighbours who hogged the limelight.

That evening we sat on the balcony drinking wine and smoking cigars. The air was exceptionally still and warm. A blazing bonfire cast moving shadows of revellers celebrating Midsummer Night. It was just possible to see the outline of the Untersberg against a dark sky, and we decided to go there the next day.

Getting into the cable car involved the ascent of two flights of stairs. With help I was manoeuvred into the cable car and I didn't feel too bad, even as it swayed about at a great height over rugged rocks. Getting out at the top was tricky because I had to alight in the wheelchair at right-angles to descending steps. A helpful tourist pulled me out but tipped me over; as I rolled out of the chair I was conscious of the barrier at the bottom of the steps and the 1500-metre drop to Salzburg. However, I was assisted back into the chair and managed to bear the incident with equanimity in spite of the laughter from some who should have known better.

The mountain air was chilly, a stark contrast to the heat below, but it was fresh and invigorating. The view over the surrounding mountains was worth the effort, and after a brief lunch of soup, bread and coffee we were ready for an afternoon touring.

The city of Salzburg is a nice size, and the pedestrian precinct – really a

collection of *platz* or squares – imparts a feeling of space and concise geometry. The older part of the city, especially around the Getreidegasse, is more crowded, with narrow, cobbled streets, quaint shopfronts and ornate signs. Some houses, dating from the fifteenth century, back onto the sheer rockface leading up to the castle. We found the most relaxing parts of the city along the banks of the Salzach river. Late in the afternoon, before returning to the hotel in Wals, it was pleasant to sit and watch the world pass by while Scott fed the swans.

"The official shook his head ruefully when we told him how long we were spending in Vienna"

The fine weather broke and we left for Vienna in a torrential downpour. But it had brightened considerably by the time we reached *Hotel Zur Post*, 43km west of the city in the Vienna woods and not far from a small brewery (again!). A fine meal of venison set us up for the expedition the following day to the old capital of the Austrian Empire, the city of culture, music, science and spies. This was the furthest point east on our grand tour, and I had a special reason for including it: my great-grandfather came from Vienna to Scotland sometime in the last century – I was going back to my roots.

With a map supplied by the helpful Austrian National Tourist Office in London, Neil managed to drive precisely through the city and park beside the brown Danube. There we left the car and began our exploration on foot. Near the giant ferris wheel (featured in *The Third Man*) we were almost run down by thirty Hell's Angels. Undaunted, we reached the Stadtpark and stopped for refreshments; Germany is the land of the beer garden, but here the wine garden ruled and we adopted the local custom.

With so many attractions in the city the choice was difficult. We elected to visit the Natural History Museum, avoiding a multitude of steps with the help of an official who took us to a lift at the rear of the building. This was no ordinary museum. The spacious entrance hall was built more like a cathedral. While Neil and Scott examined the wildlife displays, I was more interested in the remains of Bronze-Age settlements found to the south of Vienna. The official shook his head ruefully when we told him how long we were spending in Vienna. By the time we had surveyed the Imperial Palace of the Habsburgs it was getting late, and we returned to the car by taxi. One day was not enough.

We drove west along the Danube, then followed the Neckar river to Heidelberg, on the Rhine. Leaving Heidelberg the next morning brought us into the vast jungle of concrete and steel that is Mannheim/Ludwigshafen (on opposite banks of the Rhine). We got lost. For a couple of hours we drove round and round, looking for a way out northwards. Eventually we escaped and made 60km or so before we broke down.

Neil contacted the rescue service and after a few hours hanging about, during which we had a chat with the locals, a transporter arrived to take us back to Mannheim. I couldn't get into the high cab up front, but this enabled me to enjoy a good view of the countryside from inside the car on the back of the transporter. Passing over the Rhine at Worms and through the industrial complexes around Mannheim and Ludwigshafen, I was impressed by the sheer size and spread of it all, especially the BASF works.

Little was amiss with the car. A Polish mechanic, after deriding me for buying a Japanese car, took the carburettor to bits and reassembled it. The engine started first try! It was getting late by then but the garage directed us to local accommodation, where we obtained a welcome dinner and a glass or two of beer.

The following day we reached Brussels by mid-afternoon and had sufficient time to go up the Atomium, a massive construction of aluminium spheres in the shape of an atomic nucleus, built for the World Fair in 1958. A rapidly ascending lift took us to the top for a view of the city, but this was marred by badly scratched transparent panels; the cathedral was seen through somebody's initials carved on perspex. On this, my third visit, Brussels still seemed a charmless place, unlike many other areas of Belgium.

Our ferry from Zeebrugge left at 11pm and the crossing was uneventful. We made it back to Scotland by early evening, with only a few pence left in our pockets, and an assortment of foreign coins. Altogether we spent twelve nights in Europe and covered 5150km. It had been a giant buffet and we'd sampled each main dish. It was an adventure which we may never repeat, but we enjoyed every minute. I haven't mentioned a great deal about the problems of travelling with a disability; the truth of the matter is that there were none that warranted real concern, and minor difficulties were easily overcome. For this I have the people of eight countries, who helped in various ways, to thank, not to mention my companions. But perhaps most important was our attitude: we didn't go looking for things to go wrong, nor did we worry if they did.

Coming Home

Michael Turner and his wife Julie are both 27 years old and both have cerebral palsy. In 1985 they set off on a six-week trip, camping in five European countries.

As the patter of rain developed into what sounded like an avalanche, and lightning lit up the inside of the tent more brightly than our gas-lamp, I began to wonder, "What the hell are we doing here?" Home seemed like a million miles away, and at that moment I'd have given a million pounds to have been there.

This was our first night under canvas. Julie and I were both at university and we had been impressed by our friends' tales of travels in various parts of the world. Many of them had been round Europe by train, and while we felt that we wouldn't get very far on trains and with backpacks, we were confident that we could manage camping with a car.

We left home with a roughly circular route planned that would take us through Belgium (for a short visit to relatives in Brussels), West Germany, Austria, Switzerland and France. Our tastes were for the scenic aspects of central Europe, particularly the Alps, rather than the heat of the south. However, part of the attraction of camping is being able to plan things as you go along. This proved its worth when we became fed up with being rained on in Switzerland, and decided that the hot south might not be such a bad idea after all; we packed up and went to Antibes in the south of France.

Freedom has its price. Camping was undoubtedly very hard work. We had a small, three-person ridge tent (though where the third person was meant to go remains a mystery) which we'd only previously put up in a soggy back garden in spring. The dry ground of summer (except in Switzerland) proved a fair bit harder. This caused us some difficulty in a number of places, although people nearly always appeared and gave us a hand.

The only time we got into real trouble was the night we arrived in Antibes. We'd driven virtually solidly for two days to get away from the Swiss rain, and we arrived quite late. By the time we'd eaten it was gone 11pm. A combination of rocky and sandy ground meant that some of the tent pegs just would not go in, and others slid out as soon as they did. By 1am we had reached the point where it would probably stay up, and we just had to hope it wouldn't rain (much of the work in putting up a tent is to make it sure it stays waterproof).

As well as the actual putting up and taking down of the tents, camping involves a lot of lugging things around – gas cooker, chairs and table, pots and pans – and all have to be put away as soon as you've finished with them. The combination of this and the fresh air certainly made us sleep very soundly.

"I'm sure that our disabilities were actually an advantage on this trip"

Campsites are not the best equipped places for disabled people. We found only one site on the whole journey with any specific facilities – a wheelchair-accessible shower and loo. At many sites there were steps into toilets, and shower cubicles were fairly cramped. They were also, with a couple of exceptions, segregated on the basis of sex.

We both walk (with difficulty), so we didn't worry too much about physical barriers, but we had wondered about language barriers. We're rather typically British in that we speak only our own language, but we also have speech impairments and were concerned about the potential for problems with communication. Our fears were unfounded. We are well used to having difficulty making ourselves understood, which meant that a language barrier wasn't anything new to us, and we are also used to backing up what we say with gestures and expressions. More often than not, pointing to the appropriate line of the phrasebook worked perfectly well.

There was one occasion when we were caught out. We were in a restaurant in France and Julie was eating an omelette with a side order of chips, which arrived on separate plates, while my order was held up for reasons unknown. The Frenchman on the table next to us decided that the chips were mine and that I was unable to feed myself; without a word he proceeded to attempt to feed me Julie's chips. It took the timely arrival of my order to convince him that the chips were not mine and I was a dab hand with a spoon and fork!

"Mile after mile of breathtaking scenery and air that remained cool and fresh even in the hottest weather"

Apart from this incident, I'm sure that our disabilities were actually an advantage on this trip, since we were not just more English tourists who couldn't speak the language; people were more willing to take the time to understand us.

One of the very interesting things we were able to experience by travelling through several countries was the varying attitudes and understanding of disability. Obviously it is impossible to draw any firm conclusions, since we saw only a small part of each country and we were mainly in rural areas, but there were some clear differences between some countries.

Austria was a curious mixture: while virtually every shop in Innsbruck had a "happy to help" sign in four different languages, this was undoubtedly the country where our disabilities drew the most attention. On one occasion we went into a bar/restaurant in a village and literally every head in the bar turned to look at us – it was like a scene from a Western. Judging by the amount of staring that people did, it seems that unaccompanied disabled people are far less common on the continent than they are here.

Travelling from Austria into Switzerland was quite remarkable. Suddenly the staring stopped, there were better facilities and we even spotted some disabled people around. In the areas that we visited, the Swiss appeared to be very much more aware of, and more comfortable with, disability. But for the rain, we would have stayed longer, as we thoroughly enjoyed what we did see of the country, in between the low clouds. Lucerne was one of the most pleasant places we stopped at, with its situation on the lake, the many old buildings along the banks of the river, and the intricately decorated old bridge across the river. It was quite touristy, but maintained its charm and atmosphere in spite of the hordes.

Our other favourite country was Germany. We found a marvellous campsite on the banks of the Rhine, a little south of Coblenz, where the river runs through a high-sided, tree-covered valley (spoilt only by the noise of military jets and helicopters). There was level access to the showers and to the site shop, and only one or two steps to the loos. The Black Forest was another high point on our tour, with mile after mile of breathtaking scenery and air that remained cool and fresh even in the hottest weather.

It was in Obersdorf, a town in southern Germany on the edge of the Alps, that we had our strangest experience. We'd decided to have a couple of nights' break from the rigours of camping and indulge in a guesthouse or hotel. It was early August, and everywhere we tried was fully booked. Driving out of Obersdorf, towards a campsite we'd passed earlier, we saw a small hotel by the road and decided to have one last try. To our amazement there were rooms available, it was very cheap, and there was a marvellous view of the mountains.

In time it became apparent that we were the only people staying there, although there were many members of the family who lived in and ran the hotel. It also became apparent why we were the only guests. During the night the family rowed and shouted, babies cried and there were crashes and bangs. The following morning we were told that the toilet on our floor was not working. We presumed this was something to do with the plumbing, but found that the toilet had been smashed with a hammer! While this was all very strange, we didn't feel at all threatened, so we made the most of our break from camping.

France was at the end of our circular route, the warmth of Antibes a pleasant relief from the Swiss rain. It was, however, very busy with lots of English tourists, which encouraged us to move on quickly. Making our way up through France we spent time in Avignon, which has a medieval feel despite the onslaught of cars and coaches. This is an old, walled town and quite difficult to get around – finding a parking place was only the first hurdle.

From Avignon we moved on to Le Puy, a small town in a dramatic setting amongst the hills and lava pinnacles of the Auvergne. The town is dominated by a massive, hill-top statue of the Madonna. Having trudged up the hill we found that it is possible to climb up inside the statue to a viewing platform in its crown, but the steep steps and my lack of head for heights got the better of us and we had to make do with the views from the hill.

We indulged ourselves with a hotel for our last night on the continent. It was chosen very carefully as we were getting short of funds – so short that we didn't have wine with our evening meal and didn't even dare to order water for fear of getting expensive mineral water!

After six weeks on the road, the return home to comfortable beds, hot baths and just knowing where we were was very welcome, and an important part of the journey. Much of the value of travelling, for us, was to arrive home and see it in the light of what we had seen and experienced while touring.

Cruises

A Dose of Romantic Escapism

In May 1988 Terence Wilson made his third attempt at a trip on the sail training ship *Lord Nelson* (the voyages are very popular and it can be difficult to obtain a place at the right time, at the right price and for the required duration). Although he'd been sailing for about 25 years in smaller craft, he wasn't sure how he'd manage with the problems of multiple sclerosis in a larger vessel, even if the ship was designed for disabled crew, so he booked a berth on the two-day, Antwerp to Lowestoft voyage, accompanied by his daughter Sarah and her husband Timothy.

The coach set us down at the *P&O* terminal in Dover, and after a short wait in reception while the party assembled we set off for customs and the departure lounge. This was my first mistake. Thinking that it was just a short distance, I started to walk, but it turned out to be several hundred metres of corridor which I only just managed to negotiate before collapsing into an armchair. Fortunately we had quite a long wait here while our ferry was serviced. Next, a bus transported us across the docks to the ferry and we were on our way.

Around 8.30pm we disembarked at Ostend and a friendly Belgian bus driver shepherded us onto another coach. It was a good job he did! The others had to walk miles to the customs hall with their bags, while we were whisked in and out and back to the waiting coach before you could say "Jaques Robinson". One of our fellow passengers, John, was raised on a special wheelchair lift into the back of the coach and our luggage was piled into the trailer towed behind.

When we left England it was a pleasant, sunny spring day; now it was 76°F, humid, and after fourteen hours of travelling I was beginning to wilt. Bumping over the cobbled wharfs in Antwerp, the coach pulled into a small lane between two brick buildings and there she was – the *Lord Nelson*. The 400-ton barque shone in the bright lights around the harbour, the sails brailed up to the yards which towered above the quayside. We climbed out of the coach, grabbed our bags and descended a long, steep gangway to the river level and the waiting reception. A short wait while the crew signed ship's articles in the best seafaring tradition, and we were allotted our berths and watches below.

Sarah and I were Starb'd Aft Watch, while Tim was in a foc'sle berth on Port For'd Watch. Sarah and I shared a wheelchair-berth, with me on the lower bunk and she as my "buddy" on the pipe-cot above me. (Everyone in the crew has a buddy, someone to keep a weather eye on you, to make sure you are wearing your safety line, and to clip you on if things look bad.) We assembled in the lower mess deck where we met the professional crew. Watch leaders were assigned to each watch, then we were given the bad news. First watch on duty was Starb'd Aft Watch, from midnight to 4am, the Middle or "Graveyard" Watch. I came here to discover my limit and this was it! I went to see the Medical Purser and told her my problem.

"That's all right. Go and tell your watch leader and then go and get your head down." What a relief!

Next morning, things looked decidedly better. I awoke to the strum of diesel engines and the tannoy calling all hands off watch to the lower mess deck for breakfast. Here we met all the shadowy figures of last night and introduced ourselves properly. Each day – in our case, on this short voyage, at every meal – two or three crew members are given mess duties, setting the tables, handing out the food from the lift connecting us to the galley, and clearing away afterwards.

When we were not "on watch" we were lectured on safety at sea, man-overboard drill, and "learning the ropes". We were also introduced to that *Lord Nelson* institution, delightfully misnamed "Happy Hour": dusters, buckets, scrubbing brushes and cleaning materials were handed out and everybody was assigned to clean something. There were very few occasions when disabled and able-bodied crew were segregated but this was one of them. Disabled crew were relieved of the more onerous duties, such as cleaning out the "heads" (toilets), but we were all encouraged to help out with any small job during Happy Hour and at mealtimes. I cleaned the brass.

"I had no problem getting around, either below or on deck, with my elbow-stick, Long John Silver style"

Soon the *Lord Nelson* was well down the Westerschelde and on her way to the North Sea. Volunteers were called to climb the rat-lines onto the yards to prepare the large sails for sea. Tim was among a small party up aloft and they were joined by several others eager to try their hand. I went below for a well-earned siesta after lunch and when I came on deck again we were heading for the open sea, a strong breeze drawing the main and fore courses, tops'ls and t'gallants. The fore and aft stays'ls, jibs and spanker were also set and the *Lord Nelson* came alive.

I had no problem getting around, either below or on deck, with my elbow-stick, Long John Silver style. There were two wheelchair lifts up the main companion-ways, and a single chair lift for crew like myself who had difficulty walking upstairs. Along the sides of the cabins there were small, tie-up seats to perch on, and convenient bollards and machine-housing to squat on, with hand-holds everywhere.

The next watch for Sarah and me was 4am to 8am – the Morning Watch – so after a pleasant drink in the duty-free bar we turned in. I woke several times in the night and secured my lee cloth to stop me falling out of my bunk. When we were woken to stand watch we came on deck to find a grey dawn over the North Sea, with a Force 6 north-easter blowing straight down the Arctic Circle and the *Lord Nelson* pitching and rolling over the spume-blown waves. I was very glad I had brought my thermal underwear.

The first job, according to Paul (First Mate), was to reduce canvas. Our watch consisted of ten crew members, of which only one (myself) was disabled. It was logical for me to take the helm while the others shortened sail. Starb'd Aft Watch disappeared forward to start with the jib and I felt very much alone – like the Flying Dutchman, at the helm of a 400-ton square rigger bound God-knows-where. Because of complications, the task of taking in some of the sails took longer than anticipated, and I found myself at the helm for the entire watch. Every few minutes Paul's head would pop up over the edge of the bridge with a new course and bearing as we careered into the maze of offshore sandbanks lying west of the Norfolk coast. I wouldn't have changed those four hours for anything.

"We met in the bar and sang sea shanties until we were all too tired to stay awake"

When I went off watch to breakfast that morning, I sat watching the crew tumbling downstairs to the mess deck. Many had succumbed to the dreaded mal-de-mer, but instead of the group of tourists and travellers we met at Dover, here were a bunch of hardened seafarers, with oilies and life jackets, their faces red from wind-burn and salt-spray, hair dishevelled by the nor'easter, and ready for their kippers and boiled eggs. What a transformation!

As a result of the strong favourable wind, our crossing was so fast that we arrived outside Lowestoft harbour far too early to get in. The anchor was let go just beyond the North Pier while we waited for the tide. That night, tied up to the quay, we met in the bar and sang sea shanties until we were all too tired to stay awake: old songs about Australia and the great Southern Ocean, about girls of easy virtue preying on young sailor lads fresh from the sea – a rollicking end to a sea voyage.

Of course I would do it again. The feeling of achievement, the sense of adventure, the comradeship will stay with me for many years to come. For once, disability did not matter, yet – unlike many everyday-life situations – it was not entirely overlooked. At all times there was a friendly helping hand ready to assist when asked, and disabled sailors were simply part of the crew. Each person's contribution depends on their knowledge of the sea, not their degree of physical ability. For example, watch leaders are the only crew members with any real responsibility (apart from the professional crew) and they must hold the RYA Yachtmaster Offshore Certificate or equivalent practical sailing experience. On this voyage one of the watch leaders was paraplegic: what he couldn't do in a wheelchair isn't worth mentioning. More important, he knew the names of the hundreds of ropes and could give orders for them to be handled by the rest of us. That's what's meant by responsibility.

There is a saying in the Navy, "First turn of the screw pays all debts". Once you are on board the *Lord Nelson*, all debts are paid, the life you lead ashore is behind you and you can look forward to a few days of romantic escapism and nautical nostalgia, serving before the mast.

To the Edge of the Polar Icecap

For the last four years, Betty Parkin has been partially sighted (registered blind). Initially thinking that this must restrict her choice of holiday to a fortnight on a seaside hotel balcony, she now takes a yearly cruise – "expensive, but bread and only a little jam is the answer for the rest of the year". In July 1989 she joined the *Canberra* for a cruise to Norway.

I had always regarded cruising as a holiday for stick-in-the-muds or bridge fans – no adventures, no visits to unknown or extraordinary places. But a short trip to the Canaries then two weeks in the Mediterranean and I was hooked. The third cruise took me up the coast of Norway to the island of Spitsbergen, in the Arctic Ocean.

Cruising requires as much planning as any other holiday. Studying the prices, the dates and destinations may be enough for some, but not for me. I need the same cabin – or one very similar – in the same part of the same ship. As far as accommodation is concerned, mostly you get what you pay for; after many years of travel I go for the very best I can afford. There seems no sense in scrimping and saving all year only to end in a holiday of discomfort – better to lower your sights, cut down the number of days and enjoy a little luxury.

Of course, this is the view of an older person; cabins for three or four occupants are adequate for the young and idealistic, but most disabled people need space. I travel alone and indulge myself with a single cabin so that if I knock anything over, spill my tea or grovel around on the carpet, looking for my pen or an earring, I am not being a nuisance to anyone else.

Wanting the same cabin for another trip means booking it very early. On the *Canberra* an official comes on board for the last day of the cruise to take bookings for the next year, and many people take advantage of this. As one elderly lady said to me, "If I am spared I shall enjoy the cruise, and if I am not I shan't worry over the loss of my deposit!"

If I was more confident about my sight I might be tempted by the "Take a Chance" offer to those who can take their holiday at any time with only three weeks' notice of a vacancy and at a much-reduced price. My problem is that although I should get a single cabin it might be in a different part of the ship to that which I have grown accustomed to. But it is worth considering if this is not your problem.

Most shipping companies require passengers travelling alone to walk unaided, or with sticks, up the gangway of the ship. Wheelchair passengers (the chair must conform to their regulations) must be accompanied by an escort who can push their chair up the gangway. Totally blind persons must also have an escort. My tour agent states on the booking form, "Partially sighted but has previously had this cabin without any problems".

"Travelling from my village home in Lancashire to Southampton is one of the worst problems"

Having accepted the deposit, *P&O* send out a medical form, three months prior to embarkation, to all who are over seventy years of age (75 with some cruise companies) and to any disabled passengers. This must be completed by your own doctor and it ensures that the ship's surgeon knows of your condition and any medications used, should you require his or her help during the cruise.

Travelling from my village home in Lancashire to Southampton is one of the worst problems: should I go by train to London and take a taxi across to another station for the special boat train? Or should I risk the once-a-day train from a nearby station which, if delayed, could miss the sailing, to say nothing of having to spend the night in a hotel on my return in order to catch the early-morning train home? It is all very worrying, but on this trip I was lucky – the cruise I had booked was chosen by the district newspaper for a special tour and this meant coach travel to and from my local town. All my problems were solved.

For the *Canberra* cruise there is a special embarkation time for anyone requiring assistance with wheelchairs, or a chair from train or coach to the ship, or in my case a porter – hand baggage and a white cane leave no hand free for gangways, ticket collection or passport control. It is essential to carry a valise as luggage may not appear in your cabin until long after the ship has sailed.

Ask for assistance when making the final payment, so that help can be organised and you are not left stranded on the quayside. And some of your usual medication should be packed in your valise so that you are not waiting for that belated luggage to arrive in your cabin. There are large supplies of medications carried in the ship's pharmacy, but neither those nor treatment is covered by the NHS, so they are very expensive. Insurance may be included in the fare, but usually the first £15–20 has to be paid and the insurance covers only accidents and new medical problems.

When at last I am aboard I take my time, look around and tread carefully, remembering that most doorways have high sills. (The nursing staff tell me that before they leave the home port there are usually hacked shins to be stitched or dressed, mostly eager, excited, young passengers, rarely the more careful disabled ones.) Doors must be tried with caution as those opening onto decks often require a very strong arm to open and shut them.

I tell the cabin steward who comes to greet me that I am partially sighted but manage fairly well. Would he tell those who vacuum the corridor carpets to keep an eye out for me? I see their machines but the long, snaking flexes remain invisible. With the steward's permission I put some bright stickers on glass edges and such, then I stroll around, remind myself of the number of steps in the nearby staircase, refresh my memory about the lift buttons, and I am ready for the cruise to begin.

There are no Indian temples to explore on the *Canberra*, no Greek ruins to climb, but there is plenty to do and see – classical concerts, cabarets, discos and dancing, as well as entertainment from stage, TV and radio stars. The cinema shows recent films and a lecturer gives excellent illustrated talks on the ports to be visited on the cruise. Special places are reserved in the theatre for wheelchairs and their escorts, and the library has a goodly supply of large-print books. Tournaments are held for bridge fanatics, and classes covering everything from keep fit to soft-toy making. And the Chaplain takes regular services. For many passengers a long chair on deck suffices.

"The majesty of the mountain-ringed fjords and the tremendous force of the waterfalls overwhelmed me"

Tours are arranged, several of them in each port. They may be expensive but are good value for money and are accompanied by local guides. When *Canberra* cannot berth she anchors nearby and passengers are conveyed to shore by launches, which then keep up a regular service. If the town is any distance away a free shuttle service by coach is provided. Most disabled passengers on our trip were able to manage the gangway from the ship to the launches.

I had visited Norway twice before but the majesty of the mountain-ringed fjords and the tremendous force of the waterfalls still overwhelmed me as we cruised past villages perched high above the zigzag roads. The air was clean and bright, as I had remembered. At Narvik I chose the day trip, which included a visit to a war cemetery and the Chapel of Peace. The Krigsminne War Museum, run by the Red Cross, is an emotive documentation of the German bombing of the town and the sea and air battles which raged around it.

We next took the ore trail into Sweden, travelling along the railway track used by the wagons that carry millions of tons of iron ore yearly from Sweden for export via Narvik's docks. We passed into the land of reindeers, uninhabited by man, a strange terrain of lakes, marshes and rivers; deep valleys lay between snow-wreathed mountains. We lunched on reindeer meat at the Arisko National Park, but most of the animals had moved on to summer pastures and the main attraction of the park at that time of year was its wealth of wild flowers.

My day in Trondheim was spent visiting the cathedral, a very fine one with a beautiful rose window. At 1pm the doors are closed and the organist plays a short programme of Norwegian music – a lovely rest period from your shopping. I walked alone here and found it quite easy as Norway has such clearly marked crossings and the traffic stops dead at them. Traffic laws are very strictly enforced. There are many good shops, knitwear and silver jewellery being the favourite buys, but the prices were prohibitive for most of us. Even the fruit and flowers seemed expensive.

In Bergen, which was familiar ground, I went to the fish market at Torget where fish of all shapes and sizes are sold, including smoked salmon in packets, ideal for bringing home. There was every type of pot plant in the flower market – in Norway no window is complete without its pot

plant. Facing the harbour are the famous old wooden warehouses of Bryggen, the site of the original settlement of Bergen. After a morning spent exploring on my own (thanks again to those crossings), I joined the ship's tour which took me to the Aquarium and to the Bryggens Museum, where a collection of old boathouses and warehouses have been reconstructed.

"Mountains with sides polished bare by glaciers that spill huge chunks of brilliant blue ice into the sea"

The highlight of the cruise was our final destination, Spitsbergen, which is icebound for all but two months of the year. Here are mountains with sides polished bare by glaciers that spill huge chunks of brilliant blue ice into the sea to float like the bubbles in a bath alongside the ship. Reindeer graze on sparse vegetation at the water's edge, and sea birds, geese and puffins fly overhead.

A lecturer from Bergen had joined our ship for two days and had given a course of four talks about glaciers, which greatly enhanced our understanding of the area. The Captain took the ship to the very edge of the polar icecap which stands high and proud from the ocean like the cut white icing on a Christmas cake. It was a worrying time for the crew, with lookouts posted all around the ship, but an unforgettable sight for the passengers. I was delighted to be able to make out most of the scenery through my monocular glass.

During my stay on the *Canberra* I received every help from the ship's company, and while shopping ashore I found no problems to deter moderately handicapped, unaccompanied people. Many shopkeepers speak fluent English and nearly everyone can manage a few useful sentences. In one street where the pavement was under repair, strangers crossed the road to tell me of the hazard and on realising that I was a tourist and might not understand their instructions they accompanied me past the cavities and over the ramps. Many elderly and handicapped folk were using different walking frames from those I've seen in Britain – obviously adapted for use in icy places.

Before the end of the cruise I visited the ship's hospital (I am a retired nurse) to ask the doctors and nursing staff if they had any advice to offer prospective disabled passengers. One sister said, "If you are independent in your own home you will be able to manage aboard, but if you require daily nursing care, meals on wheels or home help, this sort of assistance cannot be provided." Anything that makes life more comfortable can be brought on board, for example a tripod instead of a stick if your balance is poor, a high seat for the loo, special pillows, even a hoist to transfer from chair to bed.

Children generally have a wonderful time on a cruise ship, with their own programme of events, their own staff of nursery workers and aides, and a club for teenagers. Few of the passengers on the Norway cruise will forget the delightful picture made by a young girl as she sat in her decorated wheelchair joining in the fun of Ascot night, with her pink parasol and matching crepe-paper hat.

Disembarkation of the walking wounded (as I think of us from my service days) was made easy. Our specially labelled baggage was stacked on the shore with waiting porters who escorted us through customs and to the trains, cars or coaches, where we sat and waited in comfort whilst the rest of the passengers hassled and queued. It was good to be in the coach, sipping hot coffee supplied by the driver, and remember the glory of the mountains and fjords, the sparkling waterfalls and the blue ice floating past the ship which carried us close to the top of the world.

And the Sun was Shining!

Betty Airlie's husband John has had two major heart operations and has arthritis in his spine. This means using a wheelchair whenever they leave home. In spring 1989 they joined a mini-cruise to Bergen from Newcastle.

Although I had never been to Norway, John had been there on a climbing holiday in his youth. Inspired by the stories of his visit, we studied the *Norway Line* (now *Color Line*) brochure. The mini-cruise sounded ideal: four days afloat,

accommodation in a two-berth cabin with its own shower and toilet, and – most important – the ship had a passenger lift between decks. All we had to do now was call *Norway Line* and ensure that the wheelchair was acceptable.

As it is difficult to handle a wheelchair and suitcases, we tend to travel light, and because this was to be such a short holiday it was easy to select just a few casual clothes; these and our toiletries fitted into a large holdall. A travel bag held tickets, binoculars, camera and medications. We also carried bottles of mineral water for use in the cabin. All these bits and pieces rested on John's knees, leaving my hands free to push the wheelchair.

As with many disabled people, our car is our main means of transport. At

Newcastle a local garage owner arranges, for a fee, to collect your car at the terminal and park it securely while you are on your cruise; he then has it restored to the terminal for your return. We found this a very happy arrangement, with no worries about the car while we were away. Details of the service are included in the *Color Line* brochure.

"Meals were a delightful experience, and we took full advantage"

Car disposed of, we were ready to start our holiday in earnest. The terminal is spacious, with adequate toilet facilities for the disabled. My dear husband suggested that I had earned a gin and tonic, so off I headed for the cafeteria. Sad to say, it was unlicensed, but we did have coffee, John's fortified with brandy from his hip flask.

It is quite a distance to travel by foot from the Newcastle terminal to the ship, but there is a courtesy wheelchair available for anyone with walking difficulties. A wheelchair is carried on board and could be used in Bergen. We had our own wheelchair, and I left John in the hands of two strong crewmen, who intended lifting him, in his wheelchair, up the gangway. Now John is quite a big man, and this feat proved too much for the two men. Instead, they pushed John, a very uncomfortable journey for him on account of the struts across the gangway (which are necessary for the safety of foot passengers). He was glad to be aboard at last.

Soon after we arrived on board, we were quickly taken in the passenger lift to our comfortable cabin, which was to be home for four days. Throughout that time, we were very well looked after by our charming, attentive Portuguese stewardess who kept the cabin spotlessly clean and supplied extra pillows for John without any fuss. We sailed on *MS Jupiter*, but from 1991 *MS Venus*

will be making the Newcastle–Bergen run; *MS Venus* has two cabins specially reserved for disabled passengers.

The passenger lift was easy to operate, and large enough to take the wheelchair without removing the footrests, but it was out of order twice during the cruise. On both occasions, crew members quickly and willingly came to our assistance, apologising for the breakdown and taking us to the desired deck by the service lift.

Meals were a delightful experience, and we took full advantage of the wide choice and high quality of foods. Evening meals were buffet-style – smorgasbord – and beautifully presented. I took John round the food table on our introduction to the dining room, so that he had an idea of all the goodies he could choose – hot and cold dishes of meats, fish and vegetables, tempting salads and gorgeous sweets. Choice was always difficult, but as we could return to the table as often as we wished we decided to opt for small and many courses. We never the left the dining room hungry! We were given a table where John could use his wheelchair yet not be in the way of other diners. Apart from the dining room, there was a well-supplied cafeteria, and coffee, tea and alcoholic drinks were always available in the two large lounges.

There was plenty to keep us entertained while at sea. We usually used the larger lounge, where there was dancing in the evening, ample seating and tables, and toilets nearby. A talented group of musicians played plenty of dance music, and even though not dancing we enjoyed the lively atmosphere; it was good to chat, over drinks and coffee, to our fellow holidaymakers. During the day this lounge, with its many windows, was an ideal place for John to watch the spectacular Norwegian coastline when we came in sight of land. For those with more mobility, the outside decks were the places to take in the scenery.

The sea was dotted with islands and the coastline pitted with inlets and small jetties. Our first port of call was Stavanger, where we stopped for thirty minutes on both outward and return journeys. The harbour is very close to the town, so we were able to admire the picturesque wooden houses from the ship. It looked very quaint, but I suspect too hilly for a wheelchair.

"Although we still love to travel, every holiday has to be carefully planned"

We found Bergen an interesting but expensive city. There was an early-morning coach tour laid on, but we opted to have a leisurely breakfast, then later, with the much-appreciated help of two fellow passengers, we ambled around at our own pace. John seldom lacked someone to talk to when I occasionally dashed off to scan the surrounding territory and find out where it was possible to take the wheelchair. As the ship was berthed very near the centre of Bergen, it was a pleasant stroll into town. The tall, ancient buildings of Bryggen, wooden, with very pointed gables, form the heart of the old town. We spent some time at the flower and fish markets on the quay; we were given generous samples of the most delicious smoked salmon and we could not resist bringing a sealed pack home.

Although Bergen is set between seven hills, it is an easy place to wander around as the city centre is reasonably flat and there is a pleasant park nearby. There is a funicular up Mount Fløyen which takes you to 320m above sea level; the view of the city is reported to be magnificent. We didn't attempt it with the wheelchair, as a fine view was to be had, both by day and by night,

from the deck of our ship. We were especially fascinated with the harbour area – so many different boats to see. And, to cap it all, instead of the customary persistent rain – for which Bergen is renowned, even in summer – the sun was shining. Indeed, we were fortunate that the weather was good and the sea calm throughout the cruise.

We were disappointed not to have time to visit some of the grand fjords. Many operators offer boat trips in the fjords in late spring and summer, and we look forward to taking a few of these on a longer cruise, when there is more time for excursions in port. Apart from this minor disappointment, the main problem we had on this cruise was using the gangway to get on and off the ship, especially if there were no crew members around to help. After our visit to Bergen we asked to be permitted to board via the car deck, which is reached by a ramp. Although the gangway in Bergen is on one level and covered (an improvement on Newcastle), it still has struts for passenger safety. Anyone with a wheelchair should arrange access by the car deck when booking their cruise. It means a longer walk but is definitely the easier and more comfortable way.

When our children left home, and we were both fit and healthy, John and I travelled to many countries in Europe. Now, although we still love to travel, every holiday has to be carefully planned: not only do I want John, who has to use a wheelchair most of the time, to enjoy it, but also I hope to make it a holiday for myself as well. Any break should be a holiday for both of us. The mini-cruise fulfilled all requirements, and we'd love to repeat this very pleasant and inexpensive break.

Working

Memories and Magic

Frankie Armstrong sings and runs voice workshops around the world, and occasionally tours with a theatre company. Her sight has been very gradually dwindling since 1957; at the time of writing she has little residual vision and uses a long cane to get about on her own. Frankie's work gives her great joy and satisfaction, so that her travels seem like one long, working holiday.

My travelling days began in 1973; before this I had holidayed with friends in Europe, but never travelled abroad on my own. It was not until my sight had reached the point that I needed help to cross busy streets, or to find my way around the Underground or train stations, that I realised it no longer mattered whether the traffic came from right or left, whether it was New York, San Francisco or London – it was no more or less difficult to get myself around.

I was invited to sing at the Philadelphia Folk Festival, one of the largest in North America, and I was lucky enough to be awarded a Ford Foundation grant to visit drug agencies around the United States: at the time I was the Coordinator of a day centre for drug addicts in south London, and there was great mutual interest in the different approaches to addiction and rehabilitation in the two countries. I arranged for several months' leave

from the centre, and began the now routine process of learning what can be packed in one rucksack to meet most, if not all, contingencies of weather and occasion.

Early one evening, in August 1973, I sat in the departure lounge at Heathrow, waiting for my plane for New York. Now I come to recall this event, I am amazed that eighteen years later I still entrust myself to airlines. I had been sat down in the lounge by a staff member but when, as far as I could make out, I was the only person left and take-off was less than five minutes away, my anxiety led me to find someone from the airline. She gave a little shriek of horror and immediately phoned through to the plane, which had closed its doors and, to my chagrin, obviously not missed me. This was my first valuable lesson: when in doubt, double check.

So I made my first solo flight with minutes to spare; I had to be put up in a hotel in Madrid overnight because of mechanical difficulties during the flight; I arrived in New York to find no one there to meet me and to witness a stand-up fight in the taxi queue at Kennedy airport. I've never had such a string of bad luck since, so I'm grateful I weathered the worst on my first trip and, while travelling has been far from trouble free, at least I am now better prepared.

In the end I spent nearly four months in the States on that visit. I crossed the country twice from coast to coast, and I did things that, looking back on them, seem courageous or crazy. I remember arriving in downtown Los Angeles at midnight off a *Greyhound* bus: I didn't know a soul; I asked the friendly bus driver to take me to a taxi; I asked the friendly cab driver to take me to a not-too-expensive hotel, and by 12.30am I was happily ensconced in the Mexican quarter in a hotel that I stayed in for a week, loving every minute of it.

"The sight of five colourfully dressed "cripples" caused amazement and curiosity"

I realise that something about my style of travelling has changed. I can recall talking to every person who sat next to me: on planes I met returned Vietnam vets, businessmen and women, children of five or six travelling on their own from coast to coast from parent to parent; on *Greyhound* buses there were lost young souls hoping to find themselves in a new life on the West Coast. I talked to strangers in cafés and absorbed at least some of the contradictions that make up the USA.

Now when I travel I look upon time in trains and planes as retreat time – no phones, no doorbell – and if I need to I can get down to some concentrated

work or reading (using library cassette tapes). This is partly a function of age and the amount of time I spend travelling. But I'm also aware of another factor: in any public space, alone with a white cane, one is very public. In some ways I'm grateful for this; I was brought up in the country, and I'm sure I'd have found London quite impossible had it not been for needing contact and help from people as I get around. However, as anyone with a visible handicap knows, it also means that you are "public property" and can be invaded by well-meaning (and sometimes not so well-meaning) strangers. I now feel the need to be more in control of these public encounters. I have learnt the art of assertively, not aggressively, presenting a "do not disturb" message to travelling companions when I want to create my own space.

During that first trip to the States I made friends with some wonderful people, including Ethel Raim who was to be the inspiration for beginning my own voice workshops. Initially, I ran workshops for friends and friends of friends, simply for the enjoyment and the fascination of experimenting with my own and others' voices. Soon I received invitations from Sweden, Denmark, Germany and Belgium, to run workshops for theatre companies, community arts festivals, folk song societies and schools.

I must admit to feeling less comfortable travelling on my own on trains in countries where my knowledge of the language extends to little more than asking for a cup of coffee or the way to the toilet. Train travel, even in the UK, is often more anxiety provoking than air travel. After all, in a plane you cannot step out of the door on the wrong side, or pass your stop because the guard failed to announce your destination. These are real fears, and when in addition I was not able to speak the language or see whether my eloquent sign language had borne fruit, I was always highly relieved to find myself at my desired destination, met by the organiser of the concert or workshop.

One of my most extraordinary trips was a tour of India with the *Graeae Theatre Company* in 1983. *Graeae* was set up as a professional company for actors with disabilities. I was asked to join a group of five actors to work with a very talented young theatre director to devise and perform a play around the issue of disability and societal attitudes towards disability, suited to an Indian audience. Nigel, the director, had spent many months travelling and studying in India, so with his help we improvised, wrote and rehearsed a piece which called upon our personal experiences and which used song, movement and magic as well as some more realistic scenes.

Two of the actors were completely wheelchair-bound; one was very small but only needed to use a wheelchair for long journeys; Jag (Indian by birth), a spastic, used crutches to walk; I made up the fifth member of the group. On the streets of Calcutta, Bombay and Delhi we created a greater theatrical impact than we ever could on stage. Most disabled people in India are either tucked away in institutions or are very visible – begging on the streets, where the aim is to make the disability as debilitating and pathos-creating as possible. The sight of five colourfully dressed "cripples" caused amazement and curiosity. We attracted crowds of Indians who had no sense of embarrassment about touching and staring at us at very close quarters. In a way it was wonderfully refreshing to experience this overt curiosity, rather than the pretence at politeness which may cover pity or even hostility in the West.

In addition to the performances in major theatre venues in the three cities we visited, we did a number of excerpts, workshops and mini-concerts in schools, day centres and employment centres for disabled people. Some of these I found quite distressing as they seemed antediluvian and even exploitative of the disabled, but I'm aware that as an outsider I may have formed the wrong impression. What I am sure about is the quality of some of the schools we visited, especially those run by the *Indian Spastics Society*. I have never before or since experienced such unsentimental love and creativity, or been filled with such hope and joy in an educational institute. The spastic children had little in the way of materials or technological equipment, but the inventiveness with which they used simple wooden sledges and scooters, and the physical freedom and energy with which they moved themselves around was both inspiring and moving.

"Through my cataract fog I could see the crimson sunset reflecting off the plain"

Nigel, Jag, Nabs and Jim all did conjuring tricks, often involving the children. Their delight and laughter is something I'll never forget. The children's energy of involvement in the little theatrical sketches which they had prepared for us leaves many a West End cast looking unexciting and unimaginative. They sang us songs, and I taught them all a Malvina Reynolds song (with actions), entitled "I've got a song". I have taught this song hundreds of times, but I doubt it will ever capture the warmth and vitality of those three or four occasions.

When I started my voice workshops I little imagined that one day I would receive a phone call from Australia, inviting me to run workshops there for several months. I must confess that I held a not altogether undeserved prejudice against Australian men; all those whom I had encountered in Europe seemed loud, crude, male chauvinist and generally fulfilled my stereotype of macho man. All the more ironic that I finished up marrying an Australian!

Since that first invitation I have become a regular visitor, and with resident status feel it to be my second home. I have enjoyed all the work I have done there but one of my most cherished memories is of a few days' real holiday spent in and around Kakadu, an area in the Northern Territory with many ancient Aboriginal sites. In the wet season, much of Kakadu lies under water, providing a glorious habitat for water birds and crocodiles. An Australian friend, Linsey, and I visited in October, before the build-up of the wet season was fully under way. Even then it was incredibly hot and humid; it reached over a hundred degrees by mid-morning, and I experienced prickly heat for the first and only time.

We left Darwin before sunrise and drove south through bush, eucalyptus and palm trees, stopping off at Jabaru, a uranium-mining town, for a cooling swim. The water was already the temperature of a warm bath, so, refreshing as it was, it was hardly cooling. We drove on, into the National Park, and found a perfect spot near the flood plains to set up camp and have a picnic lunch. The flood plains make up the area where the water has not totally receded, despite five months of drought.

The sounds were extraordinary: sea eagles and ibis were apparently among the throng, along with many that Linsey couldn't identify immediately; I heard the gentle whir of pelican wings as a flock flew overhead, the chattering of parrots, kingfishers squawking, and the evocative call of literally thousands of water birds, shimmering white in the sunlight so that even I could catch a glimmer of the sun glinting on their outstretched wings.

After lunch we went to one of the bizarre rock formations that are ancient sacred sites for the Aborigines. Happily, there are some signs that the criminal attitudes which have dominated white Australia's treatment of the original black inhabitants are changing; in Kakadu the Aboriginal elders decide which of their sites can be visited.

It is an awesome feeling, standing in the caves in front of rock paintings that reach back thousands of years, many thousands more than most European cultural sites. These paintings and carvings may go back 40,000 years, and until the invaders settled 200 years ago the Aboriginal cultures had flourished uninterrupted. Out there, hundreds of miles from any sizeable town, it was salutory to recall our alienation from our connection and interdependence with Nature. Here was a stillness, a sense of honouring what was and still is truly important for our physical and spiritual survival.

We saw hardly another soul all day and at dusk we were back at our campsite. Through my cataract fog I could see the crimson sunset reflecting off the plain. The bird sounds became more vociferous and insistent, as they do everywhere at dusk. Our fire lit up the pendulous peeling bark of the paper bark trees and, as darkness fell, with our meal completed and the fire dying down, there was a near-full moon glowing overhead. I am often asked how far I can see: "Over four hundred and eighty thousand miles, on a clear night lit by a full moon, but while looking at the moon I can easily walk into someone or something a foot in front of me."

That night was one of the most magical I have ever spent. We slept under a mosquito net, tents being unnecessary in the balmy temperatures. We could hear the snuffling of a wild buffalo from across the waters and, nearer at hand, smaller creatures, maybe wallabies. The moon danced through the trees, and I can recall falling asleep with a sense of gratitude. I hope this feeling, along with all the memories I've stored, will never desert me.

Sources of information

Automobile Association Travel Services, Fanum House, Basingstoke, Hants RG21 2EA; ☎0256/492004 (plus a nationwide network of *AA* shops). Recommended by David Bonnett for general advice, route planning and obtaining the necessary documents.

The British Motor Sports Association for the Disabled, PO Box 115, Aberdeen AB9 8RS; ☎0224/208338. Jack Davidson is Chairman; Mike Jackson is Vice President.

Tour operators

The aim of the *Jubilee Sailing Trust* (Test Road, Eastern Docks, Southampton SO1 1GG; ☎0703/631388, bookings 631395) is "for physically handicapped and able-bodied people to share the challenge of crewing a ship at sea". During the *STS Lord Nelson*'s first two seasons she carried 2000 crew members, half of whom were disabled people and, of those, 400 wheelchair users. For further information write to the Voyage Administrator.

Color Line (Tyne Commission Quay, North Shields NE29 6EA; ☎091/296 1313) advise that you discuss all your requirements before booking. The mini-cruise, or "4-day breakaway", costs from £59 per person (meals extra) and there's a 25 percent reduction for registered disabled passengers, plus free conveyance of car for members of the *DDMC* or *DDA*; departures are in May and June.

Contact *P&O Cruises* (77 New Oxford Street, London W1A 1PP; ☎071/831 1234) for details of *Princess Cruises, P&O Cruises* and *Swan Hellenic* tours and cruises. *P&O* appear to have well-established procedures for accommodating disabled passengers on board the *Canberra*, as well as for assisting them on and off the ship.

Cunard Line (30 Pall Mall, London SW1Y 5LS; ☎071/491 3930) will advise on the most suitable cabin aboard the *QE2*. Bill Robinson, who is 66 years old and has cerebral palsy, gave this verdict: "Apart from a coach trip, my cruise on the *QE2* was my first adventure alone. A friend gave me some holiday brochures and I went to *Pickfords* in Southampton to book a two-week cruise for November 1988, costing about £1400. They were very helpful at *Pickfords*. I booked a single cabin with no special features, where I managed very well using my wheeled walking frame.

The weather was gorgeous and I spent my days walking or sitting on deck, watching the other passengers. I liked sharing tables at mealtimes and met many different people. I enjoyed the food, although I heard others criticising it. The entertainment was very good; the Spanish evening was my favourite – everything was so colourful – and the African evening was lively and equally colourful. I also enjoyed meeting the ship's captain.

I made one trip ashore in West Africa, where I talked to people who described how they lived and showed me their doctor's surgery, which was in a shack. I believe the boat stopped in Portugal and I would have gone ashore more often, but I didn't feel adventuresome enough. I had no idea what to expect, so I wish someone had explained the trips carefully to me."

Holland America Line (UK sales agent: *Equity Cruises*, 77–79 Great Eastern Street, London EC2A 3HU; ☎071/729 1929) cruise the Caribbean, the Panama Canal, Mexico, the South Pacific and Alaska. Some Alaskan tours are tricky for wheelchair users, because of the transport used on shore, but otherwise this company seems to have an efficient, no-fuss approach to carrying disabled passengers. The brochure indicates which cabins are wheelchair accessible on the *MS Westerdam, MS Nieuw Amsterdam* and *MS Noordam*. In common with other cruise operators, anyone not self reliant must be accompanied, for safety reasons, and a form must be completed when booking.

Transport

For long journeys, involving many hours at a stretch on the move, the self-drive vehicle and the cruise ship with at least some accessible facilities probably offer the highest comfort levels. **Cars** can be fitted with hand controls, the seats adjusted and equipment and luggage arranged for easy access. On big **cruise ships**, larger ferries and specially adapted sailing

TOURS & CRUISES: TRAVEL NOTES

vessels such as the *Lord Nelson*, there are no problems in moving between decks, visiting the toilet or settling into a comfortable seat. On many ships, storm-sills and steps will make it difficult to move rapidly around the vessel in a wheelchair, but there are usually plenty of fit sailors to lend a hand.

Aircraft, large or small, provide a good service on short trips but seating is usually cramped and toilets are too small to make long hauls enjoyable. Getting on and off trains and buses is difficult for the majority of travellers with limited mobility, and impossible for most without help, except on a few accessible networks.

Nic Fleming, a paraplegic government scientist with many years' experience of mainly work-related travel, has used almost every form of transport imaginable, from helicopters to submarines. He finds it preferable to get out of his chair in a road vehicle, or a train for that matter, and sit in a big, comfortable seat with padded cushions, armrests and high back-rest:

"Such seats are made to support and restrain the passenger during corners, bumps and normal swaying or juddering. A wheelchair does not support you in this way, and is much more tiring. Transport authorities should understand that for many (although I am sure not all) disabled passengers it is better to get out of their chairs. Passengers should be given the choice, but often they are not."

Accommodation

It is impractical to set rigid itineraries on long tours – there are too many unknowns – and the task of ascertaining in advance the accessibility of likely stopping places, particularly when you plan to spend only a night or two in each, will probably seem too much like hard work. Of course, if every hotel directory and every tourist accommodation brochure contained reliable access information, this task would be simple. Instead, it is time-consuming and frustrating. Nic Fleming does not even attempt it:

"On trips across Europe I have stopped at **hotels** on spec with few problems. The hotel staff are almost always completely untroubled by the arrival of a customer in a wheelchair. I assure them that any potential problems are

easily solvable, and they are happy to believe it. The porter or other staff are usually pleased to help with the odd step. Lifts are sometimes too narrow, but Madame the concierge will find a small chair, onto which I can transfer and pull my folded wheelchair in beside me. Bathroom doors are often too narrow, but these can also be negotiated by transferring to a small, straight-backed kitchen or desk chair.

It may seem cavalier not to research visits to hotels more thoroughly. People who do not have strong arms could not use the chair-transfer, and would have to make more careful preparations. My reasoning is that all obstacles can be overcome on the spot in a matter of minutes. Once staff see that solutions are easily found, they stop worrying.

If you try to sort out all potential problems in advance, the time and worry is much greater for everyone. The staff have to count steps and measure doors, lifts and bathroom dimensions, then report back by phone or letter. Are there two steps or three to the dining room? Does it matter? Are there steps at the hotel entrance, and a revolving door? Does it matter? By the time these points have been checked, everyone is jittery and anxious, and you still find that the car park is 50m away, down ten steps, which nobody thought of.

If you are stopping in a different hotel every night, and passing through four countries in ten days, the labour of investigating all these access details for each hotel for one night would be ludicrous. In my experience, every hotel from Stavanger to Suva, from Pammukkale to Palermo, can cheerfully accommodate a wheelchair traveller after two minutes' thought on the spot. The biggest and most expensive hotels have wide doors, big bathrooms, smooth marble floors and huge lifts; the smallest hotels in remote mountain villages or tropical islands have strong friendly staff who will carry you upstairs. It all works out.

On serious business travel, or if you are passing through a city at fiesta time, it is essential to book in advance to ensure that you have accommodation close to your place of work, or to ensure that you have a room at all. I never warn the hotel staff that I am disabled. It is more

TOURS & CRUISES: TRAVEL NOTES

important to have a good, efficient hotel, at the right price, a few minutes from where you are working in a foreign city (or from the sights you want to explore) than a hotel with no steps at the entrance half an hour away by taxi. In more than twenty years of travel I have never been completely stumped, although on occasion I have had to look at two or three rooms before finding a convenient one."

For those who can manage chair-to-floor transfers, and cope with the physical demands of erecting the tent or lugging equipment around, **camping** provides the cheapest form of accommodation and for a long trip this is an important consideration. Lists of accessible sites in Britain, France, Germany and Switzerland are available to members of *Camping for the Disabled* (20 Burton Close, Dawley, Telford, Shropshire TF4 2BX); there's advice on suitable sites in other countries too. Other sources include tourist board guides (such as Sweden's *Holiday Guide for the Disabled*) and *Michelin* guides.

A camper van or caravan make life easier, but all forms of camping, from sleeping on the ground under the stars to towing a luxury caravan, can be made accessible — by vehicle adaptations (p.14), by carrying a small folding camp-stool for use in the showers (p.349), by using a gym stool on castors for manoeuvring inside a caravan (p.177).

Nic Fleming advises that a light, military folding bed, or a foam-rubber mattress, provides ample padding for the somewhat sensitive skin of a paraplegic. The biggest problem when camping is lavatory equipment — you need some sort of stool or chair to sit on in private. It is not difficult to adapt a folding camp-chair, with a light metal frame, into a personal "portaloo".

Nic finds the greatest pleasure in keeping equipment to a minimum: "Field projects involving dives close to the coast in remote areas require teams who are prepared to sleep out for weeks at a time. In Crete we had been living out for a month or more when the opportunity came to visit the uninhabited island of Kuphonisi, where I wanted to see an ancient Phoenician city. The fishermen at Ierapetra said that they were not officially allowed to carry

passengers, but if we went to a rocky headland a few miles along the coast, they would pick us up and take us to Kuphonisi where they would be fishing all night.

We waited on the rocks in the evening light, and I took on board just my foam rubber bed-roll, my notebooks and a washbag containing the essential medical bits and pieces. There was an incredible feeling of lightness. Leaving the world behind. We slept on the beach of Kuphonisi, explored the city the next day, and returned. It was a liberation."

Access and facilities

The more conventional trips — by car or train or large ship — posed no insurmountable problems. Two travellers were able to drive around Europe without booking accommodation in advance, although a little patience and persistence were necessary at times. Access to the tourist sights was obtained — sometimes with difficulty, aided by other holidaymakers, and occasionally via the back door, but nothing was out of bounds.

The contributors who took to the sea were pleased with the facilities on board their vessels. There is room for improvement in the arrangements for including disabled passengers in plans for shore excursions, and in making all amenities on board easily accessible, but good progress has been made by some shipping companies.

When contemplating holidays which are more accurately described as "expeditions", over rough terrain, perhaps in remote areas and with inhospitable climate, it is easy to make assumptions about accessibility and rule out ideas which are, in reality, possible. More advice from Nic Fleming, who has encountered fairly rugged conditions on oceanographic projects:

"Much of my work is in rough terrain, away from roads, and on rocks or sandy beaches. Sometimes we have to ford rivers, traverse mountain paths, or get through thick scrub. Backwheel balance (see *Practicalities*, "Health and Comfort") gives the basic mobility in rough terrain and on steep slopes or irregular rocky surfaces. This can be handled solo. Deep sand and shingle almost always require help. It can be OK going down a beach on backwheel

TOURS & CRUISES: TRAVEL NOTES

balance, but coming up again is almost impossible. River beds and cobbles need assistance; it is best to turn the chair backwards and have one or, preferably, two people simply tow you through the rough spots.

Steep mountain paths can only be traversed safely with assistance. Sometimes a track is navigable for a while, and then gets narrow just for a few metres, and you would certainly tumble sideways down the hillside if you tried it alone. Impassable ground can be dealt with by climbing onto a man's shoulders: in Crete I reached some important archaeological cuttings on the edge of a cliff after being carried along the cliff edge on a friend's shoulders, while another man carried the chair; in Cuba I was able to explore some stalactitic caves for an hour or more, carried aloft on the shoulders of a man of colossal strength.

Another invaluable manoeuvre for the paraplegic travelling rough is the chair-to-floor transfer (see *Practicalities*, "Health and Comfort"). You can use it to get down onto the deck of a small boat in which you would be unstable if you remained sitting high in your chair. You can use it get down onto the dock or bank, and then into a canoe, or to sleep on the ground when camping."

Health and insurance

Remember that as you travel further from "civilisation" – hospitals, pharmacists and so on – your first-aid kit must become more substantial and there are some extra precautions to be taken before you leave (see *Practicalities*, "Health and Comfort"). If your expedition involves any activity that could be classed as dangerous by the insurance companies, make sure your policy covers you. Check also that your 24-hour emergency medical service will cope with all eventualities.

Books

Richard Dawood's *Travellers' Health* (OUP, £5.95) is not only invaluable in itself, but also includes a useful Further Reading list.

The Rough Guide to West Africa includes some thoughts on crossing the Sahara.

A Book of Travellers' Tales, by Eric Newby (Picador, £5.95) contains some inspirational, if rather short, accounts from travellers great and small.

And to take with you, *Into the Heart of Borneo*, by Redmond O'Hanlon (Penguin, £4.99) – better to laugh at someone else's misfortunes than get bogged down in your own.

PART TEN

PRACTICALITIES

Planning

The preceding accounts show that, over the last few years, worldwide travel for handicapped people was certainly possible, if not always trouble free. One of the biggest problems for the 1990s is to ensure that access information – on all aspects of the holiday – is current, accurate and readily available. It is a daunting task to keep this information bang up to date, and most of the organisations that seriously attempt it are charities, with limited resources, so be prepared to verify details yourself. The **addresses** of organisations listed in the following sections are, where not given, listed at the end.

RESEARCH

The following organisations are all good places to start.

Holiday Care Service has ten years' experience in dealing with queries concerning holidays in the UK and abroad (mainly Europe or the USA but will have a go at anything) – independent holidays using all types of accommodation, package holidays run by commercial operators and voluntary organisations, activity and special interest holidays. The information and advice is free to anyone who needs help to find a holiday, finance it and plan it. Some 250 fact sheets are produced and updated yearly.

Mobility International (*MI*), a non-profit, non-governmental youth organisation, was set up in 1974 to offer travel experiences which promote the integration of disabled and non-disabled people. The emphasis has shifted slightly, to include the "empowerment" of disabled people, with integration optional. *MI* members include umbrella regional or disability-specific organisations in Europe, the USA, the Soviet Union, Africa and India, and some of these are useful contacts when planning a trip or when in difficulty abroad; where relevant they are mentioned in the *Travel Notes* of the appropriate country. *MI News* is the quarterly newsletter, and it will keep you up to date with some of the new developments on the travel scene.

RADAR (*The Royal Association for Disability and Rehabilitation*) offers an information service as well as producing annual holiday guides (see *Books*) and fact sheets – a good starting point for the inexperienced traveller, providing an overview of what's available, plenty of solid advice and reams of useful addresses. In addition, *RADAR* distributes transport and access guides; an access officer helps with queries about areas not covered by these guides.

TRIPSCOPE is a telephone-based travel and transport information and advice service, designed specifically to help disabled and elderly people, as well as those who care for them and organisations acting on their behalf. The service is free (they will even phone you back immediately to save your phone bill) and available nationwide. *TRIPSCOPE* is neither a travel agency nor a booking agency, but it does provide all the information necessary for individuals, families or large groups undertaking local, long-distance or international journeys.

OTHER SOURCES OF INFORMATION

Many **disability groups** gather and distribute information on holidays and transport, as well as organising holidays or managing accommodation. Although not comprehensive, these sources are well worth investigating, not least because the information gathered will be pertinent to your own disability. *MENCAP*, for example, publishes *The MENCAP Holiday Guide* to accommodation where mentally handicapped people are welcome.

Tourist boards vary widely in what they have to offer the disabled traveller. The Swedish and Danish tourist boards produce well researched, regularly updated, clearly presented guides, and their staff are helpful. The *Israeli Tourist Board* freely distributes the excellent *Access in Israel* (see Israel *Travel Notes*). Some (Austria, Finland, Netherlands, Switzerland) use the wheelchair symbol in their accommodation guides and/or offer a small booklet or fact sheet for disabled visitors. Some (Australia, Britain, Canada, France, USA) rely heavily either on organisations for the disabled within their own country, or on regional tourist offices, to supply information. Many produce absolutely no literature, and their staff look (or sound) blank when asked.

It is important to be **persistent** when phoning tourist boards: if you know there is a brochure for disabled visitors, insist that it is available (quote your source); it is not uncommon to be told at first that there is no such publication. You may also be assured that there is only one copy left – so ask them to photocopy it for you. They rarely run out of the general brochures; why should disabled enquirers be deprived of literature aimed at them?

As an example of the prevailing attitude among tourist boards, at the **1990 World Travel Market**, Olympia, London, only the *New Zealand Tourist Board* exhibited its access guide along with the glossy brochures. Staff from US state tourist boards, some (but by no means all) UK regional boards, the Swedes and a few others had something intelligent to say on the subject: on the Colorado stand, "Do you know of the disabled skiing program at Winter Park Resort?"; in the Wyoming adventure package brochure, half a page devoted to some interesting "handicapped programs"; full attention paid to disabled access in the West Oxfordshire accommodation, eating and drinking guide; on the Welsh stand, well advertised facilities for disabled visitors at the 1992 Ebbw Vale Garden Festival; the Swedes and Danes had run out of their holiday guides for disabled visitors – who says there's no demand for this stuff?

Staff on other stands were bewildered, apologetic or stroppy when questioned; they offered the standard information packs, determined that no one should go away empty-handed. Similar reactions came from representatives of tour operators, travel agents, airlines, hotel chains, car hire companies, coach operators and rail companies. Some notable exceptions are mentioned below, but too many people in the travel trade remain ignorant of – or perhaps indifferent to – the needs of a large (around fifty million in Europe), potentially lucrative group of holidaymakers.

The standard **brochures** do have some use, in that they are usually lavishly illustrated. Pictures can provide clues about the terrain if your destination is unfamiliar. A visit to the travel section of your local **library** will serve the same purpose: pre-holiday reading not only means that costly (and sometimes overcrowded) sightseeing tours can be avoided, it also gives you a preview of the area to be visited.

As well as the coffee-table picture books there are a handful of publications with travel information for disabled people which should be available in the library (see *Books*). The sixth edition of the *Directory for Disabled People* is scheduled for mid-1991 publication and contains several relevant sections. The *Department of Transport*'s guide, *Door to Door*, is another useful reference book.

FINANCIAL HELP

The cost of taking a holiday is prohibitive to many people, but it should be possible to obtain assistance. Our contributors suggest a variety of **cost-cutting exercises** (travelling out of season, booking six months in advance, sharing taxis for sightseeing, eating out at lunchtime rather than evening, or self-catering) as well as offering some thoughts on **saving or raising the money** once you've pared down the overall price – "bread and only a little jam" for the rest of the year (Betty Parkin, p.493), "try auctioning something that you can live without" (Jill Rann, p.4) . . .

Of the more conventional methods, first stop is your local **Social Services Department**, to which any disabled person or family of a disabled person may apply. If you get no joy there, try your own **disability organisation** (either national or local level), then local branches of the *Round Table*, *Rotary Club* or *Lions Club*, and the *Red Cross* or *Age Concern*. Consult *RADAR* and ask for their *Holiday Finance* fact sheet, which lists trusts and benevolent funds likely to help out, or ask the *Holiday Care Service*, who will research sources of finance for you.

The *Handicapped Aid Trust* is a small, independent charity providing grants to ease the expense of travelling with a **holiday helper/companion**. This is an important contribution – paying for a helper is a limiting factor for many disabled people who do not wish to travel with a group but are unable to travel alone. Anyone over the age of 17, with any form of disability, may approach the trust. Application forms are considered twice a year, by a committee of about six or seven members, and the size of grant is set according to funds available and individual circumstances, including the type of holiday and the destination. Closing date for summer holidays is February 1, for winter holidays August 1.

On **group holidays**, run by such organisations as *Project Phoenix Trust* or *Disaway*, there is often some provision made for those who are unable to meet the full cost of the trip. It is always worth asking, even it if goes against the grain.

The *Family Holiday Association* is the only national charity which specialises in making grants to enable **severely deprived families**, many with handicapped children, who have rarely, if ever, had a holiday, to take a week's break together. In 1990 the average grant for a family of four was £365; during Holiday Aid Week '90 the travel industry raised £100,000 and donated a number of free or discounted holidays. They hope to better this figure in Holiday Aid Week '91 (July 1–7).

Working along similar lines, the second-year pilot of the *Tourism for All Holiday Scheme* took place in 1990: 200 holidays for people on low incomes from Bristol and Birmingham were provided in the West Country. The scheme is proving successful and will continue – more details from the *Holiday Care Service*.

JOLT (*The Journey of a Lifetime Trust*) is a charity offering travel opportunities to disabled or disadvantaged **youngsters** (aged 14–19). The first expedition was in 1984 to Siberia and Mongolia, the next in 1986 across the Australian outback; in 1988 a group travelled through South America and in 1990 the destination was Africa. These are exciting and challenging adventures, with clear benefits for the youngsters, and the trust receives many applications for a limited number of places on each trip. The costs of such travels are high, but are met with help from the travel trade, usually involving services given free, plus donations; the youngsters themselves are asked to make a small contribution by fund raising.

Those whose travel plans are ambitious, long term, and perhaps involve work which will benefit others (for example, Roger Elliott's participation in Operation Raleigh, p.362), may consider seeking **sponsorship**. This requires a bit of lateral thinking – to find a link between some aspect of your trip and the sponsor, and an opening for the sponsor to promote his or her services or products. Mention the trip to everyone you know, use every available contact, and gather as many ideas as possible. Write *brief* applications, describe your project with enthusiasm, and be specific about what you need – equipment, fares, supplies.

Booking

Whether you go to a travel agent or book through the tour operator, you will probably find that you need to take the initiative in stating your needs and making sure that they are met: most are non-specialists, who deal with disabled clients only as and when they appear. Few companies give staff any training for basic skills such as communication with deaf or speech-impaired people, passing on clients' requirements to airlines or hotels, and understanding the mysteries of airline medical forms – which clients need to give only handling advice, which must supply medical details. This doesn't mean that they all fail to make adequate arrangements – many contributors report faultless service – but some certainly do.

TRAVEL AGENTS

Of the non-specialist **travel agents**, we've received good reports of *Austravel*, *Bath Travel Service*, *W.H. Smith*, *Trailfinders* and *Travelbag*.

Several small, local agents were praised by contributors, so perhaps the best general advice is to experiment in your own area until you find one who is efficient, sympathetic to your needs, willing to help with researching such things as the nature of the terrain and accessibility of hotels, and meticulous about informing all who *should* be informed of your travel plans.

Thomas Cook have set up *Charitylink*, through which you can book a holiday from any of the brochures in *Thomas Cook* branches, and have the choice of taking a discount or making a donation to a human charity of your choice. The discount/donation is disappointingly small, starting at £15 for a total holiday cost of £500–749, and going up to £150 for a £5000 holiday. Not surprisingly, the response so far has been low.

The more interesting side to this operation is still at a very early stage: *Thomas Cook* already store some basic hotel access information, and they are working with tour operators, airlines, car hire and ferry companies, hotels and others in the travel business, with the eventual aim of providing an advice service for disabled customers. This will include information on getting to the airport, transfers to resorts and accessibility of accommodation. But there is no scheduled date for the introduction of the advice service.

SPECIALIST TOUR OPERATORS

Specialist tour operators, most offering holidays for physically handicapped people, fall into two categories: commercial companies and voluntary organisations. The majority of contributors booked holidays with non-specialist operators. There are a number of possible explanations for this, and the tale of *Accessible Travels* illustrates two of them.

A joint venture between *Blue Riband Holidays* of Birmingham and *Viajes 2000* in Spain, **Accessible Travels** was set up in 1990 to offer a range of accessible hotels and apartments in mainland Spain, Mallorca, Tenerife and Gran Canaria for accompanied disabled holidaymakers.

All the accommodation was inspected in 1989 by twenty trained researchers, working under a medical specialist and backed by the Spanish care foundation, *ONCE*; a fact sheet was prepared for each property, with notes on resort accessibility, potential problems, measurements and detailed descriptions of the accommodation. Transfers and sightseeing trips were to be by adapted minibus wherever possible, and adapted hire cars were available. Flights from half a dozen UK airports meant that the chances of leaving from a local airport were good.

After a good response in terms of requests for the brochure, actual bookings were very low. Manager John Bradley found that there were two main reasons for this: many people mistakenly thought that they would be travelling with groups of other disabled people and were put off by that; and the price of all this special treatment was at least £100 more, per person, than a similar holiday booked through one of the big tour operators.

Contracting specific rooms, suitable for handicapped guests, apparently costs more than a general contract between tour operator and hotelier. It is also more expensive to provide a small, adapted vehicle for transfers or sightseeing than a seventy-seater coach (of course, if all coaches were wheelchair accessible this problem would not arise). But not every disabled person requires a fully adapted room or is unable to board a coach, and it seems unfair for those people to

pay for something they do not need. Not even the assurance that all their special requests would be granted persuaded people to book.

All the adapted vehicles are still in place and the approved accommodation available but *Accessible Travels* is now operating in modified form, on two fronts: you can inspect the 1990 brochure and fact sheets, ignoring the prices, and let the operator know your individual requirements, after which a price is quoted; alternatively, you can go to a travel agent, who will access the data concerning those properties which are included in the *Blue Riband* brochure; you can then book your holiday accordingly and obtain hard copies of the stored information. A big plus for this system is that the information is updated by a full-time inspector, employed by *Viajes 2000* in Spain.

The apparent lack of enthusiasm for what was, on the surface, carefully planned holiday provision, is probably also the reflection of a general desire to **participate in mainstream tourism**, to be catered for there rather than be segregated, forced to make "special arrangements" and – to cap it all – pay dearly for the privilege. Antipathy towards the "cotton wool treatment" has been expressed by many disabled travellers who feel that an accessible transfer vehicle should be part of the service, not a luxury item for which they must pay a supplement.

While those involved in mainstream tourism are being persuaded to work toward this goal, the specialist commercial tour operator may be the answer for some – perhaps those who have not travelled before, or those who are unwilling to ask for special treatment on a holiday not designed for disabled people, or those who prefer to feel confident that all their requests will be understood and taken care of.

Of course, this confidence may be misplaced, in which case it is galling to have paid over the odds, as Maxine Smith discovered when she travelled, fairly disastrously, to Egypt (p.252) with *Threshold Travel*, Manchester. This company ceased trading in November 1988 with a less than distinguished track record. Philip Wright (who is a wheelchair user) took over the *Threshold* tag and a comprehensive mailing list, and set up a completely new operation in County Down, Northern Ireland. He kept the name because despite its rather tatty image it still meant accessible holidays to most disabled people. The new company teamed up with *Virgin*

Holidays, selecting and adapting appropriate packages from their existing brochures, *keeping prices the same*, and they are doing well (see p.514).

VOLUNTARY ORGANISATIONS

The **specialist voluntary organisations** fare better in the opinion polls than the commercial companies. Several contributors (holiday helpers as well as disabled travellers) booked very successful holidays with these organisations, all of which have developed interesting programmes and well-thought-out facilities; in addition they seem to put the holidaymaker first and his or her wallet last, keeping the costs down as well as subsidising in cases of hardship. The charities below were all set up to provide holidays for disabled people; *RADAR* and the *Holiday Care Service* will offer more ideas.

On some trips you are on your own in a group of disabled people (plus helpers); this may not suit everyone but there are advantages, not least to severely disabled people who may otherwise be unable to take a holiday. *Help the Handicapped Holiday Fund, Holidays for the Disabled, Young Disabled on Holiday* and the *Les Evans Fund for Sick and Handicapped Children* offer a selection of holidays in the UK and abroad. *Winged Fellowship* (p.7) pack an astonishing amount into their trips, enabling quite severely physically handicapped people to reach places that would probably be inaccessible without the *Winged Fellowship* team of helpers. *Project Phoenix Trust* (p.207) provides some fascinating study tours for anyone who needs some sort of physical assistance. The *Uphill Ski Club* trips are physically challenging and their programme is unusual in that it includes mixed groups of mentally and physically handicapped skiers (p.189).

Other organisations take disabled person plus family or friends, or a random mixture of able-bodied and disabled. *Disaway* holidays (p.113) are for groups of physically disabled people and volunteer helpers are supplied, but group members may take their own helper/friend if they wish. The *Jubilee Sailing Trust* accepts disabled and able-bodied crew members on its voyages, so you can apply with friends or members of your own family (p.490). *PHAB* (*Physically Handicapped and Able Bodied*) organises holidays, mainly in the UK, for people of all ages, with and without disabilities.

NON-SPECIALIST OPERATORS

The number of **non-specialist tour operators** that claim to cater for disabled travellers is increasing and it is difficult to single out any for unqualified praise. It is becoming much more common to see some mention of clients with "special needs" in the brochure, usually with a request that these people phone for further information about the resorts and accommodation, and discuss their requirements when booking. There are also some wheelchair symbols creeping onto the glossy pages: *Hoseasons Holidays*, for example, use two symbols – one to indicate properties that have been adapted for wheelchairs, and one to show that facilities are not suitable for full-time wheelchair users.

This is a welcome beginning, but we are still a long way from widespread availability of *reliable* information. There are too many stories of fruitless phone calls, being passed from one department to another until satisfactory answers are obtained. Even then, disappointment may follow, and assurances that accommodation is accessible evaporate on arrival at the hotel entrance. Against this background of broken promises it is refreshing to see in the *Yugotours* (summer 1991) brochure the statement, "There are unfortunately no hotels suitable for clients in wheelchairs, only some hotels which are less unsuitable"!

Many tour operators make what can only be described as a **token effort** to accommodate disabled clients: staff are flummoxed when asked the simplest questions about resorts in their brochures, although the standard paragraph for less mobile holidaymakers assures us that help is only a phone call away. What is needed is to research, verify, store and update details of resort and accommodation facilities and access, to consider the accessibility of transfer vehicles from airport to hotel – in short, to anticipate the needs of all travellers.

Ideally, this information should be included in the main brochure; if limited space is the excuse, then a supplement for disabled clients should be available. ***Country Holidays*** is a model example: in addition to their main brochure, they produce a second brochure, *Holidays for Disabled People*, which contains a selection of cottages suitable for holidaymakers with disabilities – more than forty suitable for wheelchair users and a further 300 for those with greater mobility.

The wheelchair symbol in the brochure indicates that there are no stairs or internal steps and that the property has been successfully used in the past by handicapped visitors who needed wheelchairs. There is a detailed description of each property and if you cannot find one which meets all your requirements you are invited to phone the "Disabled Person's Helpline"; by asking a lot of questions the staff will endeavour to find the perfect cottage for you.

Relying exclusively on endless phone calls when trying to find a suitable holiday is both unsatisfactory and expensive for the client. *Thomson Tour Operations* have responded to this by replacing their "Care Line" with **Factfile** which is a computerised information service accessible to all travel agents who can book with *Thomson* companies (*Thomson Holidays, Horizon, Skytours, Wings, HCI* and *OSL*). The service is used by non-disabled clients, too, if they require more detail than that provided in the brochure.

There are four pages of information on every hotel and apartment in the brochure, one of which is aimed at less mobile clients. The information is gathered via a questionnaire (covering general suitability, surrounding area including access to beach and town centre, steps at entrance and within the hotel, approximate door widths to entrance, lift, bedroom, bathroom and balcony, and details of any other relevant facilities, such as grab-rails and availability of ground-floor rooms) which is sent out to the *Thomson* reps in the resorts. The only cause for concern is that the questionnaire may be filled in by hotelier or rep – hoteliers are not renowned for their accuracy in these matters, so it would be more reassuring if reps were given training and took responsibility for completing the questionnaire themselves.

Virgin Holidays have dealt with the problem by joining forces with a specialist tour company for disabled people, *Threshold* (see p.512). Using a small selection of accommodation in the existing *Virgin* brochures, a "fly-drive" holiday programme has been drawn up specifically for disabled holidaymakers, using adapted hire cars. These holidays are no more expensive than the standard *Virgin* packages, and the flight is non-stop on a Boeing 747 with aisle wheelchair.

Virgin Holidays was one of the first operators to adopt the *Tourism for All* Model Policy Statement (see p.141) and they must have got something right – by November 1990 *Virgin/Threshold* had surpassed their 1990 bookings figure even before the 1991 brochure was published. New for 1991 are fully accessible "Fly Cruises" and "Two Centre Cruises", a result of teaming up with *Norwegian Cruise Line*.

ADVENTURES AND CRUISES

Some **adventure holiday** operators accept people with disabilities, but not many have the imagination, resources and the will to say yes; it's about time these operators woke up to the fact that disabled people might like a challenge too (see *Tours and Cruises*). Since broken promises might be worse than inconvenient when struggling up the Amazon, it's probably best to select an operator with some experience of taking disabled clients on its tours, or one who is keen to try – waste no time on negative thinkers.

One company which has made efforts in this field is *Safari Interlink*. In July 1990, giving their services free of charge, they put together a tour of Zimbabwe and Botswana for *JOLT* (p.511). For the five-week Zimbabwe/Botswana tour the group consisted of twelve British and six Zimbabwean youngsters, one blind, one with hearing difficulties, some who had suffered physical, sexual or mental abuse, many using wheelchairs or crutches, and four adults.

The report of the trip shows what can be done, including a rail safari, reaching the Victoria Falls and camping beside the Linyati river, sailing the length of Lake Kariba by ferry, climbing to the top of the Acropolis of the Great Zimbabwean ruins. It also lists some of the highlights: Mark, completely blind, cuddling a lion cub at the Chipingali Wildlife Orphanage; showers under the stars from a billy can tied to a tree; a 45-minute walk, pulling the wheelchairs through the sand, when the bush-bus broke down, was "a great adventure".

A few **cruise operators** seem to be responding to the needs of mobility-impaired travellers, with new ships being built to higher standards of accessibility. *Holland America Line* even marks cabins for handicapped passengers on the deck plans in its brochure. However, what the cruise line deems suitable for handicapped people may be a long way off meeting your requirements. As with hotels, then, if you want to be sure of accessibility before setting off, you must ask lots of questions, not forgetting height of storm-sills. This throws up all the problems mentioned above (whom do you ask, can you rely on the accuracy of the answers, and why has no one thought of including in the brochure a small plan of the handicapped cabin(s), with all relevant measurements clearly marked?). As a last resort (but well in advance of your cruise) you could perhaps make the journey to inspect the ship.

As a safety precaution, most operators insist that passengers who are unable to walk unaided up the gangway are accompanied by an able-bodied companion. Thoughts of disabled passengers seem to stop at the gangway, however, so that, again for safety reasons, if the ship cannot berth (as happens in small ports) wheelchair users may not be allowed to attempt the transfer from cruise ship to launch — usually by ladder or steps. Sometimes, crew members will carry disabled passengers down to the waiting launch — again, more questions necessary.

Shore excursions will be tricky for some, usually because of the transport used; it's probably best to be independent once off the ship. Then there are the on-board activities to consider: can you reach all the public rooms? What about the cinemas? Can you use the swimming pool? It seems crazy to provide cabins for disabled passengers and then allow access to only some of the entertainment and leisure facilities, but it happens.

GOING IT ALONE

Choice of **independent versus package** and **group versus solo** travel is very much a personal thing. The attractions and disadvantages of each are discussed throughout the accounts and there is no clear winner as far as providing the formula for a successful holiday is concerned. Perhaps the only guideline is that the travel plans should first fit in with your interests, tastes and pocket, then if necessary be adapted to suit your accessibility requirements, rather than the alternative scenario in which you have to compromise to suit the demands of the holiday.

Of course there are times when compromise is appropriate: the flexibility necessary when taking part in a **group holiday for disabled people** is best described by Joan Cooper (p.7) and Charlotte Billington (p.207). Having to go along with group decisions, keeping up with a tough schedule, and getting on with complete strangers for two weeks might cause problems, but the advantages of these holidays are also clear — plenty of helpers to negotiate steps and difficult terrain, often the opportunity to learn something more than the average tourist, and the chance to make new friends.

The joys of the **organised tour group** (with no special arrangements for disabled people) are expounded by Betty Layton (pp.257, 335), the compromises by Daphne Pagnamenta (p.290). Christine Panton (p.414) and Robin Reeley (p.295) successfully combined organised tour with some individual travel. If you accept that you may not be able to participate in every activity on the tour, it is generally possible to join these groups, although some operators may be wary, especially of older travellers, if conditions are rough in the countries to be visited. For example, Daphne Pagnamenta was refused by several companies when looking for a holiday in India.

One big advantage of the inclusive tour is that the use of charter flights, contracts with local guides and transfer vehicle companies, and group discounts at hotels enables the tour operator to offer competitive prices. The advantage will be lost if you cannot find a tour that suits you in every respect, and this is not unlikely if you have some form of disability. If you want to tinker with the itinerary or make changes to any part of the package you will have to pay for it — tailor-made holidays cost more than off-the-peg ones.

If you require assistance on holiday but don't fancy a group holiday, you should be able to find a helper (see "Holiday helpers", below). Peter Stone (p.25) and Stephen Hunt (p.37) **travel solo** this way; you may also prefer to do your own reading about the sights and see them at your own pace by taxi, rather than be herded along on organised tours. If you'd rather see the sights on a guided tour, lack of mobility doesn't have to be a barrier, but discuss your abilities with the tour leader first.

A number of contributors booked standard **package holidays** without experiencing insurmountable problems. Philippa Thomas (p.199), Eric Leary (p.185), Theodora Hampton (p.32) and Ivy Geach (p.266) were well satisfied with their trips; Mairene Gordon (p.167), Rosalind May (p.21) and Enid Jasper (p.88) less so with theirs. Muriel Smith (p.51) makes a direct comparison between a *Saga* holiday in Yugoslavia and her later independent travels there, coming down clearly in favour of independence.

Muriel Smith is not alone — many contributors made their own travel arrangements: some used a travel agent to book flights only, finding accommodation (David Gray, p.374; Arthur Goldthorpe, p.403; Andrew Healey, p.348) or taking part in organised projects (Roger Elliott, p.362; Kate Margrie, p.270) on arrival; some made direct bookings with hotels (Barry Atkinson, p.82; Beryl Bristow, p.178); some took off in their car and found hotels or campsites along the way (Roderick MacDonald, p.482; Michael Turner, p.487; Enid Fisher, p.170).

These are only a few examples. The immense satisfaction to be had from masterminding your own trip is a major theme of this book. And if off-the-peg holidays cost less than tailor-made packages, do-it-yourself can be even cheaper.

Insurance

It is essential to be adequately insured, not only to cover the cost of medical treatment, but also because being in a wheelchair, or having some other visible disability, is no protection against petty thieving (p.38) or simple loss of your luggage. An adequate policy does not exclude people with a "pre-existing medical condition", offers medical expenses appropriate to the country visited, and preferably has no age loadings.

Check with the insurance company regarding pre-existing medical conditions and age limits. Travel agents should be able to advise on levels of medical cover, or the *Department of Transport* book, *Door to Door*, gives a rough guide to the minimum sums required for most places.

The following selection of policies gives an idea of the variation in prices and cover; they all stipulate that the insured must not travel contrary to medical advice, or to obtain medical treatment. As with specialist tour operators, insurance packages specifically designed for handicapped travellers tend to be more expensive than the general policies. But there may be a slightly wider range of benefits, such as special wheelchair cover or an emergency medical service linking the hospital abroad with the patient's own doctor in the UK.

In this selection, *Hamilton Barr* offer the best value for travellers without wheelchairs or other expensive medical equipment; the *Holiday Care Service* policy is good for wheelchair users. If you already have an insurance company, or trusted broker, who handles all your other insurance, ask them if they can fix you up with a travel policy.

Campbell Irvine have introduced additional conditions to their *Personal Travel Insurance*, at no extra charge, for *physically* disabled travellers only. Most of these conditions concern payments (up to £1000) if the traveller arrives at airport or hotel and finds that either the airline cannot accommodate him or her (rather unlikely if usual procedures are followed at booking), or (more

likely) that the hotel is totally unsuitable and alternative accommodation has to be found. Then there is cover for the cost of another person accompanying a disabled traveller if he or she becomes separated (through accident or illness) from the original companion. Loss of, or damage to, wheelchair is covered up to £500. Premiums are doubled for winter sports and travellers aged 70 or over, halved for children under 16, nil for infants under two. For two weeks, the rates are, in Europe £13.75, worldwide £39.50.

Europ Assistance will provide cover for travellers with pre-existing medical conditions but they insist on a letter from your doctor stating that you are fit to travel and listing the drugs you take. Their medical emergency service is comprehensive and professional, including medical expenses up to £1,000,000. There is a maximum of £150 per item of lost baggage. Those aged over 70 must have a medical certificate of fitness and cover is restricted to European countries. Rates are £21.50 for two weeks in specified countries (all in Europe), £40 worldwide; for winter sports £33.25 and £66.40 respectively; children under two go free.

Extrasure's *Complete Travel Insurance* offers up to £1,000,000 medical expenses outside the UK. If you are in hospital through sickness or injury for five or more consecutive days, you may recover a proportionate amount of any prepaid costs of your trip for each complete 24 hours hospitalised within the booked duration. This is in addition to the usual £10 per day hospital benefit. But maximum cover for accidental loss or damage of baggage is £150 – no special arrangements for wheelchairs or dialysis equipment. People aged 70 or over, and those engaged in winter sports, pay double the standard premium; insurance is free for children under 11. Two weeks' cover for European travel costs £17, worldwide £41.

M.J. Fish and Co offer policies with a number of companies, including *Commercial Union, General Accident, Sun Alliance* and *Travelmarrs*. A "Health Declaration", confirming that the disabled person is fit to travel, must be completed by a doctor, and (for the first three companies) a "Supplementary Form" by the disabled traveller. Wheelchairs are covered by *Travelmarrs* (see below); additional cover for wheelchairs can be arranged with the other companies.

Hamilton Barr arrange *The Travel Insurance*, recommended by Judy Page (p.18). Although not a special policy for disabled travellers, there are no medical limitations, other than the usual "no travel against medical advice". Medical cover is unlimited, and benefits include repatriation by air ambulance and 24-hour emergency service. The only sticking point is the maximum of £200 on any one item of baggage lost – not much good for wheelchairs. Premiums are doubled for winter sports and the over-70s, halved for children under 16, nil for infants under two. Cover for two weeks in the British Isles and Ireland is £6.80, in Europe £12.30, North America £30, worldwide £27.15.

Holiday Care Service has set up its own policy, underwritten by *Home and Overseas Insurance Company* and using a 24-hour emergency medical aid service operated by *Europ Assistance*. There is no limit on the amount of medical expenses that can be claimed. The premiums are doubled for persons aged 65 or over travelling outside Europe, and for anyone participating in winter sports; infants under two get free cover. Insurance for wheelchairs or dialysis machines is charged at a rate of £1 per £250 cover required, up to a maximum of £3000. For two weeks in Europe you'll pay £16.21, outside Europe £44.21.

Jardines have arranged a policy called *Supersure Plus*, underwritten by *General Accident* and with emergency medical service provided by *Trans-Care International*. Cover for lost baggage is £250 per article. Medical expenses are £1,000,000. Two weeks' cover costs £9 in the UK, £15.95 in the rest of Europe and £38 worldwide; children under two are insured free; premiums are doubled for winter sports and for those between the ages of 65 and 80 travelling worldwide.

Norwich Union's *Holiday Plus Insurance* uses the *Europ Assistance* emergency medical service and provides medical cover up to £1,000,000. It's no good for owners of expensive wheelchairs or other equipment – limit per article of baggage lost or damaged is £200 – but otherwise a reasonable policy. Two weeks in Europe, Jordan and countries bordering the Mediterranean Sea, for travellers of any age, costs £17.50; elsewhere the premium is £44.80, doubled for those aged over 66; rates are halved for youngsters between the ages of 2 and 16.

Travelmarrs' *HANDICARE* policy offers up to £1,000,000 medical expenses outside the UK but there are premium loadings for anyone over the age of 65 (double the rates for travel outside the EEC) and for renal patients (fifty percent load in all areas). The insurance does not cover winter sports. All UK nationals travelling in the EEC must hold the form E111. Wheelchairs are covered up to a maximum of £1000 and up to £50 per week can be claimed for hire of a similar chair. In the event of a medical emergency, the *Traveller's Medical Service* provides a phone link between foreign hospital and doctor at home; a full-time doctor at *TMS* discusses the management of the medical treatment abroad and arranges for repatriation if necessary. Premiums are set for four areas: for two weeks in the EEC expect to pay £20, in the rest of Europe £25, in the USA or Canada £52, in the rest of the world £46.

Health and comfort

PREPARATIONS

When travelling, especially if you're alone or if your condition could be made worse by treatment given in ignorance of your drug regime, it's wise to carry a doctor's letter explaining your medical condition and the treatment you are receiving. An alternative is to wear a *Medic-Alert* bracelet (from *The Medic-Alert Foundation*). If you have to see a doctor and you are unsure – perhaps because of language difficulties – of his or her knowledge of your disability, how it is affected by other conditions, and how your drugs interact with other medicines, then you should attempt to find another doctor.

Disability organisations and information centres within the country (there is usually at least one) can be contacted for help in finding a doctor or hospital with experience of your particular disability. You can also try your emergency medical service, part of most good insurance policies, or your own consultant in the UK. On the other hand, many complaints will be totally unrelated to your disability, and you may have a hard time persuading a doctor to concentrate on the cough rather than the multiple sclerosis (p.297)!

If travelling to sparsely populated or less developed regions, make a few extra preparations. Nic Fleming, a paraplegic (see p.504), offers this advice: "If you are going on a really rugged trip in arduous and remote conditions, it pays to get medical advice in advance, have a good check-up, and know the addresses of hospitals with expertise in treating your particular disability in the country you are going to. The remoter you get, and the longer the possible delay before reaching a hospital, the more medical equipment you should carry (this is a general rule, whether you are disabled or not)."

Several contributors emphasise the value of **getting into training** before a trip. David Gray, for example, practised balancing his suitcase and travel bag on his lap (p.374). Enid Fisher lost weight in order to be fit for her journey (p.170). Nic Fleming recommends that paraplegics devote some energy to perfecting three manoeuvres: "**Backwheel balance**, if you can do it, solves hundreds of problems – kerbs, steps, rough ground, steep slopes, long grass. It can also be used to get your chair onto and off escalators when there is no convenient lift. If you enjoy living rough and getting off the beaten track, backwheel balance makes all the difference.

Paraplegics use **chair-to-chair transfers** repeatedly to get in and out of bed, onto the lavatory, into a car – but it has much wider implications. Airlines may provide you with small aisle chairs, and you can quickly get onto the aisle chair and into your seat. You can transfer to comfortable, supportive seats in a train or a taxi. When faced with narrow doors in hotels (to bathroom or lift, for example) you can transfer onto any old kitchen chair placed just the other side of the opening, and the doorway is no longer an obstacle. You no longer have to worry whether or not a hotel is 'suitable for wheelchairs'.

Chair-to-floor transfers are routinely taught in paraplegic rehabilitation training, but the point is the way you use the manoeuvre. You can get down onto the deck of a small boat which would be unstable if you remained sitting high up in your chair. You can transfer to the dock or bank and then into a canoe or kayak. You can sleep on the ground when camping, or sit on the ground while you repair your wheelchair."

This last point applies to any disability – whatever manoeuvres and tricks you have mastered, use them imaginatively and they will get you out of all sorts of difficulties.

EQUIPMENT

Most potential causes of discomfort can be foreseen: if you take time to find out about the conditions you are likely to encounter, you'll be better able to equip yourself to survive them. There are numerous tips to be gleaned from our contributors, and many helpful suggestions in the *AA/SIA* publication, *The World Wheelchair Traveller* (see *Books*); you can also pick up useful ideas at *Aids Centres*, travelling aids exhibitions (for venues, contact *The Joint Aids Centres Council* and *Disabled Living Centres*). The *Holiday Care Service* publishes a fact sheet on the hire of equipment. Whether it's a roll-up carry-chair, a folding stool, a "portaloo" for the car or an ultra-lightweight wheelchair, there is a piece of equipment to deal with most situations.

But don't get carried away: keep luggage to a minimum, and remember there will be situations that you cannot plan for. One contributor packed her "helping hand" (light tongs for picking things up and assisting when dressing) to make life easier on her coach tour, and then left it at the first hotel (p.168); but improvisation will solve any problem – in this case, making do with a long-handled shoe-lift.

Remember also, if you are relying on any electrical equipment, to check the voltage of the electricity supply in the countries you plan to visit, and ensure that you have the appropriate adaptor, converter or battery charger for use with that supply.

Many wheelchair users carry an **emergency repairs** kit: small puncture repair outfit (unless you have solid tyres fitted to your chair – a good idea if you are travelling in remote areas across rough ground), two tyre levers, lightweight tyre inflator with connectors for both sizes of valve, spare nuts, spanner, perhaps a spare inner tube.

The repairs kit and the spares, of course, are carried in your hand luggage.

According to your destination you can obtain help when equipment breaks down from a variety of sources: garages, bike shops, hospital supply companies, hospitals or clinics, disability organisations; this can be researched before departure but in general is easily discovered when the breakdown occurs. Travellers usually find local people eager to help, and if you are with a good tour company the rep will sort out most problems.

DIALYSIS ABROAD

Travellers who need to dialyse face one major problem: that of finding a reliable medical centre, in which the risks of AIDS and hepatitis B transmission are minimised. The task of arranging the dialysis treatment abroad belongs to the consultant, but he or she cannot always verify the standards of equipment and hygiene procedures. Indeed, a few consultants refuse to sanction their patients' travel plans because they feel that the risks involved are too high.

The *National Federation of Kidney Patient Associations* (*NFKPA*) produces a quarterly magazine, an advisory leaflet and a booklet, *Dialyse Europa*, which lists the European dialysis centres. The *NFKPA* stresses that it is impossible to recommend any because they don't have the resources to check each one. However, patients have successfully used dialysis facilities around the world. Some UK units provide a portable dialysis machine for holiday use.

Judy Page (p.18) was very impressed with the *BKPA* centre in Mallorca, and there are other *BKPA* centres in Jersey and West Sussex. Using the facilities at a *BKPA* centre involves little paperwork and is quick to arrange. If the effort of finding a suitable dialysis clinic seems too much, and you don't fancy Jersey, Sussex or Mallorca for a holiday, it may be possible to join a group organised by your local kidney patients' association.

Those who are on CAPD (continuous ambulatory peritoneal dialysis) find travel much easier. CAPD supplies can be delivered to a holiday address in the UK or abroad, but suppliers like at least three months' notice. Given sufficient warning, the major airlines will carry mobile dialysis equipment (see p.523).

The *Holiday Care Service* publishes a series of fact sheets for people with specific medical conditions, including kidney patients, those with epilepsy, asthma or diabetes, and those who are deaf or hard of hearing, deaf/blind and visually handicapped.

MEDICINES

Probably the best known law of travel is to carry *in your hand luggage* enough of your **regular drugs** to last the duration of your trip – and never let this bag out of your sight. Carry additional supplies in the suitcase. The inconvenience of becoming separated from your holiday wardrobe is described by more than one contributor, but losing essential medicines is much more than an inconvenience. With clearly written prescriptions (using the chemical, or generic, names), you'll probably be able to obtain fresh supplies, but searching out doctors and pharmacists is not an exciting way to start a holiday.

Think also **beyond your usual drugs**, particularly in relation to the country you will be visiting. Advice on precautions with food and water, insect repellents and local health problems can be found in any *Rough Guide*, or other reputable travel guide. A good reference work, covering all sorts of medical matters for travellers – from sunstroke to snake bites – including a section on the handicapped and the diabetic traveller, is Richard Dawood's *Travellers' Health* (see *Books*).

Doctor Dawood suggests which medical supplies to take with you, although of course this varies according to your destination and your own preferred treatments. Nic Fleming again: "The minimal **first-aid kit** contains sticking plaster, antiseptic, scissors, small bandage and a foam rubber patch which can be cut and fitted over a pressure point. In tropical climates you should carry your favourite remedy for control of dysentery and stomach upsets; I prefer the non-antibiotic remedies based on kaolin, but everybody has a system which works for them. As you travel further and further from help, the medical kit expands to include items such as disinfectants, sterile dressings, splints, antibiotics, morphine, equipment for stitching up wounds, aids to artificial respiration, and so on."

You'll also be able to make some plans based on your own health history. For example, if you are prone to sinus infections and you are travelling to an area which is dusty or suffers from air pollution, it's a good idea not only to use a decongestant spray on the flight (to ease the effects of pressure changes) but also to carry a course of broad-spectrum antibiotics, or at least a note of the one you usually take.

There is no need to take a separate suitcase for your first-aid kit, but equally it's foolish to assume when reading about the problems likely to be encountered that "it won't happen to me". And seemingly minor irritations like insect bites, sunburn and diarrhoea can ruin a holiday.

CLIMATE, ALTITUDE AND FATIGUE

Perhaps the most overlooked potential problem is **fatigue**. Many types of disability cause people to tire more readily, and in the excitement of travelling to new countries it's easy to forget the need to pace yourself. If you try to do too much you'll end up enjoying nothing.

Travellers may suffer long waiting periods in uncomfortable conditions, loss of sleep, jet lag, stress-related tiredness if things don't go according to plan, or simple fatigue caused by attempting to be more active than they are in their home lives. A bit of yawning isn't serious, but a tired person with impaired balance and mobility is very likely to trip over a step, to misjudge distances, to crash into things. It's not worth risking an accident by racing round that one last museum.

Tourist offices and guidebooks give plenty of information on **climate** so travellers can judge the best time of year to suit them. Sensible clothing, footwear, and drinking and eating patterns will make most temperatures bearable; paralysed skin requires a bit more than average protection from the sun. Nic Fleming survived fierce frosts, well below freezing, in Moscow by wearing fur-lined flying boots, an old, heavy fur coat, woolly hat and industrial rubber or plastic gloves worn over woollen mittens (fancy ski gloves last only a few days before wearing through and letting in the damp snow). For more advice on coping with extremes of heat and cold, wind and humidity, including some comments on sunscreens, consult Colonel James Adam in *Travellers' Health*.

Anyone with disease of the heart, lungs or blood should consult their doctor before travelling to **high altitudes**. There may be increased risk of attacks for epilepsy and migraine sufferers. Cold and exertion may induce an attack in asthmatics, but high altitude alone will not. Mountain sickness may occur at heights over 2000m – people vary in their susceptibility – and the secret of prevention is to acclimatise. Doctor John Dickinson, writing in *Travellers' Health*, recommends "rest days" every 900m above 2700m for fit walkers.

Holiday helpers

Since 1986 *Holiday Care Service* has run *Holiday Helpers*, a successful and widely used scheme to match up individual holidaymakers with suitable helpers. In addition, *RADAR* can supply a list of care attendant agencies; some disability organisations, such as the *Spinal Injuries Association*, operate their own systems for members.

Caryl Lloyd (p.120) recommends spending some time, preferably at least 24 hours, with a prospective helper to allow both parties to assess the likelihood of hitting it off while on holiday. It's also important to agree money matters before departure. Caryl and other contributors who travelled with volunteer helpers report easy relationships and sterling work from their companions.

For those wishing to assist a disabled person on a group holiday, *RADAR* publish a fact sheet listing the available options. The vital ingredient here is the application form: the layout and wording should be simple and unambiguous; the replies – from disabled person and helper – should be full and frank. Problems that arise after that cannot be blamed on poor organisation or selection of helpers, and they can usually be seen off with a little tolerance and a sense of humour. Participation in these holidays can be immensely rewarding (pp.7, 207), and the organisations that arrange them deserve to be well supported.

ESCORT SERVICES

If you require an escort, taxi or private ambulance service in order **to reach your point of departure**, whether it be airport, railway or coach station, or sea port, consult *RADAR* or the *Holiday Care Service*; see also *Directory*, p.539. Jane Nyman offers some thoughts on the use of *Red Cross* escorts on p.197. If considering paid help the cheapest option may be a conscientious local mini-cab firm (p.105).

Red tape

Overcoming bureaucratic obstacles can be an infuriating way to start a holiday – but not half as bad as not being allowed to fly because you've failed to fill in a form. Other forms, such as applications for parking permits, are worth the effort of completing. Below are some problems you're likely to come across, and how to handle them.

MEDICAL CLEARANCE AND HANDLING ADVICE

The majority of disabled travellers should not need medical clearance before flying. The *MEDIF* (*Medical Information Form*) was introduced primarily to detect passengers with heart conditions who should not really be flying. If presented with a form, *MEDIF* will make up the second part and may usually be ignored. The important bit is part one, *INCAD*, the *Incapacitated Passengers Handling Advice* form which gives the airline details of your requirements – what assistance you need and where.

Travellers with stable medical conditions should obtain a *FREMEC* card (*Frequent Travellers Medical Card*), which is accepted by most major airlines and issued free by them. This is preferable to repeated form filling and can be produced when asked to complete *MEDIF* by a zealous travel agent or airline official who hears the word "disabled" or "wheelchair" and immediately assumes that medical clearance is required.

Very occasionally, there may be a problem with visa applications such as Lorna Hooper experienced (p.367). If this happens, the best advice is to be forceful: produce medical evidence of fitness to travel if absolutely necessary but otherwise remember that you are dealing with bureaucrats (see p.528) and explain patiently and firmly that your disability should not even have to figure in your application for a visa.

BOOKING FORMS

A large number of disabled people have found that they can travel quite happily without giving advance warning of their disability, making no "special requests" and dealing with any obstacles as and when they arise. In view of the fact that special requests stated on the booking form are often ignored anyway, this seems sensible. It is also the goal that all operators and travellers should be aiming for – the day when the arrival of a client in a wheelchair gives no more cause for concern than the arrival of a client without a wheelchair, and doesn't necessitate major upheavals, extra expenditure, specialised equipment or special staff.

There are many tour operators, transport operators and hoteliers who will make every effort to accommodate clients with handicaps. But a significant proportion of them – in particular the tour and transport operators – insist on advance warning. And there are many disabled travellers who prefer to make their requests for facilities or assistance in writing, and who prefer not to arrive unannounced.

If you do get involved in outlining your disability and asking for help, perhaps in boarding the coach or carrying your luggage, or for a high bed or accessible bathroom, then keep it brief, but include all relevant facts and measurements – typed or in very clear handwriting. In return, you should expect promises of facilities or assistance in writing, so that you can wave the evidence in front of the operator's nose when he or she denies all knowledge of the request.

PERMITS AND KEYS

The *Travel Notes* for each country mention the validity of the Orange Badge, as well as the availability of temporary parking permits, registration cards for Dial-a-Ride and similar adapted transport systems, procedures or vouchers for obtaining fare concessions on public transport, and keys for adapted toilets. These can often be sorted out in person, at the start of your holiday, but some might view this as a waste of valuable sunbathing or sightseeing hours, and it may be necessary to make applications in advance; if so, allow several weeks for an exchange of letters – initial enquiry (sometimes two, if unsure of the correct address), despatch of application form, return of completed form, processing of permit, and more. Despite the length of the section below, and the apparent complications, flying is overall one of the best organised means of transport for disabled travellers. Certainly, airports and airlines have put more action into provision of facilities that most land transportation operators.

Getting there by air

AIRLINES

For independent travellers, **choosing an airline** is usually all about comparing prices and selecting a convenient flight from a nearby airport. On the face of it, independent disabled travellers can do the same: the air travel industry would have us believe that procedures and facilities for transporting disabled passengers are well worked out and cope smoothly with any eventuality. In fact, there are differences in approach and facilities that are worth considering along with the fare.

The *Access to the Skies Committee* at *RADAR* is in the process of compiling a database on airline facilities, covering about 120 airlines; the information should be available around mid-1991, either through travel agents or from voluntary organisations such as the *Holiday Care Service*.

The *Nothing Ventured* survey was much smaller – a simple questionnaire was sent out to around forty airlines. Only twelve airlines (*Aer Lingus, Aeroflot, Air Canada, Air New Zealand, Air Malta, Canadian Airlines, El Al, Japan Airlines, Olympic Airways, SAS, Thai Airways, Virgin*) responded in full to every question; five airlines (*Cathay Pacific, KLM, Lufthansa, Qantas, Swissair*) despatched their passenger care leaflets, only one of which (*Qantas' Travel Care* series – clear and up to date) gave sufficient information; over fifty percent of airlines, including *Air France, Air India, Alitalia, American Airlines, British Airways, Iberia, Singapore Airlines* and many more, did not bother to reply.

The Gulf airlines, *Emirates* and *Gulf Air*, made brave attempts to respond but their head offices were busy with more pressing matters; *Emirates* staff at the airport desk were particularly helpful and filled in the gaps (see p.261).

Some of the airlines that ignored the questionnaire make all the usual arrangements for disabled passengers – indeed, *British Airways'* facilities and service are praised throughout this book, and tortuous phone enquiries eventually led to one man who knew all the answers – but their public relations departments could do with a shake-up. In many cases, staff at reservations offices, airport desks and customer services departments gave conflicting answers regarding facilities and procedures.

Most major airlines have their act together as far as passenger **handling at the airport** is concerned, provided that they are given instructions at the time of booking. If you haven't booked direct with the airline, and you don't have absolute faith in your travel agent, phone the airline desk at the airport a few days before departure and ensure that your details have been entered on the computer.

First-time travellers, or travellers new to a particular airline or airport, may want more advance information than that provided in the passenger care leaflets, many of which are out of date and lacking in detail. If this is the case, and you are concerned about parking arrangements, being met off your train, being allowed to remain in your own chair, under your own steam, as far as the aircraft door, or about boarding procedures (wheeled straight on, lifted manually, or carried aloft on a lifting vehicle?) then quiz the airline, and the airport if necessary, when booking.

These details would be swiftly established, or even swept aside, if every airport and airline provided flawless printed information and if all airport and airline staff relaxed and treated each individual as a customer with a mind of his/her own rather than an object to be moulded by company policy.

Once airborne, most disabled passengers have two major concerns: **seating and toilet facilities**. Although several airlines provide aisle chairs and some designate one or two toilets as accessible, visits to the toilet still require super-human contortions and economy seating is usually nothing less than an endurance test – we are a long way off flying in aircraft that have been designed for *independent* travel by handicapped passengers.

As one contributor says, "Comfort in the air is the biggest pain of all. On long-haul flights I try to travel out of season and/or on slack days, when I can lie down on empty seats. On charters, many with bolted, upright seats, I rest forward on the meal table. I'm carried onto planes that have steps. There are no seats specially for disabled people. Even the seats by the exits have to be taken by non-disabled. Using the plane toilet with a walking frame is like doing aerobics in a wardrobe, which is why I wear a leg-bag. All I'm asking for is a decent seat and a dignified pee – for every economy class to have one special reclining seat and one reasonable toilet."

Other factors that might influence the choice of airline include the requirement to fill out medical forms, the carriage of power-chairs, dialysis equipment and guide dogs, the acceptance of groups of disabled passengers and unaccompanied disabled passengers, and general attitudes amongst airline staff.

Comfortable seats and adequate legroom, especially on long-haul flights, are unlikely in economy class. No airline has a policy of upgrading a disabled passenger if there is space in business or first class and if disability (an unbendable leg, for example) and build will make life unpleasant in economy seats. *Air Canada* showed a flexible approach and arranged this for Steve Veness (p.436), and on *Virgin* charter flights to Orlando, seats with greater angle of recline can be purchased for a small supplement; on *Thai Airways* flights the captain may sanction moving a severely disabled passenger to first class if there's room.

But, in general, aircraft seating leaves much to be desired: one contributor, only five feet tall, with unbendable legs, was given a front seat on a *Brittania* 767 and had to remove her shoes in order to wedge herself into the seat. The policy of refusing to allow disabled passengers to sit in comfort by emergency exits (*Japan Airlines* is the exception here) has not been satisfactorily explained – as Enid Jasper says (p.89), why not throw the disabled passenger down the emergency chute first?

A number of airlines carry **aisle wheelchairs**, and the majority of aircraft have some seats with movable armrests to ease the transfer from aisle chair to aisle seat. *Aer Lingus* carry aisle chairs on all long-haul flights. All *Air Canada* planes, with the exception of DC-9 and Boeing 747 combi, are equipped with Wilshire chairs which have no armrests; they are also carried on the narrow-aisle aircraft operated by *Air Canada*'s regional airlines. *Air New Zealand*, *SAS* and *Virgin* use the Newton Skychair on wide-body aircraft; *BA*, *Canadian Airlines*, *Emirates*, *Qantas* and *South African Airways* also carry aisle chairs; *Cathay Pacific* will provide one on request; *El Al* allow passengers to bring on board their own collapsible narrow chair.

The provision of aisle wheelchairs is only half a solution if none of the **toilets** are enlarged to allow some room to manoeuvre inside; squeezing through the doorway is one thing, transferring to the toilet quite another. *Aer Lingus* and *Air Canada* provide screens so the toilet can be used with the door open; on *Air Canada*'s 767, 727 and A320 aircraft at least one toilet has this facility as well as fold-down or fixed grab-rail, low-level lever door-handles and a switch to turn the light on without closing the door. *Air New Zealand* cabin crew have been known to take disabled passengers to more spacious first-class toilets.

Most disabled travellers should be able to fly without completing complicated **medical forms**: unless there is a special health problem or special equipment is required (such as respirator or stretcher) the airline needs handling advice, not medical details. *Aer Lingus*, *Air New Zealand*, *BA*, *Lufthansa*, *SAS*, *Virgin*, as well as short-haul operators such as *Olympic Airways* and *Air Malta*, have a particularly relaxed attitude.

But some airlines insist on medical notes and evidence of fitness to travel. *Canadian Airlines*, for example, ask for a doctor's letter to certify fitness to travel and capability of self-care if travelling alone. When making a reservation with *Thai Airways*, a disabled passenger is invited to complete a medical form which is then forwarded to the "Sales Procedure Department" whose job it is to consider whether or not the passenger will be allowed to board the plane! Medical forms are issued by other airlines, and the best way round this is to use a *FREMEC* card (p.521).

Carriage of power-chairs, dialysis equipment and guide dogs is usually free, and guide dogs can accompany passengers in the cabin. The potential problem with power-chairs is the size of the hold: on a 737, for example, it is 107cm deep and the door is only 104cm high; large chairs have to be tipped, so batteries must be removed or tightly secured to the chair; small chairs may be loaded upright and stowed without removing the batteries. The dry-cell battery must be disconnected, the terminals insulated; the wet-cell battery must be drained of acid.

Most airlines will carry both power-chairs (wet- or dry-cell) and dialysis equipment. Some (*Air Canada*, *Canadian Airlines*) have special containers for wet-cell batteries; *Virgin* only carry gel-type batteries; a few do not accept electric wheelchairs.

Airlines with considerable experience of carrying **groups of disabled passengers** include *Air New Zealand* (used by several US travel agents who specialise in disabled travel) and *Aer Lingus* (who operate many charters to Lourdes). *Air Canada* offer special arrangements and fares to teams of disabled athletes and similar groups. *El Al* place no limit on the number of disabled passengers taken aboard any one flight. *Air India* do not accept groups of disabled people.

In general, airlines prefer passengers who cannot attend to their personal needs to travel with a companion. Some, including *Alitalia*, *Iberia* and *Japan Airlines*, go a step further and do not accept **unaccompanied disabled passengers** (*Iberia* do not, according to a couple of contributors, cope smoothly with wheelchair users). No one expects cabin crew to act as nurses, but if the toilets were fully accessible and the aisles wide enough to pass along on crutches, callipers or the aisle chair, many passengers who do not normally need help to visit the toilet would be able to travel alone.

The majority of contributors, using a variety of airlines, report courteous and attentive **service from airline staff**, at the check-in counter, in the terminal and on board the aircraft. *Air Canada* have declared **communication** a priority and are preparing an updated information pamphlet and a video to encourage more disabled people to travel. *Air New Zealand* are also in the process of revising their leaflet for disabled passengers. *BA* have a Minicom number (☎081/562 0313) for flight bookings and travel advice, and some staff are trained in signing. In addition, *BA* are working with the *RNIB* to produce a tape of a typical flight, to familiarise blind passengers with the sounds of air travel. *Virgin* have selected staff with a view to giving basic instruction in sign and deaf/blind language.

Whether by standard training procedures or special training in communication (including sign language, direct eye contact, good enunciation) and lifting techniques, the airlines seem to be producing the right results with almost all their staff, and the check-in clerk who insists on speaking to the wheelchair pusher rather than the occupant, or the passenger rep who ignores a disabled man struggling to transfer from airport wheelchair to his own chair (p.445) are rare exceptions.

Hiccups in the transit of wheelchairs are also rare but not unheard of (pp.278, 283, 313): apart from the role of the baggage handlers, mentioned earlier, the airline has a responsibility to ensure that such a vital piece of equipment, once separated from its owner, is loaded and labelled

correctly, transferred smoothly from one plane to another en route, and deposited at the same destination as the owner. One contributor, making a connection at Belgrade, insisted on locating his chair and found it abandoned in the corner of a lounge, despite all assurances from cabin crew that it had already been transferred to the new aircraft. The same traveller has arrived in Darwin with his wheelchair in Sydney, and in Glasgow with his chair in Edinburgh.

But it is cheering to hear many reports of cabin crew using their initiative to shuffle passengers about, allocate better seats, make use of spare seats and, when the need arose, carry a disabled passenger to the toilet – good cabin crew make the best of a bad job in aircraft that are still essentially designed to pack in the maximum number of slim, short, agile passengers.

The way forward must be to build on this flexibility, extending it to more check-in staff so that disabled passengers are given a choice and are in control from the moment they enter the terminal, and then to see acceptance of unaccompanied disabled travellers and groups by every airline; to make training in communication with hearing- or speech-impaired passengers more widespread, and to improve and update all passenger information leaflets.

AIRPORTS

Three factors should influence your choice of **departure airport**: the journey to and from the airport, which should be as brief and as relaxing as possible; facilities at the airport; and the airline you are to fly with. Responsibility for handling of disabled passengers is usually shared between the airline (or their handling agent) and the airport management, so ask what the arrangements are when booking.

Getting to the airport can be exhausting in itself, a problem especially if you have a long-haul flight ahead of you. *TRIPSCOPE* can advise on the best option, depending on your ability to use public transport, your schedule, and financial constraints.

Direct coach travel to **Heathrow or Gatwick** may be out of the question but if you can use the train to reach London the links to Heathrow or Gatwick are straightforward. *London Transport*'s cheap, wheelchair-accessible Carelink buses run every hour, every day of the week, clockwise through London's main-line stations, connecting with Airbus A1 at Victoria and Airbus A2 at

Euston. The Airbuses are adapted to carry two wheelchairs and shuttle between **Heathrow**'s four terminals and various points in central London.

British Rail's **Gatwick** Express is also wheelchair accessible (no advance warning necessary), and operates every 15 minutes during the day and hourly at night from Victoria. Gatwick Airport station is in the South Terminal complex, with lifts from the platforms, and you can arrange with your local station manager to be met off the train.

The problems of coping with luggage, or inability to use public transport, may mean that you have to go by car. To avoid car parking headaches, persuade a friend to take you or, if you can afford it, book a mini-cab; other possibilities are the *Red Cross*, *WRVS*, your Social Services department, or local Dial-a-Ride or similar scheme – again, consult *TRIPSCOPE*.

Belfast International is easily accessible from the city by taxi (drivers are very helpful and will lift passengers in and out of the taxi) or Airbus, which runs every half-hour, hourly on Sundays (£3 single, £6 return), stopping at the Central Railway Station and two bus stations on the way. There is a side-loading wheelchair lift, and wheelchair space can be booked in advance (☎0232/320011 ext 419).

PARKING AND ACCOMMODATION

If you drive yourself, parking charges and accessibility of courtesy vehicles from long-term car park to terminal building will be important considerations. **Flying from a local airport** has several advantages: the journey to the airport will probably be short and simple; there will be fewer people and a less frenetic atmosphere at the airport; car parks tend to be closer to the terminal buildings (only 50m away at Leeds Bradford), and parking charges are not astronomical. It's a shame that airports (apart from Cardiff-Wales, see below) have not considered reduced parking rates for Orange Badge holders – a car is a necessity, not a luxury, to someone unable to walk.

Your holiday package, however, may leave you with no choice but to fly from an airport a long way from home. If this is the case, and even though it eats into your holiday time, it may be worth considering finding **accommodation near the airport** for the night before you fly. There is scant attention paid to listing any accessible accommodation, let alone a selection to cover all budgets, in the airport information publications.

Cardiff-Wales supplies a separate leaflet on a hotel (*Arlington International*) with ground-floor rooms suitable for disabled guests. **East Midlands** passenger care leaflet states that *The Donington Thistle Hotel* (four-star) has rooms specially designed for disabled visitors. **Luton** airport's passenger information leaflet uses the wheelchair symbol in its list of hotels, providing a choice of four, the cheapest of which is the *Hotel Ibis*. *The Templeton Hotel* offers the best facilities for disabled travellers flying from **Belfast International**.

For other airports you can consult *RADAR*'s guide, *Holidays in the British Isles*, as well as the local tourist board. If you plan to leave your car at the hotel, be sure about transport from hotel to airport – the courtesy bus may refuse to take wheelchair users (see p.252).

There is no doubt that long-term **parking** at Heathrow and Gatwick is best avoided on the grounds of cost: parking charges are two or three times greater than at the regional airports. At Heathrow a special request must be made to obtain assistance for the transfer to the terminal buildings, but at Gatwick there is provision for long-term parking in the short-term car park for Orange Badge holders (with phones to call for assistance).

At many regional airports (Aberdeen, Edinburgh, Glasgow, Kent International, Leeds Bradford, London City, Prestwick) one car park is used for short and long stays, and spaces for disabled drivers are reserved close to the terminal building. These are usually on the ground floor of the car park, so that crossing to the terminal should be easy, but in some cases there is a telephone link to the information desk (Aberdeen, one planned for Edinburgh in early 1991), or an "Assist" button (Birmingham International, see below) to press, for those who need help to get from car to check-in desk.

The airports that have separate long- and short-term car parks either provide assistance to reach the terminal building (Belfast International, Birmingham International, Bristol), or allow disabled drivers to reserve spaces for long-term parking in the short-term car parks, which are nearer the terminal entrance. Stansted does both. At Birmingham International eight spaces are available in the multistorey car park, which is adjacent to the terminal building and reached via a covered walkway. At East Midlands a space in Car Park 1 (long and short stay) can be reserved by contacting *NCP* in advance. At Luton it is possible to reserve spaces next to the terminal by writing to the Airport Director. At Cardiff-Wales disabled drivers can phone and book a limited number of free parking spaces in the security car park, directly opposite the terminal. Passengers who cannot use the courtesy bus at Manchester make arrangements by phone to park in one of the short-stay car parks.

The general rule at airports, for security reasons, is that drivers are not allowed to leave their cars unattended, even for a few minutes, immediately outside the terminal building while **setting down or picking up** disabled travellers. Drivers must abandon their passengers, then park their cars, then come back to assist; if picking up disabled passengers they must park, meet the passengers, leave them at the pick-up point, collect their cars and return to the pick-up point.

These comings and goings are time-consuming, often inconvenient, and may cause some discomfort to the disabled person. Depending on airline and airport, it might be possible to leave the disabled traveller in the car, report to the airline information desk and ask for an assistant to come out to the car, but some handling agents insist that they only operate within the terminal buildings (this is less likely to happen at smaller airports). At Edinburgh the car can be left if the driver first notifies a policeman, and if he or she returns to the car as soon as possible.

A more satisfactory solution would be permitted, time-limited parking. The *Tourism for All* report recommends that spaces should be provided immediately outside the departures and arrivals halls, allowing sufficient time for setting down and picking up disabled passengers and giving them all the necessary assistance. East Midlands airport has gone a step further and marked disabled pick-up or set-down spaces immediately outside the terminal with no time limit; drivers can park on these, or in any available space, and accompany their disabled passengers into the building.

FACILITIES

Apart from accessible public transport connections and designated, reasonably priced car parking near the terminal buildings (or courtesy buses on which wheelchair accessibility is a standard feature), **facilities** at domestic airports should, in an ideal world, include the following: ramps and lifts for easy movement within the terminal and for access from railway platforms or bus stops; a good supply of wheelchairs or buggies; lowered telephones (preferably fitted with inductive coupler systems); clear announcements, both visible and audible; induction loop audio points; fully accessible toilets, bars, restaurants and shops; lowered counters at bank, check-in and post office; adequate methods of boarding the aircraft.

Staff should be well trained to deal with all manner of situations involving disabled passengers, particularly in the field of communicating; some should be trained in the use of sign language; anyone who has to lift disabled passengers must be proficient. Last but not least, easily obtained, reliable information for disabled passengers – including details of a range of accessible accommodation near the airport – should be available.

In reality, airports have many but not all of these facilities. What follows is a brief survey of who's got what, based partly on contributors' experiences and partly on data supplied by the airport authorities – much of which had to be followed up with phone calls because there were so many omissions in the literature.

The provision of **ramps**, **dropped kerbs**, **automatic doors** and **lifts** seems to be taken seriously at all airports. Among the newer terminal buildings, Stansted's is built on one level, with the *British Rail* direct line from Liverpool Street station coming in underneath the building; access from the platform, the coach station and the car park is by ramps, escalators or lifts.

Procedures for **checking in** vary according to airport and airline, and it's worth enquiring when booking – will you be nannied from the moment you set foot in the terminal, or will you be allowed to wander about in your own wheelchair, visiting the duty free and cafeteria, and make your own way to the aircraft door? Will you be given the choice? Too often, you will not.

There are few reports of problems with obtaining a **wheelchair or buggy**, although it may involve waiting for one to become free. Sometimes, at larger airports, there will be wheelchairs available but only to passengers using certain airlines; greater flexibility would solve this problem. There may also be a bit of juggling about, with disabled passengers being asked to transfer from one buggy to another. This has been experienced at Gatwick, where buggies or wheelchairs operate in restricted areas and a passenger moving through more than one area has to change vehicles.

Low-level **telephones** are provided at many airports (Heathrow, Gatwick, Aberdeen, Belfast International, Birmingham International, Bristol, Cardiff-Wales, East Midlands, Edinburgh, Glasgow, Kent International, Luton, Manchester, Stansted, Teeside International), but only Aberdeen, Belfast and Manchester advertise public phones adapted for hearing-impaired passengers; East Midlands has an amplified phone on the information desk for the use of passengers with hearing difficulties. Where these facilities are not available, airport staff will assist, but this is not the answer, and not in the spirit of independent travel.

Keeping track of **flight information** is difficult for visually impaired travellers if the announcements are unclear or drowned by high background noise levels (another incentive to fly from a small, regional airport). Gatwick has unfortunately maintained its policy of no audible announcements (except in the event of delays) so that blind or partially sighted passengers must make enquiries at the information desk. At Stansted the new terminal building (opened in March 1991) has no tannoy announcements but the screens are clear and brightly coloured. Birmingham International is alone in providing a **touch-map** for visually handicapped passengers.

Induction loop audio points are installed at Birmingham International, Heathrow and Gatwick, so that passengers with the "T" position on their hearing aids can receive announcements made over the public address system (only the delays, of course, at Gatwick). A recent addition to the information desk at Gatwick's South Terminal is a Minicom Supertel, which transmits written messages through telephone wires; this enables hearing-impaired people who have the necessary equipment in their home to contact the airport for flight (or other) information.

With only a few exceptions, all the **facilities for eating, drinking and shopping** in the terminals are accessible to wheelchair users. The provision of **accessible toilets** is good. Even better, the exceptions are pointed out in the literature. Gatwick scores a point for providing reserved seating for disabled passengers in the check-in area, where queues and crowds are likely. No mention is made in any passenger information leaflets of **lowered check-in desks**, bank and post office counters, although *British Airways* do have low-level check-in desks at Heathrow.

Boarding at Heathrow and Gatwick is nearly always direct from the terminal, with no need for lifting equipment. At the smaller airports, **boarding of non-ambulant disabled passengers** may involve being carried up the steps from runway to aircraft door, usually by airport fire service staff. This is the procedure at Kent International, London City and Teeside International, and it need not be a disadvantage – these airports are small enough to give personal service, and no reports have been received of poor handling.

Cardiff-Wales airport boards passengers either from air-bridges or by manual lifting. East Midlands uses either Ambulift or carry-chair, depending on the aircraft. Leeds Bradford is the only airport of its size that has an Ambulift. At Belfast International disabled passengers are usually boarded by "nose-loader" (a moveable corridor which extends from the passenger lounge into the aircraft), sometimes (on some *BA* flights) by high-lift ambulance, occasionally by carry-chair.

Lifting vehicles are available at many regional airports: Birmingham International, Bristol, Luton, Manchester, Newcastle, Stansted and the Scottish airports. At the new Stansted terminal international flights are boarded from satellites through covered air-bridges; the satellites are reached via wheelchair-accessible "automated track transit link" from the terminal.

IMPROVING SERVICE

Standards of **staff training** are difficult to assess because evidence is patchy. At both Heathrow and Gatwick some of the staff manning the airport information desk can use sign language, but other airports have not followed this lead. There is no other mention of specialised staff training in airport publications, and it may well be the case that the service provided is good enough – many contributors note helpful and friendly staff at a number of domestic airports.

But the vital role of airport staff as suppliers of information to people who may have difficulty in hearing, seeing or walking, and may be more distressed than other travellers by sudden changes in plan, has not been drummed in at all airports. Whether phoning in advance to research facilities and confirm arrangements, or asking at the information desk on the day of departure, disabled passengers – like any passenger – must be given accurate answers. If staff know how many bars there are in the terminal building and their whereabouts, why is it a cause for celebration if they know the number and location of toilets for the disabled, or phones which can be used by deaf people or those in wheelchairs?

Another part of staff training should involve the encouragement of a **flexible approach to standard procedures**. As far as possible, each disabled passenger must be given the opportunity to state a preferred method of reaching the aircraft, or a better way of being lifted. One well-travelled paraplegic, Nic Fleming, puts it this way:

"In my experience there is only one serious problem for disabled travellers, and that is bureaucrats and officials. Individuals all over the world seem to be almost universally kind, and the existence of kind people means that no physical obstacle is actually an obstacle at all. It may be a nuisance, but it can always be overcome. By contrast, the bureaucrat who says 'You can't do that. It's against company policy/the law/fire regulations. It's more than my job's worth' can be an insuperable barrier.

For example, I was told, 'You can't go in there alone, Sir, you are a security risk' by an armed guard at the entrance to the *BA* departure lounge at J.F. Kennedy airport, New York (1990). I demanded to be let in, and all the other queueing passengers supported me, refusing to go past me. The guard called two other armed guards by radio and put his foot in front of my wheel. I rolled over his foot (not seeing it) just as the manager arrived. He seemed nonplussed that anyone in a wheelchair should travel unescorted. *BA* subsequently promised to change practices at the terminal.

Arriving in Sydney (1981), I was informed by the immigration authorities that I would need a full medical examination before I could leave the arrivals area and meet the friends waiting for me. I asked if the rule would apply if I could walk, and said that I had entered Australia several times previously without this indignity and delay. The officer pointed to the door of the lounge and said if I could walk through it I did not need a medical. I put on my callipers, wheeled up to the door, walked through it, pulled the chair after me, and sat back in the chair. Bureaucracy satisfied.

Brussels airport has a wonderful system: disabled passengers are directed to a special service desk, where you find a remote telephone. You dial a distant office and say which flight you want to catch. You then wait indefinitely until someone feels that they have time to come and help you. This is typical of bureaucratic systems that devise 'special services for the benefit of our disabled customers', and then put you firmly in the slow track. Officials never seem to expect that wheelchair passengers have to meet deadlines and get jobs done on time like everybody else.

Of course, these are the exceptions, and most airlines and airports provide a magnificent service, but a reminder of the most perfect welcoming phrase won't hurt: 'Hullo, Sir, do you need any help, or would you like to go through to the aircraft on your own?' Then everything falls into place – honour is satisfied, efficiency maximised, and the airline saves money."

Airport facilities are described, not always in great detail, in general **passenger information** material or (East Midlands, Stansted, Teeside International) in a separate guide for disabled passengers. Full details of procedures for passengers with all types of disability should make further enquiries unnecessary. But if a service or facility is not available, this should be clearly stated, along with alternative arrangements and any plans to make it available in the future.

On the whole, facilities and procedures for handling disabled air passengers are not bad; with due attention to the rules of giving advance warning and allowing plenty of time on the day, you should have a smooth passage – described by some contributors as "VIP treatment" – from check-in to boarding.

Areas that need attention include arrangements for setting down and picking up disabled passengers, check-in procedures, the allocation of wheelchairs or buggies at the larger airports, staff training, the supply of information, and treatment of wheelchairs by baggage handlers – having your own chair removed at the door of the departing plane, carefully stowed and brought to the aircraft door on arrival is far preferable to collecting pieces of your chair, bent or broken, from a carousel at ten-minute intervals.

Passengers can make life easier for airport staff by turning up on time: delays in departure of aircraft caused by late arrivals at the boarding gate are increasing, and since it is usually more convenient (and better for the disabled person) to board disabled passengers first, it is unhelpful to arrive at the last minute.

Getting there by land and sea

If you're not flying to your destination, you'll be travelling on trains, coach or in your own car; and probably taking a ferry too.

CARS, TRAINS AND COACHES

Perhaps the least traumatic mode of transport of all is your own **car**: accessible, comfortable and adapted to suit you; few worries about coping with heavy luggage; room for portable aids and equipment that will make life easier at your destination or save the day when an accessible loo cannot be found (a common scenario as soon as you leave the autoroutes); freedom to fix your own schedule and the means to get off the beaten track.

Facilities at most ports and on most ferries are not bad (see below), and there is an increasing number of rest areas or service stations in Europe that cater for disabled travellers, with adapted toilets, flat access, room to manoeuvre in shops and cafeterias, and low-level telephones. A few countries, including France, Germany and Sweden, supply information on the availability of these facilities along major routes. A less helpful trend is the increase in self-service petrol stations: carry a "Help" pennant if travelling alone.

Possible difficulties include mechanical breakdown and tiredness. The careless service given by many so-called approved main dealers is bad enough for able-bodied people but unforgivable when dished out to someone who is unable to get out of a broken-down car and walk a couple of miles to the nearest garage. The display of the *Motability* symbol in the window of your local dealer is by no means a guarantee of good service, and you may be better off – in terms of the peace of mind, health of your car engine and your wallet – taking your vehicle for a pre-holiday service at the nearest Lucas or Halfords centre.

Take advice from the *AA* or *RAC* on continental motoring – what documents you'll need, what spares to carry, and so on. The basics are Green Card from your motor insurance company, driving licence (International Driving Permit for some countries), vehicle registration document, GB sticker, warning triangle, first-aid kit, left- as well as right-side wing mirror, black tape for altering headlamp dip, headlight bulbs.

Touring holidays (see p.471) or journeys to the Mediterranean countries involve covering very long distances, on the "wrong side" of unfamiliar roads, following strange or incomprehensible road signs, so driver fatigue is not unlikely. To avoid it, don't be too ambitious, make frequent stops and, if possible, share the driving.

Those who are unable to walk short distances or manage a few steps will require assistance if they are to travel by **train**, and many people will be put off by the general lack of accessible loos. Booking assistance in advance is not simple and by no means foolproof. *British Rail* can, in theory, organise help at stations and ports this side of the Channel; consult the *RADAR* publication *A Guide to British Rail for Disabled People* (1991, £4.50) or write to the *International Rail Centre*, Victoria Station, London SW1 1JU.

Assistance with getting on and off trains or transferring between platforms, as well as wheelchair service at continental ports and stations, must be arranged through the UK offices of the appropriate national railway. Staff don't appear to be well versed in the facilities on their networks, and the few booklets that are produced on the subject (the French, German and Dutch ones give most detail) are not available in English. The *Holiday Care Service* publishes a fact sheet, *Rail Travel in Europe*.

If you can get through the planning stage, if the promised assistance materialises, and if you can find accessible toilets at stations or on the long-distance trains – best of all, if you have some degree of mobility – rail travel can be a relaxing way to see the countryside, and there are many reasonably priced passes and "rover" tickets for travellers on a tight budget. Blind passengers travelling with an escort are eligible for fare concessions on French Motorail – an easy way to get a car down to the Mediterranean.

Plenty of **coach** companies offer wheelchair-accessible vehicles for hire to groups (consult *RADAR*'s *Holidays and Travel Abroad*, the *Holiday Care Service* fact sheet, *Adapted Coach, Minibus or Caravan Hire*, or the *Bus and Coach Council*'s guide, *Getting Around by Bus and Coach*). These coaches provide a useful service, but do nothing to meet the needs of disabled individuals who want to join mainstream coach tours.

Some tour operators carry a folding chair on their coaches, so that passengers with limited walking powers can reach all the sights on the itinerary, but such passengers must be accompanied: there is none of the friendly service given by the Australian *Pioneer* guide at Ayers Rock (p.355), where Barbara Horrocks was hauled along rocky paths in her wheelchair. Drivers and guides on continental coach tours stick rigidly to their job descriptions – no lifting on and off the coach, and no spontaneous wheelchair pushing for them.

It would be a great step forward to see coaches on these routes equipped with hydraulic lifts and a few tie-down spaces for wheelchair users. This would cause no inconvenience to other passengers, other than a few minutes' delay while the wheelchair passengers were loaded or unloaded at each stopping place. In addition, some information on accessibility of accommodation en route would be simple to acquire.

This type of holiday is popular and usually good value for money: it should be opened up to people with disabilities, along with the possibility of travelling independently by coach to any of the European capitals.

FERRIES

Travellers using the newest additions to the **cross-Channel** fleets, such as *Sealink Stena Line*'s *Stena Fiesta* and *P&O*'s *Pride of Dover*, find large lifts from car deck to main deck, and all amenities easily accessible, including some of the cabins. Access at most ports is not bad – in the newer terminals it's very good – and procedures for boarding disabled passengers, whether in cars, coaches or transferring from trains, usually work well.

If there is one area that ferry companies fall down on, it is the publication of basic access information, updated each year along with all the other details in their general brochures. The glaring omission in the heap of glossy brochures published by the ferry companies is a description of facilities for disabled passengers: airlines are guilty of relying on outdated or inadequate passenger care leaflets (p.522; ferry companies have no worries on this score – most produce no printed information.

The *Olau-Line* brochure, *Car Ferry Holiday Guide*, is the exception here: the wheelchair symbol is used to indicate which cabins are adapted and which hotels can cater for the "partially disabled or wheelchair user". There is a paragraph for the benefit of disabled readers and a large box on the booking form for "special requests".

But detailed information, such as cabin layout, height and whereabouts of storm-sills, accessibility of bathrooms and toilets, is often difficult to extract. This is not good enough for travellers wishing to compare prices/concessions, facilities in the cabins, and access on board ship or at the terminals. If they could study the brochures and make an informed decision like everyone else, life would be simple; instead they must consult guides produced by disability organisations, which may or may not be up to date, and for door widths and bed heights they must write letters that are passed from one department to another, or make expensive and often fruitless phone calls.

It is understandable that information regarding fare concessions is not printed in every brochure because this seems to encourage abuse of the system: a spokesman for one company reports that they have had able-bodied passengers booking the cabin usually reserved for wheelchair users, simply because they wanted a larger cabin at a reduced price; there have also been attempts to swing a fare discount when the "registered disability" amounts to nothing more than a glass eye or a slight limp.

In **choosing a sea crossing**, disabled travellers are likely to consider the overall route and the fitting in of departure and destination ports into that route, length of crossing, price, and facilities at ports and on board ferries. The overall route and length of crossing are matters of personal taste, not usually related to disability – many people prefer a short crossing, with perhaps a longer drive the other side of the Channel, but a long crossing can make a relaxing alternative to the tiring drive south if the ultimate destination is Spain or Portugal.

If you book one of the longer Channel crossings, such as Harwich to The Hook, and you want to get some rest, you'll need to book a cabin – lounge seating, even if reclining, allows only fairly hardened travellers to sleep comfortably (see p.200). Remaining in your wheelchair is unwise if it's a rough crossing – a sudden lurch may send you flying, with or without the brakes on.

At first glance the **fares** for Channel crossings seem high when compared with the price of air travel which is, after all, much quicker. But there are a number of special discounts — 53-hour returns, family tariffs, five-day savers, and so on — that bring the rates down significantly. In addition, many companies (including *B&I, Belfast Car Ferries, Brittany Ferries, British Channel Island Ferries, Color Line, Isle of Man Steam Packet Seaways, North Sea Ferries, Olau-Line, P&O, Scandinavian Seaways* and *Sealink Stena Line*) offer generous concessions to members of the *Disabled Drivers' Motor Club* or *Disabled Drivers' Association*, both of whom charge a £2 booking fee.

Color Line offer a 25 percent reduction on the standard fare for registered disabled passengers travelling outside June 14—August 8, as well as free car passage for members of the *DDMC* or *DDA*. *North Sea Ferries* cut fifty percent off the car rate for *DDMC/DDA* members. The other companies all carry *DDMC/DDA* members' cars free. *Sealink Stena Line* (who make a small administration charge) also make this concession to registered disabled people who apply direct to the ferry company, if they can obtain a signature from their local Social Services department. *B&I* make an additional concession (one third off the ordinary single fare) to holders of a *Disabled Persons Railcard*.

Facilities at Channel ports are briefly described in the *AA/SIA* guide, *The World Wheelchair Traveller* (see *Books*); for more detail and for information on other ports it's necessary to ask the ferry company or the port manager. The basic requirements are an easy journey by foot or wheelchair from rail station, car park or queueing area to the terminal, good general access to all parts of the terminal buildings, with lifts and ramps where necessary, and wheelchair-accessible toilets.

These facilities are provided at Dover (advance notice necessary for short-term parking next to the terminal building at Eastern and Western Docks), the Dover Hoverport, Felixstowe, Guernsey, Jersey, Harwich, Hull, Newcastle, Pembroke, Portsmouth, Ramsgate, Sheerness and Weymouth. There is no wheelchair-accessible toilet at Newhaven, Plymouth or Southampton, and a couple of steps at the entrance to Newhaven terminal; otherwise general access is good.

Further refinements, such as induction loop systems .inside the terminal buildings, phones with TDD, tactile floor markings, audio and visual announcements, and good access to the cafeteria

(counters and tables at the correct height), are by no means widespread, but may be found in some ports, particularly at the newer terminals, such as Rosslare, in Ireland (p.108)

The choice of **accessible ships** is wide, with only a few older vessels lacking facilities for wheelchair passengers: if you require a wheelchair-accessible toilet, the ones to avoid are *Brittany Ferries' Duc de Normandie* and *P&O*'s Dover—Ostend route. If you require an adapted cabin, book early — most ships have no more than one or two.

B&I Line operate ships on the Pembroke—Rosslare and Holyhead—Dublin routes. An accessible service lift can be used from car deck to passenger deck; there is an accessible toilet, and cabins with wide doors are available.

Brittany Ferries offer good access (except to the cinemas) and adapted cabins aboard the *Bretagne* (see p.5), which sails from Plymouth to Santander. *British Channel Island Ferries* provide wheelchair-accessible cabins (see p.148) and toilets aboard their ships which leave from Poole.

Color Line (formerly *Norway Line* and *Jahre Line*, and now incorporating the *Fred Olsen Lines* North Sea routes, see pp.210, 496) operate four routes: Newcastle—Bergen/Stavanger; Kiel—Oslo; Hirtshals—Kristiansand. The *M/S Venus*, which sails from Newcastle, has adapted (three-berth) cabins, with handrails in the loo and shower. There are accessible toilets and lifts to all decks. Storm-sills must be negotiated to get out on the decks.

North Sea Ferries provide lifts between all decks and specially adapted cabins on their ships. There are wide doors to the cabins and *en suite* facilities, a drop-down seat in the shower, low-level basin and alarm button. Three adapted cabins are provided on each of the vessels sailing from Hull to Rotterdam, and one on each of the Hull-Zeebrugge ferries. This company will offer advice on suitable hotels to passengers booking inclusive holidays.

Olau-Line sail two jumbo ferries, *Olau Hollandia* and *Olau Britannia*, between Sheerness and Vlissingen (Flushing). Each ship has lifts to all decks and a few cabins with no sills or steps, plus specially adapted toilets and handrails for visually handicapped passengers.

P&O's "Superferries", *Pride of Dover* and *Pride of Calais*, sail the Dover—Calais route and are fully accessible, with lifts to all amenities and adapted toilets. On the Dover–Boulogne route, the *Pride of Canterbury* and *Pride of Hythe* have toilets and a lift to the passenger deck, but no wheelchair access to the Club Class facilities. The *Pride of Bruges* is the recommended ship for Dover–Zeebrugge crossings; the *Ionic Ferry* is recommended on the Larne–Cairnryan route. All ships have accessible toilets except some of those operated by *P&O*'s Belgian partner, *RMT*, on the Dover–Ostend crossing; *RMT* will be introducing a new luxury ferry to this route during 1991, as well as refurbishing the existing fleet. In addition to lifts and accessible toilets, there are adapted cabins on the *Nordic Ferry* and *Baltic Ferry* (Felixstowe–Zeebrugge), on the *Pride of Winchester* and *Pride of Cherbourg* (Portsmouth–Cherbourg), and on the *Pride of Le Havre* and *Pride of Hampshire* (Portsmouth–Le Havre). On all vessels the lift from car deck to main passenger deck is a service lift, so advance warning is necessary so that crew can be on hand to operate it.

Sally Line's two ships, *Sally Star* and *Sally Sky*, sail from Ramsgate to Dunkirk (both ports fully accessible, with toilets) and have the rare distinction of carrying Braille menus in the restaurant. The *Sally Star* has a wheelchair-accessible lift from car deck to all decks and one accessible loo on the main deck. Adapted cabins have 70-centimetre-wide doors and a small (6cm) ridge in the doorway; *en suite* toilet and shower are said to be accessible. The *Sally Sky* has a lift only to

the main corridor, where all dining facilities are situated, so there is no access to the duty free or the top-deck Sky Bar.

Scandinavian Seaways ships have good general access, and three – the *Dan Anglia*, *Tor Brittania* and *Tor Scandinavia* – have special cabins with wheelchair-accessible bathrooms. The routes covered are Harwich or Newcastle to Gothenburg or Ejsberg, Newcastle–Bergen and Harwich–Hamburg.

Sealink Stena Line's older ferries are only partially accessible but facilities are excellent on the *Fantasia*, *Fiesta* (both operating between Dover and Calais), *Sylvia Regina* (Harwich to The Hook), *St Christopher* (Stranraer to Larne), *St Anselm* (Holyhead to Dun Laoghaire), *Champs Elysées* (Newhaven to Dieppe) and *Côte d'Azur* (Dover to Calais).

There are no wheelchair-accessible toilets on board *Hoverspeed*'s Dover–Calais hovercraft, and boarding requires some assistance, but there's a unisex toilet in the departure lounge and the speed of crossing (if not the fares) must be popular with some.

Contributors generally report very good service from ferry company staff, in particular *Sealink* (p.201) and *P&O* (p.160). It would be nice to see this backed up with some well-informed office staff, capable of answering questions on the layout of the ships, the exact nature of a "specially adapted cabin" and the facilities available at both ports.

Sleeping

Destination and type of holiday, availability of information, and your own approach to travelling will determine whether you try to locate a suitable place to stay before departure or on arrival. In many countries of the world (particularly in some parts of Mediterranean Europe, Africa, Asia, the Middle East and South America) disabled travellers have to rely on a combination of good luck, good will and their own resources in order to make the best of the available (and affordable) accommodation. Disasters are, on the whole, remarkably rare; lack of choice, inconvenience, and enforced dependence on others are more common experiences.

In the USA, Canada, Australia and New Zealand it should be possible to find accessible accommodation in all price brackets without booking in advance. In Europe, a good deal of information is provided by the *Holiday Care Service* and *RADAR*; accurate and verified accommodation listings are produced by only a handful of tourist boards, of which the Swedish Tourist Board stand out with their *Holiday Guide for the Disabled* (p.213), available in English and German.

The English Tourist Board's involvement with the *Holiday Care Service* and the *Tourism for All* project should result in more widespread use of symbols that can be relied on within the next few years. Two guides for accommodation operators wishing to improve accessibility in new and existing premises have been produced: *Providing Accessible Accommmodation* (£5, from the English Tourist Board) – the only criticism being that a bath is impractical for many disabled people with poor arm strength, and all the model bathroom layouts contain baths not showers; and *Easy Steps to Welcome Guests with Disabilities* (sponsored by *British Telecom;* free copies available from national and regional tourist boards), which suggests low-cost and no-cost modifications to hotels, guesthouses and B&Bs as well as covering staff training and attitudes.

For touring holidays it is usually impractical to book ahead; advice on this sort of travelling is given on p.504. For long-stay holidays or if visiting popular places in high season, reservation is advisable. The *Travel Notes* sections offer a range of accommodation recommended by our contributors, and list any guides produced by tourist boards or disability organisations in each country. Other sources include the *RADAR* holiday guides and *Holiday Care Service* fact sheets.

Although most central reservations staff will contact specific hotels direct to establish more precise access information, depressingly few hotel chains (the *RADAR* guide lists twelve) make any mention of disabled guests in their directories and publicity leaflets. Even fewer contain sufficient detail: a wheelchair symbol is not enough, and "facilities for the handicapped" could mean anything from a grab-rail in the bathroom to a fully accessible bedroom and bathroom, with tactile/Braille room number, visual alert, low-level light switches – the complete range of facilities. Criteria for deeming the hotel

accessible (see p.141) must be stated; *Consort Hotels* is currently the only group to do this, in their *Nice 'n Easy* brochure.

If there is no reliable published information, and no central reservations office to assist, facilities and accessibility may be researched via travel agents or tour operators, or direct from the hotel itself. But this is not always successful and often more trouble than it's worth: travel agents and tour operators may be more concerned with taking a booking than ensuring that the accommodation is suitable; enquiries by letter to hoteliers may take weeks, enquiries by phone will be expensive, and in either case there may be language difficulties.

In the end, many travellers find it unnecessary and even detrimental to give advance warning of their disabilities (see pp.249, 504. If your main concern is finding cheap accommodation this is certainly the best approach: in many countries the hotel chains that provide facilities for disabled guests are in the top half of the price range, and if you are looking at smaller, independent hotels or guesthouses in far-flung places the hassles of determining numbers of steps and doorway widths in advance will probably prove too much.

There are a number of lightweight pieces of equipment that can be carried (see p.518) in case of obstacles, but your most effective weapon is the attitude that anything can be solved with a little improvisation, and if the situation really is unworkable then there's always another motel, B&B or campsite around the corner. Owners of inaccessible properties will often point you towards something more suitable in the area, and local tourist information offices are usually very helpful – you're unlikely to find yourself on the street.

Eating and drinking

It's possible to find **wheelchair-accessible** eating and drinking places in most parts of the world. Awareness is good in North America, Australia, New Zealand, and some northern European and Asian countries; access to restaurants is described in several publications produced by disability organisations or tourist

boards, and the wheelchair symbol is used in a few restaurant and pub guides. *McDonald's* and *Burger King* score highly for accessible toilets.

But choice is limited: toilets are often sited at the bottom of a steep flight of stairs; the small neighbourhood restaurant is usually more concerned to pack in the tables than allow space for manoeuvre of wheelchairs. Tables are too low, bars are too high, and provision of low-level and TDD-equipped phones, or Braille menus, is rare.

Where temperatures allow, as in Mediterranean Europe, Africa, South America, Asia and the Middle East, eating and drinking al fresco makes access easier. It doesn't solve the problem of accessible toilets, but there may be facilities nearby, in five-star hotels, modern shopping malls or fast-food restaurants.

Coping with **special diets** should be straightforward if you are prepared for the sort of foods and drinks likely to be encountered; a good guidebook will supply the necessary information.

Contributors who report dietary experiences include vegetarian Annie Delin in Poland (p.222), coeliac Joy Schwabe in the Soviet Union (p.234) and Christine Panton and her diabetic husband in the USA (p.414).

With advance notice most airlines can satisfy a wide range of dietary requirements, and hotels will usually make at least a token effort to produce food that you can eat, but vegetarians have a hard time in several areas of the world, wherever a meal isn't a meal without meat (West African and Eastern European countries, the Soviet Union, to name a few). In these parts vegetarianism could almost be classed a disability.

Getting around

Almost all forms of transport are accessible with help, and there are reports throughout this book of travelling in dugouts, helicopters, Jeeps and cable cars, as well as the more conventional ferry, bus, train, plane, taxi and hire car. In some countries the public transport authorities are improving access to their existing vehicles and designing more accessible rolling stock for the future: a few of the systems singled out for praise by our contributors are the USA's *Amtrak* rail network, Canada's *VIA Rail*, San Francisco's *BART* and *MUNI* buses and trains, Metrorail in Washington DC, *BC Transit*'s SeaBus and SkyTrain in Vancouver.

But getting around independently is difficult in most countries for many disabled travellers, including those with visual or hearing impairment. Aircraft, ferries, hire cars and taxis present the smallest access problems. Aircraft are probably easiest for blind or deaf people. Trains are usually more tricky and buses a nuisance to anyone with limited mobility.

BY AIR

Like international flights, **domestic air travel** involves cramped seating and inaccessible toilets, but the shorter journey times make these much more bearable. For exploring large countries, such as Australia or North and South America, flying is the only way to pack a lot of

sightseeing into a short holiday. It may be expensive, but there are often special discounts and passes, and a common deal offered by national carriers is a free internal flight included in the price of the international flight.

One potential disadvantage is that there may be free-for-all boarding rather than pre-boarding of disabled passengers (see p.421). This means that disabled person and companion may be separated, which is disorientating for blind or deaf passengers relying on seeing or hearing escorts, or for a severely disabled person who needs help with eating or communicating with the cabin crew. In addition, a personal safety briefing before other passengers board is impossible. In some countries there are only basic facilities at the smaller, regional airports – boarding by fork-lift (p.348) or manual lifting (p.152), and perhaps no wheelchair service (pp.259, 336), accessible toilets or eating place.

BY SEA

Ships and boats vary enormously in accessibility. On the one hand is the modern car ferry (p.530) or hydrofoil (p.331), with facilities such as spacious passenger lifts, ramps over the storm-sills (or no sills at all), adapted toilets, space for manoeuvre in the restaurants and bars, Braille menus, and larger cabins for wheelchair users. Then there are the smaller, inter-island cruisers and catamarans (p.349), with no special adaptations – and no loos – but hefty crewmen to see you aboard, short journey times, and maybe some hot sun to dehydrate you.

At the other end of the scale there are the small boats – the jet-boats (p.441), sailing boats (p.135) and canoes (p.463) – for which the big problem is boarding or disembarking. If this can be overcome, the disabled person's lack of mobility no longer matters – you can't walk far in a dinghy. Here some lessons could be learned from Sweden and Cornwall: the Swedes have installed simple hoists and adapted canoes at a number of locations so that disabled people can enjoy some of their country's lakes; the *Churchtown Farm* centre in Cornwall has a flat-bottomed cruiser at Fowey which allows wheelchair boarding of their canoes and adapted sailing dinghies (p.135).

BY ROAD AND RAIL

Self-drive cars offer the disabled traveller the greatest freedom and flexibility but the availability of hand controls on a worldwide basis is not good, and the price of car rental is often prohibitive. Even where hand controls are supposed to be available, promises of adapted cars waiting at the airport are not always honoured by the big international hire companies (pp.409, 436). Smaller companies say that they are unable to bear the cost of having controls fitted for one client, then removed for the next.

There are a number of ways to avoid inconvenience and disappointment. If you are travelling alone or with a non-driver to the USA, *Lindo's Rent-a-Car* have a good reputation, and are used by *Virgin/Threshold* for their fly-drive packages (p.514); *Europcar/National Car Rental* should also come up with the goods. When visiting other countries beyond the reach of your own car, take a set of controls and find a local company who will fit them; disability organisations within the country you are visiting may be able to recommend someone. If accompanied by a driver, forget the hand controls. The cost per person will be lower for a group, particularly when compared with rail or air fares. You can also save money by shopping around for a local company.

On the whole there have been surprisingly few reports of problems with finding **parking** spaces close to hotels, shops or sights, and they are confined to big cities such as New York and London (seen by many as the worst culprit), or small villages such as the hill villages of Provence, where steep winding streets and lack of space leave little scope for building car parks. Some contributors found abuse of reserved spaces by able-bodied drivers to be less common abroad.

Reciprocal parking arrangements for Orange Badge holders exist in much of Europe (none in Cyprus, Gibraltar, Greece, Malta, Yugoslavia or the Eastern European countries), and the badge is recognised in parts of the States and Canada; where it is not, temporary permits can be obtained. There are concessions and reserved spaces in other countries, including Australia, New Zealand, Singapore and Hong Kong, and where there are no rules laid down the authorities will often show tolerance of visiting disabled drivers who park without causing obstruction.

Taxis are used extensively by our contributors both for getting around cities and for longer sightseeing trips. They make an easily accessible alternative to buses and organised coach tours, and taxi drivers are generally reported helpful. For travellers with sight or hearing difficulties, and for those who need to set their own pace, this one-to-one service is ideal. In most countries the vehicles used tend to be large, if sometimes ancient, so that there is plenty of room for transferring to the car seat and storing the wheelchair in the boot. Even the smaller, more colourful variations, such as Bangkok's *tuk-tuks* (p.322) and Manila's jeepneys (p.328), can be used with some assistance.

As a rule, ordinary saloon-type taxis (Mercedes, Volvos, the big American and Canadian limos) are better than the London cab. Wheelchair passengers using standard London cabs require very strong arms to hoist themselves onto the pull-down seat and then across to the main bench seat. Unfortunately the adapted Metro and Fairway cabs (used in London and Edinburgh) that allow wheelchair users to roll up a ramp and remain in their chairs are not the answer for everyone: the roof is too low for people of average height to sit without bending their heads to one side; and in an ideal world the passenger must be given the choice of whether to transfer to a comfortable and supportive seat or rock about in their wheelchair.

There are several adapted taxis available for hire in various parts of the world, their only fail-ings being expense and the need to book well ahead. New Zealand's *Total Mobility* taxi service (p.328) appears to have overcome at least one of these, acting as an affordable (through the use of vouchers) alternative to inaccessible buses and trains; advance booking is not always necessary, but advisable at peak times.

The matter of choice is equally important on **trains**. Some well-intentioned and costly alterations have been made to carriages without keeping this in mind. So wheelchair passengers are ushered into special compartments (pp.341, 381) or told that they must remain in the vestibule or goods van (p.117) instead of wheeling themselves onto the train and electing either to sit in the wheelchair space, with tie-down facility, or to transfer to a seat and stow the folded chair between the seats.

This is not to denigrate the great efforts that have been and are being made by some networks, but rather to encourage the use of adaptations that allow maximum flexibility and avoid putting disabled passengers in the slow lane – if you have to wait for assistance to get from car park to ticket office, then wait for a station porter to accompany you via special lifts to the departure platform, and wait again for someone else to help you board the train, it's all time wasted that could be more enjoyably spent settling into your train seat and reading a book or getting to know your fellow passengers.

Boarding is made difficult by narrow doors (often with awkward handles), steps and a gap between platform and train. These obstacles are being slowly removed in parts of northern Europe, the USA, Canada and Asia, but with emphasis on the "slowly", and in other countries there is no hint of change. The situation on the newer underground networks is slightly better: the trains more often come in flush with the platform and there are wide sliding doors – but even these doorways are sometimes spoiled by a vertical bar placed in the centre of the entrance (p.205).

Standard wheelchairs are useless on older trains with narrow corridors or aisles; in these cases it would be helpful if rail companies supplied narrow, folding chairs (rather like airline aisle chairs) that could be used throughout the journey. On long-distance routes, trains should be equipped with at least one toilet accessible to these chairs.

There are growing attempts to make route planning and ticket purchase easier for blind and deaf travellers, with the use of induction loops at booking office windows, TDD numbers for reservations, and Braille timetables. Tactile markers on the edge of platforms, large lettering on signs and clear announcements make the journey easier on several overland networks and underground systems – but not nearly enough.

In short, there's much to be done on the world's railways if we are to achieve independent and spontaneous travel for disabled passengers. Too often, assistance has to be requested in advance and communications fail somewhere along the line, so that the expected porter with wheelchair is not there. In view of the fact that most disabled passengers will need assistance, it seems only fair that some enlightened rail companies, including *British Rail*, *Amtrak* (USA), *VIA Rail* (Canada), *SNCF* (France) and *NS* (Netherlands), give substantial discounts to handicapped passengers and/or to those who are unable to travel without a companion.

The sorry state of the world's **buses** is mentioned in many accounts. Usually the cheapest form of city transport, buses cannot be used by the majority of mobility-impaired people because of near-vertical steps at the entrance. Modern vehicles are now designed to be more low slung, with fewer, shallower steps, big bright handrails and easily spotted "stop" buttons, and with front seats "reserved for disabled passengers".

But, except for a few US cities, the adaptations stop short of a wheelchair lift, and even where this is installed the wheelchair passenger may be thwarted by drivers who cannot be bothered to get out and operate it (p.426). The alternative is to shuffle up the steps on your backside (p.429), or ask two strong passengers to lift you aboard – Nic Fleming reports that he has never been refused help in this way, travelling solo on buses in Malta, Israel, Paris and the USA, as well as on airport buses in a number of countries. However, he says, "Buses are a bore. I probably use them two or three times a year, less if possible." In some countries (Australia, Yugoslavia), drivers on organised sightseeing tours will cheerfully provide this lifting service.

Neither method of boarding is ideal, and the introduction of special minibuses for disabled travellers is not a solution – as with adapted taxis, using them invariably involves booking at least 24 hours (sometimes more) in advance, and they often operate on restricted routes. The answer must lie in designing totally accessible vehicles that do not require a long stop in order to board a wheelchair passenger, and proper training of staff so that *all* passengers are welcomed aboard.

Work and study

Most people with disabilities will be able to participate in a wide range of projects and courses abroad, but research will be necessary in some cases. Sian Williams, for example, almost gave up hope when looking for a university campus that was both accessible and offered an appropriate course (p.164). In many countries, access for disabled students is the goal of hard-fought battles, and limited opportunities for education and training contribute to poor levels of employment among the disabled population. The situation is perhaps least depressing in the States, but if your ambitions lie elsewhere, persistent letter writing is, in Sian's experience, the key.

If you prefer someone else to do the organising, consult the *Holiday Care Service* fact sheet, *Working Holidays*. The *Mobility International* programme (see p.509) consists of a series of **educational and leisure projects** – cultural, activity-based, language courses, discussions, seminars. These are open to young disabled people (usually 18–30 years, but sometimes no upper age limit) of different nationalities and abilities. The 1991 programme includes computer tuition in Ireland, Deaf-Blind International Week in Greece, European Dialysis Week in Mallorca and ten days of Italian culture, language and cuisine at the "hundred-percent accessible" *San Felice Hotel* on the coast between Rome and Naples.

For **conservation work**, there are several options open, including Operation Raleigh (see p.362) and *Earthwatch*. Teams of *Earthwatch* volunteers work on environmental projects all over the world, from preserving sea turtles in the Yucatán peninsula to pinpointing coastal wildlands in need of protection along Britain's coastline. Handicapped volunteers have joined projects in the past, and the organisers have a very positive approach to placing people with disabilities, subject to the physical constraints of the project. All volunteers have to produce a medical certificate, giving a doctor's assurance that they can cope physically with the work involved. Each person's share of the costs is quite high, but many obtain sponsorship.

Other contributors who travelled with more serious missions than pure holidaymaking include Charlotte Billington, who joined a *Project Phoenix Trust* Study Tour of Sweden (p.207); Julie Smethurst improved her Spanish on a group holiday (p.10); Joy Schwabe studied art and architecture in Russia, on a five-day tour organised by the Royal Academy (p.234); Kate Margrie shared her skills on a Health Education Project in Sierra Leone (p.270); Carolyn Lucas was funded by the *Winston Churchill Memorial Trust* in her investigation of training and employment of actors with disabilities in the USA (p.390).

Participation in **sports or activity holidays** is a popular way to combine an interest in sport with a love of travel; useful fact sheets are available from the *Holiday Care Service* and *RADAR*. Ron Cottrell learned to ski in Austria with the *Uphill Ski Club* (p.189), and Terence Wilson joined the crew of a sail training ship (p.490). Information on sports clubs and training for disabled people can be obtained from the *British Sports Association for the Disabled*. Competition often involves travel to events abroad – see Jack Davidson's account of taking part in the Himalayan Rally (p.478).

John Bignell (p.275), Nic Fleming (pp.504, 528 and Frankie Armstrong (p.499) describe **work-related travel** experiences. It seems that the disabled business traveller remains an unexpected arrival at conferences (p.275) and on planes (p.528). Many operators are put off their stride by a wheelchair user in a hurry to get to a meeting, rather than the more common, passive variety who's on holiday and sits patiently waiting for the airport wheelchair to be delivered to the aircraft door when all the other passengers have long gone.

After your trip

At the end of your stay it's important to make the operator aware of both good and bad aspects of his or her services or facilities. If you are delighted with everything, or only one thing, say so. If the grab-rail is in the wrong place, or transfer to the toilet is awkward, if no stool is provided in the shower, mention this to the hotel management. In addition to giving the operator some sort of feedback, it is helpful to **share access information** with other disabled travellers.

One of the most frequently voiced requests is for reliable information. Only a handful of tourist boards attempt to meet this need; few tourism operators research facilities and incorporate access details in their brochures. There are excellent fact sheets and guides produced by organisations such as the *Holiday Care Service* and *RADAR*, but they cannot hope to cover every resort, hotel, campsite, tourist attraction and transport network, and lack of manpower and financial resources prevents them from verifying each entry in their publications. Likewise, this book is no access guide to the world, but a contribution to the pool of information.

The best way to update and correct this information is for travellers to report their experiences, to recommend the accessible places and point out the defects in other cases. If you are using a guide or fact sheet and you come across inaccuracies, send your comments to the publisher. Accounts will be (we hope) be required for a second edition of *Nothing Ventured*; meanwhile, any additions, criticisms or amendments concerning information given in this first edition should be sent to Alison Walsh, c/o The Rough Guides, 149 Kennington Lane, London SE11 4EZ.

If you are unfortunate enough to experience bad service, broken promises or inadequate facilities, you may feel bound to end your holiday with the tedious process of **making a complaint**. Angela Deakin (p.422) has the following advice to offer.

Make a written note of the complaint whilst still on holiday. Take photographs (rubbish in a swimming pool or a flooded flat are more convincing six months later if you have a set of photographs). Ensure that a tour rep fills out the appropriate form and signs it; ask for a copy.

On return, phone the company and make a formal complaint; note the name of the person to whom you complain. Then set out clearly in writing the exact nature of your complaint and what you expect the company to do about it. Keep a photocopy of this letter and send it, recorded delivery (the receipt is acceptable in court as evidence of delivery), to the highest official in the company – it's easier to start at the top.

Do not send any evidence with the initial complaint. Study any reply carefully: if the matter is settled immediately, be very thankful – most settlements are reached after many months or even years. More correspondence may result in an amicable settlement, but action in the Small Claims Court is usually very effective. More complicated claims will probably require the help of a solicitor – in any case a solicitor's letter often brings a more realistic response from the company.

Ask yourself whether or not your claim justifies the possible legal costs, but remember that if you go ahead and win, all your legal expenses will be paid by the other side.

Books

All the publications listed here have been recommended at some stage in this book. Probably the largest collection of **guides for handicapped travellers**, started in 1979 by medical librarian Irene Shanefield and still growing, exists at the *Jewish Rehabilitation Hospital* (3205 Place Alton Goldbloom, Laval, Quebec, Canada H7V 1R2; ☎514/688-9550). You can request information on almost any country, and relevant guide(s) will be photocopied for a small fee; if medical care such as dialysis is required while travelling, details of where this can be obtained will be included.

AA Guide for the Disabled Traveller (yearly, £3.50 or free to members), available from *AA* Distribution Services, Dunhams Lane, Letchworth, Hertfordshire SG6 1LF (☎0462/686241) or bookshops.

Access guides researched and produced by the *Pauline Hephaistos Survey Projects (PHSP)* teams: *Access in Israel* (1988, free from tourist board); *Jersey* (1986, free from tourist board); *London* (1989, but updated supplements available during 1991; Nicholson, £3.50); *Paris* (1985, but updated supplements available during 1991; £2.75). Can all be obtained from *RADAR* (see *Directory*) or *PHSP* (39 Bradley Gardens, London W13 8HE).

A Travellers' Handbook for Persons with Epilepsy, from the *International Bureau for Epilepsy* (PO Box 21, 2100 AA Heemstede, The Netherlands; ☎23/339 060).

Directory for Disabled People compiled by Ann Darnborough and Derek Kinrade (6th edition due August 1991, £19.95), published by *RADAR* and Woodhead-Faulkner (Fitzwilliam House, 32 Trumpington Street, Cambridge CB2 1QY; ☎0223/66733).

Disabled Drivers' Motor Club Handbook (yearly, free to members, £1.25 from *RADAR*).

Disabled Traveller's International Phrasebook, specialist vocabulary for European travel (£1.50, from *RADAR* or the publisher, *Disability Press*, 17 Union Street, Kingston upon Thames KT1 1RP; ☎081/549 6399).

Door to Door: A Guide to Transport for People with Disabilities (updated every other year), published by *Department of Transport*, free from local authorities and disability organisations, libraries, and £2.50 from bookshops.

Life in the Sun *A Guide to Long-stay Holidays and Living Abroad in Retirement* (1990, £6.95, from bookshops or *Age Concern England*).

Michelin guides: Benelux, France and Germany, from bookshops.

Out and About *A Travel and Transport Guide* (1990, £5.95) by Richard Armitage and John Taylor, published by *Age Concern England*.

RAC guides, updated yearly (all prices include postage): *On the Move*, for disabled motorists (£3.40); *Hotel Guide* (£10.95 to members, £11.95 to non-members); *Small Hotel Guide* (guesthouses and B&B, £4.95); *European Hotel Guide* (£8.95), available from *RAC Enterprises* (Publications Department, RAC House, PO Box 100, Croydon CR2 6XW; ☎081/686 2525) or bookshops.

RADAR publications: *Holidays in the British Isles* (1991, £4.50); *Holidays and Travel Abroad* (1991/92 edition due September, £4.50); *The Countryside and Wildlife for Disabled People* (1990, £3); *A Guide to British Rail for Disabled People* (1991, £4.50); *Motoring and Mobility for Disabled People* (5th edition due June 1991, £4.50).

Rough Guides: Forty titles, from bookshops.

The World Wheelchair Traveller (1990, £3.95), joint publication by *AA/Spinal Injuries Association*.

Travellers' Health: How to Stay Healthy Abroad by Doctor Richard Dawood (1989, OUP, £5.95).

Directory

AIRLINES

Aer Lingus, Aer Lingus House, 83 Staines Road, Hounslow TW3 3JB (☎081/569 5555)

Air Canada, 7/8 Conduit Street, London W1R 9TG (☎071/465 0090; reservations ☎081/759 2636)

Air France, 158 New Bond Street, London W1Y 0AY (☎071/499 9511)

Air Lanka, 6 Bruton Street, London W1X 7AJ (☎071/439 0291)

Air Malta, Air Malta House, 314/316 Upper Richmond Road, London SW15 6TU (☎081/785 3199)

Air New Zealand, Elsinore House, 77 Fulham Palace Road, London W6 8JA (☎081/741 2299)

Air UK, Stansted House, Stansted Airport, Essex CM24 8QT (☎0279/755950; "Linkline" reservations ☎0345/666777).

American Airlines, Trinity Square, 23–59 Staines Road, Hounslow TW3 3HE (☎081/572 5555)

British Airways: Supervisor, Incapacitated Passenger Unit, *BA* Health Centre, Queens Building (N121), London (Heathrow) Airport, Hounslow TW6 2JA (☎081/562 7070; reservations ☎081/897 4000; Minicom ☎081/562 0313; medical service ☎081/750 5616; immunisation service ☎081/759 5511)

Canadian Airlines International, 1st Floor, Rothschild House, Whitgift Centre, Croydon CR9 3HN (Reservations ☎081/667 0666; outside London ☎0345/616767)

Cathay Pacific, 7 Apple Tree Yard, Duke of York Street, London SW1Y 6LD (☎071/930 4444; reservations ☎071/930 7878)

Cyprus Airways, Euston Centre, 29–31 Hampstead Road, London NW1 3AJ (☎071/388 5411)

Dan Air, Newman House, Victoria Road, Horley, Surrey RH6 7QG (☎0293/100200)

EL AL Israel Airlines, 185 Regent Street, London W1R 8BS (☎071/439 2564)

Emirates, 125 Pall Mall, London SW1Y 5EA (☎071/930 5356)

Gulf Air, 10 Albemarle Street, London W1X 3HE (☎071/409 0191; reservations ☎071/408 1717)

Japan Airlines, Hanover Court, 5 Hanover Square, London W1R 0DR (☎071/408 1000)

KLM Royal Dutch Airlines, KLM Building, 8 Hanover Street, London W1R 9HF (☎071/750 9200; reservations ☎081/750 9000)

Lufthansa German Airlines, 23–26 Piccadilly, London W1V 0EJ (☎071/408 0322; reservations ☎071/408 0442)

Monarch Airlines, Luton Airport, Luton LU2 9NU (☎0582/398333)

Olympic Airways, Commonwealth House, 2 Chalkhill Road, London W6 8SB (☎081/846 9966; reservations ☎081/846 9080)

Qantas Airways, Qantas House, 395/403 King Street, London W6 9NJ (☎081/846 0466; reservations ☎0345/747767)

SAS Scandinavian Airlines System, 52 Conduit Street, London W1R 0AY (☎071/734 4020)

Singapore Airlines, 143–147 Regent Street, London W1R 7LB (☎071/439 8111)

South African Airways, 251–259 Regent Street, London W1R 7AD (☎071/734 9841)

Swissair, Swiss Centre, 10 Wardour Street, London W1V 4BJ (☎071/734 6737; reservations ☎071/439 4144)

Thai Airways International, 41 Albemarle Street, London W1X 3FE (☎071/499 9113)

Viasa Venezuelan International Airways, 19–20 Grosvenor Street, London W1X 9FD (☎071/493 3630)

Virgin Atlantic, Ashdown House, High Street, Crawley, West Sussex RH10 1DQ (☎0293/562345; reservations ☎0293/562000)

AIRPORTS

Aberdeen Airport, Dyce, Aberdeen AB2 0DU (☎0224/722331, ext 5312; arrange parking with Duty Manager, ext 5111)

Belfast International Airport, Belfast BT29 4AB, Northern Ireland (☎08494/22888; to book wheelchair space on the Airbus ☎0232/320011, ext 419)

Birmingham International Airport, Birmingham B26 3QJ (☎021/767 7145; to reserve parking space, *NCP* ☎021/767 7861)

Bournemouth International Airport, Christchurch, Dorset BH23 6SE (☎0202/579751)

Bristol Airport, Bristol BS19 3DY (☎0275/474444)

Cardiff-Wales Airport, South Glamorgan CF6 9BD (☎0446/711111)

East Midlands International Airport, Castle Donington, Derby DE7 2SA (☎0332/810621; *NCP* ☎0332/810621)

Edinburgh Airport, Edinburgh EH12 9DN (☎031/344 3136; arrange parking with Duty Manager, ☎031/344 3323)

Gatwick Airport, West Sussex RH6 0NP (☎0293/28822; Car Parks Manager ☎0293/503899)

Glasgow Airport, Paisley PA3 2ST (☎041/887 1111, ext 4552; arrange parking with Duty Manager, ext 4510)

Heathrow Airport, Hounslow TW6 1JH (☎081/759 4321; car park information ☎081/745 7160; Carelink information ☎071/222 5600; Airbus information ☎071/227 3299)

Kent International Airport, Manston, Kent CT12 5BP (☎0843/823333)

Leeds Bradford Airport, Yeadon, Leeds LS19 7TZ (☎0532/509696)

London City Airport, King George V Dock, Silvertown, London E16 2PX (☎071/474 5555)

Luton International Airport, Luton LU2 9LY (☎0582/405100; to arrange car parking, write to the Airport Director)

Manchester Airport, Manchester M22 FPA (☎061/489 3000; car park reservations ☎061/489 3723)

Newcastle International Airport, Woolsington, Newcastle-upon-Tyne NE13 8BZ (☎091/286 0966)

Prestwick Airport, Ayrshire KA9 2PL (☎0292/ 79822, ext 5090; arrange parking with Duty Manager, ext 5101)

Southampton Eastleigh Airport, Southampton SO9 1RH (☎0703/629600)

Stansted Airport, Stansted, Essex CM24 8QW (☎0279/502379; arrange assistance from car park to terminal with Duty Officer ☎0279/502387)

Teeside International Airport, Darlington DL2 1LU (☎0325/332811)

CAR HIRE COMPANIES

Avis Rent-a-Car, Trident House, Station Road, Hayes UB3 4DJ (☎081/848 8733)

Budget Rent a Car International, 41 Marlowes, Hemel Hempstead HP1 1LD (☎0442/ 232555 or ☎0800/181181)

Europcar/National Car Rental, Bushey House, High Street, Bushey, Watford WD2 1RE (☎0532/ 429300; reservations ☎081/950 5050)

Hertz Rent a Car, Radnor House, 1272 London Road, Norbury, London SW16 4XW (☎081/679 1799)

Lindo's Rent-a-Car, Paddon House, 12 Stortford Road, Great Dunmow, Essex CM6 1DA (☎0371/ 876076)

FERRY COMPANIES

B&I Line, Alexandra Road, Ferryport, Dublin 1, Ireland (☎0001/788077)

British Channel Island Ferries, Passenger Terminal, New Harbour Road, Poole, Dorset BH15 4AJ (☎0202/681155)

Brittany Ferries, Millbay Docks, Plymouth PL1 3EW (☎0752/221321)

Color Line, Tyne Commission Quay, North Shields NE29 6EA (☎091/296 1313)

Condor Weymouth Ltd, Weymouth Quay, Dorset DT4 8DX (☎0305/761551)

Hoverspeed, Dover International Hoverport, Kent CT17 9TG (☎0304/240241)

Isle of Man Steam Packet Company, Sea Terminal, Heysham, Lancashire LA3 2XF (☎0524/ 53802)

North Sea Ferries, King George Dock, Hedon Road, Hull HU9 5QA (☎0482/795141)

Olau-Line, Sheerness, Kent ME12 1SN (☎0795/ 580010; reservations ☎0795/666666)

P&O European Ferries, Channel House, Channel View Road, Dover, Kent CT18 9TJ (☎0304/203388); Cairnryan, Stranraer, Dumfries DG9 8RF (☎05812/276; central reservations ☎0304/203388)

P&O Scottish Ferries, PO Box 5, Jamieson Quay, Aberdeen AB9 8DL (☎0224/589111)

Sally Line, Argyle Centre, York Street, Ramsgate, Kent CT11 9DS (☎0843/595522)

Scandinavian Seaways, Central Reservations Office, Scandinavia House, Parkeston Quay, Harwich, Essex CO12 4QG (☎0255/241234)

Sealink Stena Line, Charter House, Park Street, Ashford, Kent TN24 8EX (☎0233/647047)

TRANSPORT ADVICE

Access to the Skies UK, c/o *RADAR*, 25 Mortimer Street, London W1N 8AB (☎071/637 5400)

Air Transport Users Committee, 2nd Floor, Kingsway House, 103 Kingsway, London WC2B 6QX (☎071/242 3882)

Automobile Association, Fanum House, Basingstoke RG21 2EA (☎0256/20123)

British Railways Board: Liaison Manager (Disabled Passengers), Euston House, 24 Eversholt Street, PO Box 100, London NW1 1DZ (☎071/928 5151); *International Rail Centre*, Victoria Station, London SW1 1JU (☎071/834 2345)

Bus and Coach Council, Sardinia House, 52 Lincoln's Inn Fields, London WC2A 3LZ (☎071/ 3817456)

Civil Aviation Authority, Cabin Safety, Aviation House, Gatwick Airport South, West Sussex RH6 0YR (☎0293/567171)

Department of Transport, Disability Unit, Room S10/21, 2 Marsham Street, London SW1P 3EB (☎071/276 5256)

IATA (*International Air Transport Association*), Imperial House, 15–19 Kingsway, London WC2B 6EN (☎071/497 1048)

Joint Committee on Mobility for Disabled People: Tim Shapley OBE (Secretary), 9 Moss Close, Pinner, Middlesex HA5 3AY (☎081/866 7884)

London Dial-a-Ride Users' Association, St Margarets, 25 Leighton Road, London NW5 2QD (☎071/482 2325)

London Regional Transport, Unit for Disabled Passengers, 55 Broadway, London SW1H 0BD (☎071/222 5600; Taxicard scheme ☎071/227 3588)

Royal Automobile Club Motoring Services, PO Box 100, Croydon CR2 6ED (☎081/686 2525)

TRIPSCOPE, 63 Esmond Road, London W4 1JE (☎081/994 9294)

HOTEL CHAINS

Best Western, Vine House, 143 London Road, Kingston upon Thames KT2 6NA (☎081/541 0033): worldwide

Campanile UK, Unit 8, Red Lion Court, Alexandra Road, Hounslow TW3 1JS (☎081/569 6969): Europe, mainly France

Consort Hotels and Transeurope Hotels, Rydale Building, Piccadilly, York YO1 1PN (☎0904/643151): Europe

Crest Hotels, Bridge Street, Banbury, Oxford OX16 8RQ (☎0295/67733): Europe

Days Inns of America, Enterprise House, 59–65 Upper Ground, London SE1 9PQ (☎071/633 9662): USA, Canada, Mexico

Flag International, 2nd Floor, William House, 14 Worple Road, London SW19 4DD (☎081/947 1168): Australia, New Zealand, Hong Kong, Canada, the Pacific

Golden Tulip International, Plesman House, 190 Great Southwest Road, Feltham TW14 9RL (☎081/750 9002)

Hilton International, PO Box 137, Millbuck House, Clarendon Road, Watford WD1 1DN (☎0923/50222): worldwide

Holiday Inns International, 10–12 New College Parade, Finchley Road, London NW3 5EP (☎071/722 7755): worldwide

Hotel Ibis, Hotel Urbis, Hotel Mercure, Novotel and Hotel Sofitel can be booked through *Resinter*, 1 Shortlands, Hammersmith, London W6 8DR (☎071/724 1000): worldwide

Inter-Continental Hotels, Thameside Centre, Kew Bridge Road, Brentford TW8 0EB (☎081/847 3711; reservations ☎081/847 2277 or ☎0345/581444 outside London): worldwide

ITT Sheraton Corporation, The Kiln House, 210 New Kings Road, London SW6 4NZ (☎071/731 5857 or ☎0800/353535): worldwide

Marriott Hotels, 80 Regent Street, London W1R 6AQ (☎071/439 0281): worldwide

Oberoi Hotels, 1 The Platt, Lower Richmond Road, London SW15 1DE (☎081/788 2070): worldwide

Quality Inns International, 2 Valentine Place, London SE1 8QH (☎071/928 3333): North America, Europe, the Pacific, India

Ramada, 160 Brompton Road, London SW3 1HS (☎071/225 3833; reservations ☎071/235 5264 or ☎0800/181737): worldwide

Shangri-La International Hotels and Resorts, 5 The Courtyard, Swan Centre, Fishers Lane, London W4 1RX (☎081/747 8484): the Far East, Canada, Fiji

INSURANCE COMPANIES

Association of British Insurers, Aldermary House, 10–15 Queen Street, London EC4N 1TT (☎071/248 4477)

Campbell Irvine, Insurance Brokers, 6 Bell Street, Reigate, Surrey RH2 7BG (☎0737/223687)

Europ Assistance, 252 High Street, Croydon CR0 1NF (☎081/680 1234)

Extrasure, Lloyd's Avenue House, 6 Lloyd's Avenue, London EC3N 3AX (☎071/480 6871)

M.J. Fish and Co, Insurance Brokers, 1–3 Slater Lane, Leyland PR5 3AL (☎0772/455111)

Hamilton Barr, Insurance Brokers, Hamilton Barr House, Bridge Mews, Bridge Street, Godalming, Surrey GU7 1HZ (☎0483/426600)

Holiday Care Service, 2 Old Bank Chambers, Station Road, Horley, Surrey RH6 9HW (☎0293/774535)

Jardines, Insurance Brokers, 25 Collingwood Street, Newcastle-upon-Tyne NE1 1JE (☎091/261 8002)

Norwich Union Travel Insurance Department, PO Box 6, Surrey Street, Norwich NR1 3NS (☎0603/622220)

Travelmarrs, 3rd Floor, Altay House, 869 High Road, Finchley, London N12 8QA (☎081/446 9620)

TOUR OPERATORS AND TRAVEL AGENTS

ABTA (*The Association of British Travel Agents*), 55–57 Newman Street, London W1P 4AH (☎071/637 2444)

American Express Holidays, Portland House, Stag Place, London SW1E 5BZ (☎071/834 5555)

ATS Travel (*The Assistance Travel Service*), 9 River View Terrace, Purfleet, Essex RM16 1QT (☎0708/863198)

Austravel, 20 Savile Row, London W1X 1AE (☎071/734 7755)

Automobile Association Travel Services, Fanum House, Basingstoke RG21 2EA (☎0256/492004)

Bales Tours, Bales House, Barrington Road, Dorking, Surrey RH4 3EJ (☎0306/885991)

Blackheath Wine Trails, 13 Blackheath Village, London SE3 9LA (☎081/463 0012)

Blue Riband Holidays (Accessible Travels), 13 St Paul's Square, Birmingham B3 1RB (☎021/236 3443)

Butterfield's Indian Railway Tours, Burton Fleming, Driffield, East Yorkshire YO24 0PQ (☎02620/87230)

Carefree Holidays, 64 Florence Road, Northampton NN1 4NA (☎0604/34301)

CIT (England), Marco Polo House, 3–5 Lansdowne Road, Croydon CR9 1LL (☎081/686 0677)

Color Line, Tyne Commission Quay, North Shields NE29 6EA (☎091/296 1313)

Compass General Sales Agents, PO Box 113, Peterborough PE1 1LE (☎0733/51780)

Country Holidays, Spring Mill, Earby, Colne, Lancashire BB8 6RN (☎0282/445566; disabled person's helpline ☎0282/445340)

Cunard Line, 30 Pall Mall, London SW1Y 5LS (☎071/491 3930)

Cyplon Travel and Holidays, Cyplon House, 563 Green Lanes, London N8 0RL (☎081/348 9142)

Cyprus Travel (London), 42 Hampstead Road, London NW1 2PH (☎071/580 0581)

Enterprise Holidays, Groundstar House, London Road, Crawley, West Sussex RH10 2TB (☎0293/560777)

Equity Cruises, 77–79 Great Eastern Street, London EC2A 3HU (☎071/729 1929)

Falcon Travel, 29 Notting Hill Gate, London W11 3JQ (☎071/229 5515)

Grecofile, Sourdock Hill, Barkisland, Halifax HX4 0AG (☎0422/374999)

Greyhound World Travel, Sussex House, London Road, West Sussex RH19 1LD (☎0342/317317)

Hayes and Jarvis, 152 King Street, London W6 0QU (☎081/748 0088)

Holland America Line, see *Equity Cruises*

Hoseasons Holidays, Sunway House, Lowestoft NR32 3LT (☎0502/500505)

Jetsave Travel, Sussex House, London Road, East Grinstead, West Sussex RH19 1LD (☎0342/328231)

Journey Latin America, 16 Devonshire Place, London W4 2HD (☎081/747 3108)

KD German Rhine Line, 28 South Street, Epsom, Surrey KT18 7PF (☎03727/42033)

Keycamp Holidays, Ellerman House, 92/96 Lind Road, Sutton SM1 4PL (☎081/661 1836)

Kuoni Travel, Deepdene House, Dorking, Surrey RH5 4AY (☎0306/740888)

Lanzarote Villas, Valentine House, Ilford Hill, Ilford, Essex IG1 2DG (☎081/514 4455)

Laskarina Holidays, St Mary's Gate, Wirksworth, Derby DE4 4DQ (☎062982/2203)

Meon Travel, 32 High Street, Petersfield, Hampshire GU32 3JN (☎0730/66561)

P&O Cruises, 77 New Oxford Street, London W1A 1PP (☎071/831 1234)

Safari Interlink, 27–31 Jerdan Place, London SW6 1BE (☎071/381 5229)

Shearings Holidays, Miry Lane, Wigan WN3 4AG (☎0942/824824)

Sunvil Travel, 7–8 Upper Square, Isleworth, Middlesex TW7 7BJ (☎081/568 4499)

Swiss Travel Service, Bridge House, Ware, Hertfordshire SG12 9DE (☎0920/5021)

Thomas Cook *Faraway Holidays*, PO Box 36, Thorpe Wood, Peterborough PE3 6SB (☎0733/332255); *Charitylink* ☎0733/558313

Thomson Tour Operations (including **Thomson Holidays**, **Horizon**, **Skytours**, **Wings**, **HCI** and **OSL**), Greater London House, Hampstead Road, London NW1 7SD (☎071/387 9321). Book holidays through travel agent or direct with *Thomson Holiday Shop*, Edgbaston Five Ways, Birmingham B15 1BB (Birmingham ☎021/632 6282; London ☎081/200 8733; Manchester ☎061/236 3828)

Threshold Travel, 80 Newry Street, Banbridge, County Down, Northern Ireland BT32 3HA (☎08206/26267)

Time Off, 2a Chester Close, Chester Street, London SW1X 7BQ (☎071/235 8070)

Trailfinders Travel Centres: 42/48 Earls Court Road, London W8 6EJ (☎071/938 3366); 194/196 Kensington High Street, London W8 7RG (☎071/938 3939)

Travelbag, 12 High Street, Alton, Hampshire GU34 1BN (☎0420/87877)

Twelve Islands, Angel Way, Romford, Essex RM1 1AB (☎0708/752653)

Venice Simplon-Orient-Express, Suite 200, Hudson's Place, Victoria Station, London SW1V 1JL (☎071/928 6000)

Virgin Holidays, 3rd Floor, Sussex House, High Street, Crawley, West Sussex RH10 1BZ (☎0293/551751)

Yugotours, Chesham House, 150 Regent Street, London W1R 6BB (☎071/734 7321)

VOLUNTARY/NON-PROFIT ORGANISATIONS

Across Trust, 70/72 Bridge Road, East Molesey, Surrey KT8 9HF (☎081/783 1355). "Jumbulances" for organised European holidays or for hire to other groups

Age Concern England, 1268 London Road, London SW16 4EJ (☎081/679 8000). Holiday fact sheets and books

Arthritis Care, 6 Grosvenor Crescent, London SW1X 7ER (☎071/235 0902). Holiday accommodation in the UK

AFASIC (*Association for All Speech Impaired Children*), 347 Central Markets, Smithfield, London EC1A 9NH (☎071/236 3632). Activity holidays

Association for Spina Bifida and Hydrocephalus, Asbah House, 42 Park Road, Peterborough PE1 2UQ (☎0733/555988). Activity and leisure courses at residential centre in Yorkshire

BREAK, 20 Hooks Hill Road, Sheringham, Norfolk NR26 8NL (☎0263/823170). Free holidays in Norfolk for mentally and physically disabled people and families with special needs

British Deaf Association, 38 Victoria Place, Carlisle, Cumbria CA1 1HU (☎0228/48844 voice; ☎0228/28719 Vistel). Some organised holidays

British Diabetic Association, 10 Queen Anne Street, London W1M 0BD (☎071/323 1531). Activity and study courses

British Kidney Patient Association, Bordon, Hampshire (☎04203/2021). Runs three holiday dialysis centres and may offer financial help

British Nursing Association, 82 Great North Road, Hatfield AL9 5BL (☎0707/263544) and local branches. Trained nurses for escort, residential or visiting assistance in Britain or abroad

British Red Cross, 9 Grosvenor Crescent, London SW1X 7EJ (☎071/235 5454), and local offices. Holidays, escorts, helpers, loan of equipment within the UK

British Ski Club for the Disabled: Mr H.M. Sturges (Chairman), Spring Mount, Berwick St John, Shaftesbury, Dorset SP7 0FQ (☎0747/88515). Holidays and instruction abroad

British Sports Association for the Disabled, 34 Osnaburgh Street, London NW1 3ND (☎071/388 7277). Information on sports and training

Camping and Caravanning Club, Greenfields House, Westwood Way, Coventry CV4 8JH (☎0203/694995). Information to members on site facilities in Britain

Camping for the Disabled, 20 Burton Close, Dawley, Telford, Shropshire TF4 2BX (☎0952/507653 evenings; ☎0743/75889 day). Advice on campsite facilities in the UK and abroad, organised weekends in the summer

The Caravan Club, East Grinstead House, East Grinstead, West Sussex RH9 1UA (☎0342/326944). List of club sites in England, Scotland and Wales with adapted toilet facilities

DIAL UK, Park Lodge, St Catherine's Hospital, Tickhill Road, Balby, Doncaster DN4 8QN (☎0302/310123). Disability helpline

Disability Now, monthly newspaper, published by *The Spastics Society*, 12 Park Crescent, London W1N 4EQ (☎071/636 5020)

Disabled Drivers' Association (*DDA*), Ashwellthorpe Hall, Norwich NR16 1EX (☎050841/449). Manage fully accessible

Ashwellthorpe Hall Hotel, arrange ferry concessions for members

Disabled Drivers' Motor Club (*DDMC*), Cottingham Way, Thrapston, Northants NN14 4PL (☎08012/4724). Information for disabled motorists, ferry concessions, travel and access reported in magazine, *The Disabled Driver*

Disabled Living Foundation, 380/384 Harrow Road, London W9 2HU (☎071/289 6111). Advice on equipment, clothing, continence aids

Disaway Trust, 2 Charles Road, Merton Park, London SW19 3BD (☎081/543 3431). Group holidays in the UK and abroad

Down's Syndrome Association, 12/13 Clapham Common Southside, London SW4 7AA (☎071/720 0008). Some holiday information

Earthwatch Europe, Belsyre Court, 57 Woodstock Road, Oxford OX2 6HU (☎0865/311600)

Family Holiday Association, Hertford Lodge, East End Road, London N3 3QE (☎081/349 4044). Grants to severely deprived families

Handicapped Aid Trust: applications for grants to Janet Marshall, 21 Malden Hill, Surrey KT3 4DS (☎081/336 2064); donations to The Treasurer, *Handicapped Aid Trust*, c/o *The Spastics Society* (see below)

HEADWAY (*National Head Injuries Association*), 200 Mansfield Road, Nottingham NG1 3HX (☎0602/622382). Some holiday information

Help the Handicapped Holiday Fund, 147a Camden Road, Tunbridge Wells, Kent TN1 2RA (☎0892/547474). Free holidays for physically disabled people who are otherwise unable to take a break

Holiday Care Service, 2 Old Bank Chambers, Station Road, Horley, Surrey RH6 9HW (☎0293/774535). Information on all aspects of travel

Holiday Helpers, 2 Old Bank Chambers, Station Road, Horley, Surrey RH6 9HW (☎0293/775137). Matchmaking service for helpers and disabled or elderly travellers

Holidays for the Disabled, 12 Ryle Road, Farnham, Surrey GU9 8RW (☎0252/721390 evenings). Group holidays

Horticultural Therapy, Goulds Ground, Vallis Way, Frome, Somerset BA11 3DW (☎0373/64782). Information and advice on all aspects of recreational and therapeutic gardening, and access to public gardens

John Grooms Association for the Disabled, 10 Gloucester Drive, London N4 2LP (☎081/800 8695). Accessible hotels and self-catering accommodation throughout the UK; room rate concessions at the *London Tara Hotel*

Joint Aids Centres Council, 76 Clarendon Park Road, Leicester LE2 3AD (☎0533/700747). Information on travelling aids exhibitions

Journey of a Lifetime Trust (*JOLT*): Mrs D.K. Dalton (Chairman), Vincent House, 32 Maxwell Road, Northwood, Middlesex HA6 2YF (☎09274/25453). Adventure holidays for disabled or disadvantaged youngsters

Jubilee Sailing Trust, Test Road, Eastern Docks, Southampton SO1 1GG (☎0703/631388; bookings ☎0703/631395). Voyages on the specially designed *Lord Nelson*

Les Evans Holiday Fund for Sick and Handicapped Children, 65a Crouch Street, Colchester, Essex CO3 3EY (☎0206/47120). Holidays for chronically sick and severely disabled children (8–15 years)

Medic-Alert Foundation, 17 Bridge Wharf, 156 Caledonian Road, London N1 9UU (☎071/833 3034)

MENCAP (*Royal Society for Mentally Handicapped Children and Adults*) *Holiday Services Office*, 119 Drake Street, Rochdale, Lancashire OL16 1PZ (☎0706/54111). UK holiday programme for unaccompanied children and adults; guide listing accommodation where mentally handicapped guests are welcome

Mobility International, 228 Borough High Street, London SE1 1JX (☎071/403 5688). Travel information and advice, plus own programme of leisure and study holidays

Multiple Sclerosis Society, 25 Effie Road, London SW6 1EE (☎071/736 6267). Holiday information and UK accommodation

National Federation of Kidney Patients Associations, Laurentian House, Stanley Street, Worksop S81 7HX (☎0909/487795). Advice on travel

Operation Raleigh Headquarters, Alpha Place, Flood Street, London SW3 5SZ (☎071/351 7541). Expeditions worldwide

Parkinson's Disease Society, 36 Portland Place, London W1N 3DG (☎071/255 2432). Holidays in the UK and Venice, advice and help with holiday finance

Physically Handicapped and Able Bodied (*PHAB*), 12–14 London Road, Croydon CR0 2TA (☎081/667 9443). Programme of holidays, some abroad, for all ages and abilities

Project Phoenix Trust, 68 Rochfords, Coffee Hall, Milton Keynes MK6 5DJ (☎0908/678038). Group study tours, some help with finance

RADAR (*The Royal Association for Disability and Rehabilitation*), 25 Mortimer Street, London W1N 8AB (☎071/637 5400; Minicom ☎071/637 5315). Information on all aspects of travel (as well as many other matters)

Riding for the Disabled Association, Avenue "R", National Agricultural Centre, Kenilworth, Warks CV8 2LY (☎0203/696510). Riding and driving holidays

Royal National Institute for the Blind (*RNIB*), 224 Great Portland Street, London W1N 6AA (☎071/388 1266). Information on their own holiday hotels. Books available on cassette or in Braille can be obtained from Customer Services, PO Box 173, Peterborough PE2 0WS (☎0733/370777)

St John Ambulance HQ, 1 Grosvenor Crescent, London SW1X 7EF (☎071/235 5231). UK ambulance, escort, nursing or care attendants arranged through county offices (listed in telephone directory)

Spastics Society, 16 Fitzroy Square, London W1P 5HQ (☎071/387 9571). Runs the *Churchtown Farm Field and Studies Centre*; publishes *Disability Now* (see above)

Spinal Injuries Association, 76 St James's Lane, London N10 3DF (☎081/444 2121). Full adapted caravans and narrowboats; Care Attendant Agency; co-production (with the *AA*) of *The World Wheelchair Traveller* (see *Books*)

Uphill Ski Club, 12 Park Crescent, London W1N 4EQ (☎071/636 1989). Programme of winter sports holidays abroad

Winged Fellowship Trust, Angel House, 20–32 Pentonville Road, London N1 9XD (☎071/833 2594). Group holidays for severely physically disabled adults at adapted UK centres and abroad

WRVS (*Women's Royal Voluntary Service*), 234–244 Stockwell Road, London SW9 9SP (☎071/733 3388). Non-medical escort service on public transport or for journeys to and from local stations or airports

Young Disabled on Holiday, 33 Longfield Avenue, Heald Green, Cheadle, Cheshire SK8 3NN (☎061/499 3639). Holidays for 18–30s